HISTORICAL AND
COMPARATIVE LINGUISTICS

Second Revised Edition

RAIMO ANTTILA
University of California, Los Angeles

JOHN BENJAMINS PUBLISHING COMPANY
AMSTERDAM/PHILADELPHIA

1989

Original title
An Introduction to Historical and Comparative Linguistics
MacMillan Publishing Co., Inc, New York
Collier MacMillan Publishers, London
1972

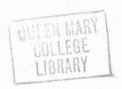

Library of Congress Cataloging-in-Publication Data

Anttila, Raimo.
    Historical and comparative linguistics.
(Amsterdam studies in the theory and history of linguistic science. Series IV, Current issues in linguistic theory, ISSN 0304-0763; v. 6)
Originally published under title: An introduction to historical and comparative linguistics. New York: Macmillan, 1972.
Bibliography: p.
Includes index.
1. Historical linguistics. 2. Comparative linguistics. I. Title. II. Series.
P140.A58   1989   410'.9   88-36035
ISBN 90 272 3556 2 (hb) / 90 272 3557 0 (pb) (alk. paper)

HISTORICAL AND COMPARATIVE LINGUISTICS

AMSTERDAM STUDIES IN THE THEORY AND
HISTORY OF LINGUISTIC SCIENCE

General Editor
E.F. KONRAD KOERNER
(University of Ottawa)

Series IV - CURRENT ISSUES IN LINGUISTIC THEORY

Advisory Editorial Board

Second Revised Edition

Volume 6

Raimo Anttila

Historical and Comparative Linguistics

PREFACE

In any course of historical and comparative linguistics there will be students of different language backgrounds, different levels of linguistic training, and different theoretical orientation. No textbook has fully overcome the difficulties raised by this heterogeneity, and probably none will; but this book attempts to mitigate the principal problems in the following ways.

Since it is impossible to treat the language or language family of special interest to every student, the focus of this book is on English in particular and Indo-European languages generally. This convention accords with the most commonly successful practice. To these languages are added Finnish and its closely related languages for an indispensable contrast. The remaining examples are drawn from other parts of the world but have been selected for their utility rather than to preserve any geographical balance.

The tenets of different schools of linguistics, and the controversies among them, are treated eclectically and objectively; the examination of language itself plays the leading role in our efforts to ascertain the comparative value of competing theories. The history of linguistic thought looms in the background, if for the most part implicitly, and no particular school is ignored. Of course, the instructor can move to his own theoretical tilt from the equipoise of this book and introduce whatever additional arguments he chooses.

The different levels of academic attainment in the typical class have been taken into account by composing the book as though it were a handbook in hopes of saving the more advanced students from frustration while still providing the essential background. For a really basic introduction, therefore, some chapters or parts of chapters can be omitted, but this suggestion should not be construed as an indication that they are superfluous. All the principles presented are significant (including cultural and biological parallels), but whether it will be thought desirable for students to attempt to learn them all within the limits of a given course will depend on the instructor's judgment. Some instructors, for example, may find it useful to begin with comparative linguistics (Part III), because this allows for constant practice with the various methods all through the course.

At least two innovations may be mentioned here. On the one hand, the various concepts have been broken down into their separate components to facilitate learning; on the other, a much greater effort has been made in this text than in other introductory texts to relate the different concepts to each other. In my experience, students have found this combination to be very helpful.

The bibliography is by necessity an abbreviated one, and will not serve the needs of every reader. Most of its titles are in English, German, and French, the languages students are most likely to know. Works of great historical importance are often listed in translation, or in a recent reprint; thus the dates in the bibliography lie mainly in the 1960s despite the concern with the history of linguistics. I have listed works that have actually influenced this text by their relation to my personal background, other elementary material, and some more advanced works for further study.

The omission of an author index is alleviated by the fact that mention of authors is avoided as much as possible in the text itself. Most names are gathered into the reference sections at the end of the chapters.

The influence on my thinking of over a century and a half of scholarship in the area of historical linguistics is obvious and freely admitted. But of particular importance has been the instruction and inspiration drawn from many teachers in many countries, above all Bernard Bloch, Warren Cowgill, Isidore Dyen, Floyd Lounsbury (all at Yale), and Robert Austerlitz. Colleagues who have given me guidance and encouragement in connection with this book are Henning Andersen, William Bright, Mati Hint, Erkki Itkonen (whose book *Kieli ja sen tutkimus* profoundly influenced the following pages), Guy Jucquois, Kostas Kazazis, J. Peter Maher, Hanns-Peter Schmidt, and Michael Shapiro. Andrew Sihler, of the University of Wisconsin, provided invaluable advice and assistance, especially in the matter of style. I am indebted to a great number of students who over the years have seen my ideas develop and who have influenced them—in particular the class at UCLA in the spring of 1970, the first one to have this manuscript in their hands, and especially Lyle Campbell and Bruce Pearson, who have responded beyond the call of duty. The valuable qualities of my undertaking have been enhanced by these sources of influence; whatever is of doubtful value is solely my own responsibility.

[1988] The continued demand for this text has been gratifying; its enlarged reissue should meet a real need, even though there is a strict space limit to the additions permitted. In essence, the bulk of the text remains the same, with only minor adjustments. An introduction (dealing mostly with the semiotic basis of change) has been added, as well as a chapter at the end (Chapter 23, "Genetic Linguistics and Metatheory," which covers aspects of explanation, particularly in historical and human disciplines). The intended elementary level of the first edition turned out not to be so in practice, and the book is generally considered to be a rather "advanced" presentation. For this reason, "An introduction to" has been deleted from the title and the exercises (at the end of chapters 8, 10, and 11) have been removed. The latter has provided space for the addition of a section on comparative syntax in Chapter 11. There is also a brief addition on the semiotic status of the comparative method to Chapter 13. The bibliography has been updated with a selection from the overwhelming amount of material which has appeared in the intervening years. The index has been redone to take account of the additions. As with the first edition, many colleagues have again supported me in this undertaking, above all Sheila Embleton, who also set the new text with her Macintosh SE.

CONTENTS

PART IV
LINGUISTIC RECONSTRUCTION: A SYNTHESIS OF
VARIOUS LINGUISTIC AND CULTURAL
NOTIONS

PART V
CONCLUSION: LINGUISTICS AS PART OF
ANTHROPOLOGY

INTRODUCTION 1988

> *The first edition of this book appeared (1972) just when many aspects of the linguistic scene started to change. It predicted many of the coming needs, but now (1988) the text can be adapted better to the requirements initiated then.*

APOLOGIA PRO REEDITIONE SUA

[0.1 Changing Times] The linguistic scene was quite different in 1970, the closing date for the writing of the first edition of this book, from what it is today. There was a general lack of interest in *history*. Further, formal means for "accounting for" change (cf. Chapter 6) predominated whenever historical linguistics was acknowledged. Then, at the beginning of the 1970s, changes, or shifts in emphasis, started to take place. Analogy again became respectable, and this was tied with a resurfacing of morphology (cf. Chapter 5). In the 1980s these aspects, together with general systems theory (deriving from similar concepts) have also led to artificial intelligence and catastrophe theory. The mathematics of lexicostatistics (cf. §§22.13-14) was extended. Sociolinguistics gathered momentum; interest in pidgins, creoles and contact phenomena and their implications for historical study burgeoned. Abductive explanation (cf. §§9.16-18, 23.4) started to win ground over the earlier descriptive formalisms. Explanation of phenomena related to language arose again in terms of philosophy of science, meaning hermeneutics, pragmatics, action theory, teleology, and historical explanation and philology in general (Chapter 23). But most importantly, semiotic concepts gradually became cornerstones in understanding language structure and its change. In the 1980s this line had produced two variants, independent of each other but deriving from the same notions (of iconicity): natural morphology and functional syntax. Toward the end of the 1980s the resurgence of interest in historical linguistics has become overwhelming (see pp. 29-30).

[0.2] Because the book has met the needs of many of the avenues mentioned above, or has in fact helped establish them (e.g., the isomorphy relation and the notation for it, §§5.14, 5.21, 6.23, 7.9, 9.3-4, 23.7), there has been steady support for its reissue. But there are also features that some find lacking. Chief among these are syntax and word order typology. Some of this is now alleviated by adding §§11.21-30, but word order typology cannot be addressed here due to space constraints on this reissue. Fortunately this material is fairly easily available elsewhere, and interest in it seems already to be waning. On the other hand, analogy has turned out (again) to be the main mover in syntactic change, a position well represented in the original version (cf. §§11.21-30). The most confusing factor in this context seems to have been the fact that syntax did not have a *chapter of its own*. Contrary to frequent claims, historical syntax has not been neglected in traditional theories, and it is in fact surprising that the classics of syntax are hardly ever quoted in more recent theoretical statements or claims. In a way there is little real "progress" since Apollonius Dyscolus, as far as the concepts go.

The so-called "glottalic theory", the ejective reinterpretation of Proto-Indo-European voiced stops, has reasserted itself since the beginning of the 1970s. At the same time tonogenesis received considerable attention. The "great English vowel shift" (§4.8) is under new scrutiny, the Irish secondary endings (§19.10) have fallen into doubt, and the Uralic family tree (Fig. 15-1) has undergone significant changes both in its structure and chronology.

SEMIOTICS AND CHANGE

[0.3 The Subtypes and Classes of Signs] A full (true) sign is composed of nine subtypes, which can be ordered the following way:

THE NINE SUB-TYPES OF SIGN	1 sign as possibility	2 sign as actuality	3 sign as rule/law
I sign in relation to itself signans	qualisign (tone)	sinsign (token)	legisign (type)
II sign in relation to object (referent) signatum	icon	index	symbol
III sign in relation to interpretant signification	rhema	dicent	argument

The first two rows represent the Saussurean sign (signifiant -- signifié), and the second row will be discussed in Chapter 1 (§§1.10-16). The third row supplies the interpretant, the idea that arises in the interpreting mind. *Type* and *token* are well known, but not *tone*, the mere quality aspect of the sign. This is why it is technically called *qualisign*. Similarly, the actual *singularity* of an occurrrence gives us *sinsign*, and sign as law is (Latinate) *legisign*. A *rhema* supplies the concept aspect without truth value, whereas a *dicent* is actually true or false. There are now ten basic classes of sign, which can be visualized as lines going through the rows choosing one box from each (this is the triadic sign). These lines can move only upward and right, not backwards (left). Thus, always starting from **III**, we have e.g. rhematic-iconic-qualisigns (1. below), etc. In many cases there is now redundancy, e.g. here, since a qualisign can only be at the top of a straight line, thus be necessity rhematic-iconic. The argument similarly can only go straight up, and does not need **II** and **I** in its name. The ten classes (with some examples) are:

CLASSES OF SIGN

1. (III1-II1-I1): A color as a sign of quality.
2. (III1-II1-I2): An individual fever diagram, e.g. a fever curve of a patient.
3. (III1-II2-I2): A spontaneous cry (of pain, rage, joy).
4. (III2-II2-I2): A weather cock.
5. (III1-II1-I3): A general diagram, e.g. a fever curve of a sickness.
6. (III1-II2-I3): Demonstrative pronouns, numerals, adverbials, prepositions (cf. §§5.15, 7.13, 11.23).
7. (III2-II2-I3): A traffic sign, an imperative sentence.
8. (III1-II3-I3): Any common noun, words in a dictionary, the open concepts of classical logic.
9. (III2-II3-I3): A normal declarative sentence, e.g. *The rose is red.*
10. (III3-II3-I3): The argument, a sign of perfect lawful connection, as in reasoning (syllogism, relations that are 'necessarily true'.

The corners with least (I1) and most semioticity (III3) remain solitary, but note that six classes partake of both III1 and I3. These corners give reason for change. Reality is funneled into concepts (III1) through abduction (§§9.16-17, 13.9, 23.4). Concepts are just possible -- they have to be used in contexts (II2 and I2), or sentences (III2). Such an open class is fuzzy on both ends, and leads to change. But more important is the fact that types can be manifested only through tokens replicating them in concrete contexts (e.g., English has one type *the*, while this page has many tokens of it). Thus again, one starts from below (III), in which only Class 10 replicates with Class 9, then 9 and 8 replicate with distance in II, through 7 and 6 respectively, and finally, at the top of the chart (I), 5, 6, and 7 get their tokens through 2, 3, and 4. Sign-use and sign-interpretation thus need indexical and iconic elements in a crucial way. This pulsation, this stretching, between symbols/types vs. indexes/tokens and icons by necessity creates change; change is the very essence of meaning and language use (§23.5). The following chapters will bear this out in concrete detail.

[0.4 Division of Linguistic Signs] Linguistic signs divide into content and diacritic signs. The former comprise lexical and grammatical signs and the latter the sound units, phonemes, that keep the other signs distinct between themselves. The lexical items can be further grouped into neutral and expressive signs. The following hierarchy reflects this state of affairs:

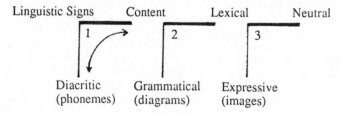

Linguistic Signs	Content	Lexical	Neutral
Diacritic (phonemes)	Grammatical (diagrams)	Expressive (images)	

The top (thick) line represents the main symbolic line. Branching 1 cuts off phonology from the rest, but, as diacritics (D), these must be employed within the rest. Phonological structure is inherently diagrammatic, i.e. hierarchical, and not just segmental (§9.15). Part of the reason for sound change is reinterpretation of such hierarchies in context. All linguistic signs have to be interpreted (since they are symbols), and such action leads to change. But phonemes are not only diacritics, they also carry strong indexical function in two ways: 1) through their allophones or as parts of morphophonemic alternations they integrate adjacent units, they show diagrammatically togetherness, they dissolve parts for the benefit of a larger unit. This way they typically blur minor boundaries and enhance lexical items, words, but sometimes also phrases. This is a paradox, diagrammatic forces deny themselves as it were, and obliterate iconicity (motivation) to sharpen the symbolic efficiency of a word, a lexical item (cf. cell differentiation in biology; §17.1, p. 325). 2) A particular pronunciation is also an index of a region, social class, and so on (Class 3). But note that such an index is already a symbol, since it means 'New Yorker', 'educated person', 'man', or 'woman' (§§3.1-3, 9.11, 11.21). It is a symbol of class membership and thus close to the integrative function of the index. But pronunciation also segregates if it reveals that the speaker is a New Yorker, and not e.g. from Boston, or if it is John, and not Michael, etc. Diacriticity does not get eliminated by the symbolic aspects. The phonemes as diacritics are also symbolic, after all, they mean 'otherness', segregation from the others (phonemes). This is the semiotic (theoretical) reason for the regularity of sound change: As all sounds are synonymous, there is no reason for competition between them on that level (of course, interference does then enter from other levels with richer meaning contrasts).

Branching 2 is typically effected through diagrammatic selection from the diacritic inventory (D), e.g. dentals only in the productive inflectional suffixes of English (§1.14). Particularly striking is the division in Semitic, with consonants for lexical morphemes and vowels for grammatical (§9.15). Here a major feature contrast matches the major grammar contrast. In the diagrams of syntax (the syntactic patterns, sentence schemes, or whatever we call them) lexical items act as diacritics. This fact makes it possible that with relatively few diagrams one can talk about an infinite number of states of affairs (§§11.21-22). Such a switch of "responsibility" is typical of semiotic systems and indicates crucial interdependence (cf. p. 199).

On the whole, grammatical and expressive signs share the same diagrammatic means. Thus English *drink/drank/drunk* (G) is "identical" to *clink, clank, clunk* (E), although the former displays diagrammaticity vs. the images in the latter (shown by a diagrammatic gradience). Similarly, the Finnish illatives *pää-hän, puu-hun, pii-hin, suo-hon, yö-hön, maa-han* (§4.16) contain a vowel that integrates the ending with the root (G). In this vowel harmony is always morphophonemic (=indexical). This is not true of the nature sounds mirrored in e.g. *käh-is-tä* 'wheeze', *kuh-is-ta* 'swarm', *kih-is-tä* 'fizz', *koh-is-ta* 'roar', *köh-is-tä* 'rasp', *kah-is-ta* 'rustle' (E), although the frame *k-h-* clearly means 'a kind of fizzing/wheezing/rustling sound/noise'. The vowels indicate the more exact onomatopoeic meaning in that the quality of the vowel represents the quality of the noise in more detail. This is a tone, an image, not an index, diagram, as in the case of the morphophonemes. The former refers directly to nature, the latter to an adjacent morpheme, more particularly, its vowel. But in a way *k-h-* is a general diagram, *köh-* etc. individual diagrams. (As for the diacritic/contrastive functions of the vowels, see p. 209.)

Grammatical and expressive vocabulary also share other means provided by the diacritic signs. Particularly prevalent devices here are reduplication, "intonation", and relative shortness of words (e.g. in hypocoristic forms like *Ed, Tom, prof, lab, ma, sis*). This homophony is not "insidious" (§9.3), since the forms occur in different object domains (II above) and interpretant fields (III); they just share the I-repertory. The most "colorless" grammatical markers do not interfere with the most "colorful" elements in language, even if they both serve iconicity. There are different kinds of iconicity.

[0.5 The Rise of the Quasiphoneme] Sounds in general adapt to adjoining sounds, otherwise there would not be any conditioned sound change. This is in fact general field behavior. An allophone is always an iconic index. Sometimes it refers only to the neighboring sound, and if this remains within a monomorphemic domain (with conditioning within that morpheme), we get something like the order of the development of Latin *k* into French *k, s,* and *š* (§4.4), schematically (A):

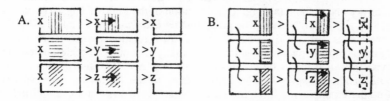

The shading indicates different environments, arrows and diacritics/letters signal adaptation of the initial to those environments (anticipatory assimilation). Finally, the merger of the environments establishes phonemic contrasts in the initial position. But when the assimilation occurs over a morpheme boundary (or otherwise in different contexts; cf. Rotuman §4.6) we get morphophonemic alternations (B), e.g. in medial position in OE *mūs/mȳs* (§4.5): At stage II the frontness of the allophone [ȳ] in **mȳs-i* is an iconic index of the segment (= front vowel *i*) to follow. In Lapp we get lengthening of stops in open syllables (§§10.14-15). Thus nom. sg. **kȅle* 'tongue' develops a half-long liquid vs. gen. sg. **kȅle-n* (cf. p. 224) in pre-Lapp. Length in the **l* is now an index of the syllable structure to follow, length being nicely iconic to the sequence of sounds mirrored. [ȳ] and [l̀] in these contexts are variants to be eliminated in classical synchronic analysis. But they cosignal following suffixes and carry considerable semiotic weight: [ȳ] tells that the following suffix contains a front element, and [l̀] informs that there is either no suffix or the suffix begins with one consonant. Selection is meaningful information. Units of this kind, allophones according to their distribution, but phonemes for carrying selective indexical information, are called *quasiphonemes*. In such cases the source meaning is likely to creep forward along its index and take it over by establishing clear phonemic contrast within a morphophonemic alternation, thus *mūs/mȳs* and *kiella/kiela* (cf. Finnish *kieli/kielen*), with drop of the endings. Note how different the segment-index and the sequence-index are. "Weak consonantism" in the Lapp suffix strengthens the medial consonant in the root by a balancing action (=diagram), which is general between vowels and consonants in Lapp (§§10.14-15), whereas the English umlaut contains a direct image (color). Iconic indexicality is quite clear in anticipatory assimilation like *il-legal, impossible*, etc. (§4.14), or the Slavic palatalization (§§5.3, 6.16f). Umlauts are different in that we notice the independence of the index more easily, e.g. **mūs-i > *mȳs-i > mȳs*:

The index goes the other way in vowel harmony (lag):

This index (i.e. in D) does not generally become independent -- rather the contrary. Note the total lagging assimilation of the Finnish 3 sg. *-v* (from *-vi*, §19.6), e.g. *anta-v > anta-a* 'he gives' (*määki-i, kieku-u*, etc.; §1.11). Now the invariant is just *-V* (E), a cover symbol for a relation (which is the raison d'être of morphophonemic notation). Finally it should be remembered that these indexical forces tie phrases together, e.g. note the Finnish imperatives with original 2 sg. **-k*, which assimilates to the following stop (§4.14). Another example would be the initial mutations of Irish, not exemplified in this book. In these the conditioning comes from the preceding word, and hence pattern A would reflect that preceding word as a morphophoneme (*x/y/z*).

[0.6 Iconic Indexes] Membership or togetherness need of course not be indicated through morphophonemic processes. On the phrasal level togetherness is normally indicated through agreement or congruence morphology or intonation, e.g. in Latin *illum bonum dominum* acc. sg. 'that good master' the marker *-um* indicates parts that go together. The *-um* of *dominum* is repeated in the adjectives, or the adjectives assimilate totally to the ending of the noun. Thus the index is iconic (cf. Italian *i grandi giornali italiani*, German *die großen italienischen Zeitungen* 'the big Italian newspapers', Finnish *tälle pienelle pojalle* 'to this little boy'). But such indexes can be suppletive also, i.e. perfectly "symbolic", e.g. Latin *pōpulus alta viridisque* 'a high and green poplar' (cf. German *-ie* [in *die*] vs. *-en* above). The reason for such symbolic elements is to build an articulated diagram. In fact suppletion (in lexicon) can be seen as an iconic index of the essential contrast between ego and 'other', between what is intimately related to selfness or impinges upon selfness in some basic ways and what does not relate to or impinge upon selfness.

Let us return to the social index, the crucial propeller of sound change (§§3.1-3, 9.11). Objects and organisms leave imprints, iconic indexes, in their environment. A sidewinder writes its twirling in sand, a tree bulges around a fence pole, and the dent remains when the pole is gone, etc. Foot prints iconically show the agent that left them. Again, the index can be rather symbolic, as in the breathing hole that the seals keep open in the ice. Animal sounds are indexes of the animals that produce them (and bird calls and bee language have different dialects). Similarly, dialects (pronunciation) are indexes of the speakers (like particular clothing or other insignia). They are often statistical indexes, i.e. diagrams as in Fig. 3-1. In these one has to use the right proportion of the index. Sound change is now somebody's (conscious or unconscious) assimilation to somebody else's pronunciation index. One tries to reproduce the index as iconically (perfectly) as possible (and if one overdoes it, it results in hypercorrection). And as already mentioned, such an index is a symbol of class or regional meaning. Prestige borrowing is also an attempt to create an iconic index towards the reference group (§8.15). (For explanation of actions, see §§23.6-9.)

Rhyme and alliteration in poetry are artistic means of tying words together in various patterns. We easily recognize the same iconic indexes as above. Even drastic vocabulary change must use iconic and indexical forces, as comes out in Cockney rhyming slang, e.g.

BASE ITEM	RHYMING SLANG
wife	*drum and fife*
	trouble and strife
stairs	*apples and pears*
tale	*weep and wail*
(table) mate	*china plate*
drunk	*elephant's trunk*
hat	*tit for tat*

Rhyme connects the two forms, but it can be lost through elliptic (indexical) shortening, giving us *trouble* (for *wife*), *apples* (for *stairs*), *china* (for *mate*), *elephant's* (for *drunk*), and *titfer* (for *hat*). Again, the end point is pure symbols.

REFERENCES

General semiotics and change: Armstrong 1986, Bentele 1984, Shapiro 1983, C. Lehmann 1974, Plank 1979, Lüdtke (ed.) 1980, Posner (ed.) 1980, Mayerthaler 1981, Dressler 1985, Bailey 1985; **0.1** Cram 1979, Wildgen 1985, Merrell 1987; Mayerthaler 1981, Wurzel 1984, Dressler 1985; Haiman 1980, 1985; **0.2** Hawkins 1983; Vennemann (ed.) 1987; Hombert et al. 1979, Weidert 1987; **0.3** Walther 1979, Shapiro 1983; **0.4** Walther 1979, Anttila 1977a; **0.5** Korhonen 1969, Anttila 1975, in Fisiak (ed.) 1978, 1980; **0.6** Anttila 1975, 1977ab, Markey 1985, Fishman 1985.

PART I

BACKGROUND:
GENETIC LINGUISTICS
IN RELATION TO
GENERAL LINGUISTICS AND
RELATED FIELDS

CHAPTER 1

LANGUAGE AND LINGUISTICS

A brief review of linguistics is presented, followed by a delineation of the domain of genetic linguistics (that is, historical linguistics and comparative linguistics). The background ideas for the book are given.

[1.1 The Descriptive Prerequisite]   For any discussion of language change (or reconstruction) a basic description of language itself is obligatory. In order to study change in an object, one must first know the object itself; and the underlying principles of historical and comparative (or genetic) linguistics can be understood only in terms of the basic characteristics of human language. In fact, before venturing into historical linguistics, most students have taken courses in descriptive linguistics. A second group, however, tries to study both aspects concurrently; and a third group never studies descriptive linguistics in an explicit manner, but deduces its knowledge of language structure from historical treatments. The last group has tended to disappear from the modern academic scene. The first approach is the most beneficial one for the majority of students: the more one knows about language, the easier the study of language change will be. It is always advisable for the student to review and refresh his basic linguistics before and during his study of historical linguistics. We shall often have to refer both to history and to synchronic description in the following chapters, though a complete treatment of what the student has done (or should have done) elsewhere is of course impossible. Still, a short skeletal review of the basic features of language is useful; in fact, it is a necessary bridge to genetic linguistics, and will therefore be given here.

[1.2 Language and Its Levels]   Human language is a particular kind of sign system which bridges two areas of the nonlinguistic universe. One of them can be called the "nonlinguistic real or imagined world" (hereafter the "real world"), the things we talk about; and the other end of the bridge is connected to physical speech sounds, for example, noises that can be produced by human speech organs. This concept is graphically represented in Figure 1-1, where the serrated line signifies the link, rather unclear (in terms of present knowledge), between language and the nonlinguistic universe. The arrows show the directions of movement in the mechanism: the speaker starts with a selection of the real world and ends up with speech sounds, whereas the hearer perceives these sounds first and then goes the other way through the mechanism. In other words, language is a mechanism that connects meaning with sound. *This is one of the factors*

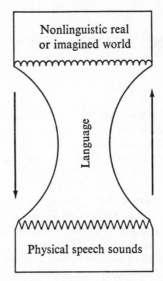

FIGURE 1-1. Language as a bridge between meaning and sound.

that make comparative linguistics possible. Figure 1-1 should be kept in mind throughout this book, because it diagrams the basic structure of language. But this graph shows only that language is a funnel with two wide ends connecting sounds with meaning and vice versa. In addition, it should be remembered that the speech sounds are actually as much a part of the same nonlinguistic universe as the things we talk about; after all, one can talk about speech sounds themselves even without being a linguist or a phonetician. Furthermore, linguists have found it useful and necessary to divide the monolithic funnel 'language' into various subsections. Taking these two facts into consideration we may now revise our graph as shown in Figure 1-2. Language is divided into three main subsystems: (1) *semology*, which is connected with all of the real world (through universal semantics); (2) a central section here called *grammar*, comprising morphology and syntax; and (3) *phonology*, which completes the bridge back into part of the real world, the speech sounds. Semology is linguistically organized semantics, semantics being the link between semology and the real world. The relation between phonology and phonetics is the same. Phonology is the linguistic counterpart of phonetics (Chapter 10). The arrows still indicate the two directions of travel within the mechanism. Further divisions can be made: it is, for example, quite common to distinguish at least two levels within the phonological part (i.e., morphophonemic and phonemic), both of which are intimately connected to the phonetic level. Usually one refers to all the levels above the speech sounds as abstract. The notion of abstractness, however, breaks down in the link between semology and semantics, because semantics is as concrete as the phonetic end of the system. Linguists are still not equipped to talk

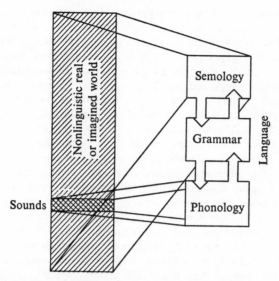

FIGURE 1-2. Figure 1-1 drawn in more detail. Experience is funneled into semology, and the speech sounds, which are part of this experience, into phonology. [Modified with permission from Wallace L. Chafe, "Phonetics, semantics, and language," *Language*, **38**, 335–344 (1962).]

about semantics, and the term 'abstract' has been used as a justification for ignorance. Positing separate subsystems does not imply clear-cut boundaries; they are still integrally connected with adjoining sections, as shown in Figure 1-2 by the interlocking arrows. Of all these levels, we know the phonological one best; this means that we know its changes best, too. The higher we go on the scale, the less definite our knowledge is, and the results of our historical work clearly reflect this defect in our knowledge.

[1.3 **Language and Its Units**]   Semology, grammar, and phonology all have units. Thus phonology is usually divided into the different degrees of abstraction corresponding to *phones, phonemes,* and *morphophonemes.* (The unit one chooses as the foundation of the historical treatment determines the nature of the changes themselves.) Traditionally the phoneme has been defined as a class of sounds in a given language that operate as one and to which the speakers react as one sound. The members of this class are allophones, which occur in mutually exclusive phonetic environments, and they share, in addition, at least one concrete phonetic feature (e.g., velar or labial, above and beyond shared negative features like [–vocalic]). Two different sounds contrast only if they occupy analogous positions in two different morphemes or words (Chapter 10). We shall see that for sound change (allo-)phones are of primary importance, and these are the sound units closest to phonetics.

Morphophonemes lead us to the buildup of grammatical units, which we may quite well call *morphemes*. Even though the morphemes *vine* and *fine* require two different initial phonemes, this opposition does not necessarily hold on the morphophonemic level (e.g., *wife/wive-s*). Such allomorphs, which are connected by regular alternations, belong to the same morpheme. These regular alternations define morphophonemes, and 'regular' means that there are at least two instances of each. Thus, for example, the alternation /ey ~ æ/ represents one morphophoneme in the following material: *sane/sanity*, *vain/vanity*, and *Spain/Spaniard* (see § 2.4). Allomorphs are not only held together by morphophonemes on the phonological side, but they are also linked to the same semantic unit; for example, the shapes *wife* and *wive-* are semantically the same. A very widespread view has been that morphemes are established solely on a semantic basis. Thus, curiously, the formal units are actually semantic; for example, *go* and *wen-*(t) are grouped together into one morpheme 'go', as are (ox)-*en* and (cat)-*s*, because both mean 'plural'. There is, however, no regular morphophonemic tie between the forms, and they should consequently not belong to the same morphemes, 'go' and 'plural'. In other words, different morphemes can represent the same semantic unit, and different semantic units can be represented by the same morpheme; for example, the entities 'third person singular', 'possessive', and 'plural' are all represented by the morpheme -*s* /s ~ z ~ iz/. Morphemes thus do not 'have' meanings, they represent them. The morpheme and *sememe* (unit of semology in language-specific semantics rather than in universal semantics) are independent units that are necessarily *linked* together in the *linguistic sign*. For example, we have *one* morpheme, *bluff*, and *two* meanings, 'trick' and 'precipice', and thus there are *two* linguistic signs: *bluff* 'trick' and *bluff* 'precipice'. Similarly, we have *one* morpheme -*s* and the *three* linguistic signs. Or, we can say, the *one* meaning 'plural' and the *two* forms -*s* and -*en* establish *two* linguistic signs, -*s* 'plural' and -*en* 'plural'. Because genetic linguistics depends on such a link between form and meaning, it will be based heavily on the linguistic-sign aspect of morphemes and sememes. No matter how the linguist establishes his units, he will have such units; and for our purposes, he will also have corresponding linguistic signs, because that is what language is—a connection between sound and meaning (Figures 1-1 and 1-2). This view is a minority opinion, because in actual practice most linguists refer to -*s* and -*en* as variants of the same morpheme. But the position adopted here will give the best foundation for treating linguistic change (see, in particular, Chapter 7). We shall have to return to the linguistic sign later, because it is of utmost importance; but before that we should look at the makeup of the units themselves.

[1.4 The Components of Units]   The units are "composed" of smaller components. In phonology these are called *distinctive features*; sound units (phones) are combinations of such features (e.g., *b* is an arrangement of *closure* (stoppedness), *labiality*, and *voice*: replacing the first feature by *friction*, we get *β*. Various schemes for handling distinctive features have been devised, either acoustic or articulatory. In this book, articulatory features will be used because they provide the most convenient common ground for philologists and linguists. Thus the vowels are defined by three parameters: tongue advancement and tongue height (both with continuous scales), and lip position (either rounded or unrounded). Height is normally subdivided into three levels; high, mid, and low (with at least two subdivisions each); and tongue advancement, into three categories: front, central, and back. Figure 1-3 tabulates the vowel scheme, with only the most frequent combinations of features represented. The unfilled boxes could be filled with symbols already used, distinguished by various diacritic marks. When we have to talk about such vowels, we may state the defining features (e.g., a central lower-high rounded vowel) and then use any convenient symbol for the situation at hand. Vowels also involve the activity of the vocal cords, but voiceless vowels have not been indicated here (they are better known as *h*-sounds; § 10.2). Similarly, murmured vowels have been omitted.

Lip position			Tongue advancement					
			Front		Central		Back	
			U	R	U	R	U	R
Tongue height	High	H	i	ü=y	ɨ		ï=ɯ	u
		L	ɪ	ʊ̈	ɪ			ʊ
	Mid	H	e	ö=ø	ə			o
		L	ε	ɔ̈=œ			ʌ	ɔ
	Low	H	æ=ä					
		L	a		ɑ		ɒ	

FIGURE 1-3. Basic vowel chart defined by three articulatory parameters.

[1.5] An articulatory classification of consonants can also be done on the basis of three elements: manner of articulation (including six possibilities, if flaps and trills are taken as vibrants), place of articulation (seven possibilities, apico-dental and apico-alveolar being separate, but combined in the table), and voicing (two possibilities). The most frequent combinations of features are given in Figure 1-4; again, the unfilled boxes may be labeled when the need arises. We have here a scheme that enables us to define most consonantal speech sounds. Semivowels have not been specified; normally one needs only two, *w* and *y*. The latter was included as a fronto-palatal voiced spirant, but often it can be equally well defined as a nonsyllabic high front unrounded vowel. This is exactly what 'semivowel' means. Similarly, *w* is a nonsyllabic high back rounded vowel, and it is a lesser degree of lip-rounding that separates it from *β*. For nasals and

Position (point) of articulation

Manner of articulation		Activity of vocal	Bilabial	Labio-Dental	Apical / Dental Alveolar	Frontal / Palatal	Dorsal / Velar	Faucal / Glottal
stop (closure)		voiceless	p		t		k	q = ʔ
stop (closure)		voiced	b		d		g	
affricate		voiceless	pɸ	pf	ts = c	tš = č	(kx)	
affricate		voiced			dz	dž = ǰ		
spirant = fricative	slit	voiceless	ɸ	f	θ = þ	ç	x	(h)
spirant = fricative	slit	voiced	ß	v	ð	y	γ	(ɦ)
spirant = fricative	groove	voiceless			s	š		
spirant = fricative	groove	voiced			z	ž		
nasal		voiced	m		n	ñ = ɲ	ŋ	
liquid — lateral	vibrant	voiced			l	ʎ = l'	L, ł = ʟ	
liquid — trill	vibrant	voiced			r		R	
flap		voiced			ᴅ = ɬ			
glide		voiced	w			y	w	

FIGURE 1-4. Basic consonant chart defined by three articulatory parameters. A row for glides is added to emphasize the frequent patterning of [y] and [w]. Note that both occur twice in the diagram. Note that [ɰ] will be used for the glottal stop and not for a back velar.

8

liquids the voiceless counterparts have not been written in, although they are by no means infrequent sounds in the languages of the world.

The two tables now *roughly* characterize the possibilities of all sounds made by human articulating organs. They map in more detail the part of the real world labeled 'sounds' in Figure 1-2. Any one language "chooses" only a small part of all the possible speech sounds defined or definable in the tables. And even if two languages use a *p*-sound, it does not mean that the *p*'s would be phonetically identical. The tables define cardinal points only, because the phonetic truth is that the sounds are indefinitely varied, even in the pronunciation of a single speaker, not to speak of different languages.

[1.6]   *Semantic components* are parallel to phonetic components. Whether there is one semantic unit (sememe) 'uncle', represented by the morpheme *uncle*, is doubtful; but in *uncle* there is at least a sum of the three components 'first ascending generation', 'first degree of collaterality', and 'male'. (These, at least, are sememes.) Thus the semantic makeup of *uncle* (or the composite 'uncle') is structurally quite similar to the phonetic makeup of *b*. In general, then, a certain configuration of semantic units or components is represented by a certain configuration of formal units (morphemes), which, themselves, are certain configurations of sound units, the latter, finally, being arrangements of distinctive features (phonetic components).

It was relatively easy to map the speech sounds, because all languages produce them in a relatively confined and clearly determined area. The same is not true of the total experience of the "real world" of Figure 1-2. Different cultures divide reality into different semological units, partly as a consequence of culturally relevant experience. There are semantic areas in which it is very difficult to decompose the semantic structure into its components, sememes. However, certain subsections of vocabulary have been very amenable to componential analysis, and we see basically the same structure as on the phonetic side. Consider the combinations of the meanings 'male', 'female', and 'young' with the generic meanings of animal species in Figure 1-5. We have here a striking similarity to the phonetic tables. All rows contain the same meaning, but the last three columns contain forms representing two meanings. The independence of form and meaning comes out very clearly indeed. The table shows that a perfect arrangement of *forms* breaks down here and there, in that the same form can represent two combinations (*goose, dog, cat*, and *man*). This is not surprising; we have seen the same situation before with completely unrelatable meanings (*bluff, -s*). The table shows farm animals predominantly, since gender differences are important in terms of cattle breeding. It is often difficult to discover a generic name, for example, for English *bull–cow–calf*. One could perhaps speak of a *bovine animal*; *cattle* will not do, however, as it may include other farm animals (sheep) and exclude calves and heifers. *Livestock*, on the other hand, covers all together. Outside the category of domesticated animals there is more of a one-to-one relation between form and meaning, for example, *tiger—he-tiger* (*male tiger*)—*tigress* (*she-tiger, female tiger*)—*tiger cub* (or *young tiger, baby tiger*),

Generic meaning and corresponding form	Generic meaning plus meanings		
	'male'	'female'	'young'
horse	stallion	mare	foal
sheep	ram	ewe	lamb
pig	boar	sow	piglet
goose	gander	goose	gosling
dog	(he-)dog	bitch	puppy
cat	tom-cat	(she-)cat	kitten
man	man	woman	child

FIGURE 1-5. A table of semantic combinations showing parallelism to Figures 1-3 and 1-4.

where *cub* again covers the young of certain mammals only. Languages differ greatly in the semantic combinations represented by one formal unit. This fact leads to various ethnocentric value judgments. One often reads in early treatments that in a certain "primitive" language there are different words for 'black cow', 'brown cow', and so on, but no generic word for 'cow' (Zulu). Similar situations are quoted for 'potato' in Aymara, 'snow' in Eskimo, and 'camel' in Arabic. 'Primitive' here really means 'different' (often it just refers to the nontechnological culture of the speakers using a certain language), since the link-up between the semantic and formal configurations is different. No language is primitive; they are all of the shape portrayed in Figure 1-2 (see § 22.5). English would also be "primitive," looked at from the point of view of the very languages that are branded that way. It does not have a single generic term for 'bovine animal' and what is "worse" by far, it has almost a hundred animal group names (not necessarily American or Modern English), restricted to one or a few species only. In addition to the rather general (but still not generic) *flock, herd, pack,* and so on, there are also *cast* (of hawks), *husk* (of hares), *fesnyng* (of ferrets), *gaggle* (of geese, on ground or water), *skein* (of geese, in the air), *shrewdness* (of apes), *skulk* (of foxes), *sleuth* (of bears), *wisp* (of snipe), and so on.

In general, a term whose extension is larger than that of another is *abstract*. In contrast, the latter term is *concrete*. Thus the notions 'abstract' and 'concrete' are relative notions.

[1.7]   The areas in which the arbitrary division of reality by a particular language first became extremely clear to scholars were the *color and kinship terms*. The physical facts are identical for all cultures, that is, the wavelengths of the spectrum and the biological relations of the ego in a population. But how these facts are segmented into relevant units within a particular culture is culture-specific, and this is then normally reflected in the language used by the culture.

Examples of these best-structured areas are provided in many introductory textbooks of linguistics. What is important to remember is the independence of form and meaning in any particular language and the different linguistic divisions and selections of the real world both within phonology and semology (Figure 1-2). English *p* and French *p* are different phonological selections from universal phonetics, and English *green* and Hopi 'green' are different semological segmentations of the universal color spectrum—not to speak of intralinguistic and interindividual variation: the chances are that your *green* is different from my *green* to some degree.

[1.8 Form, Meaning, and Classification] The particular nature of the link between form and meaning has been an important criterion for typological language classification. A language in which words contain one morpheme each and have a one-to-one correspondence between formal and semantic units is called *isolating*. If the words of a language are built up of a number of clearly segmentable morphemes, which again have a one-to-one correspondence between form and meaning, the language is *agglutinating*. When the relation between form and meaning is one-to-many, which is the general case, the language is *synthetic*. If words of a language represent an unusually high number of semantic units, the language is called *polysynthetic*. These again are cardinal points only, since there are no pure types (Chapter 16). They just show that different languages make the meaning-form link-up differently—but they all make it. This clearly shows, also, that meaning is basically independent of form (one-to-many relation). It is curious that this kind of typological classification was popular at a time when morphemes were defined semantically, that is, when linguists operated with the assumption of a one-to-one relation between form and meaning. Certain idioms, for example, *to kick the bucket*, 'to die', obviously invalidated the assumption of one-to-one relation, but they were somehow squeezed into the model anyway.

[1.9 Units and Rules] Linguists differ in the number of language levels or subsystems they posit, as well as in the number of units they assign to each level. The framework we have been characterizing here is only the common core of various conceptions of the particular shape of linguistic structure. We have referred to distinctive features, phones, phonemes, morphophonemes, morphs, morphemes, and sememes or semantic components. One must remember that the morpheme is not the only grammatical unit; there are others of different rank, where we also have various conglomerations of different size and rank (i.e., word, phrase, clause, and sentence). Each level has various rules (now often called transformations) for the combination of the units. These determine the types of constructions that occur or could occur. There are also rules that link the different levels with the adjoining ones. All these, taken together with the units, give us the sum total of language as represented in Figure 1-1.

But a linguist is a mechanic of language who tries to take the machinery apart: Figure 1-2 was a first crude step, which we followed by the establishment of units (both discussed earlier and mentioned here in connection with rules). Units without rules and rules without units cannot exist in language. Both are necessary, and consequently they cannot be hierarchically ordered; they are both equally important in the actual functioning of language. Both the units and the rules are subject to change, as we shall see, no matter what the linguist's predilections are in his assumptions about the structure of the language mechanism. But the way in which the change itself is described is, of course, dependent on the kinds of rules and units the linguist posited in the first place. Absolute change may be acknowledged differently by different linguists, therefore, because they may have disagreed on the starting point and on the exact details posited for the structure of language.

To emphasize how a change and its results can to a great degree depend on the structure we adopt as our framework, let us refer to two hypothetical examples. Let us assume that two linguists describe one and the same language, each according to his own principles. One arrives at a grammar that is a square, the other posits a circle; but both get a definite form (which is always the target of the linguist). The two grammars may be equally workable. Now comes a change that divides the grammar exactly in half. The square grammar gives either two triangles or two trapezoids of various shapes, whereas the round grammar always gives two half-circles. The impact of the change depended on the configuration on which the change operated.

For the second example, suppose that one linguist posits more units of a certain kind than another does. Say that we have two tables, one with four legs and the other with three. Both are recognizable as tables, exactly as two different grammars might be recognizable as grammars of the same language (as they should be, of course). Then a historical change removes one leg from both. The change is exactly the same in both tables, but the result is quite different indeed; again, the results depend on the structure of the starting point. (These metaphors can be translated into the grammars of different schools; see § 6.6.)

This brief characterization of language as a bridge between "reality" and speech sounds has proceeded from the more general toward the more detailed. But this is only a presentation of the findings of descriptive linguistics and in no way reflects the order in which the facts have been or should be discovered.

[1.10 Classification of Signs and Language]   Let us now look at a generally accepted definition of language:

A language is a system of arbitrary vocal symbols by which the members of a speech community (social group) cooperate and interact (communicate).

In other words, language is a system for communication. Language is *systematic* (rule-governed, nonrandom; it shows predictability) and *systemic*, which means that the total system is divided into subsystems (Figure 1-2). The definition includes the attribute *vocal* to emphasize sound over writing, which is a (historically) secondary representation of the primary speech. The remaining term, *arbitrary symbol,* brings us back to the linguistic sign and its importance for genetic linguistics. Only a full understanding of the notion 'linguistic sign' makes both change and reconstruction comprehensible and theoretically explainable.

A given entity is a *sign* of a given referent (thing meant) if it elicits at least some of the responses elicited by the referent, or as normally put, a sign stands for a thing. There are three types of signs:

1. An *icon* expresses mainly formal, factual similarity between the meaning and the meaning carrier; that is, there is physical resemblance between the shape of the sign and the referent. Thus a photo is an icon of what it represents. Also many sounds by which one tries to imitate the sounds of nature are highly iconic, because the simple qualities of the meaning are contained in the form (e.g., English *peep, thump, gulp,* and so on).
2. An *index* expresses mainly material relation (factual, existential contiguity) between meaning and form. It is based on psychological association and/or physical juxtaposition of different events and things. For example, the cause-and-effect relation is indexical; smoke is a sign of fire, or footsteps in snow are a sign of a walker. The index-like features of language include relational concepts of time and place, the deictic elements or shifters (e.g., *now, here, I,* and *this,* which all depend on other elements in the discourse).
3. A *symbol* is based on a learned conventional relation, ascribed contiguity, or colligation, between form and meaning. This relation is completely arbitrary, and this is exactly the basic characteristic of the linguistic sign (as especially stressed by de Saussure). All symbols are "arbitrary" in this way, and hence the term is superfluous in this context. Actually the term *arbitrary* is slightly misleading. We have already seen that, owing to the structure of language as a mechanism connecting sound to meaning, this link between the concept and the sound image is *necessary.* Saussure himself compared it to a sheet of paper: one side is the meaning, the other is the form. It is rather awkward to separate the two, for it is a very close symbiosis indeed. The mind does not seem to cherish empty forms or unnamed concepts, nor is it easy to talk about matters for which there are no words. Such situations require long circumlocutions. Thus the makeup of the linguistic sign is not arbitrary, but necessary. It reflects the same link between sound and meaning as the total language does.

What *is* arbitrary is that a particular sign be connected with a particular element of the "real world." *The connection itself is not arbitrary.* The connection between sound and meaning is necessary for a sign system like language. We do not and cannot deal with things in themselves; we must deal with signs pointing toward things. The necessity of the linguistic sign may be even biologically obligatory (§ 22.3), but the *shape* of the linguistic sign is arbitrary. The degree of arbitrariness that remains is crucial for much of genetic linguistics, especially comparative. This arbitrariness is *outside* the nucleus of the sign itself—it is in the outer shape and the semantic range, and it is clearly seen in looking at *different* languages. That is, it is arbitrary that different languages have such and such formal shapes for, say, the meaning 'horse' (e.g., English *horse*, German *Pferd*, Swedish *häst*, Finnish *hevonen*, French *cheval*, and so on). But when we look at linguistic signs in terms of *one* language, we can see that there is a tendency for a speaker to assume complete sameness between linguistic form and reality. The sign captures and controls reality; in fact, it *is* reality in the extreme case (*nomen est omen*, verbal magic, and so on). This is one source of conflict between the speaker (who has not been linguistically trained) and the linguist (who knows better) (see § 18.7). Later we shall see how the obligatory (nonarbitrary) aspect of the linguistic sign creates change (Part II) and how the arbitrary side makes reconstruction possible (Part III). But before that we have to go back to the other signs. (Cf. §§0.3-6)

[1.11]   The three types of signs (icons, indexes, and symbols) are only footholds in the hierarchy of signs. In this sense, they are just cardinal points, not unlike the cardinal vowels in the notation of the International Phonetic Association (IPA). Photos and animal cries are also heavily indexical in relation to the object and the source of the cry. The best signs are mixtures of all the ingredients, a situation that is often clearest in poetry, where a symbol with associative power (indexical) and sound symbolism (iconic) is very effective. It should be noted that 'sound symbolism' means exactly the opposite of the technical term 'symbol'. Onomatopoeic words, words that imitate nature sounds, are often naïvely thought to be completely iconic, that is, perfect replicas of the actual sounds they refer to. But that they are also symbolic is immediately evident in a comparison among different languages (third person singular endings separated from the root/stem):

	ENGLISH	GERMAN	FINNISH
the cow	moo-s	*muh-t*	*ammu-u*
the sheep	baa-s	*blök-t*	*määki-i*
the goat	bleat-s	*mecker-t*	*mäkättä-ä*
the pig	grunt-s	*grunz-t*	*röhki-i*
the cat	miaow-s	*miau-t*	*nauku-u*
the pigeon	coo-s	*gurr-t*	*kujerta-a*
the cock	crow-s	*kräh-t*	*kieku-u*

The cock goes *cock-a-doodle-doo* in English, *kikeriki* in German, and *coquerico* (or *cocorico*) in French, whereas in Finnish it always utters the well-formed sentence *kukko kiekuu*, 'the cock crows'. Many languages show velar stops for the word for 'cock', but it is quite clear that the animal cannot produce the same sounds that human speech organs can. The columns given are taken as very iconic within each of the three languages, and, in fact, they do agree among themselves considerably more than the rest of the respective vocabularies. The agreement is by no means perfect, however, a fact that immediately establishes the symbolic aspect of the terms. English and German are closely related languages, but they still differ. And it is only natural that Finnish diverges more, because its sound system is very dissimilar from Germanic. In some related material the agreement can be even greater; for example, the cat "says" *miau* in Finnish, even though the verb is *naukua*. On the other hand, English pigs go *oink*, the Finnish ones *röh* or *nöf*; the symbolic elements are still considerable.

[1.12] The same is true of *art*. Most art in most cultures is highly representative (except for music, perhaps), or what could be called nonabstract—in other words, very iconic—because the necessary physical resemblance between the referent and its formal marker (the signified and the signifier) exists. But art is also based on many conventions, depending on the time and place of its origin. In medieval art, for example, certain colors carry symbolic meaning. The representation of, say, perspective depends on various conventions. In short, for a full interpretation of a work of art one has to know certain conventions, and these are symbolic. In general, one could say that the more "stylized" art is, the more symbolic elements it contains. A "normal" piece of art is a symbolic icon, exactly like the onomatopoeic words in a language. In both cases the imitation of nature (the real world) is not perfect. Art gives the most concrete example of the range from iconic to symbolic representation. It shows the hierarchical character of the three basic types of signs—first, purely iconic relations between the picture and its topic, second, more abstract and stylized pictures, and, finally, completely conventional forms of decorations that still show definite meaning. But this meaning has to be specifically learned; it cannot be deduced from the physical shape of the picture. This level is, then, largely symbolic, exactly like the linguistic sign. The latter must also be learned, because the meaning and the form have to be connected by a special rule which holds for one particular case only. In Chapter 2 we shall see examples of this in the development of writing.

One area of (artistic) signs showing various degrees of symbolicity and iconicity is heraldry. It had its own rules in addition to the conventions of medieval art in general. A form of heraldry has survived in trademarks. Many companies have devised signs that blend all three sign elements, and if the mixture is successful, the trademark is very effective. A frequent form of design is one in which the initial letters of the name of a company are shaped so that together they form a picture of the product of the company, its main tools of manufacturing, or its raw materials (all these standing in indexical relation to the company). Thus the abbreviation *IP*, the registered trademark of the *International Paper Company*, is a kind of index of the total name (Figure 1-6). The shapes of the letters are completely symbolic in English; there is nothing intrinsic in the fact that *I* is /i/ and *P* /p/ and not vice versa. These two letters are written and arranged so that they form a very stylized picture of a tree. Thus two symbolic letters represent iconically a tree, which itself is an index of the company; the principles involved hold for the other cases in Figure 1-6.

International   Finnair   Southern California   Certina
Paper Company   Edison Company

FIGURE 1-6. Four company trademarks that blend iconic, indexical, and
symbolic elements. The arbitrary symbolic shapes of the letters stand in
indexical relation to the company name and form an iconic picture of an
index of the company that gives a symbol for the company. (*IP* = tree,
F = airplane, *SCE* = electric cord, and *C* twice = watchwork.) [Reproduced
by permission from the International Paper Company, Finnair, the Southern
California Edison Company, and Certina-Kurth Bros., Ltd., respectively.]

[1.13 Subdivision of Icons]   The word *icon* means literally 'picture'. The
discussion of artistic representation showed that there are different kinds of
pictures (as everybody knows); it is therefore necessary to divide icons into three
distinct subclasses: images, diagrams, and metaphors. *Images* are characterized
by a relation between form and meaning in which the former contains the simple
qualities of the latter; this is the kind of icon we were referring to above. *Diagrams* are characterized by a similarity between form and meaning that is
constituted solely by the relations of their parts (Chapter 5). And *metaphors*
embody the representative character of the form by exhibiting a parallelism in
the meaning (Chapter 7). Linguistics, like any other science, has to rely heavily
on both diagrams and metaphors. A diagram is predominantly an icon of relation, and to interpret such icons one needs conventions. Thus two rectangles or
circles of different size, used to show a quantitative comparison of steel or coffee
production in two countries, make up a diagram in that the relations in the form
correspond to the relations in the meaning. The symbolic (conventional) aspect
here is that one has to know that it is steel production we are comparing and
not, say, coffee. A diagram is a symbolic icon. As far as language is concerned,
such diagrammatic relations are its essence. Language is very frequently referred
to as a system (or network) of relations. Linguistic units are more important as
end points in various relations than as entities in themselves.
    In fact, we have already seen the usefulness of diagrammatic icons in this
background treatment. Figure 1-1 is a crude diagram of language, but it was
made more precise in Figure 1-2, which shows many relational aspects. It would
be impossible to draw an image of language, but it is quite feasible to have an
icon of the experience of the linguists. Such icons are often called models, and
they are important frames of research in all sciences. Parts of Figure 1-2 were
drawn as even more detailed diagrams (Figures 1-3–1-5). The purpose of these
phonetic and semantic tabular arrangements is precisely to show relationships;

for example, the relation of *d* to *ð* is the same as that of *g* to *y*, and *gander*:*gosling* as *ram*:*lamb*. Many more diagrams will be given later.

[1.14]   The relational character of language permeates all levels of grammar, but it has been recognized above all in morphology and syntax, where one has to deal with the distribution of symbols. In other words, such distributional elements are largely iconic (i.e., diagrammatic). This is a very important fact. Thus vocabulary is predominantly symbolic, and the rules of the language, iconic or diagrammatic (e.g., word order). The lexical tool is based on unmotivated arbitrary signs, the grammatical instrument on constructional rules. The diagrammatic relation between parts and wholes is often formally represented in this dichotomy of lexical and grammatical morphemes. They occupy fixed different positions within the word as a whole. Further, affixes, especially inflectional suffixes, generally differ from the other morphemes by a restricted and selected use of the sound units and their combinations. Thus, in English, the productive inflectional suffixes are represented by dental stops, dental spirants, and their combination in -*st*. Of the twenty-four obstruents of the Russian consonantal pattern, only four function in the inflectional suffixes. In morphology it is easy to find relational correlates between form and meaning. In Indo-European, the positive, comparative, and superlative degrees of adjectives show a gradual increase in length corresponding to the increase on the semantic side, for example, *high–higher–highest*, Latin *altus–altior–altissimus*. This is not a perfect universal, however, because there are also languages where this relation does not hold, for example, Finnish *korkea–korkeampi–korkein*; but even here the positive is the shortest one, and the inflected stems of the comparative and the superlatives are actually equal in length: *korkeampa-, korkeimpa-*. In German *hoch–höher–höchst* the comparative is the longest by syllable count, but the superlative is longest by sound count. On the whole this is how forms reflect a corresponding gradation in meaning, and this is parallel to the diagram of comparative steel production.

[1.15]   What we have seen here is that symbols need not be iconic, but that symbol complexes are arranged in iconic relations with object complexes (see also the trademark example). This situation is much better known in algebra, where every equation is a diagrammatic icon. In algebra one has to define certain symbols, but after that, the rules take care of the iconic arrangements. Iconicity is particularly clear in, say, analytic geometry. But remember that language is often referred to as a kind of algebra, and, in fact, linguistics has strived to develop algebraic notations to represent the relational aspects of a grammar. This approach has been very successful in the description of syntax, which can be almost totally represented with graphs. Thus we are able to separate the iconic (diagrammatic) forms from the conventional (symbolic) features of one and the same system.

Metaphors need not be discussed any further at this point. They are also relational, but rather than exhibiting mere part–whole relations, they concentrate on the similarity of function (e.g., the *foot of the mountain*, the *leg of a table*, and so on) (see Chapter 7).

[1.16] We have now characterized three basic types of signs as cardinal points in a hierarchy, further dividing the icons into three subtypes:

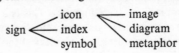

These notions will be basic to both change and reconstruction, as has been stressed already. Let us conclude this classification of signs with an observation by Charles S. Peirce, on whose work this characterization of signs is based. By referring the different kinds of signs to temporal aspects he stresses the creative power of language:

> An icon has such being as belongs to past experience. It exists only as an image in the mind. An index has the being of present experience. The being of a symbol consists in the real fact that something surely will be experienced if certain conditions be satisfied. Namely, it will influence the thought and conduct of its interpreter. Every word is a symbol. Every sentence is a symbol. Every book is a symbol. The value of a symbol is that it serves to make thought and conduct rational and enables us to predict the future. Whatever is truly general refers to the indefinite future, for the past contains only a certain collection of such cases that have occurred. The past is actual fact. But a general law cannot be fully realized. It is a potentiality; and its mode of being is *esse in futuro* (to be in the future)—(Jakobson 1965).

This quotation also delineates the two necessary aspects of historical linguistics, facts and general laws. Both are likely to be controversial in any particular case, but an understanding of signs makes the situation more comprehensible.

In *semiotics*, the study of signs and sign systems, one calls the relation of the signs to their referents *semantic*, that of signs to other signs in the code *syntactic*, and the relation of signs to their users *pragmatic*. Linguistics is but a part of semiotics (the dominating one), but it is clear that semantics has a correlate in language, syntactics has a linguistic counterpart in syntax, and pragmatics points to the social setting of language (e.g., sociolinguistics [Chapter 3], psycholinguistics, ethnolinguistics, and so on) (see § 21.2). (Also Chapters 0 and 23)

> *The discussion of the sign types (§§ 1.10–1.16) will give the basic background for the treatment of change (through Chapter 9). It is important to understand the nature of the sign types, for they provide the underlying, unifying factor in the various mechanisms of change and reconstruction (Part III and Chapters 18–20).*

[1.17   Change and Sign Types]   Genetic linguistics is a cover term for both historical and comparative linguistics because both deal with languages showing genetic affinity: historical linguistics treats linear relationships, and comparative linguistics treats collateral relationships. Historical linguistics treats change of various kinds; comparative linguistics sees through change as best it can and establishes earlier stages when much of the change had not yet taken place. In short, historical linguistics takes us downstream on the time axis, comparative linguistics upstream. The two types of genetic linguistics correlate with different types of the linguistic sign. Change occurs within one language and is thus largely independent of the changes in any other language (ignoring borrowing, of course). Within one language the linguistic sign is not arbitrary, but necessary, and assumes considerable iconic character.

We shall see that most change is due to the iconic features of a language (Part II). This is true both of phonological (Chapter 4) and analogical change (Chapter 5), just as semantic change is to a large degree based on the indexical contiguity of signs (Chapter 7). Reconstruction, on the other hand, rests solely on the symbolic side of language (Part III). Because the shape for a given meaning in any language is arbitrary, it follows that if two languages exhibit pervasive similarity in the *forms* that correspond to similar *semantic features* (diagrammatic relations in fact, but this time *between two languages*), then the link between form and meaning is one only; each language continues one and the same form–meaning set, with some alteration or other. In other words, *change, based on iconic relations, causes languages to resemble one another less and less* (Part II), whereas *the unmotivated, arbitrary nature of the linguistic sign maintains resemblances between related languages* (Part III)—resemblances that can often be unmistakably discerned even after sizable changes have taken place in the languages. These are the two diametrically opposed forces that operate on linguistic signs. These facts support the statement that only symbols enable us to predict the future. If icons and indexes point to past and present, respectively, their value for reconstruction is limited, because reconstruction occurs in the future relative to a past point of time. Since symbols are more enduring and directed toward the future, they give us the reverse perspective of "predicting" the past. The present is the future seen from the point of reference that we attempt to reconstruct. Of course, all linguistic signs are symbolic to some degree, and the more this is true, the more reliable they are for reconstruction. Thus iconic elements are the least valuable for comparative linguistics, however great their importance in other areas of language (language use, literature, and so on). In connection with the durative aspect of symbols, it is interesting to note that culture, also, depends on symbolic structure. Language, of course, is part of the total culture, and an important part (Chapter 21), since among other things it allows for division of labor. This fact is clearly based on symbolic behavior, which separates the sign from its referent in time and place. Systematic planning becomes possible. In contrast, most animal signs are indexical *ouch!*-type sounds, indicating that something is happening here and now. Culture is learned sign behavior, that is, symbolic, and it is learned from previous generations, exactly like language. Culture is man's primary adaptive mechanism, and it supports and shapes man's biological continuity (Chapter 21). But language, as a carrier of culture, itself has a biological basis, that is, man's species-specific capacity to speak and learn a language, as well as the biological presence and shape of the organs that produce speech as their by-product (Chapter 22). Thus the strong cohesion between culture and language, both of which are based on symbolic sign behavior, has connections in human evolution. To sum up, symbols make human language possible, language is an integral part of culture, and culture supports biological survival.

[1.18 Division of Linguistic Research] Linguistics is traditionally divided into three branches: descriptive, historical, and comparative (genetic linguistics is the cover term for the last two). The task of descriptive linguistics is to ascertain and formulate the structure of a language at a particular given time. Thus one can perfectly well write a descriptive grammar of Old English or Classical Latin. The term 'synchronic' is generally a synonym of descriptive, although it often includes, in addition, what might be called diatopic aspects: dialectology, sociolinguistics, and the like. Synchronic is the antonym of diachronic: no time sequences are taken into consideration, and the frame of reference covers an idealized single case or cut only. Diachronic is very much a synonym of historical, referring to the study of language as it persists through time. Comparative linguistics has two tasks: establishing the fact and degree of relationship for two or more languages (Chapter 16) and reconstructing earlier (prehistoric) stages, called protolanguages (Chapters 18–20). The first task can be done alone, but it must be settled before one can carry out actual reconstruction. One of the justifications of comparative linguistics has been that it gives a starting point from which one can deduce the histories of all the daughter languages.

Structural linguistics is not synonymous with descriptive linguistics. Structural is a point of view; it means a treatment in terms of the whole system, and its opposite is an atomistic, piecemeal treatment of parts without regard to the whole. 'Structural', to be sure, covers various conceptions of structure. Thus the generative–transformational approach adopts one kind of structure, better called the transformational one; other current theories are also generative. Also well-known structural frameworks are the Trager and Smith model; tagmemics; the Prague school, with its distinctive features both in phonology and semantics; stratificational grammar, which is an outgrowth of glossematics (the Copenhagen school); and the system-and-structure or scale-and-rank models adhered to mainly in England. A typical example of an atomistic historical treatment is plotting a Latin vowel with its modern outcome in, say, a French dialect, without any attention to the whole sound systems. In a structural approach, the whole network of the relations between the different sound units is the object of the historical linguist.

[1.19] A serious terminological difficulty has arisen from the fact that genetic linguistics has preempted the term 'comparative'. Any kind of comparison for any other purpose (e.g., translation, classification of languages by their structural characteristics, language teaching, language universals, and so on) has to be referred to by a different term (see §§ 21.14, 22.8). Sometimes the words 'typological' or 'contrastive' serve this purpose (nonhistorical comparison), but often they are not inclusive enough. The Greek counterpart to 'contrast' and 'comparison', *syncrisis*, has been proposed for this task. Others, in order to avoid confusion, use the compound 'historical-comparative' for the highly technical notion of 'comparative' in genetic linguistics.

[1.20]   Comparative linguistics has also often been called comparative philology, especially in England. The reason for this is that comparative linguistics was practiced mainly with regard to the older Indo-European languages, where philological screening of the material was a prerequisite (Chapter 17).

Means of getting at data

| Frame of reference | Either A or B or both prerequisite to C | | C |
	A Contact = field work	B Philology	Reconstruction
1 Synchrony (idealized single case, past or present)			
2 Diachrony (change through time and reconstruction, i.e., geneticism)			
3 Diatopicality (variation in space and social strata)			
4 Syncrisis (typological, contrastive, and generic aspects)			

FIGURE 1-7.   The frames of reference for linguistics. Shaded areas show that all are involved in genetic linguistics. Row 3 is an important basis or prerequisite of row 2. [Based on Dell Hymes, "Linguistics: the field," modified with permission of the Publisher from the *International encyclopedia of the social sciences* (David L. Sills, ed., 9, 358b © 1968 Crowell-Collier and Macmillan, Inc.)]

In the philological study of language the total cultural setting (customs, artifacts, social structure, and so on) is considered in connection with texts; linguistics is used in connection with various kinds of history, archaeology, geography, botany, folklore, numismatics, comparative religion, law, and the like. Linguistics, in principle, studies language for language's sake, but the total cultural setting has entered nonhistorical linguistics as well, in the form of sociolinguistics, anthropological linguistics, ethnolinguistics, and psycholinguistics (Chapter 21). These are in a way modern 'synchronic philologies', although the name philology is used only for a situation where an interpretation of texts is involved (e.g., 'classical philology' for antiquity and 'modern philology' for more recent texts). Closely connected with philology is literature, that is, language used as a medium of art; its subdivisions are stylistics, poetics, metrics, narration, oratory, rhetoric, and drama (see § 17.1).

Linguists can explore the approaches mentioned above (and even others, e.g., mathematical linguistics, lexicography, phonetic sciences, and semantics) in connection with different languages or language families, or within geographical areas, or in connection with semiotics, the science of signs. Thus an enormous number of possibilities are available for study, and no linguist masters all the combinations. Figure 1-7 sums up the different frames of reference of linguistic investigation and the different means of compiling the material. Again, these are cardinal points only; in the actual work everything is complementary. In genetic linguistics rows 2 (change) and 3 (variation) are the central ones, but the other areas also influence its course. One must also remember that each box of the diagram (Figure 1-7) raises questions of theory: what kind of features one should use, what kind of rules and units, whether the rules should be ordered and how, and so on. Such theoretical considerations have no parallel in the gathering of material (data), but they offer guidelines for handling the facts (we shall return to this shortly).

[1.21 History of Linguistics]   Historical linguistics should not be confused with history of linguistics. The only thing they have in common is that both involve change through time. Part of the confusion between the two derives from the early importance of historical linguistics, so that histories of linguistics have to deal heavily with it. By the nineteenth century, there were good descriptions of Latin, Greek, and Sanskrit available; historical linguists implicitly assumed that the structures of the other languages they worked with were adequately described, as indeed they basically were, since most scholars were native speakers of modern Indo-European languages. Crude analogizing from these well-established structures led to workable results in other, mainly Indo-European, languages; and up to the 1920s linguistics remained predominantly historical and Indo-European.

It has also been mentioned that any aspect of linguistics can be applied to any particular language or language family. But the early prominence of the study of Indo-European languages has led to another very widespread misconception—that historical linguistics can be equated with Indo-European linguistics. This is utterly wrong. The linguistic description of any language family is a sufficient condition and a prerequisite of genetic linguistics in that family.

[1.22 "Dead" Languages]   Another frequent misconception is that historical linguistics deals primarily with languages transmitted only through historical records, that is, the 'dead' languages. Such languages are traditionally, say,

Sumerian	Ancient Greek
Akkadian	Sanskrit
Hittite	Latin
Etruscan	Old English
Tocharian	Old Icelandic

It is clear that the languages in the two columns are not equally dead; those in the second one are still spoken in an altered form, whereas those in the first column are actually stone dead. A dead language is no longer spoken in any form; it has no speakers. This is only an accidental fact and is in itself not directly connected with historical linguistics. Of course, it has serious consequences in that our knowledge of such languages tends to be quite fragmentary, because no further fieldwork or checking is possible. Dead languages can be the object of descriptive linguistics, with the same limitations, of course. (All this was implied in Figure 1-7.)

[1.23 The Nature of Scientific Discourse, History, and Language]   The nature of *scientific discourse* displays two distinct parts: (1) factual statements about data, which rest on observation and which are either true or false, and (2) a hypothesis, a statement put forward in explanation of the facts. A fact is an empirically verifiable statement about phenomena in terms of a conceptual scheme; a fact is not an object in nature but a statement about nature. The hypothesis must be formulated so that it can be shown to be either inadequate or substantiated to a high degree of probability by further facts. A single contrary case may disprove the hypothesis, although it need not. The hypothesis must be based on the facts available, and the facts should not be made to fit the hypothesis. The problem is that even the establishment of facts can be highly controversial in genetic linguistics, as in any science. The facts of history are generally not perfectly clear. Eyewitnesses to such a "simple" event as a traffic accident can disagree substantially. Everybody is familiar with the tedious court procedure of establishing the facts. The same problem recurs in historical linguistics, where the evidence tends to be equally fragmentary. The facts and the explanatory truth are very elusive indeed. The linguists themselves determine the facts, as well as what they do to the facts, and they themselves decide what is significant about them. There is no universal truth given in advance. Significant statements about facts, the hypotheses, must rest on reality and not vice versa. However, the data considered to be relevant often depend on the aims and goals that the science has at any particular time, or the aims that some leading practitioners convince others to be primary. In other words, new theoretical breakthroughs require a reexamination and reinterpretation of facts. More fundamental for an empirical science like linguistics is that new facts require a revision in the theory, because a science must be able to cope with phenomena with scientific adequacy; that is, a theory must account for facts exhaustively, consistently, and economically. When the theory no longer satisfies these conditions, it must be recast. Thus a linguist, like any other scientist, works between the devil and the deep, between rationalistic hubris and empirical banality. There are periods in the history of science when one aspect carries the day: one can characterize the first half of this century as predominantly empirical, and the present time as heavily rationalistic. This kind of polar alternation is frequent in other areas of culture as well. Both ends of inquiry must be kept in mind. As for 'theory', one starts to speak of it when the fit between facts and hypothesis does not need an adjustment. The reader, however, should be careful of this word in linguistic literature, because it is used in a wide variety of meanings. In fortunate cases the context will specify its denotation.

[1.24]   Also *history*, if it is not written as a chronicle, a mere annalistic record of the past, shows the difficulties of combining facts with hypotheses. Subjective judgment necessarily creeps into the scholar's ordering and explanation of events. In other words, there can be no unbiased history. The reason is that, like theory, history is never directly observable; we never have all the evidence we should like to have. In general, relevant history tries to explain the interconnections of the events. Thus 'history', in the narrow sense, fits into the scheme as follows:

1	facts	chronicle
2	hypothesis	history

All historical sciences are very complicated and present extra procedural problems for the philosophy of science. General laws do not exist or, at least, are not within the range of our ability to observe; one has to work with individual events. One has to make the "right" selection of the documents, make statements about the facts yielded by this first step, and only then proceed to explanatory statements. Selection, interpretation, and historical criticism precede the ultimate explanation; by comparison, in natural sciences the ultimate explanation is connected almost directly to the facts. Further, the historical explanation contains at least three features that make it different from explanations in the natural sciences:

1. The lack of general laws makes induction impossible.
2. Experimentation cannot be used, because we deal with past individual phenomena (this is one of the main reasons for the relative indeterminacy of the historical sciences).

3. Historical explanation is almost always genetic; that is, a state of affairs *A* is explained by an earlier state *B*, which in turn is explained by a previous state *C*, and so on. (§9.2, Chapter 23)

Many of these problems recur in historical linguistics, of course, but fortunately there are also differences. As mentioned in connection with Figure 1-7, the four main frames of reference complement each other and thus lessen the problems inherent in pure historicity (row 2). For example, induction is the main characteristic of comparative linguistics (§ 10.6), which is often referred to as the most scientific branch of linguistics or of humanistic study in general (see § 18.17). This is because reconstructions have high predictive power; they can often be supported or even verified with further material (Part III). But on the whole, historical linguistics repeats the stages of the study of history. One cannot remain with the facts, but must strive step by step toward ultimate explanations. Here lie the real challenges for the human intelligence in science.

[1.25]   It has been said that genetic linguistics is actually an art rather than a doctrine of exact science. But all scientists must exhibit imagination and intellectual sensitivity as well as self-discipline and exactness in their work. Consequently, no two scientists are identical, and the outcome of their studies will differ accordingly. It should also be clear that the ability of different individuals to make historical inferences varies a great deal. Different individuals are simply not equal in any activity. Thus, of those who know the rules of chess, some are able to carry out the game markedly better than others, and only a few truly excel. The same obtains in the use of language. All speakers know much the same basic grammar, but some use language better than others. This is true not only of such areas as literature, but also, say, speech perception: in noisy situations, adverse to easy communication, some people understand better what is said than others.

As in anthropology, archaeology, paleontology, and the like, which also try to reconstruct the past, a successful worker in genetic linguistics must possess a flair for piecing together fragmentary bits of information. As in any other empirical science, we do have a body of exact procedures and guidelines, but this does not in itself ensure proper or correct application. The actual *practice* of genetic linguistics may seem like a special skill, an art; and it is perhaps more so than descriptive linguistics is because of its more lacunary material and other difficulties encountered in the study of history, as we saw above. But, by the same token, *some* degree of "art" is required in the successful practice of other sciences as well. The difference may still be very great, but it is one of degree only. (§13.9, Chapter 23)

It is universally agreed that regardless of the linguist's future area of specialization, his training should include the principles of genetic linguistics. He might never actively apply them, but they will deepen his understanding of language. Although everybody may not contribute to genetic linguistics, genetic linguistics contributes to every linguist. This book will provide basic concepts and principles; in their subsequent application the (student) linguist is on his own. Whether this study will lead to fascination or frustration depends on human factors outside our science proper.

[1.26 The Origin of Language]   A prime challenge for man has been speculation about the origin of a communication system like that in Figure 1-2. The topic has long been in disrepute, and once (1866) it was even prohibited in French learned societies, but in quite recent times it has been discussed anew by linguists together with anthropologists and evolutionary biologists (Chapters 21, 22). Although the area lies outside genetic linguistics, a brief paraphrase of the newest speculation illuminates some of the basic characteristics of human language as well as the independent bases of semantic and phonological change.

Animal communication, the transfer of information (a message) from one nervous system to another, occurs through various media and various channels (i.e., sound, sight, smell, taste, and touch). Although man receives and conveys information through all these channels, sound is the most essential for language. According to Hockett there are thirteen characteristic design features that are used in one kind of animal communication or another:

1. Possession of a vocal/auditory channel.
2. Broadcast transmission and directional reception, which enables the signal to travel a certain distance in all directions and be localized by binaural direction finding.
3. Rapid fading of the signal so that it does not clog the channels (unlike animal tracks or writing).
4. Interchangeability between sender and receiver; the sender can also receive what he sends and vice versa; that is, the user of the communication system is a speaker–hearer.
5. Total feedback of the message sent; the sender hears his own message.
   These five features characterize all mammal communication; the next three are peculiar to man and other primates.
6. Specialization in sending sound waves just for the purpose of communication, in contrast to sounds that animals emit in performing biological functions (e.g., the panting of a dog).
7. Semanticity, a relatively fixed association between the sound in the message and the situation in the real world.
8. Arbitrariness (noniconicity) of the association; we have discussed this before (§ 1.10).
   The rest of the design features are common to all human languages.
9. Discreteness, in that any two linguistic units selected at random are either 'the same' or 'different'. There is no intermediate grading. For example, the sound units have a fixed range. In English the initial sounds in *gap* and *cap* are sharply and functionally different from each other. There is nothing in between (e.g., no word *$\overset{c}{g}$ap 'a cap with gaps [holes]'). Gradience is only possible in paralinguistic features (e.g., different loudness of

shouting as an index of anger; gibbons are also said to possess this feature).

10. Displacement, in that the message is not tied to time and place, as we have seen in connection with symbols.
11. Productivity, the ability to produce and understand utterances which are novel, a feature often called creative.
12. Traditional transmission of the system from earlier to later generations. Only the *capacity* to learn language is biologically inherited (§ 21.3).
13. Duality of patterning. This last one is the most important single feature; for example, the thousands of words in any language are built up by arrangements of a relatively small number of sound units, which themselves do not mean anything.

Human language can now be defined by productivity, displacement, duality, arbitrariness, discreteness, interchangeability, complete feedback, specialization, rapid fading, and broadcast transmission and directional reception. These features make further achievements possible, for example, false or imaginary messages, or talking *about* speech, as we linguists do. Bees iconically convey messages of distance and direction, an example of displacement, but a dance about a bee dance is impossible.

[1.27] The hierarchical order of the above design features and man's biological characteristics point toward the primates as a source of information for the origin of language. Primates possess call systems, which contain some kind of holistic "calls" for a limited number of units of experience. Such units are, for example, 'threat, danger, desire for group contact', and the like; the corresponding holistic sound contours are describable as roars, barks, grunts, and so on. There is only one-to-one symbolization: a limited number of meanings corresponds to a limited number of sound units, each being monopolized by one meaning only. If one indicates meanings by capitals and sounds by lowercase, the signs are A/x, B/y, C/z . . . , and the primate call systems contain only from a half dozen to two dozen of them. Their use is very indexical (i.e., here and now); there seems to be no displacement.

The protoprimates or the protohominids must have had a call system of this kind. Thanks to environmental changes (i.e., living away from the trees) bipedal motion became possible. This, in turn, left the hands free for carrying, with enormous cultural consequences. At the same time, the articulatory apparatus was changing, because upright posture separated the glottis from the velum, making room for more flexible manipulation of speech organs. The expansion of human experience within the "real world" required more and more formal sound contours. One way to ease the pressure was to resort to composite calls (i.e., blends of the already existing calls). These composite parts would gradually get a special meaning of their own, and the initial stages of syntax (word order) would be in the making. The system was now on its way toward productivity. Hockett calls this stage "pre-language." Some change was already possible, and thereafter new blends might have increased in number. Speech perception was, by necessity, directed toward receiving the total calls, because the end parts of the calls could not be predicted by their beginnings. This system had to be learned by tradition, and thus required a firmer cultural setting. This is a mechanistic approach to the problem, even though it is quite clear that the mechanistic position cannot explain all of evolution (Chapter 22).

[1.28]   With the expansion of experience, further blending of utterances produced an ever-increasing stock of premorphemes, which had to be holistically different from one another in phonetic contour; the articulatory-acoustic space must therefore have become more densely packed. This probably led to a collapse of the system a number of times, but at least once it was rescued by the principle of duality. Morphemes were now identified by smaller sound units in varying arrangements (e.g., *tin* vs. *nit*). The one-to-one correspondence between sound and meaning was broken, and a true language came into being. An immediate result was that sound change became independent of semantic change. Two sound units could now merge without any effect on the semantic side. Semantic components may coalesce into new idioms and metaphors without any reflection on the phonological side. Or, if a contrast were blurred, the speakers could replace resulting ambiguity by paraphrase, or "analogy." The system finally had a safeguard against disorder resulting from change, which could now be accommodated easily (see § 22.5). All this must have taken tens of thousands of years, and duality may well have arisen once only.

But this is not the place to speculate further about details. Language evolved in intimate symbiosis with culture and biological continuity (§ 21.3), and we shall see later how the cultural aspect (i.e., man's social setting) directs its further change (see, in particular, Chapters 7, 9). In Chapter 2 we shall see how the development of writing followed this outline of the origin of language, with one difference: because language already had duality, it did not have to be invented anew for writing. In genetic linguistics we need not know more about the origin of language; we take the existence of language (of the type in Figure 1-2) for granted and study its changes or reconstruct its earlier stages (§ 22.5). With our normal linguistic methods we fall very short indeed of reaching the origin of language—by some hundreds of thousands of years, perhaps (see Part V).

[1.29]   The main defect in nineteenth-century speculation about the origin of language was a complete separation of culture and biology from language. The thinkers of the time assumed that a modern man had evolved without language, but within the structure of some kind of society. Thereafter, he proceeded to invent language, imitating nature sounds (the bow-wow theory), or laboring under physical stress in group work (the yo-he-ho theory), and so on. This line of thought, however, does not provide a satisfactory total framework, although it might hit the target in individual cases of later vocabulary creation. Considering the psychological unknowns of evolution, one has to admit that even the blending theory is, in a way, a modern bow-wow theory (Chapter 22).

REFERENCES

1.1 General introductions: Bloomfield 1933, Hockett 1958, Gleason 1961, R. Hall 1964, Robins 1964, Bolinger 1968, Lyons 1968, (ed.) 1970, O'Grady and Dobrovolsky (eds.) 1987; **1.2** Hockett 1961, Chafe 1962, Gleason 1964, Trnka 1964, Sgall 1964, Lamb 1966; **1.3** Ebeling 1962, Lamb 1966, Hammarström 1966, Trnka 1967 Krámský 1969, Sigurd 1970; **1.4-1.5** Phonetics in §1.1 and, e.g., Malmberg 1963a, Denes and Pinson 1963, Smalley 1963, Ladefoged 1982; **1.6-1.7** Hjelmslev 1963, Chafe 1962, Lamb 1964, 1966, Bendix 1966, Sørensen 1968, Lehrer 1969, Goodenough 1956, Lounsbury 1964, Fox 1967, Burling 1970, Chafe 1970; **1.10-1.15** Peirce 1955, Jakobson 1965, Andersen 1966, Shapiro 1969, Wescott 1971; **1.10** Saussure 1959, Benveniste 1939, Bolinger 1949, Valesio 1969, Lyons 1968, Zawadowski 1967, L. White (ed.) 1956, Ogden and Richards 1923, Fox 1970; **1.15** Chao 1968; **1.18-1.20** Hymes 1968a; **1.18** Hill (ed.) 1969, Lepschy 1970, Z. Harris 1951, Coseriu 1988, Blansitt (ed.) 1967, Cook 1969, Brend 1970, Vachek 1966, Hjelmslev 1963, Lamb 1966, Starosta 1969, Graur (ed.) 1.211-547, 2.715-1158; **1.21** Jespersen 1964, Bloomfield 1933, Ivić 1965, Robins 1967, Mounin 1967, Arens 1969, Graur (ed.) 2.227-342; **1.23** Beveridge 1950, Kaplan 1964; **1.24** Kirn 1963, Bocheński 1965, Kraft 1955, Robins 1967; **1.26** Hockett 1958, 1960, Hockett and Ascher 1964, Sebeok (ed.) 1968, 1968; **1.27** Chafe 1967; **1.29** Jespersen 1964.

Journals: Among the hundreds of journals that carry articles in genetic linguistics one should note the following: *Language* (Lg.), *Word, Lingua, Linguistics, Journal of Linguistics* (JL), *Glossa, Orbis, Die Sprache* (with its bibliography on Indo-European), *Norsk Tidsskrift for Sprogvidenskap* (NTS) [now *Nordic Journal of Linguistics*], *Indogermanische Forschungen* (IF), *Zeitschrift für vergleichende Sprachforschung* (KZ) [now *Historische Sprachwissenschaft* (HS)], *Zeitschrift für Mundartforschung, Kratylos*, not to mention journals in the various philologies (e.g., Romance, Germanic, Slavic, Semitic, Oriental, etc.). Numerous journals have been launched recently, e.g. *Forum Linguisticum* (1976-), *Sprachwissenschaft* (1976-), *Zeitschrift für Sprachwissenschaft* (1982-), and series like *The first* [2nd, etc.] *LACUS Forum* (1974-), or *Cahiers de l'Institut de Linguistique de Louvain* (CILL) (1972-). Purely historical content is found in *The Journal of Indo-European Studies* (1973-), *Historiographia Linguistica* (1974-), *Folia Linguistica Historica* (1980-), *Diachronica* (1984-), and *Journal of Historical Linguistics and Philology* (1984-). Sociolinguistic aspects come out in e.g. *Language in Society* (1972-) and *Language and Communication* (1981-). Particularly notable are semiotic journals, e.g. *Transactions of the Charles S. Peirce Society* (1965-), *Semiotica* (1969-), *Versus* (1972-), *Semiosis* (1976-), *Semiotic Scene* (1977-), *Kodikas/Code* (1979-), *Zeitschrift für Semiotik* (1979-), *Recherches Sémiotiques/Semiotic Inquiry* (1981-), and *American Journal of Semiotics* (1982-). A related strain of research is pragmatics, e.g. *Journal of Pragmatics* (1977-). Many of the series which already existed in 1972 continue strongly in the historical

30 BACKGROUND: GENETIC LINGUISTICS AND GENERAL LINGUISTICS

vein (e.g., *Innsbrucker Beiträge zur Sprachwissenschaft*), and new series with a large historical component have begun (e.g., *CILT*, the series in which this book now appears).

Other tools: Useful compilations are the *Linguistic Bibliography*, the *MLA Annual Linguistics Bibliography* (published by *General Linguistics*), and *The Analecta Linguistica* (published by the Hungarian Academy of Science). One should also note various encyclopedias, for example, the *International Encyclopedia of the Social Sciences* [Macmillan (Free Press), 1968], *Current Trends in Linguistics* (Sebeok, ed.), or other series, for example, the *Georgetown Monograph Series on Languages and Linguistics, Sammlung Göschen, Que sais-je?*, the *Bobbs-Merrill Reprint Series* and the *Proceedings* of the International Congresses of Linguists, e.g. Graur (ed.) 1969-70, and more recently Hattori et al. (eds.) 1983. Among dictionaries of linguistics one can note Crystal 1985, Nash 1968, Marouzeau 1961, Hofmann and Rubenbauer 1963, Knobloch 1961f., Axmanova 1966, and for rhetorical terms, Lanham 1969, and Lausberg 1967.

Many Festschriften contain a significant number of historical contributions, e.g. more recently those for Madison Beeler, Gordon Fairbanks, Jacek Fisiak, Marija Gimbutas, Henry Hoenigswald, Ernst Risch, Werner Winter, and Oswald Szemerényi; and some Gedenkschriften, e.g. in memory of Angus Cameron and Warren Cowgill. Similar collections abound (e.g. van Coetsem and Waugh (eds.) 1980; Rauch and Carr (eds.) 1983).

Because the bibliography is only a short selection, all works in the category of Paul 1920 and Wartburg 1969 are not listed. For practical reasons, many anthologies or collections will be mentioned under the editor's name only, in spite of the injustice to the actual authors. This practice is even more pronounced in the material added in 1988 due to stringent space limitations. A few items, particularly those which have been almost totally superseded by later research, have been deleted. The additions are just a meager selection from the ever-increasing literature.

Conferences: There are now regular conference series in many language families or geographic areas, etc. (cf. above), e.g. in English Historical Linguistics (Davenport et al. [eds.] 1983, for the second conference), or New Ways of Analyzing Variation (NWAVE) (D. Sankoff [ed.] 1986, for the twelfth conference). Important in this context are the International Conferences on Historical Linguistics (1973-); see 1. Anderson and Jones (eds.) 1974, 2. Christie (ed.) 1976, 3. Maher et al. (eds.) 1982, 4. Traugott et al. (eds.) 1980, 5. Ahlqvist (ed.) 1982, 6. Fisiak (ed.) 1985, 7. Giacalone Ramat et al. (eds.) 1987, and 8. Thomas Fraser (ed.) to appear. Jacek Fisiak has organized historical conferences in Poland and edited the results: 1978 (historical phonology), 1980 (historical morphology), 1984 (historical syntax), 1985 (historical semantics and historical word-formation), and to appear (historical dialectology).

Textbooks: A number of new textbooks have also appeared, including Arlotto (1972), L. Palmer (1972), Boretzky (1977), and Jeffers and Lehiste (1979); at more advanced levels Bynon (1977) and Hock (1986).

CHAPTER 2

WRITING AND LANGUAGE

The development of alphabetical writing is used to exemplify the sign types. Writing and its changes are presented as a microcosm of linguistic change and as support for reconstruction.

[2.1 Writing As a System of Signs and Its Connection to Language] Writing is a system of signs that represents language. The definition of language often specifically excludes writing, because it is a secondary representation of the primary speech. Furthermore, writing is a very recent innovation and is not a necessary accompaniment to language. But in societies that possess it, the influence of writing is all-penetrating and decisive. The often-heard term 'written language' is legitimate if one remembers its historically secondary status and takes it to mean 'language represented through writing'. It is here that laymen err most. The importance of writing in modern society has often led to the notion that only writing is true language, because it is normally used in connection with prestige dialects or norms, and because writing can often bypass phonology in such societies.

Grammatology, the study of writing, deals with the shapes and distributional regularities of graphic signs and tries to establish the exact link between these and the linguistic units they represent. This is particularly important when the languages are no longer spoken and we have to go by written records alone. Writing would seem to have five possible links with language, represented by double lines in Figure 2-1, which repeats Figure 1-2 in a slightly different form. The figure does not indicate a direct link between the two channels; in a way such a link does exist in sound spectrograms, which are pictures of acoustic "noise." But this is a very recent development in phonetics and can be left out of a discussion of typical writing. Pictures show a direct iconic relation of graphic representations to the real world, and this is why one often speaks of 'picture writing' (pictography, ideography). This is represented by link 1 in Figure 2-1. Picture writing, however, is not real writing but a form of artistic expression; it serves as the starting point of writing, exactly as leather is not a shoe but an important ingredient or prerequisite of shoes. Maps come closest to being genuine picture writing; but they cannot qualify as writing, because there is no direct connection with language. When artistic representation is stripped down to its bare essentials in order to transmit a communication, or when a picture is used for mnemonic purposes, we come closer to real writing, especially in the latter case (the former situation still closely follows the conventions of art). If

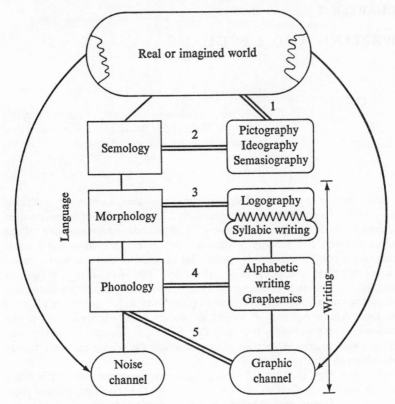

FIGURE 2-1. The relation between language and writing.

one wants to memorize or identify an object with a picture, one wants to retrieve the linguistic counterpart of the sign. The connection may be quite loose; for example, a picture with a tree and an ax might be read off as *the felling of a tree*, *to hit the tree with an ax, cutting wood*, and so on. In other words, the semantic experience is much more definite than the corresponding formal expression in language. This situation, if it exists, can appropriately be called *semasiography* (writing meanings), but it is still only a forerunner of writing, because the reader has so much leeway (as does the writer in encoding his messages, but to a lesser degree). Semasiography is roughly represented by link 2 of Figure 2-1. In practice, it is impossible to distinguish between ideography and semasiography, because the semological units in language are hard to identify. Only when the connection between the graphic sign and the linguistic unit is definite and constant do we have real writing. The graphic sign has to be connected with sound. If the sign holistically covers a sequence of sound units (e.g., a word), we have *logography* (which is often mistakenly called ideography). The important difference between link 2 and link 3 is the strict conventionalization of the picture and its reading. If the graphic sign represents a syllable, we have *syllabic writing*, and if individual sound-units, *alphabetic writing* (the study of which is often called *graphemics*), as represented by link 4. All the nonsemasiographic systems are called *phonographic*, because they represent the phonological side of the linguistic sign. The theoretically possible link 5 does not seem to be realizable: phonological units often co-occur in one (temporal) segment, whereas writing must convert this simultaneity into two-dimensional space. Thus special tactic conventions are necessary, and these must be handled in a separate graphic system (link 4, graphemics). In graphemics, the procedures are parallel to phonemics (§§ 10.1–10.5). An invariant grapheme may have positional allographs; for example, the Greek sigma, *Σ*, has lowercase variants *σ* and *s* (word-finally); and instead of the sequences *π–σ* and *κ–σ*, or *π–s* and *κ–s*, unit symbols *ψ* and *ξ* occur, respectively.

[2.2] Most writing systems include signs that are not phonographic; for example, in Europe, a star preceding a date means 'birth', and a cross, 'death'. The sign *1* is not peculiar to any given language, but can be read as *one, eins, yksi*, and so on. A writing system may have 'determinatives' that label abstract semantic or syntactic categories, as in Hittite: appropriate words are prefixed with signs meaning *god, wood, country, man's name, nation*, and the like; these are purely graphic and do not reflect any trait of the spoken language. In English, similarly, names are written with capital initials; in German, all nouns are; and so on. Many systems combine both logographic and alphabetic (or syllabic) elements. Thus English orthography is mostly alphabetic but is to some extent logographic, since the relation between sound and graphic symbol is not one-to-one; different ways of writing the same sound differentiate homophonous morphemes. For example, the diphthong /ay/ can be written (among other ways) *igh* and *iCe* (where *C* represents any consonant), and the letter *w* is not pronounced in an initial cluster with *r*. Possibilities of this kind are not used whimsically, but with specific linguistic signs: *right, rite, wright*, and *write*, all spell /rayt/. The alphabetic constant is *r-i-t*; the rest is determined by the particular word. The system is haphazard and accidental, being the result of etymological spelling, and does not represent any conscious effort to reduce ambiguity. Note that logographic writing represents words and morphemes, as the name implies; logograms are linguistic signs that embody both the formal morpheme and the semantic unit it represents. Basically, all four words (*right*, and so on) are the same morpheme /rayt/. In general, one can know when orthographic *i* represents /i/ as in *win*, and when it is /ay/; there are a few exceptions like *wind*, which is either /wind/ or /waynd/. Compared with other European orthographies, the English one is heavily logographic, although always on an alphabetic skeleton (e.g., *pane–pain, rain–rein–reign, bare–bear, cite–site–sight*, and so on). This system has definite advantages in communication, because it differentiates between homophones, and it accommodates easily great dialect diversity, but, of course, learning the system is a burden. In writing systems, where the logographic symbols are holistic (not built up from alphabetic parts), phonetic indicators are used to distinguish between morphemes. By way of illustration, let us assume that there were an English logographic writing system which used the picture of the sun for the morphemes *sun*, *day*, and *bright*. Pronunciation could now be specified with phonetic markers *n*, *i* and *t*, for example, SUN*n* 'sun', SUN*i* 'day', and SUN*t* 'bright'. In principle this is the system of Sumerian cuneiform writing, for example. It is more logographic than, but structurally similar to, the Modern English system. Both systems lie between morphology and phonology, if morphology is taken as a collection of words or linguistic signs. Real morphemic writing is seen when a logographic sign is transferred to other linguistic signs that use the same phonological shape, for example, when the picture of the sun (in our imaginary English) is not only the sign of *sun* but also of *son*, or when the picture of the eye represents both the noun *eye* and the pronoun *I*. Such signs write sequences of sounds rather than words or meanings.

[2.3]   There is, generally, no exact one-to-one correspondence between language and writing, as we have seen from *wind*, which represents two forms, and *write–right*, and so on, which represent one form. This is the general principle in English (e.g., /red/ = both *read* and *red*; and *read* both /riyd/ and /red/, and so on). This imperfect match between sound and graphic sign makes the changes in either one independent of each other, just as in the linguistic sign, the lack of one-to-one correspondence between sound and meaning makes sound change independent of semantic change. Thus a change in spelling (e.g., *through* > *thru*, or *night* > *nite*) does not necessarily reflect a change in pronunciation directly. (But, of course, such spelling changes are often made possible by pronunciation changes somewhere in the history of the language. Thus *write* and *right* faithfully record an Old English contrast between [wr] and [r], while *right* currently has a spirant [x] in some English dialects even though it was lost in Standard English in the fifteenth century.) In some cases there is no change in the spoken language at all, despite extensive orthographic changes. Thus when Turkish replaced its Arabic orthography with a Roman one, there was no change in the language; and when Norman scribes introduced new spelling practices for the writing of English—the many French loans of the period aided this process—the language remained the same (§ 8.9).

[2.4]   Alphabets can refer to different levels of phonology, that is, to phones, phonemes, or morphophonemes—in other words, to various segmental units. In Middle High German the syllable-final devoicing of stops was generally written as follows: *grap/grabes*, *lop/lobes*, *tac/tages*, *sic/siges*, *leit/leides*, or *zeigen/zeicte*, and so on (glosses below), although toward the end of the thirteenth century *g* replaces *c* [k] in these words. Thus the writing of these stops represents the phonetic/phonemic level. In Modern High German the nominatives are written *Grab* 'grave', *Lob* 'praise', *Tag* 'day', *Sieg* 'victory', *Leid* 'pain', and the past tense *zeigte* 'showed', although the pronunciation of the stops has not changed. The stops are now written morphophonemically; that is, morphophonemically voiced stops are always written with invariant symbols, because the voiceless variants can be predicted from their environments. The link between sound and writing has moved up the hierarchical scale; this is supplemented by the capital letters, which indicate the category 'noun', a category even more abstract than the morphophoneme. These orthographic customs do not reflect any change in the language itself.

In English, morphophonemic spelling generally arose from a different source: the orthography remained the same, whereas the language changed. The stressed vowels of pairs like *sane/sanity*, *divine/divinity*, and *serene/serenity* were once pronounced as well as written the same (see § 1.3). When the vowels changed, the orthography remained unchanged and thus became morphophonemic (that the vowels are contrastive, and not allophones, is proved by pairs like *vain:van*, *fine:fin*, *feed:fed*). The same outcome has two histories: in the German case, orthography was pulled up to a higher structural level; in the English case, the sound system dropped away from the orthography, which remained higher up in the hierarchy (see Figures 1-2, 2-1). (As in all other matters, English orthography is not quite consistent and has respelled a few items, for example, *vain/vanity* and *Spain/Spaniard*.)

[2.5 Writing As Evidence of Change and Variation]   Since writing mirrors language, however variously, it provides us with clear *evidence of linguistic change* in gross outline. Although the linguistic changes that occur in the lifetime of a single speaker remain largely unnoticed, written records from a longer period of time attract even a layman's attention to change. A sampling of English texts would yield the following specimens:

ANGLO-SAXON CHRONICLE (Tenth Century)

Se cyning het hie feohtan ongean Peohtas; and hie swa dydon, and sige hæfdon swa hwær swa hie comon. (The king ordered them to fight against the Picts; and they did so, and had victory wherever they came.)

ANONYMOUS SONG (Thirteenth Century)

Sumer is icumen in,
Lhude sing cuccu!
Groweth sed, and bloweth med,
And springeth the wude nu—
Sing cuccu!

SIR GAWAIN AND THE GREEN KNIGHT (Fourteenth Century)

Hir brest and hir bryȝt þrote bare displayed,
Schon schyrer þen snawe þat schedeȝ on hilleȝ (955–956) . . .
Þat noȝt watȝ bare of þat burde bot þe blake broȝes,

Þe tweyne yȝen and þe nase, þe naked lyppeȝ (961–962) . . .
A mensk lady on molde mon may hir calle,
for Gode!
Hir body watȝ schort and þik,
Hir buttokeȝ balȝ and brode,
More lykkerwys on to lyk
Watȝ þat scho hade on lode (964–969).

(Her breast and her bright throat, displayed bare, shone clearer than snow that falls [is shed] on hills . . . That nothing was bare of that lady but the black eyebrows, the two eyes and the nose, the naked lips . . . A worshipful lady on earth one may call her, by God. Her body was short and thick, her buttocks smoothly swelling and broad, more delicious to taste was what she had with her [on load].)

The selections show semantically "simple" basic material as in the description of body parts, in which vocabulary change occurs slowly. The readers may be familiar with the language of Chaucer, Shakespeare, or the King James Bible, for example. If not, they can easily verify change by consulting these early texts. In general the older a text is, the more foreign it looks; this, of course, shows that longer stretches of time can and do accommodate more changes.

[2.6]   The English situation is paralleled in all languages with written records over a substantial time span (e.g., Old High German to Modern German, Latin to Old French to Modern French, Ancient to Modern Greek, and so on). The inner consistencies within each time segment indicate that the language itself has changed and not just the writing, but it is the linguist's or the philologist's difficult task to establish the exact link (Figure 2-1). Occasional misspellings indicate clearly that language has changed. For example, a spelling *offen would indicate that the [t] in often had dropped. Similarly, if we found the verb write spelled *right, we would know that at that time initial [w-] and medial [-x-] were no longer in the language phonetically. This situation actually occurred when deleite was respelled delight, partly influenced by an imagined semantic connection with light. Such cases where orthography is modified against etymological justification are called inverse spellings. But writing not only provides visible proof of language changes, it also indicates linguistic variety. In modern societies, generally, a standard language is endorsed by strong central governments, and dialectal variation is suppressed, at least in writing. Formerly, there was much more flexibility; regional dialects were mostly accepted on a par, and different writers could use slightly different spellings (often influenced by their native dialects) within the same dialectal standard. These are matters that greatly complicate the study of the relation between sound and writing. Thus philologists must be able to handle writing in connection both with linguistic change and with linguistic variation, which implies the whole social setting of the time. As an example of dialectal variation let us look at the first four lines of Caedmon's

Hymn (from the eighth century) in the West Saxon version and the original Northumbrian:

WEST SAXON		NORTHUMBRIAN	
Nu we sculan herian	heofonrices	Nu scylun hergan	hefænricæs
Weard,		Uard,	
Metodes mihte	and his modgeþonc,	Metudæs mæcti	end his modgidanc,
weorc Wuldorfæder,	swa he	uere uuldurfadur,	sue he uundra
wundra gehwæs,		gihuæs,	
ece Dryhten,	ord onstealde.	eci Dryctin,	or astelidæ

(Now we shall praise the guardian of the kingdom of heaven, the might of the creator, and his intelligence, the work of the father of glory, as he, eternal lord, established the beginning of each of the wonders.) The situation is exactly the same in other languages (e.g., Old High German, Classical Greek, and so on), but the Old English example will suffice.

[2.7 The Development of Writing: From Iconicity and Indexicality to Symbolism] The selections from English in § 2.5 showed change in writing (and language). The origin of such an alphabetic system, unlike that of language, is well documented, because writing is a recent development and because its very purpose was, of course, the permanence of records. It is useful to review the history of writing in connection with the sign types treated in the first chapter (§§ 1.10–1.17), because the history of writing provides many parallels to linguistic change.

Writing started as iconic art, and whenever the artistic conventions prevailed, true writing did not develop. A reduction in iconicity led to semasiography, which represents the beginning of nonartistic conventionality (i.e., symbolism). At the same time, indexical relations played a prominent role. It is inconvenient to draw pictures of certain notions and thus some kind of contiguity or juxtaposition could be used. A picture of a weapon gave a ready symbol for the meaning and form '*to kill*', the picture of the sun could be used for words like *day* and *bright*, and so on. A frequent type of indexical transfer is that a characteristic part was used for the whole. Thus, for example, the Sumerian cuneiform signs for the words *man* and *woman* represent the pictures of the corresponding genitals, simplified in the form of roughly a stick and a triangle. The symbolic element of such signs is clear by comparison with our Western tradition, where the respective signs are drawn as figures with trousers and a skirt (of course this is outside normal writing). The different iconic shapes of the Sumerian and European symbols depend on the different indexical connections. The Sumerian sign for GAŠAN 'lady, mistress' represents an elaborate female hairdo and is thus closer in spirit to the European trousers–skirt convention. There is often, as here, considerable room for indexical relations; we saw this earlier in connection with the design of trademarks, whereby either the raw materials, the tools, or the end product could be chosen for the symbol (§ 1.12). These developments bring us to logographic signs, which combine iconic, indexical, and symbolic elements.

[2.8]   Pure logographic systems seem never to have existed. Even if indexical relations made the drawing of pictures possible for many items, there still remained words like *to be*, proper names, and the grammatical morphemes. What happened was that the graphic sign was used independently of meaning and started to represent form alone. This happened through homophones. Thus the Sumerian word *ti* 'arrow' was written with a picture of an arrow, but the same sign was used also for *ti* 'life'. In English the verb *be* could be written with the same symbol as the insect *bee*, and we have already seen another hypothetical example in English, *sun–son*. Now the symbol does not represent a word (linguistic sign), but a form, a morpheme. The step that produced this new relation is called the *rebus principle*, or the *principle of phonetization*. It is interesting to note that this step depends on an iconic relation between sound and its graphic symbol. Similarity or sameness on the phonic side establishes similarity or sameness also on the visual side. This is thus a diagrammatic relation, which underlies one of the most powerful forces of linguistic change, analogy (Chapter 5). Here, then, an iconic first stage produces a more conventionalized symbol, whose iconic elements may become totally obscure. Similarly, in language, when metaphors become fossilized, they become symbols without analyzable parts.

Once phonetization had taken place, semantically empty syllabic signs arose automatically, because many of the morphemes thus written would be monosyllabic, in fact heavily so in Sumerian (some 56 per cent of the vocabulary), Chinese, frequently also in Egyptian, and Hieroglyphic Hittite (Luwian). All these languages had syllabic signs in addition to logographic signs. Thus the so-called logographic writing systems are actually logosyllabic. A purely logographic writing system would be very unwieldy indeed, because each word would require its own symbol. One other way in which the pressure arising from the need for so many symbols was alleviated was the use of compound symbols (i.e., iconic arrangements of the existing symbols). For example, the symbol for Chinese *wŭ* 'military' combines the characters of *chĭh* 'to stop' and *kō* 'arms'. This is exactly what language does with its relatively limited number of morphemes, combining them into compounds, idioms, and other arrangements (e.g., *man of war*).

[2.9]   A word-syllabic writing system gives rise to a *pure syllabary* when the logographic signs are dropped. Thus the system loses most of its iconicity; but this is a cheap price, because the thousands of signs are reduced to a hundred or so. Such a number of symbols can easily be learned and used, and their shapes can be greatly simplified. All four logosyllabic systems, Sumerian (which may have influenced the creation of the others), Hittite, Chinese, and Egyptian, did develop syllabaries. This happened when foreigners took over the word-syllabic systems. They could more easily break traditions (see § 21.6), and the logographic signs were discarded as dead weight. Let us look at the development of the Egyptian system, which underlies all the European systems. The Egyptian syllabic signs did not indicate vowels, and in this form the syllabary was adopted by the West Semitic peoples. (The adoption was basically one of principle, because many of the symbols were newly created and did not continue the original Egyptian shapes.) In the West Semitic syllabary *b* was, in effect, a syllabic sign for *bi*, *be*, *ba*, *bo*, and *bu*. To indicate the vowel exactly, additional signs were sometimes used, e.g., *b-q* (*q* = aleph ', glottal stop) for $b^a q^a = ba$. The sign q^a does not stand for an independent syllable here; it just signals that the preceding sign is read *ba* rather than *bi*, *be*, *bo*, or *bu*. Similarly, the sign for y^i was used to secure a reading like $b^i y^i = bi$. This practice remained unsystematic, but it clearly shows a tendency toward vocalic writing.

[2.10]   When this system was passed on to the Greeks, they reinterpreted a sequence like *bq* the "logical" way. As the two signs stood for the sequence of two sounds, *ba*, it was reasonable to make the segmentation directly *b-a* rather than the original *ba(-a)*. The Semitic syllabic sign for a glottal stop plus vowel became thus the Greek letter *a*, and the Semitic sign for *bi*, *be*, and so on, was stripped of its vowels to give the Greek letter *b*. The *alphabet* was born. Now each letter represented a single sound segment, either a consonant or a vowel. Single symbols for a cluster of two consonants did exist (e.g., $\psi = ps$, exactly like Roman *x* = *ks*), as they still do in modern alphabets, but these are peripheral "aberrations." Only the Greeks are known to have developed an alphabet, and it has now spread all over the world, mainly through the Roman adaptation. (The impetus for the rise of the Korean system is not known; it may be original.) In more recent times, linguists have applied the alphabetic principle to develop universal phonetic notations, which are, of course, known to the readers of this text from introductory descriptive linguistics (a basic sketch has already been given in §§ 1.4–1.5). Suprasegmentals are the last phonological features to be accommodated by alphabets; their inclusion is mainly due to modern linguists, although there were antecedents in Greek Alexandria and India. For languages in which tone and pitch play an important phonological role, there is the additional possibility of writing the suprasegmentals to the exclusion of the segmental features. In a way, the drum and whistle 'speech' reported from West Africa and Mexico convey suprasegmental units only. But such systems are not instances of writing; rather they are parallel to radio broadcasting with a poor signal, which lets only parts of the sounds through.

[2.11]   Thus we have seen how a predominantly iconic visual representation underlies the *symbols of the alphabet*. When one turns the letter *A* upside down, it still shows the frame of the original picture of the head of an ox. Similarly, the horizontal strokes of the letter *F* continue the two horns of a snail; but all this can be known only through special study. As far as modern languages go, the alphabet is completely symbolic in its shapes. There is nothing inherent in the shape *H* which makes it especially suitable for the sound [h]. This is the value it has in the Roman tradition, although it is also used for indicating length (German *Lehm*), spirants (English *this, alphabet, shin*), affricates (English *chat*), or nonaffricates (Italian *che* [ke]). In Classical Greek *H* symbolizes [ε·], in Modern Greek [i], and in Russian [n]. Then again the sounds [h, e·, i, n] are written with completely different shapes in the Indic Devanāgarī, which also derives from Semitic sources. This clearly shows that the modern letters are symbols; but their arrangement within any particular language is iconic. Writing is a map of sounds or morphemes. Chartographic maps contain symbols that stand for woods, forests, bridges, swamps, mountains, houses, and so on; these symbols represent diagrammatically (iconically) the relations between these features, once we know the rules to read them off (e.g., where north is, and so on). Similarly, once we know the rules for interpreting letter sequences, we can read the relations between the sounds. Letter order represents the sequence of sounds iconically. This is like language, as we have seen, where the symbolic units are arranged iconically. It is interesting that alphabets use compound symbols (e.g., *sh, th*, and *ch*) exactly like logography or language in general.

The development from iconic to symbolic shapes can also be dictated, in part, by writing materials. Thus the use of clay tablets and the stylus transformed the iconic pictures of the earliest records into completely symbolic arrangements of dents. The Sumerian symbol for UMBIN 'wheel' is a stretch of some twenty impressions in the clay, having no similarity whatsoever to the original picture, although, of course, the large number of wedges still represents the spokes and the rim, in an unassembled or dismembered state, as it were. Similarly, the Germanic runes have no curved strokes, because they were incised in wood with a knife. In China the use of paper and brush resulted in graceful characters, and, in fact, calligraphy is an important aspect of Chinese writing. Again, there are parallels in language, where external influences also cause change—mainly in the form of borrowing, but also because of changes in the material culture.

[2.12 Writing of Writing]   Various communication needs have led to the use of tertiary symbols for the secondary symbols. Thus the Morse code symbolizes the graphic letters by means of sound or light (or even graphically through dots and dashes). The code is simply an alphabet of the alphabet; it does not represent sounds directly—just the letters, whose phonetic values depend on the particular language used and not on the code. The system of flag signs used in navies is structurally of the Morse type: it also represents the alphabet. An alphabet of an alphabet meant for tactile reception is Braille. Although stone inscriptions can also be read with fingers, the difference is that Braille symbolizes the letters, whereas inscriptions contain the letters directly. (Cuneiform impressions in clay were suitable for tactile reception by the blind, but their small size and the enormous number of different signs probably would make perception impossible through the fingertips, as would the cultural context: writing was the art of a few.) Shorthand systems can be based on the standard orthographies, but they can be geared directly to the pronunciation as well, or represent various compromises, like the English Pitman and Gregg systems.

Requirements of speed and space have led not only to shorthand systems, but also to abbreviations and acronyms. These, again, are developments where a part stands for the whole. In this century there has been a sharp increase in these, for example, *dorm(itory)*, *prof(essor)*, *exam(ination)*, *Gestapo* (*Geheime Staatspolizei*); *USA*, *NATO*, *USSR*. Originally such abbreviations occurred in writing only, and spread from there to speech. Now the practice is so popular that abbreviation can be carried out directly on the spoken forms. Normally initial parts are used; and this is an obligatory rule in making monograms. Thus a person called *Charles Wright* acknowledges a monogram *C.W.* This is based solely on the orthography, because in sound the names begin with [t], (t-š), and [r], respectively, exactly as in, say, *Tim Right*.

[2.13 The Influence of Writing on Language]   Nowadays the influence of abbreviations and acronyms on language is enormous. They give new forms that can be used as bases of derivation (e.g., Italian *le udine* 'members of the U.D.I.' [*Unione Donne Italiane*]); and when uppercase writing is given up, "normal" linguistic signs result (e.g., *radar* [*radio detecting and ranging*]). Thus here again indexical developments produce largely symbolic elements, which for only some speakers retain their indexical and iconic (linguistic context) features. The symbolic aspects are immediately apparent to foreigners who can read a language well enough but stall on acronyms; and even natives can no longer handle all of them, so special dictionaries have to be written.

The mere shape of the letters is the basis of many descriptive terms, for example, I- and L-beams of iron (cross section), A-frame houses, T-shirts, U-turns, and so on. The last one differs in principle from *U-Haul* or *IOU*, which represent a modern development of the rebus principle or phonetization. For the logo-syllabic system of writing this step was a necessity, whereas for modern English it is just facetious—although it does save writing space at the same time. Syllabic writing is exemplified by forms like *Bar-B-Q*. Writing has led to all kinds of "word" games, which are generally known under the name of logology. These have a long history under such notions as abracadabras, cabalisms, palindromes, anagrams, cryptograms, ciphers, word squares, crossword puzzles, and so on. Their influence at different times in different societies has been great, with corresponding effect on language and literature. We have already referred to the artistic potential of letters in connection with trademarks (§ 1.12); but artists, in general, and especially cartoonists, transform the shapes of letters freely to iconic shapes for particular needs; in addition, there is calligraphy. Interestingly, communication has produced not only shorter and faster forms for the letters, but also longer ones; the modern communication channels which created the Morse code have also necessitated more redundant symbols, the so-called 'pro-words': *Alfa, Bravo, Charlie*, and so on (see § 9.5). This phenomenon provides a further example of "reverse development" in the history of writing.

[2.14]   The above was a brief reminder of the rather extensive influence that writing exerts on language in various ways which are not obvious to the uninitiated. A better known case is *spelling pronunciation*. Orthography is more conservative than pronunciation (which, of course, is its raison d'être). Since sounds change independently from spelling, the fit between sounds and letters may become bad, or inadequate. Now, there are two possibilities for correcting the situation if things cannot stand as they are: either reform the spelling, or change the pronunciation. As we have already seen in the *right, rite, wright, write* example, English spelling has generally remained unchanged for a long time. Another instance of this is the loss of initial /k-/ before /n/ without spelling modification: *knife, know, knee*, and so on. (English orthography has not been altogether without change, of course; for example, Old English /h-/, lost before /r, n, l/, is no longer spelled: OE *hring, hnappian, hlūd* > *ring, nap, loud*.) Alternatively, we get a spelling pronunciation when the sound is adapted to conventional writing. Thus *often* lost its [t] before the eighteenth century, and British English seldom pronounces it. In America, however, the [t] is frequently reintroduced from the spelling: /ɔftən/. Similarly, the past tense of the verb *eat* is /et/ in Britain, having thus a poor fit with the spelling *ate*; in America the spelling pronunciation /eyt/ is the norm, which reestablished a perfect fit with the orthography (§ 5.3). Around the eighteenth century [dy] became [dž], thus *Indian* /indžən/, which is still heard among older people in certain social circles in England. This pronunciation was remodeled after the spelling back to /indiən/, and the affricated pronunciation acquired a new spelling, *Injun*, as well as a new connotation (see §§ 5.7–5.9, 7.9). On the other hand, a word like *soldier* continued with [dž]. A curious instance of spelling pronunciation is the reinterpretation of the sign þ (thorn) as *y*, and hence the spelling *Ye* for *þe* 'the' (§ 19.8) and the subsequent pronunciation /yiy/. Spelling, especially in learned vocabulary, has blocked or reversed many sound changes in English. Again, there is a linguistic counterpart to spelling pronunciations—hypercorrect forms (§§ 3.3, 5.3).

[2.15] The spelling of particular words can also be influenced by the spelling of other words. This is *spelling spelling*. Thus the "past" tenses of *shall* and *will* write the *l* which was once pronounced: *should, would*. The past tense of *can* has been influenced by these, being spelled *could* (compare *delight* § 2.6). Similar things happen in pronunciation, where words in particular semantic subsets influence each other (blends and contaminations). These kinds of changes have also been called analogical; the analogy may come from another language or an earlier stage of the same language. Thus the English word *island* never had an [s] in it; the Old English form was *īegland* (German *Eiland*, Swedish *Öland*). Similarly, Modern English *debt* comes from ME *det(te)*, which was borrowed from French without a [b] (and the French spelling is still *dette*). The prestige of Latin, however, was strong enough to modify the English spellings, making them more iconic with the Latin counterparts *insula* (which is altogether unrelated to English *island*) and *dēbitum*, decreasing the iconicity between the English sound and the corresponding spelling. In Latin, of course, the words did contain [s] and [b], respectively.

[2.16]   It is important to note that in all three cases mentioned—spelling reform or "pronunciation spelling" (§ 2.3), spelling pronunciation (§ 2.14), and "spelling spelling" (*could, debt* § 2.15)—the driving force is iconicity (for 'pronunciation pronunciation' see § 9.10). In the first two, it is the iconic relation between sound and letter. The letter is a symbol of a certain sound, and the iconic tendency would always have it as a symbol of the same sound. This drive toward *one-to-one correspondence between sound and letter* can result in changes at either end of the relationship. Spelling spelling transcends the relation between sound and writing, because it refers back to semantics or other linguistic signs, or to the wider social context of prestige dialects or languages. But such convergence is still iconic: functional counterparts become more similar on the formal (written) side, resulting in a better "fit." In spelling mistakes and inverse spellings we see clearly how the conventionality of writing tends to be broken in favor of iconic representation, and we get a spelling reform when the 'mistake' is accepted as the norm. 'Mistake' gives the point of view of tradition. On the linguistic side, every change is a mistake of this kind, although linguists avoid value judgments by speaking of 'innovations'. Such innovations generally "make sense"; that is, they are iconic.

[2.17   The Influence of Writing on Comparative Linguistics]   So far we have reviewed those aspects of writing that explain the principles of, or give parallels to, linguistic change. All these are important for people who decode or decipher writing systems whose fit to their languages is unknown. Classical philologists need these principles for epigraphy (the study of inscriptions), and more modern philologists for paleography (the study of medieval cursive alphabets). Before any written material can be used for linguistic purposes, philological screening has to establish its fit to the real language, as well as its fit to the real cultural situation, if semantic material is needed. Thus writing is often the substance from which material for historical and comparative linguistics is drawn, as contrasted with direct field work (Figure 1-7). But it is the manner in which texts were multiplied before the advent of the printing press that teaches comparative linguistics an important principle.

Before printing, texts had to be copied by hand from earlier copies. In antiquity, this was often a large-scale operation, with a number of slaves copying the same text from dictation. Single copying was later one of the characteristic activities of the medieval monasteries. It is easy to see how mistakes would creep in, because even today we are familiar with such hazards: a certain amount of hand copying still occurs in anybody's education. Different manuscripts of the same text are by no means equally valuable renderings of the original. Modern scholarship has established a set of principles for determining the most faithful copy. If a number of manuscripts display the same unusual mistake or peculiar omissions, one should assume that the mistakes were faithfully copied from the same original copy. In other words, rather than assume that the same aberrant mistake had occurred many times independently, one assumes that it had occurred only *once*. Thus one can establish the hierarchy of existing manuscripts and their succession of copying, called the tradition (i.e., handing down) of the text. This activity belongs to textual criticism. One of its famous principles is that the more difficult reading (*lectio difficilior*) establishes the direction of copying: when two texts differ on a certain point, the one that is more complicated or obscure, thus providing motivation for a simplifying mistake, is taken as the original; mistakes usually simplify complexities, rather than introduce them.

[2.18]   Thus manuscripts can be grouped into family trees showing daughter and sister relations. Three manuscripts can show five different relationships (shown in Figure 2-2). The missing links have been labeled with asterisks. In principle, the situation is the same for a greater number of manuscripts, although then the bifurcations look more complicated, and in actual practice more work will be involved.

In Figure 2-2 we see the model which was also useful for drawing family trees for language families and which influenced and reinforced the Darwinian theory of the origin of species (Chapters 15, 22). In language, the counterpart of the mistake in textual criticism is a linguistic change, an innovation, which corresponds in turn to mutation in evolutionary biology. Language and biology seem to be parallel, in that small shifts can ultimately lead to great differences. Newest results from both fields reveal extensive structural parallels between linguistic and biological change; the danger of making false comparisons lies only in loose terminology, or in taking the terms of such comparisons too literally (Chapter 22).

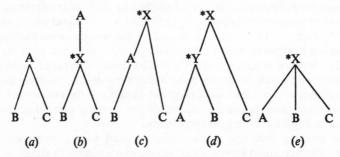

FIGURE 2-2.   Five possible derivation trees showing the copying relationship between three attested manuscripts A, B, and C.

Thus we have seen that writing does not only affect language, but that a study of textual traditions has provided a useful model for comparative linguistics.

[2.19 The Importance of Writing for Genetic Linguistics]   Without writing, society as we know it today would be quite impossible. Its role in the development of the city culture from the ancient Near East through the Industrial Revolution up to the conquest of the moon is enormous. In more recent times its tasks have been eased by electronic recording devices, but its importance will hardly diminish. This is an area peripheral to the central issues of historical and comparative linguistics, however, and, consequently, we must leave it at this juncture to anthropologists and culture historians in general. Still, there remain two important contributions of writing to genetic linguistics: writing shows how iconicity and indexicality create change, and it extends our observations on language change into the past by a few thousand years.

The first aspect of the importance of writing has been emphasized throughout this chapter. Writing and the development of the writing systems are a microcosm of language change. The development of pictographs into alphabets shows the same trend as the origin of language (i.e., from bigger holistic units to an arrangement of smaller units). The chapter provided further exemplification of the different sign types and showed that iconic and indexical relations create, change, and reorganize symbolic units, and that symbolic elements are not directly responsible for change. Such notions will be important in the remainder of the book, even though linguistic parallels were only briefly referred to here.

Although writing has been used during just a fraction of the history of language, it provides so much antiquarian information that it is difficult to imagine genetic linguistics without the support of written records. Sumerian writing started around 3100 B.C., Egyptian perhaps a century later. Around the middle of the second millennium B.C., there was an upsurge of writing systems in the Near East, as well as the appearance of the Chinese system. The Phoenician syllabary is rather late, only about 1000 B.C., and a century later it gave rise to the Greek alphabet and Aramaic writing, which was to serve as the source of the writing systems of India, Iran, the Caucasus, and Arabia. Roman writing begins about 600 B.C., and the rest of Europe follows much later indeed. This is not long, compared with the 100,000–500,000 years man is assumed to have had language (or maybe even from one to fifteen million years). Writing is not necessary to the practice of genetic linguistics, but because the methods have proved to be valid in cases where we do have written records, we can often check the reliability of our methods. The investigation of three language families —in particular, Indo-European, Semitic, and Chinese—has profited from the availability of very early written records. The first two, especially, have shaped the development of genetic linguistics. It is no wonder that they still hold a prestigious position among the achievements of genetic linguistics.

Recorded linguistic changes must number in the thousands, providing us with valuable material for making statements about universal change. Later we shall apply the comparative method without any regard to earlier stages of the languages used (Chapter 11). We can then check the results of the method. This will teach us about the reliability of the methods even in cases where we cannot check the results. Usually the value of written records comes out most clearly when we do not have them; this is the case with most of the languages of the world. Records only a hundred years old usually contain very valuable information about change, or they may confirm inferences independently made.

REFERENCES

General: Pulgram 1951, 1965, Gelb 1963, Diringer 1968, M. Cohen 1958, Jensen 1969 -- Barber 1974, Gaur 1984, Sampson 1985, R. Harris 1986; **2.2** Venezky 1970; **2.5** Frey 1966; **2.7** Wescott 1971; **2.8** Chao 1968; **2.10** Th. Stern 1957; **2.12-2.13** Malkiel 1968; *2.17-2.81* Maas 1958, Dearing 1959, Hoenigswald 1960a, 1966, Stevick 1963.

CHAPTER 3

LINGUISTIC VARIATION

An understanding of regional and social variation of speech is necessary for the study of linguistic change (Figure 1-7, row 3).

[3.1 Ubiquitousness of Variation—Basis of Change] Any speech community shows that idealized, single, static, synchronic grammar (Figure 1-7, row 1) is unreal. Its relation to the actual situation is like that of a fossil to a living specimen. There is no language without variation, and this is true of nature in general: no two natural items are exactly alike. Such variation does not always attract our attention, but it has its uses; this is the principle that makes fingerprinting possible for identification purposes. Linguists always stress the point that no speaker pronounces the same sound twice in exactly the same way. If this is true of one speaker, there is even more variation between two speakers, and so on, until we reach the whole language, or even a language family. But in this sea of infinite variability, some variations are rule-governed, specifically by socially shared rules. And variation does not manifest itself only in sound, but in all areas of language. Any study of language variation belongs to dialectology, which falls into two distinct parts: dialect geography and social variation (Figure 1-7, row 3). The latter is the central target of sociolinguistics, which studies the covariance of linguistic structure with social structure. But a brief summary of both is necessary for genetic linguistics, because dialect geography is particularly important for comparative linguistics, just as social variation is for historical linguistics. Once more, the two sides of genetic linguistics correlate with similar polar concepts in an adjoining sphere of linguistic inquiry. Dialect geography will be treated later (Chapter 14), but social variation must be included in the background as a necessary prerequisite for understanding change. (In a situation where each branch of linguistics ties in with the others [Figure 1-7], one runs into an organizational problem, because presentation must be linear. Thus the fact that certain topics must be presented in two contexts is not fragmentation, but a sign of the unity of linguistics, where fields intersect in wide configurations.)

[3.2 Synchronic Dialect Correspondence] Meillet characterizes a dialect as diversity in unity and unity in diversity. There is no way of telling when a "dialect" ends and a "language" begins, and often an exact boundary between two dialects is equally evasive; but the notion of dialectal variation is quite familiar and useful. The sound *system* of two dialects can be identical even though the actual manifestations are utterly different (see § 3.5). Thus all the dialects of English share more or less the same underlying system, although their surface variety is immense. In American English alone the vowel of *grass* can be [ɛə, æə, æɪ, æ, a, aə], not to speak of English on other continents. Such differences do not impede communication at all, because people who come into contact with any of these variants learn the proper correspondences; for example, my [æə] corresponds to *X*'s [ɛə] and *Y*'s [aə]. *Every* speaker builds such correspondences into his grammar, depending on the dialects he hears, since he is more likely to go on speaking his own variant (e.g., [æə]) than to adopt the variants of each interlocutor. (Often there is no *noticeable* difference between two dialects, although, in fact, there must be.) For a striking example, let us look at a few items from the so-called "Fox dialect" (spoken in the community of Fox, north of Red Lodge, Montana) in juxtaposition with "General American" forms. Keeping the notation of the published report (even though it looks very odd to professional linguists), we can emphasize those correspondences that show differences between the dialects by boxing them in:

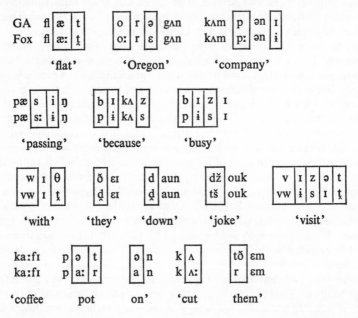

The speakers in and around that locality know these correspondences, although they are likely to speak one dialect only. The Fox dialect, extreme as it is, is a derivative of General American in the sense that it can be mapped from General American with a few rules: lengthening in certain environments, devoicing, the merger of the dental slit spirants with dental stops, merging [v] and [w] in one sound transcribed [vw], and so on. Merger—the situation where two or more contrastive features of one dialect correspond to a single feature of another—

is well known from those Southern dialects where *pen* and *pin* have the same vowel. In contact with this dialect and with others, speakers learn the proper correspondences *e–i*, and *i–i*. The real sound substance of an actual grammar are these interdialectal sets of correspondences (diaphone[me]s, see § 14.3) and not the segments in the speech of one speaker only (§§ 13.7, 13.8). Nobody speaks only with himself; at the very outset—in the language learning process—one needs other speakers.

[3.3]   The examples have so far referred to regional variation. But any speech community displays systematic variation on other scales—social layer (occupation, ethnic background, and so on), age, sex, and social context. The last is known as 'style', or more technically as 'register'. Most speech communities have at least three varieties: the normal conversational, plus something above it (formal) and below it (substandard, slang). All these factors are systematically incorporated into the speaker's use of the language, and thus should be spelled out in our grammatical descriptions. Practically no descriptions satisfy this requirement. Of course, the notation and the amount of work necessary create immediate practical problems. Figure 3-1 correlates the pronunciation of [θ] in

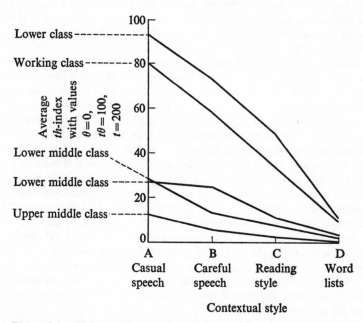

FIGURE 3-1.   Class stratification diagram for *th* in New York City. [Reprinted with modification from William Labov, "Phonological correlates of social stratification," *American Anthropologist*, **66**: 6, pt. 2, 169 (1964) (© American Anthropological Association).]

New York City (where it alternates with an affricate [tθ] and a lenis (unaspirated) stop [t]) with different social strata in different contexts. The upper middle class is closest to having spirantal pronunciation (the prestige form) in every style. The lower middle class comprises two groups: those who are able to shift considerably toward uniform spirantal pronunciation in careful speech and those who cannot. The lower working classes are clearly distinct from these by using fewer purely spirantal pronunciations. But within each class pure spirantal pronunciation increases with greater formalization of style and context. The same kind of orderly variation can exist between sexes and age groups.

Pronunciation/language is one of the strongest social indicators; it tells about the speaker's occupation, income, education, and social attitudes and aspirations. Speakers who want to climb the social ladder must know quite well the sets of correspondences that obtain between their speech and that of the prestigious class. Hypercorrect forms clearly show that speakers are using correspondences rather than individually learned items (e.g., in the case of the little girl who moved from an r-dialect into an r-less one, where her playmates said [ya·d] instead of [ya·rd]. She overdid this relation when she reported to her parents about a giant she had heard about called [ga·rd]. The prestige factor is, of course, rather special here, as the girl tried to use the parents' norm when talking to them; but it is prestige, nevertheless). One single rule handles the correspondences automatically only when there is a two-way bidirectional mapping relation between the dialects, as between the [t] of the lower class and the [θ] of the middle class in New York City. Once this relation is learned, no mistakes arise. But when there is a one-way mapping relation into a dialect with fewer contrasts, speakers at the "impoverished" end have to learn every item separately. Thus a Fox speaker learns that his [ṭ, ḍ, vw, tš] each take part in two correspondences, with [t, θ; d, ð; v, w; tš, dž], respectively; and an r-less speaker finds out that his [ga·d] corresponds to both [ga·d] and [ga·rd]. This operation—the matching of corresponding segments between two formal varieties of the same meaning—is known as the comparative method. This method enables one to discover the single sound system underlying the variations that show diagrammatic relations of sounds against the same semantic background. In General American and Fox, for example, the meanings 'because' and 'busy' show the correspondence b–p for the first consonant and z–s for the last consonant. The comparative method will be treated later; the notion of the correspondence is introduced here because it is a relevant concept in a multidialectal synchronic grammar, which is the general kind of grammar for any speaker (§§ 8.16f., 11.2). Throughout the remainder of the text, two conventions of writing the sets of correspondences will be used: horizontally, as b–p, or vertically, in a boxed-in cartouche as above. The former saves space, but the latter brings out maximal clarity for analysis.

[3.4]   Variation exists not only in sounds, but also in *morphology and syntax*. One of the most obvious features of slang or occupational jargons is of course a special vocabulary. In some languages women use special vocabularies among themselves in addition to special phonologies, and this has led to reports that they can have a special language altogether; although this is doubtful, it shows the extent of the differences. But in any language, women, at the very least, would use certain items more often than men (e.g., *terribly beautiful*). Nursery words are an exceptionally clear instance of the differences in age gradation. Variation in morphology exists on exactly the same scale as the sounds. The items can be completely unrelated, like *pail* vs. *bucket*, or can have some formal relationship, as in I *saw* it vs. I *seen* it. Differences, of course, reach syntax also, such as *I haven't got any money* vs. *I ain't got no money*. This is a general situation; for example, in Brahmin Tulu the negative tenses of the verb distinguish between gender, number, and person, whereas non-Brahmin Tulu lacks all this in its negative forms. But we have to leave the matter with these brief hints.

[3.5]   Often variation appears to be more significant than it really is. Non-standard Negro English has traditionally been heavily stigmatized, even to the point of declaring that it is not language at all. Superficially, the differences from General American are large: [bol] 'bold', [fayn] 'find', [æk] 'act', [fɪs] 'fist' show phonological variation, with morphological consequences in forms like [pæs] 'pass; passed; past'. Syntactic variation includes things like [hi wayl] 'he is wild'. But the relation between General American and Negro English is as orderly as among the dialects mentioned previously. The Negro English forms mentioned here can be derived from the Standard English ones with rules that apply in definite environments. The difference from the Fox situation is that the rules here obey statistical laws (see § 9.8); there are no speakers who always apply these rules, and none who never applies them. Some rules would escape casual analysis; for example, in general, wherever Standard English can contract the copula (*He's wild*), Negro English can delete it (*He wild*), and wherever Standard English cannot contract, Negro English cannot delete (as in the last word of *That's what he is*). Dialects are apt to differ chiefly in low-level rules, and superficial differences tend to be greater than those found in their deep structures, if there are any. On the other hand, it seems that some features of Negro English are not derivable by one-way mapping from Standard English (e.g., *he done told me, he be sleeping*, which involve aspectual contrasts absent in Standard English).

[3.6]   Differences in *semantic orientation* which correspond to different social strata are not always easily observable, but from India, where the caste distinctions are rather fixed, we have striking examples. Thus in Tamil, the Brahmins and the non-Brahmins divide the area of male affinal kin as in Figure 3-2:A. Sometimes one dialect shows different connotations for items that are in free variation in the other (Figure 3-2:B). In other words, regular systematic variation correlated with facts outside the linguistic system itself exist in every level of grammar. Linguists cannot explain linguistic events by linguistic events alone but must look into the total social network in which the language is used.

	Brahmin	Non-Brahmin
A. son-in-law	maaple	marumahã
younger sister's husband		
elder sister's husband	attimbeer	maccãã
wife's brother	maccinã	

B. food (neutral)	saadõ	sooru ~ saadõ 'food'
[food (pejorative)]	sooru	
eat (neutral)	saapḍu	tinnu ~ saapḍu 'eat'
[eat (pejorative)]	tinnu	

FIGURE 3-2.   Different semantic segmentation in two areas in the dialects of Iyengar (Brahmin) and Mudaliyar (non-Brahmin) of Tamil. [Reprinted with modification from A. K. Ramanujan, "The structure of variation: a study in caste dialect" (Milton Singer and Bernard S. Cohn, editors), *Structure and change in Indian society* (Chicago: Aldine Publishing Company, 1968); © 1968 by Wenner-Gren Foundation for Anthropological Research, Inc.]

We have returned to the semiotic situation, especially its pragmatic side (§ 1.16). Sociolinguists now hold that speech should be studied in terms of the whole speech community, and that the object of such study is a sociolinguistic system, not mere language.

If the variations in different social contexts in the speech of the same speakers are related, but very different, one speaks of *diglossia*; if the context requires the use of distinct languages by the same speakers, the situation is known as *bilingualism*.

[3.7 Variety, Change, and Reconstruction]   We seem to have avoided genetic matters completely by showing only that rows 1 and 3 of Figure 1-7 must be combined in actual practice. And when we did encounter a situation where the comparative method, the prime tool of comparative linguistics, was needed, we did no more than refer to its treatment elsewhere. But it has already been mentioned that rows 2 and 3 belong together also, and this is why they were shaded in. In other words, variation and change are interdependent, exactly as in biology. Variation is a prerequisite of change, and regular change is a prerequisite of the comparative method (Chapter 11). Thus this is the best order of treatment. We always have noncontrastive fluctuation within the structurally relevant parts of language, before change. Sound change never creates fluctuation from static unity, but replaces earlier variation with new variation.

Social dialects can become regional and vice versa. Parts of Australia and the southern United States, for instance, were populated from the London prisons, which of course detained people mostly from the lowest classes; they left a definite imprint in the language of the new regions. The same situation obtained in Roman colonization. The Latin that spread out was not that of the higher classes and of literature, but the dialect of the people; further, it was taken to the provinces at different times. Conversely, when a region becomes culturally dominant its dialect becomes the socially prestigious one. This is the general situation in Europe: London for English, Île de France for France, Castilian for Spanish, and so on. But nonnational cases also show this development. The Fox dialect was once simply a regional variant of American English. Now, with the young generation sticking to the more prestigious form supported by teachers from the outside, by television, and so on, the Fox dialect has become a social one; it is now the dialect of older people and is correlated with farming as an occupation. Similarly, many of the southern American regional features have become ethnic in the North, where Negroes have been moving in great numbers and where they have met the inevitable social barriers of American society.

When social meaning is attached to variation it starts to play a role in the language, and imitation of the prestigious forms takes place (the details depending on the configurations of social forces). Because of the interplay of such forces, one model may engulf other distinct variants (§ 9.10). A shift in society may assign immediate prestige to a new variant. The dialect of the older speakers may perish with the death of the speakers themselves, leaving room for some other variation elsewhere. Regular change thus results from elimination of variation in social interplay and from the rise of new variation in some other subgroup of society, where new social meaning is assigned to random variation. This is also how change occurs in biology. It is the species that persists through time, not individual variants. Similarly, language persists, not individual utterances, which always show variation within and among speakers. A static system does not explain change; a language that has ceased to change is dead (see Chapter 22).

[3.8 Conclusion] This chapter has shown that synchronic dialectal diversity must be treated by the same method as related languages, although the method itself was left for later discussion (Chapter 11). It was briefly stated that change and reconstruction are ultimately connected with variation, and it became clear that Figure 1-7 does indeed represent cardinal points only. Chapters 1–3 have delineated the place of genetic linguistics within other branches of the total science of language, providing valuable guidelines for the following discussions of change and reconstruction. Going more deeply into synchronic linguistics is not possible in this context, although synchronic linguistics is part of the necessary background for genetic linguistics, as our constant references have shown and will show.

REFERENCES

General: Hymes (ed.) 1964, Bright (ed.) 1966, Lieberson (ed.) 1967, Fishman (ed.) 1968, Alatis (ed.) 1969, Graur (ed.) 1.549-773; Fischer 1958, Gumperz 1958, 1961, 1968, Bright and Ramanujan 1964, Hymes 1968b, Bolinger 1968, Burling 1970, Katičić 1970, Dahlstedt 1970; **3.2** Pilati 1969; **3.3** Joos 1962, Labov 1964, 1966, Fónagy 1956-57, Kazazis 1970; **3.4** Burling 1970, Loman 1970; **3.5** Labov 1969, 1970, Houston 1969, 1970, Wolfram 1969, 1970, Loflin 1969, Fasold 1969, 1970, Burling 1970; **3.6** Ferguson 1959, Ramanujan 1968, Kazazis 1968.

More recent dialectology: Giglioli (ed.) 1972, Bailey 1973, Hymes 1974, Blount and Sanches (eds.) 1977, D. Sankoff (ed.) 1978, D. Sankoff and Labov 1979, Kay and McDaniel 1979, G. Sankoff 1980, Chambers and Trudgill 1980, Petyt 1980, Ureland (ed.) 1980, Trudgill 1983, 1986, Francis 1983, Fasold 1984.

PART II

HISTORICAL LINGUISTICS: HOW DOES LANGUAGE CHANGE?

CHAPTER 4

SOUND CHANGE

The description of sound changes and their various classifications provide the terminology central to most of genetic linguistics. Allophonic environment and grammatical conditioning are discussed.

[4.1 Evidence for Changes—Mere Change in Pronunciation or Distinctive Structural Phonemic Change in Number or Distribution] There is no doubt that the sounds of all languages change, given a long enough period. Traditionally one classifies such change under two structural headings: (1) mere change in pronunciation with no effect on the sound system, and (2) structural phonemic change, which affects the number or distribution of phonemes. In Figure 4-1 we have no structural change between the first and the second stages because the contrasts remain intact; only the outer garb of the units has changed. But between the second and the third, and the third and the fourth stages we have changes in distribution and number of units.

Time		
First stage	a a a x x y y y y	} Mere phonetic change
Second stage	b b b x x z z z z	
Third stage	b b b x x x x z z	} Change in distribution of units
Fourth stage	b b b x x x x x x	} Change in number of units

FIGURE 4-1. Changes in number and distribution of phonemes.

The fact that most English dialects have replaced a trilled (initial) *r* with a retroflex spirant *r*, as in *red*, is a case of mere phonetic change. Similarly, English *t* and *d* used to be dental; now they are alveolar, and no structural change has taken place. In Dutch all (or most) *l*'s are 'dark' (much like in *sill, bottle*), a change of no systematic consequence even though most of the other Continental Germanic languages have 'bright' *l*'s. As in the case of the dialect correspondences discussed in Chapter 3, there is regularity through time. For example, Old English *ā* repeatedly corresponds to Modern English /ow/ (which can be spelled three ways):

OE	*āþ*	*āgan*	*bāt*	*bān*	*hām*	*rād*	*stān*	*hāl*
NE	oath	own	boat	bone	home	road	stone	whole

This regularity between the sounds of an earlier stage and a later stage is called

57

a phonetic (or sound) law. The term 'law' is to be taken in a physical sense, as a statement of regular behavior. We write this 'law', this correspondence between two stages of one and the same language, as OE $\bar{a}$ > NE /ow/, where > means 'changes into'. (Note that this is different from the dialect correspondence, for example, General American alveolar d–Fox dental $\d{d}$, where we use the dash for the synchronic relation. The wedge is used only for variation through time, for example, earlier English dental $\d{d}$ > alveolar d.) The law $\bar{a}$ > /ow/ does not hold, however, if the $\bar{a}$ occurs after a w-cluster: $hw\bar{a}$ > who, $tw\bar{a}$ > two. But the exception is regular, because it occurs in one environment only, where the rest of the law does not apply. This is the general situation; for example, we have the two correspondences in time

OE	ā	ā			C	wā
NE	ow	uw	or			uw

which occur in mutually exclusive environments: the second (stated twice above, the second time with conditioning shown) after a w-cluster in Old English, the first elsewhere (i.e., $\bar{a}$ > ow, except that $Cw\bar{a}$ > Cuw). Sound laws are not as exact as physical laws, and linguists should not be startled to find exceptions (e.g., $sw\bar{a}$ > so; this change, however, is quite regular if w is first lost after s-, whereafter $*s\bar{a}$ > so) (see § 5.7).

[4.2 Allophonic Variation and Splits]   Old English /f, þ, s/ were phonetically [f, þ, s] until about A.D. 700: fif 'five', $wulf$ 'wolf', $ofer$ 'over', $þorn$, $weorþan$/$wearþ$ 'become/became', $þing$, $sendan$, $nosu$ 'nose', $wesan$/$wæs$ 'to be/was'. About A.D. 700 a mere change in pronunciation occurred in that a voiceless spirant between voiced sounds after stressed vowel became voiced: [over, weorðan, nozu]. Spelling remained the same, and the phonemic contrasts were not disturbed; only the number of allophones doubled: /f/ [f, v], /þ/ [þ, ð], and /s/ [s, z]. These voiced allophones became independent phonemes through later, unrelated changes:

1. Borrowings from Kentish (and other Southern dialects), which had also initial voiced spirants (readers may be familiar with the speech of Squire Western in *Tom Jones*), replaced inherited items like *fæt* 'barrel' (compare German *Fass*) and *fyxen* (compare German *Füchsin*) with *vat* and *vixen*. This process was also reinforced by French loans, as in *vile*. Since *fætt* (compare German *Fett*) gave *fat*, we have now minimal pairs *vat/fat*, *vile/file*. The speakers had to learn that some morphemes contained inherent *v*'s which always remained as such, although the old *f*'s alternated morphophonemically with *v*'s in certain environments, as they still do.
2. Intervocalic long spirants /ff, þþ, ss/ were simplified into [f, þ, s], and these of course contrasted with [v, ð, z], which had been the intervocalic voiced variants of the old short /f, þ, s/.

3. Upon the loss of final -ə in Middle English we get voiced spirants in final position, e.g., ME [bāðə] > [bāð] (> /beyð/), contrasting with the noun [bæþ] (see Figure 4-3, line 4). The -ə is still written as -e, but now it means the preceding spirant is voiced: bath/bathe, wreath/wreathe, tooth/teethe, and so on.

Here then we see how allophonic variation, which initially had no impact on the contrast system, was phonemicized by later developments: borrowing and sound change. The number and distribution of sound units changed. English developed morphophonemic alternation between voiceless and voiced spirants after the original endings were dropped. In French the development is the reverse, although the result is the same. Latin masculine novu(m) and feminine nova(m) 'new' started out with the similar v ('same' in French) but different endings. When the masculine ending dropped, the feminine one was still retained as -ə: masc. neuv, fem. neuvə. Final v was devoiced, neuf, and then with the drop of the -ə we get [nœf, nœ·v], an exact parallel to the English grammatical alternation safe/save, and so on. In French it is masculine versus feminine, in English, noun versus verb; in French, v > v ~ f, in English, f > f ~ v.

[4.3 Latin Rhotacism As a Historical Event]   Latin has a fair amount of allomorphic alternation between s and r: nefās/nefārius 'impious', flōs/flōris 'flower', ūrō/ūstus 'burn', querī/questus 'ask', est/erit 'be' (pres./fut.), and so on. Earliest Latin documents, and documents in closely related languages or dialects, show further that many of the r-forms originally had s, a fact confirmed by comparative evidence from other Indo-European languages. Forms like flōs, ūstus, and est show that some s's did not change into r's (some forms, like mīror 'wonder', always had an intervocalic r); the evidence shows that s > r only in intervocalic position. We can now state the law:

By about 600 B.C., Latin s between vowels became r (all s's between vowels became r's).

To emphasize that sound laws are historical events that occur at a certain time in a certain language under certain conditions, Edgar Sturtevant compared the above statement about Latin rhotacism to another possible hypothetical historical event, which he called "The Law of Waterloo":

All Prussian soldiers six feet tall were killed in the battle of Waterloo.

The Latin law as formulated does not seem to be completely true, since there are still words with intervocalic s's: dīvīsus 'divided', causa 'cause', caesus 'cut down', vīsus 'seen'; nisi 'unless', dēsinō 'desist', and so on. Morphophonemically the first four words have s's that are |d + t| (dīvidere 'divide', vidēre 'see' + past passive participle ending -tus: scrīp-tus 'written', amā-tus 'loved', etc.), and, in fact, Old Latin orthography shows a double ss in these words; for example, *caussa*. That is, at the time when intervocalic *s* changed, these words did not have *s* but *ss*, which later became short after long vowels and diphthongs. As for *nisi* and *dēsinō*, they are compounds that apparently had not yet been formed at the time when *s* changed, and thus the *s*'s in question were word-initial: *sī* 'if', *sinō* 'allow'. These cases do not fall under the conditions of the law; they are *Prussians not yet born at the time of the battle*. Another set of words shows intervocalic *s*'s after short vowels without these two possibilities of explanation: *asinus* 'donkey', *casa* 'hut', *rosa* 'rose'; *genesis, basis*. However, we can easily establish these as loans from other Italic languages and Greek. Hence these did not exist in the language at the time of the change; they are *Prussians naturalized after the battle of Waterloo*.

Thus the first formulation has withstood quite well the apparent discrepancies in Latin words showing intervocalic *s*'s. A more serious attack comes from two words: *miser* 'miserable' and *caesariēs* 'hair'. But note that here the environment of *s* is different, in that it is followed by an *r*. Now our law needs an additional clause:

except when followed by *r*.

These are *Prussians under six feet tall* and hence not subject to the law of Waterloo. According to this clause, the word for 'sister', *soror*, should be **sosor* (compare *sister*, Skt *svásar-*). Here one notices that the *s*, which has, in fact, changed before a following *r*, is preceded by *s* earlier in the word. We must add a further clause:

except when also preceded by *s*.

In other words, this *Prussian is six feet tall* after all, although his posture appeared bent. Now the law covers the facts quite well. There is only one exception, *nāsus* 'nose'. But one exception against hundreds of regular cases does not invalidate the law. In historical linguistics one always finds a certain number of unclear cases or irregular changes.

This and the English and French *v* ~ *f* case, as well as many of the following examples, will show how sound change creates morphophonemic alternation. Looked at from the point of view of analysis, they are examples of internal reconstruction, because internal reconstruction is based totally on morphophonemic analysis (§§ 10.7–10.17, Chapter 12).

[4.4 The Split of Latin *k* in French]   Latin *k* develops three reflexes in French:

I		II		III	
cor > *coeur*	'heart'	*centum* > *cent* 'hundred'		*cantāre* > *chanter* 'sing'	
clārus > *clair*	'clear'	*cervus* > *cerf* 'hart'		*carbō* > *charbon* 'coal'	
quandō > *quand*	'when'	*cinis* > *cendre* 'ashes'		*causa* > *chose* 'thing'	

That is, k > k (k remains before o and in a cluster), k > s before front vowels, and k > $š$ before a. These are three correspondences through time, complementary in terms of their environments in the earlier stage:

Environments in Latin

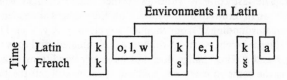

This is what regularity means; it is the reliable predictability of the outcomes of the later stage in terms of the total situation of the earlier stage. After anC and enC give $ãC$, and CwV > CV, we have examples of the French outcomes in identical environments $kã$ 'when', $sã$ '100', $šã$ 'song', and thus clear structural change, even without looking into other mergers elsewhere in the language (see § 6.2). In sound change there is a one-way mapping relation from earlier to later stages only. There is no way of knowing on the basis of French alone that the [s] in *cent* was originally different from the [s] in *sentir* < Latin *sentīre* 'feel'.

[4.5 Umlaut Phenomena]   Umlaut, which is attested in all the Germanic languages except Gothic, was also a very trivial change at the outset, whereby back vowels become fronted by an $ī$ or j after a following consonant. This can be exemplified by a very small selection from English (* = not directly attested, but inferred through reconstruction; Part III):

I	II	III OE	IV NE
*hāl	hāl	hāl	'whole'
*hāl-iþ	*hǽliþ	hǽlþ	'health'
*hāl-jan	*hǽljan	hǽlan	'heal'
*dōm	dōm	dōm	'doom'
*dōm-jan	*dȫmjan	dȫman > dēman	'deem'
*gōs	gōs	gōs	'goose'
*gōs-i	*gȫsi	gȫs > gēs	'geese'
*mūs	mūs	mūs	'mouse'
*mūs-i	*mȳsi	mȳs > mīs	'mice'
*fūl	fūl	fūl	'foul'
*fūl-iþ	*fȳliþ	fȳlþ > fīlþ	'filth'
*fūl-jan	*fȳljan	fȳlan > fīlan	'(de)file'

Umlaut itself is thus the creation of front allophones [æ, ȫ, ȳ] to the phonemes /ā, ō, ū/ (the step from column I to II). Such sounds did not exist earlier, and even now they are just automatic variants, when $ī$ or j follow: /ā/ = [ā, æ], /ō/ = [ō, ȫ], and /ū/ = [ū, ȳ]. This was a mere change in pronunciation, which later acquired structural significance only through an unrelated phonetic change —the loss of those high front vowels in unaccented syllables (i.e, the step from column II to III)—which had originally conditioned the front allophones. Now we have minimal pairs between front and back vowels, which proves that they are different phonemes, although they are still related by morphophonemic alternations. The last column witnesses further (later) changes which are all regular, but we shall return to them below. Note the changes appended to column III, that is, the unrounding of front rounded vowels ($\ddot{o} > \bar{e}, \ddot{y} > i$). They remain at the same tongue height when lip-rounding is eliminated, and thus merge with the existing $\bar{e}$ and i. This change does not have any conditions attached to it; the change is the same in every environment. (Velars still tell the two sources of the front vowels, for example, *cinn* > *chin* vs. *cynn* > *kin*.) (Cf. §0.5)

[4.6]   Similar umlaut processes, whereby following vowels affect preceding ones and then drop, are very common in the languages of the world. Perhaps one of the most striking cases comes from Rotuman. Like many of the Oceanic languages, Rotuman originally had five vowels, as it still does on the morpho-phonemic level: *i, ε, a, ɔ, u*. (We write the mid vowels with open symbols, for reasons that will become clear, and the glottal stop with *q*.) Now, *a* develops a back variant *ɒ* when it occurs before *q* and *h* followed by *ɔ*: *fɒqɔ* 'nail' and *mɒhɔ* 'to become old'. It gives a higher and backer *ɒ* when followed by *i* or *u* (the high vowels): *fɒqu* 'back' and *jɒji* 'to shape'. When followed by *ε*, *a* gives *ä*: *äfε* '1,000' and *pärε* 'protect'. Mere changes in pronunciation have occurred; /a/ has three new allophones, [a, ɒ, ɒ, ä], conditioned by *qɔ/hɔ, i/u*, and *ε*, respectively. The high vowels also raise the mid vowels by one notch, and thus we get a narrow *e* before *i/u*: *hefu* 'star' and *fepi* 'slow', and also a narrow *o*: *folu* 'three' and *mori* 'orange'. Now /ε/ has two allophones, [ε, e] and /ɔ/ [ɔ, o]. The same initial five vowel phonemes remain, although they have doubled their sum of allophones. Then, in a grammatical environment, which Churchward calls the "incomplete phase" (a kind of indefinite aspect; see § 4.26), final vowels drop, and the result is an enormous number of minimal pairs based on the earlier allophones:

fɒqɔ → fɒq	'nail'		*pɒqu → pɒq*	'eel'
fɒqu → fɒq	'back'		*pɔqɔ → pɔq*	'to blister'
asa → as	'name'		*afa → af*	'to mark'
ɒsu → ɒs	'smoke'		*äfε → äf*	'1,000'
ɒsi → äs	'to go to see'			
			εfε → εf	'coconut-pulp'
sεrε → sεr	'knife'		*ɔfɔ → ɔf*	'to announce'
seru → ser	'comb'		*ofi → öf*	'to be finished up'

The allophones have split up into ten phonemes. There was a clear hierarchy to the catalysis. First the mid vowels served as catalysts to /a/ and then the high vowels were catalysts to all the others, remaining intact themselves. But this is not the whole story. When final -*ε* is dropped, a preceding *ɔ* gives *ö*: *mɔsε →* *mös* 'to sleep', *tɔrε → tör* 'to remain'; and similarly *i*, although disappearing,

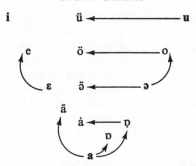

FIGURE 4-2. Rotuman vowel triangle showing the splitting up of vowels through raising umlaut (upward arrows) and fronting umlaut (left pointing arrows).

umlauts a preceding *o*: *mori* → *mör* 'orange' and *tori* → *tör* 'to use extravagantly'. Similarly, *furi* → *für* 'to turn', *fuqi* → *füq* 'thunder', and *psi* → *äs* 'to go to see', and *jpji* → *jäj* 'to shape'. In other words, we end up with fourteen vowels on the phonetic surface, although, again, the morphophonemic groupings are not affected. Scholars differ on the number of phonemes they posit for Rotuman; the number has been variously posited as 5, 7, 10, 12, and Churchward's 14 (presented here). The derivation of the vowels can be summed up as in Figure 4-2, where the curved upward arrows indicate the first raising umlaut (↑) caused by *i* and *u* and the straight arrows the fronting umlaut (←) caused by *i* and *ε*. The splitting up of the vowels is still a synchronic mechanism in the language, since eight of the vowels are unambiguously analyzable as sequences of two morphophonemes: /ä/ = |a + ε|, /à/ = |a + i|, /ɒ/ = |a + ɔ| before *h* and *q*, /ɒ/ = |a + u|, /o/ = |ɔ + u|, /ö/ = |ɔ + i|, /ɔ̈/ = |ɔ + ε|, and /ü/ = |u + i|. This analysis is strongly supported by the fact that the sequences with high and mid vowels followed by the mid and low vowels, *iCε, iCɔ, iCa; uCε, uCɔ, uCa; εCa; ɔCa* (where *C* represents any consonant), do not drop the final vowel at all. Instead, the final vowel is transposed to the other side of the consonant: *ieC, ioC, iaC; ueC, uoC, uaC; εaC: ɔaC,* for example, *sikɔ* → *siok* 'to be untrue', *pija* → *piaj* 'rat', *purε* → *puer* 'to rule', *hula* → *hual* 'moon', and *hɔsa* → *hɔas* 'flower'. These diphthongs represent single syllables, exactly as /ü/ = |u + i| in *füq*, and so on. Note further that when the mid vowels get next to the high ones, the raising umlaut occurs (as it does also for *a* sometimes, but we have to ignore it here). Because the front umlaut and the metathesis are so closely related, one might try to interpret the vowel drop the same way (i.e., *sεrε* > **sεer* > *sεr*, and so on). No vowel transposition or drop occurs if the word ends in two vowels, but, again, the second vowel from the end is affected, because it is shortened in the "incomplete phase": for example, *pupui* → *pupŭi* 'floor', *lelei* → *lelĕi* 'good', *keu* → *kĕu* 'to push', and *jaɔ* → *jăɔ* 'spear'. Thus even here we have ultimately a slight reduction in length, although not the loss of a whole syllable as in the above cases.

All the above changes are still living morphophonemic processes in Rotuman, and this is why the arrow → (§§ 6.7, 6.8) rather than the wedge > was used in the examples. There are also a certain number of exceptions to the above changes/ rules, but such things are to be expected in every language. The overwhelming regularity is the factor that counts, and it was presented as regular here. Two aspects of the Rotuman case are unusual. It is noteworthy that the ɛ-umlaut of a raises the a much more than the (second) i-umlaut. The corresponding ɔ- and u-umlauts of a remain in the more usual proportion: the high vowel raises the a one step higher than the mid vowel. The reason for the asymmetry is that the first raising umlaut pulled a into the back vowels and only the second fronting umlaut brought the a among the front vowels. This is how a lost ground in the i-fronting. And when the latter occurred, the ɛ- raising was a completed fact.

[4.7]   Even more curious is the fact that the fronting umlaut operates only when the front vowel is dropped. In those environments where the final vowel remains, the preceding vowel shows the shape at the tail ends of the straight arrows (Figure 4-2). That is, the drop of the vowel and the fronting are simultaneous processes; there is no gradual contact influence that would produce fronting before the drop of the vowels. Linguists usually would like to posit a single step at a time, for example, first metathesis, *fuqi* > **fuiq*, and then **fuiq* > *füq*, and so on. We have no direct evidence for the middle term; rather, by all appearances, the metathesis and the fronting could as well have been simultaneous. The same paradoxical situation is known also in Old Norse i- and u-umlaut, as well as in Livian (a Baltic Finnic language in Latvia). When a Livian final -i drops, it causes fronting of a preceding back vowel, e.g., [nom. sg.] *tammi* > *tämm* 'oak' and [gen. sg.] *tammen* > *tamm*. No umlaut results if the front element remains in the word, either as a vowel (e.g., *vanhim* > *vanim* 'oldest', *vasikka* > *vaʔšʼki*, *vaʔiški* 'calf'), or as palatalization (e.g., *patja* > *padʼà* 'mattress'). A nominative singular like *nurmi* drops its final -i and gives *nürm* 'lawn', whereas the partitive plural retains its i and remains as *nūrmidi*, with a back vowel. Again we have one apparent exception, *kaksi* > *kakš* '2', but š instead of s still reflects the i as a feature of palatalization.

We have seen a typical case where, as the words of a language get shortened, the number of sound units multiply; and mere changes in pronunciation were given a different structural status through a different change, the loss of the original conditioning factors.

[4.8 The English Vowel Shift]   The great English vowel shift, which affected all long vowels, had very little structural significance when it first happened, because the nuclei remained, on the whole, separate from each other, as shown in Figure 4-3. "Long vowels" are here analyzed as long rather than diphthongs to begin with, merely for the sake of simplicity. The important point is that although the vowels shift places, they all remain distinct until the time of Wordsworth, when there is a reduction and redistribution in the number of "long" vowels. The shift is still going on in English. But before the time when

	Chaucer			Shakespeare	Wordsworth	Modern English
	bite	ī		bite	əi	ai	ai
	bete	ē		beet	ī		ī
	bete	ǣ	'strike'	beat	ē		ī
[OE ă]	name	ā		name	ǣ	ē	ei
[OE ā]	foal	ɔ̄		foal	ō	ō	ou
	fol	ō		fool	ū	ū	ū
	foul	ū		foul	əu	au	au

FIGURE 4-3. The great English vowel shift.

the long vowels started to shift, long vowels were shortened when followed by two consonants or one consonant and two unstressed vowels, thus:

	-CC	-CVCV
ī	filth	divinity
ē	kept	serenity
ǣ	health	
ā	cranberry	sanity
ɔ̄	[æ] (see below)	
ō	gosling	
ū	husband, hussy	

Umlaut, unrounding, vowel shift, and vowel shortening produce forms like *whole* ~ *health* ~ *heal*, *foul* ~ *filth* ~ *(de)file*, and *sane/sanity*. As always, such vowels still tend to go together morphophonemically, although not to such an automatic degree here as in Rotuman. When OE *ā* was shortened before it became ME *ɔ̄*, the result was a complete separation of the variants: for example, *stone* and *staniel* < *stān-gella* 'stone-yeller, a kind of hawk'; *home* and place-names like *Ham-den* (compare [-əm] at the end of names like *Nottingham*); and *goat* and *Gatton* 'goat-town' in Surrey (compare, also, *holy* [which belongs to *whole*] and *hallow[e'en]*). The single element *ā* in column I in § 4.5, umlauted, shortened, and otherwise conditioned, has the following outcomes in Modern English: /ow/ in *whole*, *stone*, *clothes*; /æ/ in *staniel*, *hallow*; /ə/ in *Nottingham*; /uw/ in *swoop*, *two*; /a/ in *hot*, *holiday*; /o/ in *cloth*, *broad* (this is a dialect borrowing); /iy/ in *heal*, *speech*; /e/ in *health*, *next*; and /i/ in *silly*, *nimble*. Again there are also "irregular" cases (e.g., *folly* [*fool*], *scholar* [*school*], and *zealous* [*zeal*]), where shortening occurs before one consonant only. But such an irregularity is regular in the sense that there are many cases of it.

[4.9 The First Germanic Consonant Shift]   The first Germanic consonant shift, known as Grimm's law, is another good example of a sound 'law'. Note that Germanic is not a directly attested "historical language" like Latin or Old

English, but inferred through reconstruction (Parts III and IV). Pre-Germanic had the following stops: *p t k*, (*b*) *d g*, and *bh dh gh* (see § 11.12) of which the last three might have been murmured (breathy phonation). The voiceless stops were replaced by spirants: *p t k* > *f þ x* (with *h* in some environments at the attested stages; see §§ 11.3, 11.7) (e.g., Latin *ped-*: English *foot*; *trēs*:*three* (and *tooth*, below); and *cord-*:*heart*). The voiced stops shifted into the position vacated by the above change: *b d g* > *p t k* (e.g., Lithuanian *dubùs*:*deep*; Latin *dent-*:*tooth*; and *foot*, *heart*, above; and Latin *ager*:*acre*). And, finally, the last series filled in the new vacant slot: *bh dh gh* > *b d g* (e.g., Sanskrit *bhárāmi*:*bear*; Skt *rudhirá*:*red*; and Greek *khēn*:*goose*). Latin, Lithuanian, Sanskrit, and Greek are standing in for Pre-Germanic merely for convenience—and Greek not too well at that—because we have no direct attestation from the protolanguage, although the comparative evidence is quite solid. English, for its part, is standing in for Proto-Germanic here. So far nothing much has happened, because all three series are still distinct; but this is the nucleus of Grimm's law. (Such "mere phonetic" changes seem much less trivial from the point of view of distinctive feature analysis, which concentrates exactly on this level of phonology; see § 6.9.)

But, as usual, there is one environment in which the shift did not take place: when the sounds *p t k* occurred second in a voiceless cluster, they remained as stops, for example,

Latin	*stāre*	'stand'	Latin	*captīvus*	'captive'
English	*stand*		OE	*hæft*	

Latin	*piscis*	'fish'	Latin	*spuere*	'spit'
Gothic	*fisks*		OHG	*spīwan*	

Thus there was a change in distribution after all, because these unchanged *p t k* were identified with the outcomes of older *b d g*.

One further set disturbs the operation of the law as developed so far: in some cases the outcomes of *p t k* are not voiceless spirants but *b d g*:

Greek	*hupér*	'over'	Greek	*patér*	'father'	Greek	*hekurá*	'mother-
OHG	*ubar*		OE	*fæder*		OHG	*swigur*	in-law'

A related fact is that instead of an expected *s* in West Germanic we sometimes get an *r*: Sanskrit *snuṣá* : OE *snoru* 'daughter-in-law'. The expected voiceless spirant and the voiced stop alternate in paradigms, like OE *weorþan–wearþ–wurdon–worden* 'become'. As we have seen above, paradigmatic alternation is very likely to derive from an earlier identity differently altered in different environments. Latin *k* gave *s š k* in French (§ 4.4), and here we have the same multifariousness: Pre-Germanic *t* gives Proto-Germanic *þ d t*. The environment for the voiced outcomes (*b d g*) baffled scholars for a long time and was supposed to be haphazard, until Karl Verner saw that it was, after all, conditioned by clear phonetic facts—the position of the accent, which has been preserved in Greek and Sanskrit. His solution is now known as Verner's law. In all the cases where we have voiced outcomes, the accent in Greek or Sanskrit follows the sound in question. Note further the Sanskrit paradigm in juxtaposition with Old English:

| Sanskrit | *vártate* | *vavárta* | *vavṛtimá* | *vavṛtāná* | 'turn' |
| Old English | *weorþan* | *wearþ* | *wurdon* | *worden* | 'become' |

Thus the position of the accent enables us to predict exactly when the outcomes of *p t k* are *f þ x*, and when *b d g*. If the sound is in initial position or immediately preceded by the accent, we get *f þ x*, otherwise *b d g*. After this difference arose, the accent (stress) moved into the root syllable, although the original position is still indirectly reflected in the morphophonemic alternations *þ* ~ *d*, and so on. In the umlaut phenomena we had the same situation; the original sounds were reflected in the results.

[4.10]   There is still some controversy about the order of the stages in the consonant shift. In addition, we have treated the Germanic sounds *b d g* as though they were simple structural entities that contrasted with the other two series. Actually, they were spirants phonetically and changed into stops rather late (if at all, in some Germanic languages; see §§ 6.3, 9.9). Let us now sum up Grimm's and Verner's laws, taking the dentals as a model, and using a sequence different from the above. Figure 4-4 is one possibility. We write one change at

	I PIE	II	III	IV	V PGmc	VI OE	
1	dhúr-——→ðúr-		ðúr-	ðúr-	ð/dúr-	duru ⎫	1
	⎧pətér	patér ——→	faþér ——→	faðér	fáder	fæder ⎭	
2 ⎨	tréyes	trís ——→	þrís	þrís	þrís	þrie	2
	⎩stáyn-	stáin-	stáin-	stáin-	stáin-	stān ⎫	
3	dwóy	dwái	dwái	dwái ——→	twái	twā ⎭	3

FIGURE 4-4. A possible sequence of steps in Grimm's and Verner's laws.

each stage. First we have *dh* > *d*, then *t* > *þ* (*p* > *f*); up until stage III no structural change has occurred. We have the same phonemes, but number 2 now has two allophones: a stop in voiceless cluster, and *þ* elsewhere. Between III and IV Verner's law applies: the voiced outcome of unit 2 is the same as unit 1, and after *d* > *t*, the stop allophone of 2 goes together with unit 3. We started out with three units and we end up with three units, but with a new distribution, and hence a change in structure (for further tabulation see § 6.3 and Figure 6-2).

[4.11 Excrescence of Sounds]   We have seen how sounds drop out or change into other sounds. The reverse is also possible: in some clearly defined phonetic environments, new sounds may appear. The Old English word *þūma* 'thumb' is the base for a derivative *þȳmel* (in which *ȳ* shows that the suffix originally had an *i* underlying the attested *e*). In the inflected stem the *m* and *l*

	A		B		
	[m]	[l]	[m]	[b]	[l]
Lips	closed	open	closed	⟶ open	
Tip of tongue	down	up	down	⟶ up	
Velum	down	up	down	up ⟶	

FIGURE 4-5.   Rise of excrescent [b] caused by readjustment of articulatory movement.

were in contact, (e.g., *þymle*); the sequence of articulatory adjustments in the cluster *ml* is shown in Figure 4-5:A. By raising the velum too early to the position that it takes for *l*, we get an automatic *b* after *m* (i.e., lips closed, tongue down, velum up, that is, closed). The *b* next gives way to *l* when the lips and the tongue are readjusted (Figure 4-5:B); the whole ensemble underlies English *thimble*. If the lip position is not relevant, as in the case of OE *þunrian*, the stop that develops is different, here a *d: thunder* (compare German *Donner* 'thunder', where this did not happen). The stop is homorganic to the preceding sound. This change is very frequent when liquids and nasals come together either with *s* or with one another (*sr > str, ms > mps, nl > ndl, mr > mbr, ns > nts*).

The reverse is also possible. If the velum is lowered too late, the nasal grows a homorganic stop in front of it. Thus in West Lapp we get **ruma > robme* 'ugly', **sōne > suodnâ* 'vein', and **poŋe > buogŋâ* 'bosom'. When the lips and the tongue had already taken the position for the nasal, the velum remained up (and this defines a stop); the nasal segment commences when the velum is lowered. In the Lapp change **tuppe > tohþpa* 'sheath', the transition from the vowel to the *p* involved a difference in voicing. Here the vocal cords were deactivated too early, during the last part of the vowel; thus the vowel ended as voiceless, and a voiceless vowel is an *h*. An automatic *h* preceding a stop is called preaspiration (for examples of **k > hkk* and **t > htt* see §§ 10.15, 11.15). And again, if the vocal cords remain at rest too long in the transition from a voiceless stop to a vowel, we get aspiration after the stop (e.g., *t > th, p > ph,* and *k > kh*, however we were to write it).

In English there is even alternation based on excrescent sounds. Owing to the loss of a vowel, nasals and liquids became contiguous in words like *humble*, whereas the original sequence remains in *humility* (also *tremble ~ tremulous*, and so on). These are later developments than OE *þymble* (where also *mVl ~ mbl* alternated in the beginning). This excrescence is a persistent characteristic of English, because even today, when the same sounds come together, we may get the same development: *fam(i)ly > fambly, mem(o)ry > membry* in substandard speech. *Re-member* (like *thunder*) developed *-mbr-* (> *-mber #*) at an earlier period.

In the above cases the ultimate result was an addition of a whole segment, although it arose by "sloppiness" in only one feature, which created a new combination of features as a transition between two sounds. But a whole new segment full of features can be added in statable environments; for example, Latin initials with *s* + consonant develop an *e* in Spanish and French, and French further loses the *s*: *sponsu* > *esposo, époux* 'husband'; *scola* > *escuela, école* 'school', and so on. Excrescent sounds involving more than one feature can be consonants as well; in Kekchi (a Mayan language), initial *y*- and *w*- develop into *ty*- and *kw*-.

[4.12 Structural Classification of Changes]   We have now seen the empirical evidence for sound change. In fact, the chapter started out in anticipation of classification; this was to draw attention to the subsequent treatment, which specified the two possible results in the system: either mere phonetic change or a change in the system's structural relations. Both, however, are change, and for many purposes the distinction is not very useful. It must be mentioned, however, both because so much of linguistic literature observes this classification, and because it teaches us about language and linguistics, in particular, that the specific structure that the linguist posits will determine his account of the result of the changes (§§ 1.9, 6.17). Actually, it should become quite clear that the first type of change is the normal kind, and that structural changes are triggered only when enough phonetic change has piled up.

Changes in the number and distribution of phonemes are basically of the following few types:

1. *Complete loss*

$$/x/ \text{------} \emptyset$$

is rather infrequent, but it occurred in the development of Latin /h/ into nothing in Romance. A more frequent situation is (diagrams to be read from left to right only)

2. *Partial merger*

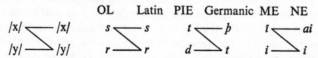

with examples already discussed above. A subtype of this would be

3. *Partial loss*

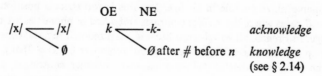

(see § 2.14)

4. *Complete merger*

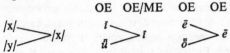

is also frequent. And we have already seen many examples of

5. *Split*

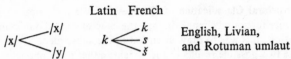

The diagram includes a split in two only, but the examples have shown that it can be multiple. Further, we saw that

6. *Excrescence*

$$\emptyset \text{——} /x/ \qquad OE\ p\bar{y}mle > NE\ thimble \qquad \text{(and so on)}$$

does not really come out of completely nothing, because the environment is phonetically specified. One can also look at loss as merger with zero. Thus every split becomes a result of merger, and excrescence is a split of zero.

But such classification is too general to be of practical value. Types 2, 3, 5, and 6 produce alternations and thus generally continue to play a role in the synchronic grammar, unless subsequent changes ultimately eliminate the alternations; these four changes are thus the prime support of internal reconstruction (§§ 10.7–10.17 and Chapter 12). The same classificatory scheme can be used for morphophonemes, although there, structural changes are much more infrequent. A good example is the Rotuman vowel splitting which leaves the morphophonemes intact. Later in the chapter, however, we shall see cases of morphophoneme splitting (morphophonemically conditioned sound change; § 4.27). Cases like 5 are referred to as *phonologization* or *phonemization* of an earlier (allophonic) variation; correspondingly, the loss of contrast in 4 is *dephonologization*.

This leads directly to the question of the role of the (classical) phoneme in sound change. As we have seen so far in this chapter, sound change characteristically does not occur by phonemes, but generally allophones get phonemicized by changes independent from the earlier allophonic distribution (compare §§ 4.21, 6.22, 7.15). The prevalent opinion in recent times has been that the phoneme plays no role in change. But this is too strict a position. There are indeed cases where the surface contrasts embodied in phonemes are relevant in change. In French, all vowels once became nasalized before nasal consonants, for example, /bɔn/ masc., /bɔnə/ fem. 'good' (compare § 4.2) > [bɔ̃n], [bɔ̃nə]. Then the nasal was deleted before a pause or another consonant, giving a masculine [bɔ̃]. But now nasalization is no longer an automatic allophonic feature, because a contrast is established between nasalized and oral vowels: /bɔ̃/ *bon* 'good', /bo/ *beau* 'beautiful'; /bɔ̃te/ *bonté* 'goodness', /bɔte/ *botté* 'with boots'. Such a contrast is found only before a pause or a nonnasal consonant; before a nasal consonant nasalization remains predictable (allophonic). Now, denasalization takes place precisely where there is no surface contrast, thus [bɔ̃nə] > [bɔnə] (> [bɔn]), as if accentuating the fact that nasalization is now distinctive on the surface and not merely "extra elegance." The general principle in this sequence of events is that if, on the surface, a feature is contrastive in some environments but not in others, that feature is lost where there is no contrast. Such phonemic contrasts can also be relevant in analogic change (§ 5.3).

[4.13 Articulatory Classification Changes] The most useful classification of changes is the one that uses the same parameters as the definition of sounds (Figures 1-3, 1-4). We have seen raising the tongue height in Rotuman (e.g., ɔ > o, and English *ǣ, ē* > *ī*), fronting of the tongue advancement in Rotuman, English, and Livian (e.g., *u* > *ü*), and unrounding in English (change in lip position), *ü* > *ī*. A change in the activity of the vocal cords affects both vowels and consonants. We saw devoicing in PIE *d* > Germanic *t*, and voicing in Verner's law and OE *þ* > *ð* in voiced environment. The development of Lapp preaspiration was an example of too early devoicing, and the Germanic aspiration of the type *t* > *th* is a case of prolonged turning off of the vocal cords. Consonantal changes may include a shift in the place of articulation (i.e., a shift in the columns of Figure 1-4), or in the manner of articulation (i.e., a shift in the rows of the same table). Merely by looking at the table one can see what the changes can be, and examples will, in fact, be given later.

The usefulness of the frames of the phonetic tables as an overall matrix for sound changes lies in the fact that it provides convenient names for talking about change, for example, *spirantization, affrication, nasalization, palatalization,* and *glottalization*. These are names based on the end result of the changes, (i.e., sounds becoming spirants, affricates, nasal, and so on). There are some obvious gaps in this nomenclature; for example, there is no handy term for a continuant sound becoming a stop, as in German *þ* > *d*, or Germanic **ð* > *d* (if not *despirantization*, then the closest term is perhaps German *Verschärfung*). This frame of reference concentrates on what happens to the sound irrespective of its place in the speech chain. Different information is provided by other classifications which also take into account the environment of the change, and we can proceed to them now. The following main types can be given diagrammatically in advance (*a* and *x* are any two sounds or features).

1.	assimilation	*ax* > *xx* (anticipation)
		ax > *aa* (lag)
2.	dissimilation	*aa* > *ax, xa*
3.	metathesis	*ax* > *xa*
4.	haplology	*aa* > *a*
5.	contamination	*yax, zbx* > *yax, zax* or *ybx, zbx*

[4.14]   One of the most frequent changes is *assimilation*, whereby a sound adopts features from another sound (i.e., literally, 'to become similar'). This usually happens only when two sounds are in contact. In Latin, consider the negative morpheme *in-*, and the preverb *com-* 'together' (e.g., *in-elegant* and *com-itative*; we can take examples which have been borrowed into English, where the whole mechanism is still a morphophonemic one). When these nasals occur before stops, they adopt the corresponding place of articulation but remain constant for the other features (nasality, voice) for example, *im-possible*, *iŋ-coŋ-gruent* ([in-koŋ-] also occurs), *in-discreet*, *com-plete*, and *con-tingent*. Such an assimilation is called partial, because all the composite features of the sound did not change. Before liquids, where the assimilation comprises both manner and place (e.g., *il-legal*, *col-lateral*, *ir-relevant*, and *cor-roborate*), the result is complete identity of the two sounds; the assimilation is total. In Finnish there is a glottal stop at the end of certain words, although it is neither written in the standard orthography nor pronounced in all varieties of Finnish; the presence of this "phantom" sound is very apparent, however, for another reason: it assimilates totally to any following consonant. From the imperative *teeq!* 'do!' we get *teem m(in)ulle* 'do for me', *teet taas* 'do again', *tees se* 'do it', *teev vain* 'go ahead and do', and so on. The excrescent preaspiration in Lapp is also a partial assimilatory process, because the vowel adapts to the stop in voicing. Voicing assimilation, in general, is very frequent indeed (compare examples in German, § 2.4). Sometimes in word or sentence-final position we get extra stops when the articulatory organs adapt to the following silence. When one cuts short the pronunciation of *no* [now] by closing the lips and shutting off the vocal cords, both occurring in anticipation of the following silence (which means that the lips are closed and the vocal cords still), we get *nope*, a fairly frequent expressive pronunciation among the young. The same thing (stoppedness plus voicing) happened in *vermin* > *varmint*. Such assimilation leads into excrescence (§ 4.11). A total assimilation to following silence means that the silence begins early, in place of the sound in question (e.g., *old* > *ole*, *slept* > *slep* [§ 3.5], Pre-English **mysi* > OE *mys*, and ME [bəlĩvə] > NE /bi'liyv/ *believe*). One does not speak of assimilation for the loss of final sounds; it is so frequent that linguists have given the phenomenon a name of its own, *apocope* (chopping-off). By contrast, loss of medial sounds is called *syncope* (e.g., *family* > *famly*, *memory* > *memry*).

[4.15]   The spirantization of stops can often be viewed as assimilation to a neighboring continuant sound (elimination of stoppedness). A very frequent type is *assibilation*, a stop becoming a sibilant, namely an *s*-sound (e.g., Greek *t* > *s* in some environments, compare *osmosis* and *osmotic*). Figure 1-4 shows that this must occur in the apico-dental/alveolar and fronto-palatal positions of articulation, the area of *palatalization*. The latter is an assimilation of a consonant to a high front vowel, usually following; it is an assimilation of tongue position. The vocal tract is narrow for the front vowel, and the stop is shifted into or toward this area, as in English [ǩi·p] vs. [ku·l] (or [ǩiyp] vs. [kuwl]) *keep* vs. *cool*. A palatalized [ǩ] can shift further front and give [t̯]. When this affricates, the result is [tš] or [ts]. In other words, palatalization is movement between the columns, and assibilation between the rows, of Figure 1-4. We stated above that Latin *k* assibilated into *s* in French (before front vowels). This was a shortcut, because in reality *k* palatalized first into *ǩ*, and this gave a *ť = tʸ*. Then the narrow transition from stop to vowel [y] was assimilated to the voicelessness of the stop part and the groove tongue shape of the following vowel, giving *ts*. The assibilation was completed when closure disappeared altogether, yielding *s*. (Different Romance languages have gone different ways with regard to this point.) In English we get basically the same assibilation from [ty] > [tš] (e.g., *won't you*), except that the point of articulation is farther back. Although palatalization and assibilation often intersect, they are distinct phenomena (columns versus rows in our diagram!).

The umlaut phenomena of English, Rotuman, and Livian exemplify a somewhat less common event, assimilation at a distance. They were generally partial; in Rotuman, the tongue height was raised before high vowels, and in all three languages back vowels were fronted before *i* (and so on), but these changes never yielded total identity of the conditioner and the conditioned.

[4.16]   In the cases mentioned so far the sound that changed leaned to a sound that followed. This is called *regressive* assimilation. The opposite is accordingly *progressive*. The drawback of these terms, however, is that it is very difficult to remember which is which. A simple remedy is to call the first type *anticipation*, because one or more (even all) features of the following sound are anticipated in the production of the preceding sound (whether in contact or at a distance). The opposite is *lag*, in which some or all features of a sound persevere into the next or following sound; for example, [sevn̩] > [sevm̩] *seven*, in which the labial articulation of the preceding labio-dental is maintained for the nasal. *Compensatory lengthening* is a case of lag. In this event a consonant is lost as far as the articulatory adjustments go, but its place is taken by (the bundle of features of) the preceding vowel. A Pre-English nasal was lost before a voiceless spirant, as in **tonþ*, **fimf*, and **gons* (compare Swedish *tand*, Gothic *fimf*, and German *Gans*), giving its place over to the vowel and yielding OE *tōþ*, *gōs*, *fīf* (as it were, *tooþ*, *goos*, and *fiif*; that is, the assimilation is total, and at contact). Lagging assimilation is common in inflectional and derivatory suffixes, which lean backward toward the stem or root. The English past-tense marker /-d/ generally assimilates in voicing to the stem-final consonant of the verb, for example: /kik-t/ *kicked*, *slep-t*, /rəš-t/ *rushed* vs. /həg-d/ *hugged*, /stæb-d/ *stabbed*, /stər-d/ *stirred* (compare, however, *mean-t*). We have here partial lagging contact assimilation. The original vowel of the Finnish illative case was *e*, as it still is in one word only, *sii-hen* 'into it'; otherwise the *e* assimilates to the preceding vowel, for example, *pää-hän* 'head', *päi-hin* 'heads', *puu-hun* 'tree', *maa-han* 'land', *suo-hon* 'bog', *kyy-hyn* 'viper', *yö-hön* 'night', and *tie-hen* 'road'; we then have total lagging assimilation at a distance. Whether total or not, this is what generally occurs in *vowel harmony*, as in Finnish, Hungarian, Turkish, and so on.

74   HISTORICAL LINGUISTICS: HOW DOES LANGUAGE CHANGE?

If a diphthong is monophthongized so that the result is a long vowel of the tongue height intermediate between the two components (e.g., *ai* > *ē*, *au* > *ō*), we have anticipation and lag at the same time, a "fusion" that produces an average (*ai* > *ei* or *ī* = anticipation alone, and *ai* > *ae* or *ā* = lag alone). Consonants also can show similar mutual conditioning. In Sanskrit we get *cch* when *d* and *ś* come together over a word boundary: *tac chṛṇoti* 'he hears that' (*tad śṛ-*).

In actual speech morphological boundaries are replaced by phonological syllable boundaries in many languages, depending on the favored syllable types. In English this is most apparent in place names, which are functional units irrespective of their component parts, for example, [nu'wɪŋglənd] *New England* and [row'dailənd] *Rhode Island*, or even semantically opaque compounds like [hælə'wiyn] *Halloween*. Such phonological syllable boundary assignment, irrespective of morpheme boundaries, is characteristic of many languages (e.g., French, Hungarian, and Finnish).

It has become clear that assimilation is one of the most important kinds of change. Neighboring sounds accommodate each other, which is the general reason for allophonic variation, of course, and, in this sense, assimilation is well known from synchronic linguistics. In summary we can note that there are three basic axes for classifying assimilation:

lag/anticipation

partial/total ——————————|—————————— contact/distance

ASSIMILATION

This does not explicitly treat articulatory space (Figures 1-3, 1-4), which is the frame for other changes as well.

[4.17]   The reverse of assimilation is *dissimilation*, in which a sequence of the same or similar sounds becomes further differentiated. In many areas of human muscular activity, repetition of the same movement is difficult. This is the operative principle of tongue twisters (e.g., *Theodore Oswaldtwistle, the thistle sifter, in sifting a sack of thistles thrust three thorns through the thick of his thumb*), which apparently exist in all languages. It may well be true that dissimilation is due to neural ease, in the same way that assimilation is connected with articulatory simplification. The former often sporadically affects sequences of liquids and nasals so that a liquid is replaced by a nasal and vice versa (e.g., Finnish *rälssi* > *ränssi* 'tax exemption', *kumppani* > *kumppali* 'companion', Italian *venēnu* > *veleno* 'poison', and Hittite *naman* > *laman* 'name'). A sequence of the same liquid can be differentiated by replacing one with the other, a lateral with a trill or vice versa (e.g., Latin *peregrīnus* > *pilgrim*, and Cheremis *lölpö* > *lörpö* 'alder'). Or just a sequence of dentals is differentiated (e.g., Lithuanian *nīzdas* > *līzdas* 'nest' and Finnish *nysi/nyde-* > *lysi/lyde-* 'handle'). Dissimilation need not be sporadic; it can be quite regular throughout the whole phonology. In Sanskrit and Greek, when a sequence of two aspirate stops occurs within a root, the first one dissimilates into the corresponding plain stop, e.g., Pre-Greek *thrikh-ós 'of hair' > trikhós and Pre-Sanskrit *bhuddhá > buddhá 'awake'). In Ngaju-Dayak (Borneo), an original sequence s . . . s is dissimilated into t . . . s. Using Malay and Tagalog as stand-ins for the protolanguage, we have

		N.-D.	
Malay	sisik	tisik	'fish-scale'
	susu	tuso	'breast'
Tagalog	sisid	teser	'dive'
	suksok	tusok	'press in'

When a repetition of the same (or similar) sequence of sounds is reduced to one occurrence only, we have *haplology*. Latin *nūtrī-trīx* > *nūtrīx* 'nurse', *stipipendium* > *stipendium* 'tax, contribution', German *Superintendent* > *Superindent*, or even English *haplology* > *haplogy*. Note that this last example is completely iconic, as the term shows the phenomenon for which it stands. *Morphophoneme* is generally known as *morphoneme* in Europe.

[4.18]   When a sequence of sounds is reversed we speak of *metathesis*. Latin *periculum* gives Spanish *peligro* 'danger' and *parabola* > *palabra* 'word'. This mechanism is very frequent with liquids: ME *brid* > NE *bird*, OE *wyrhta* > NE *wright*, and OE *be(o)rht* > *bright*; and, in fact, Germanic languages are full of such reshufflings. Metathesis is most frequently just a lapse and seldom gets established as a norm. Even whole morphemes get metathesized in lapses; for example, a linguist (Lounsbury) once lectured " . . . we can *predictly correct* . . . "; he did not notice this at all, and neither did the audience, it seemed. But, contrary to the general opinion, metathesis can also be a regular change which affects a particular sequence throughout the phonotactics of a language. If we indicate the liquids (*r*, *l*) by *R*, vowels by *V*, and consonants by *C*, we can indicate a regular Slavic metathesis by a formula (C)VRC > (C)RVC, which occurs in most Slavic languages. Compare English *robot* (from Czech) with *orphan* (from Late Latin) and German *Arbeit* 'work', the latter two showing the original place of the *r*; *gordŭ* > Old Church Slavic *gradŭ* 'city', *melti* > OCS *mlěti* 'to grind', and so on. From Ilocano (in the Philippines) we can note a metathesis which is definitely more than sporadic: *t . . . s* > *s . . . t* (this can also be stated as a metathesis of *closure* and *spirantness* in connection with *dental* plus *voicelessness*). Using the corresponding Tagalog forms as representatives of the earlier sequences, we have Tag. *taŋis* : Il. *sa·ŋit* 'weep', *tubus* : *subbot* 'redeem', *tigis* : *si·git* 'decant', *tamis* : *samqit* 'sweet', *gatos* 'trillion': *gasut* 'hundred', and *tastas* : *satsat* 'rip' (the last two in terms of syllables). And most important, the Rotuman metathesis (§ 4.6) affects all words that satisfy the formal requirements; exceptions are rather sporadic. The Rotuman case, furthermore, is rare, in that metathesis also continues as a synchronic grammatical mechanism (compare § 5.11).

[4.19   Contamination and Blending]   If the assimilation is toward another word in the semantic field we have *contamination* or *blends*; meaning, and other linguistic signs, now enter as factors of change. The related word can be semantically opposite as readily as the same. Thus English *femelle* /fiyməl/ was replaced by *female* after the opposite, *male*. Similar antonymic influence took place in Vulgar Latin; for example, *gravis* → *grevis* 'heavy' after *levis* 'light', *sinister* → *sinexter* 'left' after *dexter* 'right', and *reddere* → *rendere* 'give up' after *prendere* 'seize'. It is possible that *yep* for *yes* after *nope* belongs here, if it is not produced by "clipping," *yeah* > *yep*, exactly like *no* > *nope* (§ 4.14). According to the usual correspondences, we would expect the initial of English *four* to be *wh-*, matching Latin *quattuor* (like *what–quod*). The Germanic outcome in this number might well have a purely phonological explanation, but it has also been plausibly explained as an anticipation of the next numeral, *five*, as the two would have frequently occurred together in counting situations. The Russian numeral for 'nine', *devjat'*, would normally have had initial *n* (as it does in English *nine* and in the other Indo-European languages). Again *d* is due to the anticipation of the *d* in *desjat'* 'ten'. The Latin word for 'five' should be **pīnque*. The attested *quīnque* either is an anticipation, within the word, of the following labiovelar *qu*, or else is a lag from *quattuor* (i.e., the reverse of the English case); or rather both. Some German dialects replace *elf* 'eleven' by *ölf* after *zwölf* 'twelve', and so on in other languages. The influence of synonyms is exemplified by Finnish *viipale* 'slice', replaced by *siipale* after *siivu*, also 'slice'. Old French had two words for 'native inhabitant', *cite-ain* and *denz-ein*. In Anglo-Norman the first one "took" the *z* from the second, *citizein*, and the second, the *i* from the first, *denizein*, and we end up with English *citizen* and *denizen*.

The discussion introduced contamination to show that the environment of pure sound change can include morphology and semantics. When this happens, however, we no longer have mere sound change. In Chapters 1 and 2 (in particular, §§ 2.15–2.16) we discussed diagrammatic icons, which are better known as analogy. We shall return to grammatical conditioning shortly and to analogy in Chapter 5.

[4.20   Features and Segments in Change]   It has become clear from the survey and classification of sound changes that change applies to anything from one feature to a whole segment, that is, a certain bundle of features (compare the end of § 4.12). Partial assimilation shows the former, total assimilation the latter. Most frequently, however, features change one at a time. In one part of the Germanic consonant shift, *p t k* become *f þ x*; but this is one change only—closure is replaced by spirantization in certain environments. When Rotuman *ɔ* > *o* at the same time that *ε* > *e*, or when Sanskrit *ai* > *e* [e·] and *au* > *o* [o·], there was only a one-feature change in each language. On the other hand, if a segment is added or lost, a whole bundle of features must be accounted for, as in Latin *scola* > Old French *escole*. The symmetry of the above one-feature changes has also been called analogy, that is, diagrammatic (*p:f* as *t:þ* as *k:x*). There is not always complete symmetry, however. The Latin medial stop *d* is lost in Spanish, *cadere* > *caer*; but *b* is not, *habēre* > *haber*, [b] > [ß]. On the whole, there is more play in the dental and velar areas than in labial articulation (see §§ 11.5–11.8, 18.13 and Figure 18-2).

[4.21 Abruptness and Gradualness of Change]   Another disputed question is whether sound change is gradual or not. Phonemic changes are abrupt, and this fact may have influenced the notion that phonetic change must, in contrast, always be gradual. Vocalic changes do tend to be gradual over long periods of time, but on the other hand many changes cannot possibly be (e.g., the change of [θ, ð] to [f, v], independently and at different times, in Cockney and Black English). Any metathesis must also be an abrupt change. The abruptness of these articulatory leaps is different from the structural classification in which the relevant changes are *always* instantaneous, because mere allophonic shifts are not counted at all. The latter is parallel to ignoring the termites and their gradual influence until the house collapses, which is counted as an instantaneous relevant structural change. There is no answer as to the exact scope of the abruptness or gradualness of sound change in every detail, but sound change is characteristically gradual (see § 6.22).

[4.22 Grammatical Conditioning of Sound Change]   We have so far adhered to the classical traditional approach to sound change, which was dominant up to the 1960s, where only phonetic environments are permissible in formulating sound laws. This restriction contrasted with synchronic morphophonemic analysis, which allowed for any grammatical information to be used in phonology. Because language is one organic whole of the type represented in Figures 1-1 and 1-2, where everything depends on everything else (où tout se tient), it is logically thinkable that some sound changes would start from the grammar. It is common knowledge that sound change leads to new grammatical configurations (e.g., *doom/deem*, *goose/geese*, *belief/believe*, and so on); today these are grammatically conditioned alternations, but we know that their origin was phonetic (§§ 4.2, 4.5). Speech sounds do not exist for the sake of speech sounds, but as carriers for semantic units, embodied as linguistic signs, which are handled according to the grammatical rules of the language. Scholars have, to be sure, generally accepted grammatical conditioning by way of analogy, a type of change where meaning and grammatical machinery shape the outer appearance of linguistic signs. Thus the plural of OE *cū* 'cow' was *cȳ*. After the unrounding of *ȳ* we get *kī*. This shape was subsequently modified on the basis of the semantic antonym *ox* and its plural *oxen*. Here both meaning and a particular grammatical marker exert their influence on *kī*, which ends up as *kine*. We cannot question the occurrence of sound change that takes place under phonetic conditioning alone without reference to grammatical information (e.g., OE *ȳ* > *ī*, although to start with *ȳ* itself did occur mainly in certain grammatical contexts), and we can certainly subscribe to the existence of analogy in which meaning and grammar play the central role (Chapter 5). The question is: Is there something between the two, that is, either analogy within mere sounds or sound change dependent on grammatical categories and/or meaning? The answer is yes, regardless of what we want to call this border area. To be sure, this answer is not universally accepted. Figure 1-2 was drawn with separate sections for phonology and grammar, but it was emphasized that there is no such clear boundary. Linguists, however, have often taken such a model too literally and have not allowed any grammatical influence on sound change. One of the reasons for denying the influence of grammar is the principle of not "mixing the levels" in linguistic analysis, a principle that reigned in American linguistics from the 1930s through the 1950s. To deny grammatical conditioning implies that only hearers are allowed to create change—not speakers, who come to sounds through the rest of the grammar.

[4.23]   Actually a certain amount of grammatical information for sound change always was smuggled into historical descriptions, under the disguise of word boundaries. Thus one used (and still uses) word-initial, -medial, and -final positions as conditioning environments. Words are linguistic signs, and often their boundaries are not phonetically marked at all. In Czech, for example, there is no overt phonetic word boundary in křeči 'cramp' (dat.) and k řeči 'to speech', but the pronunciation is still different: in the first one, k and ř belong to the same word, and ř assimilates in voicing to the preceding k, [křeči]; in the second case, we have a preposition that always leans to the following word. Here k assimilates over the word boundary, the reverse of the first case, giving [gřeči]. Thus it is clear that the unity of the total linguistic sign plays a role.

In Sanskrit short i and u are lengthened before a y of some suffixes. The passives of mi 'fix' and su 'impel' are, therefore, mī-ya-te and sū-ya-te. The compound gerunds of su and kṣi 'destroy' are -sū-ya and -kṣī-ya. The perfect optative of śru 'hear' is śu-śrū-yā-s, but the lengthening does not occur if the u is part of the present suffix -nu- (e.g., su-nu-yā-m 'I would press out'). The lengthening is thus conditioned by a certain phoneme in the environment, but not by every occurrence of the phoneme. In other words, one can state this in the reverse order, too: the u of the present marker -nu- does not lengthen; this particular linguistic sign is not subject to the change/rule. Also in Sanskrit, a word-initial m induces assimilation of a preceding d (e.g., tan manyate 'he thinks this' [tad]), but the sequence remains as such within a morpheme (e.g., padma 'lotus' [compare the Czech example]), or between a root and a suffix (e.g., sadma 'seat' [sad 'sit']). In Sanskrit the passive marker -ya- and the present marker -ya- (man-ya-te) are phonetically identical. The corresponding morphemes in the East Middle Indic dialects of the Aśoka inscriptions are different. The present -ya- merges with the preceding stop, giving an affricate pad-ya-ti > paja-ti 'he goes', whereas the passive -ya- splits up pat-ye > patiye 'I fly' and khād-ya-te > khādiyati 'he chews'. If the y belongs to the linguistic sign 'passive', it does not assimilate; otherwise it does (Note also satya > sace 'truth'). Now of course there is a possibility that it was Sanskrit that had lost an earlier phonetic difference between the two signs, because there is no reason to believe that the language of East Middle Indic is a direct continuation of Sanskrit. For practical reasons, we derived these forms from Classical Sanskrit, just as one is accustomed to derive Romance from Classical Latin. On the other hand, it is equally likely that we have a case of genuine grammatical conditioning.

One frequently finds a different treatment of the same sound on the categorical verb–noun axis. Thus in Chinese we sometimes have different assimilation phenomena for the tones of verbs and nouns, even where their etymological tone is identical. In Oneida, a morphophonemic sequence |awa| always gives /u/ [ü] in the verbal prefixes (§ 16.3) but remains as /awa/ within noun morphemes. In Finnish a morphophonemic sequence |tahto-mme| gives a verbal *tahdo-mme* 'we wish', but remains as *tahto-mme* in a noun 'our wish' (§ 10.13). Perhaps in some such cases we have different chronology rather than real grammatical conditioning (in other words, we do not know the correct history). After all, English *belief/believe*, and so on, would appear to have grammatical conditioning for the spirants, if we had no knowledge of the earlier developments.

[4.24] Clear evidence for grammatical conditioning comes from Baltic Finnic and Lapp; and, in fact, Finno-Ugric scholars have always used such information, even while it was theoretically undesirable in the mainstream of linguistic inquiry. Thus, in Karelian, word-final nasals have dropped unless the nasal is the sign -*n* 'gen. sg.', as in *venehe-n* 'of a boat'. In the illative, however, where the ending was -*hen* (§ 4.16), *vete-hen* > *vedeh* 'into water'. The -*h* still remains to mark the illative, whereas the gen. -*n* could not afford to lose anything. This is clear grammatical conditioning, because, phonetically, the endings of *venehen* and *vetehen* (these forms are the historically earlier forms, and they occur still in archaic or poetic Finnish) are exactly the same. The same situation obtains in Onega Veps; the gen. sg. -*n* remains in the singular, where it is the sole marker of the category, *lehma-n* 'of a cow', but drops in the plural morpheme, **lehmi-ðen* > *lehmid'e* 'of cows', which could spare some sounds, as it were. Estonian and Votian drop the final -*n*, even as a genitive marker, but in North Estonian and West Votian the -*n* has been retained if it means '1 pers. sg.'. Thus the verb 'I carry' *kanna-n* > *kannan*, but a noun gen. sg. 'of a base' *kanna-n* > *kanna*. Again, these forms are phonetically identical, to begin with, as they still are in Finnish (both *kannan*). Note that there is no way of predicting why Karelian would retain its -*n* and Estonian would lose it; this is the actuation problem of linguistic change (compare §§ 9.16–9.18).

But another warning is in order. Even if it is easy to formulate a grammatically conditioned sound change, it need not be historically correct. When looking at the total evidence from Estonian the above case looks somewhat different, though it is still an example of grammatical conditioning. In the beginning of the seventeenth century, the final -*n* was about to disappear everywhere, but it was still retained if the following word began with a vowel. From such positions it could be generalized back into every position in the first person singular, partly (presumably) to avoid homonymy with the imperative *kanna* 'carry!'. In South Estonian the -*n* dropped everywhere, but here the imperative had a final glottal stop *kannaq*, at least in the Võru dialect, and no homonymy resulted with *kanna*

'I carry'. Incidentally, there is one compound in Estonian in which a word-final gen. -*n* has been retained, and it is the single exception: *maan-tee* 'highway' (literally 'land's road').

We also have cases in Lapp where sounds behave differently if they are the sole markers of certain grammatical categories, and where sound changes stall if homonymy would result. In the Western dialects of Finnish, case endings shed (apocopate) their vowels, but stem-final vowels remain. Thus *taka-na* > *takan* 'behind' (but *pakana* 'pagan' remains), *mu-lta* > *mult* 'from me' (but *multa* 'earth, dirt' remains). The hyphens, here and elsewhere, have been added for grammatical analysis and carry no phonetic meaning whatsoever. Similarly, final palatal consonants were depalatalized in Russian inflectional endings; for example, *dá-m'* 'I give' > *dám*, but *lós'* 'elk' remains as such.

Sometimes sound change is governed by different syntactic positions. In Livian the final -*n* 'gen. sg.' has generally dropped, as in *izà kōrand* 'father's house', but it is retained in the predicative function, as in *s'e kōrand um izàn* 'this house is father's'. Here, however, such a distribution can be explained as resulting from different stress (which would have the virtue of maintaining strictly phonetic conditioning). This could be exemplified also in English, for example, *my house* and *the house is mine*. A similar phenomenon occurs in Inari Lapp. The genitive -*n* has been dropped in nonmonosyllables, as in (nom. sg.) *räjgi/rääjgi* (gen. sg.) 'hole'. But as an adverb meaning 'asunder', the form retains the original genitive -*n*: *rääjgin* (*sukkà lii rääjgin* 'the sock is worn out').

[4.25]   It is interesting to note that the only relic in French of the Latin accusative ending -*m* occurs in the pronominal *rien*, a grammatical particle. In English, also, adverbs preserve endings that have been dropped from the nouns. A well-known example is *whilom* 'in former days', which derives directly from OE *hwīlum*, dat. pl. of *whīl* 'while, time'. This is, in fact, directly parallel to *rääjgin*, but a closer parallel is that English also used genitives as adverbs (e.g., *whiles*). A closure in the tongue position at the end of the word produced *whil(e)st* (§§ 4.11, 4.14). The excrescence occurred only in adverbs (*amidst*, *against*) and not if the -*s* was the marker of a "real" nominal genitive. The Middle English adverbial genitives *ones*, *twies*, and *pries* had the same fate: they were also cut off from the normal genitive. When the genitive ending assimilated in voicing to the stem, only the productive genitive was involved (e.g., *dog's* /dogz/), whereas the adverbial genitives remained voiceless and required a new orthography to ensure the correct voiceless reading: *once*, *twice*, and *thrice* (these now satisfy the environment for excrescence, and *oncet* /wənst/, *twicet* /twayst/ occur). The new voiced genitive has also been introduced in some adverbs (e.g., *Sundays*, *always*, *besides*, *betimes*); but in any case, syntactic–semantic factors were clearly at work. (Note that a collective *pence* also retains /s/ against the productive plural *pennies* with /z/.)

[4.26]   Let us return to the Rotuman formation of the incomplete phase (§ 4.6). As was mentioned, the drop of final vowels with or without fronting umlaut, metathesis, and vowel shortening occurred in a specific grammatical environment, in contrast to the raising umlaut, an allophone development of pure phonetic conditioning. The grammatical conditioning is a complex of syntactic and semantic factors. The incomplete phase occurs mainly in compounds or larger phrases of various degrees of complexity, that is, in specifiable syntactic environments, but also in a semantic context of indefiniteness or incompleteness (e.g., *famör qɛa* 'some people say'). The unmodified full form occurs when the meaning is definite, complete (e.g., *famori qɛa* 'the people say'), or when positiveness, finality, emphasis, or desire to be certain is involved. Such aspectual conditioning is clearly grammatical (semological) and even more "abstract" than the syntactic factor (e.g., *famori feqen* 'the people are zealous', but *famör feqeni* 'the zealous people, zealous people in general', *qɛpa la hɔaq* 'the mats will be taken', vs. *qɛap la hɔaq* 'some mats . . .'; from *hɔqa* 'to take').

[4.27 Morphophonemic Conditioning of Sound Change] In almost every case we have reviewed, change led to morphophonemic variation; that is, there was seldom any change in the structural relations of the units. The units just acquired more alternants on the surface, in clearly defined environments. This was true both for the phonemes (surface units) and the morphophonemes, and it made no difference whether the conditioning was phonetic or grammatical. The reverse is also possible: morphophonemic alternation can lead to change that eliminates variation. Morphophonemic conditioning of change is grammatical, because morphophonemes presuppose paradigmatic sets as the frames for change, and can never be mere sounds irrespective of the grammatical machinery. In Middle High German the syllable-final devoicing of voiced stops is proved by the writing (see § 2.4); thus the nominatives of *bunt/bunte* 'motley' and *bunt/bunde* 'league' were identical, as they still are in the pronunciation of Modern Standard German. In some Yiddish and Swiss dialects all those voiceless stops that alternate with voiced ones are replaced by the voiced alternant. Thus *bunt* 'league' > *bund*, but the phonemically identical shape *bunt* 'motley' remains unchanged. The change does not affect every /t/; it "looks around" in the total grammar, and if /t/ alternates with /d/, we get /t/ > /d/. This could be diagrammed as follows (wavy lines indicate paradigmatic alternation; certain historical shortcuts will be taken):

$$d$$
$$\wr$$
$$t > d$$

If there is no alternation the /t/ remains intact, as in *bunt/bunte* 'motley'. As another example of this, Old High German had a preposition *aba, ab(e)* 'away from'. The form without the final vowel underwent devoicing and became /ap/ (which is still spelled *ab* in Modern German purely for etymological reasons); such a form remains unchanged in the same dialects that replace *bunt* 'league' by *bund*. Similarly, the Middle High German adverb *enwec* 'on the way, away' gives *(a)vek* and the like (Standard German *weg* /vek/, again spelled etymologically). Like /ap/, /avek/ is an indeclinable adverb that does not alternate in any way, and it keeps its voiceless stop. The noun from which it is derived, MHG *wec/wege* 'road, way', did alternate, and accordingly the word-final /k/ was replaced by /g/:

$$
\begin{array}{c} g \\ \wr \\ k > g \end{array}
$$

and the nominative became *veg*. Thus semantic specialization and the lack of inflection in the adverbs cut them loose from their earlier morphophonemes. In Standard German, also, the adverb was cut off from the noun, but with different consequences. Starting from the MHG noun paradigm *vek/veges/vege* we first get lengthening in open syllables, which gives *vek/vēges/vēge*. This was a normal phonetic change which occurred in one phonetic environment; it increased variation in the paradigm, because in addition to the *k* ~ *g* alternation there was also *e* ~ *ē*. Similar alternations occurred in innumerable paradigms where a short vowel in closed syllable alternated with a long vowel in open syllable (e.g., *tak/tāges* 'day'). In Standard German, all such short vowels which alternate with long ones have been lengthened; that is,

$$
\begin{array}{ccc}
\bar{e} & \bar{a} & V \\
\wr & \wr \quad\quad \text{etc.} = & \wr \\
e > \bar{e} & a > \bar{a} & V > \bar{V}
\end{array}
$$

This gives us now nominatives /vēk/ and /tāk/ ⟨Weg, Tag⟩ (angular brackets indicate spelling). The adverb ⟨weg⟩ was outside the paradigm and did not alternate, and remained with a short vowel, /vek/. When morphophonemic information plays a role in such changes, the result is always a surface sound which is closer to the underlying unit. In all the cases given so far, the outcome was actually identical to the "upper story" member of the morphophoneme (the basic or most frequent alternant), but it need not be. In Ukrainian those *ž*'s that alternate with *d*'s become affricates, while others remain as *ž*'s, that is,

$$
\begin{array}{c} d \\ \wr \\ ž > dž \end{array}
$$

The outcome is not identical to the "upper story" member, but it does appropriate closure from the latter. The result is a compromise between the two variants, and the old alternation *d* ~ *ž* is replaced by *d* ~ *dž*. Normally, however, the alternation is eliminated altogether, as most of the above examples have shown; in addition, these examples have shown the prevailing replacement of the conditioned variant by the basic variant. There are exceptions to this, however. In Estonian, the sequence *ks* which alternated with *s* has been replaced by *s*:

$$
\begin{array}{lll}
ks > s & teokse > teose \text{ (gen.)} & \\
\wr & & \text{'work'} \\
s & teos \text{ (nom.) (§ 6.14)} &
\end{array}
$$

Another case is the Latin replacement of the inherited stem-final *s* in the nominative singular of *s*-stems by the *r* which was the outcome of earlier *s* between vowels (§ 4.3). The inherited pattern is transmitted undisturbed in two classes of nouns. The preservation of *s* in *flōs/flōris* 'flower', *mōs/mōris* 'custom', and *rōs/rōris* 'dew' can be phonologically described: final *s* is preserved in monosyllables. A morphological condition states that neuter nouns keep their original variation, for example, *corpus/corporis* 'body' and *genus/generis* 'kind'. (This type is very numerous and, not surprisingly, there are a few exceptions: the neuters *rōbus* 'oak' and **fulgus* 'lightening' appear as *rōbur* and *fulgur* in Classical Latin.) Otherwise, that is, in polysyllabic masculines and feminines, the word-final *s* has been universally replaced by the *r* of the oblique cases (e.g., *amor* 'love', *labor* 'work', *timor* 'fear', and so on). Here too one can find a stray exception among the numerous members of this form class: *honōs* 'honor' is not uncommon in Classical authors.

[4.28] These changes affected certain members of alternating paradigmatic sets, but such alternating sets can also act as conditioning environments to sound changes. The most famous case of this is Lachmann's law, which has become a standard example, though in most discussions it is wrongly interpreted. The situation is as follows. The past passive participle of Latin *făciō* 'do, make' is *făctus*, whereas the corresponding forms of *ăgō* 'drive', *lĕgō* 'read', *rĕgō* 'direct', and *păngō* 'agree upon' all have a long vowel: *āctus, lēctus, rēctus, pāctus*. The Romans themselves knew about this variation and commented on it; they mentioned that it usually takes place when the verb root ends in a voiced consonant that is devoiced before the morpheme *-tus* of the participle. In modern terms this could be explained by the plausible argument that short vowels in Latin had a longer allophone before a voiced consonant, and, when this "half-length" occurred before a voiced consonant in the past participle, it fell together with the phonemic long vowels of Latin. The difficulty, however, is that this lengthening is clearly a Latin phenomenon, whereas the assimilation **gt* > **kt* occurred in Proto-Indo-European. To account for the lengthening, we need access to the whole complicated paradigmatic system of the Latin verb. The starting point remains the contrast between the participle stem in /k/ versus the remaining forms in /g/, but lengthening takes place only if there is also a long-vowel perfect tense (e.g., *ēgī, lēgī, rēxī,* and *pēgī*). Thus *făciō/fēcī/făctus* does not lengthen the participle vowel, nor do *fingō/fīnxī/fīctum* 'stroke, mold', *findō/fīxī/fīssus* 'split', *stringō/strīnxī/strīctus* 'draw together', and so on. The actual spread of length to the participle is, therefore, an ordinary instance of analogy in the traditional sense.

[4.29] The Finnish paradigm for 'water' includes (nom. sg.) *vesi*, (gen. sg.) *vede-n*, (essive sg., another case) *vete-nä* 'as water', and so on. The stem-final vowel is *i* in absolute final position, *e* elsewhere; and the preceding consonant is *d* in closed syllable, *t* in open syllable, and *s* before *i* (see § 10.12). These alternations are very regular and occur in a great number of nouns. The *e ~ i* alternation is thus phonetically conditioned, although "word-final position," of course, is actually a grammatical condition. The $t \sim d \sim s$ alternation appears also to be phonetically induced, but it is not. The change $t > s$ occurs only before a stem-final i which alternates with e, that is,

$$t > s \quad \text{before} \quad \begin{matrix} e \\ \iota \\ i \end{matrix}$$

No assibilation occurs in words like *neiti/neidin/neitinä*, where the vowel is an unalternating i all the way. In some cases like this, however, the actual history may be quite different (see §§ 6.10, 10.17, 11.17, 11.18); for example, many scholars assume that the dental in *neiti* was earlier *δ rather than *t. Cases like this indicate that grammatical or morphophonemic conditioning in the synchronic grammar need not mirror a grammatically conditioned sound change.

[4.30]   As a conclusion to the sections on grammatical and morphophonemic conditioning of sound change, we can indeed acknowledge that such phenomena exist, although we have also seen warning signs that not every case that looks like them may be correctly so interpreted. This is one of the complications of history and reminds us of a well-known maxim based on natural phenomena: all is not gold that glitters. Of course, grammatical conditioning of alternations is one of the basic characteristics of synchronic grammar, but most of the time this is an incidental consequence of the piling up of pure phonetic changes (e.g., English *weorþan/worden*, *mouse/mice*, *safe/save*, *doom/deem*, French *neuf/neuve*, Livian *tamm/tämm*; other examples will be introduced later). Further, morphophonemic conditioning of sound change has taken us into the domain of traditional analogy. We have to return to this topic in the next chapter, and once more we can see that there need not be clear-cut boundaries in the grammatical apparatus and its changes. One glides almost imperceptibly from one area into another on the surface of it. This is why it has been so difficult to establish the underlying exact conceptual boundaries between various mechanisms (see § 6.25). Therefore, our chapter divisions are cardinal points only.

[4.31 Change and Variation]   This chapter has been purely descriptive, as is very often the case when we deal with linguistic change; this is a limitation dictated by the historical circumstances. That is, we describe facts that (we believe) happened. This is, of course, a necessary prerequisite to explanation, which will be treated later (Chapter 9). Even without taking the speakers themselves into consideration yet, we have seen how variation and change are interrelated. In most cases mentioned, synchronic variation was the source of change, and change led to new synchronic variation. A description that ignored allophonic variation would be very inadequate for our understanding of change. Most changes remain evident in the synchronic workings of a language for quite some time; a linguistic state is to a large degree a partial summary of the history of the language. The result and source of the change generally continue to function in the morphophonemic rules; only in a very few cases did change actually eliminate variation at certain spots. The Romance developments of Latin *k* were conditioned by its environmental variation; but in French, all outcomes occur in exactly the same environments, *kā*, *sā*, and *šā*, and no synchronic alternation remains between these (§ 4.4). In Yiddish the adverb *vek* fell outside the paradigm of its nominal origin and did not undergo the change to *veg*. These two forms do not alternate any longer, and perhaps for most speakers no mental connection exists. The same happened in Standard German, but there, the separation occurred through the vowels, /vek/ vs. /vēk/. This does not mean that variation was eliminated everywhere; e.g., the German syllable-final devoicing of voiced stops (*vēk/vēges*) is still an automatic phenomenon in the language. New loans undergo it, for example, *Job* [yop] and *Trend* [trent]. In most other cases change is variation and variation, change. Generally, then, change leads from variation to variation. Sound change is largely unobserved, because speakers interpret it as variation. Every speaker must be able to handle variation if he wants to communicate at all (Chapter 3), and speakers have no reason to know that one aspect of variation is change.

[**4.32 Regularity of Sound Change**] The startling regularity of phonetic changes was the main rallying cry of the Neogrammarian practitioners of genetic linguistics, who were actually the founders of modern linguistics. When each occurrence of a sound under the same conditions became another given sound, this was enough regularity for it to be called a law. This concept was aided by the same regularity in variation (e.g., when every *n* became *ŋ* before a velar). In fact, in allophonic variation the regularity is even more compelling than from the historical point of view, although one must perhaps say that all grammars contain some irregularities, or as Sapir put it, all grammars leak. Intolerance toward irregularity in linguistic change is unjustified, although the working hypothesis that every irregularity has its reason led to closer scrutiny of trouble spots. Many hidden regularities were found when systematic conditioning emerged from apparent disorder, and the ultimate regularity of change was saved. But sooner or later a historical linguist can expect to encounter sporadic changes. He has to live with them exactly as with gaps in historical attestation. Often irregularity mixes in equal amount with regularity (in § 4.8 see *zealous*, and so on). In such cases one just has to try harder. For instance, for a century or so a Lithuanian outcome baffled Indo-Europeanists. PIE **oi* gives either Lithuanian *ie* or *ai*. The outcomes are regular in that we have many cases of both, but there was no reason for one rather than the other in any particular word. Now, such a regular irregularity can be convincingly resolved by regarding *ai* as the native outcome and *ie* as a pronunciation borrowing from Slavic (§ 8.8). The Neogrammarian *absolute* regularity (100 per cent) of sound change is untenable, and this has always been recognized by most practitioners. The French phoneticians and the Finno-Ugric linguists have, in fact, suggested that the notion of the sound "law" has to be downgraded to a "tendency" only. In any case, it is the regular aspect of sound change that gives backbone to genetic linguistics, no matter how much the slipped discs of sporadic change may annoy the linguists.

Irregular sound change tends to occur in certain areas of grammar and phonology more frequently than elsewhere. Iconic signs (onomatopoeia and similar descriptive forms) resist regular phonetic change best. Although these categories have their symbolic aspects—they depend on the particular language —scholars, on the whole, agree as to where they expect such forms, for example, in names for all kinds of noises, scraping, quick movements, slow movements, tabu or unpleasant notions, and so on. The [ī] in ME *pipen* 'to chirp' is expected to turn out with [ai] as we saw (§ 4.8). But the vowel has not changed uniformly and there is still a kind of [ī] verb, spelled *peep*, although the phonetically regular /payp/ *pipe* also occurs and the instrument *pipe* also has the regular outcome. OE -*cwȳsan*, ME *queisen* 'to crush' should end up as /kwayz/ or /kweyz/ in Modern English. The word, however, is *squeeze* with /iy/ (not to speak of the extra *s*-, assumed to come from Old French *es*- < Latin *ex*-, as in *espresser* 'squeeze out' and similar words: *extract*, *extort*). Expressive vocabulary does not invariably resist change, but it can. In Classical Greek the sound that sheep gave was appropriately something like [bæˑ] or [bɛˑ]. This form has undergone the "regular sound changes" in the modern reading of the classical word, ending up as [vi], clearly a far less iconic shape; but the normal modern form is still [beˑ].

The Proto-Germanic word for 'cuckoo' was **gaukaz*, which in due time gave MHG *gouch*, OE *gēac*, ON *gaukr*, and Swedish *gök* [y-]. In English and German the words have again become more iconic, that is, *cuckoo* and *Kuckuck*. This is obviously not regular sound change but "analogy" from the actual sound of the bird. One should also note that in synchronic grammar descriptive vocabulary often contains sounds not found in the rest of the language.

Frequent forms, such as pronouns and grammatical morphemes, are also prone to undergo irregular changes. Without giving examples, we can note here that the Rotuman changes delineated above (§ 4.6) do not take place so consistently in the pronouns. On the other hand, we saw that in certain syntactic or grammatical contexts a form can regularly remain unchanged (adverbs *once* [§ 4.25], *vek* [§ 4.27], *rääjgin* [§ 4.24], compound *maantee* [§ 4.24], and pronouns *rien* [§ 4.25], *siihen* [§ 4.16]). Once more, there is regularity in the irregularity. Then again, there are exceptions like *nāsus*, *folly*, and *scholar*, although there are many cases of the latter, and hence (incipient) regularity.

What aids this heterogeneity of sound change is the way it spreads. Speakers adopt the changes at different times both in terms of social layers, individuals, and vocabulary sets. This provides enough room for irregularities to spring up (Chapters 6, 9).

REFERENCES

General: Hockett 1965, Koch 1970, Baldi and Werth (eds.) 1978, Fisiak (ed.) 1978; **4.1** Sturtevant 1947, Penzl 1957; **4.2** Penzl 1957, Hoenigswald 1964a; **4.3-4.4** Sturtevant 1947 -- Collinge 1985; **4.5** H. Bennett 1969; **4.6** Churchward

1940, Biggs 1965; **4.7** Posti 1942, Wickman 1958-60; **4.8** Wolfe 1972, R. Krohn 1969, Stockwell and Minkova in Kastovsky et al. (eds.) 1988; **4.10** see §6.3; **4.11** E. Itkonen 1966; **4.12** Hill 1936, Moulton 1967, Fairbanks 1969, Benediktsson 1970; Schane 1971, Lehmann 1971, Nurse 1987; **4.13** Lehmann 1964; **4.14** Kent 1936, Sturtevant 1947, Andersen (ed.) 1985; **4.15** Wang 1969; **4.17** Sturtevant 1947, Dyen (private communication), Hock 1985b; **4.18** Hockett 1967, Thompson and Thompson 1969, Dyen (private communication); **4.19** Hockett 1967; **4.21** Hoenigswald 1964b, Hockett 1965, Bhat 1968, Andersen 1972, T. Itkonen 1970; **4.22** Sapir 1921, S. Moore 1927, 1928, Collinder 1937-39, Pike 1947, Kiparsky 1965; **4.23** Jakobson 1949, Janert 1961; **4.24** E. Itkonen 1966, Kettunen 1962; **4.25** Greenough and Kittredge 1929; **4.27** Kiparksy 1965, 1968a, Newman 1968 -- L. Campbell in Anderson and Jones (eds.) 1974; **4.28** Kuryłowicz 1968, Watkins 1970, Strunk 1976; **4.29** Anttila 1969a; **4.31** Fónagy 1956-57, 1967; **4.32** Specht 1952, Senn 1953, Katičić 1970.

CHAPTER 5

GRAMMAR CHANGE: ANALOGY

Analogy is a function of the relational aspects of grammar and a mental striving for simplicity or uniformity.

[5.1 Proportional Analogy]   The term 'analogy' is used in many senses, all having to do with some kind of regularity. The earliest linguistic context of the word was the Ancient Greek controversy as to whether language was controlled by regularity or analogy, as against irregularity or anomaly. This controversy itself was an extension of an earlier dispute as to whether the relation between words and their meanings is natural or conventional. These questions gave the impetus to rigorous investigation into language, and by now we have a compromise answer. The nature–analogy position falls within the notion of iconicity, and the convention–anomaly position reflects symbolic aspects. Both forces play a role in the functioning of language, as we have seen (Chapter 1), and we have already observed various aspects of analogy (§§ 1.13, 2.2, 2.8, 2.14–2.16, 3.3, 4.19). A widespread characterization of analogy and sound change is that the former involves meaning, the latter, form only. This is valid for most instances, but is by no means absolute. We saw in the principle of phonetization (the rebus principle) a case of analogy that did not involve meaning (§ 2.8), although here, of course, we are not dealing with language directly but with its secondary representation. Nevertheless, meaning can be a factor in sound change, especially grammatical meaning. Further, the regularity of sound change is also analogical: when a sound x changes under conditions y in a word A, it also changes in word B under the same conditions.

Although the domains of sound change and analogy overlap to a degree, the latter is predominantly conditioned by morphology and other areas of grammar. A grammar is largely a system of relations, and analogy is a *relation of similarity*. We have already seen a two-term analogy, $A:B$, in the case of *citizen/denizen*, in which two nouns meaning the same thing converged on the formal side (§ 4.19). Well known is the three-term analogy of the geometric mean, $A:B = B:C$, which (in a way) operates in the case of Lapp $htt:\eth = \eth:X$, where the third term is $\eth\eth$ (§§ 10.14, 10.15, 11.15, 13.3). This Lapp analogy is not as perfect relationally as the mathematical formula, but it has the same number of terms. The most famous type of extraphonological change is the analogy of proportionality, $A:B = C:D$ (with four terms). Any system of grammatical description (§ 1.18) can be reduced to analogical terms based on the kind of relations used in each such system, and formal descriptions are based on proportional analogy. In the traditional immediate constituent approach, positive intersentential

88

analogies were used, giving what *does*, in fact, appear in grammatical constructions. In the transformational approach, the intrasentential relations between deep and surface structure provide the bases for analogies, with the extra dimension of giving information on what *might* appear in grammatical constructions. Readers who are not very well acquainted with formalized grammatical description need only accept the assertion that all these different theoretical frameworks use the same principle of analogy but on different terms and axes (see §§ 5.21, 6.24). This is just a reminder that the basic structures of all formal descriptions are, in fact, analogical. Thus it is no wonder that analogy operates mainly in the structure of grammar.

Proportional analogy is, of course, diagrammatically iconic, an icon of relation (§§ 1.13–1.15). Language has a general iconic tendency, whereby semantic sameness is reflected also by formal sameness; this force underlies contamination. We often can predict the areas where analogy will enter, if it does enter, by noting such things as formal imbalance in a semantically symmetric situation.

[5.2] Sometimes a speaker who creates a new analogical form completes the proportion. Children, especially, who have to defend their creations against the conventions of the speech community, resort to this. We have the case of the Danish child who formed a past tense *nak* 'nodded' for the present *nikker* instead of the "correct" weak conjugation form *nikkede*. When corrected, the child responded with the formula *stikker:stak* 'sticks:stuck' = *nikker:nak*; that is,

$$\frac{stikker}{stak} = \frac{nikker}{X} \quad \text{or} \quad \frac{stikker}{nikker} = \frac{stak}{X}$$

In other words, the child referred to an existing pattern by means of an example, as he obviously could not say "why not make the verb a strong one?" or the like. Such shifts in subpatterns have occurred in all Germanic languages (e.g., English *drive:drove* = *dive:X*, where *X* is *dove*). In Modern English only about one third of the Old English strong verbs remain so; the rest have shifted into the weak class. A proportion given by an English-speaking child is *sing:sang* = *swing:swang*, where two subtypes of the strong verb are at stake. In these cases, then, one can assume that one word is chosen as a model for a whole class (§ 5.18f.), but there are also cases where a single unique paradigm can serve as a model. The Elean Greek word for 'Zeus' was inflected thus: nom. *Zeú-s*, acc. *Zên-a*, gen. *Zên-ós*, and dat. *Zên-í*. The oblique stem is not inherited, but was built on the old accusative *Zên*. There was only one other noun with a similar oblique stem: *mēn-* 'moon', whose expected nominative would be *mei-s* (which actually occurs in many dialects). But the Elean form is *meús*. Both paradigms shared an oblique stem in *-ēn-* and a nominative in an *e*-diphthong. Both were unique inflections, and they converged on the model of *Zeús*; that is, *Zēn-*: *Zeús* = *mēn-*: *X*. The formula does not imply that the old form is lost instantaneously when the new one comes about. For a time they occur side by side, until one is assigned to a clear social or stylistic context, or until one variant is lost. Thus both *dived* and *dove* still exist, as well as an older *brethren* and a newer *brothers*, with clear stylistic and social differentiation. On the other hand, the original paradigm (sg.) *book*, (pl.) *beech* was given a new plural *books*; and after a time the old one was lost. Because the word shifted into the majority pattern, it is easy to give a proportion: *pen*:*pens* = *book*:X (see § 5.19). Note that the example is one of principle only, to avoid Middle English complexities of spelling.

[5.3]   Many of the iconic developments we saw in the first three chapters show proportional analogy or at least *can be* described through it. The rebus principle shows this in Sumerian orthography,

meaning	'arrow'	'life'
form	ti	ti
writing	$\succ\rightarrow$	X

$$\frac{ti}{\succ\rightarrow} = \frac{ti}{X}$$

where the proportion exists between the last two rows and X was solved with a spelling $\succ\rightarrow$. This is a case of "spelling spellings" (§§ 2.6, 2.15). The 'past' tenses of *will* and *can* were ME *wolde* and *coude*, in which the *n* had been lost already in OE *cūðe* (< **kunþe*; compare *tooth* < **tanþ*; § 4.16). After the loss of *l* we get (using modern forms)

$$\frac{\text{/wud/}}{would} = \frac{\text{/kud/}}{X} \quad \text{or} \quad \frac{\text{/layt/}}{light} = \frac{\text{/di'layt/}}{X}$$

pronunciation / spelling

and the outputs *could* and *delight*. Similarly,

$$\frac{fate \text{ (etc.)}}{\text{/feyt/}} = \frac{ate}{X}$$

spelling / pronunciation

produces the spelling pronunciation /eyt/. The mechanism of hypercorrect forms shows the same relation:

$$\frac{ya\cdot d}{ya\cdot rd} = \frac{ga\cdot d}{X} \qquad \text{God} \quad (= \text{Gard})$$

Dialect 1 / Dialect 2

This is very frequent in all languages. In Sicily medial *ll* had been replaced by apical *ḍḍ* (*stella* > *stiḍḍa* 'star'). New immigrants into the area extended the *ḍḍ* also into initial position:

$$\frac{stella}{stiḍḍa} = \frac{luna}{X}$$

Dialect 1 / Dialect 2

and we get Hyper-Sicilian *ḍḍuna* 'moon', and so on. Such examples could be multiplied by the hundred.

Hypercorrect forms show relations between regional and social variation, but the same formal situation may obtain between variants in the same norm. When British English lost the *r* in forms like *better* before pause or another consonant, variation /betə ~ betər-V/ resulted. This now serves as a model for words with final ə's:

$$\text{Environment 1} \quad \frac{bet\partial}{bet\partial r} = \frac{ay'di\partial}{X} \quad \begin{array}{l}\text{(before } C\text{)} \\ \text{(before } V\text{)}\end{array}$$

Environment 1 (before *C*)
Environment 2 (before *V*)

and phrases like *the idea-r of it* and *America-r and England* result. After Estonian *k* had been lost medially at the beginning of closed syllables, as in *kasket* > *kased* 'birches', we get alternation, that is, sg. *kask* ~ pl. *kased*. Words that originally had a stem-final *s* look now the same in the plural, for example, *kuused* 'firs'. Instead of the expected sg. *kuus* we have *kuusk*, arising from a proportion like the following one:

$$\text{Environment 1} \quad \frac{kased}{kask} = \frac{kuused}{X} \quad \begin{array}{l}\text{(nom. pl.)} \\ \text{(nom. sg.)}\end{array}$$

Environment 1 (nom. pl.)
Environment 2 (nom. sg.)

In both English and Estonian, alternation has been extended into words where it did not exist before. Such paradigmatic sets can even create new phonemes. Russian nonstop consonants (continuants) were palatalized before front vowels; when these vowels dropped, there was a split (e.g., *v* vs. *v'*, *r* vs. *r'*, and so on), and both can alternate within paradigms. A stop like *k* was affricated into *č* (*tš*) and later, in some new environments, into *c* (*ts*); this morphophonemic alternation *k* ~ *č* ~ *c* remains (compare the Old French outcomes of Latin *k* without paradigmatic alternation; § 4.4). But paradigms in which *v* and *v'* and so on alternate have called into being a new phoneme /k'/ for an expected *č*:

1st sg.	*rv–ú*	*vr–ú*	*tk–ú*
2nd sg.	*rv'–óš*	*vr'–óš*	*tk'–óš*
	'tear'	'tell lies'	'weave'

Similarly, the instrumental of *kto* 'who' is *k'em*, for an expected *čem*. The form *čem* is found as the instrumental of *čto* 'what'; thus it appears that the *k*- of the animate paradigm was restored (with automatic palatalization before *e*) as an indirect marker of 'animate', while the original form was semantically specialized as 'inanimate'. The analogical origin of *k'* in Russian is clearly revealed by its restriction to position before a morpheme boundary (see § 5.13), at least in native vocabulary, although loans like *k'inó* 'cinema' have extended its distribution into other positions. Here we have extension of an alternation, and, at the same time, leveling of an alternation that would have been much more pronounced if analogy had not occurred.

[5.4 Nonproportional Analogy]   Proportional analogy is only one kind of analogy. Often proportions do not exist, for example, in contamination or analogic lag and anticipation (§ 4.19). The last two types show an important point: the prime area of nonproportional analogy is the sentence or some other juxtaposition. In other words, indexical elements are very important in addition to iconic ones. Strong evidence against the necessity of proportional analogy were forms where the older shape was just covered over by new material without being replaced in toto. Thus the expected plural of cow, "*ki*" [kai], was adapted to the pattern of its antonym *ox* by the addition of the plural marker *n*: [kai-n] *kine*. The old plural still lurks in the word. Similar forms are frequent in the speech of children (e.g., *feets*, or with past tenses like *camed*). Similarly, in German, there are *hielt-e* 'held' and *ging-te* 'went', where the forms have been modified so that the characteristic weak preterite -*te* results. In English the noun *seamster* was already feminine, but one more marker has been piled on, giving *seamstress*, although in this case proportional influence from *mister/mistress* is also possible. The German *Hinde* 'doe' was also feminine, and again the characteristic feminine marker of the language has been attached: *Hindin*. In German the past passive participles have a prefix *ge-* (e.g., *ge-mach-t* 'made'). A verb like *essen* fused *ge-essen* into *gessen*. The resulting form was deviant, as it seemed to lack the syllable *ge-*; it was consequently supplied with it again, giving *ge-gessen*, the current form.

In these cases we have seen the iconic tendency for semantic similarity to be reflected by formal similarity; cases that get out of line are likely to be rehabilitated.

[5.5]   Another distinct case of iconic remodeling is *folk etymology*. The term is quite technical, because it is neither folk nor etymology. It means that unfamiliar shapes are replaced by more familiar ones. Thus the phenomenon is related to contamination, and should perhaps best be called *reinterpretation* or *adaptation*. Loanwords are often subject to this, because they are unanalyzable in the adopting language and have forms unusually long compared with the established morphemes of the language. A word like *asparagus* is rather long for one morpheme in English and gave way to *sparrow grass*, which more or less retains the number of consonants. What is important is that the form is now a compound built up of known elements. There is even a fair amount of semantic justification in that the vegetable is a kind of grass. Similarly, Latin *margarita* 'pearl' was replaced by *mere-grota* in Old English, a perfectly iconic compound in terms of the language, that is, *mere* 'sea' and *grota* 'grain'. English-speaking tourists used to refer to a kind of Finnish brandy called *jaloviina*, literally 'noble liquor', as *yellow wine*. Again the semantics is not completely arbitrary, although the color is not really yellow nor is the drink a wine, but wines and spirits form one semantic field in Western culture. An Indian lady was referring, quite seriously, to Ku Klux Klanners as *scrupulous clowns*, which indeed supplies an amount of topsy-turvy iconicity to the term. And for her the organization was foreign enough to be reinterpreted.

Semantic justification is not a prerequisite, because form is after all independent of meaning. When *cucumber* gives *cow cumber*, or Ojibwa *otchek* → *woodchuck*, part of the arbitrary form still remains, but the arbitrary part is shorter and the total seems to fit the rest of the vocabulary better because of the native passport in the first part. A native element that has become obscure is equally prone for replacement; thus an expected *samblind 'half blind' (Latin sēmi-'half') has given sandblind, where, in some situations, sand can be even semantically justified. An often quoted case in which semantics was also affected is ME schamfast, which in Old English meant 'modest' (literally 'firm in modesty'). When the form was modified to shamefaced, we had a basis for a new meaning 'ashamed'. Proper names and the like that do not have a linguistic meaning put no constraints on the form. The American soldiers of 1918 referred to Château-Thierry as Shadow Theory, and in German the Latin name unguentum Neapolitanum 'Neapolitan ointment' was made more familiar by umgwendter Napoleon (Napoleon turned around). But such drastic formal reinterpretation can also occur with definite meaning. The American soldiers rendered the French phrase très bien with three beans, retaining the meaning 'very well'. Indeed, reinterpretation is the basis of the literary device of punning.

Reinterpretation need not change the forms that have been reinterpreted at all. When Sturtevant's little son underwent treatment of the ear by irrigation with warm water, the situation made him connect the word ear with the first part of irr-igate. This was an inductive change (see § 9.16), aided by the situation, and falling under contamination and folk etymology at the same time. The change increased iconicity in the vocabulary of this child. But this new analysis did not show anywhere. Only a later change made it visible, when the child took his inductive reanalysis as a basis for a new deductive derivation. When his nose was treated the same way, he used the new relation ear:irrigate = nose:X, which gave nosigate, and this uncovered the earlier reanalysis. That is, proportional analogy reveals an earlier nonproportional case. Similarly, the child who saw four airplanes and learned that it was a formation made the "logical" (iconic) reanalysis for-mation (instead of the correct form-ation). This surfaced only when he saw two more planes and referred to them as a twomation. Again, the initial inductive change surfaced with a regular derivation four:formation = two:X. New formations like food-holic and gum-holic show that alcoholic must have first been reanalyzed as having a morpheme -holic 'addicted to'. The women's liberation movement has institutionalized folk etymology by trying to replace history and boycott by herstory and girlcott.

[5.6] Of course such reanalysis and new derivation by children is often ephemeral, but the mechanism is clearly at work. It can, however, become generally accepted by the speech community. English has synchronic ambiguity in cases like a name vs. an aim, because they can be phonetically alike. In the history of the language, there are cases where such an n (either part of the article or other pronouns or the initial of a noun) has been interpreted the wrong way. Old English efeta gave ME evete, which ends up as NE eft. The current normal shape, however, was reanalyzed from anevete → a-nevete, giving newt. Similarly, Middle English eke-name 'additional name' (compare to eke out a living) incorporated the n from the article, anekename, ending up as nickname. The Fool calls King Lear nuncle (< mine uncle), and the pet names of Edward and Oliver used to be Ned and Nol (mine Ed, and so on). The reverse has happened to OE *nafugār* → *auger*, *napron* → *apron* (compare *napery* 'linen' and *napkin*), and also in *adder* from ME *naddere* (compare German *Natter*). In these cases the *n* of the noun has been assigned to the article. In all the cases the reanalysis was not visible in colloquial pronunciation as long as the nouns occurred after the article or possessive pronoun. Only in other (syntactic) environments do we get proof of the reanalysis (*apron*, *nickname*, and so on). Again, another environment bears witness to an inductive change that had occurred earlier elsewhere, with no necessary visible reflexes (see § 9.16).

No proportions need work in such reinterpretations, even though they do in subsequent derivations. Latin had a suffix *-nus* (e.g., *domi-nus* 'master' and *fāgi-nus* 'of beech'). Applied to *ā-* stems, we get forms like *Rōmā-nus* and *silvā-nus* 'forest deity'. At some point these were analyzed as *Rōm-ānus* and *silv-ānus*, because new derivatives were formed with a suffix *-ānus* on stems without *ā*, for example, *mundānus* 'of the world' (*mund-*), *urbānus* 'of the city' (*urb-*), and *montānus* 'of the mountains' (*mont-*). The suffix grew also a variant *-iānus*, and this is still productive in English (into which it was borrowed through a horde of loanwords), for example, *Bloomfieldian* and *Humboldtian*.

[5.7 Interplay Between Sound Change and Analogy]   Typical for language change is the constant tug of war between sound change and analogy. Sturtevant phrased this as a paradox: sound change is regular and causes irregularity; analogy is irregular and causes regularity. That is, the mainly regular sound change can pull regular paradigms apart; analogy is generally irregular, in that it does not occur in every case where it could, but when it does, the result is greater regularity in morphology. In the case of morphophonemic conditioning of sound change we have a case of analogy, which is sometimes even regular, and, of course, sound change can be irregular. The paradox is not absolute, but still accurate.

As a first example of how sound change destroys paradigmatic unity, let us look at a Latin instance. For practical simplicity of handling examples, let us confine ourselves to the nominative and genitive singular cases, because these reveal the crux of the matter. A Pre-Latin paradigm (nom. sg.) *deiwos* (gen. sg.) *deiwī* 'celestial' has a constant stem *deiw-*, and the case endings *-os* and *-ī*, a type that survived into Latin.

1. The diphthong changed into a long close vowel, *ei* > *ẹ̄*, which had no effect on the paradigm as such.
2. Now a *w* before *o* drópped, making the nominative *dẹ̄os*.
3. *Dẹ̄os* is subject to another well-known Latin change: a long vowel is shortened before another vowel; thus *deos*.
4. *o* > *u* in final syllable.
5. *ẹ̄* > *ī*, and the paradigm should end up as *deus/dīvī* (in regularized Latin orthography).

These five changes are regular sound changes in Latin, and they have produced an irregular paradigm, where the stem now alternates between *de-* and *dīv-*. This kind of unique alternation is a situation in which analogy might be expected to restore balance (regularity), as it in fact did, because *deus* and *dīvī* do not belong to the same paradigm in historical Latin. Analogy eliminated the alternation by building complete paradigms to both alternants. The nominative *deus* got a new genitive *deī*, and the genitive *dīvī* received a new nominative *dīvus*. Now we have two regular paradigms, *deus/deī* 'god' and *dīvus/dīvī* 'god, divine'. This is an eloquent example of Sturtevant's paradox. The situation is parallel to the regeneration power of the planarian worm. When cut in half, its front part grows a new rear end, and vice versa (see § 22.1).

A paradigm need not split in two. Pre-Latin **ekwos* 'horse' and **parwos* 'little' should give **ekos* and **paros* (> **ecus*, **parus*) because of change 2 above, but the corresponding genitives **ekwī* and **parwī* (here again, of course, representing the rest of the paradigm) prevailed and grew or maintained new nominatives *equus* and *parvus*. The regular outcome is shown in the adverb *parum* 'too little', which was no longer connected with the paradigm of *parvus*. Such offshoots provide clear evidence for analogical interference. Another case is **sekwondos* > **sekondos* > *secundus* 'second', developing regularly by the sound laws after the word had been cut off from the paradigm of *sequī* 'to follow', which retained its [kw] in every position. English *sword* has also lost its *w* in this position, and so should have *swore*, but it was restored/maintained after the present *swear*. In Latin nouns the majority of the oblique stem generally wins out, but in the third declension noun **wōk-s* (gen.) **wōkw-is* 'voice', the alternation *wōk-/wōkw-* is eliminated in favor of the nominative *wōk-*: *vōx* [ks]/ *vōcis*. This is the irregularity of analogy (one cannot predict the direction), which may be quite regular, since Latin, after all, does not allow for an interconsonantal *w*, **wōkws*. On the other hand (nom.) **yekor* (gen.) **yekwinis* 'liver' has also adopted the nominatival *k*: *iecur/iecinoris*, as well as the *-or-* from the nominative. This is a clear case where proportional analogy is impossible but where we have a complex contamination of the two stems.

English shows clearly the irregularity of the direction of analogical leveling in the strong verb, where Old English had different vowels in the preterite singular and plural:

INFINITIVE	PRET. SG.	PRET. PL.	P.P.P.	
bītan	*bāt*	*biton*	*biten*	'bite'
rīdan	*rād*	*ridon*	*riden*	'ride'

The corresponding Modern English paradigms, like those of the weak verbs, have just one form for the preterite. Alternation has been eliminated both ways: in *bite* ~ *bit*, the plural vocalism prevails, in *ride* ~ *rode*, the singular, although there is also an archaic *rid* (see § 10.7).

[5.8]   The following Old English paradigms (two representative forms have
been chosen—the minimum number, of course) gave Middle English:

	OE			ME	
nom. sg.	*stæf*	*sceadu*	*mǣd*	*staf*	*schade* *mede*
(pl.)	*stavas*	(obl.) *sceadwe*	*mǣdwe*	*staves*	*schadwe* *medwe*

In the OE paradigm of *stæf* the nominative singular has a closed syllable (i.e.,
it ends in a consonant), but the first syllable is open in the plural (*sta.vas*). The
syllable structure is reversed in *scea.du* (open)/*scead.we* (closed), and in *mǣd*
the root syllable is the same throughout the paradigm, a closed syllable but with
a *long* vowel. In the last case we have the same vocalic developments as in
hǣlan and *hǣlþ*, that is, shortening before two consonants (§ 4.8)—*mead* exactly
like *heal* /iy/ and *meadow* like *health* /e/. This, of course, is the Modern English
result, but the short /e/ in *meadow* still shows the fact that the *w* was contiguous
to *d* in Middle English. In ME *staf* and *schade* we have a reverse development,
equally regular: the lengthening of short vowels in open syllables. This effects
the plural of *staf* and the nominative of *schade*, giving us *stāves* and *schāde*.
With the great vowel shift we get Modern English shapes *staff/staves* /stæf ~
steyvz/ and *shade/shadow* /šeyd ~ šædow/. Now regular English sound changes
have produced the above forms as well as *mead/meadow*. All started from uniform
Old English vocalism and ended up as regular alternations, because such vowel
alternations occur in hundreds of English vocabulary items. But exactly as in
the Latin case of *deus/dīvus* the paired English forms do not belong together
any more in Modern English, except perhaps for *staff/staves* (to a degree). The
resulting vowel alternations occur in different word classes, for example, adjec-
tive-noun *sane/sanity*, adjective-verb *clean/cleanse*, and noun-verb *grass/graze*,
glass/glaze, and *breath/breathe*, but not within the same word. As in Latin the
variants have split into two words, and the missing parts have been supplied
analogically, that is, diagrammatically according to the regular patterns (rules)
of the language: *staff/staffs* (new), *stave* (new)/*staves* (compare *cloth/clothes*),
mead/meads (new), *meadow* (new)/*meadows*, *shade/shades* (new), *shadow* (new)/
shadows (see § 7.9). As in Latin, semantic differentiation accompanies the
formal split; it is, in fact, a prerequisite of the survival of both forms (compare
Indian/Injun, § 2.14). Normally, only the oblique stem survives, for example,
in those words that had the *w* in Old English: *yellow* (*geolu*), *fallow* (*fealu*),
callow (*calu*), and *arrow* (*earh*). The oblique stem survived also in *thimble*
(§§ 4.11, 4.12); today, when hardly any inflection is left, the nominative singular
has a strong position (e.g., /owðz/ being replaced by /owθs/ *oaths* after the
singular *oath* /θ/; see §§ 10.16, 11.6). Formal vowel alternation survives in some
nouns only if the short-vowel variant occurs in fossilized derivatives (*seam/
seamstress, goose/gosling*) or compounds (*crane/cranberry, vine/vineyard, house/
husband*) which are independent words (not productive outputs of the "normal"
rules of the language). Actually *seamstress* is now generally /siymstrəs/, an
obvious analogical, partially productive form in relation to *sempstress*. The

original root vocalism is often better preserved in family names as in *Webster/ weave* and *Baxter/bake*.

[5.9]   We saw above how Estonian *k* alternates with nothing (at the beginning of a closed syllable; § 5.3). In intervocalic position this stop is written with *g*, and the alternation is exemplified by the inf. *püga-ma* next to the 1st pers. sg. *pöa-n* 'shear, cut (hair)'. Similarly, *d* alternates with nothing (among other things), as in *laadi-ma/lae-n* 'load (gun)' and *haudu-ma/hau-n* 'brood, hatch'. The alternation here is just one small aspect of the consonant gradation, which was originally determined by the phonetic shape of the word (closed and open syllables). This state of affairs is well preserved in Finnish (§§ 10.12, 10.13), but Estonian has eliminated alternation on a large scale. In some cases the *g* (and so on) has been generalized through an entire paradigm or through part of it (e.g., the present); in others, the lack of the stop (nothing) has been generalized. And in part of the vocabulary, alternation remains. This lack of exact goals is typical of the irregularity of analogical change, and we saw in the *kuusk* case that alternation can be extended even to items that did not have it (§ 5.3). Thus analogy levels out alternations by two means at the same time, either by generalizing one of the variants or by creating new cases of an existing alternation. The situation is very similar to the tug of war between the various classes of English strong verbs and the weak verbs (e.g., *dove/dive*). But the old and new forms can both ultimately survive, if semantic difference is attached to them. All three Estonian verbs mentioned developed analogical presents without alternation, the leveling being in favor of the stop alternant. The new analogical forms *püga-n* 'cheat, swindle', *laadi-n* 'load (freight)', and *haudu-n* 'be hatched, stew' coexist with the old ones because of the semantic differentiation, even though the infinitives remain the same. (Actually the semantic differences are not that clear for all speakers. There is a strong tendency for the new forms to be generalized in both meanings.) Compare the English verb *hang*, which has tolerated both a strong (*hung*) and a weak (*hanged*) inflection because of a similar semantic difference, as well as the English examples above (i.e., *sunk/ sunken*, *burnt/burned*; *shade/shadow*, and so on).

[5.10 Analogy and Regularity]   It is now clear that morphophonemic conditioning of sound change eliminates paradigmatic alternation by means of analogy (§ 4.27). It can be written in the form of a sound change when it is overwhelmingly regular, that is, when it occurs all through the phonology of a particular morphological or grammatical subsection. In the German case we saw that related forms that were outside the paradigms did not undergo the changes (*vek*, *ap*). This is exactly parallel to forms like *parum*, *secundus*, and *seamstress*, which remained true to the sound changes and were left behind by the analogical levelings (§§ 5.7, 5.8). Both morphophonemic conditioning of sound change and analogical change were triggered by alternation within paradigms.

Morphophonemic conditioning of sound change is not necessarily the only kind of analogy that is regular. The regularity of change is the ultimate result. While in progress, a change is not notably regular, because it spreads at different times in different environments and speakers. When analogy levels out all exceptions to a particular alternation, the result is perfect regularity, and it is difficult to know whether we are dealing with sound change or analogy. In this sense morphophonemic conditioning of sound change is both sound change and analogy. English *bite/bit* and *ride/rode* exemplify two-way tendencies within a category. This is also the case of Estonian consonant alternations, which are eliminated here, extended there. In Lapp, however, the alternations have been extended to every word (§§ 10.14, 13.3), and the result is perfect regularity.

[5.11 Relative Chronology in the Operation of Sound Change and Analogy]
Linguists have usually assumed that a sound change takes place in peace, and when it has sufficiently eroded morphological machinery, analogy comes to the rescue. Often this is true enough, as in the cases of Latin *deus/dīvus* and English *shade/shadow*, and a particularly illustrative example can be quoted from Spanish. In Old Spanish the sequence *dl* was metathesized into *ld* in certain noninherited Latin words. Thus *titulu(m)* > *tilde*, *modulu(m)* > *molde* 'mold', and *capitulu(m)* > *cabildo* 'chapter (church division)', in which the Latin forms show the original order of the dental stop plus *l*, and of course the Latin *u* was syncopated before the metathesis. Also, a sequence of the imperative *d* and a pronominal *l* underwent the same metathesis, *dad-los* > *daldos* 'give them' and *cantad-la* > *cantalda* 'sing it', and the pronominal *n* had the same fate, *dad-nos* > *dandos* 'give us'. Such metathesized forms remained current up to the classical period. This shows clearly that meaning and form are independent of each other, since the meaning remained the same and was not involved in the reshuffling of forms. Ultimately, however, the iconic basis of language, a preference for parallelism (one-to-one relation) between meaning and form, prevailed. The principle 'same meaning, same shape (imperative -*d*, pronouns *los*, *la*, *nos*)' extended to the surface disparity -*l*-d-*os*, and so on, and such forms as *dadlos* were reestablished.

Here then, sound change had destroyed the iconic order of sounds and morphemes (syntagmatic arrangements), and analogy restored the earlier fit. In *tilde*, *cabildo*, and so on, no iconic conflicts arose, because the change occurred in the middle of the linguistic signs, and the result of the sound change remained intact.

[5.12]   Greek has a general sound law whereby intervocalic *s* drops out. In most dialects *s* is the sign for future, thus (with verbs in the 1st pers. sg.), as is shown on the top of the next page.

The futures in group A are as expected, as *s* is not intervocalic here. Group B, however, violates the law *VsV* > *VV*; but linguists have assumed that, in fact, the *s* was lost in these futures also, giving **lǎō* and **poiéō*. If these forms had remained, they would have undergone a change whereby vowels are shortened before other vowels, and would have ended up homophonous with the presents.

PRESENT		FUTURE	
trép-ō	'turn'	trép-s-ō	A. root ends in consonant
deík-nū-mi	'point'	deík-s-ō	
lú-ō	'loosen'	lǘ-s-ō	B. root ends in vowel
poié-ō	'do'	poiḗ-s-ō	
mén-ō	'remain'	men-é-ō	C. root ends in nasal or liquid
stél-lō	'send'	stel-é-ō	

This was the destructive force of regular sound change, and analogy from the consonant stems had to be invoked to reintroduce the characteristic *s* of the future, that is, *trépō*:*trépsō* = *lúō*: *X*, where *X* gives *lǘsō* (a vowel before this *s* is automatically lengthened). But we have no direct evidence of an *s*-less stage in group B, and it has been suggested that the facts can equally well be covered by grammatical conditioning of sound change, that is, "intervocalic *s* drops, unless it means 'future'" (actually, some other grammatical markers are also included: the aorist, the dative plural). This takes care of group B, but group C shows that everything has not yet been considered. Here, after liquids and nasals, the future morpheme was not *s* alone but *es*, and in this form the *s* was, in fact, lost according to the sound law. The situation is the same as in some of the Baltic Finnic cases (§ 4.24): if a morpheme could afford to lose part of itself, it did, provided that something remained to mark the function. In Greek the surviving *é* distinguishes the future from the present, exactly like *-h* < *-hen* in the Karelian illative. Thus we see that grammatical conditioning of sound change and analogy can be explanations of one and the same thing; this was true of morphophonemic conditioning of sound change as well (§ 4.21f.). What this teaches us is that analogy need not merely scavenge the debris of sound change; it can prevent sound change from happening in tight-knit morphological systems. That is, sometimes morphological iconicity is so strong that sound change does not enter at all, although it may be quite general in those areas where morphology is not directly involved. (See §23.7)

[5.13] The Greek situation was presented first for historical reasons. It is interesting to see how scholars have interpreted it and to note that there is a wide margin for interpretation in historical situations not directly attested. But similar cases can also be observed while they are happening. In Russian the change of unstressed *ă* [ə] > *i* after palatal (soft) consonants, for example, *pójăs* > *pójis* 'belt', has been a living process for scores of years, although the change has not yet ousted the earlier pronunciation, and both pronunciations still occur. In the 1940s the change *ă* > *i* did not enter inflectional suffixes at all, because in these the vowel in question sometimes occurs under stress. Thus we have, for example,

gen.	*pól'-ă*	'field'	vs.	*žil'j-á*	'dwelling'
dat.	*ustój-ăm*	'foundations'		*krăj-ám*	'land'
(compare Greek *lǘsō*				Greek *trépsō*)	

We have a preventive analogy for the sound change ă > i based on the environment (stress) of the inflectional endings which are not subject to the change. The net result of this analogy is that the conditions of the change "palatal consonant plus unstressed ă" do not extend over a morpheme boundary in front of inflectional suffixes (see § 5.3). This is how a grammatical limitation of sound change is often analogical in origin, that is, alternation is actually prevented from occurring and not merely leveled out by analogy. Greek s showed the same situation: it was not dropped in certain grammatical morphemes, because it was retained in some phonetic environments in any case. The Russian situation has a further history; now the change/process ă > i has been extended also to inflectional suffixes.

[5.14 Analogy and the Relation Between Meaning and Form]   In the case of Estonian -n 'I', we apparently have a situation where sound change proceeded to completion before analogy became operative (§ 4.24). Final -n was lost in preconsonantal position and preserved before a following vowel. At this stage the change was a purely phonetic one, and it was only then that analogy entered. It reestablished the -n in every environment in those dialects where its loss would result in the same shape as the imperative. In the Southern dialects, where no homonymy threatened, the sound change just continued, with the -n dropping everywhere. In the Russian and Greek cases (§§ 5.12, 5.13), the driving force was the prevention of variation (difference) within one morpheme, and in Estonian, prevention of the same form from having two different meanings. But this is actually the same force, prevention/elimination of one-to-many relations between form and meaning:

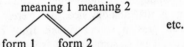

That is, both the ∧ (Russian and Greek, etc.) and ∨ (Estonian) configurations tend to be avoided by the iconic principle whose ideal is 'one meaning, one form'. Of course, all languages do have such configurations, because semology is, after all, independent of morphology, but such disparity is the characteristic breeding ground of analogy. And if analogy comes into operation, it either eliminates the alternation (i.e., establishes | -relations = one to one) or carries the alternation into other parts of the vocabulary or morphology. The important word is if, for it must be emphasized that nothing need happen. For example, in English the morpheme -s /s ~ z ~ iz/ with variation represents the meanings '3rd pers. sg.', 'possessive', and 'plural'. It can further be a variant of the morphemes is and has, thereby representing at least two more meanings.

Again, we see how grammatical conditioning of sound change is structurally parallel to analogy or the iconic tendency in that it also breaks up or forestalls these one-to-many relations between form and meaning. We have a ∨-relation in those instances where a case form represents also some adverbial element, and we have at least two meanings for one form. When change does not touch the adverbs, the meanings get forms of their own (e.g., *once* vs. *one's*, § 4.25). And as for straightening out the ∧-relation, we have seen that morphophonemic conditioning of sound change is this kind of analogy. If the ∧-relation is based on suppletion, we have simple analogy (e.g., *go/went → go/goed*). Sound change can produce suppletion, for example, Latin *oculus/oculī* 'eye/eyes' gives French *œil/yeux* [œy/yø]. When morphophonemic rules get restricted (out of productivity) original alternation can change into a kind of suppletion: *sit/seat, heat/ hot, cook/kitchen, ten/-teen*, or for some speakers, even cases like *opaque/opacity* (§§ 5.8, 6.21, 6.24 7.13, 10.7–10.9, 17.5, 18.17). The stronger the suppletive element is, the more probable is the occurrence of analogy.

Throughout this chapter we have seen this tendency of 'one meaning, one form' at work. Thus, in Yiddish (§ 4.27),

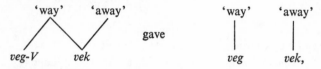

and, in English (§ 4.25), we had (in certain cases)

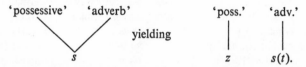

In both cases the end result was two linguistic signs with one-to-one correspondence (|-relation) between form and meaning. Meaning is decisive here; two meanings develop two linguistic signs. This is the regularity principle of analogy, which restores what sound change and syntactic combinations had diversified. Similarly, the irregular alternations *go/went* and *bad/worse* are often straightened out (by children) as

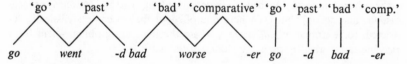

(Again, this notation shows the simplification visually.) In these particular cases the results (*goed, badder*) have not been generally accepted, because the frequency of occurrence upholds the tradition, but in countless cases it has, for example, *book/beech → book/books* (§ 5.7). It was recognized early that there is a strong correlation between analogy and frequency. A typical phrasing of this principle would be that irregular (strong) forms stand outside the general rules and have to be specially learned, thus burdening the memory; analogy is, therefore, successful where memory fails; that is, infrequent forms are prone to be changed first. This principle is generally valid, however it may be worded.

We have seen that the conflicts between sound change and grammatical analogy often result in sound changes that are grammatically limited, or sound changes affecting only certain grammatical categories and not the general sound pattern of the language. Or, in other words, a sound of certain grammatical/morphological value may resist sound laws. Grammatical conditioning of sound change and analogy are very much two sides of the same coin.

[**5.15 The Status of Old and Innovating Forms**]   When changes leave behind old forms without ousting them completely, there is a universal tendency for the innovating form to carry the primary semantic functioning of the old linguistic sign. The old form is pushed aside for some peripheral or secondary meaning. Most of the cases we have seen are clearly of this type, and it does not matter whether the driving force is sound change or analogy. Thus:

	I		II	
	OLD FORM: SECONDARY FUNCTION		NEW FORM: PRIMARY FUNCTION	
adverb	*rääjgin* 'asunder'	gen.	*rääjgi* 'hole'	Lapp (§ 4.24)
	once	gen.	*one's*	English (§ 4.25)
	vek 'away'	nom.	*veg, vēk* 'way'	German (§ 4.27)
	parum 'too little'	acc.	*parvum* 'small'	Latin (§ 5.7)
compound	*cran*(*berry*)		*crane*	English (§ 5.8)
	hus(*band*), *hus*(*sy*)		*house*	English (§ 5.8)
	shep(*herd*)		*sheep*	English (see § 4.8)
	maan(*tee*) 'highway'	gen.	*maa* 'earth'	Estonian (§ 4.24)
plural	*brethren*		*brothers*	English (§ 5.2)
	kine		*cows*	English (§ 5.4)

In every case the second column shows the regular, productive, stylistically or syntactically unrestricted (unmarked) form. The situation is different when a paradigm splits in two, because then there is a possibility that functions which earlier shared a form can become independent signs (e.g., *deus/dīvus*, *shade/shadow*, and so on), but even here one offshoot may become stylistically restricted, for example, *mead/meadow*, where the innovating oblique-stem form *meadow* carries the "normal" functions of the word.

[**5.16 Analogy and Syntax**]   We have seen how analogy works both in phonology and morphology under semantic constraints. But syntax also has been clearly involved both in sound change and analogy, for example, in the form of adverbs and predicatives, and both mechanisms also change syntax. Often they do this together. Greek had, for instance, the following forms in its verbal paradigms:

	1ST SG.	3RD SG.	INFINITIVE
'want'	*thél-ō*	*thél-ei*	*thél-ein*
'write'	*gráph-ō*	*gráph-ei*	*gráph-ein*

The endings have been separated from the root by the hyphen. The infinitive occurred in phrases like *thélō gráphein* 'I want to write' and *thélei gráphein* 'he wants to write'. Then the final *-n* of the infinitive dropped and its outer shape became identical with the third singular: *thélō *gráphei*, *thélei gráphei*. The former expression is "formally poor" for the meaning 'I want to write', because it can also be interpreted 'I want, he writes' (√-relation). And the same applies to all the other persons as well, except for the third singular *thélei gráphei*. At some point this sequence was reinterpreted as the 3rd sg. twice 'he wants, he writes' with the same 'he', that is, 'he wants to write' in a new form. As the reinterpretation of *formation* it would not show overtly here; this was an inductive change, which did not alter the outer shape produced by the sound change. The reinterpretation surfaced in the other persons; for example, *thélei gráphei* = *thélō X*, where the end result is *thélō gráphō* 'I want to write' (formally also the 1st sg. twice). This deductive analogy restores the diagrammatic relation between person and the corresponding form. Ultimately, the infinitive in Greek was lost altogether. (The change shows also that infinitives are indeed underlying sentences, or finite verbs; when sound change interfered with them they easily reverted back to their basic form. We ignore here the subsequent modification whereby the particle 'that' became obligatory, thus in Modern Greek: *thélō ná gráphō* [literally] 'I want that I write'.)

[5.17]   Finnish once had an accusative in *-m* in the singular, whereas in the plural the accusative was homophonous to the nominative. A selection of the paradigm would be (with modern orthography)

	NOM.	ACC.	GEN.	
sg.	*poika*	*poja-m*	*poja-n*	'boy'
pl.	*poja-t*	*poja-t*	*poik-ien*	

Also the 1st sg. ending was *-m*. A sentence like 'I see the boy go' went *näe-m poja-m menevä-m* (written here in a hybrid orthography where only the endings reflect the earlier sounds). The last word *menevä(m)* is a participle of the verb 'to go', and because it is an attribute to *pojam*, it agrees in case and number with it; that is, 'I see the boy, the going one' = 'I see the boy going'. The corresponding plural object can be formed with cases given: *näe-m poja-t menevä-t* 'I see the boys go'. A sound change *-m* > *-n* produced new endings: *näen pojan menevän*. The acc. sg. became homophonous with the gen. sg. (there was no such merger in the verbal 1st sg. ending). As in the Greek example, sound change made two forms identical, here *pojan* and *menevän* (both acc. and gen.). Note that, to start with, *pojan* is the head and *menevän* an adjective attribute to it. At some point the form *pojan* was reinterpreted as a genitive, and consequently as an attribute to the following *menevän*, which therewith became the head to the genitive attribute. Again, such reinterpretation is not reflected in the forms themselves; they remain *pojan menevän* (compare *thélei gráphei*), although the literal analysis is now '(the) going of the boy'. The new analysis is proved by the plural, because there the accusative and the genitive are different, and the original, unambiguous phrase has been replaced by the equally unambiguous *näen poikien menevän* 'I see the boys go'. *Menevän* is now, unmistakably, an uninflected head with the attribute *poikien* in the gen. pl. (see §§9.16f., 11.27).

[**5.18 Analogy and Speech Production**]   In the survey of the various types of analogical changes, two ways of classifying them were occasionally referred to: leveling and extension. When differences between two (related) forms are reduced or eliminated, we have *leveling*. When a form or an alternation is carried into a new environment, we have *extension*. All the examples we have seen represent one of the cases or both. For example, the differences between the originally unrelated linguistic signs *ear* and *irrigate* were partially leveled by a new semantic identification and recutting *irr-igate*. The part *-igate* was then subsequently extended to *nosigate*. The morphemes *-ism* and *-able* were borrowed into English as parts of hundreds of loanwords (e.g., *humanism* and *usable*). These endings have been extended to native stems or roots (e.g., *token-ism* and *think-able*). Extension is similar to borrowing in that a form is lifted from one environment into another, though, in borrowing, the source environment is in a different language, dialect, or even idiolect, whereas, in extension, it is within the same grammar in another grammatical environment or in another part of the vocabulary (lexicon). The parallelism with borrowing has even led to calling extension *borrowing from within* (the same grammar).

New analogical (deductive) forms are, by necessity, tied to speech production; that is, a speaker must utter them according to his grammatical machinery. The creation of such forms is independent of their subsequent fate, because they may or may not become the new norms. One of the most mystifying characteristics of human language is its productivity (§ 1.28). This is connected with man's innate ability to learn a language. Such a capacity manifests itself very early in the child's apprenticeship in speaking, as he can and does easily go beyond the sentences he has heard. Each utterance is either a parroting or a new creation. From the data he has been exposed to, the child is able to abstract regular patterns or rules; he then extends his use of these into areas that are novel to him, and maybe even to other speakers. Thus one aspect of extension of forms or patterns is clearly a function of the use of the grammar, that is, speech production.

Grammar is somehow internalized in the brain and is not directly observable except for its product, the actual utterances. Of course it is a two-way affair, as the regular patterns have to be abstracted from the utterances. But once they have been established, they need not be reinforced by concrete instances. If we heard a new English adjective *glump*, we would be automatically able to form the comparative and superlative *glumper*, *glumpest* without referring to another concrete instance like *damper*, *dampest*. If it were a noun, its plural would be *glumps*, if a personal name, a genitive *Glump's* would follow. And a verb would go *he glumps, he glumped,* and so on. These forms have now been created by frequent productive patterns. Such patterns tend to prevail over unproductive types. Instead of the unique *good/better,* the speaker may lapse into a comparative *gooder,* or instead of an irregular weak *brought,* he may come out with *bringed.* Adults usually quickly correct themselves, whereas children tend to make an effort to stay with these. Only such irregularities as *good/better* and *bad/worse* have to be learned form by form, otherwise the patterns are enough. Thus in highly inflected languages, speakers do not in every case store hundreds of different forms for each word but create any form they need according to the patterns at their disposal (see § 18.17). Many forms are created afresh for each occurrence rather than repeated from memory. This is even more true in syntax than in morphology, because we speak and hear more different sentences than different words. Language is one manifestation of the innate faculty of analogizing, shown clearly by children even before they have acquired language.

[5.19]   As was already mentioned, grammatical patterns are not directly observable; only the surface forms produced by them are. To talk about formal systems like the grammatical speech-production mechanism, one has to use analogy (see § 5.1). Analogy is a type of reasoning that plays an important part in all scientific thought. An analogy is a resemblance between the relationship of things rather than between the things themselves (a relation of similarity; §§ 1.13, 1.14, 5.1). Analogy is particularly valuable in suggesting clues and hypotheses, and in helping us comprehend and treat phenomena and occurrences we cannot see. Grammar is exactly such a phenomenon. Proportional analogy supplies a handy model for the regular patterns. Careful linguists have always made it clear that speakers themselves need not use the proportion; rather, it is a linguist's way of describing the action of the speaker. Further, the proportion itself is, in any case, just a crude shorthand notation for what has gone on in the process of speech production. When the speakers themselves give a proportion like *sing:sang* = *swing:swang* (§ 5.1), they imply that the same process which gives *sing/sang* could (and can) also produce *swing/swang.* One should note that for all its limitations, proportional analogy is the only model that is spontaneously formulated by speakers themselves and thus has greater psychological reality than any other model—even if some other model might be expressive of some deeper psychological reality of which the speakers are unaware. It is easy to give a proportion when we wish to exemplify a productive process, but it does *not* mean that one needs a concrete instance like *pen:pens* every time a new plural is formed, as in *book:books* (§ 5.2). The proportion means only that whatever pattern or process produced *pens* is also responsible for *books.* That is, we do not suppose that the actually occurring surface shapes *pen, pens,* and *book* are creators of *books,* but that the invisible underlying relations are the same grammatical machinery that has produced many other such forms.

[5.20]   Because the productivity of language can be described analogically, linguists speak of analogic *creation*, or simply creation. The relational side of proportional analogy has invoked another name, *relative* analogy. Productivity involves extension of items in connection with the regular patterns of the grammar, and this is in effect creation, indispensable in speech activity (which might be called reified grammar). We have spoken so far of regular patterns or processes, and analogy, in fact, means regularity (§ 5.1), that is, rulegovernedness (Latin *regula* → English *rule*). It has already been mentioned that the constructional rules of a language handle symbols exactly as an algebra (§§ 1.13, 1.14). We have come full circle now, for analogy is one form of iconicity, and so are the rules of a language. Much work has been done in making hypotheses about language, and we now know more about the possibilities of writing grammars and their rules. This knowledge is reflected in terminology, too, in that one now speaks of rules rather than patterns, though 'pattern' can still mean a collection of rules. Because the term 'analogy' was meant to cover patterns, alias rules, it has become superfluous for many linguists. The underlying notions of productivity or creation have been raised into a more central position, and, even here, there is a change of vocabulary: 'create' has been replaced by the almost perfectly synonymous 'generate', since both terms mean basically 'produce, bring into being, originate'. The connotations are now different and depend on the different theoretical frameworks, but the original substance is very much the same. If by analogy and creation, unobserved grammatical processes used to be described indirectly (with the use of surface forms), today one tries to go directly to the processes themselves, with rules and generation (generativeness). This is the crux of the different connotations; difference in emphasis has created different terminology as well. Today, grammars and linguistics are more explicitly generative, even those varieties not directly connected with the generative-transformational school.

In Chapter 6, we shall look at change through linguistic rules. Let us note here that the terms 'analogy, extension, regularity, productivity, creation, generation, and iconicity' overlap to a great degree. Different scholars give to these terms slightly different meanings, but overlapping is still pervasive. Note that iconicity is a more general concept than proportional analogy or rules. Various nonproportional cases show that the driving force is the tendency of 'like meaning, like form'. The driving force of iconicity resides in the linguistic sign as well as in the rules of the grammar. The importance of meaning is obvious, because grammars do not exist per se, but to convey meaning.

[5.21]   Finally, a short *historical note* is in order. Almost a century ago, there was controversy about the existence of analogy, and the situation was very much the same as today. It was not the *phenomenon*, but the *term* 'analogy', that was objectionable to many. The objections gradually provoked explicit psychological notions as better explanations for this phenomenon. Even the Neogrammarians stated clearly that analogy was due to a psychological process, which took place prior to the materialization of the sound by the vocal organs.

The proportions were supposed to mirror this process only retroactively, of course. There was no obvious terminology available for speaking about what went on in the brain, and linguists had to resort to hinting or alluding to various psychological associations. An important concept in this connection was *Sprachgefühl*, the language user's implicit knowledge of his language, also referred to as 'the inner language', in contrast to the actual surface form which had to be used in the proportions as substitutes or mirrors of it. One claim was that there is no analogy, because Sprachgefühl and memory (see § 5.14) are enough to explain these phenomena. Indeed; but proportional analogy was an attempt to make the process explicit. Today, however, the somewhat vague notion of Sprachgefühl has been developed into a more explicit notion of the speaker's *competence*. This is described largely through rules, and we have come back to what was said earlier (e.g., § 5.20). All these ways of looking at the problem revolve around the same substance. One can very roughly characterize the situation by noting that concentration on surface forms in linguistic description dominated American linguistics from the 1920s through the 1950s; this theoretical stance derived from the point of view which, among other things, preferred the use of analogy in talking about the invisible. Now linguistics has turned back to Sprachgefühl as a direct object of study. But the notion of analogy (i.e., regularity) is essential for both approaches, no matter what formal mechanism of description we use (§ 5.1) nor what we call it. Analogy is indispensable in scientific discourse—though this does not mean that it would automatically lead to correct results.

The higher, more general principle of 'one meaning, one form' is as old as European linguistics. It has been referred to, among other things, as the principle of optimality (Humboldt), or univocability (Vendryes), and as the canon of singularity (Ogden and Richards). M. Bréal named the two underlying forces separately: the law of specialization ($\wedge$ > |) and the law of differentiation ($\wedge$ > |, |). The principle operates in, for example, nonproportional analogy, contamination, and folk etymology, where proportional analogy or rules are inadequate. It has always been known that this principle is a tendency only, like so much in human behavior and biology that is not susceptible to rigorous formulation. No one has ever implied that it actually would lead language to a point where every meaning would have its own form, or total one-to-one correlation between form and meaning. The 'one meaning, one form' principle was also connected early with psychological factors, which "aim to eliminate purposeless variety" (Wheeler); we have seen how both leveling and extension comply with this. In the case of leveling the principle is obvious, but in extension the purpose is less so; it can be interpreted as the spelling out of a formal distinction eliminated through the loss of an earlier marker (§§ 5.10, 10.14, 13.3), so that the variety is no longer purposeless. In accordance with this terminology, the Pre-English umlaut alternation in **mūs/*mȳs-i* was purposeless, but was no longer so once it carried the singular/plural distinction in Old English *mūs/mȳs*. In German, umlaut plurals have been extended to a substantial part of the nouns; that is, this variety is made "purposeful" use of. In Modern

108 Historical Linguistics: How Does Language Change?

English, however, the umlaut plurals have become a tiny minority in relation to the *s*-plurals. They are purposeless in this sense, and a natural target for analogical realignment to the *s*-class (§ 5.14).

REFERENCESREFERENCES

General: Wheeler 1887, Hermann 1931, Trnka 1968 Kuryłowicz 1945-49, Mańczak 1958, Hoenigswald 1955, Leed 1970 -- Samuels 1972, Best 1973, Anttila 1977b, Anttila and Brewer 1977 -- Mayerthaler 1981, Dressler 1985, Wurzel 1984, 1985, Fisiak (ed.) 1980, (ed.) 1985a, Matthews 1972; **5.1** Robins 1967, Dinneen 1968, Lyons 1968, Leed 1970; **5.2** Jespersen 1964, Hermann 1931, Sturtevant 1947; **5.3** Wartburg 1969, Hogg 1979; **5.4** Thumb and Marbe 1901, Esper 1966; **5.5** Sturtevant 1947, R. Coates 1987; **5.10** Sturtevant 1947, Kiparsky 1965, Bolinger 1968; **5.11** Malmberg 1963b; **5.12** Sturtevant 1947; **5.13** Jakobson 1949; **5.14** Bréal 1964, Vendryes 1925, Wurzel 1985; **5.15** Kuryłowicz 1945-49; **5.16** Havers 1931, Wartburg 1969, Bolinger 1968, Joseph 1983; **5.17** E. Itkonen 1966; **5.18** Lindroth 1937, Sturtevant 1947, R. Hall 1964, Bolinger 1968; **5.19** Beveridge 1950; **5.21** Wheeler 1887, Bréal 1964, Vendryes 1925, Ogden and Richards 1923. (See also p. xv)**General**: Wheeler 1887, Hermann 1931, Trnka 1968 Kuryłowicz 1945-49, Mańczak 1958, Hoenigswald 1955, Leed 1970 -- Samuels 1972, Best 1973, Anttila 1977b, Anttila and Brewer 1977 -- Mayerthaler 1981, Dressler 1985, Wurzel 1984, 1985, Fisiak (ed.) 1980, (ed.) 1985a, Matthews 1972; **5.1** Robins 1967, Dinneen 1968, Lyons 1968, Leed 1970; **5.2** Jespersen 1964, Hermann 1931, Sturtevant 1947; **5.3** Wartburg 1969, Hogg 1979; **5.4** Thumb and Marbe 1901, Esper 1966; **5.5** Sturtevant 1947, R. Coates 1987; **5.10** Sturtevant 1947, Kiparsky 1965, Bolinger 1968; **5.11** Malmberg 1963b; **5.12** Sturtevant 1947; **5.13** Jakobson 1949; **5.14** Bréal 1964, Vendryes 1925, Wurzel 1985; **5.15** Kuryłowicz 1945-49; **5.16** Havers 1931, Wartburg 1969, Bolinger 1968, Joseph 1983; **5.17** E. Itkonen 1966; **5.18** Lindroth 1937, Sturtevant 1947, R. Hall 1964, Bolinger 1968; **5.19** Beveridge 1950; **5.21** Wheeler 1887, Bréal 1964, Vendryes 1925, Ogden and Richards 1923. (See also p. xv)

CHAPTER 6

RULE CHANGE

Sound change and analogy are restated under one unified convention of notation which emphasizes the inner invisible parts of language and grammar. Such a notation deals with before–after relations and may skip the actual history altogether, as well as psychological reality.

[6.1 Relative Chronology]   We know that every language is a product of history, an end point in a series of changes of the kind that we have seen in the two preceding chapters. All changes occur in absolute historical order, whether we can observe them or not. Thus any two changes in a language have occurred one after the other, in partial overlap (i.e., one change begins before another has ended), or simultaneously (complete overlap). Although change can perhaps be abrupt in the grammar of the innovator (how abrupt it is depends on the scoring mechanism adopted), it is often very slow in getting established as a new norm in the speech community; and thus partial overlap occurs easily. When the output of one change is the input of another, we can establish *relative chronology* between them, even when we cannot tell their exact dates. The establishment of relative chronology between changes has been one of the prime goals of historical linguistics as well as of internal reconstruction (Chapter 12). Of course, when there is no such interference between two changes, relative order cannot be established without direct historical attestation. For example, if we knew only Old English and Modern English (and nothing in between), we could not establish the relative chronology of the changes (1) dental d > alveolar d (§ 4.1) and (2) $\bar{y}$ > ($\bar{\imath}$ >) *ai* (§§ 4.5, 4.22), because they take place in different parts of the phonology. We would not have record of any intermediate stages either, but our experience would certainly make us doubt a direct leap from $\bar{y}$ to *ai*. As it happens, we know roughly how the process went (§ 4.8). Similarly, even if we knew only Latin and Modern French, we would still have to assume the intermediary stages of k > $t\check{s}$ > $\check{s}$ and k > ts > s (§§ 4.4, 4.15, 5.3) on the basis of our knowledge acquired elsewhere (from other languages). Thus our historical presentations often skip intermediate stages, and contain free order between changes, owing to historical ignorance. The actual historical sequence is necessarily absolute; our presentation, largely random.

[6.2]   In favorable cases we have enough interference to posit relative chronology. Before the English vowel shift occurred, two other changes had to have taken place: shortening of certain long vowels (§ 4.8) and lengthening of certain short vowels (§ 5.8). These two changes are independent of each other, because they apply to mutually exclusive environments, that is, long and short vowels, respectively; but they interfere with the vowel shift, because the one takes away long vowels that would have undergone the shift if they had remained long, and the other provides new long vowels that subsequently do shift. The relative chronology here is only partial, in that both the shortening and the lengthening have to occur before the shift, but whether they themselves occurred simultaneously or sequentially is unknown. (Direct historical attestation often mixes with relative inferences; for example, we know that umlaut occurred before shortening and lengthening.) This is summed up in Figure 6-1:A. In other words, both the shortening and lengthening occupy the same slot in the relative chronology, although, in absolute historical chronology, they could have been centuries apart. But that does not matter; only the interference with the vowel shift is of interest. In the case of the shortening, this interference is called *subtractive*, because it takes material away from the domain of the vowel shift; in the second case, it is *additive* (Chafe), because the change adds new material to the vowel shift (the terms 'bleeding' and 'feeding' are also used [Kiparsky]). In Rotuman, we saw the same relationship between the raising umlaut and the fronting umlaut. The former had to occur first to provide, for example, a closed *o*, which then gave *ö* through the latter. Fronting umlaut itself is complementary to the other two changes, metathesis and shortening, and all three thus occupy the same position in the relative chronology, as shown in Figure 6-1:B. Raising umlaut is seen to be additive to the three other changes. In the passage from Latin to French, we must first have the change *k* > *tš* (*kantāre* > *tšanter*), and only then *w* > *Ø* (*kwandō* > *kand*), whereas the change *tš* > *š* is free in regard to *w* > *Ø* (but, of course, it must occur after the first change that feeds into it, § 4.4). If *w* had been lost first, we would have had the sequence *kwandō* > *kand* > **tšand* > **/šã/*, which is obviously contradicted by the attested form /kã/ *quand* 'when'.

A. English vowel changes

Time	1.	umlaut		
	2.	shortening (−)	3.	lengthening (+)
	4.	vowel shift/diphthongization		

B. Rotuman vowel changes

Time	1.	raising umlaut	
	2. fronting umlaut and vowel drop	3. metathesis	4. vowel shortening

FIGURE 6-1. The relative chronology of these English and Rotuman vowel changes is inferred, except for the English box 1, whose relative chronology is guaranteed by written records.

	A	B	C	D	E
1.	dh > ð	t > þ	—	t > þ, ð	t > ð
2.	t > þ	d > t	—	—	t > þ
3.	þ > ð	þ > ð	—	—	—
4.	d > t	dh > ð	þ > ð	—	—

FIGURE 6-2. Possible relative chronologies of Grimm's and Verner's laws.

[6.3]   When describing shifts one usually takes one change at a time. Grimm's and Verner's laws (§§ 4.9, 4.10) thus require one of the relative chronologies in Figure 6-2. Possibility C lists *þ > ð* as the latest change, and what precedes can follow either the order of A or B. Thus altogether four alternatives have been tabulated in A–C, and D and E add further possibilities (these are not exhaustive). This mirrors the indeterminacy or randomness which is characteristic of our retrieval of history, but note that there is still a fair amount of relative chronology in the arrangements. Change *d > t* must occur after *t > þ*, because otherwise it would add to the latter, which in its turn does, in fact, add to Verner's law *þ > ð* and can occur before it, or simultaneously with it (D), and, indeed, even E is a possibility. Change *dh > ð* is free in respect to others, as long as we interpret *ð* as phonetically different from the starting point *d*. If, however, we operated with *dh > d*, it would have to occur after *d > t*, because otherwise it would add to the latter; that is, we would have basically (1) *t > þ*, (2) *d > t*, (3) *dh > d*, and (4) *þ > d*, where the last two changes could be also reversed. In this case, the relative chronology would be rather definite or strict.

   Another way of presenting consonant shifts would be simultaneous chronology, which gives also the desired result. The problem is, however, that such changes have not been unambiguously attested in observable cases, especially when more than two terms are involved in the shift. Thus it is very likely that in historical fact the Indo-European consonantism was transformed into the Germanic at one stroke:

$$\text{Proto-Indo-European} \begin{cases} dh \longrightarrow ð \\ t \longleftarrow þ \\ d \longrightarrow t \end{cases} \text{Germanic}$$

(Of course, it is always possible to describe shifts at one stroke on paper.) Latin medial stops on the whole develop as follows into Spanish: (1) *d > Ø* (*cadere > caer* 'to fall'), (2) *t > d* (*tótum > todo* 'all'), and (3) *tt > t* (*gutta > gota* 'drop'); the reverse order would give *Ø* for everything. Shifts of this kind are common in the languages of the world. Here one could devise, for example, a feature 'closure' plus various degrees of it; writing one degree of 'closure' with each dash, we have the following in Latin: *d = [−], t = [=]*, and *tt = [≡]*. The Spanish shift can now be described in one step—loss of one degree of closure—and the outcome is right.

[6.4]   Even though it is quite possible to use such tricks for presenting shifts as simultaneous jumps, their value as historical indices is highly questionable. We have presented the shifts above as chain reactions, that is, one sound moves away and another takes its place. The question has also been raised whether the shift can be caused as well by one sound invading the allophonic range of another, thus pushing it out of its earlier place. These two ways of looking at the shifts are known as *pull chain* and *push chain* changes, and in general it seems that the former has more support in linguistic literature, although the latter cannot be ruled out (§§ 9.3, 9.6, 9.7). It is interesting to note that push chains would give a relative chronology with considerable overlapping between the steps (see also § 9.16).

A case of shift where two steps must be simultaneous is a switch between two sounds, a change known also as a *flip-flop*. Until quite recently, historical linguists considered this kind of change impossible, and it is still controversial; but evidence for it is believed to be accumulating. Whether this *evidence* represents the *facts* correctly cannot always be determined, which is a general deficiency in historical explanation (compare the court procedure in which the evidence may be quite clear, but the facts are not). However, a switch seems to have taken place in the southwestern United States (e.g., Utah), where the vowels in words like *card* and *cord* have switched places (also *far/for, ardor/order*). Here the change is so recent that it seems to be true without intervening stages. Often, of course, we simply do not have the total historical knowledge of a shift, and even though the end points seem to point to a switch, it need not be historically true. More than likely it never (or very seldom) is.

[6.5 Synchronic Order]   Sound changes take place in exact historical order, although we cannot often tell what the order was at all, or we can only posit partial relative chronology. Another area of language where we have a similar hierarchy is language acquisition by children. After a babbling period during which babies of any speech community produce any sound possible, the child loses such articulatory facility and starts from scratch. This is the threshold for learning the phonology of the language to which the child is exposed. Independent of the particular language, the order in which the child tends to learn sound distinctions is about the same. First comes the distinction between labial nasals and stops (*m–p*), then labials and dentals (*p–t*), to which the velars are added later (*k*). Similarly, among vowels the axis dark-bright (*u–i*) is basic to openness (*a*). Stops are learned before spirants and affricates, front rounded vowels after other vowels, and so on. Such universal facts must be connected with man's innate capacity to learn a language (§ 9.14), but what makes them really important are certain speech disturbances. Such empirical data are important evidence for the theory of markedness (§ 6.20) in generative grammar. Several types of aphasia dismember language in the opposite order from which it was learned. This seems to show clearly that there is relative depth in the brain, because those items which were put in last are lost first. In the same fashion, a bilingual may lose his more recently acquired language through aphasia but retain the first one. We have the same antonymy here as between historical and comparative linguistics, because comparative linguistics tries as best it can to unwrap the historical changes that have piled up. There is a certain parallelism between phylogeny (evolutionary development) and ontogeny (passage of time in which the inherent potentialities of an individual can be realized). Ontogeny would be reflected in language acquisition, and the consequent relative depth of the components of grammar (§ 6.6). The universal features of sound systems correspond rather well with the order of acquisition; that is, languages that have affricates also have stops, languages that have voiceless or nasal vowels also have oral voiced vowels, and so on. Also, anything that a child tries to do to his language while learning (mainly analogical formations) can also be taken as a possible sound change. In this connection it is interesting to note that a little American girl who was exposed only to Finnish at home tried to introduce a switching metathesis into the sequence of certain consonants. Thus $k-p > p-k$ (e.g., *piike-* for *kiipeä-* 'climb') and $p-k > k-p$ (*koipa* for *poika* 'boy' and *kyyppi* for *pyykki* 'laundry'); $k-t > t-k$ (*teikki* for *keittiö* 'kitchen') and $t-k > k-t$ (*veikitta* for *veitikka* 'little rascal'); $ks > sk$ (*yski* for *yksi* 'one') and $sk > ks$ (*yksä* for *yskä* 'cough'). This seemed to be rather consistent between the ages of two and four (but may quite well have been more apparent than real). As in most such cases, her parents were able to wipe it out; but it still seems to support the reality and possibility of a switch, even though it was abortive here. It looks as if she had perceived vowels and consonants from different ends.

[6.6]   It was already noted how change is dependent on the particular form of grammar the linguist adopts (§ 1.9), and we saw an example of this in the Spanish consonant shift (§ 6.3). We had either a sequence of steps, or with the feature *closure* (in various degrees) we could describe the whole shift in one stroke. In Chapter 4 we saw that most historical changes leave behind alternations that stay in the grammar indefinitely. But for this reason and because the brain seems to be capable of hierarchical ordering (language acquisition/aphasia), the practice has become prevalent of presenting phonological derivations from the underlying invariant morphophonemes with similar ordering. In other words, the historical sequence of changes is supposed to be reflected, to a degree, in the synchronic order of *application* of phonological rules. This synchronic order ("brain order") used to be called *descriptive* order in contrast to historical order or relative chronology. Historical order thus tells us about the relative history of how the language came to be as it is at the time of attestation (or now), and descriptive order reflects what—perhaps—goes on in the brain of the speaker every time he utters something. The former is a fact, unknown to most speakers, of course, whereas the latter is a hypothesis; it is easily forgotten, however, that it is a hypothesis and is often taken as a fact. The parallelism between the history of a grammar and the present functioning of grammar is attractive and reminds us of the similarities between phylogeny and ontogeny, but here also the similarity is not absolute. As in culture, in general, *all* of history cannot function forever, although a substantial part can, in some form or other.

Let us return to the partial paradigm of Finnish *vesi* 'water', *vede-n* 'of water', and *vete-nä* 'as water' (§ 4.29). The underlying invariant shape is *vete*, to which the speakers apply the following rules to get the actually occurring surface forms: (1) *e → i* in word-final position, (2) *t → s* before *i*, and (3) *t → d* in closed syllable. Again, the arrow indicates a synchronic process. This rule order could be the same as the historical order of the corresponding sound changes. The same is true of the crucial ordering of raising umlaut first before the other changes in Rotuman (§ 6.2). But we shall see how the synchronic reflex of a change need not repeat history this well. This kind of a description of phonology has led to new terminology, so that sound changes, too, are called 'rules', and relative chronology becomes 'ordering of rules'. The term 'rule' itself, however, is rather old, although it was used only sporadically some hundred years ago.

[6.7 Form of Rules]   To be able to observe and describe rule change, one must give the rules a definite form; and as has been stressed, this form has an effect on the structure of the change itself (see §§ 1.1, 1.9). The general form of a synchronic rule is *sound* a *becomes sound* b *in environment* c, that is *a → b/—c*. The environment can be anything and need not be a segment following *a*, as this general structure would seem to indicate. Such a rule can be read *ac → bc*; or if the environment flanks *a*, for example, .../*d—c*, we get *dac → dbc*. Sound *a* is the *input* to the rule that operates in environment *c*, and the *output* is *b*. Sections *a* and *c* belong together by virtue of the fact that they are the targets that the rule seeks out to operate on, and *b* is the output. Thus *a + c* represents a hierarchical upper level with respect to *b*, and it has been useful to have separate names for this dichotomy, *structural description* (*a + c*) and *structural change* (*b*) (Kiparsky). How *a* and *c* are, in fact, related will be further clarified by an example.

An English speaker must have a systematic way of distinguishing items like *chief/chiefs*, and *faith/faiths* from pairs like *knife/knives*, and *sheath/sheaths*. That is, in some words, spirants get voiced in the plural and, in others, they do not. Thus the voicing rule must be able to discriminate between such items. This must be done somewhere in the structural description. Traditionally, one established different kinds of spirants, those that underwent voicing and those that did not. For example, $|f_1|$ and $|\theta_1|$ undergo voicing and $|f_2|$ and $|\theta_2|$ do not; in other words, the subscript 2 subtracts the spirants from the voicing rule. Or we can put the conditioning into the environment by labeling those words that do not voice by a feature like [−native]. Now *voiceless spirant* (*a*) → *voiced spirant* (*b*)/—[+native] (*c*). By manipulating either *a* (units) or *c* (environment, with classificatory features) we get the same desired result. This shows clearly the interdependency of units and features, and especially units and rules. Both have to be adjusted to each other, and they are complementary to each other (§ 1.9). Another way of blocking the voicing in words like *chief* and *faith* is to label them directly, with [−voicing rule], whereby the rule jumps over such items. What was paraphrased here is, of course, morphophonemic analysis (see § 10.16), and we can leave it at this point. It showed, however, that different paths can lead to the same results. After all, we do not really know what goes on in the speaker's head, but we do know that he is able to handle words like *chief* vs. *sheath* correctly (i.e., differently).

[6.8] Because the rules must be able to describe social variation (Chapter 3), they can contain considerable depth, for example,

$$a \rightarrow b/\text{—educated formal style}$$
$$b'/\text{—young speakers}$$
$$b''/\text{—women's speech}$$
$$\text{etc.}$$

where the grammatical environments have been omitted altogether; and they, of course, would include many more possibilities. In other words, the rules have to spell out the correspondences to be found in a speech community (§§ 3.2, 3.3). A grammar that does not include such information is not a real grammar of a speech community.

Then there is the question whether different outputs and grammatical environments like

$$a \rightarrow b/\text{—}c \quad \text{(or with combinations like } b\text{—}c', b''\text{—}c', b'\text{—}c, \text{ etc.,}$$
$$b'/\text{—}c' \quad \text{if we let the } b\text{'s represent social variation and } c\text{'s}$$
$$b''/\text{—}c'' \quad \text{grammatical environments)}$$

represent one rule with three *subrules* (the rows) or whether they are different rules $a \rightarrow b/\text{—}c$, $a \rightarrow x/\text{—}z$, and $a \rightarrow m/\text{—}n$, and so on. Actually, it all depends on the particular situation and linguist. In the case of the social variables we would seem to have just one rule. Whichever interpretation one chooses will, of course, be reflected in the description of the changes.

[6.9] It must be noted further that the parts a, b, and c of a rule must often be decomposed into the relevant distinctive features, to get the maximal linguistic generalizations (§ 4.20). Here again the exact shape of the rules depends on the features used. Thus, using normal articulatory features, part of Grimm's law would look like

$$\begin{bmatrix} \text{stop} \\ \text{voiceless} \end{bmatrix} \rightarrow \begin{bmatrix} \text{spirant} \\ \text{voiceless} \end{bmatrix} / \begin{matrix} [\#]\text{—} & \text{(word initially)} \\ [\text{accent}]\text{—} & \text{(after accent)} \end{matrix}$$

$$\left(\begin{bmatrix} \text{spirant} \\ \text{dental} \\ \text{voiceless} \end{bmatrix} \right) \begin{bmatrix} \text{spirant} \\ \text{voice} \end{bmatrix} / \begin{bmatrix} \text{no accent} \\ \text{voice} \end{bmatrix} \text{—[voice]}$$

Grimm's law is, of course, a historical change; but if the voiceless stops shifted first, this would have been a synchronic rule as well, because such stops would remain unshifted when second in a voiceless cluster. This particular formulation takes Verner's law simultaneously with Grimm's law. Since the Indo-European *s* also takes part in the former, it has been written in the rule separately. If we ignore for the moment the so-called laryngeals (§§ 12.3–12.5), *s* and the voiceless stops could be combined as [obstruent, voiceless]. Of course, the output of the first subrule could be a later input for a voicing rule (§§ 6.3, 11.20).

[6.10]   In Chapter 4 we saw historical changes written in a notation emphasizing the unity of structural description. When the sound (morphophoneme) was its own environment in some other grammatical category or form, we wrote the environment as alternating with the input proper. This is morphophonemic conditioning (§ 4.27f.), for example,

$$\text{German } \begin{matrix} d \\ \wr \\ t > d \end{matrix} \qquad \text{or Estonian } \begin{matrix} s \\ \wr \\ ks > s \end{matrix} = \begin{matrix} \emptyset \\ \wr \\ k > \emptyset/\!-\!s \end{matrix}$$

This notation has a utilitarian exactness and flexibility, because what is easily written as a simple alternation can be a many-sided, complex, paradigmatic situation. The complete grammar can act in the environment (*c*); we saw this in the Finnish assibilation (§§ 4.29, 6.6), which was more complex than presented above in this chapter, namely,

$$\begin{matrix} e \\ \wr \\ t > s/\!-\!i \end{matrix} = \begin{matrix} e \\ \wr \\ ti > si \end{matrix}$$

By replacing > with → we get the corresponding synchronic rule. (It must be again emphasized that this is characteristic of what linguists try to do with their notation. The actual history shows quite different things. We have been looking only at stem-final syllables in inflection. Elsewhere the change **ti* > *si* has indeed happened: **tinä* > *sinä* 'thou' [compare *te* 'ye'], *silta* 'bridge' [borrowed from Baltic, compare Lithuanian *tiltas*], *morsian* 'bride' [compare Lithuanian *marti*; § 8.2], even in derivation: *pit-kä* 'long'–*pite-mpi* 'longer'–*pis-in* 'longest' [compare §§ 1.14, 19.4 B]. All this shows that rule manipulation can obscure the real history. Words that do not assibilate in a stem-final syllable are somehow late [*neiti* § 11.18], for example, analogical offshoots like *koti/kodin/kotina* 'home' [from *kota* 'hut'; compare § 13.3], or loans [with original spirants]: *äiti* 'mother' [§ 8.2, compare § 4.29]. As in the case of Lachmann's law [§ 4.28], the total evidence shows that such rules are largely achronological restatements [of analogy and borrowing; compare § 10.17].)

We have seen that information about the environment can be written in either of the parts of structural description (*a* or *c*), but actually some of it can as well be included next to the output (*b*) to specify, for example, social variation. This would leave part *c* free for phonetic and grammatical environments, for example, *a* → *b*(= f [style, age, etc.])/—*c*, that is, *a* becomes *b*, which is a function of style (*b'*), age (*b''*), and so on, in the (grammatical) environment *c*. No matter how much we have to decompose any of the parts of the rule for our purposes, its basic structure is always $a \rightarrow b/\!-\!c$, a structure that is already familiar from sound change (Chapter 4).

Having thus delineated the form of synchronic phonological rules, we can go on to observe what happens to them through historical change. It is useful to keep in mind that we took a similar position with regard to phonemes (§ 4.12). Phonemic changes were not agents but results of sound change, given a certain theoretical position on sound units (i.e., the phonemic principle, §§ 10.1– 10.5). Given a similar position on the structure of rules and their application, we get a new vantage point for observing change.

[6.11 Change of Rules] In Chapter 4 we saw that most of the time sound change did not disrupt the underlying invariant morphophonemes, although the actual phonetics could change drastically. A perfect example is the Rotuman case, which retained the five vowel morphophonemes all through the various reshufflings (Figure 4-2). The underlying structure of morphemes tends to remain the same, although new paint jobs here and there modify the appearance. Sound changes just add new layers of paint on top of the earlier ones. Rules are accordingly modified only in that the final outputs (*b*) are different, or that their number increases. When the earlier English realization rule of the dentals (e.g., $d \rightarrow$ [dental ḏ]/ . . . [everywhere]) was affected by the sound change ḏ > alveolar *d*, the new rule came to be: $d \rightarrow$ [alveolar d]/ . . . (§ 4.1). Such a rule change is rather trivial, of course, but a sound change did, in fact, modify a rule; we shall see more drastic changes below. As for additions of rules, all those Rotuman changes added quite a few, the exact number depending on how we write them (§ 4.6). Earliest German had a rule whereby voiced stops were brought out as voiced stops, that is, a rule of the above English type: $d \rightarrow$ [d]/ . . . . Then a sound change devoiced syllable-final voiced stops, for example, [d.] > [t.]. This meant an addition of a rule like $d \rightarrow$ [t]/—[.] to the phonology, and the result of both the sound change and the interdependent rule change is, for example, *bunt/bunde* 'league'. Here dentals are just standing in for the real change [voice] $\rightarrow$ [voiceless]/—[.] (or [voice] $\rightarrow$ Ø, if loss of voicing would automatically mean its opposite, voicelessness). These two simple cases show that when a sound changes in all its environments the corresponding rule is also modified; and when a sound splits, corresponding rules are created. Thus the number of rules increases (see § 4.12). Rules increase to handle the more complex relations between the surface sound units and their greater number. The two cases show also that the historical change had a direct reflex on the rule; in short, that history and synchrony were practically identical, whatever theoretical philosophical considerations there might be.

[6.12] The Pre-English umlaut that fronted back vowels created alternation and added its reflex as a synchronic rule [back] $\rightarrow$ [front]/—[high, front], for example, **mūs-i → *mȳs-i* (§ 4.5). Again synchrony repeats history directly. When the environment was lost, that is, [high, front] > Ø, the change was to have a repercussion in the rule, because the information on where the rule must operate was wiped out. But since this was a mere phonetic change, the rest of the grammar retained the syntactic and semantic relations as they had been before, and the umlaut vowels were by necessity related to these facts. The phonetic environment was at some point replaced by a grammatical one, that is, [back] → [front]/—[PLURAL, CAUSATIVE, and -þ-NOUN], or the like. Not all plurals had umlaut—only those that had *-i earlier; that is, such items had to be specially learned, as before. The rule has now been modified. Its environment needs a more complex specification in terms of the total grammar and not only phonology. The umlaut rule in English has basically retained this structure, although many other rules have piled up subsequently (unrounding, shortening, vowel shift, §§ 4.5, 4.8, 6.2).

[6.13]   Oldest English had only voiceless spirants; that is, all spirants were realized as phonetically voiceless in every environment (e.g., *f* → [f]/ . . .; § 4.2). A change

$$\begin{bmatrix} \text{spirant} \\ \text{voiceless} \end{bmatrix} > \begin{bmatrix} \text{spirant} \\ \text{voice} \end{bmatrix} \Big/ [\text{voice}]\text{—}[\text{voice}]$$

added its replica at the end of the already existing rules (replace > by →). Borrowings from Kentish and French established initial voiced spirants, and long consonants (and thus also voiceless spirants) were shortened. The balance between units and rules was upset. For synchronic purposes, rules have a reason only if they handle alternation. Now, some of those words that had had a short intervocalic spirant, for example, *always* showed voice only, as did the loans. There seemed to be no reason to carry this voicing rule in these words any longer. It could be dropped by changing the underlying units into voiced ones, for example, |v| in *over*. Such partial unit merger, of course, brings another rule with it of the straightforward type |v| → [v]/ . . . which does not create or carry alternation. Typical, in this case, is that when a rule is lost the underlying units get rearranged. This process is called *restructuring*; that is, the end result is that, for example, the old |ofer| was restructured into |over|. The voicing rule and old |f| remained, of course, in those items that preserved alternation between /v/ and /f/ ([v] and [f]). This is one more example of the interrelations between units and rules and how they adapt to each other as part of the tendency toward 'one meaning, one form'. This tendency is hostile to alternation and thus also to rules that carry alternation. Such rules are usually dropped, and when rules drop, underlying units are also overhauled. We can continue with this example, the material for which has already been given. By 1200, short vowels had been lengthened in open syllables, and then ə in final syllable dropped. As in the umlaut case, ə was the phonetic environment that induced voicing for those spirants that were voiceless in other environments. And, again, the conditioning of the new voicing rule had to refer to the grammatical environments: *voiceless spirant* → *voiced spirant*/—[VERB, PLURAL] (e.g., *bathe*, *staves*). Note that the voicing rule now always occurs with the lengthening rule (unless, of course, the base form already has a long vowel), and it might be possible to combine them, for example, → *voiced spirant with preceding length*, or the like. Further, one could take the voiced variants as the basic units and reverse the rule with the units, giving a devoicing in the environments [NOUN] and [SINGULAR], because words where this occurs have to be especially learned anyway. Now we see that the voicing rule starts to become historically dead, although, of course, ultimately triggered by history. Synchronic rules can skip historical stages or combine them into one. In cases like *staff/staves* the rule has been dropped with concomitant *restructuring* of the earlier form |staf| into ME |staf| and |stāv|. Again the drop ensures invariance of morphemes. Perhaps for many Modern English speakers this has happened also for |glæs| and |gleyz| or |græs| and |greyz|, where the vowels also alternate and the verbs have a technical meaning. The rule apparently still works fine in items like *wreath/ wreathe*. It is equally clear that alternation has been eliminated in cases like *whole/hallow/heal*, where indeed the meanings have also separated (§ 4.8). The sequence of changes within the rule is, in a way, a kaleidoscopic process. In these cases, the environmental part (*c*) of the rule shifts from phonetic to grammatical reference, and from there it jumps to the units (*a*), and the jump eliminates the rule. This is another indication of the complementary nature of units and rules, or *a* and *c*. Rules keep variants together within one morphophoneme. When the variants are scattered enough they become independent, and unity is achieved within each linguistic sign by dropping the rule. Paradoxically enough, regularity is established by dropping the rule, but this is true only of unproductive infrequent rules. The voicing rule started out as a most productive rule and is now merely a relic. The reason is the grammar's adaptation to historical change.

[6.14]   When a change affects one member of a variation by making it identical with the other, the result is, of course, loss of the corresponding alternation rule, with concomitant restructuring. We have already seen cases of this in the morphophonemically conditioned sound changes (§ 4.27). After German had added syllable-final devoicing, we had alternations $d \sim t$, $g \sim k$, and $b \sim p$. The voiceless variants are the outputs of the devoicing rule. Now when the "sound change" converts all such voiceless stops which alternate with voiced ones back to voicing, the devoicing rule loses its motivation and drops. At the same time, items that are no longer semantically connected with the living alternation paradigm restructure their voiceless stops into underlying voiceless stops, for example, |veg| splits into |veg| 'road' and |vek| 'away'. Now, an underlying |d| is also realized as /d/ = [d]. In this German case, the sound change eliminated the derived variants with the restructuring of the units in unmotivated derivations. If change eliminates a variant that is the base of phonological derivation, the derivation rule has no motivation either and drops with the underlying unit. Thus in Baltic Finnic, a *k* drops out before an *s* followed by a boundary # or a consonant, for example, Finnish *teoks* → *teos* 'piece of work', where it is still a living rule (before a vowel, *ks* remains: *teoksen* 'of a work'). The example does not reveal the total structure, because other rules have already operated on these forms; we are looking only at the $k \sim \emptyset$ alternation before s. We have already seen that Estonian loses a k which alternates with zero (§§ 4.27, 6.10); k is lost from this item completely, and the underlying form becomes *teos-* in contradistinction to the Finnish *teoks-* (ultimately something like |teko-kse-| and |teko-se-|, but this is irrelevant here). The Finnish synchronic rules reflect history, Estonian no longer does at this point. Since this change happened only in a clearly specified environment, an underlying |k| remains in the language elsewhere (some dialects do retain *-ks-*). But both the German and the Estonian cases show how a "sound change" leads to the drop of a synchronic rule with concomitant restructuring.

[6.15]   After the addition of the devoicing rule, German |ding| 'thing' was realized as *diŋk*, gen. *diŋg-əs*. Then *g* is dropped after *ŋ*, and the paradigm goes *diŋk/diŋəs*. This is the correct historical sequence and still the synchronic state of affairs in the Northern dialects (note the similarity to the Finnish $\emptyset \sim k$ alternation in *teos/teoksen*). In the standard dialect, a *k* that alternates with nothing drops out, giving *diŋ/diŋəs* (compare now the same kind of morphophonemic change in Estonian yielding *teos/teose*). We can interpret this situation so that |g| was now dropped after |n|, which itself became an independent |ŋ| in this position (i.e., the restructuring of |ding| into |diŋ|); this item now skips the devoicing rule completely, because there is no longer any stop to undergo it. This is no doubt the correct synchronic state of affairs for most "innocent" standard German speakers, exactly as there is no *k* for the Estonian speakers in *teos* either. The problem is that linguists are not innocent speakers; they know too much (see § 18.17). Even without referring to the actual history, they would notice that |ŋ| has a very precarious domain in German, because normally [ŋ] occurs only before velars, for example, *daŋk* 'thank' ← |dank|. They would try to write rules which keep a velar stop there long enough to get |n| → [ŋ] and then drop it. The only free velar available in this position is *g*, so we would come back to the underlying |ding| purely on the basis of filling a gap in the patterning. Thus we apply our rules in the order

    1. $n \rightarrow ŋ/$—[velar, stop]   (*daŋk, diŋg*)
    2. $g \rightarrow \emptyset/ŋ$—   (*diŋ*)
    3. devoicing   (*lo·p, bunt* 'league', *ta·k*)

The order of the drop of *g* and devoicing is exactly the reverse of the historical order (relative chronology), which was retained as such in the Northern synchronic order:

    1. devoicing   (*diŋk, lo·p, bunt*)
    2. drop of *g*   (*diŋəs*)
    3. drop of *k* (when $\sim \emptyset$)   (*diŋ*) [does not apply in the North]

A historical change of dropping a *k* when it alternated with nothing triggered a *reordering of rules*. Here history and synchrony differ widely. Note again that whatever we are not willing to do with separate units has to be done with rules.

We do not know when speakers shift from rules to units, but it is clear that they do it earlier than linguists. Reordering is largely due to the linguist's reluctance to modify the underlying forms and, as we shall see, the reluctance to modify the rules. Most cases of such reordering can be handled with loss and concomitant restructuring or by modifying the environmental part of the rule. The only mechanism that seems to be historically real is the addition of rules (e.g., sound change, analogy); loss and reordering are effects in the particular notation used (see § 22.9).

[6.16] We have already referred briefly to the Russian alternation of *k ~ č ~ c* (§ 5.3). Slavic underwent two main palatalizations; in the first one, velar stops became fronto-palatal (hushing) affricates before front vowels, thus **vlŭke > vlĭče* 'wolf' (vocative). Then the back diphthong *ai was monophthongized into *ě* or *i*, producing new front vowels which subsequently caused a second palatalization. Thus (nom. pl.) **vlŭkai > *vlĭki*, but this time the palatalization gives apico-dental (hissing) affricates, **vlĭki > vlĭci*. The nominative retains its *k* because no front vowels occur there, *vlŭkŭ*. The final outputs here are Old Church Slavic (compare Old Russian [nom. sg.] *volk*, [voc. sg.] *volče*, and [nom. pl.] *volci*), and the relative chronology is quite clear:

1. First palatalization
2. Monophthongization
3. Second palatalization

Synchronically, however, it is simplest to apply the monophthongization first and then to combine the palatalizations as subrules of one rule:

$$k \rightarrow c/\text{---}+\begin{Bmatrix}i\\ě\end{Bmatrix}+$$

č/—(+)[front vowel]
k/—   (elsewhere)

The environments (all of which are not exemplified here) can now be specified with morpheme boundaries (+). The second palatalization takes place first in the environments where front vowels *i* and *ě* are the sole markers of a morpheme, the first palatalization follows in other environments with front vowels, and, finally, we get the *constant* subrule *k → k/* in other environments. When subrules are ordered, they specify less general cases first and give the most constant part last. The subrules then show strict descriptive order. With the notion of the generality of the constant rule among ordered subrules, descriptive order is by expectation very different from relative chronology, as it is here. In the case where all the realizations are phonetically different, for example, *p t k* from the Greek labiovelar |k^w|, the most general one is the one with widest coverage (here *p*).

[6.17] In Finnish, long mid vowels diphthongize, thus *tee* (still the Estonian form, §§ 4.24, 5.15) > *tie* 'road'. Then comes consonant gradation, whereby stops at the beginning of closed syllables give corresponding voiced spirants, as in *teke-q* > **teɣeq* 'do!', and the spirant ultimately drops out in this environment, *teeq!* (§§ 4.16, 10.12, 10.13, 18.13). In other words, underlying contiguous |ee| give *ie*, whereas an underlying sequence |eke| shows up as *ee*; the underlying *k* blocks the diphthongization. Standard Finnish has the same synchronic order:

1. diphthongization: *tee → tie*
2. consonant gradation: *tekeq → teeq*

Note that the synchronic rules may now quite well skip the intervening **ɣ*, at least in this situation. In the Eastern dialects, there is another diphthongization, so that *teeq > tieq*. Synchronically, however, both diphthongizations can be combined by reversing the above order into

1. consonant gradation: *tekeq → teeq*
2. diphthongization: *teeq → tieq, tee → tie*

Structurally, this situation is exactly identical to the German *Ding*-case (§ 6.15): in those dialects where an additional change modified the output of the earlier shared rules, the new relation between the dialects could be *described* by reordering. Description by this procedure has become popular in dialectology. In the German case, there was another possibility of explanation, however: loss of a rule with concomitant restructuring. In the Finnish case, there is no such possibility. Clearly it could combine the diphthongizations, because in both cases an *e* gives *i*. But we have already seen this situation in the paradigm of *vesi* 'water' (§§ 4.29, 6.6). Synchronically, it is better to try to connect the diphthongization to the raising. In Standard Finnish, we would now have

1. $e → i/—\begin{Bmatrix} \# \\ e \end{Bmatrix}$ (*vete → veti* [→ *vesi*], *tee → tie*)

   $e/—$ (elsewhere)

2. $k → \emptyset/V—VC$ (*tekeq → teeq*)

   $k/—$ (elsewhere)

These rules have been simplified to include only what is needed for the present example. Now we can describe the *tieq*-dialects as having added one more subrule for the realization of |e|, which is intuitively much better—since this is what happened—and the *k*-rule does not enter here at all:

$e → i/—\begin{Bmatrix} \# \\ e \\ keC \end{Bmatrix} ⟫$ (*tekeq → tikeq* [→ *tieq*])

$e/—$ (elsewhere)   [← N.B.]

Synchronically, this rule should not interfere with consonant gradation, because the latter takes place within open or closed syllables, and the *e*-rule does not interfere with that. Now the situation is parallel to the one in Old Church Slavic in that a small portion of the environment of the constant subrule is lifted up among the cases that have to be specified first. The subrule is, in other words, expanded into the environment *k in the beginning of closed syllable followed by e*, which was earlier in the domain of the constant subrule. The rule says now: in looking for the following vowel, ignore |k| in this position. One can also devise rules that are not ordered, but the subrules always have to be (§ 9.19).

This discussion has shown that there is considerable margin in interpreting rule changes, and many of the matters connected with them are still unknown or controversial. One thing is clear, however. The linguist's account and explanation of them depend on the particular structure of the rules that his theoretical preferences lead him to accept (§ 1.9).

[6.18 Classification of Rule Changes] At the end of the previous chapter it was pointed out that new ways of looking at things and attempts at new explanations of phenomena often lead to new terminology. This is a common occurrence in the sciences generally. This chapter has provided new mechanisms whereby both sound change and analogy can be described very much on the same terms. We saw indications of this earlier, for example, in morphophonemic conditioning of sound change, which, like regular sound change in its regularity aspect, was analogy as well (§ 5.1). Analogy represented the grammatical machinery, and grammar could also condition sound change. Rules must be set up wherever there is alternation; and when alternation is modified, so are the rules. In a way, Chapters 4 and 5 were like observing a piano keyboard and its relationships from the outside. In this chapter we have looked inside the piano to see how it works.

In transformational grammar, classification of rule changes is connected with the notions of *competence* and *performance*. Competence is the speaker's internalized grammar, and the linguist's grammar is a model (icon) of that competence. Grammar and actual competence do not necessarily match. Performance is language in connection with actual speech activity, the use of the competence, the individual concrete utterances. The realization of this dichotomy between the underlying productive mechanism and the actually observable product is well over a century old, although the terminology has varied with the exact details of definition. The dichotomy *deep* structure versus *surface* structure falls roughly within competence. The notions are useful as relative terms, because, whereas the surface is clearly observable, the deeper part of the structure must be somewhere in the brain and, therefore, not directly accessible. The problem is further complicated by the fact that language is like the color spectrum, without clear break-off points (Figure 1-1); but break-off points are posited by the linguist for purposes of description (e.g., Figure 1-2). We do not know where competence ends and performance begins and cannot, therefore, give priority to one or the other. Similarly, it is arbitrary to draw a line between deep and surface structure.

We saw that in the structuralist classification of sound changes only those that affected the number or distribution of units were counted (§§ 4.1, 4.12), whereas articulatory changes were not, even though they triggered the structural ones. Structural classification of analogy also embodied changes in distribution, that is, leveling and extension, as well as analogies that were parallel to the articulatory grouping: proportional and nonproportional (contamination, folk etymology, and so on). Transformational grammar and related positions take a similar stand in looking at changes, because only those changes are counted that affect competence. Thus changes are of two kinds, those that affect performance (not counted), and those that touch competence. This division is even more arbitrary than the phoneme classification, because the two areas cannot be divided. However, in science it has usually turned out to be more useful to have some classification than none. After English *d* had become alveolar, the corresponding feature [dental] was replaced by [alveolar] in the rule; this fact was now part of "proper" English. A rule was modified, but since it changed a surface feature into another surface feature without otherwise affecting the grammar, it is not counted as change. This is exactly parallel to the position of not counting allophonic changes.

[6.19]   Now, relevant change itself is classified under two headings: *primary* change, which affects the rules and represents an *innovation*; and *restructuring*, which changes the units or underlying representations (sequences of units, i.e., distribution of units). When restructuring means split, and not change in distribution, one member of the split is the innovation, the other a *relic*. We saw examples of this in grammatical and morphophonemic conditioning of sound change (see also § 5.15). Restructuring is then the exact counterpart of change in number or distribution of units. Allophonic changes are often antecedents of phonemic changes, and we saw above that the rule changes (which handle variation changes) are intimately bound with restructuring. When phonetic change creates (allophonic) variation, a rule is established to describe it, because rules handle systematic variation. When analogy (that is, tendency toward regularity) eliminates variation, the rule is of course lost, or otherwise modified, and at the same time relics create restructuring. Rule addition is chiefly connected with sound change; rule loss and reordering, with analogy. In fact, the former are basically restatements of the latter. At the end of Chapter 5 we saw that analogy was one way of speaking about the creative aspect of language, the total grammatical machinery, in other words, the rules. And analogy, of course, originally meant 'regularity', that is, 'rule-governedness'. Rule loss turned out to be the same as paradigmatic leveling in the German revoicing example (that is, morphophonemic conditioning of sound change), and the same with the split of *staff* vs. *stave*, and so on, that is, $\wedge > |, |$ (see § 5.14 for notation). Modern Russian has dropped the historical palatalizations from the word for 'wolf', *volk/volk'e/volk'i*, and the Old Russian multiplicity has given unity, $\wedge > |$ (we have already seen how analogy gives palatal /k'/ before front vowels; § 5.3). The reordering of the German drop of *g* after *ŋ* (*diŋ*) is also paradigmatic leveling, $\wedge > |$ (Chapters 6 and 15). Reordering of the Finnish diphthongization and consonant gradation, on the other hand, did not involve leveling but extension of the diphthong *ie* into words that did not have it before (*tieq*; § 6.17). In the Finnish case, a new environment is added (fed) into the diphthongization; in the German case, an environment is subtracted (bled) from the final devoicing and no alternation could result, although it was there before.

Modification of the structural analysis of a rule (*a* + *c*) results in extension of the rule, and shows again its unity. Thus, if a rule like

$$\begin{bmatrix} \text{stop} \\ \text{voiceless} \end{bmatrix} \rightarrow \begin{bmatrix} \text{spirant} \\ \text{voiceless} \end{bmatrix} \Big/ \underline{\quad} \qquad (p\ t\ k \rightarrow f\ \theta\ x)$$

in a language that has voiced and voiceless stops drops the feature [voiceless], the rule becomes more general. Fewer features need be specified, for example, [stop] → [spirant]/—(*c*), and the result is an extension of the domain of the rule, because all stops undergo it: $p\ t\ k\ b\ d\ g \rightarrow f\ \theta\ x\ \beta\ \delta\ \gamma$.

[6.20 Marking and Rule Change]   Every language has both symbolic and iconic/indexical elements. The lexicon is largely connected with the former, the rules with the latter (see § 1.14). Not everything in a language can be generated with the regular rules; some things have to be learned as separate units. Thus there is a clear difference between compounds like *dog meat*, which can be accounted for in terms of a productive pattern, and *nutmeat* and *sweetmeat*, which cannot. Because of semantic change, the compounding rule has been dropped from the latter, making the old compound a new single linguistic sign which has to be learned as a unit (restructuring!). All languages show similar "relics." All languages are composites of tradition (conventional symbolic elements) and creation, and only the latter can be handled easily with rules. Of course, every child learns the creation or rule aspect together with the unproductive conventions. Such unproductive relic mechanisms have to be especially *marked*, which is another way of saying that they have to be learned separately, that is, that they cannot be generated with the usual rules.

On all levels of grammar, one makes the distinction *marked* vs. *unmarked*, when there is an opposition. For example, in English, the singular/plural contrast is normally marked by some overt plural marker, as in *boy*:*boy-s*, *cat*:*cat-s*, and so on. Within the plural itself, some patterns are further marked formally against the regular *-s*, for example, *mouse*:*mice*, *ox*:*oxen*, and so on. It is always the more general, less restricted member (in the case of two) which is the unmarked one. Marking, however, need not be overt at all. Figure 1-5 contains semantically unmarked terms in the first column, for example, *horse*, against words marked for sex (*stallion*, *mare*) and young age (*foal*). *Horse* is clearly the most general term, because it can be used for the others if the marking is eliminated, that is, if the situation does not warrant such detail.

If a language has many declensional and conjugational patterns, all words have to be marked for one, and it might be difficult to have an unmarked type at all (e.g., Latin and German). Lexical marking like that belongs to the dictionary; it acts as the address, which takes the word to the appropriate rules in each case. In other words, the marking is a catalyst that triggers the rule. 'Irregular' or 'strong' forms are the traditional terms for formally marked items in morphology, and they mean exception from the most general rules. The English verbal inflection includes the unmarked weak conjugation, the marked weak irregular, and the various strong ones. Thus *bring* would have to be marked [+weak irregular], although, from its phonetic shape, it might seem to belong to the *swim*-type (see §§ 5.2, 5.19, 10.8), which we can call here the [+ablaut] group. And, indeed, children try to introduce ablaut *bring/brang* into this verb. In other words, the analogical shifts between classes can be spelled out with features. The motivation is apparently the formal presence of a nasal in *bring*; that is, like forms should have like treatment in the grammar. If, however, marking is dropped altogether, the verb shifts to the unmarked class, as in *bring/bringed*. The dropping of marking eliminates irregular forms by assigning them to the productive types. Marking is no more than a restatement of traditional analogy, because marking notation does not add to our understanding of such shifts; for example, it gives no insight into the reason why *dreamed* and *kneeled* were reassigned to the pattern of *dealt*, so that we get *dreamt, knelt*. This is a complication in the grammar, and a similar, more recent one is *dove* for *dived*. On the other hand, languages seem not to go one way only, that is, become simpler and simpler all the time. Thus the plural formation of OE *cū* 'cow' was marked as something like [+umlaut], giving *cȳ*. Later, apparently, the semantic antonym *ox* influenced the feminine, and another overt marker was piled onto the word, [+n-pl.] = *kine*. Note that the mere additional marking [+n-pl.] does not "explain" the reason behind it, which is more to be found in iconicity in the forms of this bovine set (§ 5.4). Now, when all the marking has been dropped, the outcome is *cows*, according to the regular pattern.

[6.21]   Marking with respect to a rule can be positive or negative; that is, some items are marked as subject to a rule, others as exceptions to a rule. Morphemes that satisfy the environment of a rule without undergoing it are marked negatively with respect to that rule. Loans often establish this situation; for example, when French loans like *chief, faith*, and so on, were adopted into English, they had to be marked [−voicing] for the plural formation. Similarly, recent loans in Finnish are marked [−consonant gradation] (§§ 10.16, 10.17), one such word being *auto* 'car', (gen.) *auto-n*. On the other hand, morphemes subject to a rule that is not predictable from their shape are marked positively for the rule. Thus, already in Old English, words like *mūs* 'mouse' and *bōc* 'book' were marked [+umlaut], which ensured the corresponding plurals *mȳs* and *bēc*. Elimination of negative marking expands the domain of the corresponding rule, because exceptions to it diminish. Similarly, elimination of positive marking restricts the domain of a rule, because all items positively marked for a rule are exceptions in the total grammar. Marking is, as has been said before, something that has to be learned by special effort, and children in particular, while learning the language, try to omit it. Thus Finnish children omit the [−consonant gradation] marking, whereby the outcome is *auto/audon*, and English-speaking children, the [+umlaut] with the results *mouses*, *foots*, and so on. Many of these have been accepted in English, for example, *beech* → *books*. Usually, in such frequent words, the speech community is able to drill the "correct" marking in after a while. But both the extension of a rule and the restriction of a rule are based on the same mechanism: loss of marking. And loss of marking means automatic simplification in the lexicon, because exceptions to the general rules diminish in number.

Let us return to the case of *sheath/sheaths* /θ ~ ð/ vs. *faith/faiths* /θ ~ θ/. The opposition here has always been [+voicing rule] vs. [−voicing]. When the loans started being adopted, it was the negative value that was marked (and hence the exception). After enough of these exceptions had been accumulated, *they* became the regularity, and this made the positive value the marked one. Today one has to list *sheath* as [+voicing], and, indeed, this is shown by the further restriction of the rule when the marking is dropped in words like *oath*, pl. /owθs/ (see §§ 10.16, 11.6).

The tradition versus creation dichotomy manifests itself among the rules as unproductivity versus productivity. The unmarked morphemes are subject to the productive rules, and the marked forms undergo unproductive rules if they are positively marked (*cat/cat-s* vs. *jinni/jinn*, a unique plural in English borrowed from Arabic). In negative marking, the matter is more complicated in that if neologisms are exempt from a rule, the rule is no longer productive, but rather the exception is. But if their number is small, their impact in the total grammar does not look like productivity. In a strict sense, the phonological rules which apply in every word of a language are productive, and loan words, for example, are generally adapted to them fast (loan substitution; § 8.4). When such a phonological rule no longer refers to the relations within the phonological system but to the distributive regularities (alternations) of specific morphemes, it has become a morphophonemic rule. The border between these two need not be clear cut; for example, in our Rotuman selections it would seem that the rules remain strictly phonological. However, it was mentioned that the changes did not take place in certain forms (e.g., many pronouns) and, in this sense, the rules are morphophonemic. We have, indeed, seen in many cases how a strictly phonological rule becomes morphophonemic (e.g., umlaut). Morphophonemic rules, on the whole, get more and more restricted (e.g., English umlaut plurals, voicing plurals, strong verbs), and may disappear altogether (e.g., consonant gradation in Veps, one of the Baltic Finnic dialects). The other possibility is that the rule is extended into every word of the language (e.g., consonant gradation in most Lapp languages) (see § 5.21). Morphophonemic rules may be dropped with a concomitant change in morphology (i.e., in the shape of the morphemes, as we have seen above).

[6.22 Cause and Effect]   Even if we have a certain scoring board for recognizing and counting changes, something like what we have observed in this chapter, the question of cause and effect is still open. The point of view that changes would first occur in the program, in competence, and only later would change the utterance without having anything to do with performance is clearly inadequate, although popular. This notion is a result of the scoring mechanism for changes. Language is learned and hearers interpret utterances largely from performance, that is, real concrete speech situations. Causes have to be sought in the totality of language and the relation of its use with the total culture and individual speech acts. If the surface forms are ambiguous, in the sense that they can be produced in two different ways, we have a potential source for reinterpretation, which may change the competence. Most changes seem to be triggered by performance; only grammatical conditioning of sound change and related phenomena are aided from higher up (in a hierarchy as in Figure 1-2). And, indeed, one cannot separate performance from competence. We have seen how ambiguous surface forms have been inductively reinterpreted. This has changed the program, because the reanalysis comes to light deductively in the outputs of this modified program (§§ 5.5, 5.6). Thus changes can originate from both ends, which is indeed logical, because language is used from both ends; that is, there are both hearers and speakers (Figures 1-1 and 1-2). Language is a system that tries to keep an optimum balance between form and meaning. Languages are there to be used; if a language is no longer used, it ceases to change. Hence usage and the actual situation must play a role in the changes, wherever the first impetus originates (see § 9.16f.).

We have not yet mentioned changes in the social registers of the linguistic rules, although linguistic rules are always society oriented (Chapter 3, § 6.8). Age characteristics change when people grow up or die, or when a social group emigrates as a whole. We have first the particular social or historical change in the community, which has a reflex in the rules of the total grammar of the community. It would be ridiculous to maintain that the rules changed first, thereby killing off old people and exiling particular sects. In cases of this kind we see clearly how rules are changed from the outside, by history in general, and this is perhaps true in most cases.

Proto-Indo-European had no infinitive in its verbal paradigm, but most of its daughter languages grew one. Thus we can describe the situation as the addition of an infinitivization rule. In Greek, if the second half of the sentences 'he wants, he writes' is the object of the first, and *he* has the same referent in both cases, a rule operates that deletes the second *he* and replaces the present with the infinitive (which is the most unmarked neutral verbal form), for example, *thélei gráphein* 'he wants to write'. Because infinitives are derived from underlying full sentences, it is clear that we need this rule, and, historically, it was added in Greek (see § 5.16). The same rule applies to *thélō gráphein* 'I want to write', and so on, where there is more formal divergence between the verbs on the surface. We could say that Modern Greek lost the infinitivization rule again when the sentences come out as *thélei (ná) gráphei, thélō (ná) gráphō*. But the situation is not this simple, as we have seen. The motivation for the loss was that sound change had eroded the output of the infinitivization rule, and this triggered a reinterpretation of the surface ambiguity. The same is true of the

Finnish head and attribute switch (§ 5.17), which as a change in a purely syntactic rule would have hardly any motivation.

It is relatively easy to devise rules for mapping the transition from what was earlier to what comes after—to say, for example, that Greek dropped its infinitive rule and the rest followed. As we have seen, the historical changes are, to a great degree, independent from the synchronic rules. What the rule changes always describe, then, is the before–after relationship. They give a mechanism for description, not a historical explanation, except in accidental cases. This fact is often forgotten. Phonemic changes follow suit, because they, also, could occur only between two stages (before–after), whereas phonetic change occurred within the same system. If we count changes in competence only, we jump from what was before to what comes after when we have a new grammar. And the similarity between tallying phoneme changes and rule changes is no wonder, since both use such rigid scoring rules. Moreover, the proportional formula is heavily before–after oriented, because here one actually writes both parts in the formula. All this is indication again of the basic unity of structural change, whether presented as phonemic, analogical, or rule change. Every such concept exemplifies a form of structural change.

The difference between gradual change through time and the linguist's statements on before–after relations leads easily to misunderstanding. For example, phonetic change is primarily gradual (see § 4.21), but the linguist's phonological notations allow mostly for abrupt leaps. It is hasty to say, therefore, that all change is abrupt, because that is a consequence of the notation. The mistake is generally twofold. If, for example, a phonological notation is binary, all features must manifest either as [+] or [−], and any change described through this will look abrupt. This mistake is a deductive one. On the other hand, if some changes are abrupt (e.g., metathesis), it is inductively wrong to argue that all other changes must be the same. It is of utmost importance to distinguish between the actual change and the before–after relations manifested in our notation and rules. The latter can be called *diachronic correspondences*; they need not reflect the actual history at all, but they are always "abrupt" (see § 9.14).

[6.23 Simplification]   The main characteristics of analogy have always been regularization, simplification, generalization, and that is what, in fact, the Greek term originally meant. A claim has arisen that there is no such thing as analogy, which is at best too vague to be useful; instead, we need only the grammar (with its rules) and *simplification*. It is true that analogy is a wide term, indeed, and we have seen that it did, in fact, cover all of grammar and its regularities (§§ 5.18–5.21); for example, rules and marking are the more sophisticated counterparts of Sprachgefühl and memory (marked forms have to be especially learned). The notion of simplification is a direct development of analogy in certain aspects. The terms do not match perfectly, but even analogy was a different concept for different linguists. At this state of the art, it is also not so clear where simplification ends and other mechanisms begin, but, basically, simplification overlaps with analogy. Simplification has a different theoretical connotation, however, and this tends to obscure the substance. The various types of "primary change" affecting the rules (addition, loss, reordering, and modification) are often cases of simplification. But so is restructuring. Both have their ultimate motivation in the principle 'one meaning, one form', which eliminates diversity between form and meaning. We have seen this before:

subtractive reordering $\wedge > |$ restructuring and loss of rule $\wedge > | |$

Here the diagrams represent just the links between form and meaning, although end points have been spelled out before (§§ 5.14, 6.19). Subtractive reordering means leveling, whereas additive reordering extends alternations. The first case in the above diagram is the counterpart of merger, the second a split. This is exactly the kind of simplification in the sign system that happened through analogy. It should be noted that when restructuring does not split the paradigm in two we have just $\wedge > |$, the same leveling of alternation as with subtractive reordering. In other words, we have come back to the effects of morphophonemic conditioning of sound change (analogy). When the base variant of the alternation is affected, we get leveling $\wedge > |$, whereas when the derived variant returns back to its base, we have $\wedge > |$ and $|$, if relics cut loose and establish a split. In every case we have $\wedge$-relations before and $|$-relations afterward. Sound change is largely responsible for changing the one-to-one relations into one-to-many relations; analogy (alias simplification) tends to restore $|$-relations. When alternation is extended to every word (e.g., Lapp consonant gradation), the net result is still unity for diversity: $\wedge, | > \wedge$.

[6.24 Rules and Surface Forms]   The question of the form of rules (and their change) is still very much an open one. This chapter has delineated a central position from which further investigation has to take off. Emphasis was put on the obvious connections with the traditional analogy whose *mechanisms* the rules make more precise, although not their motivation. Rules themselves are posited on the basis of the (morphophonemic) alternations, or in syntax with similar formal correspondences that show semantic similarity or identity (transformational relations). The rules are there to bring out the actually occurring surface forms. Thus the ultimate justification of rules includes very much the same kind of surface linguistics as analogy, especially proportional analogy (see § 5.1). Rules represent another hypothesis about the inner form of grammar based on the actual surface alternations. In other words, rules belong as much to competence as to performance, and after all, no boundary can be drawn between the two. The material in this chapter, as in Chapter 5, has shown the underlying unity of the attempt to elucidate the unknown. The rules are also hypotheses and can quite well be wrong, exactly like, for example, proportional analogy. Indeed, the number of mistakes made in the writing of rules is perhaps as high as those made in applying other forms of analogy earlier. The errors are chiefly seen in the general tendency to write rules for unproductive fossilized connections of the type *drink/drench, bake/batch, hallow/whole*, and so on. In short, regularity has been pushed into the irregular parts of grammar that are unproductive (i.e., symbolic rather than iconic aspects).

[6.25 Conclusion] In spite of the emphasis throughout this chapter on the limits of rule manipulation as a historical process, a further warning must be added because of the importance of the issue. Rule change is not a primary change mechanism, but an effect (on a notation of the "right" kind) resulting from sound change, analogy, and so on (§ 6.22). The form of rules (§§ 6.7, 6.10) was originally derived from sound change (Chapter 4, § 6.6) and such rules were expanded in synchronic description. From there they were illegitimately taken back into diachrony. It was sound change (history) that gave a useful *model* for phonological rules, not the other way around. If the trend-like character of sound change (and the existence of analogy; see § 6.23) is ignored, maximal simplicity through ordered sets of rules is unattainable for sound changes as historical events. On the other hand, if synchronic simplicity is our prime aim, ordering may not produce it at all (compare § 18.17). A theory that combines the mechanisms of classical sound change (§§ 4.1–4.20) and analogy (Chapter 5) into one type (Chapter 6) is deficient in many ways: It tends to become a game on paper, and it may destroy the systematic relations within a language. It provides no motivation or explanation for most changes, that is, such a theory is in essence antimentalistic (compare Chapter 9). It ignores simplicity and psychological reality (§§ 3.3, 5.2) and does not give a useful mechanism for treating distinctive features in an obvious way (see end of § 5.3). It lacks the indeterminacy of a natural language and thus fails to account for the multiplicity of historical changes (see Chapters 7 and 8), as well as social variation and competing forms (Chapter 3). It further destroys relative chronology by ignoring shared innovations and the "secondary" nature of analogy, which provides essential service in various seriation methods (see §§ 14.5–14.7). Thus we are hampered in retrieving drift or reconstructing language splits (Chapter 15). Now, after all, our look inside the piano was just that (§ 6.18); we saw certain movement, but the real impetus came from the outside (see § 9.16f.).

Only phonological rules were discussed, because they provide some ground to stand on. This is not true of syntax or grammar in general (see § 19.5), although marking conventions illuminated the borderline between grammar and lexicon (§§ 6.20, 6.21). (See further §23.10)

REFERENCES

General: Halle 1962, Saporta 1965, Kiparsky 1965, 1968a, Sigurd 1966, Chafe 1968, Chomsky and Halle 1968, Weinreich et al. 1968, Labov in W. Lehmann and Malkiel (eds.) 1982, Wang 1969, King 1969b, Leed 1970, Newton 1971, Kiparsky 1982, Anttila in Anderson and Jones (ed.) 1974 [repr. in Baldi and Werth (eds.) 1978]; **6.1** Bremer 1894, Götze 1923, Hermann 1907, Hoenigswald 1960a, Hořejší 1964, Chen and Hsieh 1971, Chen 1976; **6.3** Voyles 1967, W. Bennett 1968,

Bergmann 1980; **6.4** Martinet 1958, 1964, King 1969a, Kiparsky 1965; **6.5** Jakobson 1968, Fudge 1969, Stampe 1969; **6.6** Lenneberg 1967, Luria 1967, Oldfield and Marshall (eds.) 1968, Martinet (ed.) 1968, Whitaker 1969, Graur (ed.) 3.201-321, 683-779; **6.7** Kiparsky 1965, Chomsky and Halle 1968; **6.8** Fischer 1958, Weinreich et al. 1968, Labov in W. Lehmann and Malkiel (eds.) 1982; **6.10** Weinreich et al. 1968; **6.12** Leed 1970; **6.13** Huntley 1968, Leed 1970; **6.15** Saporta 1965, Vennemann 1970; **6.16** Zeps 1967, D. Cohen 1969; **6.17** Anttila 1969a; **6.18** Andersen 1969, Vachek 1968, King 1969b; **6.19** Schuchardt 1928, Kiparsky 1965; **6.20** Lyons 1968, Maher 1977; **6.21** Andersen 1969, Maher 1977; **6.22** Grace 1969, Terho Itkonen 1970, Andersen 1972; **6.23** Nyman 1987; **6.25** Leed 1970, Newton 1971, Bailey 1982, 1985, Lüdtke (ed.) 1980.

CHAPTER 7

SEMANTIC CHANGE

> *Semantic change highlights the iconic and indexical forces of change. More than the mechanisms seen so far, it stresses the importance of the cultural and social setting for change. And, finally, semantic change shows the mental or psychological factors of change in their purest form.*

[7.1 Changes in the Linguistic Sign]   Although semantics has been a target of scholarly investigation since the activities of Ancient Greek philosophers, we still do not have adequate ways of talking about it. As for semantic change, we still rely basically on the terminology of Greek literary rhetoric. We know much more about phonology in relation to phonetics than about linguistic semology in relation to semantics in general. Semological structures have emerged most clearly in areas where the referents also show measurable structure (e.g., color terms and kinship terminology). The very reason for language is semantic, that is, communication or the carrying of messages; the general buildup of language shows this clearly (Figures 1-1 and 1-2). Semantics is the "deepest" level of grammar, and, basically, all languages are the same on this level, no matter how their formal realization is effected.

Even if we do not have an exact apparatus for describing semological structures, the mechanisms of semantic change are reasonably clear, and we can concentrate on those aspects that must be known as a basis of further investigation. It is possible to discuss semantic change with a vague term 'meaning', if we remember that it is a variable of many dimensions indeed.

Central to semantic change is the nature of the linguistic sign, that is, the connection and independence between form and meaning. There is no one-to-one relation between form and meaning, which means that either end is free to change without affecting the other (see §§ 1.3, 1.26). But we have already seen how semantics can induce formal changes and how the form of the linguistic sign can affect the meaning, because there is a tendency toward a one-to-one relation between form and meaning. This interaction was clearest in analogy (Chapter 5), and now we shall see that semantic change can be analogical.

[7.2 Pure Semantic Change]   Changes in the linguistic sign are more obvious than changes in the semantic structures alone. Figure 1-5 arranges the semantic relations on exactly the same principles as those by which Figures 1-3 and 1-4 handle sounds, and such examples can be multiplied; see, for example, Figure 7-1, in which Spanish semantic experience is divided in a different way from Latin, and this is parallel to what happens in the relationships in a sound system, as emphasized with the boxes of the diagrams. Some of the Latin forms do survive in Spanish outside the system, for example, Latin *novellus* > *novillo* 'young steer, calf'. For pure semantic structure and change, one has to observe the configurations of the boxes, as it were, and not the names of the boxes. Thus the distinction between Latin 'horse' and 'mare' has remained semantically unchanged until Modern French, for example,

1. | *equus* | *equa* | Latin

2. | *cheval* | *ive* | French (early)

3. | *cheval* | *cavale* | French (later)

4. | *cheval* | *jument* | French (modern)

The meanings themselves remain the same, although the names change. However, this kind of a situation is also called semantic change, because the word *jument* meant 'pack horse', before it came to be connected with the meanings 'female + horse'. These meanings are connected with the form *mare* in English (Figure 1-5). These examples show the two possible ways of looking at the form–meaning links, that is, we can concentrate on the name/form and see what meanings it has represented through time, or we can take the meaning as the base and see what forms have represented it at various periods of a language. The former is called *semasiology* 'study of meanings', and the latter *onomasiology* 'study of names', that is, forms. In both cases, the linkups of linguistic signs change. When the form *jument* shifted its colligation from the meaning 'pack horse' to 'mare', we had a case of semasiological change and the result was a new linguistic sign, often loosely referred to as a new *word*. When the meanings 'horse + female' ('mare') replaced their form *equa* by *ive*, only sound change had occurred, which might be regarded as a slight form of onomasiological change. But when *ive* was ousted by *cavale* we have a normal case of name change, and it is repeated in the shift from *cavale* to *jument*. Semasiological changes are accompanied, at least somewhere in the grammar or lexicon, by onomasiological ones, for example, overt increase or decrease in names, and so on. This is indeed what makes discussion of pure semantic change so difficult, and why one tends to remain with the total linguistic signs, that is, both semasiology and onomasiology. In other words, the lexicalization rules, the rules that link form to meaning, may change without any change in the semantic structure itself. In addition to the Latin terms *āter* 'black' and *albus* 'white', there were also two terms marked for the feature 'shining': *niger* 'shining black' and *candidus* 'shining white'. When the semantic notion of 'lustre' is lost as an obligatory feature, the units merge into one name for 'black' and 'white', respectively, in Romance, for example, French *noir* 'black' (which continues

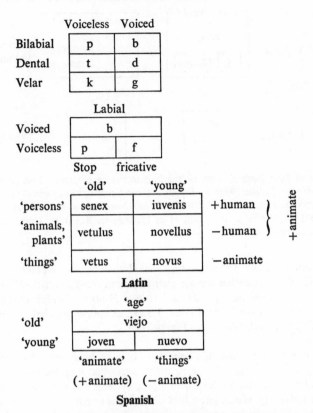

	Voiceless	Voiced
Bilabial	p	b
Dental	t	d
Velar	k	g

	Labial	
Voiced	b	
Voiceless	p	f
	Stop	fricative

	'old'	'young'		
'persons'	senex	iuvenis	+human	⎫
'animals, plants'	vetulus	novellus	−human	⎬ +animate
'things'	vetus	novus	−animate	⎭

Latin

	'age'	
'old'	viejo	
'young'	joven	nuevo
	'animate'	'things'
	(+animate)	(−animate)

Spanish

FIGURE 7-1. Parallelism between phonology and semology (compare Figures 1-3, 1-4, and 1-5). [Reprinted with slight modification from Eugenio Coseriu, "Pour une sémantique diachronique structurale," *Travaux de linguistique et de litterature*, II, No. 1 (1964) (© Centre de Philologie et de Littératures Romanes, Université de Strasbourg).]

the old marked term) and *blanc* 'white' (with no formal connection with the old terms). Of course, the possibility of speaking about 'lustre' or 'shine' was not lost; only its obligatory indication was. Semantic merger was here accompanied by a reduction of forms as well. With semantic split, the number of forms increases, at least in part of the vocabulary, for example, when Latin *avis* 'bird' gives Spanish *ave* 'big bird' and *pájaro* 'little bird'. When we look at this semasiologically, *avis* has restricted its semantic range, and *pájaro* has expanded it, since the form continues Latin *passer* 'sparrow' (§ 7.12).

Latin had a generic term *homō* 'man', with sex marked in *vir* 'man' and *fēmina* 'woman' (compare Figure 1-5). French and Italian have eliminated the masculine marking, thereby giving a skewed system as shown in Figure 7-2:A.

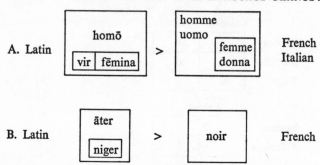

FIGURE 7-2. Loss of semantic marking in the development from Latin to French and Italian. [Reprinted from Eugenio Coseriu, "Pour une sémantique diachronique structurale," *Travaux de linguistique et de littérature* II, No. 1 (1964) (© Centre de Philologie et de Littératures Romanes, Université de Strasbourg).]

French thus continues the old Latin forms, but Italian has replaced the female term with what was earlier a more restricted term *domina* 'mistress'. Note that Latin is of the German type: *Mensch* (*Mann–Frau*) vs. English *man* (*woman*), which is just like French and Italian. This is, of course, parallel to a total loss of marking like in the *āter* area (Figure 7-2:B).

[7.3 Reasons for Semantic Change]   It is probably true that meaning is least resistant to change. Most semanticists agree that meaning is always vague, and this has indeed led to the use of logical systems and notation to lessen the inherent ambiguity. We all know how difficult it is to communicate. In a normal situation, the hearers have to ask for more information, and the speakers must paraphrase their messages. Only in simple situations like *Pass the salt, please!* can one easily reach complete understanding. This is why most students need a teacher in addition to a textbook. Many words have more than one meaning, and sometimes ambiguity results in spite of the context. Indeed, the context itself can be ambiguous. Further, the structure of vocabulary is open; linguistic signs come and go. Thus the possibilities for semantic reinterpretation are greater by far than for formal reanalysis. The more elements and relations there are within a system, the more complex it is, and such a system is, a priori, more likely to change than a simpler one. This applies very well to lexicon in contrast to morphology. In mechanical terms: the more complex a machine is, the more likely it is to break down.

    To understand a semantic change, one often requires thorough historical knowledge of the situation. The formal apparatus of language is much more conservative than changes in culture or human experience, which expands constantly and necessitates new semantic divisions. In short, there are always more meanings than words, and one of the impressive facts about language is its ability to adapt to such a semantic challenge, which, of course, is made possible by the syntactic rules (e.g., compounding, and semantic creation, e.g., metaphors). Semantic change due to change in the material culture is called 'thing change' or 'referent change' (German *Sachwandel*). English *pen* originally meant 'feather', and in Pre-Latin days it was a motivated derivation from the root **pet-* 'to fly' (this indeed still lurks in the English word *feather*), that is, 'a flying aid' or the like. When quills were used for writing with ink, the old name was appropriate. And it was retained even after pens were no longer feathers; that is, the material culture got away from the original situation, leaving the form behind. As a consequence *pen* means now only 'writing tool' and semasiological change has taken place. English *mint* and *money* derive ultimately from Latin *moneō* 'admonish'. We can explain this, because we know the total historical situation. *Monēta* 'The Admonisher' was one of the surnames of Juno, in whose temple in Rome money was coined. This shows at once the value of the principle 'words and things', which states that in etymological studies one should not separate the two (Chapter 17). Another interesting case is Latin *prōclīvis* 'sloping downhill', which is also used in the meaning 'easy'. Such a metaphorical leap seems quite natural and immediately acceptable without question. The problem is, however, that, in early Latin, the word also meant 'difficult', and this appears to defy reason. An attempt to try to alter the meaning so that it would also mean 'uphill' (i.e., going the slope the other way) is out of the question. The basic meaning is simply 'downhill'. The solution is provided by the linguistic and cultural context. The meaning 'difficult' is contrasted with *plānus* 'flat, level' (i.e., *plain*), and we can assume that the metaphor arose when Roman vehicles did not have efficient brakes. For many such changes, we have no knowledge; for example, how did Italian *fiasco* 'flask, bottle' acquire the meaning 'complete (ridiculous) failure'? One story goes that a comedian, who was famous for never failing to come out with the right comment, was given a bottle at one of his performances. This time he could not find anything to say and in angry exasperation he finally threw the bottle to the floor saying *fiasco!* All this could be true (at least the meaning seems to refer particularly to a theatrical context), and it would show how a mere historical accident can influence semantic change. But we do not know the true history.

[7.4]   A case where change was due to an ambiguous context is the meaning of English *bead*. The word originally meant 'prayer' (compare *bid*, and German *beten* 'pray'). Medieval and modern religious practice holds it important to keep track of the number of prayers, and the scoring device is the rosary with its small balls. Praying with this device was called literally *counting one's beads*, that is, *prayers*. The balls just represented prayers as symbols, and praying and counting the balls were contiguous activities, the former being the cause of the latter. Now the more obvious referent to *counting one's beads* was the physical activity of tallying the balls and the situation was interpreted this way, whereby *bead* came to mean 'small ball' (also *boon* has shifted its meaning from the 'prayer' [compare Swedish *bön* 'prayer'] to the 'thing asked for, a welcome benefit'). Without knowledge of this religious practice, the change from 'prayer' to 'small ball' would be completely incomprehensible.

[7.5]   Habitual linguistic collocation may become permanent, and if part of the collocation is lost, the remainder changes meaning, when it takes on the semantics of the earlier phrase. The Latin negative *ne* was emphasized as 'not a thing' (*rem*), 'not a step' (*passus*), 'not now more' (*iam* + *magis*), 'not a person' (*persōna*), and so on. These gave ultimately the French negatives *ne* . . . *rien* 'nothing' (compare *no thing*), *ne* . . . *pas* 'not', *ne* . . . *jamais* 'never', and *ne* . . . *personne* 'nobody'. All these are in a way discontinuous compounds, as they represent the negative *together*. After this, the *ne* can be omitted without change in the meaning of the earlier juxtaposition. Thus *personne* can mean alone 'nobody' as well as 'person', which gives a situation parallel to Latin *prōclīvis* with opposite meanings. Here, however, the reason is syntactic. In other words, *prōclīvis* acquired its antonymic meanings metaphorically (iconically), whereas *personne* reached the same situation through ellipsis (indexically). A parallel case is English *but* < *be-ūtan* 'outside', where the negative *ne but* 'not outside' retains its meaning after the drop of *ne*: *I have but five apples*, that is, 'only' = 'not beyond'.

In earlier French *traire* was the general verb for 'pull', also used in phrases like *traire les vaches, traire le lait* 'to milk'. When *tirer* replaced *traire* as the general verb, the latter was retained as a farming term 'to milk', and its object could be omitted. This is how social groups omit grammatical objects that are the normal unmarked ones for them, whereby the verb changes meaning. Latin *pōnere* 'to place' could have the object *ova* 'eggs', that is, 'to lay eggs'. In French and English farming circles, the object can be omitted: *pondre* 'to lay eggs', *The hen won't lay*; similarly, in Hillbilly style, *He is a-pickin'* 'he is playing a string instrument'. Completely motivated iconic compounds often face the same fate, for example, *airplane → plane, drive-in theater → drive-in, swimming pool → pool*. This same process can even create completely "new" words, if earlier boundaries are not observed. When *automobile* 'self-moving', a descriptive term for car, was shortened to *auto* in many languages, *auto* changed its meaning from 'self' to both 'self' and 'car'. In Swedish, however, only the end of the compound was retained giving *bil* 'car', a completely unmotivated single sign. The bus was also descriptively named *omnibus*, Latin for 'for everybody', and later it was shortened to the last syllable. In this way, a Latin case ending (dat./abl. pl.) became a regular noun. Note that we are dealing with loanwords, which implies partial bilingualism in those circles where the words were coined (§ 8.15). A well-known truncation is Greek *om-mátion* 'little eye', where *om-* represents the original root and the rest is a sequence of suffixes, which gives Modern *máti* 'eye'. The earlier ending is now the noun itself.

In all these cases we have seen that ellipsis induced loss of motivation. Compounds and phrases are motivated when they are built up according to the productive rules of the grammar, in other words, they are iconic. When the formal side was truncated, an unmotivated sign (symbol) resulted, which had to be specifically learned, because of the semasiological shifts. Loss of motivation is always beneficial to semantic change, even when sound change is primarily responsible for it. A symbol has to be learned anyway, so it does not matter for what referent it is learned. Old English *hlāford* was already a slightly obscured compound *hlāf-weard* 'bread warden', but when it became *lord*, all motivation was lost.

[7.6]   Thus, with cultural expansion, there is a constant need for new names, and this is often quite explicit. Mostly one resorts to perfectly iconic (motivated) descriptions, for example, *radio detecting and ranging* (§ 2.13), *lunar-exploration module*, *drive-in theater*, and so on. Often some kind of shortening is the result, as in *radar*, *LEM*, and *drive-in*. Very seldom, indeed, does one coin something out of the blue, for example, *gas*, *kodak*; even a word like *gobbledygook* has a considerable onomatopoeic basis. But under the right sociolinguistic conditions such creations are indeed possible; Estonian has incorporated dozens of them since the 1910s. The following belong to the active vocabulary of contemporary Estonian: *laip* 'corpse', *relv* 'weapon', *laup* 'forehead', *roim* 'crime', *kahur* 'cannon', and *veenma* 'to convince'.

The process of giving new names to either old or new things is called *nomination*, and it characteristically implies the extension of the machinery already available in the language. It is, at the same time, both onomasiological and semasiological change. Often nomination can be carried out with loanwords, and we shall return to this both in this chapter and in Chapter 8. The need for a new name need not be a consequence of a new meaning/thing. There are all kinds of social and psychological reasons for renaming things, for example, euphemism and tabu in general. All such restrictions depend on the particular culture and the particular speakers. For instance, the old Indo-European name for bear has been replaced by a euphemism (hunting tabu) 'the brown one' in Germanic, and the Germanic word for wolf gave way to *varg* 'out-law' in Swedish, *varg*, in turn, being replaced by descriptions like 'grey-foot'. Other European languages have used circumlocutions like the 'honey-eater', the 'honey-paw', or the 'apple of the forest' for bear. The tabu of obscenity is well known, although the notion itself varies quite arbitrarily. For example, at one point the word *leg* acquired indelicate connotations in America, which would clash with good taste at Thanksgiving dinners, for example. Euphemisms like *dark meat* or *drum stick* saved the day. Sometimes the correction itself would seem to be more objectionable than the original term; for example, in some American dialects, the highly tabu word *bull* was replaced by *top cow*. All this shows the unpredictable social forces at play. And man does indeed play with his language (e.g., *kisser* for 'mouth'). The world wars immediately produced rich soldier slangs, which were useful in releasing emotional pressure. Weapons were called with household words, for example, 'coffee mill' or 'sewing machine' for a machine gun, 'repair shop for comrades-at-arms' (Finnish *asevelikorjaamo*) for the first aid depot in the field, and so on. On the other hand, the use of war terms for familiar household items was also able to lessen the grim connotations of the former, for example, 'wire obstacle' for beard and 'hand grenade' for potato, and so on. The first steam drills in the Rocky Mountain mines were known as *widow makers*, where again humor lessened the grim realities. Similar euphemism exists also in those social layers which practice deceit in one form or other, as in the underworld; but, linguistically, merchants and politicians also fall into this class, with their advertising propaganda (e.g., 'ultimate solution' for genocide or 'home' for house). Literary style also requires new names for old notions; as Aristotle said, if one uses too little metaphor, language becomes plain and dull, and if too much, language becomes enigmatic.

[7.7]   One way of handling nomination is to borrow a word, especially when one borrows the referent at the same time. But native morphemes may be substituted for the foreign ones, and we get what is called a calque or *loan translation*, that is, semantic borrowing only. Various types of loan translation can be distinguished, but the essence is clearly analogical: language A has a form *z* with meanings 'm, n', and language B has a form *x* with the meaning 'm'. Symmetry is attained by language B borrowing the meaning 'n' for its form *x*. In Finnish, *harja* is a brush used for cleaning or tidying up, whereas any paintbrush is *pensseli* or *sivellin* (literally 'stroker', 'stroking tool'). Because English *brush* covers both meanings, Finnish Americans tend to use *harja* the same way, and occasionally even *pensseli* for 'pencil' (which is *lyijykynä* in normal Finnish). In bilingual situations, one often "speaks one language with the words of the other" (see § 8.17f.). French *arriver* and English *arrive* matched more or less in their semantic range, except that the French verb meant also 'attain success'. Ultimately, this meaning was also borrowed into English. Of course, the word itself had been borrowed earlier. English *earl* meant originally 'man of noble rank'. Subsequently, it assumed the meaning of Scandinavian *jarl* and thus replaced the native *alderman*. Phonetic similarity between the two cognates was an obvious factor. Later still, *earl* borrowed the meanings of *count*, and this time there was no phonetic support at all (the first instance is of the type American Finnish *pensseli* 'pencil'). German has tended to translate foreign phrases morpheme by morpheme, for example, *Schöngeist* for French *bel esprit* and *Geist des Jahrhunderts* for *esprit du siècle*. Also, English has such phrases from French: *gilded youth, castle in Spain, goes without saying, marriage of convenience*, and so on. Old English was very much like German in this respect, because many foreign notions were rendered by native morphemes (e.g., *eorþcræft* (earth-craft) 'geometry', *tungolwītega* (star-knowing) 'astronomer, -logist', *godspell* (good-tidings) 'ēvangelium', *gewritu* (writings) 'scriptures', and so on). This phenomenon is quite parallel to such German words as *Wasserstoff* (water-stuff) 'hydrogen' and *Fernsehen* (far-seeing) 'television'. Of course, Modern English still has this possibility for motivated (self-explaining) compounds and derivations: *railroad, farmer, eatable*, and so on. Various aspects of loan translation show how analogical and iconic relations reshape the semantic content of native morphemes. The Middle English adverb *faste* had acquired the meaning 'swiftly' by about 1300, whereas the adjective *fast* retained its meaning 'firm' (compare German *fest*). Toward the end of the fourteenth century, *fast* borrowed the meaning from the adverb, hence 'rapid, swift', though the original meaning also survives, *he is fast asleep* (compare *fasten*). Thus the borrowing can occur within the same language between different categories which display formal similarity. Here also the principle at work is analogical, that is, 'one form, one meaning', in other words, borrowing from within is analogy (see § 5.18).

[7.8 **Semantic Change, Iconicity, and Indexicality**]   In sound change, we saw that change was a function of speech production and a result of synchronic variation. Analogy, too, is intimately connected with speech production and grammatical rules, and change is thus a function of synchronic aspects. In addition to referent change, semantic change is tied to synchronic linguistic variation, which we can call style. Important in this connection are the so-called *figures of speech* (tropes). These are the elements of literary rhetoric: metaphor, metonymy, litotes (negation of the contrary: *not a few*, that is, *many, in no small measure*), hyperbole (exaggeration), emphasis, and irony; these are the more basic types, though there exist hundreds of ways of classifying and combining these. We can touch here only on the very essential characteristics.

The subject matter of the *metaphor* alone is practically inexhaustible. Metaphor is based on a perception of a functional resemblance between two objects. It is one of the most important phenomena in human linguistic communication. Although any utterance can be used metaphorically, current linguistic theory has tended to regard the metaphor as something unnatural and ungrammatical; this view is a consequence of neglecting semantics. Metaphor is an important kind of analogy, or vice versa, and we have seen that both are subtypes of icons (§ 1.16). One could even say that man has an innate capacity for analogy and metaphor, and that language is only part of this. Like analogy in general, metaphor is quite suitable for scientific and philosophical terminology (§ 9.16f.).

Metaphor was an important ingredient in Germanic poetry. Particularly characteristic were two-part compounds for single items, for example, OE *mere-hengest* (sea stallion) for 'ship' and *hron-rād* (whale road) for 'sea'. These are known technically as *kennings*.

The indexical counterpart of metaphor is *metonymy*. When one uses parts for wholes or vice versa, one refers to this as *synecdoche*, for example, *bread* for 'food' and *army* for 'soldier'. Metonymy is wider and covers any other contiguity or causal relation, as in *throne* or *scepter* for 'king' and *White House* for 'the President'. A thing may be named by any of its accompaniments, or indexes, that is, instruments for agents, containers for the thing contained (even *trousers* for a man and *skirt* for woman) and effects for causes. Other relations possible are equipment for a person (*ensign*), action for agent (*aid*[e]), place for service (*church*), and place for inhabitants (*the City*), and so on. We saw these same principles in the development of writing systems and in the design of trade marks (§§ 1.12, 2.7).

Metaphor is semantic transfer through a similarity of sense perceptions. A subtype of it is *synaesthesia*, a shift of terms between the physical senses, as in a *sharp smell*, a *soft color*, and a *bright sound*. If a comparison is spelled out with *as* or *like* one speaks of *simile*, for example, *he roared like a lion, you eat like a pig*, versus a metaphor like *I do not tolerate pigs at the table*. If a metaphor is expanded through a discourse one gets *allegory* and *parable*.

Metonymy comprises words that are already related by contiguity in the same semantic sphere, and it can be classified according to spatial or temporal fields, for example. Inventions are often named after their inventors (e.g., *ohm*, *ampère*, *watt*, *sandwich*, *mauser*), products, by the place where they are first characteristically produced (e.g., *bordeaux*, *champagne*, *madras*, and *china*).

Similarity of names leads to folk etymology and blends. In cases like *sandblind* (§ 5.5), there was a change only in the connotative meaning, not in the referent. Similarly, German *vrīthof* 'an enclosed court' and *sinvluot* 'a general flooding' were connected with *Friede* 'peace' and *Sünde* 'sin' giving modern *Friedhof* 'cemetery' and *Sündflut* 'deluge', with no change in the actual referent. In *shame-faced*, we saw a change both in meaning and referent. The situation is repeated by English *belfry*, which meant 'a movable tower used in attacking walled positions'. But the first syllable was associated with the noun *bell*, and the basic meaning is now 'bell tower'.

And we saw in our discussion of French negatives that words that frequently occur side by side influence each other semantically so that one of them can drop without semantic consequences. Such deletion is called *ellipsis*, and it is often difficult to distinguish it from metonymy, for example, *a daily* (paper), *the main* (sea), Latin *prōsa* (ōrātiō) 'straight speech', *oriēns* (sol) 'rising sun', *ovīle* (stābulum) 'sheepfold', French *à* (main) *droite*, *à la* (manière, mode, façon) *française*; *a* (painting by) *Picasso*, *a burgundy* (wine), *a Winchester* (rifle), and so on.

The order of importance of the four mechanisms of change is metaphor, metonymy, ellipsis, and folk etymology, the latter only peripherally important. These are again only cardinal points; in real situations, they interlock extensively. Particularly delicate is the boundary between metonymy and ellipsis. For example, is German *Schirm* 'umbrella' a straight metonymy from the meaning 'shelter', or is it an elliptic form for the self-explaining compound *Regenschirm*?

	Iconicity (similarity)	Indexicality (contiguity)
Meaning (sense)	metaphor	metonymy
Form (name)	folk etymology	ellipsis

FIGURE 7-3. The interrelation among four mechanisms of semantic change. [The essence of the diagram reprinted with permission from Pierre Guiraud, *La sémantique* (Que sais-je?) No. 655 (1955) (© 1962 Presses Universitaires de France).]

We can relate metaphor, metonymy, ellipsis, and folk etymology through Figure 7-3.

[7.9 Simplification in Semantic Change]   Lasting semantic change occurs when the figures of speech lose their stylistic value and become the unmarked, normal representatives for a meaning. First, it should be noted that metaphor, metonymy, loan translation, folk etymology, and the development of different syntactic categories all add to the complexity of the grammar. They are, in a way, 'rule additions', which increase the one-to-many relations between form and meaning, as shown in Figure 7-4. All the mechanisms mentioned add the right side to the diagrams A–D. These contrast in shape with E–G, where the formal side is the more varied one. We already know case F from sound change which splits up paradigms in this way, and case G represents phrases that were completely motivated to begin with, but where the parts have fused into one semantic unit. As with other innovations, the development of a new meaning does not immediately oust old meanings. For a time the new and old meanings exist side by side, and this situation is characterized in the diagrams. Those that open upward represent semasiological aspects, the reverse ones, onomasiological ones. This synchronic variation (one-to-many relations) is the basis of change.

We have already seen how case F becomes simplified through analogy (or rule manipulation). Forms that are semantically the same tend to be leveled out also formally, for example, $\bigwedge$ > | (*cow/cow-s*), or else the paradigm splits in two, $\bigwedge$ > |, | (*deus, dīvus* and ˜*shade, shadow*). In this case we have a formal split that˜leads to a semantic split. The underlying principle here is that the mind tends to eliminate purposeless variety (§ 5.21), that is, 'one form, one meaning'. This is shown also by a well-known fact of synonymy (E), that exact synonyms are hard to come by. Either one form is lost, as in $\bigwedge$ > |, or differentiation takes place, $\bigwedge$ > |, |. In other words, case F is just a subtype of E; their formal relations in change are the same, although F belongs to the grammar (paradigm) and E to the lexicon to begin with. English is rather rich in synonyms, and, nearly always, there is some differentiation in that one term is stylistically marked as more abstract, emotive, emphatic, technical, or colloquial (*help–aid, reject–decline, bloody–sanguinary, turn down–refuse*, and *daddy–father*). The old term for 'animal' was *deer*, which became restricted to the animal as the main target of hunting in contrast with the general *animal*. This is indeed quite common in semantic differentiation: the old term takes on a special restricted meaning and a new term becomes the normal unmarked one (§ 5.15). The Savoyard dialect borrowed the words *père* 'father' and *mère* 'mother' from Standard French, and these clashed with the old *pâré* and *mâré*. Again differentiation took place: the old terms became restricted to cattle; that is, they became technical, professional terms.

Case G is the starting point of ellipsis, which is simply the loss of one of the formal constituents, $\bigwedge$ > |. Either the attribute or the head can be omitted (*swimming pool → pool* vs. *drive-in theater → drive-in* and *ne . . . pas → pas*). Here belong, also, those compounds that become fused together rather than

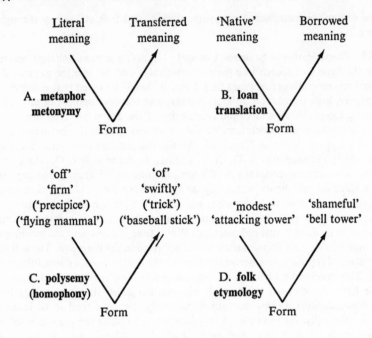

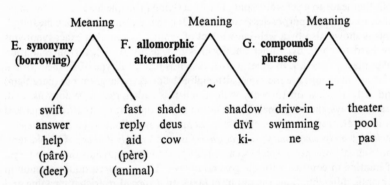

FIGURE 7-4.   Elaboration in the meaning-form links as a basis for simplification and semantic change.

dropping one part, for example, *hlāford > lord, hussy, shepherd* (see § 5.15). These have to be learned as single signs; in other words, a motivated relation has yielded |, one symbol.

In polysemy (case C), meaning is the trigger of change, contrary to F. Depending on the different grammatical categories, the same form becomes differentiated or leveled (see § 5.14), that is, $\bigvee > |, |$ or $|$. Thus the more emphatic adverbs retain forms like *thorough* and *off*, whereas the less stressed prepositions yield *through* and *of* (compare further *convey–convoy, clothes–cloths, costume–custom, conduct–conduit, alternate–alternative, masterful–masterly*, and so on, and similar cases in other languages, e.g., Swedish *klädning* 'clothing'–*klänning* 'woman's dress' and Latin *relīgēns* and *religiōsus*, both originally 'pious', in *relīgentem esse oportet, religiōsum nefās* 'It is proper to be *religious*, wrong to be *superstitious*'). Latin *homō/hominem* yields both French *on* 'one' and *homme* 'man'. On the other hand, if a variant borrows its meaning from a different category, we get $\vee$ > | as in the case of *fast* with its meaning 'rapid' borrowed from the adverb, where it had developed creating elaboration of the type $\vee$ (ignoring here relics of the original, and derivatives like *fasten*; § 7.7). We have already seen that this kind of borrowing from within is a type of analogy (§ 5.18). Here, borrowing leads to simplification, in case B, to elaboration. The reason is the different basis of simplification; in C, it is agreement (correspondence, iconicity) within one and the same grammar, and in B it is agreement between two different grammars (languages), that is, cultural influence rather than purely linguistic (compare spelling changes, § 2.15).

Sometimes the split occurs in writing only, for example, *flower/flour, born/borne, metal/mettle*, French *dessein* 'design, purpose' (God) vs. *dessin* 'design, drawing' (artist), German *Mann* 'man' vs. *man* 'one', which also are different in stress (compare French *homme/on*). This is one indication of the importance of writing in communication, and the parallelism of changes in writing to those in language.

When the phonetic shape of a morpheme leads to a new meaning (case D), the innovation is likely to survive, since it increases iconicity. When the old meaning vanishes, the situation is again simplified as $\vee$ > |. And this is the configuration also in metaphor and metonymy (A), when their literal interpretation is lost and the transferred meaning becomes the normal unmarked one. This process is called *fading*, and it occurs with all figures of speech (e.g., *awfully nice, ne . . . pas*). Repetition itself is not enough for fading, because in certain semantic spheres metaphors may stay alive. This has, in general, been true of Western religious metaphors. The Latin metaphor *pastor* 'shepherd' for the *head* of the *congregation* ('herd') has faded outside Latin and Italian, but, in all languages, the metaphor of a shepherd and sheep lives on. In communication without emotional overtones, metaphors lose their association with the primary meaning more easily if the referents do not normally have emotive value for the speakers. As long as both meanings are present, the metaphor has both cognitive and emotive value. If the metaphor does not catch on, there is really no change, but if it does, and this leads to the disuse of the original meaning, only the marked reading remains. But a marked value without a corresponding unmarked one is not possible, and hence the remaining connection becomes the normal one. A metaphor for a weeping person was *maudlin* (Magdalene, because she was often depicted in that state). When this extralinguistic connection was lost, *maudlin* became a normal adjective meaning 'weeping, foolish, sentimental'. This is also how euphemisms tend to become the normal symbols for the referent, and thus necessitate new euphemisms, for example, Swedish *ulv* 'wolf' → *varg* 'outlaw' → *gråben* 'grey-foot'. A new euphemism could occur when the old metaphor or metonym had faded and become the normal sign for 'wolf'. In Old English, the antecedent of *wanton* meant 'undisciplined, unruly' and the word was euphemistically used for 'lascivious, lewd', which, indeed, became one of the habitual meanings of the word. Different social layers handle euphemisms quite differently. In high style, a euphemism can remain as such (e.g., *outhouse*), whereas in low style it easily becomes the normal word for the referent; then it has to be avoided as a vulgarism even by the higher circles (in favor of *toilet, restroom*, and so on).

All the cases show that fading is simplification in the meaning–form relations. It is a shortcut between form and meaning in the colligation of the linguistic sign. It is a by-product of the tendency 'one meaning, one form'. (§23.7)

The mechanisms presented here represent only the very basic core of semantic change. The subject is enormous if all the possible distinctions are drawn. It is easy to see why semantic change is so uncertain and unpredictable. Every utterance can act as a metaphor in the right situation. All the faded figures of speech can enter new living ones, which in their turn may again fade, and so on. Thus *pioneer* meant originally 'foot soldier', whose task it was to clear the terrain for the more prestigious troops. It was applied metaphorically to the forerunners of colonialization and civilization, which is now the basic meaning in English (but, in Russian, 'member of the communist youth organization'). A further metaphor, such as *pioneer in linguistics*, could therefore spring up. Semantic change takes place in terms of the total cultural situation. Isolated words do not change their meanings (unless they are so isolated that reanalysis becomes easy), but words in clear syntactic contexts in sentences and the relation of these sentences to the physical environment are often decisive. The diagrams (Figure 7-4) emphasized again the similarity of semantic change to analogical change (or rule change) (§§ 5.14, 6.19, 6.23). Both are different ends of one and the same force, the adaptive power of language to meet the needs of communication. Analogy and the rules of the grammar are exactly those mechanisms that allow for metaphor, and so on, when the need arises. And the tendency toward 'one meaning, one form' restores balance when either the formal or semantic marking becomes highly loaded. Change is a function of language as a system of communication; analogy and rules are the mechanism for it but not the driving force.

[7.10 Semantic Shifts]   Because linguistic units are not isolated, any change in one item may lead to changes in other items within the same semantic sphere (e.g., *jaw* used to mean 'cheek' and *cheek* meant 'jaw'). Such shifts may be so regular and far-reaching that they look like shifts in the sound systems. One of the best cases reported comes from Latin legal terminology. In the older period, we have the following terms: *damnum* 'legal obligation, trust', *noxia* 'damage', *culpa* 'guilt', *cāsus* 'negligence', and *fortūna* 'chance'. In the later period, the form–meaning links have shifted one notch:

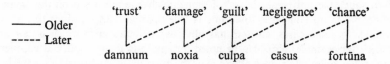

	'trust'	'damage'	'guilt'	'negligence'	'chance'
—— Older					
---- Later					
	damnum	noxia	culpa	cāsus	fortūna

The semantic system as such has not changed much, only the form–meaning pairings.

[7.11 Laws of Semantic Change]   It has not been possible to formulate truly general laws of semantic change, because the latter is often so intimately bound with the historical events (*fiasco!*). This is a general difficulty with history (§ 1.24). There are, however, universal tendencies. Aside from the general anthropocentric way of looking at the world and of making metaphors, which is common to all mankind (see § 1.15), there are also other parallel developments. One of the most interesting cases is Stern's study of English adverbs meaning 'rapidly', which all (some twenty-five of them) develop the meaning 'immediately' before 1300. The development has three stages, illustrated by the following examples: (1) *He wrote quickly*; (2) *When the king saw him, he quickly rode up to him*; and (3) *Quickly afterward he carried it off.* In (1), the verb is imperfective and the adverb means 'rapidly' (speed in space); in (3), the verb is punctual and the adverb is 'immediately' (speed in time); and (2) the verb is ambiguous, because it can be taken as action in progress or the action as a punctual unit. The reverse development 'immediately' > 'rapidly' does not occur.

Similar cases can be found in fairly well known semantic systems. But certain metaphors and metonyms are also widespread all over the world. The sun is often called *day's eye*, or *sun* gives 'day' and *moon* gives 'month'. Language is often named after the *tongue*; that is, man has always given preference to the speaker, and this has been repeated by modern linguists. No language seems to have made a metonym *ear* for 'language'. The mouth seems to be the dominant organ; that is, its activity is the most visible one (compare the counting of beads), because, for all appearances, the brain and the ears do not do anything (compare, also, German *Mundart* 'dialect', i.e., 'mouth-fashion'). It is also very common to name one's own language 'language' and a foreign or neighboring language 'nonlanguage' or the like. The Austro-Bavarian dialect of Sauris in the Carnian Alps is called *taitš* 'German' or *inzəra špro·xe* 'our language'. *Cheyenne* is from Sioux for 'to speak unintelligibly or in a foreign language'. The Russian word *nemec* 'German' is a derivative from a word for 'mute'. But in semantic change the relation can hold in the reverse order as well, for example, Russian *jazyčnik* 'heathen' (having a language [of his own]) and American Finnish *kielinen* 'English-speaking' (provided with language), in which particular sociolinguistic factors are responsible for the formations.

The concept of property is also fairly universal, and it often happens that words denoting 'cattle' come to mean 'money', and vice versa. In North America, and apparently also Finland, the development from 'fur' to 'money' is attested.

In short, the universal "laws" of semantic change are based on the figures of speech in all languages (the same is true of other classifications to follow below). In some cases, an item has obvious attributes after which it can be called; for example, birds can be noted for eggs and flying. And, indeed, they are rather commonly named after one or the other in the languages of the world. German *Vogel* and English *fowl* derive from 'fly/wing', although the latter is no longer connected with flying; compare Finnish *lintu* 'bird' with *lentää* 'to fly', and the Sanskrit words for bird *aṇḍaja* 'egg-born' and *dvija* 'twice-born', which refer beautifully to eggs.

[7.12   Classification of Semantic Change According to Range and Evaluation]
It has been customary to classify semantic changes quantitatively according to their ranges, that is, *extension* and *restriction*. This is exactly what we saw with analogy and rules. It is another variant of labeling before–after relations and does not explain anything; it just states a fact. Restriction is the more common direction, since everyday life is directed toward the concrete. Thus *deer* has changed from 'animal' to a particular kind of animal, *hound* from 'dog' to a particular kind of dog, and *fowl* from 'bird' to domesticated edible birds (German *Tier*, *Hund*, and *Vogel* retain the original meanings). English *starve* is a particular way of dying in comparison with its German cognate *sterben* 'to die', and so on. Semantic extension is rarer, but still easy to find (e.g., Latin *panārium* 'bread basket' > French *panier* 'basket', and *target* 'small round shield, shield-like device for shooting practice' now has a much wider range). Similarly, *batch* which meant loaves baked at the same time, now means any set that goes together (this is generally true of faded metaphors). The last two changes can also be classified as a change from concrete to abstract meaning. One axis of classification is evaluation, that is, either pejorative or meliorative developments. Latin *villānus* 'inhabitant of a farm' gives English *villein* 'serf' and *villain*, both lower in value than the original term. English *knave* meant 'boy, servant' (German *Knabe*) and was thus higher than the modern meaning. The reverse happened in *knight*, also originally 'servant' (German *Knecht*), and the melioration occurred during the age of chivalry when horse-related activities became prestigious (compare *marshal* from 'horse servant'). A word meaning 'exile' has given both English *wretch* and German *Recke* 'warrior, hero', with opposite developments in the two languages. Hungarian *szemrehányás* 'reproach' meant once literally 'vomiting on the eyes', and Low German *Hunsvott* 'rascal' is still, formally, the original 'dog's cunt'.

The value of tabulating restrictions, extensions, pejorations, and so on, is rather limited. All they show is that figures of speech do, in fact, fade and that different indexical collocations can lead to different directions; for example, exile meant both misery and daring deeds of war and *caitiff* 'a mean, cowardly person' is the same word as *captive*. In this semantic area of Medieval society and warfare belongs also *vassalage*, originally 'the state of being a vassal to somebody'. Inferiority of status in relation to the overlord led to a meaning 'servitude, bondage', but bravery in such service also to the now obsolete meaning, 'valorous deeds of war'. German follows the development of English *wretch* in *Elend* 'misery', which originally meant 'foreign country, exile'. The "cultural" context is obvious; what is heroic to the doer can be criminal to the sufferer; that is, different parties look at the same event differently. This is the basic fact in the development of occupational jargons, for example. Words denoting women often go down in evaluation. We have already seen *housewife* > *hussy*. German *Dirne* meant originally 'virgin'; in the literary language, it is now 'whore', although in dialects, just 'country girl'. French *fille* can mean, depending on the context, 'daughter', 'girl', or 'prostitute'. Much more seldom is there melioration in this area, but even here one can note that the Swiss German (Küssnacht) word for 'whore', *huore*, could, at least around 1956, be used quite generally, for example, by children for their mother, without bad connotation. Once more we see that the meaning developments remain in a clear semantic field, that is, women in their different contexts. It would again be absurd to posit the rule change as occurring first; that is, "change the colligation *Dirne* 'virgin' to *Dirne* 'whore', whereby those women not on their guard would lose their virtue." The total context leads to an abrupt new interpretation.

What classification of this kind shows is the universality of the total cultural and historical contexts in shaping linguistic change. Lists on these lines may also be helpful for comparatists when there is doubt about a naturalness of a particular semantic leap that has to be assumed.

[7.13 Grammaticalization and Lexicalization]   The distinction between grammar and lexicon is a well-established one, although the exact border is not clearcut. In fact, traditionally, one treats these areas in separate volumes, with some overlapping. Lexicon corresponds to the symbolic sign aspects, grammar to the iconic ones, that is, rules. Restriction of the semantic range of a word may lead to a complete loss of lexical meaning. The inflectional suffixes of agglutinative languages are often independent words that have been grammaticalized. A Hungarian noun *bél* 'guts, core' (the inside) gave, in its lative case, *bele*, *belé*, compounds like *vilagbele* 'into the world' in Old Hungarian. In Modern Hungarian, this has been shortened into *be*, *ba*, and it acts as a mere case ending, *világba*. A Baltic Finnic inflected noun **kerða-lla* 'at a turn, on time of', used with genitive attributes like *koira-n keralla* (Finnish) 'with the dog', has yielded pure comitatives in the Eastern dialects, with a shortened form *ke* (compare the Hungarian): Karelian *velle-ŋ-ke* 'with the brother', Lude *vere-ŋ-ke* 'with blood', and Veps *kirvhe-ŋ-ke* 'with the ax' (the hyphens separate the original genitive ending). Note that in these examples the original head and attribute have switched places, because the head has become a mere appendix to the attribute, which retains its lexical meaning. There are many other clear cases in Finno-Ugric; for example, Finnish *kohta* 'place, spot', in the adessive *kohdalla* 'on the place', and *talon kohdalla* 'on the spot of the house' becomes just 'at the house', and *kohdalla* is now a postposition with the earlier genitive attribute *talon* as its head. Here semantic fading produces a similar switch to the one caused by sound change and reinterpretation (§ 5.17). Indeed, Old English compounds with *hād* 'state, quality' and *līc* 'body, form' give the suffixes *-hood/-head* and *-ly* (*motherhood, tenderly*, and so on). In Finnish, a similar noun-forming suffix develops from the word *vuosi* 'year' > *-uus*; compare *uusi vuosi* 'new year' vs. *uut-uus* 'novelty'. The French counterpart to English *-ly*, *-ment*, was, in Latin, the nominal head; for example, *dulce mente* 'with a sweet mind' > *doucement*, and thus etymologically identical to *ment* 'mind'. Spanish still retains independent accent on the adjective, as in *rápida-mente* 'rapidly', although no space is written. German *Drittel* '3rd part' and *Viertel* 'quarter, fourth part' contain a variant of *Teil* 'part'. (See §11.23)

All this is quite parallel to the grammaticalization of the emphatic attributes of the French negative. Forms that go together habitually become reinterpreted as a unit, and semantics and forms adjust to the situation. Free nouns become adverbs, and adverbs become affixes, prepositions, and postpositions, as well as conjunctions. This is how grammatical morphemes often originate. We have already seen the development of adverbs from the formal side (§§ 4.24–4.27, 5.7, 5.15), but even then semantics had to be considered as we are now consider-ing form (*bél/-be, keralla/-ke, like/-ly, Teil/-tel, vuosi/-uus*). In other words, we see that sound change, analogy, and semantic change represent a whole, which must be split up only for expository purposes (see Figure 9-1). And syntactic change, also, forms a part of the whole—as a result of these other changes; it is not an independent mechanism (see § 19.5).

In Indo-European languages noun stem-forming suffixes rarely have any clear meaning. But when inflectional endings are apocopated, their meaning sometimes is reassigned to the (originally meaningless) stem formant that remains. Thus PIE *$*uk^w sē$* 'ox' (nom. sg.) and *$*uk^w senes$* 'oxen' (nom. pl.) are typical *en*-stems: *$*uk^w sen$-* is the stem, and *-es* is the ending for the nominative plural. These forms appear in Old English as *oxa, yxen* and Old High German as *ohso, ohsen*; the nominative singular without *-n* is an ancient form, but the cases have disappeared from the ends of the other forms, leaving the *-en* to be reinterpreted as a case or number marker (English *ox, oxen* shows a minor adjustment of the vocalism—*yxen* would have given **ixen*—but German *Ochs, Ochsen* is quite regular). This also happened in the German weak feminines like *Kirche, Kirche-n* 'church', where the bare stem (neutral with respect to number) still occurs in compounds like *Kirche-n-spiel* 'parish'. In the same way, the German plural ending *-er* is an original *s*-stem (as in Latin *gen-us/gen-er-is*, N.B., by both Latin rhotacism and Verner's law *s* > *r*); and the Russian genitive plural *-ov* represents the Indo-European *u*-stem from which the original Proto-Indo-European genitive ending had been lost (see § 9.13). These cases are just regrammaticalizations. In English, there is a tendency to reinterpret final *-s* /z/ as 'plural', especially if the meaning supports this. Thus *cherry* ← OF *cerise*, where the mass noun was obviously plural ('many berries'), and ME *pese*, *pees* → *pea*, where the old form *pease* still lives on in certain dialects and archaic contexts (e.g., nursery rhyme *pease porridge*). The result in all these cases is a shift in morpheme boundary along the chain of sound units.

Actually, the development of adverbs from nouns is also a case of lexicalization. When an adverb splits off from a noun, it has to be learned separately and is thus a new lexical item. Whenever a linguistic form falls outside the productive rules of grammar it becomes lexicalized. We have seen examples of this in ellipsis (*drive-in*) and shortening (*bus, bil*) and in loss of motivation in general. Often compounds go their own way (e.g., *lord* and *hussy*, which have become lexicalized), whereas the simplex parts remain intact and can still enter productive (motivated) compounds: *loaf warden* and *housewife*. On the other hand, compounds may retain the original meaning as in *nutmeat, sweatmeat* ('food'). These are now lexicalized units quite different from *horse meat, dog meat* ('flesh'), and so on, which display the productive meaning. Similar relics are *Holy Ghost* ('spirit'), *widow's weeds* ('clothes'), and *fishwife* ('woman who sells fish'). The reason semantic change seems to go so haphazardly in all directions is that there are more semantic environments than phonetic environments in sound change. Lexicalized compounds can, of course, enter productive compounds, and so on. And change always occurs in a concrete environment.

One form of lexicalization is particularly clear in English, where many common suffixes or end parts of Greek-based compounds have become independent words (as in *bus*). Although this is not very general, one can note the following cases, some of them rather literary or technical: *ism, ology, onomy, ocrasy, ade* (lemonade), *itis* (bronchitis), and also, from native materials, *teen* (teen-ager). Other languages also show this phenomenon, but we shall leave the subject with these examples.

Deeper syntactic reinterpretation also leads to lexicalization. We have already seen cases of the development of adverbs from inflected nouns. Adverbs may then further shift and become conjunctions. In other words, we have different degrees of fading. Conjunctions develop often from pronouns, for example, *I think that; You come tomorrow.* 'I think this/that. You come tomorrow', German *Ich vermute das; Du kommst* (the odd English represents here the typical early Indo-European situation). The two coordinated sentences merge together, and the pronominal element fades and joins the following sentence, giving subordination *I think that you come tomorrow.* and *Ich vermute, dass du kommst.* Fading meant a shift in the syntactic boundary; and note the difference in German orthography, which was introduced on the principles discussed earlier. Finnish follows this same pattern: *Minä luulen että. Sinä tulet* 'I think thus. You come'. > *Minä luulen, että sinä tulet* 'I think that you come'. Thus conjunctions are often very intimately bound with pronouns, or other adverbs (compare *while* § 4.25; *Wait while I do it!*).

We have seen how semantic change can also be due to reinterpretation. Here the speakers play a role, as, in metaphor and so on, it is the speaker who first perceives a similarity between two things and then uses his analysis deductively in forming his figure of speech. Perception is recognition of qualities and relations. The hearer may not always completely understand such figures and requires further clarification. The most important message of this chapter, which can hardly do justice to the enormous topic, is that the main forces that operate in semantic change are iconic and indexical, exactly the same ones that operated in analogy and rules, as well as in the development of the writing systems. These are the forces of change in historical linguistics. Culture and society are particularly clear in this respect, because the referents have so many connections and similarities of function, and so on (see § 9.16f.).

We have now seen that on all levels of grammar we have iconicity, part of which is known under the term motivation. Onomatopoeia show phonetic iconicity, and metaphors show semantic iconicity. The former show the nature of images, the latter that of diagrams, exactly like analogy. Grammatical or morphological iconicity resides in the rules of a grammar, for example, in the motivated compounds like *steam engine*, *raincoat*, and *armchair*, which all show indexical connections in addition; that is, steam is the energy for the engine, the coat is against rain, and the chair has arms (itself a metaphor) (see Figure 1-6).

[7.14 The Role of History]   The accidental nature of history and its influence on language (semantic change) cannot be overstressed. Etymological research has discovered many semantic leaps just by the availability of accidental historical knowledge. Although the case of *fiasco* was chosen as a possible example, it, of course, is not conclusive. But there are many others, although perhaps not of such stark character. In 1956, in a Finnish army unit, one of the women kitchen workers was known as *Risteilijä* 'Cruiser'. Such a nickname is metaphorical, as nicknames and names often are (if they are not indexical, e.g., son of . . ., names after the trade of the person, after individual physical characteristics, which is also iconic, and so on). As the town had navy units, the most obvious conclusion would have been that her promiscuous behavior had been labeled by a direct metaphor from the naval vessel. But closer familiarity with the total "cultural" situation proves that the assumption would be false. Mess-hall tables had a bowl where one could deposit potato peels, bones, and so on. This bowl cruised regularly between the eaters and was known as *risteilijä* 'cruiser'. The nickname was a second metaphor based on this garbage bowl! In another example, at the time of the first atom explosion on the atoll of Bikini, a contemporary bathing suit was metaphorically named after it, that is, something that has startling effects, leaves very little cloth there, lays things bare, or the like. When, in the mid-1960s, the topless fashion set in, the word *bikini* was reinterpreted as having the same *bi-* as, for example, *binoculars*, because the item did, in fact, consist of two pieces (compare *formation* § 5.5), and the newcomer could be named a *monokini*. It is perfectly irrelevant that *bi-* is originally Latin and *mono-* Greek. This is how metaphors and other analogical changes combine and pile up, when language adapts to the needs of communication. After the passage of a few thousand years many such steps will necessarily always remain beyond our grasp. Current history is being recorded in more detail than in the past, so future etymologists will have it easier on this score.

[7.15 Semantic Change and Speech Production]   We saw that both sound change and analogy were intimately connected with speech synthesis. Change is a function of language use. In phonology, speaking means variation, which becomes socially interpreted, and, in social interplay, change results. Analogy is based on the mechanism of the very rules of grammar. Change results when the rules win over tradition (symbolic aspects). Semantic change has shown all this in a much clearer profile, because the role of society and history is unmistakable. The phenomena of culture, in general, elicit various responses to nomination, for example, metaphor, metonymy, or other figures of speech, and, as a result, synchronic variation increases. This variation is the basis of semantic change, when fading in the marked values takes place. Fading is, of course, loss of stylistic marking, style to be understood in its widest sense and not as literary style only. Change is always a result of variation and speech production. A language that is not used does not change.

Semantic change can be as abrupt mentally as other changes. The cultural environment, of course, shows smooth gradience between situations and objects (referents), but the semantic reinterpretation can be abrupt. It would be difficult to imagine a gradual change from 'prayer' to 'small ball'. There was a contiguity in the physical situation only. Characteristically, semantic change is gradual for the speaker or the innovator, for example, in the formation of metaphors. The shifts can be very small indeed. But the hearer may drastically reinterpret such metaphors, and, in any case, the diachronic correspondences appear to witness abrupt changes (see § 6.22). This exemplifies the two mechanisms of change that a natural human language can undergo: evolution (more frequent) and mutation. In contrast, artificial languages are subject to mutation only.

REFERENCES

General: Bréal 1964, G. Stern 1931, Ogden and Richards 1923, Thorndike 1947, Ullmann 1959, 1962, Sørensen 1967, Leumann 1927, Sperber 1930, Meisinger 1932, Öhman 1951, Kronasser 1952, Graur (ed.) 2.343-714, Fisiak (ed.) 1985a; **7.2** Coseriu 1964, Hjelmslev 1963, Wiegand 1970; **7.3** Bréal 1964, Shands 1970, Scancarelli 1986; **7.4** G. Stern 1931; **7.6** Tauli 1968; **7.8** G. Stern 1931, Söhngen 1962, Todorov 1967, Lausberg 1967, Lanham 1969, B. Campbell 1969, Reddy 1969, Shapiro and Shapiro 1976; **7.9** Menner 1936, 1945; **7.10** Oertel 1901; **7.12** Andersen in Anderson and Jones (eds.) 1974 **7.13** Tauli 1956, Ullmann 1962, E. Itkonen 1966, Szemerényi 1968, Stein 1970 -- C. Lehmann 1982, Heine and Reh 1984, Heine and Claudi 1986, M. Harris and Ramat (eds.) 1987, Kahre 1985. (See also p. 388)

CHAPTER 8

EXTERNAL CHANGE: BORROWING

Borrowing reflects contacts between languages and cultures and is thus of importance for historians and anthropologists. Its mechanism, however, is highly diagrammatic, as in any other kind of linguistic change.

[8.1 Relation of Borrowing to Other Mechanisms of Change] Various aspects of borrowing have already been referred to in the preceding chapters, for example, spelling spelling, in which a word borrows its spelling (or part of it) from another word (§§ 2.6, 2.15, 2.16), and hypercorrection, where the borrowing dialect goes beyond the model (§§ 3.3, 5.3), that is, the borrowed feature goes beyond its original range. This was also true of analogy as borrowing from within (§ 5.18), because, here, an element expands its distribution within one and the same grammar. Then, of course, loan translation showed semantic borrowing, in connection with an analogical situation (§§ 7.7, 7.9). Borrowing is not a change all by itself, as the term 'external change' might suggest. It is intimately tied to other mechanisms of change, one of which is analogy, as mentioned. In fact, at some point, the difference between inheritance and borrowing disappears, since one might as well say that language learning is borrowing it from those who know it. The same is true of dialect borrowing, which indeed can result in sound change. However, one usually speaks of borrowing only when the item borrowed crosses a more noticeable barrier. If the transmission occurs within the same language, one usually speaks of inheritance and sound change. Also, if one lifts an item from an earlier stage of the language, one calls it an *archaism*, but if it is early enough, it is a regular loan. Thus if Modern French borrows a word from Latin, it is regarded as a loan, but if it borrows from seventeenth-century French, it is an archaism. But dialect borrowing restricted to vocabulary items means loans, for example, Savoyard *père* and *mère* from Standard French (§ 7.9). If, ultimately, the pronunciation of a neighboring dialect is adopted in toto, sound change results. The spread of any feature is borrowing as long as it is happening. Curiously enough, learning and adopting another dialect may be called borrowing, but not learning another language. However, if foreign language learning is typical of the whole speech community, one speaks of bilingualism, and of adstrata, when learning is not perfect (§ 8.16).

Thus borrowing is a notion that fuses into other mechanisms of change, and it competes with the figures of speech as an important source of new nomination.

[8.2]   Loans are the easiest to observe in vocabulary if they represent tangible objects, tools, utensils, and ornaments. Such items diffuse easily from culture to culture. Any new item necessitates new nomination, which can be met by loan translation (loanshift), metaphor, or straightforward borrowing. The necessity for new nomination is often referred to as the need-filling motive. Cultural items and notions also diffuse, but generally the more abstract the element is, the more difficult is the transfer. For concrete items, English has borrowed freely, for example, *gnu, aardvark,* and *sputnik,* whereas borrowed abstract terms are more limited, although English has borrowed them with less constraint than many other languages (e.g., *tabu, Weltanschauung,* and *hubris*). Of course, there is less need for abstract items in any language.

The need-filling motive is just one reason for borrowing; an equally important motivation is prestige. Of course, prestige is itself a rather elusive notion, although it is clearly the driving force in social interaction and linguistic change. As one dialect (whether social or regional) may be regarded prestigious compared to others, so certain foreign languages may exert the same influence. This happens often if the ruling class speaks a different language from the subjects, or if the speakers of a foreign language represent a culture that is being imitated. The Baltic Finnic tribes must have lived in rather close symbiosis with the Baltic tribes, and a little later with the Germanic ones. Hundreds of loans were adopted, among them items for which there was clearly no other motivation than the prestige factor. Even if such a word as Finnish *morsian* 'bride' might reflect new wedding customs, there is hardly any such reason for *tytär* 'daughter', *sisar* 'sister', and *äiti* 'mother' (Germanic), as well as *hammas* 'tooth', *napa* 'navel', and *kaula* 'neck', *reisi* 'thigh', and *karva* 'fur, body hair'. It would be ridiculous to maintain that Finnic speakers did not have native, inherited names for female relatives and body parts. If "prestige" itself is not the right term, then the examples indicate very close cultural contacts and intermarriage.

[8.3]   Often borrowing increases synchronic variation, which solidifies into stylistic contrasts at least (see § 7.9). Such style contrasts embrace not only snobbish overtones, as in the so-called inkhorn terms of English, but also derogatory connotations. The Finnish word *koni* 'jade, nag' is originally a Slavic word for 'horse', and the Russian dialectal *varža* 'a bad or very young stallion' is borrowed from Finnish *varsa* 'foal'. Similar borrowing, both ways, occurs at many language boundaries, for example at the German–Czech one. Foreign words are often felt to be descriptive/suggestive, even if they are not used with negative or snobbish overtones. Thus at the Finnish–Russian boundary, Russian has Finnish names for many tools, activities, and agricultural products, and vice versa, without necessarily having borrowed accompanying techniques.

In short, loanwords can be stylistically neutral or marked (high style, low style, intense forms, and so on). In Finnish, the Germanic word *huusi* (house) is a "low" or colloquial word for 'outhouse' with respect to *ulkohuone* 'out-chamber' or various circumlocutions, and the same is true of *pottu* vs. *yöastia* 'night bowl', that is, 'chamber pot'. Similarly, *ruuma* (←room) is a technical term for the section of the stable where dung is collected. On the other hand, *pissa* is the "nice" children's word for 'urine', with the native *kusi* having very vulgar overtones.

[8.4 The Retailoring of Loans]   Loanwords may be taken over with the foreign morphemes unchanged, as in the above examples. Sometimes, part of the word, especially if it is a compound or derivative or interpreted as such, is substituted for by a corresponding morpheme from the borrowing language. An often quoted example is the Pennsylvania Dutch substitution of the native *-ig* for English *-y*, for example, *bassig* 'bossy', *fonnig* 'funny', and *tricksig* 'tricky'. American Lithuanian, also, substitutes native suffixes, as in *bossis* 'boss', *fòniskas* 'funny', and *dòtinas* 'dirty'. This type can gradually grade into a loanshift, for example, American Finnish *lukkoruuma* 'locker room', formally a compound of *lukko* 'lock' and *ruuma* 'ship's hold' (cf. above in nonnautical context). Both words are earlier Germanic loans in Finnish, but the new meaning was triggered by the phonetic similarity to the English model (see § 7.7). The scale and interrelationships between different types of borrowing can be represented roughly as in Figure 8-1. Sound substitution can range from zero to

	Morphemic importation	Morphemic substitution	Sound substitution
Loanwords	+	−	±
Loanblends	+	+	±
Loanshifts (loan translations, semantic loans)	−	+	−
Pronunciation borrowing	−	−	±
Sound change	−	−	±

FIGURE 8-1. A table defining various types of borrowing through three features. Note how the last row indicates that borrowing can blend into sound change.

such a degree that the original model is no longer discernible to the uninitiated. English loans in Japanese are usually standard examples (*bus* → *basu*, *taxi* → *takushii*, and *baseball* → *beisuboru*), but similar situations obtain elsewhere, for example, English loans in Hawaiian: *laiki* 'rice', *palaki* 'brush', and *Mele Kalikimaka* 'Merry Christmas'. Considerable sound substitution has occurred in the following American Finnish loans from English: *runnata rilisteettiä* 'to run real estate', *taippari* 'diaper', and *karpitsi* 'garbage'. The amount of sound substitution depends on the level of bilingualism (which is a prerequisite for borrowing). In a prebilingual period substitution is heavy, but with succeeding generations (as in the American immigrant situation) it becomes less and less, and ultimately one switches to English altogether. Pronunciation borrowing like /iyðər/ for /ayðər/ and /dæns/ for /dɑns/ can be spotted when it is dependent on particular words, but when a British English speaker switches completely to the American pronunciation, he has borrowed the whole dialect (discarding cases like *lift–elevator*, and so on). But even here there may be sound substitution; that is, the imitation is not perfect.

In some languages, phonetic substitution must be accompanied by inflectional adjustment and gender alignment. Words ending in a consonant are given a final vowel *-i* in Modern Finnish, as in *posti* 'mail', *tulli* 'customs', and *jeeppi* 'jeep'. In the last item, the long *pp* gradates in the inflection: the plural, for example, is *jeepit*. An English plural may give the stem, for example, *pointsi* 'point', *keksi* 'cracker' (cakes), and American Finnish *kukiiksia* (partitive plural) 'cookies'. Here the final /z/ of *cookies* was interpreted as /s/, which is normal, and this further as an alternant of the *-ks-* stem, as in *teos/teoksen* (see § 6.14). Other immigrant loans show the same phenomenon, for example, American Norwegian *kars-er* 'cars' and American Italian *pinozz-i* 'peanuts'. In these two, however, a native plural just overlays an English plural (compare *kine*, and so on, §§ 5.4, 6.20, 6.21), whereas in *kukiiksia* there is a further stem adaptation. As an extreme example, the Finnish word *tituleerata* 'to address with a title' contains the original French infinitive ending as *-eer-*, then the Swedish infinitive in *-a-*, and finally the Finnish infinitive in *-ta*. Such stratigraphy tells part of the route the word has traveled.

These alignments are often impossible to predict though the language may have set morphological classes where loanwords are accommodated. German must assign one of its three genders to any loanword. Often the gender of the lending language is retained, as in *das Drama* (Greek), *die Mensa* 'student restaurant' (Latin), and *die Chaiselongue* (French), but also *das Chaiselongue*. Some other times, the gender of a native equivalent seems to prevail, as in *das Baby* from English (*das Kind*), *das Sofa* from French (*das Bett*), and *der Smog* from English (*der Rauch* 'smoke', *der Nebel* 'fog', *der Dreck* 'dirt'). But why *die Sauna* from Finnish (against *das Bad*[*ehaus*]) and *die Couch* from English (against *das Bett*, *das Sofa*)? In short, every alignment cannot be reasoned away, and, anyway, such reasoning starts after the fact.

A striking example of substitution and adaptation is shown by Spanish loans in Chiricahua (Apache), for example, *jabón* → *hà·γóń* 'soap', *rico* → *žî·gò* 'rich', and *loco* → *lô·gò* 'crazy'. Assignment of tones is obligatory in addition to the various sound substitutions. Further, the distribution of sounds in Chiricahua is changed, as *ž* and *l* occurred only in medial and final position in native vocabulary. Moreover, there are no adjectives of the Spanish type in Chiricahua, and *rico* and *loco* were interpreted as third person verbs and equipped with paradigms according to the native pattern of prefix and stem, for example (with partial paradigms):

	NI-····-CÀ	*HÀ-····-ČÀ*		LOANS
Sg 1	*ñščà·*	*hà·ščà*	*lô·šgò*	*žî·šgò*
2	*ñcà·*	*hàñčà*	*lóñgò*	*žîñgò*
3	*ñcà·*	*hà·čà*	*lô·gò*	*žî·gò*
	'to be big'	'to burst into tears'	'to be crazy'	'to be rich'

Similar things happen in other languages as well (see reanalysis § 5.5); for example, English *film* fits into the Semitic triconsonantal pattern quite well, and gets an Arabic plural *ʾaflām*.

[8.5]   Native speakers are aware of the distinctive features of their phonology. Thus English doggerel and Mother Goose rhymes reflect the psychological reality of componential features in phonology, witness nasality in *a stitch in time saves nine, one for my dame,* and *one for the little boy who lives in the lane,* or voiceless stops in *Little Tommy Tucker sings for his supper* (next: . . . *butter*), *If the ocean was whisky and I was a duck, I'd go to the bottom and never come up,* and *he catches fishes in other men's ditches,* and so on. In sound substitution, the borrowers apparently make a kind of distinctive feature analysis of the foreign sounds and assign them to the closest native bundle. In oldest Germanic loanwords, an *f-* is reflected by Baltic Finnic *p-* (§ 8.6), as [voiceless, labial]. There were no voiced stops in Finnic at that time. Later *f* is rendered by *-hv-*, that is, [voiceless] = *h* and [labial, spirant] = *v*. Splitting a bundle of features into two segments like that is not infrequent. French [ü] was replaced by [u] in English, but [ü] gave a decomposite [iu] or [yū]. Similarly, Russian borrowings render Baltic Finnic [ü] by [u], or more often with *palatalization* + [u], *sysmä* → *s'uz'om* [or s-] 'thicket'. And Russian [ɯ] has a similar fate in Baltic Finnic, as in *mylo* → Karelian *mui̯la* 'soap'.

Attempts at using borrowing as a window to the psychological reality of abstract phonology have not yielded valid universals. The above shows, however, that in particular *cases* it may yield useful information. As other changes can support abstract mechanisms, borrowing can be expected to do the same.

[8.6   Criteria for the Direction of Borrowing]   Sometimes an item occurs in two neighboring unrelated languages without any certainty of the direction of borrowing. A classical case has been Finnish *laiva* and Lithuanian *laĩva*, both 'ship'. There is no way of telling whether Baltic Finnic borrowed from Baltic or vice versa, because the forms are isolated in the derivational morphologies of both languages, although, generally, Baltic Finnic is on the receiving end. Handbooks, on the whole, have taken both directions as equally probable, or rather that Baltic is the borrower. In a situation like this one, it may, of course, turn out that both languages have borrowed the word from a third. And closer scrutiny does, in fact, show that the origin must be Germanic *flauja- 'ship' < *plowyo- (> Greek ploîon 'vessel'), which gives Old Norse fley, from where the word was borrowed into Old English as flæge > ME fley. The word shows the same root as float. In Baltic Finnic, an expected sequence *lauja metathesizes into laiva. Consequently, Baltic is indeed the borrower from Baltic Finnic, which itself had borrowed this and many other navigational terms from Germanic. The sound correspondence Germanic fl- : Baltic Finnic l- leads us to phonological criteria for determining the direction of borrowing.

It was noted early that Baltic Finnic shares hundreds of words with Germanic. Many scholars cherished the idea that such items had been borrowed from Baltic Finnic into Germanic, with the assumption that much of Europe had had a Finnic substratum. Here, however, the matter can be settled with a phonetic criterion, namely, sound correspondences (written horizontally in Figure 8-2). The table contains an English word where possible, that is, English and Finnish represent their respective families. The direction of borrowing is decided quite simply. One can predict the Finnish sound, given the Germanic one, but not vice versa, and thus one has to choose the Germanic column as original. The same kind of mapping relation will be important in comparative linguistics (Part III), where the original roster of sounds is always chosen so that from it one can predict all the outcomes in the various languages that are being used in the reconstruction.

Another criterion for the direction of borrowing is morphological and grammatical. If a word occurs in two unrelated languages, and it is an unanalyzable

(English) **Germanic**			**Baltic Finnic** (Finnish)		
flat	strand	$(C_1)C_2C_3$	C_3	ranta	lattia 'floor'
pound	(Go)paida	p	p	paita 'shirt'	punta
beard	ball	b	p	pallo	parta
Friday	field	f	p	pelto	perjantai
turf	token	t	t	taika 'magic'	turve 'peat'
(Go)paida	field	d	t	pelto	paita
(Go)aiþei	death	þ	t	tauti 'sickness'	äiti 'mother'
kettle	token	k	k	taika	kattila
gold	garden	g	k	kartano 'manor, yard'	kulta
heifer	hen	h	k	kana	kauris 'goat'

FIGURE 8-2. Consonant correspondences between Germanic and Germanic loans in Baltic Finnic. English stands in for Germanic, Finnish for Baltic Finnic. The words are arranged symmetrically from the middle.

sign in one and a motivated compound or derivation in terms of the grammar of the other, the situation is quite clear: it is a loan in the language where it is unanalyzable, for example, English *aardvark* (Afrikaans 'earth pig'), *smörgåsbord* (Swedish 'sandwich table'), and Finnish *hunsvotti* 'rascal', which is a metaphorical compound in German (§ 7.12). Similarly, Finnish *aura/atra* 'plough' is a loan in Finnish, because on the Indo-European side it is a derivative from a verb 'to plough' (*ara-tro-*, and so on). The languages can, of course, be related as well. Slavic and Baltic share a word for 'hand', OCS *rǫka* vs. Li *rankà*, respectively. The word is isolated in Slavic, without other morphological connections. In Baltic, however, it is a derivative of a verb, Lithuanian *riñkti* 'to gather' and occurs in a compound *parankà* 'gleaning of ears of corn' as well. Thus it is likely that the Baltic word meant originally 'gatherer, palm [of hand]'. It seems that the word was consequently borrowed from Baltic into Slavic. Of course, it is possible that folk etymology interferes with this principle. Thus English *sparrow grass* is newer than *asparagus*, and it would be wrong to say that German *Spargel* 'asparagus' is borrowed from *sparrow grass* (see § 5.5).

Sometimes semantics tells us the direction of borrowing, even if we are not able to understand morphological motivation in one language. Certain words occur both in American English and in some Indian languages, as in *wigwam*, *moccasin*, and *squaw*. Clearly, these are not motivated in English; but we do not need that information from the other side, since the meanings 'Indian house', 'Indian shoe', and 'Indian woman' decide the issue. The "objects" belong integrally to Indian culture, and this tells us that the words were borrowed from there. But, of course, such cultural differences are not always available, for example, between the groups speaking many American Indian languages themselves.

[8.7 Borrowing As Evidence of Change and Earlier Stages]   Once a form has been transplanted from one language into another, it usually is no longer influenced by its original source, although it can be (e.g., spelling spelling—even from beyond the original source, *det* > *debt*; § 2.15). Even if the entrance fee in the form of sound substitution is high (e.g., *brush* to *palaki*), radiation from the source language into various other languages records some phonetic detail. And, of course, a source language can, on its part, be the receiver, and this mutual borrowing will tell something about both languages. When languages go down the stream of change, they throw clues to the shore, which the linguist can interpret. (§13.9)

We saw above (§§ 4.4, 4.15) how Latin *k* > *tš* > *š* and *k* > *ts* > *s* in French. The earliest stage is confirmed by words like Greek *Kaîsar* and German *Kaiser* (← *Caesar* 'emperor') and would thus be certain, even if some Romance dialects had not preserved the *k*. Similarly, Latin *cellārius* gives German *Keller* 'cellar'. Later, however, we get *cella* → *Zelle* [ts-] 'cell', and *Zäsar* 'Caesar', borrowed apparently during the stage of affrication. The earliest French loans in English retain the stage *tš* in words like *chair* and *chase*, and thus the change *tš* > *š* is subsequent to this period. Newer loans, of course, have *š* as in *chevron* and *champagne*. As in the above German examples, the "same" word can be borrowed at different times; thus, for example, *chief* with *tš* is older than *chef* with *š* (compare *Charles* with *Charlotte* or with *Charlene*). Similarly, the shapes *jaunty*, *genteel*, and *gentle* betray three different borrowings from French, although here the consonantism is rather constant *dž-nt-(l)* (compare *saloon* with *salon*, *liquor* with *liqueur*, and so on). Characteristically, the meanings are different also when the "same" sign has been borrowed twice; compare further Finnish *patja* 'mattress' (Gothic *badja-*), which attests to a stage before umlaut. Later, the same word was borrowed again, but after umlaut: *peti* 'bed' (with an automatic -*i* at the end of newer loans). Now, even if Gothic *badja-* had not been attested, Finnish would confirm the Germanic reconstruction **badja-*. This is what Finnish, in fact, often does (e.g., *kuningas* for 'king', for the reconstructed **kuningaz*, and *rengas* 'ring, loop' for a Pre-Germanic **hrengaz* (before the change *eNC* > *iNC*; see §§ 12.2, 13.2). In this way, loans can tell us much about relative chronology and earlier shapes of items.

[**8.8 The Effect of Borrowing on the Structure of Lexicon**]   New-coming words generally change the preexisting semantic relationships, because complete free variation with a previous word does not go on indefinitely (tendency toward one meaning, one form). If the loanword ousts a previous word completely, no semantic shifts need occur. We have seen already that very often an innovation within a language renovates only the primary function of a form, leaving the secondary functions on their own (§ 5.15). This is true of borrowing as well (e.g., *animal–deer*, *père–pâré* [§ 7.9]). In these cases, of course, the semantic fields change, if either the native or the new term becomes somehow stylistically or semantically marked (Figure 8-3, where in the first two cases the loanword assumed primary function; in the last two, the loanword is the marked term).

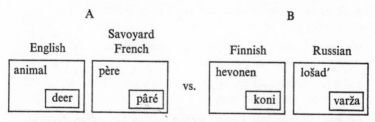

FIGURE 8-3. Changes in semantic marking through borrowing. In A the old term becomes the marked one. In B the borrowed term becomes the marked one.

It is interesting that borrowing shares many of the characteristics of other mechanisms of change, especially the liability of leaving secondary functions alone. When Finnish adopted the Baltic word for 'tooth', the old word *pii* and its derivatives remained untouched in metaphorical usages (the 'teeth of a rake').

In this way, borrowing knocks the feet from under the metaphor, and "immediate" fading is the result. Pronunciation borrowing, too, can affect primary function only (e.g., the Lithuanian word for 'snow' is expected to be *snaīgas). Extensive Slavic contacts led to a replacement of the native ai with the Slavic 'e = ie (OCS sněgǔ > Russian sn'eg, Polish śnieg) yielding sniẽgas. In some derivatives, however, the old ai remained: snaīg(ū)lė 'snow flake', snaigýti 'to snow a little', and įsnaiga 'snow hanging from trees'. Of course, the derivatives based on sniẽgas have ie.

Borrowing is one of the main factors behind changes in lexicons. In English, its effects are enormous. Borrowing has contributed to the many stylistic levels and it has led to a considerable loss of motivated compounds and derivatives (as we shall see). Metaphors and metonyms strive for novelty. With time they fade, necessitating new metaphors, and so on. Loans are not very different; they carry considerable stylistic loading but are subject to fading like other mechanisms, thereby increasing synchronic variation. And the stock can be replenished by new loans, and so on.

[8.9 Borrowing As Evidence of Cultural Contacts]   In many documented cases throughout the world, it is possible to observe borrowing situations that take shape when a foreign upper class imports or imposes its way of life on speakers of other languages. Of closest concern for English are the Norman conquest and the subsequent centuries. The Normans represented what is referred to as a "superior" culture. Among other things, "superior" means the official grip of the Norman government, church, legal system, and various aspects of social and economic life. Hundreds of loanwords were introduced in these areas, among them

government and social order: *baron, noble, dame, servant, government, crown, state, reign, court, tax, subject, duke, manor, vassal.*

ecclesiastical sphere: *religion, sermon, homily, prayer, chapter, faith, virtue, ordain, divine.*

law: *justice, crime, bar, suit, judge, attorney, inquest, verdict, bail, sentence, prison, plead, pardon, tenant, heir.*

social life: *fashion, dinner, supper, victuals, venison, beef, salad, boil, chair, towel, garner, marriage.*

the arts and skills: *art, music, painting, poet, prose, grammar, gender, ointment, balm, poison, metal, mason, labor, tailor, powder.*

These lists could be easily expanded to book length. Similar situations obtain with Arabic loans in Persian, Turkish, and many African languages (including even Spanish); Turkish loans in the Balkans; Nahuatl loans in the Mayan languages; and Russian loans in Soviet Asia. Indeed, even Alaskan Eskimo bears witness to Russian loans in the areas of food, housekeeping, clothes, housing, techniques, domesticated animals, religion, politics, and intellectual life in general. Especially well represented are all kinds of terms connected with trade items. In all these situations we know from history that the loanwords reflect what went on quite accurately.

[8.10] Thus grouping of loanwords into semantic spheres can give valuable support for historical inferences even when no other documentation is available. (Of course cross-language comparison must first establish which words are loans.) Germanic loans in Finnish cluster into roughly the same areas as the French ones in English:

> government and social order: *airut* 'messenger', *hallita* 'to govern', *joulu* 'Yule', *kihla* 'security', *kuningas* 'king', *kunnia* 'honor', *laina* 'loan', *murha* 'murder', *rikas* 'rich', *ruhtinas* 'prince', *sakko* 'fine', *tuomita* 'to judge', *kartano* 'estate', *raha* 'money', *lunnas* 'ransom', *vakoilla* 'to spy', *vuokra* 'rent', and so on.

> religion: *peijaiset* 'funeral banquet', *siunata* 'bless', *taika* 'magic', *hurskas* 'pious', and so on.

> tools and skills: *kaira* 'auger', *naula* 'nail', *mitta* 'measure', *saha* 'saw', *lukko* 'lock', and so on.

> housing and housekeeping: *lato* 'barn', *lattia* 'floor', *leipä* 'bread', *saippua* 'soap', *patja* 'mattress', *kattila* 'kettle', *tupa* 'living room', and so on.

A justified inference from all this is that the Baltic Finnic speakers apparently absorbed a Germanic-speaking upper class, although, of course, borrowing can take place without absorption of peoples. At least the other available evidence, mainly archaeological, does not speak against this hypothesis but rather supports it, in that there seem to have been Germanic trading posts in the Baltic. In this way, assessment of loanwords is an important tool for anthropology and history, as such words record cultural contacts.

[8.11] One can also derive certain indications about the *geographical position* of a language family in relation to other families by plotting corresponding borrowings. Thus, for Finno-Ugric, we have the situation given in Figure 8-4. When this type of a table is used in connection with the family tree (§ 15.1, Figure 15-1), many inferences can be made. The importance for considering the subgrouping and the particular phonological shape of the words comes out in the first two rows. All the languages have loans from Old Iranian and Slavic, but they must be assigned to different depths in the tree. Old Iranian loans go into the protolanguage, whereas Slavic loans generally enter each individual language separately. The splits in the tree are clearly reflected in the table; for example, Hungarian does not have early Germanic loans and Baltic Finnic does not have Turkic ones. Both contacts were obviously made in different locations after the split. Sometimes the exact passage is not clear,

Loans In From	Finnish	Lapp	Mordvin	Cheremis	Zyrien	Votyak	Ostyak	Hungarian
Slavic in general	+	+	+	+	+	+	+	+
Old Iranian	+	+	+	+	+	+	+	+
Proto-Baltic	+	(+)	?	−	−	−	−	−
Proto-Germanic	+	(+)	?	−	−	−	−	−
Old Norse	+	+	−	−	−	−	−	−
Scandinavian in general	+	+	−	−	−	−	−	−
Old Chuvash	−	−	−	−	−	−	−	+
Chuvash	−	−	−	+	(+)	+	−	−
Volga and Irtych Turkic	−	−	+	+	−	+	+	−
Other Turkic	−	−	−	−	−	−	−	+

FIGURE 8-4.   The sources of loans for the Finno-Ugric languages. [Reprinted
from Robert Austerlitz, "L'Ouralien," *Le langage*, Encyclopédie de la Pléiade,
25 (Paris, 1968 © Editions Gallimard).]

e.g., there is doubt whether the Baltic and Germanic loans entered Lapp directly
or came through Baltic Finnic (the latter is more likely, perhaps).

[**8.12 Internal Criteria for Borrowing**]   Dialect borrowing, such as
/griyziy/ for /griysiy/ *greasy* or /rut/ for /ruwt/ *root*, are very difficult to spot if
the dialects are close. Because there is no clear boundary between dialect and
language, it is obvious that the same obtains between closely related languages.
In the following pairs

NATIVE WORDS   shirt   rear   'em   yard   whole
SCANDINAVIAN LOANS skirt   raise   them   garden hale (or Northern)

certain phonological features betray the loans (*sk-*, *-s-*, *th-*, *g-*, *-a-* in these
words), because, otherwise, they are completely acclimatized in English. The
situation is completely different from the Latin and Greek loans (which normally
carry technical meaning). Note the following short sample where in each grouping the radical parts come ultimately from the same Proto-Indo-European
root:

NATIVE	*tooth*	*sooth-sayer*	*three*	*five*	*ten*
LATIN	*dent-ist*	*essenc-e*	*tri-nity*	*quin-tet*	*dec-imal*
GREEK	*odont-ology*	*ont-ology*	*tri-ad*	*penta-gon*	*deca-de*
				punch (Hindi)	

NATIVE	*hund-red*	*foot*	*sun*	*know/can*	*be*
LATIN	*cent*(*i-grade*)	*ped-al*	*sol-ar*	*i-gno-rant*	*fu-ture*
GREEK	*hect-ograph*	*pod-iatrist*	*heli-ocentric*	*a-gno-stic*	*phy-sical*

NATIVE	father	mother	brother	dough	kin
LATIN	pater-nal	mater-nal	frater-nity	fig-ure/fic-tion	gen-itive
GREEK	patr-iarchal	metr-opolis	phratr-y	tich-odrome	gen-otype
			pal (Romany)	(para)-dise	gender
				(Persian)	(French)

NATIVE	yoke	naked	quick (the q. and the dead)
LATIN	junc-tion/con-jug-ate	nude	viv-id
GREEK	zeugma	gymn-astics	bi-ology
	yoga (Sanskrit)		

NATIVE	murd-er	wolf	feather
LATIN	mort-al	lup-ine	pet-ition/pen
GREEK	a-mbros-ia	lyc-anthrope	petr-ify/petr-ol

Sometimes one of the corresponding classical words is not cognate with the whole set, or the English word is not, for example,

NATIVE	tongue	fish	fire	work/wrought/wright
LATIN	lingu-istics	pisc-atorial	[igni-tion]	[labor]
GREEK	[gloss-olalia]	[ichthy-ology]	pyr-omania	org-an/en-erg-y

NATIVE	queen/quean		[horse]	[engine (< French)]
LATIN	[femin-ist]	vs.	equ-ine	machin-ation (< Greek)
GREEK	gynec-ology		hippo(-potamus)	mechan-ical

but it still takes part in the configurations and adds to the semantic fields of English. When large-scale borrowing occurs between related languages, we get regular sound correspondences between the items; note t–d–d (TOOTH, TEN, FOOT, HUNDRED), th–t–t (TOOTH, THREE, FATHER, MOTHER), f–(p)–(p) (FOOT, FATHER, FEATHER, FIRE, FISH), k–(g)–g (KNOW, QUEEN, YOKE, but see KIN with affrication before e), b–f–(f) (BE, BROTHER), m–m–m (MOTHER), n–n–n (KIN), r–r–r (FATHER, MOTHER), and so on (this of course clearly exemplifies Grimm's law; §§ 4.9, 4.10, 6.3). Such correspondences are curious in that, formally, they are like morphophonemic alternation, but, psychologically, they need not be connected at all, because there is *no rule* for the alternations. No clear environment for them can be specified (just try to write rules even for a simple case like *E-gypt/Copt-ic/Gyps-y*!). Similar correspondences obtain in the Romance languages through loans from Latin, for example, Spanish *leche* 'milk' vs. *lactar* 'lactate', and *noche* 'night' vs. *nocturno* 'nocturnal' ($t\check{s}$–kt), or French *croire* 'believe' vs. *crédible* and *loi* 'law' vs. *légal* (wa–e + *voiced stop*). Such situations originate easily when a language borrows from a literary norm of its own past, for example, Old Church Slavic loans in Russian and Sanskrit loans in Hindi. Scandinavian loans in English, Low German loans in Swedish and High German, and Iranian loans in Armenian give the same configuration.

[8.13   The Notion of Correspondence in Linguistics]   It will be useful to make a detour into the notion of the correspondence. It is one of the central concepts in linguistics and has been used throughout this book. In addition to the sound-meaning correspondence (which is basic to a sign system like natural language, as well as to its change, as we have seen) and the sound-writing correspondence, transformational relations rest on similar correspondences. The type *shooting of the hunters* corresponds to both *the hunters shoot* and *the hunters are shot*. Since we can unambiguously map from the full sentences to the nominal phrase, we take them as the basis of derivation. Such a notion was familiar in Latin grammar; for example, the semantically ambiguous phrase *amor deī* 'the love of God' was either the "subjective" genitive (from *deus amat* 'God loves') or the "objective" genitive (from *deum amat* 'he loves God'). In these cases, one can then establish transformational direction exactly on the same principle as borrowing direction. On the same principle, dialectal sound correspondences could be mapped unambiguously one way but not the other (e.g., from General American to Fox). In such cases it is the "richer" side that is again more "original" (see §§ 14.5, 14.6, 21.22, 21.23, 22.11). The essence of sound change was a correspondence between the sounds of the earlier and later stages. The dialect correspondences, however, are psychologically real, as is shown by hypercorrect formations (a type of analogy); and the morphophonemic alternations that result from sound change are quite regular for a long time, even if they ultimately split (e.g., *bake/batch*). Typically such native splits occur between different parts of speech without marked semantics other than archaic (see also § 5.15).

The above sound correspondences are thus without statable environments, and one cannot definitely predict their manifestations, (e.g., there is no Latin *p* in the FIRE set and no Greek *p* in FISH, and so on). Still, such sound correspondences always point to historical connections. If conditioning cannot be found within *one* grammar, it means that we have interference between *many* grammars, though in the form of lexical items only. The highly technical meanings in these sets support this analysis. The whole array further reveals that borrowing occurred between related languages. Situations like this are of great interest because they seriously interfere with comparative work. Vocabulary comes and goes and one cannot trust it in comparative studies; instead one also requires sound correspondences in grammatical elements, although they can also be borrowed, but not so easily. Note that if English had borrowed substantially from an unrelated language, no sound correspondences would have resulted *within* English (just as, e.g., there are no obvious sound correspondences between *liver* and *hepatitis*). But they would, of course, exist *between* English and the original source (e.g., between English *hepatitis* and Greek *hêpar* 'liver'). Given enough time, borrowing would not be so easily recoverable; but if such similarities occurred chiefly in (technical) vocabulary, the likelihood of borrowing would be great, as it always tends to be.

We have seen here that, in favorable cases, internal evidence can point to borrowing, especially from a related language or languages. This can be shown with sound correspondences without regular (stable) environments, in connection with semantics. But loanwords often do not comply with the rest of the rules of the language and can be spotted accordingly. At the time when English spirants alternated generally like *knife/knives, sheath/sheaths* [θ/ð], newcomers like *chief/chiefs* and *faith/faiths* without such alternation stuck out of the grammar (see §§ 4.2, 6.21, 10.8). Of course, borrowing can be proved in this case; but the situation is typical of borrowing and would have invited the linguist's closer scrutiny.

[8.14 Borrowing and Different Levels of Grammar]   Sometimes, the description of a language must recognize a special phonological layer of foreign forms. The more recent loans in Modern Finnish (since about 1800) have established four new phonemes: /b, g, š, f/. In addition, the distribution of the earlier /d/ has been extended to initial position. The following pairs are kept distinct in educated (standard) Finnish and in the speech of most young people:

/b/	*Kuuban* 'of Cuba'		*baari* 'bar'	*betoni* 'concrete'
	kuupan 'of a lampshade'		*paari* 'bier'	*petoni* 'my beast'
/g/	*liiga* 'league'	*goottiin* 'into Gothic'		*Golgata* 'Golgotha'
	liika 'surplus'	*koottiin* 'was gathered'		*kolkata* 'knock out'
/š/	*šakki* 'chess'	*šekin* 'of a check'		*paššaan* 'into a pasha'
	sakki 'gang'	*sekin* 'also it'		*passaan* 'I serve'
/f/	*fasaani* 'pheasant'		/d/	*dyyni* 'dune'	*duuri* 'major key'
	vasaani 'my fawn' (part.)			*tyyni* 'calm'	*tuuri* 'luck'

The lower word in each pair is the older one and shows the shape in which the upper word would have entered Finnish at an earlier date (except for /f/, see § 8.5). For those who still use the old system these pairs are homophones.

There is also a drastic change in the distribution of old and new phonemes. The old native words did not allow an initial consonant cluster. As we saw, loanwords with original $(C_1)C_2C_3$- were always adopted under C_3- (Figure 8-2). But now loans have introduced new clusters, both initial and medial: *struktuuri, frekvenssi*, and so on. Even the vowel harmony breaks down: *polygamia, papyros, kalypso* (y = ü). Earlier, front and back rounded vowels did not occur together in the same word.

If we include /b, d, g, f, š/, and so on, in our description, it is easy to state simple rules of replacement for dialects with the old phonemic system. This is impossible in the other direction. This kind of mapping relation is characteristic of dialect relations, as we have seen (§§ 3.2, 3.3). Note that in the earlier loans there was more sound substitution than here in the educated norm, but the conservative dialects follow the old pattern. It is also significant that the innovating pattern is connected with a social layer where knowledge of foreign languages or bilingualism is extensive.

Mordvin used to have only medial voiced stops and spirants in voiced surroundings, but no initial ones, for example, *jalgo* 'on foot' (compare Finnish *jalka* 'leg, foot'), *p̂ize* 'nest' (*pesä*), *kandoms* 'to carry' (*kantaa*), *kargo* 'crane' (*kurki*). Russian loans have introduced initial voiced sounds, and these have spread even beyond the original model, for example, hypercorrect *bauk* 'spider' (Russian *pauk*). Often such rare foreign sounds have considerable descriptive force, and they are preferred in onomatopoeic, descriptive, or suggestive forms, or in intense forms and nonsense forms, whatever we call them. In Mordvin the voiced sound has spread to native *guŕńems* 'to growl' (*kurnia*) and *guj* 'snake' (*kyy* 'viper'), enhancing their emotional color. Similar spreads of rare sounds that had entered originally through borrowing occur in all Baltic Finnic and Lapp languages. The same phenomenon is well attested elsewhere also; the Berlin dialect of German spreads its *ž*, originally confined to loanwords like *genieren* [ž-] 'to embarrass, bother', to descriptive vocabulary, e.g., *kuželn* 'to cuddle' and *wuželig* 'unkempt'. Other languages could be cited as well; note in this connection the *šm-* "reduplication" in American English, for example, *doctor šmoctor* and a few other words with *š(m)-*, *schmalz, schlemiel*, mainly from Yiddish.

Earlier it was shown that loans helped to establish English /v, z/, and the same is true of /dž, ž/ (§ 4.2). Foreign sounds thus typically come in as parts of whole words, even if the words are imported precisely because their sounds are felt to be expressive. This is true of bound morphemes as well. The hosts of Latin/French words in *-able, -ism, -ize, -tive*, and so on, were the basis for expanding these into new creations, for example, *eatable, tokenism, macadamize*, and *talkative*.

It is customary to say that English has borrowed a great many Latin/Romance phonological rules, as the essence of the Latin stress rule and the Romance softening of $k > s$ in certain environments (*opaque/opacity*). Such a statement sounds as if the rules were borrowed without the actual items on which they operated. In reality, the rules are a result of the importation of the units, the individual words. Sound change had produced the French morphophonemic alternations in clearly definable environments (§§ 4.4, 4.15). When both items, such as *opaque* and *opacity*, had been borrowed into English, a synchronic rule could be formulated. Because it had to cover the "same" facts in the "same" environments, it turned out very much like the original French rule. Such rules may well be different for different speakers, and it may take quite a while before a child is exposed to all the necessary facts. Similarly, English has in many cases borrowed both singular and plural formations of the Classical languages, for example, *phenomenon/phenomena* and *alumnus/alumni*. The level of bilingualism made this possible, and, also, English had the categories of singular and plural to begin with. The pluralization rules were not borrowed but rather the actual forms. The rules, whatever they are here, were just a by-product.

The borrowing of intonation, which is frequent in convergence areas (§ 8.18), would seem to come closer to straight rule borrowing if it carries a meaning like 'question'. But note that intonational contours can as well be regarded as "morphemes," and hence it is not primary rule borrowing. In American Finnish, the question intonation has been borrowed from English, and it sticks quickly, even to Finns who speak normal Finnish. Finnish yes–no questions are marked by the particle -*ko* with no characteristic intonation; this can be replaced by a suprasegmental unit ⌐⌐.

[8.15] Borrowing in vocabulary results when foreign words are adopted into native syntactic patterns. Interference can go the other way as well; that is, one takes native words into foreign syntactic patterns, and, of course, both types can be mixed together. The latter type requires an advanced degree of bilingualism, whereas the first case is possible with a more superficial knowledge. Both are potential results of a society's shift of languages after a period of bilingualism. When the Normans finally adopted English, they retained thousands of words from French, as is easy to demonstrate. In syntax, however, exact determination of borrowing is much more difficult, because the chances of parallel development are great. This fact has led many linguists, especially in more recent times, to the position that syntax is not easily borrowable and is likely to be always inherited. Others maintain that syntax is most vulnerable to foreign influence.

The evidence as we have it today shows that syntax can be borrowed as easily as other parts of grammar; grammatical morphemes show the greatest resistance to borrowing, but it still occurs. (The reason is, perhaps, the great frequency and abstractness of such units. They are unconscious and "too obvious" to draw attention.) Closely related to syntactic borrowing is loan translation, where native elements are joined according to the foreign model (see § 7.7). Latin exerted considerable syntactic influence on the languages of Europe, as well as pervading their vocabularies. The development of German and English interrogatives (*welcher*, *which*, and so on) into relatives is an imitation of Latin. So are the free participles like *generally speaking*, *taken literally*, which render Latin ablatives absolute. These have caught on in English, whereas the construction was abortive in German: *dieses Geschäft berichtigt* 'this transaction corrected' (Schiller), *nach aufgehobener Tafel* 'the dinner party having adjourned', and *nach gestillter Blutung* 'after the bleeding had been stopped' (Carossa 1943). Similarly archaic today are some German imitations of *accusativus cum infinitivo*: *mich gewesen sein in grosser Not* 'me having been in great peril'. In the eighteenth century, the purists were also able to establish the Latin ban on double or multiple negatives in literary English (see § 3.4). It is also likely that the rise of periphrastic conjugations (use of auxiliaries) all over Europe irrespective of the language (family) is hardly altogether independent in each case; considerable mutual influence must be assumed.

One language family where syntactic borrowings are quite obvious is Finno-Ugric. Relics of the original syntax can be found in varying degrees in all languages of the family, but the following facts are significant. Finnish syntax is largely Indo-European (Baltic and Germanic, apparently Swedish for the most part). Lapp syntax in Finland is strongly Finnish—in fact, almost like Finnish with Lapp words, but in Norway is markedly Norwegian. Turkic influence is obvious in Cheremiss and Votyak syntax, Russian in Veps and Zyrien. Historical reasons and the bilingualism necessary to account for this are amply attested (see Figure 8-4). A lack of bilingualism may necessitate translation, which serves the same end. The sacred Buddhist texts in Burma were written in Pali, an Indic language. Because the knowledge of Pali was very limited among the people, Pali words and phrases were glossed in Burmese. Such bilingual texts, known as Nissaya Burmese, are known at least from the fifteenth century and subsequently increase in number. With time, the Nissaya style became established: each Pali morpheme was matched by a Burmese one. This is parallel to "Lapp being virtually Finnish with Lapp words"; Nissaya is highly artificial Burmese with native vocabulary and Pali grammar. In due time, the original Pali was omitted; the prestigious position of Nissaya secured it as the literary model, and, since then, Pali syntax has seeped into more colloquial styles as well.

The loss of the Greek infinitive (§§ 5.16, 6.22) has had repercussions throughout the Balkans. It has been lost in various degrees in most Balkan languages, and there is a clear correlation between its loss and the proximity of the language to Greece. The Greek pattern has thus diffused northward. In Southern Calabria the Greek speakers finally switched to Italian, as often happens to minority enclaves, but in place of the Italian syntax of the infinitive, they retained their old rule. A sentence like 'I cannot see you', which requires an infinitive in Italian, is rendered instead *non pozzu mu ti viju* (*e mu ti sentu*) 'I cannot that I see you (and that I hear you)'. In other words, *this* sentence is Greek with Italian words, or Italian with Greek syntax. The *total* dialect shows, however, that the dialect is Italian, and hence this syntactic feature is borrowed from Greek. The end result is that a syntactic *rule* is borrowed; but such a rule borrowing in syntax is not an abstract occurrence—it is based on bilingualism and a *correspondence* between the two languages. Like loan translation, it is *analogy* between two languages. The situation is clearly diagrammatic:

MODEL   Semantics A forms X syntactic rule Y

BORROWER   Semantics A forms M syntactic rule N

If X replaces M we have morphemic borrowing, if Y replaces N we have syntactic borrowing. Bilingualism is just another kind of synchronic variation for the speaker with code switching occurring in certain situations. This variation goes through the whole language, both grammar and vocabulary. From the psychological (if not from the social) point of view, this is an enormous burden, hostile to the efficient principle 'one meaning, one form'. When social forces permit, simplification results in the two complete codes ending up as only one. Ultimately, in vocabulary, the word of one language wins out, or else semantic differentiation takes place; most English speakers would admit that there is a slight difference between *freedom* and *liberty*. As for grammar, one language wins out, possibly with patterns from the other. It is useful to realize that bilingualism is indeed one aspect of synchronic variation, and often there is, of course, no way of drawing a line between dialect variation and bilingualism (see § 3.6). Once more, we have an indication that borrowing shares characteristics with the other mechanisms of change and variation. The transfer from bilingualism to monolingualism is another aspect of simplification, or the movement toward 'one meaning, one form'. And this situation is the most fertile breeding ground for borrowing. Bilingualism can be of two main types (1) coordinate (in which the speaker keeps his two systems apart), and (2) compound (in which systems interfere). The latter is particularly conducive to borrowing.

[8.16 Borrowing and Wider Configurations of Language Contact and Use] Language switches produce *adstrata*, that is, the adoption of features of the old languages by the new one. This is often given as a reason for particular phonetic developments, and sound change in general. One distinguishes a *substratum* when speakers abandon their language for another, a prestige language; and a *superstratum*, in which conquerors take up the language of their new environment. Thus French is said to have a Gaulish or Celtic substratum and then a Frankish or Germanic superstratum.

Let us now return to the Fox dialect mentioned in Chapter 3. It shows a clear Finnish substratum. Germanic loans in Finnish given in this chapter have demonstrated the general phenomenon that voiced sounds are replaced by voiceless ones, and a voiceless one by a voiceless geminate, for example, *rilisteetti* 'real estate', *paikki* 'bike', *spiikkeri* 'announcer' (*speaker*), *partti* 'party', *taippari* 'diaper', *jeeppi* 'jeep', and many earlier loans (§ 8.6). This replacement principle is clearly visible in the Fox dialect, as are other Finnish features. In this case, we need not rely on inference alone, as a community with a predominantly Finnish base (drawn mainly from two locations in Finland) is historically documented from 1900. In the heyday of the dialect, 1920–1940, the school records show about 70 per cent of the students to be from Finnish families (the percentage was higher in 1967, but the numbers are too small to be significant). The dialect was spoken by persons of other backgrounds also, but this fact is irrelevant for the substratum; it shows merely that the Finnish element was strong enough to establish the norm for the community (as was mentioned, the dialect now has age and occupational meaning).

Similar cases of substrata have been attested in all parts of the world, but the American society is, of course, particularly conscious of substrata; in fact, there are even handbooks on theater dialects to enable actors to imitate proper ethnic "accents." A well-known case from New York City is the Yiddish substratum feature [-ŋg] in *coming*, for example.

[8.17] The various kinds of borrowing, that is, vocabulary, adstratum phonetics, and syntax, have led to the notion of a *mixed language*. This concept has remained undemonstrable to the present day. In bilingual situations, there is frequent code switching even in the middle of the sentence, for example, nineteenth-century "Aristocratic Russian" 'on se réunit le matin au breakfast, et puis *vsjakij delaet, čto xočet*'. The sentence begins in French and has one

English loan, and then shifts into Russian. The French part is totally French, so is the Russian, Russian. This is no mixed language, but two languages used jointly. Similar sentences can be found in America and Russia among the linguistic minorities, and, of course, elsewhere. On the other hand, sentences like American Finnish *Menin norttiin muuseja hunttaamaan* 'I went north to hunt moose' or Lude *D'uod'ĭ pivad, d'uod'ĭ vĭnad, paịatet't'ĭ, plÿ̈šit't'ĭ* 'One drank beer, one drank liquor, one sang, one danced' are hardly mixed. In the first, all but one word are loans from English, but the grammar is clearly Finnish, and the same is true of the Lude sentence: the grammar is all Lude, although, in vocabulary, only *d'uodĭ* is, the rest coming from Russian. The Gypsy dialects are also often referred to as mixed, but, here also, much of the vocabulary and phonetics is borrowed from the "host language." Consider the following "pure" old English Gypsy sentence: *Komóva te jal adré mi Duvelésko kēri kana meróva* 'I'd like to come to my Lord's house when I die'. In modern English Gypsy this goes *I'd kom to jal adré mi Duvel's kēr when mandi mers*. This is English in grammar except that it has an extra set of vocabulary, which is characteristic of social jargons. Actually, classification by syntax or vocabulary is an arbitrary decision; for example, Nissaya is considered basically Burmese with Pali syntax and not Pali with Burmese vocabulary. Considerations of continuity, and the social status or attitudes of the speakers, play a role in such decisions.

The only certain conclusion that can be drawn is that all languages are mixed, if mixing merely means borrowing. Some are, of course, more mixed than others. Over half of English vocabulary is borrowed, which is also true of Swedish (both about 75 per cent). But because Swedish has borrowed mainly from Low German, it does not show so readily. Albanian, on the other hand, has borrowed more than 90 per cent of its vocabulary, and even if Finnish has borrowed only 20 per cent, it is still mixed in the same sense. The same mixing is true of syntax, but there is no workable way of measuring that because of the universal features prevalent in it.

In a puristic context, one speaks of "pure" and "hybrid" languages. Pure language should avoid or even uproot loans from the outside, but encourage them from the past of the same language (archaisms). Such concern is schoolmasterly and has value for genetic linguistics only insofar as it may provide a sociolinguistic setting for certain innovations. The distinction between "pure" and "hybrid" languages is untenable, of course.

[8.18]   When adjoining and overlapping languages give and take, the result can be what is called *convergence* (Sprachbund). In such convergence areas, different languages may develop identical phonetics, similar phonological systems, and very similar grammars, even if the lexical items and phonotactics remained different. Famous convergence areas are, for example, India, the Balkans, the Caucasus, and the Pacific Northwest. On the Marathi–Kannada boundary one can find villages that have one basic grammar with two sets of morphemes, one Marathi, the other Kannada. This leads to the startling position that it is the lexicon that does indeed determine genetic relationship, and not grammar! The reason is, of course, that lexicon (including grammatical markers) is heavily symbolic, whereas grammar is iconic and largely universal. Vocabulary comes and goes, but when it is retained, it remains symbolic. Now, is modern English Gypsy still Gypsy with English syntax?

Maybe there was a convergence area in the Baltic as well. We have seen a few examples of far-reaching borrowing in Finnish from both Baltic and Germanic. Although grammatical influence can at present only be guessed at, there seems to have been a complete upheaval in the sound system. The two thousand or so years preceding and following it have apparently been relatively stable in comparison. Thus feeding Pre-Baltic Finnic into the convergence area and taking it out, we get the configuration in Figure 8-5. Note that Germanic had Verner's law alternation between $f \, \flat \, x \, s$ and $\beta \, \eth \, \gamma \, z$, which is a startling parallel to the Baltic Finnic consonant gradation between $p \, t \, k$ and $\beta \, \eth \, \gamma$ and $s \sim h$ (*viisas*, (gen.) *viisahan* > Modern Finnish *viisaan* 'wise'). All the individual phonological changes between Pre-Baltic Finnic and Late Proto-Baltic Finnic are commonplace; but the cumulative effect makes the convergence hypothesis impossible to ignore. If convergence areas can guide phonetic change like this, it means that loss can be one side of borrowing. In this vein, it has been observed that less prestigious languages avoid native forms that resemble obscene forms in the prestige or upper language.

Such filtering does indeed seem to happen, and it is the reverse of adstratum influence: one keeps one's language and borrows only the prestige phonetics. It has been noted that Welsh has an "English" type of phonetics and phonology, whereas Breton shows "French" features. Surely English and French, respectively, are responsible for this.

[8.19] Convergence areas and adstrata are not the only situations referred to as mixed languages in layman classification. Other candidates are various trade jargons known as *pidgins*, which arise in superficial, often short-termed, and limited cultural contact. They have sprung up since the European expansion from 1500 onward, based on the languages of the maritime powers, that is, English, French, Portuguese, and Spanish. A rarer phenomenon is a native-based pidgin, as in the Chinook Jargon of the Northwest, Police Motu in Papua, and Kituba in the Congo.

The belief that a pidgin is a mixture of the grammar of one language and the vocabulary of another is oversimplified but very practical and fits quite well the examples already mentioned. Pidgins are no more mixed than some other languages, although they are drastically simplified in grammar and in the size of their vocabularies. The aiding factors in the formation of a pidgin are the very limited vocabulary, which is sufficient in such situations, and the universality of syntax. This vocabulary is largely directed toward universal human experience (see Chapter 21), which makes syntax a side issue only. The concentration on learning such key words can be verified in modern refugee or tourist situations. Both sides try to let syntax take care of itself; for example, sentences

| Pre-Baltic Finnic | Sprachbund filters | | Late Proto-Baltic Finnic |
	Baltic	Germanic	
p	p	p	p (ß~b)
t	t	t	t (ð~d)
k	k	k	k (ɣ~g)
	b		
	d		
	g		
ð		ß(b)	
ð'		ð(d)	
ɣ		ɣ(g)	
		f	
		þ	
		h(x)	h
š	š		
s	s(z)	s	s
ś			
	ž	z	
m	m	m	m
n	n(ŋ)	n(ŋ)	n(ŋ)
ń			
ŋ(ŋ́)?			
l	l	l	l
l'			
r	r	r	r
v	v	v	v
j	j	j	j
c = ts			c = ts
č = tš			
ć = t'ś			
kt	kt		
		ht	ht
pt	pt	ft	
mt	mt		
nt	nt	nt	nt
ln	ln		
		ll	ll

FIGURE 8-5. The filtering of the Baltic Finnic sound system through the Baltic and Germanic ones. [Reprinted from Lauri Posti, "From Pre-Finnic to late Proto-Finnic." *Finnisch-Ugrische Forschungen*, **31**, 1–91 (1953).]

such as *me eat coconut* (*coconut me eat*, and so on) or *you catch train* (*train catch you*, and so on) cannot be misunderstood in a practical situation in which philosophizing is incongruous. It is also normal that the pidgins developing in slavery situations in the New World would resort a great deal to African syntax, although it is often difficult to spot. This is a solution of least effort. The masters would also imitate this, for various (scientifically false) reasons, but the result is a system that does the work. Drastic simplification is characteristic even in Kituba, even though the neighboring languages are quite similar to its base, the dialect of Marianga. Pidgin formation implies elimination of morphophonemic alternations and suppletion, reduction of grammatical classes, and emphasis on single unaltered forms of lexical units. In short, practically all inflection is stripped off; this mirrors an attempt to improve the efficiency of the system, and it especially helps the person with a limited experience of the dominant language. By concentrating on and hearing one form of any item, both encoding and decoding are greatly simplified. One result is the "baby talk" effect, which, incidentally, shows that speakers do, in fact, implicitly know how to simplify. In other words, they are knowingly applying the principle 'one meaning, one form', and this is done so easily in these situations because of the limited content the sign system has to handle. Note that here also, as in similar "analogical" changes, there is a break in tradition. Against analogical simplification is opposed the total community, which upholds linguistic conventions; but, even so, analogical changes sneak in. In a pidgin situation, however, there is no community or tradition, because the whole language is largely a makeshift for economic profit (for at least one of the partners). In more recent times it has become obvious that economic motives erode traditions in other areas of culture as well. Note a certain parallelism to the lack of tradition in the Greek adoption of writing, which was very conducive to the rise of a simple and efficient orthography. The social status of a pidgin is generally very low indeed, below the less-valued dialects of the standard languages; and often a gradual shift to one of the standard languages occurs. In areas where many native languages are spoken, a pidgin may provide the most convenient *lingua franca*, a common language for communication; in such a polyglot area Melanesian Pidgin English, for example, has remained vigorous. A pidgin is always a lingua franca, but a lingua franca need not be a pidgin; for example, English is a lingua franca in India, and, to an increasing degree, throughout the world. The original lingua franca was pidginized Romance, mainly from the Riviera area, and it served in the Mediterranean in various forms at various times during and after the Crusades.

Artificial languages are pidgins coined in the calm of the study. The most famous and successful one is Esperanto (contrived in 1887 by L. L. Zamenhof), which can be classified as a kind of pidgin Romance or Neo-Latin, with loans from other European languages; in other words, European Pidgin Romance. A similar version of individually "pidginized" English is Basic English (contrived by Charles K. Ogden [1889–1957]). The name is an acronym of *B*ritish, *A*merican, *S*cientific, *I*nternational, and *C*ommercial, and the "language" is intended for international communication and as first steps into English, that is, for typical pidgin purposes. It has not caught on very well (it is so modern as to be copyrighted, which would seem to be inimical to the very idea of a contact language).

We have seen that, generally, when words shorten, units multiply. English and French have lost most of the Indo-European inflection, but this has been compensated for by syntax (prepositional phrases, word order). The great reduction of pidgin phonology, morphology, and vocabulary must likewise be compensated for in syntax. Elaborate periphrasis must be used, that is, metaphors and metonymy. Children are capable of the same, even with very limited vocabulary; this is one side of the human capacity to analogize (Chapters 5 and 7). Thus Melanesian Pidgin English has the metonymic (indexical) phrase *woman he brother belong me* for 'my sister', *he no got money* for 'poor', and, for example, metaphoric *grass belong face* 'beard' and *grass belong head* 'hair'. Basic English with its 850 words is more "wasteful" in that it includes the words *sister* and *poor*, but not *beard* or *hair*. "Technical" terms like *thyme* must be paraphrased as in *goodly* (note the regularity) *smelling and tasting grass, smelling grass tasting good*, or the like. Pidginization is always directed toward greater redundancy. Free pronouns rather than affixal forms result in longer phrases; independent adverbial particles instead of tense morphemes, for example, do the same. (Redundancy is another factor that facilitates communication and that must be prominent in an efficient sign system.)

[8.20]   When a pidgin becomes the first language of a community, one speaks of *creolization*. This happened often on the plantations of the New World, where slaves from different language backgrounds were forced to use a pidgin among themselves, and between themselves and the masters. After escape, freedom, or revolution the pidgin was all they had, and it had to become the first language of the community. Creoles can approach the source language by continued borrowing. A typical creole would have some 5,000 words, which is about five times the number in Chinook Jargon, whose 1,100 words are in the bracket of Basic English. In some families, Esperanto is handed down to children as a first language, but no true speech communities have arisen; this is why creoles are often also referred to as *marginal* languages, but such a name for Haitian Creole French, for instance, is very misleading, because it is the colloquial norm throughout the country.

In conclusion, pidgins and creoles are usually taken as very aberrant dialects of their source languages and not as "mixed languages." The source language is the dominant language. We have seen that it is often rather difficult to draw exact lines for classification. Speaking of dominant languages implies social values, and these are very important in the definitions of pidgins, creoles, and so on. A kind of lingua franca with prestige overtones is the *standard language* of a stratified society (see Chapter 3). Then, a kind of standard for business purposes without necessarily having social overtones is a *koiné*, which often carries considerable simplification, but with no such drastic breaks in structure as in the pidgins. For instance, the Greek *koiné*, based on the Attic dialect, remained mutually intelligible with the Greek of the Greeks themselves. In a way, the notions "mixed language," pidgin, creole, trade language, lingua franca, standard dialect, and koiné overlap extensively, because so many criteria enter into their definitions. As always, classificatory schemes run into difficulties (see Chapter 16). We simply do not know all the facts yet. Since all languages are mixed, the notion "mixed language" is not very useful in classification. The task is to find out what happened in the histories of languages, and our concern need not be whether such events can be put into neat classificatory pigeonholes.

It is interesting to note that in pidgins and Sprachbund situations it is the vocabulary or morphology that decides the genetic language alignment, not syntax (see § 16.10). It would seem that the characterization of a pidgin as having been filtered through universal syntax is correct. Universal syntax cannot be used for classification. After the syntax has been pumped empty, it gradually fills from the languages involved. In this sense a pidgin might be called a new language (admixture) altogether, because a language has been stripped and filled again around a few symbols. Because genetic linguistics is concerned with genesis, origin, and continuum through time, pidginization is a legitimate problem that has not been solved (see § 21.3). Note now that in the cases of American Finnish, Lude, and modern English Gypsy the morphology was Finnish, Lude, and English, respectively, and this decided the issue.

[8.21 Conclusion]   Basically, borrowing is no more external change than semantic change is. In both cases the cultural setting and cultural change induces grammar change. In borrowing, however, it is more obvious. Even if borrowings often complicate the grammar, especially in phonology, it can still be seen that the total communicative situation becomes more iconic in that more of the language moves toward the greater efficiency of 'one meaning, one form'. As the primary function of grammar is to serve communication, the "naturalness" of the earlier grammar is sacrificed. We have seen this before. Iconicity in one part of the grammar (e.g., *-n-* plural for bovines of both sexes [*kine, oxen*]) results in a highly marked plural from another angle (*kine* with *umlaut + n*) (§ 6.20). Similarly, spelling spelling, like *island* and *debt*, increase iconicity toward Latin, but they, of course, complicate spelling rules in that *s* and *b* are arbitrary parts of these words in terms of English. Loans are mainly introduced by bilinguals who, of course, have a mental reason to level out the vocabularies of the respective languages (usually in one direction only). And characteristically, the loans then spread to monolinguals. Similarly, persons who knew Latin introduced the spellings *island* and *debt*. When a group does not want to communicate with another and tries to maintain cultural independence, borrowing is greatly impeded.

REFERENCES

General: Haugen 1950, Weinreich 1968, Deroy 1956, Martinet (ed.) 1968, Petrovici 1969, Alatis (ed.) 1970 -- Le Bourdelle et al. (eds.) 1980, Janhunen et al. (eds.) 1983, Koivulehto 1981, Hofstra 1985, *Suomen väestön esihistorialliset juuret.* Helsinki, Soc. Sc. Fennica 1984; **8.2** Tabouret-Keller 1969; **8.3** Kalima 1915, 1936; **8.4** Aron 1930, Hoijer 1939, Yannay 1970; **8.5** Raun 1968, Maher 1969a, 1972, Hyman 1970ab; **8.6** E. Itkonen 1966, Koivulehto 1970, Bernštejn 1961, Halldórsson 1970; **8.8** Senn 1953, Patterson 1968; **8.9** Baugh and Cable 1978, Jespersen 1956, Hammerich 1954, H. Vogt 1954, Doerfer 1967, Kazazis 1972; **8.10** Hakulinen 1961; **8.11** Austerlitz 1968, Jacobsohn 1922, Joki 1973; **8.13** Katičić 1966, 1970, Krahe 1970; **8.14** Ravila 1952, Specht 1952, Petrovici 1957, 1969; **8.15** Bach 1956, E. Itkonen 1966, Okell 1965, Burling 1970, Rohlfs 1922-1923; **8.16** Nielsen 1952, Szemerényi 1964, Herman and Herman 1958; **8.17** Mueller (ed.) 1954, Fokos-Fuchs 1962, Havránek 1966, Petrovici 1969; **8.18** Becker 1948, Posti 1953, Emeneau 1956, C.F. Voegelin 1945, Weinreich 1958, Pisani 1966, Burling 1970, Martinet (ed.) 1968, L. Campbell et al. 1986; **8.19** R. Hall 1966, Nida and Fehderau 1970, Welmers 1970, Ogden 1968, Uotila 1986; **8.20** Nida and Fehderau 1970, R. Hall 1958, Martinet (ed.) 1968.

8.19-8.20 More recent pidgin and creole linguistics: Hymes (ed.) 1971, Heine 1973, Voorhoeve 1973, DeCamp and Hancock (eds.) 1974, Todd 1974, Meisel (ed.) 1977, Valdman (ed.) 1977, Bickerton 1973, 1975, Hill (ed.) 1979, Day (ed.) 1980, Nelde (ed.) 1980, Valdman and Highfield (eds.) 1980, Bailey 1983, Boretzky 1983, R. Posner 1983, Woolford and Washabaugh (eds.) 1983, Versteegh 1984, Mühlhäusler 1984, 1986, Samarin 1985, Nelde et al. (eds.) 1986, Muysken and Smith (eds.) 1986 (starting a *Creole Language Library*), Thomason and Kaufman 1987.

CHAPTER 9

WHY DOES LANGUAGE CHANGE?
LINGUISTIC AND SOCIAL FACTORS

Summary of the first eight chapters in which the unity of the mechanisms of change is emphasized. Linguistic and social factors are mediated by a psychological one, the principle of 'one meaning, one form'.

[9.1 All-pervasiveness of Change and Language]   The previous chapters have shown the complementary positions of the mechanisms of language and the change of language. Without synchronic variation, change would not have a launching pad. Change is not peculiar to language alone; evolution pervades the whole of "reality," that is, the inorganic/cosmological, the organic/biological (Chapter 22), and the human/psychological (Chapter 21). The whole question of variation and change in language has a direct parallel in life, which is complex self-reproducing and self-varying matter. Of course, language is a parasite on the biological and psychological factors, but it can be viewed as a sign system that perpetuates itself through time. If biological change can be largely characterized as coming from behind, by automatic natural selections, and cultural evolution from in front, from a conscious purpose, where does language fit in? Language serves the sociocultural ends and its task is thus to keep itself in an enduring state, to keep functioning, adapting itself to new environments. We clearly have to start out from the Heraclitan statement that everything changes. Cosmological change is very slow, and so is biological; this leaves language with culture, where change is more readily observable. In short, since everything changes, it would be truly phenomenal if language did not. This, of course, is no issue; language does indeed change, and it shows variation like any living matter. And, of course, culture allows for great variation and duplication of items on its part as well. The question to be asked is: *Why* does language change?

[9.2] Problems of Explaining Change and the Structure of Change]   It has been almost impossible to separate the factors and mechanisms of change from its causes; indeed, even the consequences of change, that is, various classifications of change, have been given as explanations. We have seen all the basic mechanisms and factors (and, in fact, their similarities are considerable), but are they causes? Linguists have always fallen easily into the trap of circularity. When it turns out that certain changes can be *described* as rule loss or rule reordering, it is easy to shift to stating that change occurred *because of* rule loss, and so on—an easy way of changing a how into a why. In this chapter we shall see that much of the why can be answered. In historical explanation, one has to use the so-called genetic explanation, which states that things are now as they are, A, because earlier they were B; and they were B, because before that they were C, and so on (§ 1.24). Certainly much of historical linguistics has been explained this way. One of the difficulties has been the tendency to look for one cause only, which is hardly advisable when one is dealing with such a complex system as language. Further, there is hardly any bottom to causes. For instance, why do we have a particular change? So that language gets simpler. Why does it get simpler? So that it will better serve communication. Why do we need communication? So that people interact better. Why do they have to interact? Because their survival is linked with culture. Why do they have culture? Because . . . , and so on, and so forth. In this sphere, of course, no answers can be given to satisfy everybody. What is explanation for one is just description for another.

One usually speaks of internal and external causation of change. These are extreme poles, a situation we have encountered often before, as it is difficult to draw a line where one ends and the other starts. Language is so integrally connected with the speech community that one has to look at the grammar of the community when studying change, and not at the grammars of individual speakers, the so-called idiolects. Semantic change due to "thing change" would seem to be caused by external factors, even historical "accidents," whereas

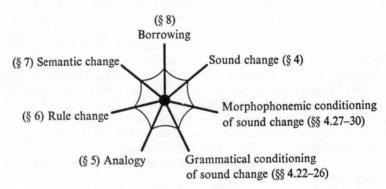

(§ 8)
Borrowing

(§ 7) Semantic change

Sound change (§ 4)

(§ 6) Rule change

Morphophonemic conditioning
of sound change (§§ 4.27–30)

(§ 5) Analogy

Grammatical conditioning
of sound change (§§ 4.22–26)

FIGURE 9-1.   The different mechanisms of change share a common analogical core. The change types blend into the adjacent ones.

semantic change due to euphemism and other metaphors have psychological and emotive factors as the driving force. Other changes that we saw were connected with linguistic factors, as in the ellipsis of one of juxtaposed units. Various analogical changes, or rule changes (if corresponding notation is used), resulted in simplification. This simplification itself is not the cause of the changes, but it is triggered by the mental constraints on a maximally efficient sign system of the type of natural language; that is, the mind shuns purposeless variety (§ 5.21). This is connected with constraints on the capacity of memory. Frequent forms do, in fact, resist change, whereas infrequent forms are prone to be caught by change much more easily. We have seen that this ultimate mental cause for simplification creates either leveling or splits in terms of signs, or leveling or extension in terms of the grammar. The slogan 'one meaning, one form' refers to this force. This reason is one of the causes of borrowing as well, in addition to the prestige factor. And borrowing for descriptive usage is also psychologically motivated, because it is *felt* to be iconic (image) to the thing meant. Throughout the preceding chapters it was stressed that all changes share the analogical mechanism, and one change type gradually gives way to (or shifts into) another, as shown in Figure 9-1. Some of these types are, of course, subtypes of others; for example, grammatical conditioning is analogy, and rule change is a restatement of analogy. But it is still true that *all* have the same "analogical" mechanism; that is, the mechanism is diagrammatic, based on one kind of iconicity. In former times one said that analogy permeates everything; today, when analogy is rewritten as more explicit rules, one repeats that all change is rule change. This reiterates that the basic mechanism of change is iconic, and diagrammatic, in particular. In other words, language is an intricate system of relations. Whatever we call these relations, grammar, patterns, inflectional paradigms, derivational groups, and so on, these are not the causes of change. They just supply the patterns (or rules) according to which change takes place. The driving force is the mental striving to adapt language for communication with least effort, that is, the psychological motive and the necessity of fulfilling the functions of speech. These same patterns work both for clarity (e.g., in analogical changes), or for concealment in secret jargons, and so on, because the same relations (rules) provide the mechanisms for metaphors, metonyms, and so on. In the latter case, we still have communication, though not meant for the total community. Of these changes, sound change occupies a peculiar position, and we shall return to it. (Cf. also §§0.4, 11.21)

[9.3 Manifestations of the Principle 'One Meaning, One Form']   A maximally efficient system avoids polysemy (forms with many [related] meanings, especially if these occur in the same semantic sphere) and homophony, two (unrelated) meanings getting the same form. Again, the border between polysemy and homophony is not always clear, because in ultimate analysis it depends on the psychological reality or awareness of the speaker (see § 18.17). Either of these one-to-many correlations between form and meaning are easily tolerated, if they have to do with different parts of speech or different semantic spheres. Avoidance of homophony and polysemy provide clear evidence of this mental force of 'one meaning, one form'. We have seen that the apocope of the past marker *-ed* in Negro English led to homophony between present and past only as a statistical variable in some verbs, not in strong or "irregular" ones (*give–gave, tell–tol'*, and so on; § 3.5). In Trinidad English, however, the invariant forms *roll, give*, and *tell* are used for the simple past. Homophony with the present is avoided by the use of the auxiliary *do*, *He does give* 'He gives' vs. *He give* 'he gave'. The present has become the formally marked form, unless one wants to derive the past by deleting *does*. Similar cases exist in many other well-known languages.

The most famous case comes from Southwestern France in the history of the Latin *gallus* 'rooster' and *cattus* 'cat'. In this area two sound changes worked toward the merger of the two forms: (1) Latin *-ll-* > *-t*, and (2) initial *c-* > *g-*. Both 'rooster' and 'cat' should now end up as *gat*. But in a farming situation, such a homophony is "insidious" and detrimental to an efficient sign system. And, indeed, one of the forms was replaced by another, namely, 'rooster' by *bigey* 'village judge, deputy (vicar)', *azã* 'pheasant', or *put* 'young chick'. An "intolerable" homonymic clash resulted from the merger of Old English *lætan* 'allow' and *lettan* 'hinder'; one had to go, and it was the latter. It survives only in the phrases *without let or hindrance* and a *let ball* (tennis term), which has been folk-etymologized into *net ball* (though, in strict terminology, there is still a difference between *let* and *net* balls). In a similar way, Old English *cwēn* 'queen' and *cwene* 'wench' end up as /kwiyn/. Of these, *queen* has stood its ground, whereas *quean* is strongly limited. It is also natural that the latter has receded, as it has dozens of synonyms to replace it.

Even if the semantics are unrelated, homonymy is still avoided if it has obscene overtones, because this is another impediment to communication. Speakers react to embarrassment (either ridicule or annoyance) by avoiding the homonyms to the tabu words. This has been observed in many languages, for example, in American English, *rooster* and *donkey* are much more prevalent than *cock* and *ass*. Finnish *kuti* 'spawned' does not assibilate *t* > *s* as expected, apparently because of *kusi* 'pissed'.

Borrowing can be the mechanism to correct polysemy. In Finnish, *kutsua* means 'to invite' and 'to call'. In the dialect spoken in the Province of Värmland, Sweden, *kuhtua* is retained in the first meaning, and *kalloa* has been borrowed from Swedish for the second.

[9.4]   Polysemic clashes are also revealed through dialect geography. If the same form—especially a technical term—has different meanings in adjacent geographical areas, a difficulty arises at the borderline, where both meanings would meet, resulting in polysemy. A buffer zone may now develop to bar either meaning and thus keep the sign system unambiguous. In the central German speaking area, *Korn* means 'rye', in the southwestern corner, 'spelt'. The two areas are kept apart by a narrow strip going northeast of Bodensee, looping around Stuttgart, and petering out at the Black Forest, where the 'rye'/'spelt' line runs southwest to cross the Rhine north of Basel (Figure 9-2:A). In the buffer zone, *Korn* retains its original meaning 'grain' and, as a generic term, covers both sides. Note that the meanings 'rye' and 'spelt' abut along the Black Forest; but this is not a farming area, and it is thus natural that this isogloss separates the Rhine valley from the Neckar and Danube valleys.

In the standard terminology of dialect geography, the Black Forest is a natural barrier to communication, especially for farming. Another clear example comes from the Belgian province of Limburg (the following matter is slightly simplified). In the western section the word *Opper* (quoted in Standard German form) means a 'big heap of hay' in the north, and a 'row of oat sheaves' in the south. In the eastern half, the farthest northern corner with the meaning 'small heap of hay' is adjacent to the western part, and the southeastern meaning an 'unbound half sheaf' would clash with the meaning in the adjacent southwestern sector. The clashes all through the territory are prevented by a strip of no man's land running all through the province (Figure 9-2: B) in which the form *Opper* is missing. In the *Korn* case, the form itself could remain, with retention of the old meaning of the word not giving way to the innovations of either side, whereas in the *Opper* case the form had to go, in any meaning, in favor of other, "neutral" carriers. In both cases, the efficiency of the system in the expected clash area was preserved.

A   B

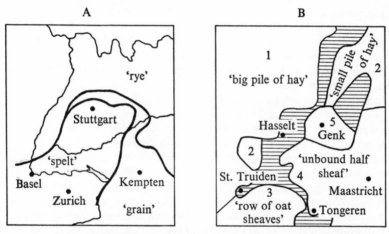

FIGURE 9-2. Geographical distribution of meanings. A, the meanings of German *Korn* in the southwestern German-speaking area. B, the meanings of German *Opper* (standing for the Flemish variants) in Belgian Limburg. [Reprinted with modification, by permission, from Jan Goossens, *Strukturelle Sprachgeographie*, Heidelberg, 1969 (© Carl Winter Universitätsverlag).]

In the tabu cases, we saw that uncalled-for connotations and reactions may lead to the elimination of a term, even when there is no danger of ambiguity. A similar case can happen also in polysemic clashes. Again, in Belgium, in the Brabant area, *läufig* (Standard German form) means 'in heat' (of cows), whereas in the East (Limburg–Rhine) it is applied to bitches. The two areas are separated by a no-man's-land. The reason is not cognitive, but apparently avoidance of ridicule (compare how funny it sounds when a foreigner says *squeeze* instead of *press*). Interference with communication for other than semantic reasons does indeed occur; imagine a stockbroker who worked in pajamas. His "actual" working capacity would not be impaired, but the disturbance created in our cultural setting would render all work impossible.

[9.5 Preservation of Redundancy]   One aspect of an efficient sign system like language is redundancy, to ensure proper decoding in adverse conditions (see § 2.13, and end of § 8.19). It has been maintained, on this account, that excessive shortness necessitates replacement of a term to increase redundancy. But clear examples are hard to come by; the most persuasive are French *é* 'bee' < *apem*, and *hui* 'today' < *hodie*, which have been replaced in various ways (in Standard French by the outcome of a Latin deminutive *apiculam* > *abeille*, and a compound *aujourd'hui*, of which the original short form itself is a part). The problem, however, is that French retains many forms just as short, for example, monovocalic nouns like /u/ *août* 'August', /ü/ *us* 'custom', and /o/ *eau* 'water'. Note also that *hui* 'today', *huit* 'eight', and *huis* 'door' (all /ɥi/) represent different parts of speech, and thus the homophony is not insidious. But compounds like *aujourd'hui* are on occasions demonstrably a way of avoiding ambiguity; for example, in certain areas of Scandinavia, the form for 'potato' and 'pear' is the same, let us say *X* (e.g., Swedish *pär*). One of the signs is now explained by a compound like *apple X*, *tree X*, or *earth X* (compare logographic writing and pidgins § 8.19).

In the previous chapters we saw many examples of avoidance of homophony in paradigms (analogic resistance to sound change), or therapeutic removal of homophony (by analogy, borrowing, or grammatically conditioned sound change). But all languages have homophony to different degrees, and one can never predict with complete confidence when a community or speaker will find it inconvenient enough to be corrected, although certain guesses have a high probability of being right. And even when avoidance or correction of homophony does occur, there is no way of telling by what mechanism of change it will happen (the possibilities are metaphor and borrowing, and subtypes of them). Further, it is not always possible to predict which of the homonyms will be replaced.

[9.6 Holes in Patterns]   From this internal cause we can move to another: the symmetry or asymmetry of phonological systems. The hypothesis is that systems strive toward perfect symmetry, that is, gaps tend to be leveled out. Language is normally full of gaps of all kinds, and not only phonological ones (e.g., in derivation, all possible combinations are never used), and this skewedness is, of course, a prime target of analogy. Similarly, all possible combinations of distinctive features need not be used in one language. If in the middle of an otherwise perfect pattern an "expected" unit is missing, one speaks of a hole in the pattern. In English, there is a gap in the combination of the forms *good* and the comparative *-er*. When the "expected" combination is made the gap is filled by *gooder* (§ 5.14).

The vowel system of Middle High German was the following, after the umlaut and before the lengthening of short vowels in open syllables:

$$
\begin{array}{ccc\quad ccc}
i & ü & u & \bar{\imath} & \bar{\ddot{u}} & \bar{u} \\
e & ö & o & \bar{e} & \bar{ö} & \bar{o} \\
\varepsilon & & (\,) & & & \\
\ddot{a} & & a & \bar{\ddot{a}} & & \bar{a}
\end{array}
$$

Here we have a twofold asymmetry, one between short front and back vowels and one between short and long vowels. Balance can be achieved by eliminating one front vowel or creating a new back vowel. In certain parts of Switzerland ε has indeed been eliminated by merging with e, in other localities by merger with $\ddot{a}$, with the result that the long and short systems correspond exactly. In areas where four unrounded front vowels remained, there was a split:

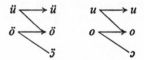

and the hole was filled. In the lengthening of short vowels, a is integrated in three ways (in different areas):

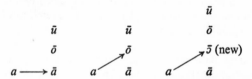

The last alternative obtains only in those areas where the short vowels have four degrees of height.

A striking development toward symmetry is the first-syllable vocalism of Proto-Baltic Finnic, in which the short vowels had one degree of height more than the long ones, and contained the only rounded front vowel in the whole system:

PROTO-BALTIC FINNIC									FINNISH		
i	$ü$	u	$\bar{\imath}$	$(\,)$	$\bar{u}$	i	$ü$	u	$\bar{\imath}$	$\bar{\ddot{u}}$	$\bar{u}$
e	$(\,)$	o	$\bar{e}$	$(\,)$	$\bar{o} > e$	$ö$	o		$\bar{e}$	$\bar{ö}$	$\bar{o}$
$\ddot{a}$		a	$(\,)$		$(\,)$	$\ddot{a}$		a	$\bar{\ddot{a}}$		$\bar{a}$

Finnish has filled every single gap and ended up with perfect symmetry. Another asymmetry is known in the Serbo-Croatian system of velars:

$$
\begin{array}{cc}
g & (\,) \\
k & x
\end{array}
$$

The gap is a missing combination of features (parallel to the missing combination *good* + *er*), viz., [voice + spirant]. This gap has been filled, depending on the dialect, by splitting either the *g* or the *x*, that is,

$$g \rightarrow \gamma \text{ (Čakavian dialects of Istria) or } g \quad \gamma_\uparrow \text{ (dialects of the}$$
$$k \quad x \qquad \qquad \qquad \qquad \qquad k \quad x^\uparrow \text{ Montenegrian coast)}$$

This is the kind of evidence thought to show internal causality of sound change, but all linguists do not agree that this furnishes satisfactory evidence for cause; after all, it is quite clear that most sound systems contain gaps and that perfect systems become skewed (compare Rotuman § 4.6). But what the Swiss mergers and splits do show is that the spread of certain innovations are favored by internal factors, and that certain sound changes can mutually exclude each other. (N.B.: Internal structure of a language may easily adopt borrowing or resist it.)

Taken negatively, this same principle would say that a system would resist the development of a hole in its pattern. This would, of course, work against some mergers, whereas the positive side calls for splits to fill the gaps. The dual concept is the same as that behind analogy in its role of either preventing sound change or straightening out its results. Note that the negative side of this principle would be the basis of push chains, the positive, of drag chains (§ 6.4). Sound shifts do, in fact, occur, although we cannot always say whether they are push or drag chains. Some consolation is given by the fact that both chains represent one and the same underlying force, even if this is controversial and not perfectly established as yet.

[9.7 Articulatory Balance]   Chain shifts would further show one aspect of the principle of maximal *differentiation*. There seems to be a universal tendency for phonological space, as defined by the articulatory possibilities (Figures 1-3 and 1-4), to be divided evenly among the units so that each has maximal elbow room. Languages with one *s*-sound show [ś]- or [š]-type phonetics for their /s/ (e.g., conservative Finnish); languages with three vowels would normally display *i*, *a*, and *u* (see § 6.5); and so on. Further, a universal tendency in vowel shifts is that tense vowels rise and lax ones get lowered. Hence push chain shifts are in principle quite possible. Another regularity in the idea of maximal differentiation is that languages with skewed vowel systems have more front vowels than back vowels. This is a consequence of the shape of the mouth and articulatory organs, which provide more room in the front area. Although this factor is internal with respect to the human head, it should be classed as an external one as far as the actual language is concerned. Then there is the problem of "perceptual space," which may be relevant. Unfortunately, not much is known about it as yet (§ 9.16).

Note how frequently linguists rely on the principle of articulatory balance by using arguments based on holes in patterns. We saw above a case in which German *diŋ* was anomalous in its final *ŋ*, because elsewhere it occurred before velars only, *daŋk*. The hole could be filled by *g*, *diŋg*, which is then automatically dropped by a phonetic realization rule (§ 6.15). Here the linguist tries to fill the hole that sound change is trying to create (or has created, depending on one's vantage point; see § 19.6).

[9.8   Tendencies, Statistics, Universals, and Frequency]   In speaking about causes of change, one has often to refer to tendencies. Some linguists feel that it is below the dignity of their subject to resort to such a notion. This dissatisfaction stems from a more ambitious goal—that of wanting to be able to predict everything in linguistic change. This requirement ignores completely the fact that language is perhaps closer to anthropology and behavioral science than to philosophy and logic. It is certainly clear that language is not all logic, and, as in the social sciences in general, statistical inference is often all that we have to base predictions on. Note also that arguments based on language universals are statistical in nature, and so are the universal kinds of changes described in the previous chapters. In other words, language universals represent a sophisticated kind of interlanguage inference of statistical tendencies.

One of the factors in sound change is frequency of occurrence. Frequency is by no means a mere mechanistic concept, as it has repercussions in association formation and memory. High frequency presses forms into memory, and we have already seen how this was a factor in analogic changes (§§ 5.14, 5.21); that is, infrequent forms are replaced more easily, or they merge more easily with others. Frequency is also a factor in ellipsis (§§ 7.5, 7.6, 7.8). In Parisian French, /œ̃/ and /ɛ̃/ tend to merge into /ɛ̃/, and have largely done so, but the frequency of *un* and a few other forms retain /œ̃/ in the system.

One of the results of high frequency is exceptional wear, which is common in grammatical forms like auxiliaries, negatives, pronouns, and particles (see the Finnish apocope in case endings; § 4.24). Of course, in these cases one could maintain that grammatical conditioning is enough, or that the generally unstressed phonetics of such forms could do as well. These factors are indeed valid candidates, but why should there be just one force of change? We do not know to what degree grammatical conditioning is tied to frequency, because, by necessity, grammatical markers are always more frequent than other signs. Similarly, there are apparently more unstressed forms in the speech chain than stressed ones. Frequency is a function of grammar and thus a legitimate "grammatical conditioning." But frequency is also a function of social intercourse, which requires more frequent use of certain signs, depending on the particular culture, subculture, or social group. Frequent wear occurs also in greetings, titles, and names (where, of course, hypocoristic forces also operate), or basic vocabulary such as *come, go, be, can,* and *know.*

It is this area of wear that is mainly responsible for irregular sound changes (see § 4.32). From English, we can mention, for example, Old English *ne willan* > *nyllan* 'not wish' and *nān wiht* 'not a creature = no one creature' > *nāwiht,* *nānuht, nāuht, nāht, nōht,* and so on, 'naught' and 'not'. With the negative, this is later repeated in *will not* > *won't,* and the like. In German, *sk-* gives /z/ in *sollen* 'shall', instead of the regular /š/ as in *Schiff* 'ship', and so on. From the nongrammatic area we have already seen forms like *hussy* < *hūswīf, lord* < *hlāford, lady* < *hlǣfdige*; others could be added, for example, *head* < *heafod*. (*Lord* and *lady* fall basically into the area of titles.) From the sailor's vocabulary, one could name similar forms, for example, /bowsən/ *bosun* ~ *boatswain* and /stənsəl/ *studdingsail*. Developments like *Eboracum* > *York* occurred all over Europe, where we have old records to prove the cases.

Another aspect of frequency in linguistic theory is the claim that sounds that distinguish very few forms from others are more likely to disappear than those with a higher functional yield. In English, the contrast *š* ≠ *ž* is rather peripheral, and its elimination (say, through merger into *š*, or *ž* into *dž* would not disturb many signs, whereas it would be quite a different matter with *s* ≠ *z*, or with any of the other consonants, especially stops. The pairs *k* ≠ *g*, *t* ≠ *d*, and *p* ≠ *b* differentiate among a host of words in English. In a way, a low functional load is the same as a hole in the pattern, that is, a hole in the distribution of sounds in the lexicon or morphology. The inbalance can be eliminated by increasing the load of the precarious sound (e.g., by borrowing) or eliminating it. Here again, scholars do not agree on the extent of the phenomenon, or even on its existence.

There is one further area where frequency plays a role in change, namely, resistance to pronunciation borrowing. Words with high local frequency tend to be the last ones to be changed. Now if high local frequency acts as a barrier to change from the outside, it is also supposed to initiate change from the inside. The hypothesis goes that the most frequent sounds can get away with less precise articulation. This variation goes one way, for example, toward less marking, and sound change results. Thus one would say that the relative frequency of the voiced stops *d g* in Indo-European launched Grimm's law. These were marked with [+voice] in contrast to *p t k*. As the most frequent stops they tended to lose their marking and move toward *t k*, which in turn had to shift out > (*f*) *þ x*. We do know that variation is the basis of change, but the exact role of frequency in this connection is unknown and unknowable. On the other hand, speakers themselves seem to know statistics connected with speaking, because in certain sociolinguistic situations the proportion of the cases in which a rule applies is rather consistent considering all the possible cases in which it could apply (Figure 3-1, §§ 3.3, 3.5, 9.3, 9.11).

[9.9 Marking and the Naturalness of Systems]   Various schemes of markedness can be easily devised to explain shifts. If we interpret Indo-European *t d dh* as plain (voiceless), voiced, and murmured, respectively, we have a hierarchy of marking, as murmured sounds are highly unusual in the languages

$$t$$

of the world. If [murmur] is replaced by [spirantness], we get *t d dh* > *d ð*, where *ð* is doubly marked for [voice] and [spirantness]. It is unusual to have voiced spirants without voiceless ones in a language that has the feature [voiceless],

$$þ$$

and thus *t* > *þ* would correct that, yielding *d ð*. But now the system is even further skewed, because there are no unmarked sounds. This is an impossibility,

$$t \ \flat$$

and *d* has to shift > *t*, that is, *ð*. Now the *ð* is again in the air, until it becomes

$$t \ \flat$$

a stop in some environments, *d ð*, and the system is finally symmetric. There is the least reason for the change *t* > *þ*, because it increases markedness. If we assign this step to a substratum, then we get

$$
\begin{array}{ccc}
þ & t \ þ & t \ þ \\
d & > dh & > d \\
dh & &
\end{array}
$$

quite easily if we further interpret the Germanic *d* as a stop only, and then

$$t \ \flat$$

Verner's law completing the symmetry *d ð*. Now, substratum influence exists in phonology, that is, sound substitution when borrowing a whole language (as well as influence in other areas of grammar). Language-learning situations, in general, are responsible for various simplifications (or analogical developments; see § 9.14). Because of the same mental requirement that meaning and form should be connected in a maximally simple fashion, a child, for example, tries to make shortcuts accordingly. And we formalize these shortcuts with analogy or various types of rule manipulation (loss, reordering, and so on; for such shortcuts in *Ding* and *tieq*, see §§ 6.15, 6.17).

Another very popular explanation of cause is ease of articulation. Here one would say that the spirants require less effort than stops and consequently that *p t k* > *f þ x* in Grimm's law. But ease is a highly subjective concept and clearly dependent on the specific language. If spirants are easier to pronounce than stops, why would the Baltic Finnic speakers have replaced them with stops (Figure 8-2)? On the other hand, the results of assimilation indeed often require fewer articulatory movements (§§ 4.14–4.16). But this requires us to maintain that the result is the cause. Once alternation is produced by the vacillation between the unassimilated and the assimilated sequence, the simpler sequence may be favored for the final adoption. Cases where cause and result are intricately connected are known by the term 'teleology.' One should note, however, that simplification is not the same as ease and, further, that all sound changes do not produce simplification. Even if analogy is always simplification in some respects, sound change is not. If it were, all languages would now be maximally simple phonologically, that is, a mumble or silence. But this would not serve the function of language, where signs have to be kept separate and redundancy maintained.

It does not seem advisable to review other combinations or various (still developing) theories of markedness and change. Suffice it to note that they are variants of the notion of a hole in the pattern.

[9.10 Sound Change and Indexicality] We have constantly seen how change is intimately connected with variation. Change is the struggle of variants;

without variation, one could not understand change, and without change, one would not understand synchronic variation. Sound change shows the social factors of change, in addition to the phonetic/physiological (determined by the articulatory organs), phonological (determined by the pressures of the system), and psychological factors (e.g., tabu).

The starting point of sound change is index formation. The articulatory basis of pronunciation always ensures a certain amount of random variation. Culture allows for the same, for example, in the area of clothing. Striking random fluctuation (in pronunciation) has been quoted for example, from Papuan, where the velar in *voka* 'coffee' varies (or varied) between *kh*, *kx*, *g*, and *γ*, or the French of the Ardennes, where *l'eau* 'water' can (or could) be [loɔ], [lou], or [lao]. When a particular variant is given social interpretation, it becomes an index of that group. In the same way, animal sounds are indexes of the corresponding animals, and this index is often reproduced iconically in language in naming the animal (onomatopoeia). Similarly in culture, variation can become a social index, as in a particular clothing fashion. If a group which shows social cohesion through pronunciation indexicality has wider appeal, its pronunciation will be imitated; that is, others try to produce the index as iconically as they can. This represents the combination 'pronunciation pronunciation' which was missing in §§ 2.14, 2.15 (see end of § 21.4). Again, the same happens in culture, say the imitation of fashions if it is not proscribed (e.g., the imitation of royal insignia, and so on). If on the other hand a group is stigmatized for its pronunciation by a more prestigious group, it may ultimately give up its index for the prestige model. Such indexes need not be absolute but can be statistical parameters; that is, one throws in the index at the proper frequency (see Figure 3-1, §§ 3.3, 3.5). This easily results in hypercorrection by those who try to belong to the prestige group. They overdo the index. A similar reaction in nonlinguistic culture (and scientific schools) is typified by the aphorism: "The Irish are more Catholic than the Pope." This is also why upstarts, or social climbers, are often easily spotted.

Much of this index identification is subconscious, but at times it reaches the level of awareness. Even linguistically naïve speakers can brand pronunciations as vulgar, soft, hard, coarse, and so on. (N.B.: To do this they thus use indexes/metonyms and icons/metaphors!) Indeed, misinterpretation of the index can lead to serious misunderstanding among different groups. Young people may interpret the pronunciation of older people as pompous and authoritarian, and older people that of the young as provocative and irresponsible. An American can interpret the British intonation as patronizing and insulting. Practically every "major" sound change since the seventeenth century was explicitly discussed by French orthoepists. This shows the struggle of variants and their social implications, and, of course, reveals that the whole situation could be observed. The first occurrence of English labialization *wa* > *wɔ* is attested from 1640. In 1766 Buchanan used *ɔ* in some words (*ward, warn, want*) and *æ* or *a* in others (*wabble, wad, wallop*). In 1780 Sheridan connected the pronunciation of *quality* with *ɔ* with the meaning 'people of high social rank', whereas, in its abstract meaning, the old *æ* remained. In 1633 there was apparently no difference in the vowels between *good* and *blood*, both with *u·*. Later in the seventeenth century, when short *u* > ʌ, the long *u·* was in the process of being shortened (attested already in 1569 for *good*). Now this variation *u* ~ *u·* interfered with the change (variation) *u* > ʌ. Those words where the long variant was more frequent were not affected, except by the later shortening (*good*), but those in which the short *u* was dominant underwent *u* > ʌ (*blood*). Thus the apparent double outcome depends on the overlap of two sound changes, which went on as synchronic variation in the grammars. In 1747 Johnson sometimes had difficulty in deciding the proper pronunciation for his rhyming dictionary, for example, whether *great* rhymed with *state* or *seat*. The best speaker in the House of Lords decided without hesitation for (st)*ate* = (gr)*eat*, and the best speaker in the House of Commons likewise for (s)*eat* = (gr)*eat*. These English examples have shown three facts: (1) variation and change can spread from word to word and need not be simultaneous throughout the vocabulary, (2) statistics/frequency does play a role, and (3) identification with a social layer exists.

In French, many grammarians have recorded the alternation *wɛ* ~ *wa* (*loi* 'law', and so on). The variant *wa* occurred in monosyllabic words, and in polysyllabic words before *r* and *l*. The upper classes condemned *wa* and regarded *wɛ* the only acceptable pronunciation. Toward the end of the eighteenth century, both pronunciations were almost on equal footing. When Louis XVIII, who had fled in 1791, came back in 1814, and uttered: *C'est moè le roè* (i.e., *wɛ*), he was quickly told that in his absence this pronunciation had become vulgar and provincial. In other words, the complete social upheaval of the French revolution reversed the social value. This is often true when new social classes come to political power.

[9.11]   Information on the interrelationship between variation/change and social meaning can be gleaned not only from the orthoepists of the past. William Labov has shown in studies of Martha's Vineyard and New York City that the same situation obtains everywhere. There is a close correlation between a speaker's ethnic background, profession, age level, and so on. Let us review briefly the pronunciation of the diphthongs |ai| and |au| in Martha's Vineyard.

The phonetic characteristic of these diphthongs is centralization of the first part, maybe all the way to [ə]. At the time of the New England dialect survey, 1933, |au| showed very little centralization, whereas |ai| was [əɪ]. This situation had apparently existed a long time before that. The island is divided into two social sectors, a rural up-island, and a down-island with three small towns. Up-island is characterized by a high degree of centralization in both |ai| and |au|, but centralization occurs in one of the down-island towns in a more restricted measure, particularly in words such as *right, white, wife*, but not so much in others, for example, *time, while, I, my*. Both phonetic conditioning and particular words are involved, exactly as in the English and French examples already quoted. A centralization index is calculated by assigning the value 0 (to [a]) and 3 (to [ə]), with two steps in between. Centralization indexes by age groups are as follows:*

	|AI|	|AU|
over 75	0.25	0.22
61–75	0.35	0.37
46–60	0.62	0.44
31–45	0.81	0.88
14–30	0.37	0.46

In 1933 the centralization for |ai| was about 0.86, for |au| only 0.06. For |au|, centralization has been steadily rising. There is a clear difference in the geographical distribution as well:

	|AI|	|AU|
Down-island	0.35	0.33
Up-island	0.61	0.66

or occupation

	|AI|	|AU|
Fishermen	1.00	0.79
Farmers	0.32	0.22
Others	0.41	0.57

Labov gives such indexes for ethnic groups also, but the most revealing is the correlation of centralization with the attitude of the speaker toward the island. The indexes for four 15-year-old high school students are: down-island and leaving 0.00–0.40 and 0.00–0.00, up-island and staying 0.90–1.00 and 1.13–1.19. With those people who feel very strongly about the island, the index can go even beyond 2.00. In general the attitude test gives the following centralization averages:

NO. OF PERSONS	|AI|	|AU|
40 Positive	0.63	0.62
19 Neutral	0.32	0.42
6 Negative	0.09	0.08

The immediate meaning of centralization is 'Vineyarder'; it indicates group cohesion. The total distribution of such index shapes correlates quite well also with other factors of social interaction on the island. Here again we see that statistics is a factor in the measurement of social indexes and that symmetry has been achieved for the phonological space by letting |au| go the same way as |ai|. Similar findings are recorded from New York City (see Figure 3-1, § 3.3; compare § 14.4).

* The tabular material in § 9.11 reproduced by permission from William Labov, "The social motivation for sound change," *Word*, **19**, 273–309 (1963).

[9.12 Change and the Social Setting] The social setting shows a common mechanism of change. A feature is adopted by a group as a social index. Now, understanding why a particular feature should be involved at a particular time is beyond us, exactly like predicting fashions. If a group becomes a reference group for some other, the latter will accept the index and exaggerate it. Hypercorrection further spreads the feature, perhaps in combination with structural symmetry. This establishes a new norm when the social situation stabilizes, which again can serve as a model for other groups. Equally important is the acknowledgment and realization of the heterogenousness of the transmission of a change. It may be individual or occasional and it may first affect women or young people, sailors or farmers, individual words or word classes (e.g., verbs or certain semantic fields), and so on (see § 6.8). All this makes it possible for many irregular forms to come into being "regularly," for example, the pronunciation of *good* vs. *blood*. That is, grammatically irregular forms have a regular explanation in terms of the relations in the speech community. Linguistic change cannot be understood without data from the speech community, because language exists for the community, is maintained by it, and refers to the culture of the community. Sublinguistic (e.g., allophonic or individual) fluctuation is given noncognitive social meaning, and this results in sound change. When one variant wins out at the end, ultimate regularity is produced, if one excepts certain irregularities here and there.

The particular cultural setting may involve a long history of writing. This creates the additional possibilities of spelling pronunciation and archaisms, which are loans from earlier stages of the same language. Semantic change, in particular, emphasized that linguistic structure alone is not sufficient for the unfolding of linguistic change. The causality of change resides in a complicated texture of social, physiological, psychological, phonological (and other systemic) factors. It is clearly wrong to seek only one factor which would explain everything. One must acknowledge the psychological factor to be the strongest one— that is, the general tendency toward simplicity and symmetry. It is also clear that this chapter has been a general summary of the preceding ones, and that we have continued to discuss more the 'how' than the 'why' of change. Nonetheless, the factors that have been delineated are all we have at the moment, and, on the whole, it seems plausible that such factors combine to give causes of change.

[9.13 Teleology of Change] In fact, it has not been enough to refer to only 'how' or 'why' (for what reason) in linguistic change. We have also asked the question 'for what purpose'. The same combination of questions must also be used in biology, in the study of living organisms (Chapter 22). It is the nature of the organism to be oriented toward the change that occurs. This "nature" influences the range and direction of change that can occur. Possible changes are added to others, which together are the 'causes' toward which the developing organism is drawn. In other words, the 'causes' are the results, the purpose. In cases like this, one speaks of goal-directed behavior, teleology, or entelechy (having the end in itself). And language is also a teleological or goal-directed system, exactly like human culture, that is, all aspects of the specifically human environment. (§23.4)

The "purpose" of language is to keep functioning through time and in any new cultural environments within the boundaries of human mental capacities. Causes and results entwine to ensure both the survival of the system and the self-reproduction of the system. In other words, finalistic and causal influences are closely connected. (As in biology, outside factors also play a role.) The mechanisms of this teleological purpose are various kinds of iconic (diagrammatic) or indexical relations. In linguistic change, an observable tendency toward a goal is known as *drift*. As in biology, it takes a form of complex synchronization, for example, loss of inflection with increased use of prepositions and word order in English. It is also understandable why two related languages can go different ways. If they both start out from a particular imbalance, say, a "hole" of some kind in any level of grammar, one may fill it, the other may eliminate the odd term. Or they can independently resort to the same remedy, and the result will look as if it had been inherited in both. A good formal imbalance is the indication of the Slavic genitive plural. Proto-Slavic (and Old Church Slavic) had three forms, -ŭ, -ovŭ (see § 7.13), and -ĭjĭ, the first being the most frequent and widespread in declensions. With the loss of -ŭ, the most frequent marker became zero, creating literally a hole in the system. Now, in every Slavic language zero has lost ground and is no longer the dominant form in any of them. The languages inherited the triggering for the same drift, and although the individual replacements have been different, they are, nonetheless, similar to a great degree. (Cf. §23.9)

[9.14   Sound Change and Language Learning]   It has been mentioned that language is one manifestation of an innate ability to analogize (§ 7.8), and that children, in particular, introduce analogical creations (§§ 3.3, 5.2, 5.4, 5.14). The contribution by children to linguistic change may be quite considerable; it is difficult to know its exact scope, however, because tradition usually prevails. Linguists stated early that one of the chief factors of sound change is 'imperfect learning' by children. The reason for this might well be biological/psychological; that is, there may be an innate natural system of phonological processes, manifested particularly in the postbabbling period. This innate system is gradually modified by linguistic experience so that the child comes closer and closer to the standard; if he fails to any degree, change results. An innate system would also explain the implicational laws or scales presented in § 6.5.

Such a 'natural phonology' (Stampe) is the first language of the child, a kind of "innate speech defect," which automatically produces a substratum effect in the acquisition of the pronunciation of the community. The child masters the underlying phonological units earlier than he can produce all the contrasts. Surface contrasts are eliminated through the application of the processes of the innate system. Thus there is a "biological" pull toward the language-innocent state of affairs and a social pull toward the language of the community.

Many linguists believe that the former is the more important factor and often state it in the slogan: "Children simplify (restructure) grammars, adults complicate them." The way adults "borrow" phonetic change (§§ 9.10, 9.11), however, is no different in mechanism from language acquisition. In both cases there is regular sound substitution (see § 8.4; Figure 8-1), although the interference comes from different sources. The regularity of substitution, of course, results in the regularity of sound change. Such an innate sound system is also compatible with the fact that sometimes change is very radical indeed.

When the child fails to suppress some innate process that does not apply in the standard language, phonetic change occurs which looks like an addition to the standard grammar. One of the natural rules appears to be that word-final obstruents are devoiced, and English speakers must unlearn it (in contrast with German speakers, for example). If they fail in this, the language gets an "addition," for example, $d > t$: [bɛ·d] > [bɛ·t] 'bed' (which, in fact, has become standard in some Appalachian dialects). The word still remains distinct from [bɛt] *bet*, because the lengthening of the vowel before voiced stops carries the contrast /be·t/ vs. /bet/. The lengthening had been copied correctly (see § 10.4), which automatically "orders" it before the devoicing in the synchronic application of rules. The innate application is unordered (strives toward perfect unmarking), and thus synchronic order would result from the order in which particular distinctions are copied from the standard language. (This is parallel to the possible different chronology in dialect borrowing; § 14.8.) An unordered application of vowel lengthening and devoicing would produce [bɑt] for both 'back' and 'bad', but when vowel lengthening is applied first we get [bɑt] 'back' and [bɑ·t] 'bad', as above. Here again we see that our descriptive mechanisms of change (or rather diachronic correspondences, § 6.22) look totally different from the point of view of language acquisition; that is, they are not historical explanations. The apparent addition, generalization, and unordering of processes arise in the child's *failure* to suppress, limit, or order processes of the innate system, to the extent required by the standard language.

Such a natural phonology is the exact opposite of the empirist tabula rasa. In spite of the "neatness" and the dramatic appeal of the hypothesis, it is highly controversial; it serves, however, as a modern example of bold reasoning into the causes of sound change. (We have not discussed those earlier attempts now proved unfruitful—climate, geography, and so on.)

[9.15 Rules, Sound Change, and Iconicity]   Because all the different mechanisms of change are so heavily diagrammatic (analogical), and because change is, in general, connected with iconicity and indexicality, the traditional interpretation of sound change as something very different would, if true, be quite noteworthy. On the contrary, it is notable that sound change is indexical, and iconic (especially in its spread). Since rules are largely iconic, and since phonological rules handle the commutations, associations, and distributions of distinctive features, they are iconic as well. They represent the relations in the hierarchy of distinctive features and are thus diagrammatic (see §§ 1.13–1.16).

The function of phonological rules within the phonological system is to produce overt signs of the distinctive-feature relations that define the phonemes. Allophonic variation and neutralization are such overt signs (at the time they are introduced). Ukrainian assimilates its obstruents to following voicing, for example, [s] → [z] / —[b], [proz'ba] 'request', but not to following voicelessness: [dužka] 'handle'. Russian does both, in addition to utterance-final devoicing. This shows that the Ukrainian opposition is [tense] vs. [lax], Russian [voiced] vs. [voiceless]. Serbo-Croatian is like Russian except for its lack of final devoicing and thus provides no evidence for the nature of its distinctive features. Pure phonetic evidence might still tell the features in question. The fact that English initial voiced stops show delayed onset of voicing characteristically indicates that the relevant feature is [lax] and not [voice] (§ 10.3). In contrast Russian voicing starts immediately and represents [voice]. In this way we do indeed have diagrams of the feature hierarchies. (Note that this diagrammatic axis is different from lexical or semantic representation through a limited number of phonemes [§ 1.14]. The most striking case of the latter is Semitic in which consonant sequences represent lexical meanings and vowels grammatical meanings, for example, Arabic /k-t-b/ 'write', /kataba/ 'he wrote', /ka·tib/ 'writing [person]', /kita·b/ 'book', and so on [see the end of § 8.4], although there are of course also affixes, for example, /ma-ktab/ 'place for writing, study', and /katab-at/ 'she wrote'.)

The diagrammatic aspect of sound change is clearest in phonetic analogy (sound analogy), which takes place irrespective of meaning (see §§ 4.20, 5.1, 5.3). This is the factor that makes sporadic sound change regular in the end (compare § 9.10), that is, a particular outcome in a particular environment is *generalized*. The process is the easier the more natural the rules involved are (§ 9.14). Note that the rebus principle is also a particular kind of analogy without conceptual meaning, unless we want to speak of visual meaning (§ 5.3).

In the following we will see how distinctive-feature hierarchies are subject to reanalysis in the same way as other linguistic hierarchies are.

[9.16 Abduction, Language Learning, and Change] The references to induction and deduction in change (e.g., § 5.6) need refinement, because there are actually three modes of reasoning or argument. The natural order of the logic of the syllogism is the following (cf. §23.4):

D   **I   A**

RULE: All men are mortal.   (major premise)
CASE: Socrates was a man.   (minor premise)   VS.
RESULT: Socrates was mortal. (conclusion)

This inference is deductive. Now, induction is inference with the order of the procedure reversed: we infer the rule from the case and the result. But the most common type of reasoning is *hypothetical inference*, in which the rule and the result are given and we infer the case. This is abduction, the everyday logic par excellence. It is extremely fallible (all modes of reasoning are, to some degree), but people go on using it even though it gives correct results only part of the time. Man seems to have an instinct for abduction. Abduction is a reasoned guess as to how a surprising observed fact may have come about and is consequently an 'explanation'; it is an act of insight, coming to us in a flash. It is the idea of putting together what we never thought of connecting before. It suggests that something may be; unlike the other modes of inference it introduces a new idea. Any learning or understanding must be by abduction. Its purpose is to stand as the basis for, or to represent, predictions. The purpose of deduction is to infer those predictions, and the purpose of induction is to test them. These are the steps for solving any problem by the methods of science. Abduction is always a gamble, whereas deduction, with little risk and low return never introduces anything new. In short, abduction suggests that something is the case, that something *may be*; deduction proves that something *must be*; and induction tests to show that something *actually is*. (Cf. columns 1-3, p. x)

Thus the various changes usually called 'inductive' in this book and elsewhere are actually 'abductive'. This is how a grammar or language is learned. Everybody has to abduce his own grammar from the output of other grammars; in this situation ambiguities can be newly resolved. The essential link (which repeats itself indefinitely) can be diagrammed thus according to H. Andersen:*

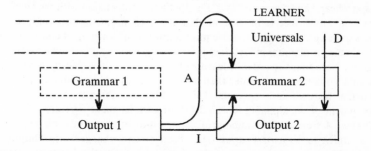

Grammar 2 is inferred from Universals (the major premise) and Output 1 (the minor premise) by abduction; if Grammar 2 is different from Grammar 1, we may speak of abductive change. Output 2 is inferred or derived from Universals and Grammar 2; if Output 2 is different from Output 1, we may speak of deductive change. Note that deduction is always an experiment. In language the test is whether Output 2 is acceptable to speakers who produce Output 1. If it is, the general rule has been verified: the two grammars are the same for practical needs, although they may be drastically different in structure (I).

Although the exact nature of the language universals is still unknown, their existence is a certainty, and they are connected with man's innate capacity to learn a language. We have at least seen some of the cornerstones of the universals, scattered throughout the preceding chapters. The most important one

* The diagram reproduced by permission of Henning Andersen (with modification).

is 'one meaning, one form' (e.g. § 9.3), which need not be repeated here. We have seen various assimilation phenomena and other phonetic processes (Chapter 4; see also § 16.8) and marking conventions which somehow represent universals (§§ 6.20, 6.21, 9.8, 9.9). Then, there is a universal phonetics (§§ 6.5, 9.14) and articulatory balance between units (§ 9.7).

Many linguists have posited a particular 'language acquisition device' (LAD) that would handle language learning alone. But there is no need for a separate learning device or autonomous mechanism like that. Language acquisition is a process of socialization and not verbalization alone. Language is just one facet of the human capacity for analogizing (§§ 7.8, 9.14), in other words, the human capacity for abduction. Significantly, diagrams for language learning devices (to process the speech signals) tend to have compartments corresponding to abduction, deduction, and induction. Perceptual differentiation comes earliest and this leads to a discovery of perceptual values (abduction). Then these values are given an articulatory optimization to find and produce the favored contrasts; this is discovery of articulatory values ("creative behavior," deduction), aided by a device that handles articulatory balance (§§ 6.4, 9.3, 9.6, 9.7, 9.9). The principle of perceptual differentiation maximizes the degree of perceptual contrast, and the principle of least effort minimizes articulatory expenditure. The balance between these two factors keeps the phonology natural, "easy-to-hear" and "easy-to-say." Finally there is interaction with the environment and adult speech in general that leads to normalization (induction). This is quite correct, except that we must allow for the learning of culture at the same time. Our diagram in fact does this; it is a general acquisition and learning diagram. Note that the order of learning phonology is hierarchically ordered in that first come sentence units, then words, unanalyzable syllables, and last, distinctive features and segments. This exhibits a striking parallelism to the development of the alphabet (§§ 2.7–2.11), or even language (§§ 1.27, 1.28).

Chapter 4 treated the mapping of sounds into other sounds, for example, $t > \theta$, which looks as if Output 1 has been directly changed into Output 2. But this was just a convenience of description. Similarly, the diachronic correspondence rules of Chapter 6 took Grammar 1 directly to Grammar 2. Historical change actually must go through abduction; this was more clearly seen in our discussion of morphology and semantics (e.g., §§ 5.6, 5.16, 6.13–6.15, 6.19, 6.22, 6.23, 7.4), but the same is true of sounds also. Sounds cannot be shifted *directly* on the articulatory scale (Chapter 4, and Figures 1-3, 1-4) in spite of the convenience of such terminology. The child cannot learn all the articulatory facts—many are simply not visible—but he has to abduce the sounds from his perception. Here the child is well equipped since he can distinguish rather early between features and things he cannot yet produce (primates and some other animals have this ability as well). Articulatory space and ease do produce random variation on which social forces feed (§ 9.11), but this happens through abduction. Only in this way can we give a natural explanation for changes like $x > f$ (*genoh* > *enough, hleahhan* > *laugh*), $f > x$, $\theta > f$ (§ 4.21); the child reinterprets the acoustic signal. Thus, after the Pre-Greek $*k^w$ gave $*k^{\ddot{w}} > *k^y$

before i (§§ 6.16, 18.13), we had more or less the following acoustic scale with p, t, and k: [t − k^y(i) | k − k^w(u) | k^w(o) − p]. At some point somebody inferred that [k^y] could be taken as a variant of a dental, [k^{w}u] as [ku], and [k^{w}o] as [po]. This abduction was successful; we end up with $p − t − k$ as indicated by the vertical divisions above. Of course there is a fair amount of "articulatory justification" in this, but as cases like $x \gtrless f$ show, the auditory justification is more powerful. This is why a reduction of an acoustic scale [t − p′ | p] in a Czech dialect into $t − p$ is not so exotic after all (in the standard dialect $p′$ merged with p, which is more "normal" or natural). In general, near homophony can easily lead to a merger, also in terms of words. We have seen how the Old English high vowel scale [i − y | u] was reduced to $i − u$ by merging i and y (§§ 4.5, 4.12, 4.13, 4.22). This is a reversal in the distinctive feature hierarchy. As long as y was a clearly derived unit, rounding was the primary feature. At some point frontness was inferred as basic, and this led to i quite naturally through Universals (front vowels are characteristically unrounded). To take another example, the voicing of intervocalic consonants is a natural assimilation (articulatory ease, the speaker's "lazy tongue") that can easily catch on. Once [voice] is interpreted as the primary feature, voiceless variants are likely to disappear (compare § 6.13).

Reversal of basic and derived features is particularly clear in the fading of metaphors and so on (§§ 7.9, 7.15). The cultural situation allows for the learning of base and derived forms separately or in the reverse order of the actual history (*irrigate* [§ 5.5], counting one's *beads* [§§ 7.4, 7.15]). We see again that culture change is parallel to linguistic change: there too boundaries shift through abduction (§§ 7.3, 21.8). More generally, culture and human semiotic systems show markedness reversal in marked contexts. As an example, consider the distinction between formal and casual dress. In the everyday situation formal wear is marked and casual clothes unmarked, but in the marked context of a festive occasion, the values of formal and casual clothes are reversed (compare other reversals in § 21.13). Similarly, in the marked context of the underworld or war killing can be unmarked activity. We have already seen how such facts guide semantic change in terms of social jargons (§ 7.5). But the same phenomenon is operative in syntax also. In the marked subjunctive mood, the past vs. present opposition (*they knew* vs. *they know*) is neutralized; the normally marked past tense is used to the exclusion of the present (*I wish they knew*). The number opposition (*they were* vs. *he was*) is also neutralized here so that the normally marked number is used to the exclusion of the unmarked number (*I wish he were*).

Now we can profitably return to the German syllable-final devoicing. We saw that devoicing was a sign of neutralization into the unmarked voiceless member in Russian (§ 9.15). German manifests the features [tense] vs. [lax] and hence the unmarked member should be [lax]. But note that this phenomenon occurs in syllable-final position. This position is marked in respect to syllable-initial position. The order of learning syllable types goes (1) CV, (2) CVC, (3) VC, and (4) V. Voicing is learned earlier in syllable-initial position;

for example, when an English-speaking child can already produce [buk] 'book' he goes on saying [pik] 'pig' (compare § 9.14). We see now that in the German case the usually marked member of the opposition takes up unmarked behavior in the marked position of the syllable. Thus "devoicing" turns out to be another misnomer which has to be taken as a traditional term.

Another universal factor in change is *syllable structure*. We have seen its influence as a conditioning factor in terms of open and closed syllables or various cluster rules. The assignment of syllable boundaries (and not only the learning of syllable types) tends to be rather universal, although there are language-specific differences (§§ 4.6, 4.7, 4.16, 11.19). Syllable structure does not only guide sound change, it can also be its target. The most unmarked syllable structure is *CV* (open syllables only). Slavic seems to have had a "conspiracy" toward *CV* (drift, teleology) in its passage from Proto-Indo-European to Proto-Slavic. Three changes are mainly responsible for producing open syllables: (1) metathesis of liquids, *CerCV* > *CrĕCV* (§ 4.18), (2) monophthongization *CeyCV* > *CiCV*, *CewCV* > *CuCV*, and *CenCV* > *CęCV*, and (3) cluster simplification, for example, Pre-Slavic **supnos* > *sŭnŭ* 'sleep, dream', where both closed syllables drop the final consonant. The language ends up with open syllables only (compare the Rotuman loss of one syllable or length; §§ 4.6, 4.7, Figure 6-1:B). On the other hand, all the modern languages have reverted to complicated clusters (by syncope), that is, a marked state of affairs.

[9.17]   Of course, it may take a long time before the change gets established for good. Let us look at one more example of restructuring (§§ 6.13– 6.15, 6.19). Many English dialects have an underlying diphthong |yū| after dentals: /tyuwn/ *tune*, /nyuw/ *new*, and so on. In some dialects the glide is considerably weakened, so that it has been inferred as being an irrelevant accompaniment to the dental. This leads to restructured forms like |nū| without the glide: /nuw/ *new*. If this output is not acceptable to the community, it can be corrected into the "proper" |nyū|. Another possibility is to keep |nū| and to add a patch-up rule $\emptyset \rightarrow y$ after dentals to pacify the community. Now the outcome is again an acceptable /nyuw/ *new*. But the problem is that the rule applies only in certain words which have to be specially learned (compare § 3.3), and thus hypercorrection can creep in: /nyuwn/ for *noon* (which never had |yū|). As time goes by, such a patch-up rule is gradually eroded, because a person who was forced to put it up has little or no reason to require it from his own children, and so on. Somewhere on the line the patch-up rule can be omitted, as our predictions would tell us.

Let us look at another typical readjustment. An English-speaking child learns early a base form *foot* and a pluralization rule with *-s* (frequency and basic meanings). He can now predict a plural *foot-s* (§ 6.21; the grammar gives the *-s* rule, and the universals, 'one meaning, one form'). But this deduction is not accepted by the community, and he has to redo it. Normally he does not want to abandon his first attempt completely, but patches it up as *feet-s* (compare § 5.4). Finally he learns that this is one of those cases that "defy reason." This is a case without any danger of changing the underlying form. Note that a reinterpretation of distinctive features is obligatory for an adult borrower (§ 8.5). This shows that features are more important than segmental units (which must be combinations of features).

[9.18]   Folk etymology and semantic change show most clearly the short-cuts abduction helps to make; even completely "unjustified" extrapolation can become successful. The reversals in base and derived values we have seen are by no means rare. If the historically derived form is the most frequent one or otherwise represents basic morphological, syntactic, or semantic categories, it is natural for the learner to take it as basic and derive the original form from it in reverse (if alternation is not leveled out altogether). This is *inverse derivation* (compare "inverse spelling" [§ 2.6] and "inverted reconstruction" [§ 18.14]), the exact reverse of the original history, that is, history: $a > b \mid -c$, inverse derivation: $b \rightarrow a \mid -$ non-c (see the form of rules in §§ 6.7–6.10), which is a synchronic process.

In the Yiddish revoicing phenomenon we saw how a base form (voiced stop) asserted itself also on the surface (§ 4.27). Similarly, the German vowel length-ening in the nominative singular proves that the derived long vowel in the majority of the paradigm (one kind of frequency) had apparently been reanalysed as basic, and it thus surfaced everywhere. Note also the role of frequency in the reversal of markings in the pluralization of final-spirant nouns in English (§ 6.21). When alternation is eliminated no inversion remains. But it is clearly there in cases where the alternation is extended beyond the original items. The preconsonantal /betə/ *better* is more frequent than the prevocalic /betər/, and was clearly taken as basic whereby the /r/ became an automatic transition sound, and thus spread (§ 5.3). Of the various final -*n* deletion cases let us look at English *mine* /mayn/ (§ 4.24). Like /betə/, *my* was the original preconsonantal derived form which came to be taken as basic, whereby the /n/ in *mine* was reinterpreted as a derived predicative marker. And again, in some dialects it has spread into other persons: *his'n*, *her'n*, *our'n*, and so on (the alternation is made "purposeful use" of; § 5.21). This is the same process that gave the final stop in Estonian *kuusk* (§ 5.3). Some Estonian words even switch consonants after $d > \emptyset$ and $g > \emptyset$ (§ 5.9). The derived form, $\emptyset$, is taken as basic and we get a reversal $\emptyset \rightarrow d$ and $\emptyset \rightarrow g$. We know this from the fact that sometimes the wrong stop is reestablished: $d > \emptyset \rightarrow g$, and vice versa.

Proto-Indo-European had a large number of roots of the shape *CeRC* (§ 4.18), for example, Greek *derk-* 'see' (or English *help*), but relatively few roots of the type *CReC*, for example, Greek *trep-* 'turn' (or English *break*; see § 12.3). From such shapes another root variant was derived by the deletion of the vowel, $e \rightarrow \emptyset$, whereby both *CeRC* and *CReC* result in *CRC*. Thus in Sanskrit, where $e > a$, we have the deletion as $a \rightarrow \emptyset$: *darś* → *dṛś* 'see', *kalp* → *kḷp* 'be adapted', *myakṣ* → *mikṣ* 'mix', and *mrad* → *mṛd* 'crush', and so on. These derived forms without *a* hold the majority in morphology, and came to be taken as basic. The deletion rule was reversed in that now the vowel had to be inserted in the grammatical environments where it had originally belonged. But the vowel was inserted according to the majority pattern *CeRC*, and thus goes *always before* the medial resonant: *mikṣ → *maykṣ > mekṣ, mṛd → mard*, and so on. The old base form, if not ultimately lost, is often relexicalized into a separate root not subject to vowel alternation at all, for example, *myakṣ* 'join, belong to' (compare § 17.9).

One of two possible word orders is often called 'inverted'. This implies that also linguists take the other one as basic. Reversal of word order easily occurs if the frequency and the semantics are right. Even more peculiar are cases like the Finnish head and attribute switches (§§ 5.17, 6.22, 7.13), although they can be explained through abduction, the main force of syntactic change (§ 19.5). In syntactic change a single case leads to a new syntactic pattern, whereas the matter is quite different elsewhere in grammar, because a single direction may be lacking. Linguists (and other scientists) have not been willing to acknowledge abduction because of its unpredictability. Only when its results are regular have they been happy to formalize the situation post facto, bypassing the actual abductive link. But such regularity is "accidental" and does not represent the essence of abduction (e.g. §§ 5.9, 5.10). (Cf. §§11.21f., 23.7)

[9.19 Conclusion and Transition]   Reasoning is basically diagrammatic, and this is why analogy must be used in all sciences (§ 5.19), in all the modes of reasoning: abduction, deduction, and induction. For Peirce the three modes of reasoning complement each other, which is quite parallel to his triad of sign types (§ 1.16). This works out very well in genetic linguistics, as we will see in turning to comparative linguistics, which is basically inductive. We will no longer refer to these matters, except in passing (e.g. § 10.6), and no distinction between induction and abduction will be drawn (to lessen complications for those who start with Part III). Why comparative linguistics is inductive is this: We have a hypothesis that certain facts can be explained from a common origin. If this is so, we can predict certain things (e.g., certain similarity, certain correspondences), and finally put the predictions to test (e.g., through the comparative method). Thus we put the universals of Part II to test in connection with certain languages. We quite legitimately expect that languages behave like languages.

Abduction is certainly psychologically real, although we might get to know the particular cases only accidentally. It also explains why the actuation problem of change cannot be perfectly solved (compare § 9.5), because it is not a purely linguistic question, but a much wider one of human perception and reasoning. On the other hand, it explains the common core of change mechanisms (§ 9.2) and analogy in analysis (§ 18.16). Note that like folk etymology such analysis can be "wrong" (*ride/rid* [§§ 10.7, 10.16], *serps* [§§ 17.5, 17.6]).

At present we do not know how much a speaker *knows* about his language, and thus we cannot draw a clear boundary between synchrony and diachrony (compare § 18.17). Whenever a phonemic rule becomes a morphophonemic one, that is, loses its phonetic motivation (§ 6.21), it is prone to lose its psychological reality altogether (restructuring). Since our purpose is to retrieve history, our emphasis has been throughout past-oriented in that historical relics have been pointed out beyond conscious associations. Synchronic grammar is not past-oriented to that degree, and thus cases like *clean/cleanse*, *heat/hot*, *opaque/opacity*, and so on (§§ 5.8, 5.14, 6.21, 6.24, 7.9 [Figure 7-4 : E-F], 7.13, 10.7–10.9, 17.5, 18.17), can become a form of suppletion, similar to borrowings from related languages (§ 8.12). Such forms may belong together through various degrees of association (§ 5.14), but need not. This is another feature of abduction, difficult of formalization. It is parallel to the difficulty of formalizing folk etymology, in fact, both represent one and the same thing. Folk etymology, however, is at least future-oriented like linguistic change or language in general (§§ 1.16, 9.13, 18.16). Much confusion has arisen from the fact that linguists have tried to use past-oriented models to predict change (Hjelmslev [§ 12.6], Chomsky and Halle).

Very doubtful is also synchronic rule ordering as a psychological reality (§§ 6.5, 6.6, 6.15, 6.16, 6.25, 10.15), because the real momentum seems to be abduction and perhaps unordering (§ 9.14; some rules are *persistent*, whether biologically or in a language-specific manner, e.g., diphthongization in *tieq* [§ 6.17]). Again, attention to such ordering questions highlights our difficulties with relative chronology (§§ 6.1–6.4), a prime goal in genetic linguistics. Another warning of inadequate synchronic theory will be given in the form of diacritics like [+ native] which were fashionable in the 1960s (§ 10.16).

As we now turn to the historical methods we must remember that we will press them beyond the point where speakers themselves stop, because we are learning how to retrieve history, and not psychological reality in a more limited frame. Language learners are indeed to a degree internal-reconstruction machines and comparative-method machines (§ 13.7). It is the linguist's task, especially in synchrony, to find out where speakers stop using the methods. Thus in the English examples to follow (§§ 10.7–10.9) the method goes beyond synchronic reality, but seems to remain within legitimate synchronic bounds for Finnish and Lapp (§§ 10.11–10.14).

REFERENCES

9.2 Stern 1931, Vachek 1962; 9.3 Menner 1936, Jespersen 1941, Labov 1970, W. Coates 1968; 9.4 Goossens 1969; 9.5 Dressler 1969b; 9.6 Martinet 1958, 1964, Moulton 1960, 1961, 1970, Sieberer 1964, E. Itkonen 1966, P. Ivić (private communication); 9.7 Labov 1972, Labov et al. 1972, Liljencrants and Lindblom 1972; 9.8 Zipf 1965, King 1967, Mańczak 1968, 1969, Weijnen 1969, Onishi 1969, Greenberg 1969b, L. Campbell in Traugott (ed.) 1980, Herbert 1986; 9.9 J. Harris 1969, Cairns 1969, Vennemann 1972; 9.10 Joos 1952, Fónagy 1956-57, 1967, Wang 1969, Chen and Hsieh 1971; 9.11 Labov 1963, 1965, Wang (ed.) 1977; 9.12 Weinreich et al. 1968, Labov in W. Lehmann and Malkiel (eds.) 1982, Labov 1970 and in Sebeok (ed.) 1963f. vol. 11, Anshen 1970, Malkiel 1967; **9.13** Sapir 1921, Sčur 1966, Greenberg 1969a, L. Campbell and Ringen 1981, Shapiro 1985; **9.14** Halle 1962, Stampe 1969, Martinet (ed.) 1968, Graur (ed.) 3.127-200, Locke 1983 -- (See also p. 411); **9.15** Andersen 1966, 1969, Shapiro 1969, 1972; **9.16** Peirce 1955, Knight 1965, Andersen 1969, 1972, 1973, in Anderson and Jones (eds.) 1974, in Fisiak (ed.) 1978, Savan 1980, Raffler Engel 1970, Lindblom 1972, W. Coates 1968, Vennemann 1988; **9.17** Andersen 1973; **9.18** Anttila 1969b; **9.19** Knight 1965.

PART III

COMPARATIVE LINGUISTICS
(GENERAL NOTIONS AND
STRUCTURE):
HOW CAN CHANGE
BE REVERSED?

CHAPTER 10

PRELIMINARIES TO THE
HISTORICAL METHODS

*Comparative linguistics bases itself on the regularity of
sound change either to classify languages or to reconstruct
earlier stages (§ 1.18). Because sounds develop regularly,
it is possible to use well-defined methods to bring them back
together regularly. These methods are variants of the
normal synchronic methods of establishing sound units,
phonemic and morphophonemic analysis, which will later
be taken into historical contexts and renamed.*

PHONEMIC ANALYSIS

[**10.1 The Rise of Phonemics**]   As a countermeasure to the generally
rather inadequate orthographies of most languages, phoneticians, around the
turn of the century, developed transcription systems intended to be truly phonetic.
Such alphabets were supposed to accommodate any speech sound encountered
in the physical appearance of any language, and they are still, of course, a
must in linguistic analysis. But it was soon realized that one could never reach
the ultimate logical goal of one symbol for each sound in the sum total of all
known languages. This obstacle results from the fact that nobody pronounces
the "same sound" twice; that is, one would have to have a separate symbol for
each token in all the languages and not only for each type. A transcription that
records as much phonetic detail as possible is said to be *narrow*. It was further
noticed that no language taken on its own terms required a completely narrow
transcription. Such a transcription could be replaced by a *broad* one in which
most of the detail could be dropped while still maintaining an unambiguous
representation of the actual pronunciation of the language. The narrow transcription belongs to the realm of general or universal phonetics, phonetics for
its own sake, whereas the principle of the broad transcription is language-
specific. A variant of it has in more recent times also been referred to as systematic
phonetics.

Thus, for a human analyst, a perfect narrow transcription was a dead end,
although (sound) spectrograms (visible speech) now render similar service.
The other end of phonetics, however, has been more amenable to linguistic
treatment. Here we encounter the question of how broad a phonetic transcription
can be without violating the functional distinctions made by the language.
Phonetics in this framework was called *functional*, and an enormous amount

of work has been directed toward the principles and procedures for arriving at this level of phonetics. These principles are generally known as *phonemic analysis*, and the functional phonetic surface units as *phonemes*. Contrary to general belief, the phoneme was intended as a practical (rather than theoretical) help in writing down and analyzing the utterances of a language, with a minimum of symbols and without sacrificing the relevant distinctions, because a key permits an unambiguous mapping of the phonemes into the actual sounds and vice versa. A phonemic notation is one that does not write any phonetic detail that can be predicted from this notation. In other words, phonemic analysis is a handy storing procedure when we do not want or need to carry around minute phonetic detail in our operations. The key converts the phonemes back to sound when necessary. This technique is similar to the dehydration of food, also for practical purposes: water can be put back when needed. That is, these procedures do not replace phonetics or water, they just do without them for some purposes.

[10.2 Contrast and Minimal Pairs]   The structure of phonemic analysis will be very important in the other analytic techniques to be treated in subsequent sections, and thus it will be useful to paraphrase it here briefly. (The procedures we shall be discussing are also available in most elementary textbooks of synchronic linguistics.) As was mentioned above, one correlates sound with meaning to find out what sounds are used to differentiate meanings. Sounds that occur in the same environments and distinguish words/morphemes are said to contrast, for example, English [kʰæp] *cap* and [gæp] *gap*. Sounds that occur in the same environment without meaning or word differentiation, for example, [gæp, gæpʰ] *gap* are noncontrastive and belong to the same phoneme. In this case, where the final labial of *gap* can be either aspirated or not, we have a case of free variation. Often the distribution of the sounds is environmentally restricted; for example, we have a front (palatal) [k̑ʰ] in *keep* before a front vowel, a neutral [kʰ] in *car* before a low central vowel, and a back liproundish [kʷʰ] in *cool* before a back rounded vowel. In this case, we have complementary distribution. Exchanging one *k* for another in these words, if for some reason one would want to, does not make any functional difference in English; all are members, variants, or (allo-)phones of one phoneme /k/. However, one would indeed produce unnatural pronunciation, as the reader can eaily verify, by positioning (placing) his tongue for *keep* and then pronouncing *cool*. Similarly, the bright [lʹ] in *light*, the dark [ł] in *tell*, the dorsal [ʟ] in *milk*, and the voiceless [l̥] in *play* occur in one lateral phoneme /l/ in English, but not so in Russian, where the bright and dark *l*'s are not interchangeable, [stolʹ] 'so', [stoł] 'table'— hence separate phonemes /lʹ/ and /l/. The *h*'s in *hut, hot, hat,* and *hit* are all quite different, [hₐ, hₐ, hₐₑ, hᵢ], in fact voiceless nonsyllabic vowels, [ʌ̥, ɑ̥, æ̥, ɪ̥]; what is distinctive here is the voiceless glottal friction, its timbre being determined by the following vowel. There is thus only one phoneme /h/, which has even more allophones than listed here.

Minimal pairs like *cap* vs. *gap* are very helpful to have, and English is full of them. The same is true of Finnish, in which all eight vowels can be defined with a minimal octuple:

	(1)		(2)		(3)
tikin	'of a stitch'	*tykin*	'of a cannon'	*tukin*	'of a stock'
tekin	'also ye'	*tökin*	'I push'	*tokin*	'with reindeer herds'
		täkin	'of a quilt'	*takin*	'of a coat'

The situation requires eight different units (see Rotuman, § 4.6).

To sum up, according to one conception phonemes are classes of sounds, sets of allophones, which contrast with other such classes (sets), for example, English:

$$/k/ \quad /l/ \quad /h/$$

$$\begin{bmatrix} K^{(h)} \\ k^{w(h)} \\ k^{(h)} \\ \vdots \\ \text{etc.} \end{bmatrix} \begin{bmatrix} l' \\ l \\ L \\ \mathring{l} \\ \vdots \\ \text{etc.} \end{bmatrix} \begin{bmatrix} \Lambda \\ \mathring{\varphi} \\ \mathring{æ} \\ \mathring{I} \\ \vdots \\ \text{etc.} \end{bmatrix}$$

keep	*leap*	*heap*
coop	*loop*	*hoop*
carp	(*milk*)	*harp*
etc.	(*play*)	

This principle of contrast is in itself quite simple and normally leads to satisfactory results. But in many cases the method (technique) of phonemic analysis brings the linguist only so far. When the method has given all the contrasts that it can, he will be completely on his own; he will then probably do some adjustments in borderline cases on the basis of his criteria of overall patterning, universals, and system slots, or his experience in general. That is, the complete final phonemic analyses of two linguists may not agree in detail, although a rigorous application of the analytic method might give both of them practically the same results. This final indeterminacy is very important to remember, not only because it has such a prominent role in linguistic literature, where a reader must always find out for himself what kind of an analysis has been used by the authors he consults, but also because it will recur in the purely historical methods. As examples of these difficulties, let us review some typical cases where the results of the method are retailored by the linguist.

[10.3 Postediting and the Role of the Linguist]   One frequent indeterminacy in the area of segmental sounds is 'one or two phonemes' (unit or cluster)? In English, [tšɪn] *chin* contrasts with [džɪn] *gin*, ([tʰɪn] *tin*, [dɪn] *din*, and [šɪn] *shin*). Because of patterning and other criteria, many linguists phonemicize these as /čin/ and /jin/, although /č/ never contrasts with the sequence /tš/. The /č/-notation is still quite unambiguous: initially it is preceded by stress onset, whereas /t/ and /š/ are separated by one (*why choose* vs. *white shoes*). Here, then, many linguists are happy to remain below the level of strict phonemics, even when this stress onset can be written as a juncture or boundary;

that is, /+ č/ vs. /t + š/ could as well and even better be /+ tš/ vs. /t + š/. Often these junctures require grammatical information, and generally they are used freely in editing the results of the method. In German, there are a few cases where the palatal and velar spirants contrast, for example, [ku·çən] *Kuhchen* 'little cow' and [ku·xən] *Kuchen* 'cake, pastry'. The occurrence of the variants can be predicted grammatically, and one generally writes the morpheme boundary in *Kuh + chen*, that is, /ku· + xən/. Such pairs are peripheral in German, it is true, and they always involve the diminutive, for example, *Tauchen* 'little rope' vs. *tauchen* 'dive', *Schlauchen* 'little sly one' vs. *schlauchen* 'to use a hose for filling a barrel', or almost minimal pairs in *Pfauchen* 'little peacock' vs. *fauchen* 'hiss' and *Frauchen* 'little woman' vs. *rauchen* 'smoke'. It is also rather difficult to find a native speaker who would acknowledge all these forms.

Linguists differ greatly in their use of such boundary markers or junctures. Many factors play a role here, for example, the tradition of the language, or the linguistic school in which the linguist was trained, or simply the linguist's preferences for theory or even for some kind of implicit elegance. Thus a junctural analysis may be rejected for one language (e.g., English above) and preferred for another (e.g., German above), even by the same linguist.

The stops in *spill*, *still*, and *skill* are complementary to both /p, t, k/ and /b, d, g/. After [s] in initial position, only a lax unaspirated voiceless stop occurs. If *that's tough* and *that stuff* can be [ðætstʰʌf] and [ðætstʌf] without indication of stress onset, as they, in fact, sometimes are, we would seem to have a contrast in the dentals. Such pronunciations, however, are extremely peripheral, and this is why one relies on the position of the stress onset, which makes the dentals complementary: /ðæts'təf/ vs. /ðæt'stəf/; stress onset correlates well with morpheme boundaries *that's + tough* and *that + stuff*, because some boundaries can always be phonetically implemented. In some varieties of English, the pronunciation of *stuff* is auditorily (at least) identified with *duff* /dəf/, if the [s] is somehow eliminated (e.g., through tape erasure). English /d/ is a lax stop in many dialects, and voice is apparently not the distinctive feature in it. Thus, in this variety of English, *still* should be written /sdil/. Very few linguists do it —apparently for orthographical and practical cross-dialectal reasons.

[10.4] It is possible to perceive five degrees of phonetic vowel length in English *bit*, *bid*, *beat*, *bee*, and *bead*. The method groups them in two functional units, *bit*, *bid* vs. the rest, that is, it tells that the vowels in *bit* and *beat* contrast. It remains for the linguist to interpret the contrast and devise a notation for writing it. In this particular case, four approaches have been taken: (1) lax /ɪ/ vs. tense /i/, (2) single /i/ vs. its occurrence twice /ii/, (3) /i/ vs. its occurrence followed by a length phoneme /i:/, and (4) /i/ vs. a diphthong /iy/. A very famous problem of English length occurs in those American dialects where both /t/ and /d/ are replaced by a medial flap [ɒ]. Now the length difference in *bit* vs. *bid* becomes distinctive, as in [bɪɒər] *bitter* vs. [bɪ·ɒər] *bidder*, and, similarly, in *writer–rider*, *matter–madder*, *latter–ladder*, and so on. (Such differences of length may, in a few dialects, be supported by other minimal pairs, for example, *adze–adds, Polly–Pāli*, and so on; compare § 9.14.) The flap itself is complementary to both /t/ and /d/, and its assignment to either one is impossible; thus, by the strict principles of phonemic analysis, it should be a phoneme by itself, /D/; compare *still*, which should be /sdil/ in some dialects, but which, contrary to such an identification is universally written as /stil/. The importance of the method is that it pinpoints the differences in [rayDər] and [ra·yDər], for example. It is at this point that the linguists usually leave the method and rephonemicize *shortness + flap* as /t/ and *length + flap* as /d/, for reasons dictated by the rest of the grammar, for example, the relationship with /rayt/ vs. /rayd/. Then, of course, many generative phonologists would say that one should not use such a phonemic method in the first place. Be that as it may, in actual practice they implicitly use something very similar.

[10.5] Another example of the problems encountered when postediting the results of the strict phonemic method, and one that also deals with length, can be taken from the Turku dialect of Finnish. It also involves the flap, which in the English problem was written with [D] to emphasize entanglement with dental stops; but, in Finnish, it is a case of *r*'s, and the flap will be written [ř], while a lengthened *r* will be written with a macron, [r̄]. In brief, we have three degrees of length in the *r*: a single flap, two to three vibrations, and several vibrations: [sořan] 'of war', [soran] 'of gravel', and [sor̄an] 'I oppress'; and [kuřin] 'knitting', [kurin] 'of discipline', and [kur̄in] 'of nonfat milk'. Of course, such minimal pairs must always be accounted for, even if we do not accept the three different *r*'s that result from the use of the blind phonemic method. Three degrees of length are not general (systematic) in Finnish; so one can indeed assign the flap to a /d/, and the resulting two degrees of length are interpreted in terms of approach (2) above, giving us the three forms, now identical with Standard Finnish *sodan, soran, sorran*, and so on. These two dialects have the "same" phoneme /d/ with different phonetics, Standard [d] and Turku [ř]. But three degrees of length are normal in Estonian: [lina] 'flax', [linna] 'of town', and [linnna] 'into town'; [koli] 'trash', [kooli] 'of school', and [koooli] 'into school'—no matter how length would be phonemicized in a final analysis. The method merely locates this situation for the linguist, who must interpret it.

One way of collapsing the number of phonemes resulting from the application of the strict method is to establish feature phonemes; for example, in the table of Finnish vowels (§ 10.2) we can combine columns 2 and 3 by positing a special fronting feature F for 2: Ftukin, Ftokin, Ftakin. This F fronts all the back vowels within one word (the definition of "word" is unnecessary here), for example, Fruusulla = ryysyllä 'with a rag' vs. ruusulla 'with a rose'. In the case of English *rider* we saw that two units, length and flap, were written by one symbol, /d/, and here we see that one unit can be written by two symbols, F, plus back vowels. Any survey of the practice of phonemic analysis frequently runs into cases of this kind.

What has been emphasized in this brief review of phonemic analysis is the method, which is there to help the analyst. A perfect narrow transcription is impossible, but the phonemic method enables us to draw a fairly clear boundary as an end point to the broadest functional phonetics. We have seen that linguists, for reasons both theoretical and practical, often do not need such clear boundaries. But linguists still must know the method and how far it can take them in any particular case. The method must remain a servant and should not take over as the primary goal in normal linguistic investigation.

[10.6 Analysis and Synthesis]   The method as presented here is necessarily analytic. The phoneme was defined above as a class of phone types occurring in mutually exclusive environments, or sometimes, in the case of free variation, even in the same environment. This fact stresses the item-and-arrangement framework in the initial stages of analysis when we aim at the units. This framework takes the items, for example, phones, as independent entities, which shun each other in complementary environments, like magnetism of the same polarity. The method lays bare the variants and their environments, which will then be the targets of synthesis, that is, the rules for mapping the units back to their manifestations, or the process framework. One must add at this point that the phones of a phoneme must share at least one distinctive feature, one phonetic quality that is constant in all the allophones of the same phoneme; that is, a phoneme is also a bundle of such features. In this sense a phoneme is a constant, and this is why it is labeled with one constant symbol. In other words, in this conception one emphasizes the constant in the variants and lets all the environmental differences be assigned to this constant unit when taking it to the environments where it occurs. Clearly these two ways of looking at variation are different aspects of one and the same thing. Much confusion has arisen from the fact that the analytic and synthetic aspects of investigation have not been kept conceptually separate. Analysis, then, is an item-and-arrangement mechanism that allows us to establish relevant units. One should not forget that these units are all-important to synthesis, the process mechanism that assigns rules to these units and brings them back to the starting point of analysis. Units are impossible without rules and vice versa (§§ 1.9, 17.6, 22.1, 22.2). Units are the end points of analysis and the starting points of synthesis; variants are the starting points of analysis and the end points of synthesis. Unfortunately, these statements about analysis and synthesis are rather crude oversimplifications, which, however, cannot be avoided in an introduction. But they are helpful guidelines for the beginner. From the point of view of the speaker, the phoneme is perhaps not always that important, because he is a synthesizer who applies rules starting with units higher than the phoneme—the morphophonemes—and ends up with physical sound tokens—the variants, that is, the allophones (compare the end of § 4.12), but we must repeat, for the hearer—the analyzer—phonemics seems to be of greater logical weight, because it is the level of phonology at which the maximum information for differentiating meanings is given; that is, it is really functional phonetics, which triggers his decoding machinery. Interestingly enough, the position of comparative linguistics is parallel to that of the hearer;

history produces an output of sound and meaning, and the linguist has to work the data backward toward the deeper origins. Reconstruction is a predictive inference; that is, we "generate" part of the past, as it were, and we do this initially with the analytic item-and-arrangement method, which is the comparative method (Chapter 11).

As a final reminder, it is very useful to remember that a coin has two sides, that is, that there are different complementary aspects of methods and their domains in linguistic investigation in general. These two aspects with their characteristic constituents can be listed in two columns (and these should, again, be taken only as helpful cardinal points that enable the beginner to organize his thinking about various aspects of linguistics):

analysis	synthesis
item-and-arrangement	process
units	rules
comparative linguistics	historical linguistics
hearer/linguist	speaker
induction (see § 9.16f.)	deduction

Some linguists believe that a native hearer analyzes by synthesis only, but the notion of "analysis-by-synthesis" is too one-sided to be of so much value. It does, of course, occur to a great degree because hearers are also speakers and can use contextual information for interpretation. A person who has to start with pure analysis is a nonnative hearer, a linguist.

This discussion of phonemic analysis is extremely sketchy; its purpose is just to recall the basic principles of the method. Many linguists, for theoretical reasons, emphatically reject the kind of analytic phoneme described here, but we must repeat once more the two main practical reasons why the concept and the method must be known even to genetic linguists: access to past publications (written in that framework) and access to the other methods. This will become clear in the subsequent sections. The better one knows phonemic analysis, the easier it will be to handle the other analytic methods.

MORPHOPHONEMIC ANALYSIS

[10.7 Inclusion of Grammatical Environments and Sets]   In the postediting examples of the previous sections (§§ 10.3–10.5), we saw that linguists have generally been ready to let grammatical criteria enter phonemic notations, but only to a small degree, because phonemics was primarily meant as a kind of (linguistic) phonetics (for one language). It would defeat its own purpose if the whole grammar should bear upon it. This does not mean that the grammar would not somehow be tied to it, but only that in a phonemic notation the aim is generally to write only details that cannot be predicted from the phonetic environment. Since we have now seen that all kinds of nonphonetic criteria usually do creep into phonemics, the question arises as to how much grammatical information should be allowed at the other end of phonology. The answer is, clearly, all there is (subject only to psychological reality in synchronic grammar; see §§ 4.5, 4.8, 6.24, 10.9, 18.17). This aspect of phonology is widely known as *morphophonemics* or *mor(pho)phonology*. A morphophonemic notation minimizes or eliminates altogether the regular or automatic alternations within the variants of morphemes; it does not indicate any phonetic/phonemic detail that can be predicted from the rest of the grammar. A phonemic level need not be a prerequisite here, because it is merely the most systematic phonetic level, and in fact many linguists skip it ('level' need not be understood literally; it may stand for any area somehow delimited, e.g., by rules of some kind). These maximally invariant phonological units of morphophonemics will be called *morphophonemes*, but they have been also called (and still are) *systematic phonemes*.

The method for arriving at the morphophonemes is the same as that used in phonemic analysis. Instead of to sound segments, phones, we apply it to sets of corresponding sound units (phones or phonemes), to units that occur in related morphs, to variants of the same morpheme. And instead of allowing only for phonetic conditioning in the distribution of the variants, we also allow for grammatical conditioning. Generally, however, what the method does is to contrast such sets to find out which sets are needed to distinguish morphemes. This means that one writes the morphemes involved with such sets and finds out whether the sets differentiate meanings or not, exactly as one does in phonemic analysis to simple sound segments. For example, in English, we have the phonemic contrasts /iy/ *seat*:/e/ *set*, /ay/ *fine*:/i/ *fin*, and /ey/ *vain*:/æ/ *van*, but these oppositions do not necessarily hold when we group the phonemes according to the paradigmatic sets of the language, for example (concentrating here on the vowels only):

A

1	**iy** / **e**	l|ea|ve / l|e|ft	k|ee|p / k|e|pt	d|ee|p / d|e|pth	ser|e|ne / ser|e|nity
2	**ay** / **i**	dr|i|ve / dr|i|ven	ch|i|ld / ch|i|ldren	w|i|de / w|i|dth	div|i|ne / div|i|nity
3	**ey** / **æ**	s|a|ne / s|a|nity	op|a|que / op|a|city	d|a|me / d|a|msel	Sp|ai|n / Sp|a|niard

B

| 1 | **iy** / **e** | r\|ea\|d (present) / r\|ea\|d (past) | br\|ee\|d / br\|e\|d | br\|ea\|the V / br\|ea\|th N |
| 2 | **ay** / **i** | b\|i\|te / b\|i\|t | h\|i\|de / h\|i\|d | etc. |

Traditional orthography has been retained, both as a matter of convenience and because it will give an example of the conservative nature of writing systems (§ 2.4). The sets of correspondences have been boxed in for maximal clarity (see § 3.2, and compare § 8.12), and the reader should make himself familiar with this convention, because it will recur in the following sections. The box notation is valuable because it makes the set similar to the sound segment (phone), and thus stresses their structural and functional identity as far as the method is concerned, although it would not really matter how we wrote these alternations. This boxed-in set captures the essence of a group that behaves like a unit.

A close look at group A immediately reveals that no grammatical conditioning is needed for the alternations, in spite of what has been stressed before, although the alternations do of course occur in grammatically identical morphs. Morpho-phonemic alternation can quite well be phonetically conditioned. Here the diphthongs occur in word-final syllables ending in a single consonant (except for the *l* in *child*), and the short vowels, before a consonant cluster or before following unstressed syllables. In group B, on the other hand, we seem to have pure grammatical conditioning, because the consonantal skeleton of these paradigms is constant (although not quite in /briyð ~ breθ/, which will be discussed below), and the vowels alternate only in terms of the grammatical categories. But appearances are here deceptive, because a comparison of A and B shows that the groups are complementary in terms of their phonemic shapes: group B contains words ending in dentals only, and the two categories occurring with short vowels here have dental stops in A (e.g., *kep-t*, *dep-th*). For example, when the morph ends in a dental stop or spirant, there is no dental ending, unless the base and the suffix have different manners of articulation (*wid-th*). However, the vocalism behaves as if there were consonant clusters in the second rows of the alternations in B. The expected clusters would be geminates (double or long stops), which do not occur in this position in the phonetic manifestation in Modern English. Here, then, the environments of the two groups are complementary in terms of the sounds and can thus be written in the same way, for example (tentatively), *read-d*, *breath-th*. It is also quite clear that the boxed-in sets of correspondences are units by themselves and can be written with one symbol (as is somewhat typical of English orthography), say, *E*, *I*, and *A* (*dEp/dEp-th*, *hId/hId-d*, *sAn-ity*, and so on; see § 2.4). Exact minimal pairs are difficult to find, but as a matter of illustration let us use an archaic past tense *rid* of *ride* (which may still be the norm in some dialects). Now we have a minimal pair with *read*:

$$r \boxed{i} de \qquad \boxed{ay} \quad vs. \quad \boxed{iy} \qquad r \boxed{ea} d \quad (present)$$
$$r \boxed{i} d \qquad \boxed{i} \qquad\qquad \boxed{e} \qquad r \boxed{ea} d \quad (past)$$

The *r*- and *d*-sets are constant, and thus the vowel sets do differentiate meanings and, consequently, contrast. This becomes clearer once we write the vocalic sets with single symbols (letters) *rId* vs. *rEd* (compare a German minimal pair,

§ 10.10). This is quite parallel to, say, /pin/ *pin* vs. /pen/ *pen*. Thus the past-tense forms *rId-d* and *rEd-d* assume the vocalism *ridd* and *redd*, and, finally, a geminate is simplified, giving /rid/ and /red/ *read*. (Historically, this analysis of *ride/rid* is wrong, because the paradigm derives from the type *drive/drove/driven*.) In other words, the vowels tell us that there is a morphophonemic dental suffix in these forms. This suffix has no other manifestation.

These same alternations do seem to occur under grammatical conditioning in, for example *-teen/ten*, *life/live* V /liv/ (the adjective /layv/ *live* has the same vocalism as the noun; the difference in spirants will be treated below), but we cannot pursue them here, because our purpose is to show the method, not how far the method can take us.

[10.8] Grammatical conditioning of morphophonemic alternation is obvious in the English umlaut plurals:

singular	uw		t	oo	th	g	oo	se		aw	m	ou	se	l	ou	se
plural	iy		t	ee	th	g	ee	se		ay	m	i	ce	l	i	ce

These cases are so few that one would not necessarily set up special morphophonemic vowels for them (see § 4.5), but more compelling evidence can be found for the following consonant alternations:

singular	f		wi	f	e	kni	f	e	sta	ff	
plural	v		wi	v	es	kni	v	es	sta	v	es

singular	θ		clo	th		mou	th		pa	th	
plural	ð		clo	th	es	mou	th	s	pa	th	s

singular	s		hou	s	e
plural	z		hou	s	es

These alternating spirants contrast with the invariant ones in *chief/chiefs*, *faith/faiths*, and so on, so that there has been reason to posit two morphophonemic classes of spirants. Here again one does run into indeterminacy, but a completely regular pattern is found in

N	f		grie	f	e	belie	f	e	sa	f	e
V	v		grie	v	e	belie	v	e	sa	v	e

N	θ		too	th		wrea	th		brea	th	
V	ð		tee	th	e	wrea	th	e	brea	th	e

N	s		gla	ss		advi	c	e	hou	s	e	u	s	e
V	z		gla	z	e	advi	s	e	hou	s	e	u	s	e

The corresponding verb is derived from the underlying noun or adjective by voicing the final spirant (this inference is, of course, based on the reversal of what happened, see § 4.2). In these cases, the voiceless variant occurs in the environment *Noun* and the voiced one in the environment *Verb*. Hence they do not contrast, although there is a clear phonemic opposition between theta [θ] and edh [ð] (*thigh/thy*). Morphophonemically, they tend to be completely complementary, in that edh occurs in grammatical environments, mainly in deictics (*this, that, hither,* and so on); a handful of exceptions like *faiths, rhythm,* and *edh* break the pattern. Clear grammatical conditioning of alternations occurs in English paradigms like *sing/sang/sung,* although this particular three-part alternation itself is limited to the position next to a nasal (*swim, begin, ring, sink,* and so on; see Chapter 12).

The method, then, is the same as that of phonemic analysis, as has been constantly stressed in this discussion. For example, the four sets

$$\text{eva}\begin{bmatrix}d\\s\end{bmatrix}\text{e} \quad \text{gene}\begin{bmatrix}t\\s\end{bmatrix}\text{ic} \quad \text{permi}\begin{bmatrix}t\\ss\end{bmatrix}\text{is} \quad \text{permi}\begin{bmatrix}t\\ss\end{bmatrix} \quad \text{opa}\begin{bmatrix}q\\c\end{bmatrix}\text{ue} = \begin{bmatrix}k\\s\end{bmatrix} \quad \text{ma}\begin{bmatrix}ss\\ss\end{bmatrix}\text{ive} = \begin{bmatrix}s\\s\end{bmatrix}$$

share an /s/, but the "upper" members of the sets make them contrast and consequently we need four different labels for the sets: |d|, |t|, |k|, and |s|. When one finds other sets that share members with these, one again tries to see whether they are variants of the ones already established or independent, for example,

$$\text{Gree}\begin{bmatrix}k\\c\end{bmatrix}\text{ian} = \begin{bmatrix}k\\š\end{bmatrix} \quad \text{spea}\begin{bmatrix}k\\ch\end{bmatrix} = \begin{bmatrix}k\\tš\end{bmatrix} \quad \text{so}\begin{bmatrix}c\\c\end{bmatrix}\text{iety} = \begin{bmatrix}s\\š\end{bmatrix}$$

The first two sets do not contrast with $\begin{bmatrix}k\\s\end{bmatrix}$, and the last is a variant of $\begin{bmatrix}s\\s\end{bmatrix}$,

although its orthography points to |k|. Note now the structural similarity of the English phoneme /k/ and its morphophoneme |k|, as exemplified in Figure 10-1.

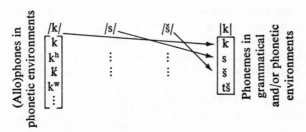

FIGURE 10-1. The parallelism between the phoneme and the morphophoneme.

[10.9] In many cases there remain peripheral alternations that are unique or extremely limited in number. In such cases it does not pay to establish special morphophonemic symbols, and linguists usually treat them as exceptions of some kind, for example, something related to suppletion. Many English speakers do not associate *bleak* and *bleach* in their synchronic knowledge of the language, in spite of the close similarity in meaning and phonetic shape of the two words. There are other examples of this /k ~ tš/ alternation, for example, *break/breach* (where the second member is a derived noun), *stink/stench* (where the second member is a derived causative), and *duke/duchess* (where the second member is a derived feminine). Parallel to these are *stick/stitch* and *drink/drench*, but these are now synchronically separate although historically the same. Of course, there are also many types of alternation in the vocalism of these forms but we shall ignore them here. Thus, in a synchronic description, one has to posit two different forms like |stik| and |stitš|. This has clearly happened, that is, it has become obligatory, for *book* and *beech*, which once were closely connected in the same way—not to speak of other more opaque cases like *wrinkle* 'clever trick' and *wrench* 'false interpretation' (both from a root originally meaning 'twist'). Such "exceptions" are a nuisance in a synchronic grammar, although they show a fair amount of regularity; but they are often the main source for historical hints in connection with internal reconstruction, the historical side of morphophonemic analysis (Chapters 12, 18). Thus the method should always be carried as far as possible, because it turns up handy stepping-stones into history. For the synchronic grammar, the debris from the use of this aspect of the method creates an area of considerable reshuffling, which surpasses that of phonemic analysis. Here, too, one eventually reaches a level where the services of the method become redundant or useless in the synchronic context (§ 9.19).

[10.10] The morphophonemic situation in English is quite typical; compare the phonetic conditioning in German,

	singular	bun|t|	bun|t|
	pl./dat.	bun|t|e	bun|d|e

where the sets differentiate minimal pairs and need different labels. Modern German orthography, in fact, uses invariant symbols for both words, according to morphophonemic principles, *bunt* 'multicolored' and *Bund* 'league'. Russian has a similar situation, both in sound and orthography. But grammatical conditioning is apparent in many German verbal paradigms, for example,

schnei|d|en sie|d|en = |d| vs. |t| = rei|t|en schel|t|en
geschni|tt|en geso|tt|en |t| |t| geri|tt|en geschol|t|en
'cut'   'boil'   'ride'   'scold'

Whatever the ultimate assignment of these sets, they contrast and belong to different morphophonemes (compare English *seethe/sodden* and *ride/ridden*). But in German also one reaches a point when a combination of alternants ceases to be profitable; for example, it is clear that we have the same alternation as in *schneiden/geschnitten* between the following sets:

'hand'	han $\boxed{t}$	vs.	han $\boxed{t}$ ieren	'handle'
'trade'	han $\boxed{d}$ el(n)		han $\boxed{t}$ el	'hand bar'

No environment could specify the conditioning of the variants (except within the first set which is of the *Bund/Bunde* type). Thus the second pair will probably contain an unalternating |t|, because otherwise the alternation would have to be listed by a special feature to secure the occurrence of /t/ or [t]. Surely a |t| to begin with is much simpler.

[10.11 Application to "Exotic" Languages]   Students tend to let the mere appearance of an unfamiliar language paralyze them so that they are unable to *apply* the method that they already know quite well. On the other hand, their native language may also seriously interfere with the *method*, because they know the material too well, and the simplistic method looks superfluous. Both aspects are important in the training of a linguist. One should apply the method to one's own language, whose raw materials one can both master and verify, because the results of the method are valid only to the degree that the facts to which it is applied are also valid. But the application of the method to "exotic" languages teaches the linguist not to be afraid of "weird" shapes. No matter how the language is written and what kind of sequences of written symbols occur, the method can be applied to them (with the exception of logographic writing). The case is quite clear with alphabetic writing, because it represents the sounds rather closely and regularly, even if not perfectly. For the application of the method, one need not know the exact phonetics of the language. As examples of "exotic" languages we shall take selections from Finnish and Lapp. Both are far simpler than English, because in English one runs so easily into all kinds of peripheral cases like *man/men*, *bleak/bleach*, and so on, whereas the alternations we shall see in the Finnish and Lapp examples pervade the whole language with overwhelming regularity.

[10.12]   Finnish morphophonemic alternations are on the whole phonetically/phonologically conditioned. Let us first look at three sets involving the front vowels /i/ and /e/, and the dentals /s/, /t/, and /d/ (all are clearly phonemes: *sitä* 'it' [partitive], *setä* 'uncle'; *suuri* 'big', *tuuri* 'luck', and *duuri* 'major key'), as they are arranged in Figure 10-2. These particular words have been chosen to represent the seven particular sets labeled 1–7, that is, three vowel sets and four dental sets. They could be multiplied by the dozens and even by the hundreds. Minimal pairs also exist; for example, the last vowel set in *nalli* 'percussion cap' is set 3 against 1 in *nalle*, and the last vowel set in *syli* 'fathom' is set 2 and the one in *syli* 'lap' is 3, or further *Pete* 'Pete' with set 1 and *peti* with 3,

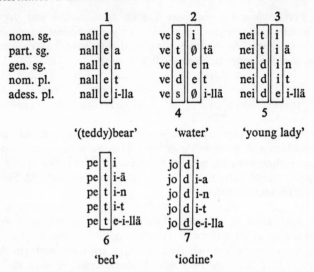

	1	2	3
nom. sg.	nall\[e\]	ve\[s|i\]	nei\[t|i\]
part. sg.	nall\[e\]a	ve\[t|∅\]tä	nei\[t|i\]ä
gen. sg.	nall\[e\]n	ve\[d|e\]n	nei\[d|i\]n
nom. pl.	nall\[e\]t	ve\[d|e\]t	nei\[d|i\]t
adess. pl.	nall\[e\]i-lla	ve\[s|∅\]i-llä	nei\[d|e\]i-llä
		4	5
	'(teddy)bear'	'water'	'young lady'

	6	7
	pe\[t\]i	jo\[d\]i
	pe\[t\]i-ä	jo\[d\]i-a
	pe\[t\]i-n	jo\[d\]i-n
	pe\[t\]i-t	jo\[d\]i-t
	pe\[t\]e-i-llä	jo\[d\]e-i-lla
	'bed'	'iodine'

FIGURE 10-2. A selection of Finnish front vowel and dental sets (limited to five forms out of twenty-eight).

and so on. For practical purposes these words have been quoted in the nominative singular only, because more of the paradigm is supplied in Figure 10-2 through other items. The sets are labeled numerically because the method has not yet shown which ones, if any, have to be grouped together. Now, because of such minimal pairs, these three Finnish front vowel sets clearly contrast, exactly like the dentals in German *bunt* vs. *Bund*. Within sets 2 and 3 the alternation is, of course, environmentally conditioned: in 3 /e/ occurs only before *i*, and /i/ occurs elsewhere; in 2 the vowel is syncopated before the plural *i* and the partitive morph *-tä*, and is replaced by *i* in final position (nom. sg.); and in 1 *e* is unalternating all the way. Sets 1 and 2 contrast only in stem-final position; elsewhere we have sets like 1, for example, the first vowels in *vesi*, *neiti*, and *peti*. This situation reminds us of the English flap problem encountered in phonemic analysis (§ 10.4), that is, there is a contrast only in one particular environment, and indeterminacy in the assignment of initial vowels (to either 1 or 2). We shall return to this, but for now let us go by the method, which gives us three morphophonemes, say, 1 = |e₁|, 2 = |e₂|, 3 = |i|.

Turning now to the dental sets we can immediately see that 6 and 7 contrast: 6 is unalternating /t/, and 7 unalternating /d/. Set 5 shares both /t/ and /d/ and thus clearly contrasts with both 6 and 7. The alternation is phonetically conditioned: /t/ occurs in open syllables, /d/ in closed ones. Thus, from the end, the sets can be labeled, for example, 7, |d|, 6, |t₁|, and 5, |t₂|. There remains set 4, which shares /t/ and /d/ with |t₂| (5), but otherwise shows an extra dimension in having /s/ in addition. Because of this /s/, it has been taken as another independent set contrasting with |t₂|, say |t₃|, but a closer look reveals that the occurrence of /s/ is environmentally conditioned. It occurs only before the morphophoneme |e₂| (2), which syncopates before the plural *i* and turns into an *i* in final position. Only these two *i*'s assibilate (in nouns); the conditioning is thus morphophonemic. In other words, set 4 is a variant of the morphophoneme |t₂| (5).

[10.13]   The /t ~ d/ alternation is part of the consonant gradation (which is simply alternation between certain consonants). Let us also take examples from velars, because this material will be important in later discussion as well. Because the alternation is conditioned by the structure of the syllable in the beginning of which the sound occurs, we can reduce the sets to only two characteristic members (two is, of course, the minimum number of members in an alternation), which will be represented by the nominative singular (open syllable) and genetive singular (closed syllable). Now, all but one of the following sets share a /k/:

	8	8	9	9
nom. sg.	jo |k| i	i |k| ä	su |k| u	ky |k| y
gen. sg.	jo |Ø| en	i |Ø| än	su |v| un	ky |v| yn
	'river'	'age'	'family'	'ability'

	10	10	11	12
	syl |k| i	jär |k| i	mu |k| i	lii |g| a
	syl |j| en	jär |j| en	mu |k| in	lii |g| an
	'saliva'	'intelligence'	'mug'	'league'

Again, starting from the end, sets 12 and 11 clearly contrast, and one can establish morphophonemes: 12 = |g| and 11 = |k₁|. Sets 8–10 share the open-syllable member with 11, but otherwise contrast with the closed-syllable variants and hence are different. These variants are completely governed by their phonetic environments, /j/ occurs between liquids /l, r/ and /e/ (10), /v/ is flanked by high rounded vowels (9), and nothing occurs in other environments (8, and others not exemplified here). Hence the sets 8–10 are variants of one unit, say |k₂|. In all these examples, it has been relatively easy to segment the sequences into sets; that is, one just cuts out the alternating part and keeps the rest of the word as it is. Basically, we have been cutting at the impressionistic seams between vowels and consonants. Segmentation need not observe such seams, as is shown by the long-stop words in which two ways of segmenting are possible:

		13
ka |t| o vs.	ka |tt| o or	kat |t| o
ka |d| on	ka |t| on	kat |Ø| on
'loss'	'roof'	

$$\begin{array}{ccccc}
\text{su}\ \boxed{\text{k}}\ \text{a} & & \text{su}\ \boxed{\text{kk}}\ \text{a} & & \text{suk}\ \boxed{\text{k}}\ \text{a} \\
\text{su}\ \boxed{\emptyset}\ \text{an} & \text{vs.} & \text{su}\ \boxed{\text{k}}\ \text{an} & \text{or} & \text{suk}\ \boxed{\emptyset}\ \text{an} \\
\text{'brush'} & & \text{'sock'} & &
\end{array}$$

The important fact is that the method does confront the minimal pairs here in either case. The second analysis definitely seems to be better for *sukka*, because it does not require any new machinery (i.e , set 8 includes this environment, too), and for *katto* we would get a new variant (13) of the morphophoneme |t₂|

$|t_2|$

(5). All this agrees with the analysis that length in Finnish is taken as a double occurrence of the single unit.

So far we have been treating Finnish morphophonemic alternations that are phonetically/phonologically conditioned, just like most of the English alternations above. But Finnish also has cases parallel to English *tooth/teeth/teethe*, *wreath/wreathe*, and so on:

$$\begin{array}{llll}
\text{tah}\ \boxed{\text{t}}\ \text{o-mme} & \text{N} & \text{'our wish'} \\
\text{tah}\ \boxed{\text{d}}\ \text{o-mme} & \text{V} & \text{'we wish' (§ 4.23)}
\end{array}$$

$$\begin{array}{llll}
\text{mä}\ \boxed{\text{k}}\ \text{-is-tä} & \text{adj.} & \text{'hilly' (part.)} \\
\text{mä}\ \boxed{\emptyset}\ \text{-i-stä} & \text{N} & \text{'from the hills'}
\end{array}$$

The surface environments are exactly the same for both alternants; that is, in terms of the sounds that actually occur, the alternation is induced in clearly defined grammatical categories. In short, the possessive suffixes (*-mme*, and so on) do not induce consonant gradation, and neither does the adjective suffix *-ise-* (whose final vowel is |e₂| and thus drops in the partitive).

[10.14] The morphophonemic alternations known as Lapp consonant gradation are grammatically conditioned in the rather limited selection we are going to look at. In Finnish, only certain stops participate in the gradation, but in Lapp, all consonants are subject to it. The sample in Figure 10-3 is from East (Skolt) Lapp (most distinctions of a narrow transcription are ignored here). Simply stripping off diacritics is not a legitimate way of making a narrow notation broad, but here we resort to it in the name of pedagogy. The transcription still looks more forbidding than did the one for Finnish, because it has more diacritic marks and longer sequences alternate with shorter ones. But linguists should not be carried away by looks and should concentrate on the underlying structure. The selection concentrates on only a few consonants, and most of the vowels have been reproduced very crudely. Thus the nominative of 'age' and the genitive of 'old woman' are given as *āhkke* even though there is actually a slight difference in the first vowels (a slightly higher front *a* in 'age'). Lapp is another language famous for three distinctive degrees of length; for example, set 18 has *kō∂∂a/kō∂a* and the lative case of the same word is *ko∂∂a* (see Estonian in § 10.5), a quantity that recurs in set 19 as well. For length we can note here only the following cases (which are by no means all those drawn in the handbooks); writing any consonant by *x*: *x* (short), *x̀* (halflong), *x̄* (long), *x̆x* (short geminate), *xx* (halflong geminate), *x̄x* (overlong geminate). These will recur below. Small capitals represent half-voiced stops. Now we are ready to start the analysis.

Set 16 contrasts with 18, and 17 with 19; the first pair has double stops, the second has overlong stops in the nominative. The genitives are the same for all and thus cannot be used for predicting the nominatives. The length difference in the nominative (16 and 18 vs. 17 and 19) is conditioned by the preceding

Dentals:

	14			15		16
inf.	koĮ D̄ eᴅ		*nom. sg.*	nieį D̄ a		kie htt a
1 sg.	kōl d am		*gen. sg.*	nie ð a		kie ð a
	'dig at random'			'young lady'		'hand'

17	18	19
ku hĩt a	kō ðð a	o ō̄ð a
kū ð a	kō ð a	ō ð a
'six'	'spawn'	'new'

Velars:

	20		20	21	22
nom. sg.	jo hꝁk a		so hꝁk a	ā hkk e	juoĮ Ḡ e
gen. sg.	jō ʏʏ a		sō ʏʏ a	ā ij e	juol g e
	'river'		'family'	'age'	'leg'

22	22
toĮ Ḡ e	tšoĮ Ḡ a
tōl g e	tšōl g a
'feather'	'saliva'

Corresponding longs:

	23			23	24	24
inf.	ka hĩt eᴅ		*nom. sg.*	nuo hĩt e	so hꝁk a	a hꝁk e
1 sg.	kā htt am		*gen. sg.*	nuo htt e	sō hkk a	ā hkk e
	'cover'			'seine'	'sock'	'old woman'

All consonants:

(other than stops)

25	26
ne m̄m a	kie ll a
nē m a	kie l a
'name'	'tongue'

FIGURE 10-3. A selection of East Lapp consonant alternations.

vowel. If the vowel is short (17, 19), the intervocalic stop is overlong; if long or a diphthong (16, 18), the stop is double. Indeed, this recurs in the rest of the material as well (20 vs. 21, 25 vs. 26). (Further evidence would show that such overlong stops occur only in nouns, not verbs, which is another interesting grammatical conditioning.) Now we can turn to sets 15 (genitive *ð* as in 16–19) and 14 (*Đ* as in 15). It is easy to see that 14 and 15 are complementary to 16–17; [htt] occurs between vowels and [Đ̄] after resonants (*palĐ̄eᴅ/pāldam* 'be afraid/ I am afraid', *kuŭ̯Đa/kuŭ̯ᴅa* (or *kuŭ̯ᴅa*) 'hay patch'), which are also long in the nominative. These same environments determine the occurrence of [ð̄] and [d] in the genitive. The consonants turn out to be always long in the nominative, and, in addition, a voiceless stop is preaspirated. All these dentals can be predicted from two units, which the method gives us, the morphophoneme |t| (14–17), and |d| (18–19). The same principles hold for the velar sets 20–22 as well: they are all environmentally conditioned and thus variants of one morphophoneme |k|. The longs are also here best taken as clusters of the single stops, |tt| (23) and |kk| (24). Also |m| (25) and |l| (26) are unambiguous starting points for the nominatives *nem̄ma* (overlong because of the preceding short vowel, which is long in the genitive only) and *kiella* (double because of the preceding diphthong). (Cf. §0.5)

Morphophonemic analysis is a method of establishing invariant sound units in the framework of paradigms or the total machinery of the grammar. We have seen how easily it eliminated consonant gradation from both Finnish and Lapp. The (mainly) phonological conditioning in Finnish and the grammatical conditioning in Lapp made no difference to the method. The Lapp situation would make one seriously suspect that the consonant alternations were originally determined by phonetic conditioning (compare *wreath/wreathe*, and so on, §§ 4.2, 4.5). And, indeed, if monosyllabic words had been included, they would have shown the genitive marker *-n:kī* 'who', *keä-n* 'whose' (compare Estonian *maa-n-tee*, the only relic of the genitive *-n* in that language; §§ 4.24, 5.15). Thus there is a section of vocabulary that retains the original phonological conditioning. This section confirms our suspicions. But the point is that morphophonemic analysis operates without such confirmation quite well; but such historical guesses need not be included in a pure synchronic context. (Cf. §11.27)

[10.15 Postediting As Adjustment Between Units and Rules]   When the method has given the units, one has to devise the mapping rules that define the shape of the units in each specific environment. That is, one has to use rules to come back to where one started out from (§§ 1.9, 10.6, 17.6). For example, in Finnish (with ordered rules) we have

(1)   Drop of |e₂| after *t* before partitive *-tä* and plural *-i-*: *vettä, vetillä*
(2) |t₂| → /d/ in closed syllable: *veden, neidin*
(3) |e₂| → /i/ before #: *veti*
(4) |t₂| → /s/ before /i/: *vesi, vesillä*

(or the like, see § 6.6)

and in Lapp,

(1) |t| → [D] in nom. sg. after resonants (and finally): nieịDa, kolDED
(2) |t| in gen. sg. and 1st sg. → [d] after resonants, [ð] intervocalically: koldam, kieða, kuða
(3) Lengthening of consonants and clusters in nom. sg.: kietta, nieịD̄a, kōðða, nuoïte, nemma, oðða
(4) Extra lengthening in nouns with a short vowel preceding: nem̄ma, ōðða, kuïta
(5) Lengthening of short vowels in the genitive and 1st sg.: kūða, nēma, kōldam
(6) Preaspiration of voiceless stops: kiehtta, nuohïte/nuohtte, kuhïta [or the like]

Note that the rules *always* turn out to rely heavily on the environments that made the analysis possible in the first place (§ 10.6). As we see, this synthetic part mirrors the framework of historical linguistics, because sound changes occur in a strict historical sequence (§§ 6.1–6.3). The difference is that in the synchronic framework one can take the shortest way even when it violates our knowledge of the actual history (§§ 6.5–6.6). Often, however, such ordering of synchronic mapping rules mirror the actual historical changes to some degree; for example, there is a fair amount of relative chronology in them. In the Finnish case, we must first have the raising of *e* > *i* to get the right environment for the assibilation *ti* > *si* and so on (§ 6.6).

It has already been mentioned that when the method encounters rare or unique alternations, for example, English *man/men*, one is hardly willing to construct special vowels for such cases. The alternation in *man/men*, however, is not completely random, since there are other vowel alternations in English. The case of *goose/geese* and *tooth/teeth* is more systematic, because there are at least two instances of it, but certainly not systematic enough to warrant a special vowel to carry the alternation (one might rather use an exception feature like [+umlaut] or the like; see § 10.16). These words will have to be somehow listed or marked as "regular" exceptions. The postediting problems of morphophonemic analysis surpass those of phonemic analysis; one hardly ever tries to apply the method up to its logical conclusion and to adopt its results without any questions asked in the establishment of morphophonemes. Postediting is the final touch in which every factor is drawn in and inductive methodology is mellowed by deductive expectations from universal theory. The results of the method were not adopted in the framework of the item-and-arrangement model of listing allomorphs, which in any case did not involve morphophonemes, and the result was that all items were exceptions in this sense. The logic of the grammar must naturally prevail over the logic of the method (§§ 5.14, 9.19).

[10.16]   As an example of postediting the results of the strict method, let us return to the Finnish morphophonemic *e*-vowels, dentals, and velars. There are two ways to adjust the contrast between $|e_1|$ and $|e_2|$ (1 and 2). First, $|e_1|$ occurs only in proper names (especially in pet names), acronyms, trade names, nursery and loanwords, and other such descriptive material (notable exceptions are *itse* 'self' and *kolme* 'three'). The two vowels merge, if the words with $|e_1|$ are marked for a special feature, say, [+affective]. This feature indicates just all those semantic areas mentioned and it blocks vowel alternation. Or, second, we may erase $|e_2|$ from the underlying forms altogether and establish a boundary marker (juncture) of some kind. At this boundary we can now write the automatic union vowels *i* and *e* where needed. We notice further that consonant gradation fails to occur in the same categories listed above. By adopting two features [native] and [foreign], we might have one dental only, $|t|$, which would be unalternating /t/ in connection with [−native] and unalternating /d/ with [+foreign]. The same is true of the velars as well, for example,

		REALIZED AS
nalle	[−native]	*nalle/nallen*
vete	[+native]	*vesi/veden*
peti	[−native]	*peti/petin*
joti	[+foreign]	*jodi/jodin*
liika	[+foreign]	*liiga/liigan*
liika	[+native]	*liika/liian*
muki	[−native]	*muki/mukin*
	etc.	

Note now that [−native] in this scheme is not the same as [+foreign]. In the same way, one has used these features to indicate the differences in English spirants, for example,

		PLURALS		
chief	[−native]	*chiefs*	[f]	
faith	[−native]	*faiths*	[θ]	
knife	[+native]	*knives*	[v]	voice
sheath	[+native]	*sheaths*	[ð]	

Now, in the environment [−native] a spirant fails to voice. One should note that such features would not necessarily reflect historical borrowing; a historically native word like *oath* has to be listed as [−native] in those varieties of English in which the plural is /owθs/ (rather than /owðz/), to ensure the voiceless spirant. In a way it creates a situation that is the reverse of the acclimatization of loans, taking away the official citizenship rights. The feature [+foreign] fails in those Finnish words with more than one stop that are different with respect to voicing, for example, *toga* and *Golgata* 'Golgotha'. Hence one seems to need $|d|$ and $|g|$ after all, but the voiceless stops can be combined with the use of features as indicated. All this is quite parallel to what we did to Finnish *tykin*, for example, by extracting a feature F(rontness) and writing the word as *^{F}tukin*. Such features as [±foreign] are rather vague as a device for blocking the operation of certain rules, and they were presented here only as historical curiosities of a procedure that enjoyed popularity during the mid-1960s. To block a rule one can use the nonoperation of the rule as the most concrete feature, for example,

> *peti* [−consonant gradation]
> *faith* [−voicing rule]   etc.

That is, rather than create a special feature that ultimately negates a rule we directly use the negation of that rule. This makes our phonology as concrete as possible. In the above case, this same desirability prescribes Finnish morphophonemes |d| and |g|. These are now always /d/ and /g/ and no special conversion rules are required.

Diacritic feature notations like [±foreign] show the extent linguists like to theorize for their own delight irrespective of "innocent" speakers whose speech they supposedly describe and explain. A child learns his language without knowing that borrowing exists; he has no use for history in any form. For him *read/read* /riyd~red/ and *breed/bred* are on the same footing as *bite/bit* and *ride/rid* (original ablaut), and in fact *hide/hid* is now conjugated exactly the same as *ride* (analogy; past passive participle *hidden*). The child is always right, as long as his output is accepted, whereas the historical linguist is wrong when he does similar things in (the [hopefully] initial stages of) his analysis (§§ 9.16, 9.19, 10.7, 18.16, 18.17). It is important to realize that both the language learner and the linguist must use abduction (§ 9.16), and are thus bound to make "mistakes" here and there. This aspect is emphasized throughout the book.

[10.17 Conclusion]   This rather lengthy paraphrase of synchronic methods serves many purposes. First, it makes the methods maximally explicit. Second, the method part of the discussion of morphophonemic analysis serves (as it is) as an exemplification of internal reconstruction (Chapter 12). And, finally, the discussion of the postediting problems of morphophonemic analysis highlights the differences between synchrony and diachrony. This reminds us that the results of the method must be polished by the linguist himself. It is here that linguists differ among themselves. Some would accept all the different units given by the method as different entities in a synchronic grammar. Others would try to combine some of the units by using various kinds of features, as we have seen. But from the point of view of internal reconstruction, such different units can be given different temporal interpretations. Words that contain units that do not undergo all the rules of the language are often recent loans; what creates a serious postediting problem in synchronic analysis often has a clear historical explanation. For example, there is independent evidence that those Finnish words with unalternating voiceless stops are loans, *muki* (mug) and *peti* (bed) (see § 8.6). They were thus taken into the language after consonant gradation had ceased to operate as a productive mechanism. Words with voiced stops are even more recent loans, *jodi* and *liiga* (see § 19.4). What is important is that the method actually gave us three dental units in Finnish, $|t_1|$, $|t_2|$, and $|d|$, all of which can be shown to be historically distinct ($|t_2|$, inherited, $|t_1|$, early borrowing, and $|d|$, late borrowing). They are also synchronically distinct, whether one collapses the first two with features or not. A notation like $|t_1|$ means exactly the same thing as $|t|$ + [−consonant gradation]. Also, those cases of spirants that do not undergo voicing in English will turn out to be borrowings or other later developments (analogy). The more familiar one is with synchrony, the easier history will be, and vice versa. Linguistics is a panchronic discipline (Figure 1-7).

REFERENCES

General: Bloch 1948 and the references in §1.1; **10.4** Schane 1971; **10.6** Sigurd 1970, Schane 1971; **10.9** Wartburg 1931, Malmberg 1969; **10.10** Vennemann 1968; **10.12-10.14** Anttila 1968; **10.14** E. Itkonen 1941, 1946, T.I. Itkonen 1958; **10.15-10.16** Anttila 1969a; **10.17** Anttila in Sebeok (ed.) 1963f. vol. 11.

CHAPTER 11

THE COMPARATIVE METHOD
(THE CENTRAL CONCEPT)

> *The comparative method dominates comparative linguistics,
> even though it is complementary to other methods. It can
> be used for reconstruction (Chapter 18), constructing a
> dialect cohesion (§ 13.8), or indicating language relation-
> ship (§ 16.9). The chapter concentrates on the structure
> and the deficiencies of the method as applied to a few
> selected languages in an attempt to reconstruct their earlier
> stages.*

[11.1 Ingredients of the Method]   The comparative method, the central
method in comparative linguistics, adds the dimension of using more than one
language to what we already know from synchronic methods. Here we need
two or more languages, exactly as we needed two or more alternating forms
(grammatical environments) in morphophonemic analysis. That is, the comparative method operates on sets of correspondences, like morphophonemic analysis;
but unlike morphophonemic analysis, which takes the members for its sets
from related morphs (from one paradigm within one language), the comparative
method builds its sets of correspondences out of elements coming from different
languages. But, like phonemic analysis, the comparative method observes
phonetic/phonemic conditioning of variants. The rather definite semantic
identity used in phonemic and morphophonemic analysis can be relaxed in the
comparative method after some initial success in establishing sound units,
but good semantic matching of the forms used is a must in the initial stages of
work. The difficulty is that there are no exact rules for handling semantic change;
the final factor here is necessarily the common sense and the experience of the
individual scholar as they contribute to his handling of the possibilities outlined
in Chapter 7.

[11.2 The Comparative Method: Swedish, English, and German Consonants]
It is best to introduce the method with languages rather closely related, so that
complications can be avoided. Let us take some material from the Germanic
languages Swedish, English, and German and organize the items so that English
is in the middle. This gives us the advantage of showing at a glance the similarity
of English either to Scandinavian or to a sister variant of West Germanic. To
underline the fact that the exact status of the sound units is irrelevant we shall
start out with standard orthography; this will also preserve the reader's familiarity with most of the forms. Such writing obscures certain things, for example,

that the vocalic nuclei of English *pipe* and German *pfeife*, English *out* and German *aus*, Swedish *bok* and German *buch*, are phonetically the same. We shall, however, be looking at the consonants and hence we need remember only that German *tz*, *z* = [ts], *v* = [f], *w* = [v], and that double stops in Swedish are phonetically long but in German only a way of writing a preceding short vowel. In Swedish also a vowel preceding a double stop is short, and we can thus ignore length at this point. Let us now observe the following items, which have been arranged so that their consonants match:

m	a	n		s	o	n		h	e	m		h	å	r		h	u	s		m	u	s	
m	a	n		s	o	n		h	o	m	e	h	ai	r		h	ou	s	e	m	ou	s	e
m	a	nn		s	oh	n		h	ei	m		h	aa	r		h	au	s		m	au	s	

How to decide which part corresponds to what is an enormous operation logically. Fortunately we do not need such rigor. It is sufficient to segment at the boundaries of consonants and vowels, and the principle almost always leads to satisfactory results. This has been done to the above material, which now gives us the familiar sets of correspondences. Only the consonantal correspondences have been boxed in, but they automatically establish the vocalic sets. Such cartouches, then, are the sound matter of the comparative method. These sets must recur in material that satisfies the requirement of semantic similarity or identity. Both aspects are clearly fulfilled in the six Germanic items; all except the *r*-set of *hair* occur at least twice and the meanings of the words are identical in all three languages. One unique set is not a regular correspondence and does not lead anywhere. Unique sets can easily be established between any number of languages, for example,

English	d	ay	Greek	th	eós	Finnish	i	t	s	e
Latin	d	ies	Latin	d	eus	Latin	i	p	s	e
				'god'				'self'		

In spite of the semantic identity and the formal similarity of the boxed-in sounds in the first two items, we do not have regular sets of correspondences; these are unique. No other items where these recur can be found between these languages. Thus the requirement of regularity diminishes the possibility of being misled by chance similarity. Actually, it eliminates chance similarity altogether, but it is no help in another kind of complication. We said that it is impossible to find another pair of words where English *d* corresponds to Latin *d*. But note Latin *dēns* 'tooth' and English *dentist*, where the semantic side is certainly acceptable and where we have another such set (see §§ 8.12, 8.13). Or consider

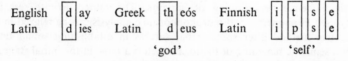

French	j	u	g	e	j	o	l	ie	g	é	l	a	t	i	n	e	t	ou	ch	er	ch	aise
English	j	u	dg	e	j	o	ll	y	g	e	l	a	t	i	n		t	ou	ch		ch	air

where we have at least two occurrences of the following correspondences: ž–dž, l–l, t–t, and š–tš. We have exactly the same regularity as in the above Germanic case. Here we know, however, that English has borrowed these words from French, exactly like *dentist* from Latin. In many cases borrowing cannot be documented, especially when dealing with greater time depths. Extensive borrowing easily creates regular sets of correspondence between the source language and the target language; such situations arise with, for example, French loans in English, Arabic loans in Turkish, Chinese loans in Japanese and Korean, Germanic loans in Finnish, Low German loans in Swedish, and so on (see Figure 8-2, §§ 8.6, 8.9–8.13). The sets are *regular* (they recur) and speak for a *historical connection* and against chance similarity. This historical connection may be due to either inheritance or borrowing, and it is the linguist's task to try to separate the two possibilities. One way to guard against borrowing is to start the comparative method with vocabulary items that come from semantic spheres not usually borrowed from, that is, basic noncultural vocabulary (body parts, natural objects, animals, plants, pronouns, lower numerals, and so on; in other words, the so-called Swadesh list is a handy starting point; see §§ 18.3–18.5, 22.14). In the case of *dentist*, the basic term *tooth* reveals both its learnèd semantic environment and the proper correspondence relation, that is, Latin *d*–English *t* (*edere–eat*, *dēns–tooth*, *decem–ten*).

[11.3]   Let us now go back to the six items from the three Germanic languages. Here we clearly have basic core vocabulary, which seems to guarantee inheritance. Excluding stops, the Germanic consonant correspondences are very straightforward, as the cartouches show: each language reflects the same sound. To apply the comparative method we treat these sets of correspondences like phones in phonemic analysis, that is, we combine all noncontrasting sets into one unit; all such sets can be written (labeled) with one and the same symbol. Thus the *m*-set and the *h*-set clearly contrast, because we have the minimal pairs *house* and *mouse*. One would not combine *m*'s and *h*'s anyway, because there is no phonetic justification for it. Phonetically there is more reason to try to see whether the *m*-set contrasts with the *n*-set (both are nasals). These sets do occur in the same environments, for example, in final position in *son* and *home*, hence contrast and must be labeled differently. For mnemonic purposes and reasons of common sense we label the *h*-sets with **h*, the *m*-sets with **m*, and the *n*-sets with **n*. The asterisk is the traditional indicator for the fact that the following symbol(s) (letter[s]) is (are) shorthand for a whole cartouche, a set of correspondences; more generally, * means 'not directly documented'. In this sense, **h* means that we have *h* in Swedish, *h* in English, and *h* in German, and so on, in other words, what we can read in a set (cartouche). These sets recur through a great amount of additional material, for example, in the numbered items of Figure 11-1 (see § 11.4), which supplies evidence for stops: **m* (5), **n* (11, 12, 15, 24, 36), and **h* (7, 16, 17). Further similar simple unalternating sets are **r* (14, 16, 22, 24, 25, 26, 31, 33) and **l* (2, 5, 6, 8, 13, 21, 34, 36), where the choice of symbol is again obvious, because these contrast with

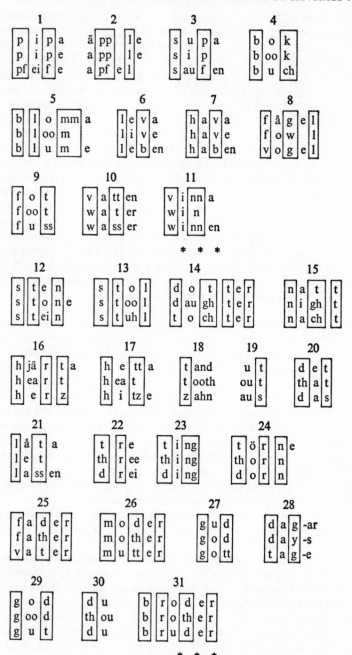

FIGURE 11-1. Swedish, English, and German consonants lined up for the comparative method.

32	33	34	35
k o k a	r å g	l ä gg a	s ä g a
c oo k	[r a y]	l a y	s a y
k o ch en	r o gg en	l e g en	s a g en
	'rye'		

36	37	38	39
n a g e l	s å g	b å g e	s ä g en
n a i l	s a w	b o w	s a w 'saying'
n a g e l	s ä g e	b o g en	s a g e

* * *

40	41	42	43
fäl t	skyl t -ar	gul d	mil d
fiel d -s	shiel d -s	gol d	mil d
fel d -er	schil d -e	gol d (es)	mil d (e)

44	45	46	47
bin d a	han d la	bör d a	mor d
bin d	han d le	bur d en	mur d er
bin d en	han d eln	bür d e	mor d (es)

FIGURE 11-1. [Continued]

the units already established (the nasals and *h). So far it has been easy to see how these sets contrast, because their phonetic makeup has been so obvious and constant within each set. Now we have to look beyond standard orthography and remember that the German s in *sohn* (and 3, 35, 37) is [z] against an [s] in *haus* and *maus*, and an [š] in *stein* and *stuhl* (12, 13). In other words, instead of the orthographic single set *s–s–s* we have actually three *s*-sets:

	1'	2'	3'
Swedish	s	s	s
English	s	s	s
German	s	z	š

Closer inspection reveals that these sets are complementary, occurring in mutually exclusive environments: 2' occurs in syllable-initial position before vowels, 3' before a *t*-set, and 1' in syllable-final position. Hence they are allosets of one and the same unit which we can label *s. So it turns out that German orthography would have given us a shortcut in this matter in any case. For the application of the method it does not matter whether one applies it to orthographic units or to phonetic units. It matters only for the correctness of the results, because sometimes orthography obscures facts (distinctions) that must be known in order to secure correct results. This phonetic check on the *s*-sets proves that at this point the orthography does not obscure relevant phonetic detail. Orthography is mentioned here in anticipation of those cases where orthography is all we have.

[11.4] When we turn to stop correspondences, the situation becomes complicated in comparison with the obvious constant sets we have seen so far. But, as we shall see, it does not make any difference for the method; rather, it is only that the challenge is greater (and more typical). Reference will be made again to the numbered items in the table. It should be noted that in a few cases the meanings are not exactly the same: *shield*–Swedish *skylt* '(shop) sign'; *bloom–blomma*, *blume* 'flower'; *sip–supa*, *saufen* 'drink heavily'; *fowl–fågel*, *vogel* 'bird'; *leap–löpa*, *laufen* 'run'; *thing*, *ding–ting* 'court (session)', and a few others. In every case the meanings are close enough to be accepted without hesitation. The only doubtful case would be *thing–ting*, but note Latin *causa* 'situation, condition, point in an argument, matter, lawsuit' > French *chose* 'thing', and OE *sacu* 'lawsuit', German *Sache*, and Swedish *sak* 'thing'. As for the segmentation, it does not matter how it goes in ambiguous cases like 14 and 15, that is, either *t–gh–ch* followed by *t–t–t* or *Ø–gh–ch* followed by *tt–t–t*. In either case the method is the same and *it will reach the same conclusion* (see § 10.13).

[11.5 Labials] Looking first at the labials we see that Swedish has *p b f v*, English *p b f v w*, and German *pf b f v*, but we have six sets of phonemic correspondence (as opposed to the relationships in the traditional orthography) in Figure 11-2. The numbers indicate the proper environment for the sets, which can be looked up in Figure 11-1. To facilitate talking about these sets, let us call the first two *p*-sets, the next two *b*-sets, and the last two spirant sets. Once again, we are going to treat the sets like phones to find out whether they contrast or not.

In phonemic analysis, phonetic similarity makes two phones potential candidates for membership in a single phoneme, and the method then checks out

	Two sets sharing *p*		Two sets sharing *b*		Two sets with continuant articulation all the way through	
Swedish	p	p	b	v	f	v
English	p	p	b	v	f	w
German	pf	f	b	b	f	v
	1, 2	1, 3	4, 5	6, 7	8, 9, 25	10, 11

FIGURE 11-2. Labial sets taken from Figure 11-1 with numbers indicating the original item.

such cases. As we have already seen with the *s*-sets, the same is true of the regular sets of correspondences in connection with the comparative method. Thus with the labial sets the best strategy is to see first whether the two *p*-sets contrast. After all, they are the same in Swedish and English and differ only in German. Exactly the same situation obtained in the *s*-sets. We have only to refer to the actual environments given in the table (Figure 11-1), and it is clear that the set with a German affricate (*pf*) occurs initially, and medially after short vowels; the set with a German *f*, after diphthongs (and long vowels). Of course, the evidence reproduced here is rather meager, but those who know German will immediately see that this is indeed true. Hence the two *p*-sets are complementary, conditioned variants of one and the same unit, and they can both be represented with one symbol, say **p*. The structure of the *b*-sets is the reverse of the *p*-sets, because here German is the same for both, and Swedish and English differentiate between stop and continuant articulation. But they are complementary also, because the first one occurs in initial position and the second medially; they can thus be written with, say, **b*. Since **p* and **b* occur in the same environments they also contrast. Another labial set can be found which has stop articulation in German:

Swedish	v		lö	v	dö	v	
English	f	in	lea	f	dea	f	
German	p		lau	b	tau	b	(devoicing; see §§ 2.4, 6.15)

This set occurs in (syllable-)final position, and thus contrasts clearly with **p* (*lopp–leap–lauf, upp–up–auf*). The *b*-sets, however, never occur in this environment but only in syllable-initial position, and hence this new set is a variant of **b*. Note that English does not supply any information for syllable position, as both *live* and *leaf* are monosyllables, but the other languages do: *leva/leben* vs. *löv/laub*. Swedish and German thus provide the information that explains the contrast *v ≠ f* in English *live* vs. *leaf* (see § 4.2). This is a typical situation in the comparative method. Obviously, the method works only when different languages have undergone different independent changes. English has lost final vowels to a greater degree than Swedish and German, but it does not matter here, because the comparative method uses the *combined* evidence from all the languages to which it is being applied. Each language can potentially supply useful information. The combined evidence has been emphasized by boxing in the sets of correspondences for enhancing the notion of unity derived from diverse sources (languages). Again, as in the case of the *s*-sets, we see that German orthography, for example, *laub* for [p], is efficient.

As for the spirant sets, they contrast with each other, and with both stop sets. It is easy to choose a label for the constant *f–f–f*, namely, **f*, but the voiced one, *v–w–v*, would seem to suggest either **v* or **w*. It is perhaps easier to derive **w > v* than **v > w*, and hence **w* seems to be preferable, both because of articulatory simplification (bilabial more marked than labiodental) and for mnemonic reasons (since the German orthography uses *w*).

We have now treated seven labial sets of correspondences, which were all regular in the sense that they occurred more than once in this material (which is just a small selection). These seven sets were made up of four Swedish and German units, and five English units. This is a general characteristic: the number of sets of correspondences can be bigger than the highest number of units in any of the languages. Also, the number of reconstructed units is independent of the number of sets with which we start out, although it obviously cannot exceed the number of the sets. For the Germanic labials we got four, *p, *b, *f, *w, a number very close to the number of units in all three languages. Notice, however, that the distribution of these reconstructed units is completely different from those of the units in the source languages.

[11.6 Dentals] The situation with regard to the dental stops and spirants is more complicated than the one with regard to the labials. The s-sets (where each language had spirants only) have already been treated. This leaves us two units from Swedish (t, d), four from English (t, d, θ, ð) and three from German (t, ts, d), but these yield seven sets of correspondences as in Figure 11-3, where

	Three sets containing voiceless sounds only			Four sets containing voiced sounds and/or interdental spirants			
				Swedish voiceless	German voiced	Swedish voiced German voiceless	Voiced dentals only
Swedish	t	t	t	t	d	d	d
English	t	t	t	θ	d	ð	ð
German	t	ts	s	d	t	t	d
	12, 13, 14, 15	16, 17, 18	10, 19, 20, 21	22, 23, 24	14, 27, 28, 29	25, 26	30, 31

FIGURE 11-3. Dental sets taken from Figure 11-1 with numbers indicating the original item.

the sets have been organized according to voicing and spirantness. These are features that we expect to be relevant, because they were important with regard to the labials. The best place to begin is with the three voiceless sets, which are differentiated only in German (exactly like the three s-sets). The first one (t–t–t) occurs only after sets with a spirant (at least in German); the second (t–t–ts) initially and after short vowels (at least in German) or after *r (16); and the third (t–t–s) after long vowels (at least in Swedish). Thus they are conditioned variants of the same unit, which we can label *t. The conditioning of the variants is generally the same as for the labials; both groupings are thereby mutually supported. In the remaining four sets, both Swedish and German agree for those sets where German has voiceless stops (t). These two sets are different because of the contrast $d \neq \delta$ in English. As for their distribution, the set with the English spirant (d–δ–t) occurs only before a vowel followed by the r-set, that is, *r. Complementary distribution based on so few examples may of course always be wrong, but here it is all we can use. With more evidence, for example, with the information that there are English dialects with [d] in *father*, we would be inclined to combine these two sets under *d. Now, the two remaining sets also have spirants in English. Because they both occur in initial position, they contrast with each other as well as with *t and *d, which both also occur in the same environment. The symbols we need to label these contrasts have to be different from the established stops, and since spirantness is present in English, spirants should be used. Thus we can label the set t–θ–d with *$\flat$ (thorn rather than θ is appropriate in Germanic, for historical reasons) and d–δ–d with *δ. It turns out that the groupings come closest to the English units.

One further dental set involving an English spirant is

Swedish	d			e	d		klä	d	-
English	θ	in	oa	th		clo	th	
German	t			ei	d		klei	d	(devoicing; see §§ 2.4, 6.15)

which occurs in syllable-final position only. Thus it is complementary to both *$\flat$ and *δ, neither of which occurs in this environment. The situation is quite parallel to the American English flap problem in cases like *writer–rider* where [ᴅ] is complementary to both /t/ and /d/ (§ 10.4). German orthography suggests *$\flat$, and in the labial situation we saw that orthography was right. German orthography is morphophonemic: it does not indicate the obligatory devoicing of voiced stops in syllable-final position (which Middle High German orthography still did). The use of patterning (from the labials) would thus follow German orthography and assign the set d–θ–t to *$\flat$. On the other hand, if we look at the same words in the plural where the dental set is intervocalic in Swedish and German, we have

Swedish	d			e	d	er	klä	d	er
English	ð	in	oa	th	s	clo	th	es
German	d			ei	d	e	klei	d	er

This is identical to *δ, and must be assigned to it by the method. The result is that we have reconstructed singulars *$V\flat$, *$klV\flat$ and plurals *$V\delta$-V, *$klV\delta$-V (where V is a cover symbol for the vocalic nucleus, which will not be further treated). Such a situation is by no means typologically impossible; in fact, it is exactly what English morphophonemics shows. But note that we made a selection from English, since the plural *oaths* can also occur with [θ]. If we had chosen this form and the plural *cloths*, we would have gotten a completely different result—*$\flat$ for all forms. The sections on morphophonemics showed that the voiced spirants are regular in old inherited material, and thus we probably chose the right variant. This shows, however, that dangers lurk at every stage in our work. Synchronic variation may impose far-reaching effects on our reconstructions.

So far we have treated the nucleus of the evidence for dental stops. With further material and similar collation, other sets emerge. Let us look at items 40–47, where the words have been given in such a form as to avoid German syllable-final devoicing. This would just complicate the application of the method, but as we have already seen, it would not block it. We get the following two additional sets:

	A		B	
Swedish	t		d	
English	d		d	
German	d	40, 41	d	42–47

Neither of them occurs in word-initial position, and hence they are potential candidates for membership in those units that do, that is, *t, *d, *þ, *ð—in other words, all the units we have so far established. Both sets A and B contrast with each other since they both occur after *l (i.e., set l–l–l). Hence they contrast also with *d, which also follows *l (English *scold*–German *schelten*). Set B, being voiced all the way, would now seem to belong to *ð, and this leaves set A as a candidate for *þ, which does not otherwise occur word-medially after *l. This is the direction in which the method points; the evidence, however, is too scanty for a definite answer.

[11.7 Velars]   Finally, let us turn to the material that shows the velar sets of correspondences, not counting the *h*-sets, which have already been dealt with. Swedish supplies *k g y* (*säga* 35), and even *t*; English, *k g y w* : (length), and German, *k g x*. Again the number of sets of correspondences exceeds the number of the units in any one language, as shown in Figure 11-4. The *k*-sets, one of which occurred also in the item *cloth(es)*, are obviously complementary: *k–k–k* occurs initially and *k–k–x* medially and finally. Hence they can both be labeled with *k. The *g*-sets provide a more complicated situation. One, *g–g–g*, occurs initially only and is thus complementary to the rest,

	Two sets sharing *k*		Five sets sharing *g*					Two sets sharing *x* and *t*	
Swedish	k	k	g	g	y	g	g	t	t
English	k	k	g	y	y	w	:	:	y
German	k	x	g	g	g	g	g	x	x
	32,	4, 32	27, 29	33, 34, 36	35	8, 38	37, 39	14	15

FIGURE 11-4.   Velar sets taken from Figure 11-1 with numbers indicating the original item.

where English participates with y, w (glides), and $:$ (length), no matter how they are written. It is impossible to establish complementary distribution with this material at hand, for example, both sets g–y–g and g–w–g occur after the vowel set $\mathring{a}$–[a]–o (8, 33), although there is a tendency for the first to occur after English front vowels. English orthography strengthens our suspicion that all the medial g-sets are somehow conditioned variants of the same unit. Length and rounding is written with a w, and in the meaning 'say', the verb is *say* (35) and the noun, *saw* 'proverb' (39). Similarly, in Swedish, [y] in *säga* is written with a g, which occurs as such in *sägen*. To have such orthographic evidence is, of course, quite accidental. But when it is available, linguists are free to use any clues it can supply. Here, then, we have clear evidence for a $*g$, certainly for initial position. But for the medial position we cannot be sure whether $*g$ is enough or whether there lurks another unit in addition or instead.

The two spirant sets seem to contrast with $*t$ and $*k$, although there is not enough material for a definite answer. They both occur in syllable-final position before a t-set ($*t$), and are thus complementary to the h-sets ($*h$) as well, which occur only word-initially. Thus these can be combined into one $*x$ (because it is easier to derive $*x > h$ than $*h > x$ if we assume that x has more friction and is more marked; of course, such arguments are more practical than valid). We can see that one must continually revise one's tentative results according to the new material brought in through the use of the comparative method. It was convenient in the beginning to establish a symbol $*h$ to cover all the initial h-sets (i.e., h–h–h). Now that this $*h$ turns out to be complementary to other sets that include velar spirants (x), one has to combine both under one symbol. Universal tendencies of phonetic change make $*x$ more preferable phonetically, although such tendencies are not absolute and $*h > x$ is possible. But phonemically there is no difference whatsoever: $*h$ and $*x$ mean exactly the same thing in terms of the relevant distinctions. Both symbols would represent those sets that contain voiceless spirants and thus contrast with all the stop sets. On the other hand, one might quite well retain both symbols $*x$ and $*h$, although they occur in mutually exclusive environments. This would, of course, be allophonic writing, which is sometimes used even in comparative linguistics (§§ 11.12, 11.14, 18.9). A fundamental principle of the comparative method is involved here: it is both simplest and most plausible to assume one conditioned change in the protolanguage ($*x > *h \mathbin{/} \#$—), rather than two (West Germanic and Swedish) or three (English, German, and Swedish) identical changes in exactly the same environment (see §§ 2.18, 15.2).

[11.8 Checking the Results of the Method] Three modern varieties of Germanic, rather than their corresponding older stages, were used above, because most languages do not have a long history documented in writing. Usually a linguist must confine his research to languages as they are at the time he is studying them, or he must at least base his comparative work on rather recent field work. Of course, it is true that most Indo-European languages have a long documented history behind them, and this has led to the general misunderstanding that the comparative linguist works chiefly with old written records or "dead" languages. Historical linguistics suffers from the same kind of misunderstanding, since obviously its entire framework is very historical indeed. This has led to a further misconception—that the comparative method is valid only for the older Indo-European languages with written records (see §§ 1.21, 1.22), with the implication that all "unwritten" languages need another method. One could easily imagine a situation in which the European languages were unwritten and, say, the American Indian languages had a long tradition of writing. Writing is a historical accident depending on the socioeconomic factors of the culture and not on the particular shape of the language. The three European languages in this sample were presented in this spirit; this is how they would appear to a Martian linguist sampling them. Traditional orthography was retained, but that was ancillary and was *not* the basis of the actual treatment (and, of course, such orthographies might also be available to the Martian linguist).

But more important, the choice of Modern Germanic languages enables us to check on the results of the comparative method: since the Germanic languages were already written down a thousand years ago, we can go at least that far toward the ultimate cutoff point and see how our groupings hold. (This will be most valuable as a reminder for those situations where documentation is not available.) Any reconstruction is valid only for those languages that have been used (i.e., included in the buildup of the sets); thus the units we have tentatively reconstructed cannot be called Proto-Germanic, because all the Germanic languages were not used. They can only be labeled Proto-Swedish–English–German, or the like. Neither is there any certainty of such an exact historical unity; it means only that we have a base from which we can derive all the languages used in the establishment of the proto-units. This always carries some historical truth; how much is another matter.

Turning now to the oldest records of English, we find that Old English *father* and *mother* did have a [d], *fæder* and *mōdor*, and that *daughter* and *night* displayed a fricative [x], as reconstructed, which was written with the same symbol as [h]: *dohtor* and *niht*. In the first instance, the method hinted at the right direction, in the second, its result is confirmed. Further, *have* and *live* come from Old English *habban* and *libban*, which in fact show *b*'s, although long ones. Those items that contained sets with German *g*'s and where English was so diverse all turn out to have orthographic ⟨g⟩'s at least, seemingly representing [ɣ] in back vowel environments and [y] in front environments, for example, *saw* < *sagu*, *bow* < *boga*, *nail* < *nægel*, *rye* < *ryge*, *fowl* < *fugol*, and *lay* < *lecgan*, *say* < *secgan* (where *cg* is probably [ddž], that is, an affricate derivable from *g*). In other words, Old English almost matches Modern German and settles the issue in favor of one medial **g*. The method by itself was able only to suggest this.

As for the dentals, Old Swedish also shows voiced interdental spirants. Old English, on the other hand, displays only a tendency toward complementary distribution of ⟨þ⟩ and ⟨ð⟩, the latter occurring only more frequently in voiced

THE COMPARATIVE METHOD 241

1 Reconstructed spirants on the basis of modern languages	2 Items	3 Check through Old English and Old High German forms		4 Adjusted reconstruction	5 A further check through Gothic
þ	thing	þing	(OHG)	no change	no change
þ	thorn	þorn		no change	no change
ð	brother	brōðor		no change	þ
ð	burden	byrðen		no change	þ
ð	murder	morðor	OE	no change	þ
þ	cloth	clāþ		ð	þ
ð	clothes	clāðas		no change	þ
þ	oath	āþ		ð	þ
ð	oaths	āðas		no change	þ
ð	gold	gold		no change	þ
ð	bind	bintan	OHG	d	no change
ð	mild	milti		d	no change
ð	handle	hantalōn		d	no change

FIGURE 11-5. Checking the reconstruction.

environments than not. Depending on the documents, both [ð] and [θ] (which are in complementary distribution) can be written with either þ or ð. Old High German bears witness to a spirant in *thing*, that is, OHG *thing* > NG *ding* and *thiob* > *dieb* 'thief' as *ther, dher* > *der* 'the' (§ 11.9). It also "replaces" some of the Modern German *d*'s with *t*'s. In Figure 11-5 we can now tabulate our reconstructed spirants, the additional older evidence, and the consequent correction of the results of the comparative method. Now *þ occurs only in initial position where it contrasts with *ð, which, however, occurs in this environment only in pronouns. As for the set *t–d–d* (*field* and *shield*), we find older Swedish spellings *fäld-* and *fäldh-* (sixteenth century). It becomes clear that there is also a word *sköld* which means 'shield', whereas *skylt* is a technical word meaning 'sign'. But also *fält* is a technical term occurring mainly in military contexts. OHG *scilt* shows that *shield* contains a *d and OHG *feld* speaks for a *ð in *field*. Swedish *fält* and *skylt* still do not fit in these, and the evidence is in all ways characteristic of a borrowing situation (compare *tooth–dentist*). The technical meanings of these two words, together with historical evidence pointing to strong contacts between Sweden and the Hanseatic states, make the borrowing hypothesis attractive; and, as it happens, the Low German forms are *velt* and *schilt*, with exactly the right dentals. These two items are typical of loans which are not spotted right away but undergo the method and may lead to chimerical reconstructions.

[11.9]   We have seen that our method was unable to penetrate completely all the changes that accumulated during a thousand years. In English, the difficulties arose partly from the changes $ð > d$ and $d > ð$, which are very complicated indeed, but more significantly from the fate of medial velars. German has undergone a tricky change $t > d$, which is not phonetically regular (i.e., OHG *skeltan > schelten*, but *milti > milde*). The comparative method rests on the assumption of regular phonetic change. Irregular change (various types of analogy and borrowing) immediately blocks its historically correct course. All three types of change do occur, and often we have no way of sorting them out. Hence the result of the comparative method is always highly tentative. Further evidence requires a revision as often as it confirms the earlier results. The Germanic case shows that in the majority of items the method did give correct results, which were confirmed by the earlier stages of the languages used. On the other hand, in the reconstruction of interdental spirants, the older evidence necessitated a revision.

If we turn now to Gothic, the "oldest" substantially recorded Germanic language, we would have to make further changes, namely, to collapse *$þ$ and *$ð$ into *$þ$ (column 5 in Figure 11-5), because now we have, say, the following two sets:

Swedish	t	örne	and	d	et	broder	ed
English	þ	orn		þ	at	brother	oath
German	d	orn		d	as	bruder	eid
Gothic	þ	orn		þ	ata	brōþar	aiþs

Gothic supplies just one $þ$ where the other languages required two, *$þ$ and *$ð$. English has been written phonemically, in terms of Old English, as $þ$. The first set occurs word-initially and the second word-medially and -finally, but also word-initially in pronouns (e.g., *du–thou–du–þū*). This grammatical conditioning of the set should be noted, because it is not normal in the comparative method. Many scholars would rather interpret it as conditioned by weak stress, or the like, to get a phonetic environment for it. But the change is still completely regular and thus enables the comparative method to penetrate it. When Gothic is brought into the picture, all major branches of Germanic are represented and the result could now be called Proto-Germanic. But note that Gothic is *not* a check on our initial use of the method; since a new language is involved, we have a new reconstruction altogether. We do not have a check on the method but on the total Germanic evidence. At the same time, the results of the first application stand up quite well indeed.

We have now seen the method, the reliability of its results, and why one should always use the earliest evidence available, because then one can eliminate many cases of unexplainable change. When we do not have early documents, we apply the method to any other material available. But we always have to allow for a certain range of confidence in the results. They need never be perfectly correct historically. They are only correct as a starting point from which we can derive unambiguously all the languages used in the method; to some degree this is also historically true. The method is very powerful and very useful, but not omnipotent.

[11.10 The Number of Units and the Number of Correspondences]   We have seen one important aspect of the comparative method: the number of reconstructed proto-units is independent (1) of the number of units in any of the languages being used and (2) of the number of sets of correspondences among the languages being used. The decisive factor is the number of contrasts within the sets; that is, all noncontrasting sets are grouped together into one proto-unit. Theoretically, two units from two languages can form four sets of correspondences. This we have already seen, as is clear from the following sets, showing Swedish and German t and d:

	a	b	c	d
Swedish	t	d	t	d
German	t	t	d	d

Now, neither the two units for each language nor the four sets by themselves determine the number of proto-units. As already mentioned, only contrasts count. Sets **b**, **c**, and **d** all occur in initial position, and thus contrast. Set **a**, which occurs only after spirants, is thus complementary to the three others. We know that there is a further set t–ts in initial position, and since this is voiceless all the way, we would be inclined to assign set **a** to it. Thus all four sets, being built up by only two units from each language, do in fact contrast, and we need four proto-units to account for them. The choice of symbols for them would be easy for **a** (and t–ts) = *t and **d** = *d, but rather tricky for **b** and **c**. A provisional answer might be *t_2 and *d_2 for **b** and **c**, or vice versa, or else *þ and *ð (either way). To choose appropriate labels, the linguist would have to use his sense of patterning and his experience. What is important is that the method lays out the contrasts, the relevant distinctions needed to derive the outcomes for both languages; it unveils the *relations* between the units, but it does not choose the labels for the units. This has to be done by the linguist. Thus, although the method is rather simple and mechanistic, the linguist is needed for the postediting of its product, as has already been noted many times.

[11.11]   We have seen a situation that is very frequent indeed: two units from two languages building three contrasting sets. Let us look at six items from European and Syrian Romany (Gypsy), both varieties having an s and an $š$, but which form three sets of correspondences:

European Romany	š	o	s		vu	š	t		š	el		de	š
Syrian Romany	š	a	s		o	š	t		s	ai		da	s
	'six'					'lip'			'hundred'			'ten'	

European Romany	s	ap	ma	s	ek
Syrian Romany	s	ap	ma	s	

'snake'   'month'

The three sets can now be lifted out as

$$\begin{array}{|c|} \hline \check{s} \\ \check{s} \\ \hline \end{array} \quad \begin{array}{|c|} \hline \check{s} \\ s \\ \hline \end{array} \quad \text{and} \quad \begin{array}{|c|} \hline s \\ s \\ \hline \end{array}$$

This small selection makes it look as if the set š–s occurred only next to a set e–a. In that case it would be complementary to both š–š and s–s, and we would look for further items to see whether the hypothesis holds or not. But further evidence shows that these sets are not complementarily distributed; rather, all occur in the same environments and thus contrast. Now š–š can be obviously labeled *š, and s–s as *s. The middle set š–s needs something different, and the best strategy is to choose a phonetic symbol that is between the two, namely, a fronto-palatal *ś. The important thing, again, is that the three contrasting sets be labeled differently, that is, by three symbols (at the same time, one tries to stick as close as possible to the phonetics actually manifested in the material). In the case of Romany once more we can check the reconstruction, because it is an offshoot of the ancient language of northern India, a related form of which, Sanskrit, was recorded quite early. The corresponding Sanskrit words are ṣaṭ '6', oṣṭha 'lip' (ṣ = š), śatam '100', daśa '10', sarpa 'snake', and māsa 'month'. These forms go well beyond Proto-Romany, because they point to sounds that were not preserved in it at all, for example, retroflex ṭ, but they confirm the existence of three different sibilants. The conclusions of the method were basically right. But once all of Romany had, for example, replaced ṭ by s, ṭ could not be recaptured on the basis of Romany alone. This is a limitation of the comparative method. We need different independent changes in different languages to be able to reconstruct earlier stages.

Exactly the same configurations of s-sets can be found in correspondences between South and East Slavic vs. West Slavic, Hebrew vs. Arabic, Georgian vs. the other Kartvelian languages, and so on. The method requires three proto-units, and it can (or should) be right, as was actually demonstrable in the Romany case.

[11.12]   Similar to the above cases is the question of the velars in Indo-European. The most famous isogloss in the world is the one that divides these languages in two groups, the *centum* and *satem* (see Figure 15-2:1). Centum languages have plain velars and labiovelars (i.e., two units) corresponding to the satem sibilants and affricates ([s, ś, z, dž], for which the cover term 'coronal' will be used in the diagram) and plain velars (i.e., again two units); but these form three sets of correspondences:

	A	B	C
Centum	velar	velar	labiovelar
Satem	coronal	velar	velar

These sets are now abstract cover symbols whereby voice and "murmur" have been ignored; that is, they actually embody distinctive features abstracted from segments in which voice, voicelessness, or murmur co-occur. These three sets are frequently labeled with three different symbols, for example (using voiceless stops), by a palatal **ḱ* (A; see item TEN § 11.13/Figure 11-6), a plain velar **k* (B), and a labiovelar *k^w (C). Sets A and C occur in the same environments and a contrast is consequently clear. Set B, however, occurs only after **u* and **s* and before **r* and **a*, that is, $^{u}_{s}\,\mathrm{B}\,^{r}_{a}$ (one environment of which must be present), whereas set A does not show up in these environments. In other words, sets A and B are environmentally conditioned variants of the same unit, and can thus be written with one symbol, **k*, again using voiceless stops. The complementary distribution is not quite watertight, however, which is hardly surprising in a time span of some two thousand years (the reason being apparently dialect borrowing); and that is why many Indo-Europeanists go on writing the allophonic variants **ḱ* and **k*—exactly as we could have done with our Swedish-English-German **h*- and *-*x*- (§ 11.7). In the selection of words for Indo-European vowels (Figure 11-6), we shall see the three voiced velars, **ǵ* (FIELD, DRIVE), **g* (YOKE), and *g^w (COME), where, to be sure, **ǵ* occurs before **r* against the rule, but **g* after **u* according to it.

This section shows that the method can be applied to abstracted features and not to segments only. But such features have to be handled in connection with meanings. They also complicate the bundling operations for getting back to the segments. It is much simpler to apply the method first to segments and do the componential analysis on the reconstructed protosegments; at the same time, one can look back at the attested phonetics of the daughter forms. The reason is that one also needs a knowledge of subgrouping for phonetic reconstruction (§ 18.8f.).

[11.13 The Comparative Method: Indo-European Vowels (and Selected Stops)]
Let us look now at a selection of Indo-European vocabulary items from Sanskrit, Greek, Latin, and Gothic (which represents Germanic in general). In a few cases Gothic is necessarily replaced by some other form of Germanic, and twice by Old Church Slavic, just to keep the sets at four items each (Gothic /ĕ/ is spelled *e* and not *ai* as in the documents themselves). Most of the vowel sets have been boxed in, which leaves the consonant sets readily legible on either side of the emphasized vowels. The meanings indicated are approximate lexical labels. The items have been arranged for a reconstruction of vowels, which will supply us material for the next chapter. But before treating the vowels let us look at a few consonantal sets.

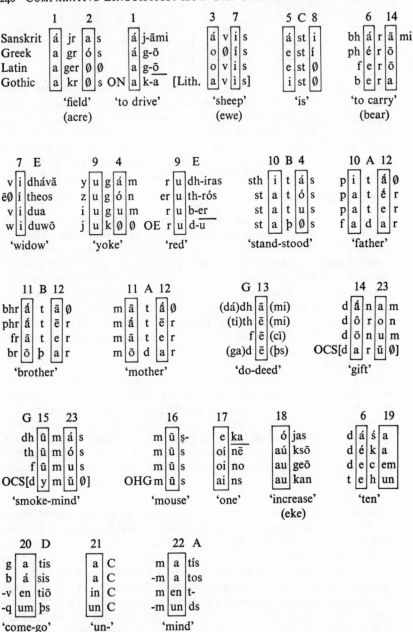

FIGURE 11-6. Indo-European sets of correspondences lined up for the comparative method.

Some of the consonants in Figure 11-6 are as straightforward as in the Germanic cases above, namely, the sets for *s (IS, STAND, MOUSE), *r (FIELD, CARRY, RED, FATHER, and so on), *m (SMOKE, MOUSE, MIND, MOTHER), *w (SHEEP, WIDOW). Let us now extract the three sets that predominantly display t's, sets A (FATHER), B (BROTHER, STOOD), and C (IS):

	A	B	C
Sanskrit	t	t	t
Greek	t	t	t
Latin	t	t	t
Germanic	d	þ	t

Set C is the constant with which Germanic (in A and B) disagrees. These are then the areas that need scrutiny. Are the three sets (A–C) complementary or not? Set C occurs after s, set A in noninitial position before an accented vowel, and set B after an accented vowel or in initial position. The accent is given by Greek and Sanskrit. However, set B does occur before the accent in STOOD; here it is part of a voiceless final cluster in Gothic. (Elsewhere a d does, in fact, occur, as we have seen in English stood; compare further (home)stead and Swedish stad 'town'.) In MOTHER, Greek and Sanskrit disagree on the place of the accent, but we have to rely on Sanskrit alone, which matches the Germanic forms in every case. All three sets are now environmentally conditioned (by other such sets) and we can label all of them with one symbol, conveniently *t. Set D is different from B only for Greek, which has s instead of t. But the s is conditioned by the following i, and hence set D is also a variant of *t (and we can reconstruct the starting point for Grimm's and Verner's laws, §§ 4.9, 4.10, 6.3).

Or, take set E from WIDOW, F from RED, and G from DO and SMOKE, which give us sets that are different only because of Latin:

	E	F	G
Sanskrit	dh	dh	dh
Greek	th	th	th
Germanic	d	d	d
Latin	d	b	f

We notice easily (when we survey the total evidence in these languages) that set G occurs initially, set F medially next to *u or *r, and set E medially elsewhere. Once more the method does its service and we can label all the sets with "one" symbol, say, *dh (we anticipate here, because there are other sets that require the symbol *d, that is, the initial sets in GIFT and TEN). This then is how one continues all through the phonology until one reaches units that can no longer be combined with each other.

[11.14]   The vowel sets are numbered with Arabic numerals. The uniform sets 1, 7, and 9 clearly contrast, and just for mnemonic purposes these are thus best labeled *a, *i, and *u. Set 3 contrasts with *a in having an o in two languages, and an o occurs also in sets 2 and 4, which are complementary to set 3 in that they occur in final syllables. The difference between 2 and 4 is confined to Latin Ø vs. u, of which Ø occurs further without a following s, and only after r (compare RED, and add sacerØØ 'sacred', virØØ 'man'). Further, this r shows up as er in this environment. But now we see that 3 does not contrast with 2/4; their differences are conditioned by the position in the word, as has already been noted. Hence the sets 2/3/4 do not contrast; they are all complementary, their distribution being conditioned by their phonetic environments (other such sets). The most sensible, unambiguous, and mnemonically good symbol for these sets is *o. In addition, set 23 is also a noncontrasting variant of this same *o, although it brings in extra variety through Old Church Slavic. Now, sets 5 and 6 contrast with the already established units in that at least half of the languages show an e, but they are different within Germanic, which has e vs. i. The two sets do not contrast between themselves, however, because set 5 is conditioned by set 8 (and other sets not included here), but 5/6 do contrast with the other sets. For these reasons, then, we label them separately, with *e. As for set 8, it is a conditioned variant of *i (7), although here we do need grammatical conditioning in Latin (a final *i drops after stops in verbal endings). We have now arrived at five short vowels:

$$
\begin{array}{llll}
(7, 8) & i & u & (9) \\
(5, 6) & e \quad o & & (2, 3, 4) \\
& a & & \\
& (1) & &
\end{array}
$$

But we still have not accommodated set 10 (FATHER and STOOD), which can be paraphrased as 'i in Sanskrit, a elsewhere'. Although the majority of the languages show a, set 10 clearly contrasts with *a, because of Sanskrit, and it also contrasts with *i, because of the languages other than Sanskrit. By the same token it contrasts with all the other vowels as well and thus requires a symbol of its own. Traditionally, the symbol *ə (schwa) has been used, which is between i and a (and the other vowels as well), and which fits in the middle of the vowel triangle.

Set 11 has long vowels only, and it thus contrasts with all the short vowels established, as it does also with sets 13 and 14. The best labels for these are obviously *ā (11), *ē (13), and *ō (14). Set 12 contains an ē in Greek, and e in Latin, and an a in Gothic, but since half of the set agrees with *ē, one must look closer for a possible ultimate identity. Indeed, 13 occurs in root syllables (i.e., we do not count prefixes) and 12 in final syllables before *r. Hence they can indeed be combined into one unit. Sets 15 and 16 do not contrast between themselves, because Slavic always has y against ū elsewhere, but they obviously contrast with all the other vowels we have reconstructed, hence *ū.

It is now clear that one continues this procedure by taking more and more material under scrutiny. Here we must leave the systematic handling of the Indo-European evidence, with a brief reference to what we would encounter if we continued. We would have to reconstruct an *i for which no material is included here, as well as i- and u-diphthongs. For the latter, just two items are given, set 17 for *oi and set 18 for *au. In some cases single vocalic segments in Sanskrit (and Greek) correspond to a sequence of vowel plus a nasal or liquid in the other languages, as in sets 19–22. Such sets obviously contrast with the others already established; but is 19 different from 20, or only its variant, or vice versa? Sanskrit and Greek agree; Latin and Germanic reverse m's and n's. But a word-final m does not occur in oldest Germanic, nor an m before t in Latin. Hence the sets do not contrast and must share one label. Here Indo-Europeanists combine the Sanskrit and Greek evidence for a single syllabic segment with that of Latin and Germanic, which point to a nasal, and write a vocalic *m̥. Sets 21 and 22 show an irregularity in Latin, where the i occurs only in this negative prefix. Otherwise, both clearly contrast with *m̥ by showing an n in Latin and Germanic. Thus the label *n̥. By the same token, one would encounter evidence requiring us to reconstruct *r̥ and *l̥, and, as in most other vowels, also length: *m̥̄, *n̥̄, *r̥̄, and *l̥̄. Here we shall completely ignore diphthongs with a long initial part, for example, *ōi.

One reconstructs nonobstruents for Proto-Indo-European as shown in Figure 11-7 (the boxed-in units have no evidence at all in our selection of data). Most Indo-European handbooks write these units as given entities. Interestingly

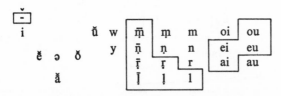

FIGURE 11-7. The inventory of reconstructed Proto-Indo-European vowels and resonants (evidence for boxed-in items not provided here).

enough, we are again dealing with a crude phonetic alphabet or allophonic writing, because the consonantal resonants y w m n r l do not contrast with the corresponding vocalic ones i u m̥ n̥ r̥ l̥. The method enables us to find this out easily, because the former always occur adjacent to vowels (although the diphthongs are *traditionally spelled* *ei, and so on, and the reverse always *yo*; compare English *say, lei*, but always *yes, yell*); the latter occur between consonants, and as we saw in TEN, silence counts as a consonant. All this will be important in the next chapter, where we shall see how internal reconstruction confirms this result of the comparative method. Students may immediately think of some cognate sets where the vowel correspondences given here do not work at all, for example, *warm* vs. Greek *thermós* (§ 8.12). But this is due to *ablaut* and will be reserved for Chapter 12.

[11.15 The Comparative Method: Finnish and Lapp Consonant Gradations]
In the case of the Finnish and Lapp consonant gradations (§§ 10.12–10.14), we saw that in morphophonemic terms there was no gradation at all; it was obligatory and easy to construct invariant units. Because, however, the gradations in the two languages are so similar, one naturally wonders whether they existed in the protolanguage underlying the two; and what does the comparative method do to alternations? Does it also eliminate them? (See § 11.6.) It is clear that we have to start out from the surface units, phones or phonemes, which actually do alternate. We get eight sets of correspondences arranged in Figure 11-8. The long stop words in 8 turn out to be crucial from the phonemic point of view, because they yield sets A2 and B1 in closed syllables, producing a contrast with sets A6–7 and B3–7, which also occur in closed syllables. The shape of the syllable is sometimes obscured in Lapp but is available from Finnish;

		1	2	3	4
A	Finnish	kä s i	tie t ää	nei t i	läh t eä
	Lapp	kie htt a	tie htt eᴅ	nieĮ ᴅ̄ a	liex t aᴅ
		'hand'	'to know'	'young lady'	'to leave'

	5	6	7	8
	ku t u	ku d un	läh d en	nuo tt a
	kō ðð a	kō ð a	lieu t am	nuo hĭt e
	'spawn' (nom.)	'spawn' (gen.)	'I leave'	'seine'

		1	2	3	4
B	Finnish	jo k i	jal k a	su v un	jo ∅ en
	Lapp	jo hk̄k a	juoĪ ḡ e	sō ɣɣ a	jō ɣɣ a
		'river'	'leg'	'family' (gen.)	'river' (gen.)

	5	6	7	8
	i ∅ än	jal ∅ an	syl j en	a kk a
	ā ij e	juol g e	tšōl g a	a hk̄k e
	'age' (gen.)	'leg' (gen.)	'saliva' (gen.)	'old woman'

FIGURE 11-8. Finnish and Lapp consonant correspondences lined up for the comparative method.

	Finnish			Lapp		
	dental		velar		dental		velar
I	katto		sukka		nuohĭte		sohǩka	sohǩka
II	katon	kato	sukan	suka	nuohtte	kiehtta	sōhkka	
III		kadon		suan		kieða		sōγγa
	'roof'	'loss'	'sock'	'brush'	'seine'	'hand'	'sock'	'family'

FIGURE 11-9. The interrelation of phonemes and morphophonemes. Rows indicate different phonemes and phones within each articulatory set (dental, velar). Columns indicate different morphophonemes. [Reprinted with slight modification from Raimo Anttila, "The relation between internal reconstruction and the comparative method," *Ural-Altaische Jahrbücher*, **40**, 159–173 (1968), (© Societas Uralo-Altaica).]

this situation is parallel to the information provided by the accent in Greek and Sanskrit that supplied environments for grouping consonant sets together. That is, we have the three-way contrasts as indicated by the rows of Figure 11-9. In other words, the rows indicate phonemic identity within each language and articulatory set (i.e., dental and velar in this material), whereas the columns indicate morphophonemic identity within themselves but morphophonemic difference with other columns. These columns contain the sets we found to contrast with each other in the section on morphophonemics, but here they have been written so that the phonetic/phonemic identity of their members match in the same rows. The phonemic contrasts between the rows are clear, because minimal pairs immediately establish them: *katto/kato, katon/kadon, tahtomme/tahdomme* 'our wish/we wish'. The table, then, is a summary and a visual comparison between morphophonemics and phonemics and their overlapping. Using these phonemic contrasts we must group the sets under three contrasting units within each articulatory set: *t* (A1–4), *d* (A5–6), *tt* (A8), *k* (B1–2), *g* (B3–7), and *kk* (B8). It must be remembered that the three units (within each articulatory group) arrived at here depend on the material used, and in no way mirror the number of units one would have to posit with fuller evidence. The method can never go beyond the material to which it is being applied. Only if the selection happens to represent the total population adequately will the result of the method have wider validity. It is always helpful, therefore, to expand the selection until it includes all the evidence.

What is of interest in this particular Finnish-Lapp selection is that the comparative method does assign consonant gradation to most of the words used, as we see by writing the reconstructed units in their proper environments, for example, (nom.) *kätV, (gen.) *käden 'hand', and (nom.) *suku, (gen.) *sugun 'family', and so on. However, in one item, where both languages have alternation, the comparative method eliminates it, (nom.) *kudu, (gen.) *kudun 'spawn'. This would be true of all those consonants that alternate in Lapp, but not in Finnish (e.g., *m, n, l,* and so on). We should expect this here, however (i.e., Finnish has no alternation but provides the phonetic environments for the Lapp alternation)—unlike the case where both languages participate.

[11.16]   We have seen that in both phonemic and morphophonemic analysis the method could be deadlocked in cases where a unit occurred in one particular environment and was complementary to two other units, so its assignment to either one was rather arbitrary or impossible. Now, the comparative method can be subject to exactly the same indeterminacy, as we see in set 7A, which is complementary both to the sets comprising *t* and to those of *d,* because it is the only set occurring in a cluster with a spirant set (10):

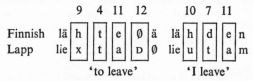

The only indication of gradation comes from the spirant set 10, which is complementary to 9 in that it occurs as a first member of a cluster that begins a closed syllable. Thus both can be combined under the symbol *x,* and A7 occurs after this where it starts a closed syllable. If one now arbitrarily assigned A7 to *d,* we would get consonant gradation for this paradigm, and if we connected it with *t,* there would be no gradation in this cluster *xt.* In this case, then, one would have to compile all the relevant material before one could reach an unambiguous conclusion. As for set 12, with a little extra evidence it would be easy to see that it is a variant of *t.*

We observed in the application of the comparative method to this Finnish and Lapp gradating material phonetic conditioning of the distribution of the sets of correspondences, which is one of its characteristics. The method did sort out the material so that it gave consonant gradation in the protolanguage for the majority of the cases. Unfortunately, the method does *not* tell us whether this result is correct! It is a well-known axiom that the comparative method is powerless if two (or more) languages undergo the same change after the split-off point. That is, it is conceivable that the protolanguage had a certain tendency toward allophonic variation in terms of open and closed syllables, with no phonemic importance, and that this tendency increased with time, ultimately giving the attested gradations. This process is called drift (§ 9.13), and the comparative method assigns its results automatically to the protolanguage, against the actual historical facts. What makes the comparative method work is that different languages usually undergo different changes, as we saw from the Indo-European material above. Another cause of great uneasiness in this matter of reconstructing consonant gradation is the crucial role played by the long-stop words, as has been mentioned. They are rather infrequent, which raises the question whether they arose after the period of unity. Here, also, the actual history and the result of the method need not agree at all.

[11.17] But there are even situations in which a change in one language can deadlock the method or derail it, as far as the real history is concerned. The Finnish *i* ∼ *e* alternation could easily be eliminated through morphophonemic analysis, exactly like the consonant gradation (§ 10.12). If we want to apply the comparative method to this material to see whether the alternation should be reconstructed in the protolanguage, a dead end is the consequence of the fact that both Finnish *i* and *e* correspond to Lapp *a*, for example, set 11 above and

13	14	14
$\begin{bmatrix} i \\ ä \end{bmatrix}$ kä hkke 'age'	käs $\begin{bmatrix} i \\ a \end{bmatrix}$ 'hand'	neit $\begin{bmatrix} i \\ a \end{bmatrix}$ niejᴅ 'miss', etc.

Sets 13 and 14 are complementary, and sets 11 and 14 both occur in the same environment (medially) and thus contrast, the method now requiring two units, **e* (11) and **i* (14), for example, (nom.) **käti*, (gen.) **käden* 'hand'. The vowel alternation turns out to be the same as in Finnish. From these reconstructed forms one can unambiguously derive the Lapp vowels, but there is no guarantee whatsoever that Lapp ever had the alternation also. From the time that Finnish (all of Baltic Finnic) shows the change of final **-e* > *-i*, the method assigns the result (*i* ∼ *e* alternation) also to the protolanguage.

Thus in both cases (consonant gradation and *i* ∼ *e* alternation) the comparative method gives us alternation, if we use surface phonology (phonemes or phones), but no guarantee of exact historical truth. This contrasts sharply with the results yielded by the Indo-European material. But even in cases where the method yields uncertain historical facts, it still gives us a possible starting point from which the languages used can be unambiguously derived. And of course such starting points will always be historically true in some sense.

[11.18 Checking the Results on Finnish and Lapp Reconstructions] In the case of Germanic and Romany, we could go to earlier records to check our reconstructions (at least in part) in order to gain confidence in the performance of the comparative method. One should never forget the fact that reconstructions are valid only for the material used, either in terms of selection or the number of languages; and since Finnish and Skolt Lapp are not the only representatives of their family, we can use wider comparative checking.

Additional material may require readjustment of earlier results, and since our samples were so restricted, we could hardly expect that they would allow us to recapture everything. Let us mention a few points. The Lapp genitive *nieða* is completely anomalous; if it were regular one would expect a paradigm *niejᴅa/*nieida* or **nieiᴅa* (like *noajᴅa/noaida* [*noaiᴅa*] 'witch'). 'Miss, young lady' represents a semantic area that often attracts irregular change (§ 9.8), and such an irregularity should not have been included in the reconstruction at this stage. Further, Finnish *neiti/neidin* was not originally an *i*-stem, because dialects and the *Kalevala* (the Finnish national epic, the model of *Hiawatha*) show an e-stem, like *käsi/käden*. The old paradigm was thus of the type **neisi/ *neiden*, and such a nominative lurks in the Karelian compounds *ńeiz-akka, neiž-akku* 'old maid' (with *akka* 'old woman'; compare English compounds *husband* and *shepherd*, which contain old shapes, § 5.15). The *i*-stems are late, and found in Proto-Baltic Finnic only; our application of the method, therefore, had to rely on Finnish. The lateness of the Finnish paradigm also explains the lack of assibilation in the *i*-stems, that is, difference in chronology (§ 4.29). But note that in spite of the Lapp anomaly, the reconstruction of consonantism was basically right.

Forms like *lähteä/lähden* 'to leave/I leave' did not have consonant gradation in Early Baltic Finnic in the cluster **kt*: **läkte-öäk/*läkte-m*. After the change **k > h* gradation was analogically extended to the word. In Lapp all words are subject to gradation in one way or another, and the Proto-Lapp paradigm went **lēktă-öēk/*lēɣìă-m*. This is a perfect example of independent drift in both languages, triggered by the common kernel of at least phonetic consonant gradation (see § 9.13). In such cases the comparative method is helpless.

[11.19]   In Chapter 12 we extend comparative reconstruction by internal reconstruction. Since we have left so much material unused (from Finnish and Lapp) we can use it to test the result of the comparative method with *internal reconstruction*. If a Finnish word has two sets of consonants expected to be subject to gradation, the stem has only the weak grade in the first set, whether the syllable is open or closed. Thus from *käsi/käde-n* 'hand' and *puku/puvu-n* 'suit' we have

nominative	kä.de-.tön	pu.vu-.ton
genitive	kä.de-t.tö.mä-n	pu.vu-t.to.ma-n
	'handless'	'suitless'

where the period indicates syllable boundaries, and the hyphen, morpheme boundaries. The genitives are as expected because the syllables *.det.* and *.vut.* are closed (< *.tet.*, (*u*).*kut.*), but in the nominative *.de.* and *.vu.* are anomalous, because here one would expect *.te.* and *.ku.*, respectively. But since the genitives show that the single *t* of the *-tön/ton* '-less' must be derived from the underlying double *tt* of the suffix |*-ttoma-*|, one must assume that a double *tt* was still present in the nominative at the time when single stops gradated. The order of gradation is thus (ignoring vowel harmony):

	NOMINATIVE	GENITIVE
(1) underlying	|käte-ttömä|	|käte-ttömä-n|
(2) gradation of single stop	kädettömä	kädettömän
(3) drop of final vowel	kädettöm	kädettömän
(4) gradation of double stop	kädetöm	kädettömän

And then at some point, final *m > n*. Thus Finnish still shows a clear hierarchy in the gradation of single and double stops. Finno-Ugric scholars use this information correctly in assuming that the double gradation is later than *t ~ *d and *k ~ *g, and they generally write a phonetic difference, for example, *tt ~ *ĭt, *kk ~ *k̆k. The method could not, of course, go beyond the material it was applied to. Because it had to rely on Finnish (and Lapp) disyllabic stems only, its result was too much like Finnish (all evidence not considered here). The moral of this is that everything in a language must be subjected to different methods for solid reconstruction, and even so, many indeterminacies will remain. But our treatment can be only so detailed, as our main purpose is to get a feeling of what is involved in applying the methods and how reliable they are.

[11.20 Conclusion] All the methods (phonemic analysis, morphophonemic analysis, internal reconstruction, the comparative method) have now been treated, and the discussion of them will go on in the next chapter, which forms an integral whole with this one. In this chapter, we have seen how the operation of the comparative method rests on two factors: the arbitrariness of the linguistic sign and regular phonetic change. Now, if two or more languages show regular correspondences between themselves in items where the meanings are the same or similar, that is, if there are diagrammatic relations *between* different languages, it means that there must be only one underlying colligation of sound and meaning (the linkup of the linguistic sign). The differences in the attested sound segments therefore depend on regular phonetic change, which has changed the sounds of the original linguistic sign; and often the meaning has also changed. This surface diversity is not at all different from dialectal variation, which also does not affect the sign aspect; that is, in cases like /iyðər/ vs. /ayðər/ *either* there is clearly only one colligation of form and meaning, although the form does not manifest itself in exactly the same shape (see Chapter 12). Whenever an innovation that does not involve regular phonetic change enters the language, the comparative method staggers, or can even be derailed. The principal stumbling blocks are either all kinds of analogy, which often make the signs more iconic in relation to the rest of the grammar, or irregular sound change, which can also be iconic with respect to sounds of nature. That is, when the symbolic aspect of the linguistic sign is tampered with, the comparative method runs into trouble. Regular sound change retains the conventional arbitrary *colligation* of sound and meaning intact; although the shapes change, they change regularly. The fact that comparative linguistics depends chiefly on the symbolic sign was stressed in the background (§ 1.17). This chapter has shown how and why.

The actual act of establishing reconstructed units is generally not visible in our standard handbooks and historical grammars, although they are all based on such comparative work. The handbooks invariably start with the starred forms and map them to the attested forms; that is, they use the framework of historical linguistics, which is the reverse of what we have done in this chapter. Thus one writes that a sound *x gives y in language M and z in language N, and so on. We have seen in this chapter that the comparative method gives us the starting point of Grimm's and Verner's laws, and that it also automatically provides the rules for them, that is,

Proto-Indo-European *t* in voiceless clusters gives *t* in Germanic, *þ* word initially and medially after stressed vowel, and *ð* elsewhere.

In other words, we just back-project the environments that provided us the reasons for combining various sets of correspondences. Of course we have seen earlier that this change is more general: (1) the feature *closure* (occlusion) remains when it co-occurs with the feature *voicelessness* after a segment containing voicelessness (when we do not have a double stop, for example, *tt* > *ss* in Germanic), (2) it changes into a feature *fricative* initially and medially after stress (Grimm's law), and (3) the feature *voicelessness* is replaced by *voice*, when it co-occurs with fricativeness (Verner's law) (§§ 4.9, 4.10, 6.3, 11.13). The formulation of these rules (1–3) is not superior in theoretical terms to the establishment of the starting points. Both are by-products of each other, that is, complementary. Regular sound change makes comparison possible, and comparison then establishes the starting points, at the same time giving the mapping rules, that is, the sound changes that made it work. Since there is no choice but to believe in the complementarity of units and rules, and since the rules have already been treated in Part II, we can leave the matter here. Sound change is the rule part of the comparative method. Historical and comparative linguistics are opposite sides of the same coin.

REFERENCES

General: Meillet 1967a, 1926, Hoenigswald 1950, 1960a, Pike 1957, Thieme 1964, Anttila 1968, Devoto 1969, Katičić 1970, Allen 1953, Ellis 1966; **11.8** Moulton 1954; **11.12** Krahe 1970 -- Glottalic reinterpretation of Proto-Indo-European stops: Gamkrelidze and Ivanov 1984, Vennemann in Fisiak (ed.) 1985, (ed.) 1987; **11.13-11.14** Krahe 1970, Szemerényi 1970; **11.18** E. Itkonen (private communication); **11.19** Leppik 1968, Anttila 1969a.

The comparative method is quite different in syntax (than above) in spite of the use of the same name. It is based on analogy (cf. §§5.16-17), not regular sound change, and falls under the concept of internal reconstruction. This is treated below (§§11.21-30), with further exemplification to come later (§§19.5-12; cf. §§20.1-6).

THE COMPARATIVE METHOD IN SYNTAX

[11.21]   Statements about reconstructing morphology, syntax, and semantics are distributed throughout this book, with warnings that the comparative
method as used in phonology does not work that well (elsewhere) in the grammar.
Under the recent hegemony of syntax many linguists have been confident in denying this stance, maintaining that the method works in syntax about as well, a few
more difficulties notwithstanding. This is not so (although fashions exert their
weight and take time to run their course). The regularity of sound change (§4.32),
the mainstay of the comparative method (in phonology), is due to the fact that all
sound units mean the same, viz. 'otherness': Sounds are diacritic marks that keep
morphemes (both lexical and grammatical) separate. Thus, on that level there is
no competition between them (interference comes e.g. from analogy and sound
symbolism; these are the disturbing factors). Many sound changes are irreversi-
ble, giving us an indication of direction (§§14.5-6). In a good case there are hundreds or even thousands of matching words giving us a solid basis of material
which can tolerate a certain amount of indeterminacy, e.g. irregular sound
change. And most importantly, we get reconstructed words (cf. §20.14) and morphology (§§19.1-2, 19.8-10), without which syntax would be helpless (nonexistent). The comparative method does not work because of "deep structure" units
(e.g. the phonemes; which are not that deep anyway), but because of contrasts;
and the units and environments are on the same level (§§10.1-6). Sounds can be
symbols, e.g. a particular pronunciation can reveal that the speaker is e.g. a
woman and/or a New Yorker (cf. §§3.1-3, 9.11), but this is in addition to the primary diacritic function. With words and morphemes the symbolic aspects are essential. And this is where relationship must be established before syntactic reconstruction can be attempted. Sentences are of course symbolic signs also (§§0.3,
1.11, 1.16), but lexical symbols act as diacritic marks between them.

[11.22]   Against the thousands of vocabulary items (open set) in which sounds
act as diacritics (closed inventories) in syntax we have only a limited number of
patterns (closed set) with limitless diacritics (words; and the closed set of morphemes). It is of course the diacritics that are crucial here; they allow us to desig-
nate practically any state of affairs. One can have words without syntax, but not
the other way around (§8.19). Syntax is a kind of algebra (§1.14) and thus strongly
iconic (diagrammatic), and like onomatopoeia problematic in reconstruction
(Fig. 16-4). Syntactic patterns are recreated whereas vocabulary is inherited with
its arbitrary symbolic moorings. Syntax strives toward types (patterns), which are
mental, whereas history and reconstruction require tokens (manifestations), with
contextual links. Furthermore, the limited number of syntactic patterns would be
parallel to (short) pronominal sequences of the type *CV* between daughter languages, if no lexical material were to be used. Often in this area there are serious
problems even with lexical support.

[11.23   Directionality/Irreversibility]   All comparative methods that allow a reliable reconstruction require systems that persist relatively unmodified through mechanisms that contain identifiable irreversibilities. The systems must be able to split into daughter systems, and the similarities among daughter systems that have been inherited must be identified from other types of resemblance. The comparative method is a machine that rakes up diagrams to this end. The lack of regular syntactic change must be compensated through elements that carry regular sound correspondences and through relics and archaisms. Lexicalization and grammaticalization processes often give directionality patterns, e.g. *noun > postposition > clitic > case ending*, and this would match the directionality of sound change. We have seen this in Hungarian *bél → világ bele > világba* 'into the world', and Finnish *kerta → koiran keralla >* koira*ŋke* 'with the dog' (§7.13). Similarly, Italian *casa*, Spanish *casa* 'house', and French *chez* prep. 'at' would indicate that French has innovated. Stylistic registers also show that archaic patterns tend to survive in frozen compounds, poetic collocations, legal and religious language, and proverbs (§19.7). When these contrast with ordinary discourse they should reflect the older state of affairs (§5.15). In favorable cases seriation thus fulfills the irreversibility requirement.

[11.24   Resemblance]   A resemblance between two independent branches (languages) (cf. §§2.18, 15.2-3, 18.8-11) tends to be assigned to the common origin (protolanguage). This is what the comparative method does, if the resemblance resides in emic units, or actually constitutes it. The extension of the method to syntax has been most explicit in the tagmemic model:

> Sets of correspondences of tagmemes [roughly: phrase slots] and syntagmemes [roughly: sentences] between two daughter languages may be considered to be continuations of respective prototagmemes and protosyntagmemes in the parent language, just as sets of correspondences of phonemes and morphemes between two daughter languages may be considered to be continuations of respective protophonemes and protomorphemes in the parent language.-- (Costello 1983)

These sets look like the ones for cases (§§20.1-3). The oldest Indo-European languages display so-called "absolute constructions" in which a noun with an agreeing participle functions as a phrase. These vary from manner to time to means, and the different languages use different cases (Sanskrit - locative, Greek - genitive, Latin - ablative, and Gothic - dative) which match those of substantival temporal adverbials. The similarity is thus clear, and according to the principle of minimizing steps in derivation (§§2.17, 15.2, 21.22) it should be assigned to the protolanguage, although the result is just participle plus head noun in a local case. The method always pushes agreements back and ignores disagreements. Recurrence is a real problem in syntactic correspondences because of the limited number of patterns to begin with. Hence the agreement in substantival temporal adverbials is telling, although it does not indicate which case. The method tends to reconstruct slots only. Unless the slots can be filled with corresponding material they do not prove the issue. There is great danger of using mere logical possibility (that which we do not know not to be true).

[11.25 Reconstruction and Typology] This is why one has to talk of morphosyntax, because (paradigmatic) morphology is the best anchoring point we can have for reconstructional syntax, or vocabulary at large if morphology fails. Without this anchoring one remains adrift among universals (§16.10). But it has become another fashion to use typological universals as determiners of change and reconstruction, especially under the auspices of the so-called typological consistency of language types (largely word order typologies). This approach is seriously misguided, however. Typology and comparative reconstruction have inherently different goals and they should not be allowed to override each other. When there is a clash between history and typology, typology loses. Or in other words, the highest human universal is history. The comparative method is intimately connected with time, which explains its predictive power. It is true that the method has its achronic aspects, but typology is totally so, a purely descriptive device or mode, although usually given as theoretical or explanatory.

[11.26 Matching Texts] In addition to the lack of commensurate syntaxes as a starting point for reconstruction (§16.10), there is the problem of matching texts (manifestations). One should use linguistic reactions to matching pragmatic situations, i.e. syntactic expression of similar thematic contexts in cognate traditions (without loan syntax). For example, we know that athletic contests were an integral part of Proto-Indo-European funeral practices for important persons. (Such funeral games ultimately give us the modern Olympics.) Take now the following set of relative sentences from Hittite (cf. §19.9), Vedic Sanskrit, and oldest Greek (cf. §§19.8-10):

HITTITE:

nu tarhzi kuis dān pedass-a kuis nu-smas II TAUGHIA ERAINMESpianzi
ptcle wins who of 2ᵈ place-and who, ptcle-to them 2 uniforms they-give
'he who wins, and he who (is) of 2ᵈ place, to them 2 uniforms they give'
LÚKAS₄.E tarhzi kuis I MANA KUBABBAR pianzi
the runner wins who, 1 mina of silver they-give

SANSKRIT:

sa   yo   na   ujjeṣyati   sa   prathamaḥ somasya pāsyati
(ptcle)-he who of-us will-win (ptcle)-he first of-the-soma will-drink
sa   yo   na   ujjeṣyati   tasya idam bhaviṣyati
(ptcle)-he who of-us will-win (ptcle)-his this will-be (cf. §§19.8-9)

GREEK:

hos nun orkhēstōn pantōn atalōtata paizei tō tode k[ ]n
who now of-dancers all most-sportively plays, his this k . (is)

These are the kinds of sentences that Indo-Europeanists should compare. The agreements are perfect (§11.24), and there is no doubt that the pattern is inherited. But it is one pattern, as a pattern. What is important is the morphology manifesting the standard paradigms as results of phonological and morphological reconstruction. Note e.g. *kwis 'who' in Hittite (cf. also Latin quis) and *yo (-) in Sanskrit and Greek as a 'dialectal' isogloss, as well as *-ti '3 sg' in Hittite and Sanskrit vs. *-i in Greek (cf. §§19.8-10). And so one proceeds, even when the lexical items do not match. The difference in method between phonology and (morpho)syntax should also be clear. When one compares sounds, morphemes, and words, correspondences between formally different constructs yield unique reconstructions. In paradigms and sentence patterns the correspondence is the identity relation to begin with. The clarity is given (found) in an archaic pattern (language) and more opaque patterns are evaluated against it. Thus when the clear pattern of Hittite and Vedic is unleashed on the complicated morphology of Old Irish we can bring it into the common mold (§19.10 [p. 361]). We uncover results of sound changes, boundary reinterpretations, and analogical levelings. This is indeed normal, and Old Irish can now be derived from Proto-Indo-European. But is this (the) application of the classical comparative method? No, the pattern was given in the daughters, and hence this is a variant of internal reconstruction (cf. §§10.7-17, 12, 19.6).

[11.27 Matching Patterns]   Let us take up the Finnish sentence(s) 'I see the boy(s) go' (§5.17) to reconstruct the original pattern for participle objects of verbs of perceiving and saying. We need three lines for the singular (**A.-C.**) and three for the plural (**D.-F.**):

A. näen	poja-|n|	mene-|vä-n|	=... ACC.SG....ACC.SG
B. näen	poja-|n| 2	mene-|vän| 1	=...ACC.SG. ...-vän-"INF."
C. näen	poja-|n|	mene-|vän|	=...GEN.SG. ...-vän-"INF."
D. näen	poik-i-|en|	mene-|vän|	=...GEN.PL. ...-vän-"INF."
E. näen	poja- t	mene-|vän|	=...ACC.PL. ...-vän-"INF."
F. näen	poja- t	mene-vä-t	=...ACC.PL. ...ACC.PL.

The relevant morphology is highlighted in boldface, then labeled grammatically in small capitals, and finally matched for number through hooked lines. This is a "cave-in" arrangement in that one starts from the identity beween **A.** and **F.** and moves towards the middle, ending up with current **C.** and **D.** In each line the analysis of the singular attracts a parallel plural. We can uncover two reanalyses in the singular form although its manifestation remains the same. The first one, **A.→B.** (1), is a fossilization of the two morphemes into a unitary -vän (loss of boundary; cf. §§5.4, 5.15, 7.9). This leaves the plural **F.** (extremely archaic or poetic) dangling, and it follows suit producing **E.** (Old Finnish and traditional poetry). Then, the acc. sg. is taken as gen. sg., **B.→C.** (2), producing the head and attribute switch (§5.17). This analysis is unambiguously reflected in the modern pl. **D.**

These two changes in the singular can be summed up through English forms "I see the boy going" (**A.**) > 1 "I see the boy go" (**B.**) > 2 "I see the boy's go" (**C.**). These are abductive reinterpretations that remain covert, but they typically surface deductively in the corresponding plural forms (§9.16). The necessity of this formal analysis is matched by the stylistic registers of **F.** and **E.**, making them the oldest and most original (§11.23). The original case marking (**A.** and **F.**) is clear with the reverse word order in the adjective-head construction *Näen menevän pojan* 'I see a/the going boy' and *Näen menevät pojat* 'I see the going boys', as well as in *Näen pojan* 'I see a/the boy'. The order in the tabular arrangement above reflects subject-predicate structure (§19.6), as is also clear from the meaning; these could be glossed with clauses '...that the boy(s) go(es)'. This is typical of how one explicates analogical forces, thereby retrieving syntactic changes also.

Such an analysis is supported by verbs of seeming and feeling, which as intransitives would not have objects but rather nominative subjects. Thus, with the same lexical items, *Poika näkyy menevä* 'A/the boy is seen going, it seems a/the boy is going' in Old Finnish is replaced by *Poika näkyy menevän*. The comparative evidence points the same way. The construction in Estonian corresponding to **A.**, with the equivalent words as partitive objects (showing object-case agreement, even if different cases; cf. the absolute constructions, §11.24), *Näen poega* (or *poissi*) *minevat*, would match a Finnish *Näen poikaa menevää*, 'I see the boy go'. There are also attestations of partitive objects in negative sentences which have been totally eliminated in the Finnish reanalyzed results, e.g. *En näe pojan menevän* 'I do not see the boy go'. South Lapp preserves the original genitive -*n* and accusative -*m* distinction, making the analysis quite certain (cf. §10.14).

What kind of evidence is this comparative evidence? As in the Indo-European material above it is actually internal evidence. Finnish is evaluated against the normal situation elsewhere and it is possible to bring it into the common mold. This is done largely through the analysis of the interplay of sound change and analogy.

[11.28 Morphological Prerequisites] To show how detailed paradigmatic reconstruction is the basis for syntactic inferences, let us look at the Finnish cases (with many shortcuts):

"GRAMMATICAL"	II INNER ('in')	III OUTER ('at')
Nominative *Ø*	Illative *-(h)Vn* 'to'	Allative *-lle* 'to'
Genitive *-n* 'of'	Inessive *-ssa* 'in'	Adessive *-lla* 'at'
Partitive *-(t)a* ('from')	Elative *-sta* 'from'	Ablative *-lta* 'from'

Internal analysis in the local cases points to -*s*- and -*l*- as ingredients in the local columns, appended with the normal essive (-*na*) and partitive (-*(t)a*) markers (for the last two rows), which are in fact the general local cases in adverbs or postpositions, hence "deeper" in grammar, in positions where archaisms often lurk. In adverbs there are also latives ('to'-cases) with -*s*, -*n* and -*k*. The local pattern can now be written as follows, with *taka*- 'rear, behind' and *ete*- 'front' (the row labels now have Uralic terms):

	I GENERAL	II INNER	III OUTER
A. Lative	taka-s/n/k	ete-s-(e)n	ete-l-en
B. Locative	taka-na	ete-s-nä	ete-l-nä
C. Separative	taka-ta	ete-s-tä	ete-l-tä

The forms are written without consonant gradation (the actual Finnish forms are *taas* 'again', *taan, taa* 'to behind', *takaa* 'from behind', etc.). For *ete-* the only missing slot would be IC. Comparative evidence shows that Column I reaches back to Proto-Uralic, II back to Cheremis, whereas III occurs only in Baltic Finnic (Fig. 15-1). It is also easy to see how II has been created out of the ingredients in I, with the two latives in IIA, and the lative *-s* and the essive (IB) and separative for IIB and C. The agglutinative freedom of combination reminds one of something like English prepositional *from within* (IIC); also the translative combines two latives: *taa-kse* 'to behind', and an exessive arose as a union of IB and C, *kotonta* 'from (at) home'. The syntactic distribution is telling. Column I is the most restricted one, occurring only as local adverbs (e.g. *olen kotona* 'I am at home'), II shows up in unproductive idioms and phrases: (e.g. *naiset menivät marjaan* 'the women went to pick berries', literally 'into a berry'!), whereas III is the general one (*miehet olivat oluella* 'the men were having a beer', literally 'at the beer'). Such a distribution agrees well with the comparative evidence for time depth (seriation, §14.6).

[11.29] It is now also clear that III has been based on II. The question is, where does the *-l-* come from? The agreed-upon answer is: from pronominal adverbs built on a derivational suffix *-la* as follows:

(1) *täkälänä*	(2) *täyälnä*	(3) *täällä* 'here'	(4) *täällä*
sikälänä	*siyälnä*	*siällä* 'there'	*siellä*
tookalana	*tooyalna*	*tuualla* 'there, yonder'	*tuolla*
muukalana	*muuyalna*	*muualla* 'elsewhere'	*muualla*

Both adjectives and nouns make nominals in *-la* with local meaning, e.g. *vesi/vete-* 'water', *vete-lä* 'watery', *seka-la* 'mess(y)'. *Täkä-lä* (1) would thus mean 'this place, place here'. In stage (1) we have locatives in *-na* (IB) which then in (2) have syncopated the penultimate vowel thereby creating a closed syllable which triggers consonant gradation ($k > \gamma$). In (3) the weak grade γ has dropped (§§6.17, 10.13, 18.13) and *$*ln > ll$* (the last column lists modern standard forms).

Note that these pronominal adverbs do not give the regular adessives, because the extra formative *-ka-* adds an extra vowel to the result (3 and 4), as compared with the pronominal adessives *tällä, sillä, tuolla* (late as adverb (4)), and *muulla*. But there is a group of local nouns that supplies *-la-* derivatives of the shape in (1):

ete-	'front'	*etelä*	'south'
lähe-	'near'	*lähelä*	'place nearby, neighboring farm'
pohja	'rear, foundation'	*põhjala*	'threshing floor' (Estonian)

When these adapt to the pattern of II through both sound change and analogy, along the lines of (1) to (3) above, the outer pattern ends up as

ete-s(-)en   *ete-lä(-)n* —▸ *ete-len* ▸—▸ *edelle(n)*
ete-s-nä   *ete-l-nä* > *ede-llä*
ete-s-tä   *ete-l-tä* > *ede-ltä*

The allative deviates more than the others, but the analogical forces from IIA and IIIB make it reasonable to infer the above. This is indeed how one goes about and continues reconstructing paradigmatic morphology. Note now that these nouns give the missing link in the development and spread of the outer local cases, because after the syncope *-lä-* > *-l-* the liquid is pulled into the ending and the base defaults to the original noun (e.g. *ete-* → *etelä/-nä* > *edellä/ete-*).

[11.30   The Syntactic Yield]   The morphological reconstruction above just skirted the various complications one actually has to handle, and the strict syntactic frame in which it was carried out remained invisible. The *-la-* nouns include also places for kin, e.g. *setälä* 'uncle's place', *appela* 'parents-in-law's place'. Consider now the following sentences (with modern Finnish orthography): **Setälänä on hevosia* 'there are horses in the uncle's place' vs. **Lähelänä on hevosia* 'there are horses nearby'. With an animate noun as the base we get the possessive construction when the derivative kicks back into the base: *Sedällä on hevosia* 'Uncle has horses'. No subject-function reading results with inanimate nouns: *Lähellä on hevosia* (meaning as above). This is typical. The load carried by morphology by far exceeds that of syntax, which in a way is an afterthought only. Furthermore, the method used is clearly internal reconstruction, not the comparative method as in phonology.

REFERENCES

General: Steever et al. (eds.) 1976, Langhoff 1980, Pilch in Fisiak (ed.) 1984, Ramat (ed.) 1981, Lehmann 1974, Hawkins 1983; **11.21** Vincent in Ramat (ed.) 1981; **11.22** Jeffers in Christie (ed.) 1976, Watkins in Steever et al. (eds.) 1976, Winter in Fisiak (ed.) 1984; **11.23** Hockett 1985, Hock 1985, Watkins in Steever et al. (eds.) 1976, Campbell 1986; **11.24** Costello 1982, 1983, Holland 1986; **11.25** Dunkel 1981, Winter, M. Harris, both in Fisiak (ed.) 1984; **11.26** Watkins in Steever et al. (eds.) 1976; **11.27** Campbell 1986; **11.28-30** Anttila and Uotila 1984, Korhonen 1979. (See also p. 363)

CHAPTER 12

INTERNAL RECONSTRUCTION

The metamorphosis of morphophonemic analysis into internal reconstruction is shown with examples that come originally from a historical frame.

[12.1 Gothic and Germanic Verbal Ablaut]   Internal reconstruction is already known to the reader, as it is exactly the same as morphophonemic analysis. Only the emphasis of the two is different: morphophonemic analysis brushes aside unproductive "irregular" alternations, whereas internal reconstruction concentrates on them (§ 10.9). As far as the method itself is concerned, there would be no necessity for further exemplification, but we shall use it once more to retrace one of the most famous cases of its application, the Indo-European laryngeal theory. It is a topic for which students seem to have an unabated interest, and it is indeed illustrative. We shall lead into the theory by the application of internal reconstruction to the Gothic strong verb (i.e., the type *sing–sang–sung*, exhibiting "ablaut").

We rewrite Gothic *ei* [i·] as *ii* to do justice to the actual sound and then look at the vocalic nuclei of the verbs *bite*, *choose*, and *bind*, according to our familiar sets of correspondences, boxed in along the seams of the flanking consonants:

	'BITE'			'CHOOSE'			'BIND'		
pres.	b	ii	tan	k	iu	san	b	i	ndan
pret. sg.	b	ai	t	k	au	s	b	a	nd
pret. pl.	b	i	tum	k	u	sum	b	u	ndum
p.p.p.	b	i	tans	k	u	sans	b	u	ndans

The first two sets are of the type in *divine/divinity* vs. *sane/sanity*, or of course like *bite/bitten*; that is, a diphthong alternates with a short vowel. They obviously contrast; but then we notice that the *i* and *u*, respectively, run through the whole set, suggesting a different segmentation:

b	i	itan	k	i	usan	b	i	ndan
b	a	it	k	a	us	b	a	nd
b	∅	itum	k	∅	usum	b	u	ndum
b	∅	itans	k	∅	usans	b	u	ndans

Now we see that the first two diphthongs contrast on account of *i* and *u* and not the alternating vowel, which now resembles the vowel set in *bind*. We had exactly the same situation with Finnish *katto* and *sukka* (§ 10.13). We further note that the set *i-a-u-u* as in *bind*, occurs only before nasals and therefore, is conditioned by the set *n-n-n-n*; it is thus a variant of *i-a-Ø-Ø*, however we would label it. What happened in the above case was that the vowel alternation tended to fuse with its environment, thus creating more possibilities for segmentation. Rather than carry out internal reconstruction in this familiar way to establish all the contrasting alternations, we shall concentrate on the *environments* of the variants of this one unit, that is, *i*, *a*, and nothing. In this way our internal reconstruction has a slightly different emphasis from that presented in Chapter 10. Such a treatment of vowels and environments means the study of canonical forms (favorite sound shapes of morphemes, e.g., *CVC*, *CVCC*, *CVCV*, and so on), and we shall see that the essence of the laryngeal theory is also a fusion of the alternating vowel and its environment. Thus this chapter will not be superfluous after the previous one, since it will show a new side to the flexibility of internal reconstruction.

To facilitate this new aim we simply turn around the above arrangement by ninety degrees, which gives us

	PRES.	PRET. SG.	PRET. PL.	P.P.P.
I.	b i itan	b a it	bitum	bitans
II.	k i usan	k a us	kusum	kusans
III.	b i ndan	b a nd	b u ndum	b u ndans

In other words, lexical meanings are represented by rows, the grammatical ones, by columns. Thus we can segment the formal markers that correspond. The first column shows the same vowel *i* all the way, the second, *a* (ignoring the unified infinitive ending *-an*), whereas the last two columns do not share sound units except, again, the endings *-um* 'we' and *-ans*. The vowels *i* and *a* alternate in clearly defined grammatical categories and thus represent in a characteristic fashion one and the same morphophoneme. The rows within themselves share the same sequence of sound units within the roots namely, *b-it*, *k-us*, and *b-nd*. The only problem is in the last two columns of row 3, which breaks the pattern by showing an extra *u*. This is a typical situation in morphophonemic analysis, alias internal reconstruction. We use widespread regularities against which we evaluate apparent aberrations. According to the regular pattern in rows 1 and 2, the "aberrant" root shape of row 3 should be an "expected" *bnd*. Such a sequence does not occur in the surface phonology of Gothic at all. This is a hopeful sign indeed, and now one has to test whether *bund* can be derived from |bnd|. We are dealing with a restricted environment, *n* between stops, and the answer is clear: an underlying |n| between consonants inserts a *u* in front of it to yield the actually occurring sequence *bund*. In other words, vocalicity is written into an extra segment, because *n* does not accommodate it directly, as *i* and *u* do, of course. Another characteristic of morphophonemic analysis/internal reconstruction has now come out. We strip off everything that can be put back unambiguously in terms of the paradigms (grammatical environments) and/or phonetic environments. Also *m*, *r*, and *l* share this particular behavior with *n*. If we label all four with *R* and other consonants with *C*, we can state that, instead of the structurally defined sequence *CRC*, we get *CuRC*. Now, including also *i* and *u* under the cover symbol *R* (although *u*-insertion does not operate on these) we get a uniform paradigmatic alternation for all three verbs: *CiRC* ~ *CaRC* ~ *CRC*. Internal reconstruction has resolved surface diversity into underlying unity, that is, one canonical form.

[12.2]   Even without all the Germanic evidence, it is interesting to compare this result of internal reconstruction with that of the comparative method. Not only vowels, but also consonants alternate, for example,

Gothic	k	iu	s	an	kaus	ku	s	um	ku	s	ans
OE	c	ēo	s	an	cēas	cu	r	on	co	r	en

The set *s–s* contrasts with *s–r*, because both occur medially, and they require different labels, *s and *z, or so (see § 4.10). Internal reconstruction in Gothic gave no hint of this. We have seen the internally reconstructed Pre-Gothic ablaut pattern *CiRC* ~ *CaRC* ~ *CRC*; the comparative method provides a different version:

$$CiiC \qquad\qquad CiC$$
$$CinC \qquad\qquad CuC_/$$
$$CeRC \qquad CaRC \qquad CuRC$$

where *R* means the resonants not already specified above it. Thus for inter-consonantal *n m r l*, the vocalicity segment *u* existed already in Proto-Germanic; and the present vowel was generally *e*, not *i*, which occurred only before another *i* and *n*. Only the past tense forms *CaRC* match for both methods. If we now apply internal reconstruction once more to the result of the comparative method, we can easily eliminate the "aberrant" *i*-forms, since they occur only with *i* and *n*. And the "extra" *u* in *CuRC* can be stripped off again. The result is a pattern *CeRC* ~ *CaRC* ~ *CRC*, a combination of both comparative and internal evidence. The principal contribution of the comparative evidence was the present-tense vocalism *e*. Gothic also has *e* (written *ai*), but only before *r* and *h* (*wairpan* 'to throw', *saihwan* 'to see', and, in the previous chapter, we saw *bairan* 'carry' and *taihun* 'ten'); *i* never occurs before *r* and *h*, so *e* is only a variant of *i* (actually there is one exception, *hiri!* 'come here!').

[12.3 Proto-Indo-European Ablaut and the Laryngeal Theory]   Our Gothic example provides a handy door to Indo-European ablaut alternations and the laryngeal theory. In the previous chapter we saw how the comparative method yielded an inventory of sound units (§ 11.14). Such inventories imme-diately establish relationship, but in themselves, otherwise, their value is limited. One has to show how the units fit into the total grammatical machinery of the language. The comparative method was applied to miscellaneous vocabulary items to give us the vowels. We ignored systematic alternations such as *sing ~ sang ~ sung* in English or Germanic in general (except for Gothic). The other languages used in the method, Sanskrit, Greek, and Latin, have very similar mechanisms. Thus there is no doubt that they all inherited this feature from Proto-Indo-European. Consequently, one must organize the reconstructed units according to paradigmatic sets, as was done with Gothic. In other words, one applies the morphophonemic analysis to the reconstructed Proto-Indo-European units.

We have seen that phonemic contrasts like /ey/ vs. /æ/ (*vain/van*) are not always functionally contrastive when morphs are grouped into paradigmatic sets. This, of course, is the basic feature of morphophonemic analysis. We reconstructed an **e* and an **o* for Proto-Indo-European (the latter corresponds to Germanic *a*), but from the Gothic example we saw that their reflexes alternated within paradigms (**e* > Gothic *i* in presents and **o* > Gothic *a* in preterites). Similarly, in Proto-Indo-European, **e ~ *o*, reflected, for example, in Latin genitive *ped-is* and Greek genitive *pod-ós* 'foot'. The vowel may also be completely lacking, for example, Sanskrit *upa-bd-á* 'foot-stamping' (**pd* assimilates automatically into **bd*). In other words, **e* alternates with **o*, and both of them with nothing. The vowel alternation is thus:

1. *e ~ o ~ Ø* (also Latin *sed-eō* 'I sit', *sod-ālis* 'companion', **ni-zd-os* > *nīdus* 'nest'; English *sit, sat, ne-st* '*sitting-down [place]')

This is ablaut. Essentially there is nothing more to it (with the exception of the environments for the variants, which we shall discuss shortly); it is only this simple alternation in terms of paradigms or words belonging together in derivation of some kind. It should be remembered that the few examples given here are just a suggestion of the actual material to which the comparative method was applied; but the method gave us the units that we handle and organize here. Obviously the total evidence cannot be reproduced in this book. When possible, we let Greek *stand in* for Proto-Indo-European vocalism. (The previous chapter showed that Greek agreed almost to the dot with our reconstructed units.) This is only an expedient, since Greek of course is Greek and not Proto-Indo-European.

When this alternating unit *e ~ o ~ Ø* occurs next to a resonant we have the same situation as in the Gothic case:

2. *ei ~ oi ~ i* (Greek pres. *leípō*, perf. *léloipa*, aor. *élipon* 'leave')
   eu ~ ou ~ u (fut. *eleúsomai*, perf. *eiléloutha*, aor. *éluthon* 'come')
   er ~ or ~ ṛ (pres. *dérkomai*, perf. *dédorka*, aor. *édrakon* 'see')
   el ~ ol ~ ḷ (pres. *stéllō*, noun *stólos*, perf. *éstalmai* 'send')
   em ~ om ~ m̥ (pres. *némō*, noun *nomé* 'divide'; Gothic *niman ~ nam ~ numans* 'take')
   en ~ on ~ n̥ (*ménos* 'mind', perf. *mémona*, p.p.p. *-matos* 'think')

The difference from pattern 1 is that when the vowel disappears, the resonant carries the syllable by becoming vocalic. But note, this happens only when the resonant is interconsonantal, as in the cases here. Otherwise, the distribution of allophonics (using again R as a cover symbol for all six resonants) is

	V—C	C—C	C—V	V—V
$R = ywr$ lmn	R	$R̥$	R	R
often written	$i\ u\ r$ $l\ m\ n$	$i\ u\ r̥$ $l̥\ m̥\ n̥$	$i̯\ u̯\ r$ $l\ m\ n$	$i̯\ u̯\ r$ $l\ m\ n$

An example is Greek acc. *patéra, -patora*, gen. *patrós* (with *r*), but dat. pl. *patrási* (with *$r̥$*, because it is flanked by consonants) 'father'. We see that pattern 2 contains exactly the same vowel alternation as 1, namely, $e \sim o \sim Ø$. Only the phonetic environments are different, mainly because of the allophonics of the resonants. The resonant may also precede the alternation $e \sim o \sim Ø$, for example, $Re \sim Ro \sim R̥/R$ (Greek pres. *trépō*, noun *trópos*, aor. *étrapon* 'turn'), and the resonant takes on the syllabicity when the vowel is gone, exactly as above.

This is the overwhelming regularity against which divergencies have to be coordinated and evaluated.

There is a pattern to the distribution of the vowels, otherwise it would not be morphophonemic at all. Characteristically—to name only a few categories—e occurs in presents and s-stem nouns, o in prefects and o-/$ā$- stem nouns, and no vowel at all in past passive participles, ti-stems, and certain aorists. Now, Proto-Indo-European has long vowels too; and when we group the long vowels according to these same categories, we get pattern 3:

1. | e | o | $Ø$ |
|---|---|---|

2. | eR | oR | $R̥$ |
|---|---|---|

3. | $ē$ | $ō$ | $ə$ | (Greek pres. *títhēmi*; noun *thōmós* 'place'; Latin *faciō* 'do')
| $ā$ | $ō$ | $ə$ | (pres. *phāmí*; noun *phōnḗ*; *phásis* 'speak')
| $ō$ | $ō$ | $ə$ | (pres. *dídōmi*; noun *dôron*; Latin *datus* 'give')

In other words, except for a few isolated cases like *$pətḗr$ 'father', the vowel *$ə$ alternates with long vowels. We remember also from the reconstructed inventory that *$ə$ is the only vowel without a corresponding long (Figure 11-7). And here it occurs in formations where only resonants show up and the other vowels do not. Such striking complementary distribution always points to ultimate sameness, and Saussure was the first linguist to juxtapose patterns 2 and 3. The first row of pattern 3 shows the same vowels as 2, and when we strip them away we are left with the frames

$$\begin{array}{llll} \text{2.} & R & R & R \\ \text{3.} & - & - & \partial \end{array} = \begin{array}{lll} R & R & R \\ \text{length} & \text{length} & \partial \end{array}$$

That is, length occurs in those categories where the resonants of pattern 2 are consonantal, and *ə, where the resonants are vocalic. Equally important is the fact that the *long syllabic resonants* occur in morphemes that elsewhere have *ə's,

$$\begin{array}{llll} \text{2.} & eR & oR & R \\ \text{3.} & \bar{e} & \bar{o} & \partial \\ \text{4.} & eR\partial & oR\partial & \bar{R} \end{array} \left\{ \begin{array}{l} \text{Sanskrit noun } bhavitar, \text{ p.p.p. } bh\bar{u}t\acute{a} \text{ 'to be',} \\ janitar, \text{ p.p.p. } j\bar{a}t\acute{a} \text{ 'be born'} \end{array} \right.$$

When the vowels are subtracted from 3 and 4 we get

$$\begin{array}{llll} \text{3.} & - & - & \partial \\ \text{4.} & R\partial & R\partial & \bar{R} \end{array}$$

But since the term *R* is a constant throughout line 4, we can ignore it for the time being; eliminating it from the table, we get a startling configuration

$$\begin{array}{llll} \text{3.} & - & - & \partial \\ \text{4.} & \partial & \partial & - \end{array} = \begin{array}{lll} \text{length} & \text{length} & \partial \\ \partial & \partial & \text{length} \end{array}$$

which clearly shows that *ə and length are strictly complementary. The only correct conclusion is that length and *ə represent one and the same thing. It is further clear from the collocations above that this unit patterns exactly like the resonants, and Saussure therefore posited a consonant *H (we do not use his orthography), which gives a *ə in interconsonantal position (parallel to *R*) and length in postvocalic position, that is,

	V—C	C—C	C—V	V—V
$H =$	length	∂	$\emptyset$	$\emptyset$

There is nothing peculiar in a morphophoneme like this. In principle it is not different from the vowel in, for example, English *sane/sanity*, which also appears under two phonetic shapes. Or similarly, the /r/ is manifested as retroflexion and length in words like *bird* in American English, and as a spirant in words like *dread*. (We shall return below to the prevocalic position, where *H gives ∅.)

[12.4]   Thus the anomaly of the vowel *$ə$ and length could be eliminated by evaluating it against the regular pattern 2:

2.	eR	oR	R
3'.	eH	oH	H
	aH	oH	H
	oH	oH	H
4'.	eRH	oRH	RH

This analysis is further supported by the fact that length does not occur with the consonants either (on the morphophonemic level) in Proto-Indo-European. The current tendency in Indo-European linguistics is to remain with this analysis. But there is one irregularity in the otherwise perfect pattern: the *e*-column has one *a and one *o, in categories where hundreds of *e-vowels occur. They can be eliminated only by assigning the vowel color to the *H's. That is, instead of three vowels and one *H, we have one vowel and three *H's: *H_1, *H_2, and *H_3, of which *H_2 assimilates an adjacent *e into an *a, and *H_3 assimilates an *e into an *o before lengthening operates. Mnemonically, the best way of writing these *H's is *E, *A, and *O. Now the pattern is perfect in terms of the vowels:

$$3''. \quad eE \quad oE \quad E$$
$$eA \quad oA \quad A$$
$$eO \quad oO \quad O$$

Only the vowel *e is affected by *A and *O; in all other environments these units lengthen the preceding vowel, whatever it is, for example, also the vocalic resonant *R.

Proto-Indo-European root structure happily accommodates our three units *E, *A, and *O. The majority of Indo-European roots begin with a consonant and end in a consonant, for example, *$bher$- 'carry', *$g^w em$- 'come', and *sed- 'sit'. Pattern 3' reinterprets the long vowel roots like $dh\bar{e}$- as this same type: $dheH$- = $dheE$-, that is, CeC-. On the other hand, there is only a handful of roots beginning with a vowel, and here also we frequently encounter the anomalous vowels *a and *o; for example, *es- 'be', *ag- 'drive', *aug- 'increase', and *ok^w- 'eye' (Latin $oculus$). Of these initial vowels, the *a and *o are remarkable in that they ablaut exactly like our *eA and *eO; that is, there is alternation *$a \sim$ *o, but *o as in *ok^w- is always *o. Here we do not need the lengthening power of the *H's, but since they lengthen only postvocalically, we can safely put them into the initial position, where they assimilate the following vowel before dropping out: *Ees-, *Aeg-, *$Aeug$- and *Oek^w-. Thus even though the H is not physically there in the attested forms its imprint is left on the next vowel. Now we can derive the comparatively reconstructed vowels from the internally reconstructed sequences in three steps:

1. ASSIMILATION	2. LENGTHENING	3. LOSS
$eA > aA$	$eE > \bar{e}$	$Ee > e$
$eO > oO$	$aA > \bar{a}$	$Aa > a$
$Ae > Aa$	$oO > \bar{o}$	$Oo > o$
$Oe > Oo$	$RH > \bar{R}$	$HR > R$

These correspond to the two reconstructive steps: extraction of length (as *H)
and extraction of vowel color (in two steps, both pre- and postvocalically).
This analysis does not mean that all surface long vowels contain an *H, but
only those that alternate with a *ə. (There is also a morphological process for
deriving long vowels from short ones in certain grammatical environments, but
we can ignore it here; compare the Modern English /v/'s in to dive and to thieve.
The first represents a |v|, the second an |f|.)

We established these *H-sounds purely in terms of the internal structure of
Proto-Indo-European. Thus their exact phonetic nature is not known, although
their position (as consonants) in the sound system of Proto-Indo-European is.
The necessity of these structural entities is traditionally called the laryngeal
theory. The name sounds unnecessarily pompous. First of all, 'theory' merely
means the hypothesis that is the end result of internal reconstruction. This
hypothesis adequately explains various apparent surface exceptions to the
overwhelming regularity of Indo-European roots. Semitic languages have a
number of laryngal and pharyngal sounds, which by an odd chain of events
provided a basis for making guesses about the phonetics of these *H's; hence
the term laryngeal. The two most general speculations about the phonetic
features of the *H's are *E = q (glottal stop), *A = h, and *O = $y^{[w]}$ ([labio]
velar voiced spirant); or, that they are just a class of spirants, *x, agreeing with
*ḱ, *k, and *k^w (§ 11.12), that is, *ẋ, *x, and *x^w (a real laryngeal interpretation
on the Arabic model would be "rough breathing" [h], tense emphatic laryngeal
spirant [ḥ], and lax emphatic laryngeal spirant [ʕ]). Three spirants in addition
to *s does not sound unreasonable in the rich inventory of Proto-Indo-European
stops; in fact, it is typologically very attractive:

$$
\begin{array}{llllll}
 & p & t & \acute{k} & k & k^w \\
(b) & d & \acute{g} & g & g^w \\
 & bh & dh & \acute{g}h & gh & g^wh \\
\hline
 & s & \boxed{\acute{x} \quad x \quad x^w} \\
\end{array}
$$

But note that this would point toward independent plain and palatal velar
series after all (and *x is better attested than *k, *g, or *gh). Anyway, it has
always been clear that the term "laryngeal" is a misnomer, if it includes velar
consonants. The important thing to keep clearly in mind is that the phonetics is
pure conjecture.

Thus we see that the laryngeal theory is just a small part of Proto-Indo-
European ablaut, where other sounds interfered with vowels. One hears it said
that the 'theory' is untenable both for its substance and for its method. Both
criticisms are clearly wrong. The substance is very impressive indeed—only a

small selection was taken for treatment here—and the method is the best there is: internal reconstruction, alias morphophonemic analysis. Of course, different scholars bring the method to different depths. As has already been mentioned, many remain happy with one *H = *h; postulating the three *H's (*E, *A, *O) still represents a central position, as it were; and others go on splitting the *H's further (even to as many as ten!). But it seems that we need three and certainly at least one. In our present discussion this particular hypothesis has explained four 'anomalies': (1) the curious status of *$ə$, (2) length, (3) unexpected *a and *o in certain positions, and (4) roots with initial vowels. We have to stop here, but it can be at least mentioned that there are further difficulties that are resolved by the laryngeals, for example, (5) the Proto-Indo-European voiceless aspirate stops (= *C + H), (6) the so-called Brugmann's law in Sanskrit, and (7) the Proto-Indo-European prevocalic vocalic resonants. (That is, contrary to the usual distribution of allophonics, one reconstructed sequences like *$CR-V$. But these typically occur only where the evidence points to the preconsonantal shape *$CRH-C$. Thus the aberrant sequence is actually *$CRH-V$, in which a prevocalic, or an intervocalic, *H drops out.) Certainly an explanation that takes care of so many different phenomena cannot be doubted, but these last points must be left to Indo-European linguistics for a full treatment. We have seen the principle, and that will do here.

[12.5. Independent Confirmation]   Saussure published his internal reconstruction of the laryngeals in 1879 (at the age of 21!). In 1915 Hittite was discovered, and in 1927 it was noticed that its h-sounds corresponded rather well with one of the structurally posited *H's (Latin and Greek standing in for Proto-Indo-European):

TRADITIONAL EVIDENCE	LARYNGEAL RECONSTRUCTION OF VOWEL	HITTITE EVIDENCE
Latin *mālum* 'apple'	eA	*mahlan*
pāscō/pāvī 'protect'	eA	*pahsanzi*
Greek *antí* 'against'	Ae	*hanti*
argḗs 'white'	Ae	*harkis*
thē- 'place'	eE	*te-*
es- 'be'	Ee	*es-*

Thus further comparative evidence, which was not available at the time of the internal reconstruction, confirms a substantial part of the results. There is at least one h, and it occurs exactly in the positions assumed. Problems do exist, however: namely, that *E has no reflex beyond the fact that *e remains as e (but compare Germanic, where the Indo-European accent leaves no evidence beyond the alternation of d and $þ$). Thus Hittite apparently confirms the existence of two laryngeals at least (possibly even three). Hittite orthography has a rather poor fit with the sounds of the language, which adds difficulties. But we can leave all this to Hittitologists and Indo-Europeanists. The important point is that Saussure's reconstruction was confirmed. (Laryngeal studies have mushroomed, often leaving all reason behind in their seeing of laryngeals everywhere and in their having them do everything. That, however, is no longer the method, but its misuse.) Further evidence for three laryngeals has been seen in Greek, where the outcome of *ə is sometimes *e* or *o* (and not *a* alone), with no analogical models to fall back on as explanation, for example, *ánemos* 'wind' vs. Sanskrit *aniti* 'he breathes' < *AenE-* (see § 11.19). But even without this point the theory was already solidly validated. The results of comparative linguistics have considerable predictive power (see § 1.24). In this sense, perhaps 'theory' is the right term, although 'hypothesis' does the same service. (§13.9)

[12.6 Conclusion] This and the previous chapters together form a single whole, the realm of the method, as it were. The chapter on the comparative method was preceded by synchronic preliminaries, and this one will be followed by the comparative method in a synchronic frame (§§ 13.7, 13.8). The argument that morphophonemic analysis and internal reconstruction are the same method seems to have been contradicted by their separate treatment in two chapters. This was done for various practical reasons, but also to emphasize the distinction between synchrony and diachrony, and the different means of getting at the data. Thus Part III covers all the columns of Figure 1-7, as well as the first three rows, with an occasional reference to the last. Surely this demonstrates once more the basic unity of different linguistic fields and the methods of analysis. The comparative method was applied to contemporaneous Finnish and Lapp, to three Indo-European languages lifted from a philological frame, and to one Indo-European language reconstructed partially from modern languages and checked by philologically preserved older stages. Internal reconstruction was applied to present-day data and, under the guise of the 'laryngeal theory', to historical material, but on the reconstructed Proto-Indo-European it was applied as a synchronic analysis. Thus the result is both synchronic and historical (Pre-Indo-European) from our point of view. Louis Hjelmslev was the first to maintain that internal reconstruction is *never* "historical," because whatever can be captured on the basis of one language is synchronically present in that language. All we get is a higher level of abstraction, in other words, morphophonemes.

Further examples of internal reconstruction were presented in Chapter 4, by way of illustrating sound change; since internal reconstruction applies to sound change in the reverse direction, the examples can serve just as aptly as internal reconstruction (e.g., Latin rhotacism and Rotuman umlauts; §§ 4.3, 4.6).

REFERENCES

General: Hoenigswald 1946, 1960b, Marchand 1956, Chafe 1959, Kuryłowicz 1964 and in Sebeok (ed.) 1963f. vol. 11, Anttila 1968 and in Sebeok (ed.) 1963f. vol. 11, Bammesberger (ed.) 1988; 12.1 Vennemann 1968; 12.3 Saussure 1879, Hjelmslev 1970, Winter (ed.) 1965, Bammesberger (ed.) 1988, Lindeman 1970, Szemerényi 1970; 12.4 Keiler 1970.

CHAPTER 13

CONCLUSION TO THE METHODS

Both the unity and the complementarity of the methods are brought out by diagrammatic summing up of the material used earlier. Genetic linguistics is shown to be part of panchronic linguistics (Figure 1-7).

[13.1   Priority and Powers of Penetration of the Historical Methods]   There is widespread agreement that internal reconstruction should be undertaken before the application of the comparative method, because this would eliminate the effects of the most recent changes which obscure earlier layers. In many cases this order of application is justified, but there is the danger that internal reconstruction antedates the split-off point which is the goal of the comparative method. The Finnish material that we have been using is a perfect case in point. By internal reconstruction (or morphophonemic analysis) one arrives at a Finnish shape *vete-* 'water', from which forms showing consonant gradation (presumably "younger" than the base-form *vete-*) can be derived. But this is practically identical to Uralic **wete*, with no consonant alternation. On the other hand, comparison of Finnish and Lapp suggests that their common ancestor (Early Baltic Finnic or the like) had some sort of consonant gradation. That is, the internal reconstruction of Finnish has here produced a form that antedates the time depth that can be claimed for the comparison of Finnish with Lapp; if internal reconstruction were to be applied in this fashion to Finnish and Lapp before any comparison of the languages was undertaken, the resulting comparative reconstructions of Early Baltic Finnic would not suggest consonant gradation. (Of course, the striking similarity between *vete-* and **wete* is largely chance; most words do not resemble their protoforms so closely, especially at such a time depth.)

The methods do not observe an inherent order of application; rather, the particular state of the languages used and the particular task at hand decide what method should be called upon. Because of the indeterminacy of the time depth of internal reconstruction compared with the temporal homogeneity given by the comparative method, their respective results must be labeled differently. Internal reconstruction gives *pre-*forms, which can reach to any depth from a given point of reference (e.g., English or Finnish), whereas the comparative method produces *proto-*forms, which cluster around a split-off point, a node in a family tree. Thus *pre-* refers to anything preceding a node, *proto-* to a node itself (e.g., Proto-Germanic). The end of a branch is also a node, although it is just a split-off point for dialects (see §§ 13.7, 13.8). Internal reconstruction on a protolanguage (e.g., Proto-Indo-European) is possible; one simply applies it to the result of the comparative method. One could even say that this is the proper order of application, because the comparative method gives us the surface structure (phonemes, and in some cases even phones), which has to be integrated with the rest of the grammar through morphophonemic analysis alias internal reconstruction. Thus, for optimal analytic clarity, linguists alternate between the two methods—if the family tree of the languages being used permits this—going farther and farther into the past (see § 11.18). However, experienced comparatists tend to use both methods at the same time, which can be confusing to beginning linguists when they consult works done in that mode. Still, the correct way is to take these two methods as complementary. The power of internal reconstruction proceeds from its utilization of the total grammar of one language, which, among other things, enables us to unravel many kinds of structure-determined changes (analogy). But from another angle the comparative method is more powerful: it does not depend on the existence of morphophonemic alternations, and it can retrieve mergers within given languages, provided that different languages have undergone different mergers. The reconstruction of Proto-Indo-European stops gave us an eloquent example of this (§ 11.13). The penetrating and retrieving powers of the two methods are simply not directly comparable, because the methods are complementary. The weight to be given to either one of them depends on what one wants to find out, and the results achieved will depend on more factors than the mere method (e.g., the structure of the languages). Usually one wants to find out anything one can, and therefore one ultimately uses both methods. But as already indicated above, in a situation where we want to find out if a protolanguage has an alternation, the role of internal reconstruction is nil, because its raison d'être is elimination of alternation without any regard to the nodes in the tree (nodes automatically mean comparative evidence from other languages).

[13.2]   We saw a clear case of the different results of the methods when reconstructing the Gothic and Germanic verbal ablaut (§ 12.2). We started from Gothic forms ($R = i\,u\,m\,n\,r\,l$; exceptions are mentioned first; that is, when r is listed above R, it is excluded from the cover symbol):

$$
\begin{array}{cc}
h & i \\
CerC & CuC \\
\end{array}
$$

A. CiRC   CaRC   CuRC

Internal reconstruction on Gothic gave us Pre-Gothic:

B. CiRC   CaRC   CRC

The result of the comparative method on all the Germanic languages ended in Proto-Germanic:

$$
\begin{array}{cc}
i & i \\
CinC & CuC \\
\end{array}
$$

C. CeRC   CaRC   CuRC

We see how the comparative method yields surface forms (i.e., A and C are very similar in structure). Internal reconstruction again on Proto-Germanic gave Pre-Germanic:

D. *CeRC CaRC CRC*

Whenever internal reconstruction operates, the result is minimal surface variety (B and D). Graphically we can compare the different time depths of the methods in Figure 13-1. The straight row of boxes represents Proto-Germanic, the raising steps, Pre-Gothic. We see that in the first column Pre-Gothic does not reach Proto-Germanic, in the middle column it does, and in the last column it penetrates beyond Proto-Germanic, all the way to Proto-Indo-European, and even Pre-Indo-European. As for Proto-Germanic, *CeRC* is also Proto-Indo-European, whereas *CaRC* is not; but this can be proved only through further comparative evidence. The different time depths yielded by the two methods come out clearly. This situation is characteristic.

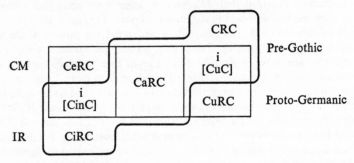

FIGURE 13-1. Relative time depths of internal reconstruction and the comparative method.

[13.3]   Schematically we can also compare and visualize the results of the two methods in terms of the Finnish and Lapp dentals used above (§§ 10.12, 10.14, 11.15, 11.16). Figure 13-2 roughly indicates the boundaries of the units (internally reconstructed ones are written with small capitals, and alternations are shown by curved lines). The diagram is drawn for the disyllabic stems used in the reconstruction and ignores the adjustment of § 11.19, which, however, is indicated in parentheses. Boundaries labeled *a*, *b*, and *c* coincide in the columns as indicated, but others do not. It is also interesting to note that *a* and *b* set off vocabulary items involving morphophonemic longs. Both methods happen to give the same number of units, but only if we include a Finnish D = |d| in column 2, based on one word only, (nom.) *sydän*/(gen.) *sydämen* 'heart' (Lapp *tšāðe/tšaððam*), because clear loans like *jodi/jodin* 'iodine' must be discarded, although synchronically they are also D-words. If we now accept *sydän* as a genuine relic of an unalternating *d*, we immediately uncover an abundance of

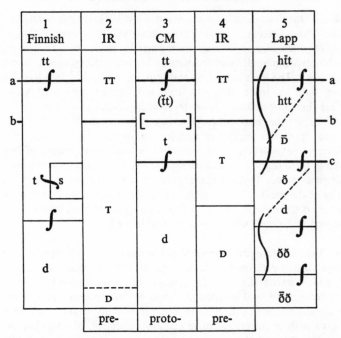

FIGURE 13-2. Relative difference in the results of internal reconstruction and the comparative method. Lines a, b, and c indicate boundaries among vocabulary items. Curved lines represent alternations. Note the alternations in column 5, which skip one whole box (§ 10.14), and the parenthetical material in column 3, which represents a modification through internal reconstruction (§ 11.19) [Reprinted with slight modification from Raimo Anttila, "The relation between internal reconstruction and the comparative method," *Ural-Altaische Jahrbücher*, 40, 159–173 (1968) (© Societas Uralo-Altaica).]

analogical cases in Finnish. That is, this relic supports the reconstruction of *kudu/*kudun 'spawn' without alternation and shows that the Finnish outcome kutu/kudun has shifted to the type vesi/veden and neiti/neidin, and so on. Such a (single) relic often gives important information; here it enables us to distinguish between analogic change and sound change. But this revelation is possible only by combining internal and comparative evidence; that is, the comparative evidence (Finnish syllable structure) showed that the Lapp length alternation was secondary in, for example, neṁma/nēma 'name', kiella/kiela 'tongue', and kōðða/kōða 'spawn', and that (because of the lack of Lapp stop/continuant alternation) the Finnish gradation in kutu/kudun was a Finnish development. The one relic sydän strongly supports this interpretation. This situation is characteristic, and linguists would always like to see such matching in the results of the two methods.

[13.4]   Our discussion has demonstrated the basic complementarity of the methods. Their different characteristics have led to contemplation of the *reality of the methods*, and linguists have generally tended to form two groups: those who favor internal reconstruction and distrust the comparative method, and vice versa. The question about reality is, in short, this: Is internal reconstruction, with its more abstract, structural domain (the total grammar), more real than the basically lower-level heuristic device of the comparative method? Or are the more concrete surface phenomena closer to reality? But again, such questions imply the complementarity of the methods. In recent times internal reconstruction has tended to be the prime concern of linguists, but, even in these cases, comparative evidence is freely used for confirmation of the inferences made. This, of course, reveals again the fundamental complementarity of the methods. Taking the two as heads and tails of one coin ends unnecessary methodological feuds. Before flipping the coin the linguist can name the side that he believes will be most profitable for him.

[13.5 The Structure and Domain of the Methods]   Although the methods are independent of each other as far as application is concerned, we have clearly seen that their mechanisms are identical. All of them—phonemic analysis, the comparative method, and morphophonemic analysis/internal reconstruction—handle some kind of sound units in connection with meaning, whether it is lexical (as *mainly* in the comparative method), grammatical (morphophonemic analysis/internal reconstruction), or both (phonemic analysis, but also the comparative method). Also, some kind of conditioning is stated, either phonetic (phonemic analysis, the comparative method) or phonetic/grammatical (morphophonemic analysis/internal reconstruction), either within one language (phonemic analysis, morphophonemic analysis/internal reconstruction) or with conditioning shifting from language to language (the comparative method). This last fact is an automatic consequence of the makeup of the sound units of the comparative method, namely, sets compiled from different languages. Because the structures of the methods are equivalent, their respective outputs are also equivalent. All methods give ultimate units from which there is a one-way mapping relation to the lower units (or to units in different languages)— in short, to the units from which one started. This mapping relation is generally expressed as a given rule component of the grammar. For example, the result of the comparative method, the protophoneme, can be mapped (rewritten) into the attested sounds depending (first) on the particular language, and (second) on the particular environment in the language. The morphophoneme or the prephoneme (the result of internal reconstruction) can be mapped into phone-(me)s depending on the particular grammatical and/or phonological environment. The more severe (strictly phonetic) constraints of phonemic analysis give units (phonemes) with a bidirectional (one-to-one) mapping relation with lower units (phones), that is, the situation known as the biuniqueness relation. Because the structure of the methods is the same, it will be illustrative to feed different units and conditioning environments into it and see where the differ-

Input				Output		
Number of languages	Phonetic units	Condition- ing		Name of procedure	Name of units	History vs. des- cription
Single	Sets of corre- sponding sound units	Gramma- tical	Contrasting Mechanism	IR	Pre- phoneme	H
a		f		Morpho- phonemic analysis	morpho- phoneme	D
Many		Phonetic		CM	proto- phoneme	H
d	e			Pandia- lectal analysis	dia- phoneme	D
		c				
Single	Phones			Phonemic analysis	phoneme	D
a	b					

FIGURE 13-3. The interrelationship of various methods of establishing sound units. [Reprinted with slight modification from Raimo Anttila, "The relation between internal reconstruction and the comparative method," *Ural-Altaische Jahrbücher*, 40, 159–173 (1968) (© Societas Uralo-Altaica).

ences originate. Figure 13-3 summarizes our discussion of the three procedures; their common mechanism is called 'contrasting mechanism'. The diagram is not an algorithm that would automatically produce a certain output, given the input, but rather a convenient approximation of what linguists do. Since the mechanism is the same for all the procedures, all differences originate in the input, which has three compartments (the columns), each allowing for two possibilities. Now, supplied with information on the number of languages, the makeup of phonetic units (sets or phones), and the nature of the conditioning allowed, the 'machine' finds out whether these units contrast or not, that is, whether these units differentiate meanings or not. All units that do not contrast in this way are grouped together by the machine, and the linguist can label such groups with one symbol. Characteristically, the machine handles the following combinations:

1. $\dfrac{a\,e\,f}{a\,b\,f}$ = internal reconstruction, morphophonemic analysis

2. $a\,e\,c$ = phonetically conditioned morphophonemics

3. $d\,e\,f$ = comparative method on morphophonemes

4. $d\,e\,c$ = comparative method, pandialectal analysis

5. $a\,b\,c$ = phonemic analysis

The graphic comparison in Figure 13-3 clearly brings out the interlocking and overlapping of the procedures. Box *a* is listed twice so that the diagram can show the three most usual combinations in as many rows. The units given by the output will then have a one-way mapping relation back to box *b*, and the output units can be fed again into the machine, for example, by putting the phonemes back into boxes *e* and *b*. Thus one usually applies the comparative method (4) to phonemes (result of 5). The exact linguistic status of these units is not so essential, and for Lapp we made no appeal to such questions. The essence of Finnish consonant gradation and most English alternations, for example, is phonetically conditioned morphophonemics (2). Internal reconstruction (1) was applied to selections from attested languages, but it can also be applied to a reconstructed protolanguage (result of 4), as is shown by the laryngeal theory. Or if we applied it to the reconstructed column 3 of Figure 13-2, we would get the same result as column 4, the Lapp state of affairs (in other words, Pre-Lapp clearly penetrates Early Baltic Finnic). If we apply the comparative method (4) to the morphophonemes (result of 1) of the languages used, the result (3) is similar to internal reconstruction. This is again made quite clear by Figure 13-2. Applying it to the material underlying columns 2 and 4 we would again end up with column 4, the Lapp state of affairs. Here then, the order of application does not make any difference; the comparative method on columns 1 and 5 gives column 3, and internal reconstruction on it gives column 4; or, internal reconstruction on columns 1 and 5 gives columns 2 and 4, and comparative method on these gives column 4. The reason for this homogeneity is of course the grammatical conditioning which always operates somewhere in the sequence of applications of the two methods. We can even keep the usual comparative method but allow for grammatical conditioning of the sets. Let us use three varieties of Lapp and Baltic Finnic that have dropped the final -*n* of the genitive, which had induced phonologically conditioned consonant gradation. After the drop of -*n*, gradation is grammatically conditioned in all the languages:

Lapp	juoĭ	Ğ	e		juol	g	e	
Estonian	jal	g	Ø	nom.	jal	Ø	a	gen. 'leg'
Finnish	jal	k	a		jal	Ø	a	

The two velar sets do not contrast, if categorial information is used; one occurs in connection with the *nominative*, the other with the *genitive*, and we can reconstruct one velar, say **k*, for both sets. If we were using phonetic conditioning, the method would automatically assign grammatically conditioned consonant gradation to the protolanguage as soon as the last language dropped the final -*n*. This would be an instance of multiple merger (exactly the same change in all the language here), which is not recoverable by the comparative method; the well-defined grammatical environment, however, might make us suspect what actually happened—compare English *wreath/wreathe* ($/\theta \sim \eth/$). The point is that once the characteristic grammatical conditioning of internal reconstruction is used, even the comparative method gives us a morphophonemic result.

[13.6]   We have already mentioned that Figure 13-3 is not an algorithm, but perhaps a more neat than real summary of actual practice. The input section contains some serious problems, especially for the comparative method. There is no way of distinguishing discrete languages, which would bear the required independent witness to the protolanguage, from dialects. But in favorable situations, dialects can be used (e.g., Baltic Finnic and Romance), and the whole matter is parallel to the permitted flexibility in the exact status of the sound units. But more serious is the necessity of weeding secondary material out of the input; that is, all kinds of screening operations and decisions have to be made before the automatic mechanism is allowed to operate. This is the most important area for future investigation: the development of criteria for pre-screening. Important steps for formalizing box *e* of Figure 13-3 have been taken, although we have been segmenting our material at such implicitly convenient boundaries as between consonants and vowels. For the methods themselves this is enough, but the notion of the sound correspondence is not a simple unit, but a rather complex one, a result of a quantification of the empirically given statistical continuum, which is also true of the obligatory meaning correspondence. Even if, so far, it is perhaps not possible to give a wholly formalized description of the procedure of establishing sound correspondences, it should be made explicit at least to the degree that linguists will become aware that what they take as given is no simple matter. Linguists usually arrive at a convenient segmentation by an implicit trial-and-error method, which is based on their experience in handling linguistic material for historical purposes. One tries to minimize both the proto-units and the rules that derive the attested forms from these. The rules play a very important role in the final establishment of proto-units; they are often the decisive factor for postediting the results given by the methods. It is interesting to note that similar segmentation difficulties occur also in phonemic analysis (box *b*), as in whether a phonetic segment or sequence is one or two phonemes, a unit or a cluster. Other prescreening decisions must also be made here, for example, whether loans (Fremdwörter) in any particular language necessitate a different phonological system from that of inherited items and acclimatized loans (Lehnwörter), or the coexistence of two phonemic systems.

Figure 13-3 also emphasizes the unity of all kinds of historical and synchronic investigations; they are different aspects of the same material (see Figure 1-7). The diagram lists the almost complete overlapping of the ultimate units arrived at by internal reconstruction and morphophonemic analysis. The units have been the concern of these analytic methods, and not the mapping rules, although both represent the two fundamental aspects of any kind of phonology and both are subject to change. The mapping rules are the arena of the controversy between historical and descriptive order and represent a prime target of contemporary research (§§ 6.1, 6.5, 6.6). But the same problem exists for the

282 COMPARATIVE LINGUISTICS: HOW CAN CHANGE BE REVERSED?

underlying units, that is, how to decide between a synchronic and diachronic interpretation; such criteria must be developed for the units and not only for the rules. Even in the absence of an algorithm here, at least there is agreement that these notions must be kept strictly separate, because they serve different purposes; this is why we label the units differently, although the names might not be the best possible ones. Thorough philological screening is important for the recovery of real history, and, interestingly enough, in etymological work we often have the same dichotomy as in units vs. rules, namely, the origin versus the history of an item. Both are important for their own sakes (§ 17.6).

Both historical methods, then, give us ultimate units as starting points for various mapping rules. There has been a choice available in the presentation of material: for example, some scholars tend to favor the units, reconstructed protophonemes (independent sound correspondences); others take the units as given and use a set of ordered rules, as many of the scholars favoring the proto-units have done in practice.

[13.7 Pandialectal Analysis]   We have seen the structural identity of internal reconstruction and morphophonemic analysis. The purpose or the use of the method dictates the final evaluation as either history or description. This decision rests with the linguist and not with the method. This situation is neatly summed up in Figure 13-3, in that the input does not recognize a difference between history and description (diachrony versus synchrony), whereas the output does. The dashed-line division of the highest row of boxes in the output section has been frequently referred to in the preceding discussion, but not the same division between history and description (H/D) in connection with the comparative method. The comparative method is also a descriptive method by which speakers handle dialect differences (see Chapter 3). In any speech community there are always dialect differences, be they between age groups, social strata, or whatever. Since the speaker must accommodate this situation in his knowledge of the use of the language, he has to apply a mechanism like the comparative method in the learning stages. A child will learn the regular correspondences between his speech and that of, say, his grandparents, his teacher, and so on. His grammar will incorporate all these differences, whether this process is explicit or implicit (as it normally is). This same situation obtains when communication is established between regional variants. Speakers devise a receptor mechanism for understanding the sounds of the new dialect, because they normally go on speaking their own way. But the psychological reality of the interdialectal sound correspondences comes out clearly in hypercorrections (§§ 3.3, 5.3, 9.10). These occur when the speakers make an effort to switch from their end of the correspondences to the other. If their end of the correspondences supplies only one unit for two or more interdialectal correspondences, the speakers are in potential trouble in their dialect switches. For example, a speaker of a dialect of English where final [ŋ]'s following an unstressed vowel have been replaced by [n]'s (*comin'*, *goin'*) learns that two sets of correspondences hold between his dialect and the other one, that is, *n–n* and *n–ŋ*. The first one presents no difficulties, but the second one does, because it is highly characterized; the speaker has to learn something new. He has to learn every single morpheme where he must replace his [n] with an [ŋ]. There is no simple mapping relation (rule) from his dialect to the other one, as there is in the reverse case: a speaker with [ŋ]'s can always replace them with [n]'s, once he has learned this correspondence. It is easy to learn that all verbal forms in *-in(g)* are affected. But the speaker who has to travel the one-to-many scale tends to overdo the "difficult" (characterized) part in cases that he has not yet thoroughly learned. Results are then "mistakes" like *coffing* and *chicking*. Such mistakes show that sound correspondences are clearly (one would like to say consciously) handled. The mistake is not due to method but to its application; the speaker makes an unjustified shortcut and secures an outcome that would look more like the target dialect. In other words, he lets some kind of proportional analogy enter his handling of the sound correspondences (§§ 5.1–5.3). The use of such analogy is quite characteristic of other language learning situations also, as we have seen. Such interference is expected, because as a synchronic mechanism the comparative method is only part of the machinery of the speaker. In comparative linguistics, however, the method is used, as it were, in "sterile" laboratory conditions and it can be kept from being contaminated by other factors, at least to a much greater degree.

Thus English speakers who communicate across the American and British dialect boundary acquire the knowledge of the following (and many other) correspondences (we have to assume that these speakers know nothing about writing):

	A	B		
1.	æ·	æ·	*mass, cad*, etc.	
2.	æ·	a·	*dance, half*, etc.	
3.	a·	a·	*father, balm*, etc.	
4.	a·ɹ	a·	*barn, barm* 'foamy yeast', etc.	
5.	a	ɔ	*pot, hot*, etc.	
6.	D	t	*writer, latter*, etc.	(§ 10.4)
7.	D	d	*rider, ladder*, etc.	

Structurally the situation is exactly the same as between mutually unintelligible but related languages. One cannot map one way from A into B because of sets 1 and 2, and 6 and 7—and not from B to A either, because of sets 2 and 4. In a pandialectal grammar one would then, sometimes, have to rely on the distinctions in American English and sometimes on those in British English. We can now set up pandialectal units that differ from both outcomes, but from which there is of course an unambiguous one-way mapping relation to both A(merican) and B(ritish), for example, (1) *æ*, (2) *æ·*, (3) *a·* (these first three sets cover two units in each language; compare §§ 11.11, 11.12), (4) *a·r*, (5) *a* (= ɔ), (6) *t*, (7) *d*. This setup is now a dialect cohesion (§ 13.8) that connects the two varieties of English, exactly as the reconstructed units connect the outcomes of two (or more) related languages.

[13.8]   The result of this pandialectal analysis can be called *dialect cohesion*, and this is the synchronic counterpart of a reconstructed phonological system. The units of dialect cohesion have been called diaphonemes in Figure 13-3. Thus we must add another characteristic combination for the method of treating sound units; *a e c* = pandialectal analysis. Structurally it contrasts with the comparative method in that its sets of correspondences have a different source; they are different dialects rather than different languages or different grammatical environments in one and the same language or dialect (as in internal reconstruction/morphophonemic analysis). It is a truism that one cannot draw a boundary between two dialects of the same language and two closely related but different languages. Thus it is also reasonable that the method is the same in both areas. It is the linguist's task to try to determine when such a dialect cohesion has no more synchronic validity but must be given a historical explanation in terms of reconstructed protoforms. This partly depends on the cultural situation and the alertness of the speakers, and of course we must exclude professional linguists altogether (see § 18.17). Children speaking, say, Swedish and German (not to speak of more closely related dialectal varieties like Bulgarian and Macedonian or the Scandinavian "languages") may quite well develop a fair number of synchronic correspondences between the two, without being able to give any historical explanation to them (and in most cases the correct explanation is actually borrowing rather than inheritance). The most startling case is reported for Lapp and Finnish. Although we have seen very clear correspondences between the two languages, the languages are definitely not mutually intelligible. They are as much apart as English and German in this respect. Still, Lapp children can map Lapp words into Finnish and vice versa, exactly as between dialects. Obviously they master the sets of correspondences, though here again they cannot give them a historical interpretation. Thus once more, this time in connection with the comparative method, we get an indication of unity within linguistics, in terms of the methods used in diachrony and synchrony.

Since we have also seen that regular sound change depends on dialect interaction, and that sets of correspondences depend on regular sound change, we see even more reason for the structural parallelism between dialect cohesion and the comparative method. Such dialect cohesion guides regular sound change (Chapters 3, 9). The comparative method, on the other hand, starts at the other end of the material and works backward in time. It is natural that both aspects have the same basic structure.

The acceptance of the comparative method in descriptive linguistics has been hindered by a fallacious concentration on uniform idiolectal grammars. Historical linguistics shows, however, that diversity is a must if we want to understand change. And it is also a logical necessity, since these fictional unified speakers at least understand other varieties of the language (see Figure 1-7).

A final remark on Figure 13-3. Phonemic analysis is the only method that remains unpaired with a historical aspect, and we have indeed seen that changes generally do not occur by phonemes (compare § 4.12). When phonemic changes occur, they are most often the results of other changes. But phonemic analysis is the school where the basic mechanism of the other methods can best be learned; it is here that the structure of all these methods is displayed with maximal clarity and simplicity.

[13.9   The Semiotic Status of the Comparative Method]   The comparative method is often taken as the closest equivalent in linguistics to the exactness of natural science, i.e. "real" science (§1.24). Such a notion would seem to be supported by the neatness of the sound correspondences, likened to the tightness of e.g. chemical formulae. But what does the method give us, what do we reconstruct? One of the standard natural-science-tinted answers is: we predict the past. This is clearly due to the prestige of the method in natural science, in which prediction and explanation are identical. In history, however, piecing together a possible past is guessing through indexes, where the laws involved somehow relate to the common experience of being human, and the results are traces of human action. Reconstruction thus means piecing together a possible chain of events, a state of affairs, i.e. inferring the case. The inference involved is abduction (and induction; §§1.24, 9.16), not deduction, and the frame is classical hermeneutic anamnesis (re-enactment through interpretation and understanding), not natural science. What we are doing here is interpreting circumstantial evidence in the manner of hunters, sailors, physicians, and particularly detectives. It is important to note that such various contexts have called forth sundry names for the indexes involved: *sign* (track, trace), *symptom, syndrome, clue* (Part IV will show what one does in comparative linguistics).

Reconstruction is not a random process, and it does not create ideas. It rather tests and modifies ideas. Thought creates an object, and not the other way around. But where does one get such an idea (of a protolanguage, common origin)? The answer is analogical argument (abstraction) from experience. Notions of growing apart have been there since the Greeks. Not only population movements but genealogy in general taught these; and, in Europe, the development at least from Latin to Romance was known. These concepts solidified in due course in e.g. (Lachmann's) textual tradition (§§2.17, 2.18) and (Schleicher's) family trees (§15.1). Such crystallizations proved that the idea was useful, productive, right. The idea of a protolanguage is adopted to begin with, and constant activity by comparative linguists determines, corrects, and modifies it. The idea calls out facts; this is called the generative power of abstraction. Collateral information comes from archaeology, loan words, and other hermeneutic disciplines. Ultimately the frame is pattern explanation (§23.10) where all parts fit, or have to fit. The best example of this is the very birth of comparative (Indo-European) linguistics. Sir William Jones adopted the idea of Proto-Indo-European (made public in 1786 in Calcutta), and within a century linguists had worked it out in its essentials (cf. §1.16).

Since the universe (and perception) is ruled by continuity, or synechism, or networks of similarities, all interpretation and understanding requires some kind of iconicity. Thus the more iconicity is involved in signs, the more direct is their interpretation. Likeness must be there, even if only through convention. This is where the comparative method comes in: it is a device to rake up faded diagrams between daughter languages (§§1.10-17). It combines what agrees and suggests a single protodiagram. The method verifies a perceived connection between languages. It is a kind of ruler for tracing correspondences, or a kind of microscope for seeing faded diagrams. Or, in still other words, the comparative method is a transposition machine for hypostatization of relations (taking relations as things) between languages.

The comparative method is also a sampling device, a selection machine, since it presents certain choices for the analyst (exactly as in phonemic analysis). The sample is not random, because it represents what matches in the daughter languages. We know that it is only a part of the total, but we take it as a representative sample. This gives us a foothold for further guesses of hermeneutic recovery. This kind of sampling is inductive, although the general frame of historical research belongs to abduction, judging circumstantial evidence. The major premise (the rule) here is human experience, human nature, culture (Chapter 23).

The efficiency of the comparative method depends on the regularity of sound change (§§11.9, 11.20-21). The other factor in its success is simply the fact that it is applied correctly or competently (§1.25). What this entails we have seen above (and will see in Part IV and Chapter 23): at every turn the method relies on hermeneutic aspects of sign behavior. The material fed into the method must be pre-screened and the output must be post-edited. Parts must be brought into uniformity with other parts (pattern explanation). Everything points to hermeneutic acts of recovery/interpretation, not to a natural-science-like situation. The method turns apparent observer's knowledge into putative agent's knowledge and in this a subjective act of knowledge typically catches objective knowledge. Thus both the input, the method itself, and the output conform to hermeneutic requirements. We work within the realm of ideas and rationality, not causality.

REFERENCES

General: Hermann 1970, R. Hall 1950, Anttila 1968; **13.4** Hjelmslev 1970; **13.6** Katičić 1966, 1970; **13.7** Dyen 1963, Bailey 1969, Anttila 1969a; **13.8** Dyen 1963, 1969, Anttila 1969a; **13.9** Eco and Sebeok (eds.) 1983.

PART IV

LINGUISTIC RECONSTRUCTION: A SYNTHESIS OF VARIOUS LINGUISTIC AND CULTURAL NOTIONS

CHAPTER 14

DIALECT GEOGRAPHY

The geographical distribution of linguistic variants may give clues to the relative age of the items. Because dialect relations have many similarities to reconstructed proto-languages, they throw much light onto our historical inferences. Finally, this and the subsequent chapters will show that genetic linguistics is not passé, but full of sub-stantive issues, which must be integrated with facts from the social setting.

[14.1 Variation and Spatial Distribution] Dialectology, the study of linguistic variation, is central to many branches of linguistics. In fact, there is no uniform invariant system as far as natural language is concerned. When operating with idealized uniformity linguists are using a working hypothesis only (see Figure 1-7). In the same fashion, a dialect is an entity based on a particular social selection of features. Language and dialect are relative concepts without necessarily clear boundaries; this is true of many other linguistic notions as well (e.g., the sign types). But they are psychologically and socially real concepts, acknowledged by laymen in various ways. Culture often includes areas that cannot be "scientifically" defined, for example, astrology and mythological concepts, and there is nothing peculiar in the notion of dialect being a "clear" concept of "folk science" rather than strict linguistics. A social definition is of course also scientific, even though it is not measurable in the same way as units in physics or chemistry. In linguistics, a dialect might be defined differently in different situations, depending on features thought relevant for the task or situation at hand. In other words, linguists follow the same practice as the naïve speakers, although what they think relevant may be different from the folk notion; both use the existence of variation as the basis of definition. It has become clear that change depends on variation and the interplay of dialects, and dialectological aspects have been constantly mentioned (Figure 1- ; Chapters 3, 8, 9; §§ 1.20, 2.6, 5.3, 7.8, 13.7, 13.8). If dialectology in its socio-linguistic aspect provides us with the basis for explaining change, it has also rendered many other services for reconstruction through *linguistic* or *dialect geography*.

Chapters 3 and 9 demonstrated the chief methods of writing variation. The most basic presentation is a list of correspondence sets, but the same information presented in a graph represents social variation succinctly (Figure 3-1); it is a map of social stratification. Alternatively, one can use numerical parameters without drawing graphs (e.g., the centralization on Martha's Vineyard, § 9.11). We have already introduced maps showing the geographical distribution of meanings for forms (*Korn* and *Opper*, Figure 9-2), but we have not seen the reverse—the distribution of forms for given meanings—and we have not yet seen maps of phonological features. (A review of Chapter 3 will help in reading this one.)

[14.2 The Rise and Impact of Dialect Geography]   In 1876 August Leskien published his famous slogan that sound laws have no exceptions, J. Winteler published the first rigorous dialect monograph, and Sophus Bugge deciphered the runes. The last half of the 1870s was the beginning of modern linguistics in many respects. Also in 1876, Georg Wenker wanted to prove Leskien's claim by checking it with the High German consonant shift (e.g., *Dorp/Dorf* 'village', *dat/das* 'that', and *maken/machen* 'make'; the first item in each pair is Low German, agreeing with English *thorp, that,* and *make*). Proof was supposed to come from the "pure" folk dialects, because the standard and the city dialects were often obviously mixtures of the surrounding dialects. Wenker expected to find a sharp boundary, on one side of which High German sounds prevailed, on the other Low German; in other words, he hoped to find sharp dialect boundaries in general. He failed in this, but found the isoglosses instead. An *isogloss* is a line that separates an item *a* from not-*a* whether this is a word, a phonetic or syntactic peculiarity, or whatever. An isogloss therefore allows us to reconstruct the spread of any linguistic feature, and dialect boundaries are defined by isoglosses, either one or more. The boundaries for the above items show the widest separation along the river Rhine. The isogloss between *dat/das* crosses the river south of Coblenz, that of *Dorp/Dorf* south of Bonn, that of *maken/machen* between Düsseldorf and Cologne, and the isogloss for *ik/ich* 'I' reaches the farthest north, crossing the river at Ürdingen. This is the famous Rhenish Fan (an obligatory example in any book on the topic, although we shall break the rule in not reproducing the map). The lines form a fan-like picture, since they merge into a common stem farther east; the situation shows that every word has its own spread. Wenker had discovered dialect geography.

Also in 1876, two Frenchmen, independently of Wenker, wanted to find the boundary line for Provençal vs. French. With a questionnaire of twenty words they walked zigzag along the expected boundary; like Wenker, they found isoglosses, or dialect geography, rather than a neat dialect boundary. Ferdinand Wrede extended the German study into every German-speaking village in Europe (44,000 points), and Jules Gilliéron organized what became the French dialect atlas. Wrede had to rely on questionnaires filled out by school teachers, whereas in France the field work was carried out (in some 640 localities) by Edmond Edmont, a student of Abbé Rousselot, the most famous phonetician of the day. The German survey could at least give reliable information on syntax, which the French survey did not include at all. Other projects have built on the French and German (and other) experiences; for example, the New England field workers were instructed by Jakob Jud and Paul Scheuermeier, who had worked with Karl Jaberg on the Italian atlas. Hans Kurath, the director of the linguistic atlas of the United States and Canada, prepared a questionnaire of 1,000 questions. A historian picked the towns so that connections with England could be studied as well, and twenty hours were spent with one informant, four to a locality, thus permitting investigation of age differences, and so on. The survey began with nine field workers, but it eventually became clear that one is better than nine, and subsequent areas were investigated by G. S. Lowman, and after his death, by Raven McDavid. After the publication of the New England dialect maps the survey was published in list form to cut costs.

The results have been the same in principle everywhere: that there is always variation, which has been described in Part II, and that there need not be "clear" dialect boundaries (i.e., tight bundles of isoglosses). Every feature can have its own spread. This seemed to be a complete denial of the regularity of sound change, and the maxim *sound laws admit of no exceptions* (Leskien) was replaced by *every word has its own history* (Gilliéron, Schuchardt), especially in the Romance field. Both positions of course have truth in them; it is too optimistic to expect that only one principle would contain the whole truth about such a complicated phenomenon as language change. The first maxim relies on a successful result of sound change, the second stresses the spread of change, which takes place in terms of individual words, grammatical categories, social layers, and so on (see § 9.10, 9.11). But most important of all, the maxim specifies *words*, which easily come and go, and do indeed have unique histories (Chapter 17). The same is true of morphological elements in general, although it is most obviously true of words. The spread of a change depends on social forces, which can shift before a particular change has attained regularity. The isoglosses also clearly show the role of communication and social interaction in change. Isogloss bundles tend to cluster along barriers that impede communication, for example, mountains, swamps, lakes, and political or religious boundaries. Many of the German dialect boundaries follow medieval diocese limits, splitting even single towns, and we have seen that social dialects are different within the same geographical spot (Chapter 3). In other words, different beliefs act "like mountains between people." From a different point of view, isogloss bundles can be looked at as lines of weakness in the network of oral communication. Although dialect geography at the outset was atomistic in orientation (i.e., it studied single items), it led to valuable results, especially when coupled with the study of the distribution of cultural artifacts. Cultural diffusion is another aspect of communication. The combination of linguistic and ethnographic data is known as the *Wörter und Sachen technique* (words and things). The value of this method is particularly great in studying semantic change; often we must know the exact cultural context to understand it (see Chapter 7). The Wörter-Sachen method is one aspect of philology and etymology; it is a prerequisite for solid reconstruction (see Chapter 17), and must be employed whenever possible.

[14.3 Structural Dialectology]   An extreme structuralist position denies structural dialectology, because when a system is defined solely by its internal relations, its items cannot be compared with those of other systems because they are likewise defined by their internal relations. Only systems could be compared with other total systems. But it is obvious that speakers and hearers can handle rather different dialects or parts of dialects without impairing communication, and equally obvious that this is usually done by taking such systems as variations of one underlying system. To solve this dilemma the so-called *overall pattern* has been suggested. This notion is best seen in phonology. An overall pattern is basically the grand total of all the sound units in the dialects. It is not really different from a general table like Figure 1-3, except that it is more limited in scope. Of course such an arsenal is practical and necessary, but it does not help in comparing systems, even if it gives a handy basis for positing a *core pattern*, an intersection of shared elements between any number of dialects. The difficulty was solved by looking outside the single sound segment in one dialect, into the sound correspondences between dialects. Such correspondences are the basic cross-dialectal sound units as has become clear in the preceding parts (see, in particular, Chapters 3, 9 and §§ 13.7, 13.8). Each contrasting set of correspondences defines a *diaphoneme*, and the system can be called a *diasystem*, the result of this pandialectal analysis (Figure 13-3). We have seen a fragment of a diasystem, from which one could derive British and American English (§ 13.7); but because no full system was developed, it was called *dialect cohesion*. A diasystem is a wider term than dialect cohesion because even unrelated languages may be combined under it. Certain kinds of bilingualism are thought to be of this type; that is, the speaker constructs a common underlying diasystem from which he derives both languages (§ 8.15). Such a diasystem has an extreme amount of unsystematic formal variation (synonymy), and we have already seen that switching from a diasystem to one language can be regarded as a move toward 'one meaning, one form'. Universal grammar, which studies the shared elements of all languages, endeavors to establish a universal diasystem for all languages of the world. All the particular languages are then derived from it with language-specific rules. The term 'dialect cohesion' is used in this book for a system that comprises sound correspondences, and this is the counterpart to reconstructed phonologies (§§ 13.7, 13.8). A 'diasystem' is a wider term covering any other relations as well. Dialect cohesion is one kind of diasystem. Reconstructions or protolanguages are historical diasystems.

[14.4]   Recently linguists have been trying to devise a common diasystem for all the dialects and to describe the dialect differences with a common rule pool, that is, an overall rule pattern. Let us look at a classical example from the. Atlantic states involving the diphthongs |ai| and |au| which we have already seen in Martha's Vineyard (§ 9.11). The vowels in the following four words in four localities are

		CHARLESTON, S.C.		NEW BERN, N.C.		WINCHESTER, VA.		ROANOKE VICINITY, VA.	
five	*down*	[aˑɪ]	[au]	[aˑɛ]	[æˑu]	[aˑɛ]	[æˑu]	[ai]	[æu]
twice	*out*	[əɪ]	[əu]	[aˑɛ]	[æu]	[əɪ]	[əu]	[əi]	[æu]

For the realization of the first element of the diphthongs one needs mainly the two rules: (1) *a → ə/ — vowel + voiceless consonant*, and (2) *a → æ/—u*. This is the common rule pool in this sample: Charleston needs only (1) and New Bern only (2); Winchester applies first (1), which of course gives the same lower row as in Charleston, and then (2), which can now apply only in the upper right-hand corner, making it the same as in New Bern; and the Roanoke vicinity undergoes first (2) and then (1), that is, it has the same rules as Winchester, but in reverse order. It has been possible to characterize four dialects with only two rules and a specification of their order of application (of course, other rules would be necessary for the facts not yet taken care of). The German *Ding* case (§ 6.15) and the Finnish *teeq* case (§ 6.17) showed exactly the same situation for dialect characterization with different rules or different rule order. If all the rules in the overall rule pool can be hierarchically ordered in a scale from top to bottom, dialects can be specified on the basis of where they appear on the scale, as shown in Figure 14-1. When no reordering of rules occurs, one can

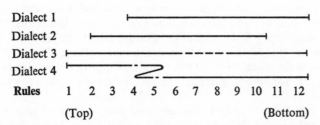

Dialect 1
Dialect 2
Dialect 3
Dialect 4
Rules 1 2 3 4 5 6 7 8 9 10 11 12
(Top)   (Bottom)

FIGURE 14-1. Four dialects characterized by a pool of twelve rules.

simply state that dialect 3 takes all the rules from R 1 on (but skipping two), dialect 2 from R 2 to R 10, dialect 4 would apply R 5 before R 4, and so on. There seems to be more order in this than in defining a dialect with a bundle of isoglosses (e.g., D 1 [I 1, I 3, I 7]), but of course it is basically the same concept. It has even been suggested that the name dialect be replaced by 'climacolect', to agree with such rule scales (C.-J. Bailey). Note that these rules apply to the underlying common units, diaphonemes or whatever one wants to call them. We have seen many times already that such units and rules are complementary concepts. It is not enough that two dialects share most of their rules; they have to have common units as well (e.g., words, morphemes, and so on). The phonological rules for two different languages in a convergence area may be about the same, but no dialect cohesion can be constructed by the speakers if there are no regular sets of correspondences (diaphonemes) (see §§ 13.7, 13.8).

[14.5 Stratigraphy and Seriation]   Dialectology enables us to understand linguistic change (Chapter 9, § 13.8) and social interaction, but it also tells us that we need not assume dialect-free protolanguages, because the comparative method gives us only a partial dialect cohesion. We can never reconstruct a real protolanguage, a complete diasystem. But in the form of dialect geography, dialectology provides information on relative chronology.

Innovations within one grammar can leave the old forms intact in certain categories, or in corners of the grammar (see § 5.15). Similarly, innovations in prestige dialects may never reach the periphery of the dialect continuum. In dialect geography one speaks of a *focal* (central) and a *relic* (marginal) area. If a focal area radiates subsequent innovations, their geographical spread may show the corresponding stratification. Figure 14-2 shows the distribution for the French words for 'mare', the outcomes of Latin *iūmentum, caballa* and *equa* (see § 7.2). The fact that the *equa* forms are separated by the *caballa* territory shows that *equa* represents the relic. But the *caballa* territory itself is split in two by the *iūmentum* area and represents a relic with respect to that. Relics characteristically cluster around the periphery of Parisian influence. The innovation of the French prothetic vowel (excrescence of *e*; § 4.11) has left small pockets around the French borders (Figure 14-2). The development of Latin *k* before *a* (see § 4.4) shows different spreads for different words (compare the Rhenish Fan); for example, *keval* 'horse' has only a small pocket in Catalonia and a bigger one north of Paris. Generally, however, the *k*-lines cluster along boundaries running roughly from south of the Channel Islands–Regneville–Beauvais–Fourmies in the north, and Bordeaux–Aurillac–Mende–Villefort–Bollène–Saint-Paul in the south. North of this southern line there is a belt of areas with *tš, ts* (or *st*). Such a configuration confirms the relative chronology of (1) *k*, (2) *tš*, and (3) *š*.

These stratigraphic configurations are quite general. Another good example is the distribution of the outcomes of the medial cluster **md* of Proto-Lapp (Figure 14-3). At the extreme ends we have *md*, which can be taken as the oldest state of affairs, then comes *bd*, and finally *wd* and *gd*. The map cannot give any clues as to the relative age of the last two. Our inference that *wd* is later than *bd* in the extreme north is confirmed by documentary evidence.

[14.6]   *Stratigraphy* is a method borrowed from geology (see § 22.7) by archaeology, and from both by linguistic geography. Linguistic stratigraphy in the French case was completely substantiated by other evidence (comparative and historical), and stratigraphy for its part confirmed another method we may call *linguistic seriation*. In archaeology, seriation is a method utilizing a gradual change of style or fashion, which permits a relative arrangement of objects in

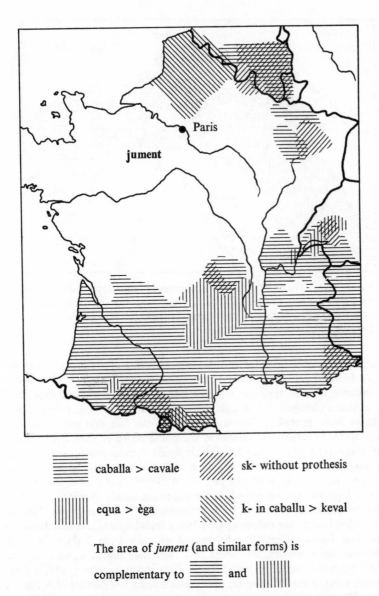

FIGURE 14-2. Geographical stratification of some items in France showing clustering of relics in the lateral areas. [The forms for 'mare' reprinted by permission with slight modification from Albert Dauzat, *La géographie linguistique*, Paris, 1922 (© Ernest Flammarion).]

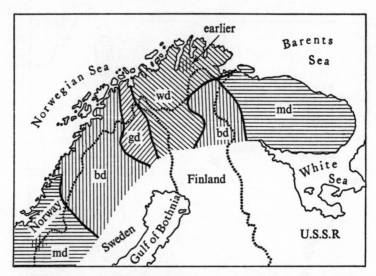

FIGURE 14-3.   The distribution of the outcomes of Proto-Lapp *md in Northern Fenno-Scandia and Kola Peninsula. [Reprinted with slight modification from Erkki Itkonen, *Kieli ja sen tutkimus*. Helsinki and Porvoo, Söderström, 1966 (by permission of the author).]

a temporal sequence (like, for example, the withering of a structure in evolutionary biology). What we know about sound change permits similar scales. For instance, if three languages have corresponding k, $t\check{s}$, and $\check{s}$, our experience tells us that a change $\check{s} > k$ is highly unlikely, and so is $t\check{s} > k$, even if $\check{s} > t\check{s}$ might be more probable. This also underlines the fact that experience is a crucial factor in actual reconstruction. We would be led to posit the following relative age: (1) k, (2) $t\check{s}$, and (3) $\check{s}$. Certain sound changes nearly always go one way only, for example, $s > h$, $h > \emptyset$, $u > \ddot{u}$, and $\ddot{u} > i$, along with various assimilations, as in $kt > tt$ and $pt > tt$. A change $h > s$ is reported from Ryukyu Japanese, but on the whole the statement stands. According to these principles one could reconstruct the antecedent of Italian *sette* and Modern Greek [eftá] 'seven' the following way. In the initial, one would take Italian *s-* as original, because Greek can be derived naturally from it ($*s > *h > \emptyset$). As for the medial consonants, Greek *ft* is older than Italian *tt*, which can be derived from the former by assimilation. This seriation gives $*seftV$, a form that falls short of the PIE $*sept\d{m}$; but at least it has a *voiceless labial* $+ t$ in the middle. Words generally get shortened rather than lengthened by sound change; thus English *kiss* vs. German *küssen* would suggest a protoform more like German than English on two counts, $\ddot{u} > i$, and $-en > \emptyset$. Swedish *kyssa* [tšüssa] has a final vowel and therefore holds an intermediate position between German and English, but its $t\check{s}$ is newer than either English or German. Indeed,

Old English has *cyssan* (*c* = *k*, *y* = *ü*), where the ending is *a* + *n*, which is older than German *ə* ⟨e⟩. The whole truth is that the vowel was *a in the antecedent form, and the umlaut was triggered by *j, that is, *kussjan. Reconstruction can never go beyond the evidence used (see §§ 11.8, 11.18), but seriation pointed toward the right direction of change. Similar universal linguistic trends exist in morphology, syntax, and semantics, and they can be used for seriation chronology. We have seen that a free word is older than a corresponding bound suffix (§ 7.13), because we can derive the suffix with wearing from a longer word (§ 9.8). This would not work the other way. Similarly, certain semantic changes tend to go one way, for example, 'to weigh' > 'to think' (see § 7.11). Pronouns give conjunctions, but not the other way around (§ 7.13). Unfortunately, we know very little about such universals of change, although these indications are suggestive (see § 16.8).

[14.7 Areal Linguistics] In other words, we have again run into the notion of correspondences and mapping relations, which are central to (genetic) linguistics. These were able to establish direction of borrowing (§§ 8.6, 8.13). If there is unambiguous two-way mapping within the members of the correspondences, no priority can be stated. But a one-way mapping relation establishes direction, as above. And when one cannot map either way, one reconstructs a diasystem from which there is a one-way mapping relation to all the systems used in the reconstruction. And whenever correspondences and mapping are involved, some kind of comparing/contrasting is being carried out. The French dialect maps, of which Figure 14-2 is a sample, not only led to results in dialectology in general, but also to a whole school of linguistics known as *areal linguistics*, practiced mainly in Italy, in which the units of comparison are languages, dialects, forms, or sounds from them. With three areal norms one can in many cases establish the relative chronology of the two sides of an isogloss line.

1. The earlier form is preserved in the more *isolated* area, for example, the mountainous Auvergne region in Figure 14-2.
2. *Lateral areas* preserve the older forms, which also was obvious in Figure 14-2.
3. The *larger area* shows the original form, except when the minor area is the more isolated one, or when the minor area represents the sum of lateral areas.

For example, by comparing the dental spirant of English *mother* against the *t* in Latin *māter*, Greek *mátēr*, Sanskrit *mātá*, and Russian *mat'* (see Figure 11-6), one would conclude that *t* was the original sound, if English cannot be taken as an isolated or lateral area. English is *geographically* lateral or isolated, but there is no further evidence for the others' having innovated together. These norms are handy rules of thumb, but like other methods of analysis they can lead to incorrect interpretations; especially when coupled with the principle of linguistic seriation in its many aspects, reliable hypotheses can often be put forward. (For example, in the example of the English dental spirant just given, any hypothesis that t is earlier than θ would receive strong support from the seriation principle, because $t > \theta$ is considerably more likely than $\theta > t$.) Note that seriation itself is not a rigid principle all the way through various subsections of grammar. In a borrowing situation one could map from the language in which the form was motivated (iconic) into the one where it was not (§ 8.6). But if the same situation, anomaly versus regularity, obtains across an isogloss, it is the anomalous form that is generally older. If two dialects have plurals like *kine* vs. *cows*, the former is the older one. Within the same grammar, plurals like *men* and *mice* are likewise older than *boys* and *horses*. We have here variations of the principle of *lectio difficilior* (§ 2.17), a principle that helps in establishing chronology. Linguistic seriation is another manifestation of it.

Areal linguistics claims that the traditional comparative method or comparison between languages was just its forerunner, because the latter also projected into the past forms and sounds (e.g., **t* in *mother*) which exist synchronically in (at least some corner of) the investigated area. Only when complex correspondence relations are used (i.e., in establishing diaforms that do not exist anywhere as such [**seftV*]), is comparative linguistics different from areal linguistics. Whether one wants to build a separate doctrine of areal linguistics in addition to dialect geography or not, the importance of spatial distributions for genetic linguistics cannot be questioned. We shall also see how dialect geography does further service for comparative linguistics in helping to establish relationship models (Chapter 15).

[14.8 Transition Area and Diasystem]   Since dialects grade gradually into others, feature by feature, transition is the general phenomenon. In general every village mediates between other villages on its sides. But if two major dialect areas have a buffer zone between themselves as a mediator, transition dialect (or language) is a convenient term. Thus one recognizes an intermediary area called Franco-Provençal between Provençal and French, and Catalan is today a transition language between Provençal and Spanish. Transition areas can be defined by the sharing of rules as well as by other items; that is, a dialect with rule 1 and another with rule 2 have a buffer zone with both rules 1 and 2. Such a geographical situation might even explain different rule order in a concrete fashion (see § 9.14). Suppose that rules 1 and 2 spread from opposite directions until they finally overlap. In the transition area closer to 1, rule 1 would have come earlier than rule 2, and vice versa. The dialects would now be defined by the following conglomerations: [1]—[1, 2]—[2, 1]—[2]. A situation like this was presented from several southern Atlantic states, and there might be some geographic justification to it, although the transition area is not physically in the middle (§ 14.4). Note that rule 1 in Charleston meant *ə* in the second row, and rule 2 in New Bern *æ* in the second column. Winchester and the Roanoke vicinity have both *ə*'s and *æ*'s: when rule 1 wins out, *æ* occurs only in the upper right corner; when rule 2 wins out, *ə* occurs in the lower left corner (§ 14.4).

In vocabulary such transition dialects often produce contaminations; for example, Low German *he* and High German *er* give *her* 'he'. The two forms may combine to give a compound; for example, *Ünne* (onion) and *Lauch* (leek) yield *Ünlauch* 'onion' (Niederrhein). A transition dialect can thus be a mixture of two or more dialects, and resemble the convergence situation. It can be an intermediate stage in seriation as the French *tš* case shows, or it may represent the most conservative area and be closest to the original state of affairs. Western and eastern Cheremis dialects are separated by speech forms which the speakers themselves call 'middle language', which is rather close to Proto-Cheremis. The reason is that the innovations from two focal areas have not overlapped totally, but have left most of the earlier state of affairs untouched in between. We then have inheritance rather than convergence. A parallel case was seen in the meanings of *Korn* in the southwestern German-speaking area. The buffer zone retained the original meaning whereas both sides had innovated (Figure 9-2).

Note now that a dialect cohesion or diasystem can be taken as a kind of transition dialect similar to an intermediate machine language in machine translation; a diasystem also helps the mapping of systems into others. In the case of the partial dialect cohesion devised for British and American English (§§ 13.7, 13.8), we come close to some existing conservative dialects. Diasystems need not have any geographical representation whatsoever, and their historical accuracy in mirroring protostages can be limited. Paradoxically, the wider apart the dialects/languages are for which the diasystem is being (re)constructed, the better the chances are for capturing actual history as well. In dialect geography as well, confident reconstruction requires discontinuity, as in the case of lateral areas. Areal and relational aspects of reconstruction and language always require close scrutiny, before the final interpretation is made by the linguist.

REFERENCES

General: Gamillscheg 1928, Bottiglioni 1954, Serech 1954, Saporta 1965, Francescato 1965, Risch 1966, Bolinger 1968, Alatis (ed.) 1969, Goossens 1969, Dahlstedt 1970, Graur (ed.) 2.1-225, Kurath 1972, Stroop in Koopman et al. (eds.) 1987; **14.1** Reichstein 1960; **14.2** Bach 1934; **14.3** Weinreich 1954, Pulgram 1959, 1961, 1964, Kohler 1967, Moulton 1968, Rensch in Sebeok (ed.) 1963f. vol. 11, Katičić 1970; **14.4** Kurath and McDavid 1961, Keyser 1963, Saporta 1965, Bailey 1969, Fasold 1970; **14.6** Bonfante 1945, 1946; **14.7** Bàrtoli 1925, R. Hall 1964, Winter in Sebeok (ed.) 1963f. vol. 11, L. Campbell in Fisiak (ed.) 1985; **14.8** E. Itkonen 1966, Goossens 1969. (See also p. 54)

CHAPTER 15

ALTERNATIVE RELATIONSHIP MODELS

Efforts toward simple models of language relationship have led to two ways of drawing pictures, because here also there are two sides, units and rules, which are complementary.

[**15.1 Language Families and Family Trees**] The variation inherent in language is so complex that a complete diasystem represented in a single diagram is impossible, at least for a human reader. Various sets of correspondences have given us mapping relations for particular items, and these have shown relationship as well. With dialects, relationship has traditionally seemed obvious, whereas metaphorical expressions have been developed for related languages. Languages connected by sets of correspondences form a language family. Thus all the Romance languages are sisters, and therefore daughters of Latin, the parent or mother language, from which they are descended. 'Related' is a technical term, exactly like the equivalent 'cognate', meaning that the items were once identical. Family terminology is of course as imprecise as the term 'dialect', as long as we do not know its defining items. More precision was introduced by the presentation of relationship through a genealogical tree which shows part of the (assumed) history as well. The tree diagram was inherited from the plotting of Classical population migrations, for example, Greek colonization, with the original colonies founding offshoots of their own; but it got important support from textual criticism (§§ 2.17, 2.18) and biology. It is of course now widely used for all kinds of derivational mapping relations, as in the derivation of sentences, in which capacity it is perhaps now best known.

The longest-studied language families are Indo-European, Uralic, and Semitic, and they have contributed enormously to the methodology of genetic linguistics. Because so many Uralic languages have been quoted in this text, it seems appropriate to use the Uralic family tree as an example (also, the first known formulation of genetic relationship involved Uralic languages, Hungarian and Lapp). The Uralic family tree is given in Figure 15-1, and it is of the type already shown in Figure 2-2. A tree like this shows many facts at a glance. Each node defines itself by the lower nodes. Thus Uralic is a cover term for the whole family since it is the highest node, but more immediately it is defined as the sum of Finno-Ugric and Samoyed (divided into a northern and a southern group). For many practical considerations, Samoyed is still often ignored and the family is just called Finno-Ugric, it, in its turn, being defined by Finnic and Ugric, and so on. 'Finno-Ugric' is typical of the compound names used when no geographical or other term has become current. Uralic is so named because the languages are spoken on either side of the Ural Mountains, that is, it names the

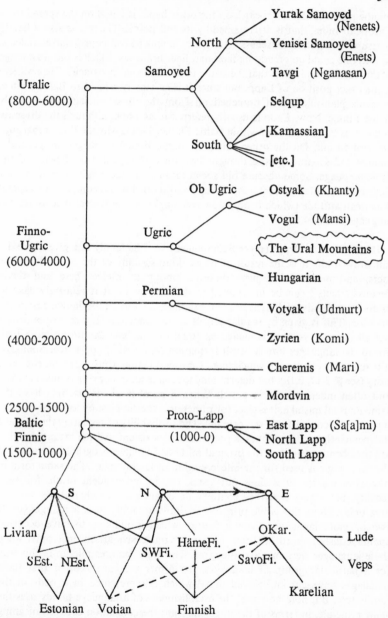

FIGURE 15-1. A family tree of the Uralic languages. The complicated relations within Baltic Finnic cannot be rendered through a tree. Converging branches indicate isogloss overlap (§§15.4-5). [Revision courtesy of Mikko Korhonen.]

middle point. 'Indo-European', on the other hand, is based on the spread from
Europe to India, that is, it is named by its end points. The tree is also a handy
measure of relative closeness. All these languages of course have dialects,
so that one could go on adding finer and finer branches, which is one advantage
of the tree diagram. Note that the Baltic Finnic node has two nuclei. The problem
is the exact position of Lapp, but since it is so closely related to Baltic Finnic,
it seems plausible that it branched off from the upper nucleus, called Early
Baltic Finnic. Now, Lapp is usually referred to as Lapp, although the diversity
within it is far greater than within Baltic Finnic. This is why the three subgroups
are written out. On the other hand, the Baltic Finnic languages are generally
enumerated separately even though they are best regarded as dialects of the
same language. Some obscure old social reasons are seemingly responsible for
this radically different treatment of Lapp and Baltic Finnic; compare the general
American attitude (which is only now receding) that the Negro dialects are not
language at all.

[15.2 How to Draw Trees: Subgrouping]   The family tree given here did
not draw itself. It is the result of painstaking scrutiny of the actual linguistic
facts, and moreover linguists disagree among themselves here and there,
because "facts" can be interpreted in different ways. It is relatively easy to
establish a family of languages, for example, all the Uralic languages in the
diagram. This is given by regular sets of correspondences. But correspondences
put all the units of each language on equal footing, and can do no more than
group the languages into a brush formation (one node), not a tree. Similarly,
it is relatively easy to see which (e.g., Classical) manuscripts represent the same
story (see §§ 2.17, 2.18), but determining the sequence of copying is much trickier
and often indeterminate in detail. When a number of manuscripts have the
same unusual mistake, it is clear (or rather, it is the simplest hypothesis) that the
mistake was copied from the original. The probability of repeating the mistake
independently so many times is practically nonexistent. All the extant mistakes
are thus continuations of the original mistake. In dialect geography we saw that
the same logic is used for the interpretation of lateral areas. The same form in
discontinuous localities does not speak for an independent origin for each
locality, but argues that they continue an original unity (when there was one
area only). Now, this is the principle in drawing family trees for languages. If
two or more languages share a feature which is unlikely to have occurred
spontaneously in each of them, this feature must have arisen once only, when
these languages were one and the same. The more features pile up in this way
for a particular group of languages, the firmer the conclusion is that these
languages represent an original unity, which is represented by a node in the
family tree. But note now that the establishment of a language family uses the
same principle, in terms of the linguistic sign: the colligation between meaning
and form is arbitrary, and if any two or more languages have compatible forms
(ascertained on the basis of sound correspondences) linked with compatible
meanings, and if borrowing is not likely, it is simplest to hypothesize that we
have relationship, that is, a language family, which will be represented by a node

in the tree. This is an important criterion for subgrouping, in spite of the danger of interference from borrowing. The more morphological signs (grammatical markers) are involved, the better guarantee we have against borrowing.

Let us now refer back to the Uralic family tree. It was mentioned that the Baltic Finnic languages are so close to each other that they can be taken as dialects of one language; their variety is roughly on the order of the Romance or Slavic languages. The total grammar of the Baltic Finnic languages is essentially identical. Hundreds of basic vocabulary items are shared as well. There is no possibility that all this could be accidental, and thus we assume that the grammars and the vocabulary arose once only, and that the slight differences are due to later change in each form. Let us mention one specific Baltic Finnic innovation, a change that breaks away from tradition (or a "common mistake"): all the languages have undergone the change of final -e# > -i (§§ 4.29, 6.6, 10.12, 11.17). All these languages and Lapp (except for Veps, Livian, and a variety of Southern Lapp) have consonant gradation, and this is one of the features defining Early Baltic Finnic, although it is not really certain in what form, if any, it existed in the protolanguage (§§ 11.15–11.19).

The same situation as in Baltic Finnic obtains in Germanic. Here again the grammars are obviously very similar, as well as the vocabulary (§§ 11.2–11.8). Even the linguistically uninitiated notice the necessity for a common node in the tree, however they word it. Consider, for example, the Germanic strong verb system (§§ 12.1, 12.2), essentially the same everywhere. It is utterly impossible that each language would have independently carried out the following innovations: shift of the Proto-Indo-European perfect into (1) a preterite, or (2) a few auxiliary "presents" (e.g., can, may, shall), and (3) the formation of the weak conjugation (with the preterite formed with dental stops). Or take the Germanic innovation of replacing the Proto-Indo-European syllabic resonant by a back vowel plus the corresponding consonantal resonant, $*R > uR$ (in certain environments we have subsequent umlauts $u > o$). Again it is more reasonable to assume that this happened only once, in the protolanguage, rather than many times. As these common innovations keep accumulating, our analysis and our reasons for positing a common node become vindicated.

[15.3 Family Trees and Comparative Linguistics]   What has emerged is that the drawing of family trees is one aspect of comparative linguistics. It is a way of formalizing the rule part of the dichotomy between units and rules. This dichotomy has been observed throughout this text (Part II dealt largely with rules, Part III, largely with units, but the mapping rules were especially emphasized in §§ 10.6, 10.15, 11.20, 12.4, 13.6). A family tree tries to convey in gross outline the basic mapping rules that bring the highest level reconstructions back to the attested forms. The principle of minimizing both units and rules necessitates that some rules are applied high enough, to work once only, in a node that splits only later. A 'shared innovation' has been recently rephrased as a *shared rule*, but the new term does not reflect any real change in substance. In the early days of family-tree construction one chose one particular innovation after another, exactly as one does with synchronic trees of derivation. The result was always bifurcations, that is, binary splits. This is how August Fick drew the Indo-European family tree, and this was made popular by August Schleicher. Schleicher first split Proto-Indo-European into Aryan-Greco-Italo-Celtic vs. Slavo-Germanic. The former was then divided into Indo-Iranian vs. Greco-Italo-Celtic, the latter into Germanic vs. Balto-Slavic. Greco-Italo-Celtic gave Italo-Celtic and Greek. Albanian somehow sprang from the stem of Greek, and as for the remaining two-part names, their final splits are obvious. A binary split is, of course, possible, and in fact the Uralic tree has many of them (some linguists posit even more than indicated in Figure 15-1). This is also why the Finnic node has two nuclei. It can be split in two by lowering Volga Finnic down the stem. But to limit oneself to binary splits only is too stiff a requirement; this became quite clear when dealing with closer relationships, where adjacent dialects share features (e.g., the Baltic Finnic languages or the Germanic languages). It is impossible, without being arbitrary, to give priority to some features, and the "tree" remains a brush-like formation with one node only. This is also how one has to draw the Indo-European family tree for the following subgroups: Indo-Iranian, Armenian, Greek, Italic, Celtic, Germanic, Balto-Slavic, Albanian, Anatolian, and Tocharian.

The drawing of trees is of course based on actual linguistic differences—in fact, isoglosses, as in dialect geography. Instead of indicating the isogloss line between two items, say, $a \mid b$, one concentrates on the actual derivation of the items, $a \wedge b$, because this can show history and the aim of the tree is to show derivational history, that is, the actual splits. Now, such splits need not be absolute, because borrowing is always possible; in a convergence situation borrowing can be quite considerable in every part of the grammar. Rather than draw splits often based on arbitrary selections of features and of dubious chronology, Johannes Schmidt proposed (1872) that changes be represented like the mesh of chain mail, or like circular ripples on water, which spread outward from the point of origin of the change. He called this way of handling the relationship the *wave theory*. A few years later, when dialect geography was well established, it became apparent that it was not mere theory, because this was the way an isogloss map behaved. Of course the choice of isoglosses for this new purpose can be as arbitrary as the selection of innovations in drawing trees. Trees can represent splits, waves the actual spread of features. Both ways of representing relationship can of course be as bad or good as the linguists make them, within the limits imposed by the models themselves.

[15.4 Wave Theory]   When no particular linguistic innovation can be given chronological priority, subgrouping results in a brush-like tree without depth (one node). In such a situation an isogloss map gives much more information because it spells out the overlapping items, and isogloss bundles indicate the relative strength of boundaries. Figure 15-2 includes twenty-four isoglosses of different value, in the spirit of Schmidt's proposal. The exact value of the isoglosses is irrelevant for our purposes, because we are looking at a principle. Note, however, that phonetic isoglosses are included, which makes isogloss 1 just

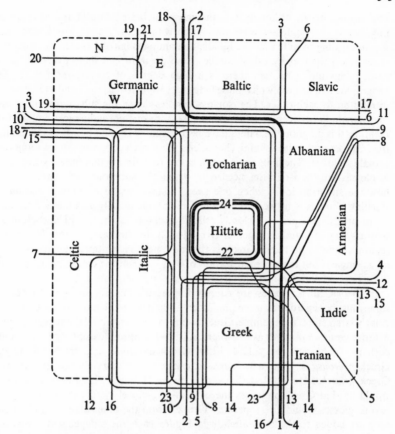

FIGURE 15-2. A dialect map of the Indo-European languages.

DEFINITIONS OF THE ISOGLOSSES

1. centum | satem [right] (§ 11.12)
2. -ss- | -st-, -tt- [right]
3. aoə | a, āō | ō [inside]
4. eao | a [inside]
5. s | h [inside]
6. CVRC | CRVC [inside] (§ 4.18)
7. kʷ | p [inside] (§§ 18.13, 18.16)
8. e- | Ø 'past' [left, outside] (§ 19.10)
9. -osyo 'genitive' [right, inside]
10. -r | -i 'present' [right, outside] (§ 19.10)
11. -m- | -bh- 'case marker' [below]
12. -to- | -mo- 'ordinal' [below]
13. -u 'imperative' [inside] (§ 19.10)
14. proti | poti 'preposition' [inside]
15. secondary endings (without no. 10 -i) [below] (§ 19.10)
16. feminine nouns with masculine endings [inside]
17. -ad 'ablative' | 'genitive' [inside]
18. new tense system from perfect [inside] (Chapter 12)
19. umlaut [inside] (§ 4.5)
20. -ww-, -jj- | stop + w, j [outside]
21. -ggj- | -ddj- [right] (no. 20)
22. laryngeals as h's [inside] (§ 12.4)
23. uncontracted reflexes of sequence *yH [inside]
24. unit pronouns | particles + enclitic pronouns [inside] (§§ 19.8, 19.9)

one among many, although it is the most celebrated line in Indo-European linguistics. The isoglosses were not chosen with an eye on isogloss 1, and thus it is interesting to note that the bundle containing isogloss 1 is weaker (contains fewer lines) than many other bundles. The diagram is a dialect map without exact geography, although there is a high degree of correspondence to the geographic situation in which these languages were first attested and are situated in relation to each other. The isogloss bundles define the subgroups, the areas that remain in between, but for practical reasons one normally picks a name for them. In this diagram the names have been given by the end points of the family tree. One can read the defining characteristics of each subgroup by scanning the actual isoglosses. The diagram is not intended to maintain that these twenty-four isoglosses are the isoglosses needed to define the subgroups; it merely shows how the situation looks when one keeps adding isoglosses. One of the most startling bundles is between Italic and Greek. One usually gets the notion that Latin and Greek are very closely related, because for historical and cultural reasons they are studied together (see § 16.12). In this sample more isoglosses separate than unite them. Greek is the most heavily wrapped subgroup here; let us single it out for a demonstration of how one can use dialect geography in the service of comparative linguistics.

In theory, all isoglosses are equally important, but, for defining purposes, some must be regarded as more fundamental than others. Unique relics are particularly interesting: for example, Greek seems to have preserved the sequence *yH without contraction to *i as elsewhere in Indo-European (except for Hittite and perhaps Tocharian; see §§ 12.4, 12.5). Greek develops ya/ia from *yH (e.g., Greek *phérousa* < *-ontya* vs. Sanskrit *bharantī* 'the carrying one' (fem.) and Greek *príasthai* 'to buy' vs. Sanskrit *krīṇāmi* 'I buy'). Another relic feature would be that Greek preserves the original five-vowel system (§ 11.14). These two isoglosses would now separate "Greek" from the other dialects, and when they are added to the ones already in Figure 15-2, the independent status of Greek is strengthened. But these isoglosses still do not tell when "Greek" became Greek; because they define relics in "Greek," they define a Proto-Indo-European dialect as well. Time depth is completely lacking. If relics can be used to define general characteristics, certain innovations give footholds for relative chronology. In Greek, one way of forming a perfect is with a suffix -k-, which occurs already in Homer but is absent in the other Indo-European languages. The k- perfects could now be used for defining the starting point of Greek. But, of course, there is always the danger that an innovation might be as old as the protolanguage. In such cases the relative chronology would be wrong, but it would still serve as a characterization of the dialect against others.

The diagram includes a few isoglosses that affect only single subgroups or part of them (6, 19, 20, 21). Some of the wider isoglosses affect just parts of certain subgroups (5, 7, 12, 14). This is exactly what a real dialect map looks like: it shows how, in favorable cases, dialectal differences can be reconstructed, because it is to be expected that *some* of the isoglosses represent divisions in the protolanguage (e.g., 11), although others can have diffused later from group to group.

It is interesting to note that Tocharian and Hittite turn out to occupy a central position in the map, although they were attested in the peripheries of Indo-European territory (Chinese Turkestan and Anatolia, respectively). But there is no contradiction, because seriation shows that Tocharian and Hittite occupy the conservative side of the isoglosses involved—they generally do not share innovations with other subgroups. Thus it is likely that they had already left the original homeland when most of the innovations were occurring in the central area. Areal notions work out quite well for isogloss 10, -*r* being retained in lateral areas. In short, Figure 15-2 has many of the characteristics of a real dialect map, which strengthens the validity of such a diagram.

[**15.5 Synthesis of the Models**]   The problem with the family-tree model was that it did not spell out the actual linguistic items defining the nodes. It did not allow for diffusion either, and this then led to the wave-theory model. And now we see that the isogloss map has a problem in handling chronology. It spells out the isoglosses, but they are all on the same flat surface without chronological depth. Seriation can be used, but only for one isogloss at a time, atomistically and without relation to other isoglosses. In short, this leads us back to family trees, which show time depth. This is an indication of the complementarity of the two models, a view championed by Leskien. Both diagrams are visual aids which show, in a single picture, interrelationships within the whole family or its subgroups. Models are, of course, icons of these relations, but since models represent certain hypotheses, they are icons of hypotheses. Overliteral interpretation is the greatest danger, since a picture (diagram) of a hypothesis cannot be more accurate than the hypothesis itself. It should also be no wonder that pictures of the same object, taken at different angles, look different, although they have a substantial common core. And both pictures tend to be fuzzy as well, because the object is vague as a consequence of many historical gaps.

How would one now lift up a tree out of the flat map of Figure 15-2? One must give priority to some isoglosses over others. Schleicher's tree (§ 15.3) would seem to take isogloss 11 as the first basic division, then numbers 17 and 4, and so on. It is not claimed that Schleicher used these very isoglosses for his tree, but the isoglosses provided in Figure 15-2 would enable one to set up Schleicher's tree. On the other hand, if isogloss 1 is given highest priority, we get the most famous subgrouping into *centum* and *satem* languages, west and east, and this is again a two-way split, as always in Schleicher's tree. Isoglosses 22 and 24 gave rise to another two-way classification: Hittite (or Anatolian) versus the rest of Indo-European. To stress the very deep-cutting nature of this cleavage (22, 24, and others not given here) a name Indo-Hittite has been proposed for the family. The term has aroused almost unbelievable rage in some linguists, although the facts have not changed at all. The dialect map remains exactly as before; the new name just emphasizes certain isoglosses. In this sense the Indo-Hittite hypothesis is based on internal analysis. Of course new names often stress old facts from a new angle; for example, rule manipulation supersedes analogy in this way. There is traditional justification in keeping old names. It

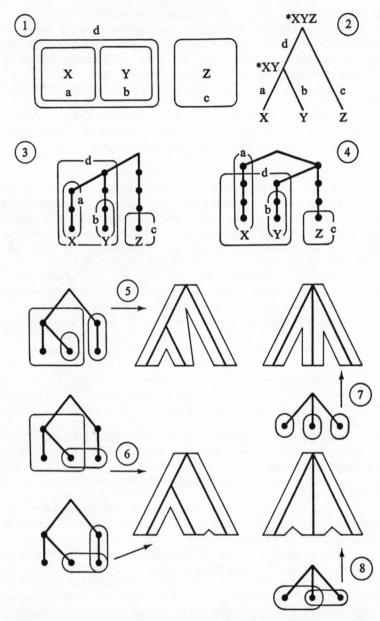

FIGURE 15-3. Combinations of trees and isoglosses. [Reprinted by permission from Franklin C. Southworth, "Family-tree diagrams," *Language*, **40**, 557–565 (1964) (© Linguistic Society of America).]

could be rather difficult (not to say pointless) to ban the word *horse* and replace it with, say, *hay burner*, just to stress the fact that horses eat hay. The term *horse* can and does cover that as well, and similarly every Indo-Europeanist knows that he can go on using the name Indo-European irrespective of the actual isoglosses that split the family.

If we choose isogloss 23 as the earliest division, we get a two-way split between Tocharian, Hittite, and Greek versus the rest. One could now postulate that after Hittite had left the scene, Tocharian and Greek vocalized *yH (Greek ya/ia, Tocharian $y\bar{a}$), and this would give another two-way split. The fact is, however, that the only solid two-way tree remains the Indo-Hittite one, that is, the one based on isogloss 24. If one does not like the name or the tree, the fact still remains that Hittite is the most aberrant dialect of Indo-European.

There is one unfortunate gap in the procedure of converting a map into a tree. There is no single way of deciding which isogloss is basic. This is why so much controversy arises. Linguists go basically by their feelings or intuitions, even to the point of trying to justify the correctness of linguistic theories. Such intuitions often brand the work of other linguists as "wrong" or "uninteresting." No wonder the Indo-Hittite hypothesis has not been "settled."

F. C. Southworth has suggested a notation that would combine the family tree and wave diagrams. In Figure 15-3:1 we have four isoglosses (*a*, *b*, *c*, and *d*) defining three languages (*X*, *Y*, and *Z*) without time depth. This map can be converted into a family tree (Figure 15-3:2) if we assume that *d* is earlier than *a* or *b*. This tree can be made more detailed by indicating successive stages with bumps in the branches and by stretching the isoglosses through the time axis: the higher an isogloss reaches, the earlier it pitched in (Figure 15-3:3). But the tree is of course different if isogloss *a* is the earlier one (Figure 15-3:4). Two different trees now represent two different histories for the isogloss situation (Figure 15-3:1). Southworth also suggests converting the isoglosses into an envelope around the family tree (Figure 15-3:5-8). If an early split is not bridged over by later isoglosses, the envelope will indicate the split accordingly (Figure 15-3:5). But if the early split is connected by later changes, the notch in the envelope is shallow (Figure 15-3:6). This now makes the distance between the highest node and the second branching significant (in Figure 15-3, compare combinations 5 and 6). In a brush-like tree (Figure 15-3:7, 8) the branching distance remains the same, but the different depths of the envelope notches indicate the absence or presence of isogloss overlap.

REFERENCES

15.1 Hoenigswald 1963, Maher 1970b, Austerlitz 1968, Korhonen (private communication), Collinder 1965, 1955-60, *Suomen* ... (See p. 178); **15.2** Brugmann 1884, Chrétien 1963, Hoenigswald 1966; **15.4** Brugmann 1884, Meillet 1967b, Porzig 1954, Birnbaum and Puhvel (eds.) 1966, Krahe 1970; **15.5** Pulgram 1953, Höfler 1958, Southworth 1964.

CHAPTER 16

CLASSIFICATION OF LANGUAGES

The chapter reviews briefly the almost hit-or-miss character of early typologizing, although typological classification is never perfect or absolute. This contrasts with the absolute nature of genealogical classification. Without typology, however, genetic linguistics would be impossible.

[16.1 The Necessity of Typology] Linguists look at language from any point of view ranging between two extreme poles. At one end each language is unique; at the other, all languages are the same. Both polar extremes deny the feasibility of typological classification, although the universalist approach delineates natural language from other sign systems. The problem is the same in all social and cultural sciences: the phenomena we study never show up in pure form. Every such event occurs in the concrete form of particular, historically conditioned cultures, languages, and so on. Individual men and communities do not dwell alone in incommensurate worlds of their unique experiences; they communicate with each other. The general human experience is that we sense simultaneously the unique and the universal in our fellowmen. This type of study is necessarily, therefore, a syncritical/comparative one. To study culture or language we must study cultures and languages. In linguistics it has always been clear that certain languages resemble each other more than certain others, as shown by dialectology and genetic relationship, for example. English dialects form a group that is distinct from German dialects, and the Germanic languages pattern correspondingly with respect to the Romance languages, and so on. And in convergence areas languages share features that unite them in structure in contradistinction to the outsiders.

[16.2 The Development of Morphological Typology and Typological Classification of Languages] Along with the genetic study of language there was always a keen interest in the typological classification of languages. Samples and descriptions of different languages were collected in the seventeenth century and at the beginning of the eighteenth century classificatory schemes started to develop.

Friedrich von Schlegel divided languages into two groups, flective vs. affixive. The term 'flection' was ambiguous because it meant not only root modification (*sing–sang*), as intended, but also inflection, which can be of the affixing type (*cat-s*). 'Affixive' referred to particles (*the paw of the cat*) as well as affixes; it encompassed any material outside the root or its modification. Friedrich's older brother August expanded this scheme into a tripartite one: (1) languages without structure (Chinese), (2) languages with affixes (Turkish), (3) languages with flection (Indo-European; *goose/geese, sing/sang/sung*, and so on). A fourth type was added later by A. F. Pott: the incorporating languages (Eskimo). This type means that the language incorporates into one word what is a sentence in the other types, for example, Oneida *kΛtsyuq* 'fish' and *kítsyaks* 'I eat fish', *swâ·yat* 'berry' and *kahyókwas* 'I am picking berries out of water' (i.e., 'cranberries'). Noun objects and adverbial phrases are incorporated into the verb. In these examples it looks as if the free nouns were completely suppletive to the incorporated objects, but actually the same base is embedded in both, because the "free forms" also have obligatory prefixes and suffixes. Incorporation need not involve suppletion. The three-way division remained the basic one, under the terms: (1) isolating (coined by W. v. Humboldt), (2) agglutinating, and (3) flectional, although there were attempts at further segmentation. Thus F. Misteli made use of six types (by splitting the first two of the above grouping into two): (1) incorporating, (2) root-isolating, (3) stem-isolating, (4) serializing, (5) agglutinating, and (6) flectional. He gives Malayan as a stem-isolating language, where the root is made into a stem by various affixes. This is essentially agglutination without inflectional affixes. English *deep* would be a root, and *deepness* an isolating stem, but *depth* would already be partly flectional. Coptic (Semitic) and Bantu are supposed to be serializing languages. For Bantu the criterion is the complicated system of agreement, for Semitic the discontinuous morphemes. F. N. Finck added two more types in his classification: (1) root-isolating (Chinese), (2) incorporating (Eskimo), (3) coordinating [serializing] (Subiya), (4) subordinating [agglutinative] (Turkish), (5) stem-isolating (Samoan, Tagalog), (6) root-inflecting (Arabic), (7) stem-inflecting (Modern Greek), and (8) group-inflecting (Georgian). The questions asked were slightly different for the different categories. There were the old questions about the inflectional shape of the word:

	ISOLATING	INFLECTING
roots	Chinese	Arabic
stems	Samoan	Modern Greek
groups	—	Georgian

but for Subiya and Turkish, syntactic criteria were used, with concentration on nouns for the former and verbs for the latter.

In addition to the above classification according to the makeup of the words in relation to form and meaning, Max Müller introduced the terms 'analytic' and 'synthetic' to refer to the segmentability of units. W. D. Whitney added the term 'polysynthetic' for cases when segmentation was especially difficult. These terms have been used concurrently with 'isolating' or 'agglutinative', 'flectional', and 'incorporating,' respectively, because such types allow for corresponding segmentation.

[16.3]   Nineteenth-century typology was disfigured by extreme ethnocentricity and lack of reliable data. Indo-European was judged higher than other types, and statements were made on undigested written material. One basic criterion for classification was always translation (into German), which figured prominently in the notion of incorporating languages. It was generally thought that isolating languages yield agglutinating ones and that these in turn yield flectional types. Max Müller connected the three types with social order as well: the isolating languages were family languages, the agglutinating ones, nomadic, and the flectional ones, state languages (see § 21.11). Schleicher supported typological history (isolating to agglutinating to flectional) because it corresponded to the biological parallel of birth, growth, and withering. Of course it was rather arbitrary to brand a language with one name only, because such types are relative. English is heavily agglutinative (*cat-s*, *good-ness*) and flection is a minority (*goose/geese*). Cases like *dep-th*, *duch-ess* are somewhere in between. And if one characteristic of an incorporating language is that the free form and the corresponding bound one are different (as in the appearance of Oneida above), English has it also in *dep-*, *duch-* versus the free forms *deep* and *duke*, or even further in cases like *horse/equine/hippology* or *woman/feminine/gynecology* (see § 8.12). Moreover, it is often possible to devise agglutinative analogs to synthetic flectional languages, through internal reconstruction alias morphophonemic analysis, which shows how sound change may indeed change agglutination into flection (compare Lapp consonant gradation, §§ 10.14, 11.15). Morphophonemic analysis makes the synthetic Oneida word *lû·yaks* 'they (masc.) eat berries' into a perfect agglutinative sequence |hla-wa-ahy-k-s| '3rd person/masc.-plural-berry-eat-continuous/present', which can be converted into the actually occurring form with six rules: (1) $aV \rightarrow a$, (2) |awa| $\rightarrow u$ in certain prefixes (§ 4.23), (3) |#hl-| $\rightarrow l$-, (4) insert *a* between a noun stem ending in a consonant and a verb stem beginning with a consonant, (5) place the accent (') on the penult, and (6) $\acute{V}hy \rightarrow \acute{V}\cdot y$. In Latin *dīcor* 'I am said' the ending -*or* is usually learned as one lump meaning '1st sg.' + 'passive' + 'present'. But in the reconstruction this is easily split up into *deik-o-A-o-r* 'show-conjugation marker-1st sg.-passive-present'. Similarly, the Sanskrit middle subjunctive 1st sg. -*āi* in *bharāi* 'let me carry for myself' is in Indo-European terms *bher-o-e-A-o-i* 'carry-conjugation marker-subjunctive-1st sg.-middle-present'. (N.B.: Latin -*r*/Skt -*i*: isogloss 10 in Figure 15-2; see §§ 19.1, 19.10).

[16.4]   To break the nineteenth-century deadlock on typology *Edward Sapir* developed an apparatus capable of a more flexible characterization of languages. Languages display four types of concepts:

   I. Basic (concrete) concepts (objects, actions, qualities)
   II. Derivational concepts
   III. Concrete relational concepts (differing from the above in indicating relations that transcend the word they are immediately attached to)

IV. Pure relational concepts (which are purely abstract, relating concrete elements to each other, expressed through word order, particles, or inner modification)

Groups I and IV are universal and must be represented in every language, whereas II and III are facultative. Of these, group III is rather obscure, but perhaps we can say that the -*um* in Latin *vīdī virum* 'I saw the man' indicates the relation of 'man' to 'seeing' (IV), which in English is given by word order. Then the second -*um* in *vīdī virum bonum* 'I saw the good man' would seem to be III, relating *bonum* to *virum*. Sapir also clarifies the old 'flectional' type by calling it 'symbolic'. He adds the term 'fusional' when underlying agglutination is modified, for example, in cases like *dep-th*, *fil-th*, and *duch-ess*. Fusion indicates the relative firmness with which the affixed elements are united with each other. The degree of (poly)morphemicity of the word is expressed by the terms 'analytic', 'synthetic', 'polysynthetic'. These terms are again purely relative; a language may be analytic from one standpoint and synthetic from another.

Now all languages can be grouped according to the concepts expressed:

A. Pure-relational nonderiving (simple) languages (I + IV)
B. Pure-relational deriving (complex) languages (I + II + IV)
C. Mixed-relational nonderiving (simple) languages (I + III + IV)
D. Mixed-relational deriving (complex) languages (I + II + III + IV)

When these types are combined with different techniques and syntheses we get a three-parameter classificatory scheme as in Figure 16-1. Chinese is now a simple

1. Fundamental type	2. Technique	3. Synthesis
A	Isolating (relating words together)	Analytic
B	Agglutinative⎫	Synthetic
C	Fusional ⎬within words	Polysynthetic
D	Symbolic ⎭	

FIGURE 16-1. Sapir's three-parameter classificatory scheme of languages.

pure-relational isolating analytic language, Turkish complex pure-relational agglutinative synthetic, English complex mixed-relational fusional analytic, Semitic complex mixed-relational symbolic-fusional synthetic, and older Indo-European complex mixed-relational fusional (with symbolic tinge) synthetic. Bantu is given as simple mixed-relational fusional analytic (mildly synthetic), although it could go under D as well.

It is obvious that this scheme is no longer so absolute as a single three(+)-partite system, because technique and synthesis can be specified with 'strongly' or 'mildly', and so on, and compounds like 'symbolic-fusional' are used. But the system is still unable to represent exact details; Sapir of course was aware of it and warned that the strong craving for a simple formula has been the undoing of linguists, and that languages cannot be pigeonholed (stated thus already by Humboldt). But Sapir's multiple-parameter typology was a definite step forward, and it has been extended by Joseph Greenberg to yield exact numerical values.

[16.5]   Taking samples of one hundred words of running text, Greenberg calculated various ratios between elements and relations. Let us look here briefly at the profiles of eight languages through ten indices of his, reproduced in Figure 16-2. The traditional nonquantitative results are on the whole confirmed. One can now draw the numerical boundaries for analytic (1.00–1.99),

Typological indices		Sanskrit	Old English	Persian	English	Yakut	Swahili	Annamese	Eskimo
Synthesis	M/W	2.59	2.12	1.52	1.68	2.17	2.55	1.06	3.72
Agglutination	A/J	.09	.11	.34	.30	.51	.67	—	.03
Compounding	B/W	1.13	1.00	1.03	1.00	1.02	1.00	1.07	1.00
Derivation	D/W	.62	.20	.10	.15	.35	.07	.00	1.25
Gross inflection	I/W	.84	.90	.39	.53	.82	.80	.00	1.75
Prefixing	P/W	.16	.06	.01	.04	.00	1.16	.00	.00
Suffixing	S/W	1.18	1.03	.49	.64	1.15	.41	.00	2.72
Isolation	O/N	.16	.15	.52	.75	.29	.40	1.00	.02
Pure inflection	Pi/N	.46	.47	.29	.14	.59	.19	.00	.46
Concord	Co/N	.38	.38	.19	.11	.12	.41	.00	.38

M = morphemes, W = words, A = agglutinative constructions, J = morpheme boundaries (junctures), R = roots, D = derivative morphemes, I = Inflectional morphemes, P = prefixes, S = suffixes, O = order, N = nexus (relation of words within a sentence), Pi = pure inflection, Co = concord.

FIGURE 16-2.   Greenberg's typological indices expressed by simple numerical values, for example, the number of morphemes divided by the number of words (synthesis). [Reprinted from Joseph H. Greenberg, "A quantitative approach to the morphological typology of languages," *Method and perspective in anthropology*, Robert F. Spencer, editor, University of Minnesota Press, Minneapolis, © copyright 1954 University of Minnesota, Minneapolis, Minnesota.]

synthetic (2.00–2.99), and polysynthetic (3.00 and over), and similarly agglutinative (0.50 and over). Perfect isolation is 1.00 (Annamese), and Eskimo comes out as expected (0.02 = 0). Similar indices can be devised for syntactic facts in addition to the last three in Greenberg's list.

It should be noted that the terms 'analytic', 'synthetic', and so on, are used in widely different meanings by different linguists; the context usually shows what is meant. The situation is no different from other linguistic terminology which displays a diversity of meanings, e.g., 'morpheme' and 'sememe'.

[16.6 The All-pervasiveness of Typology] Every descriptive scheme is potentially typological. As so often in linguistics, different approaches are complementary (e.g., internal reconstruction and the comparative method), and this is true of the descriptive and typological approaches as well. Any feature can be taken as a basis of classification, but the resulting groupings need not have much practical value (e.g., the class of all languages with rounded front vowels, or nasal vowels). Very popular is the grouping of vowel systems into triangles and squares and/or by the number of units; for example, Latin has a five-vowel triangle, Italian a seven-vowel triangle, American English (in the traditional analysis) a nine-vowel square, and Turkish an eight-vowel cube (Figure 16-3). Similar diagrams can be drawn for consonant systems, accentual

Latin
(Triangle)

Traditional
American English
(Square)

Turkish
(Cube)

FIGURE 16-3.   Characterization of vowel systems through geometric arrangements.

systems, and so on. The Proto-Indo-European morphophonemic resonant system $VR \sim R/R$ (Chapter 12) occurs in almost identical form in Proto-Kartvelian (the language from which Georgian descends). All kinds of tense and aspect systems can be plotted into pictures or can be otherwise compared. The basic features of Oneida verbal content structure are strikingly similar to those of European languages, especially Romance, although, formally, the structures are quite different. An imperfective (active) contrasts with a perfective (passive); for example, *kʌtsyáku* 'it-fish-eat-past/done' = 'the fish is done ate' = 'the fish has been eaten' (compare Spanish *está comido* 'it has been eaten'); *wakitsyáku* 'it-to me-fish-eat-done' = 'I have eaten the fish' (compare Portuguese *tenho comido* 'I have eaten'); *wanitsyáku* 'it-to itself-fish-eat-done' = 'the fish has been eating' (compare the 'middle voice', or, for example, German *der*

Fisch hat sich genährt 'the fish has nourished itself'); and *wanítsyaks* 'it-to itself-fish-eat-present' = 'the fish eats itself' = 'the fish gets eaten' (compare Spanish *el libro se vende* 'the book is sold').

Syncrisis is a generic aspect of the study of variation (Figure 1-7), and the same tools have to be used as in dialectology: diagrams (see Figure 3-1) and numerical parameters (§ 9.11).

[16.7 Contrastive Analysis and Translation] A practical aspect of typology is contrastive linguistics, whereby two languages are contrasted by dismembering them into their components and matching the components as closely as possible in the framework of semantic equivalents. Thus English nouns like *food, faith,* and *love* have to be rendered by verbal expressions in Mazatec (of Mexico); some Hopi verbs can be given by Kannada verbs, others correspond to Kannada adjectives; and so on. Names are verbs in certain languages, for example, Oneida *Kanʌstalukwa* 'Shelled Corn', *Skanyataliyo* 'Handsome Lake' (roughly 'the water is again good for navigation'), and also *layʌthos* 'he plants corn' for 'farmer' and *shakoye·nás* 'he arrests them' for 'sheriff', although the English word *farmer* was also borrowed as *lafaqmahkó* (with considerable sound substitution and gender marking). The immediate aim of contrastive analysis may be language teaching, but the same syncritical comparison is also the essence of translation. Translation is intimately tied with knowledge of the respective cultures, and linguistic typology has also been connected with culture circle theory (see § 21.19). Translation merges on one side into the notion of bilingualism, and it represents a situation that is fertile for borrowing, either in the form of loan shifts or morphemic borrowing (as in Oneida). In addition, translation was one of the basic activities that led to the development of morphological typologies. This happened mainly in connection with samples from the Bible, and it is interesting to note that Bible translation was one of the momenta for the rise of descriptive linguistics in America (Summer Institute of Linguistics, American Bible Society). In Russia, B. A. Uspenskij has developed an explicit notion of a comparison standard, which he calls *étalon language* (*étalon* French → Russian 'standard'; *standard* has already been preempted, with a different meaning, in English usage). The concrete real languages are characterized by the transform rules necessary for converting their structures into that of the étalon language. Languages are measured by their distance from the étalon language. Different étalon languages can be devised according to the purposes of typological comparison. Note that for a long time Greek and Latin (or Indo-European in general) served as an implicit étalon language (standard of comparison). The notion of such a standard or intermediate language makes typology even more similar to translation, since one way of doing machine translation is through a machine language rather than directly from one language into another.

[16.8 Language Typology and Genetic Linguistics] Language typology shows two aspects, (1) language universals and (2) typological classification, based on language-specific features. But so far we have not seen what typology can do for genetic linguistics, although the nineteenth-century belief that isolating languages changed into agglutinating and these into flectional ones has been mentioned. Indeed, this sequence is often found, or at least such a tendency is seen in the development of Indo-Iranian to Persian, Old English to Modern English, and Latin to French (see Greenberg's table [Figure 16-2] for the first two). On the other hand, Chinese used to have flection, and thus the development between types is not necessarily a one-way phenomenon. (We shall return to this question below.)

It turns out that the role of typology in diachrony is so basic that it is not usually noticed at all. All diachronic changes imply types, for example, assimilation, metathesis, analogy, fading of metaphors, and so on. Part II has shown us the true regularity of processes of change, of diachronic universals (and every chapter has had a section on classification as well). These have been empirically established through historical documentation. These processes on their part make reconstruction possible (Part III). Reconstruction itself can be viewed as the establishment of a partial étalon language for genetic comparison. Diasystems are thus members of the class of étalon languages made for a particular purpose, genetic classification. The distance of each language from this comparison standard is measured by transform rules (innovations or retentions). The distance can often be given visually in a family tree or in a combination of a tree and a dialect map, as already shown.

Also, largely through Greenberg's efforts, we now have a doctrine of dynamic comparison between language types, where the objects of comparison are the processes themselves. It is often possible to establish the relative origin of types and we might call this method *seriation of types*. There are two classes of languages, those that have nasal vowels and those that do not. There is the further implicational hierarchy that languages with nasal vowels also have oral vowels. Now, a hypothesis can be asserted about the relative origin of nasal vowels: they result from the loss of a nasal consonant, apart from borrowings and analogical creations. A typical course of events is $VN > \tilde{V}N > \tilde{V}$, but the nasal of course can also precede the vowel. This is pure *relative* chronology, because nasal vowels need not arise; when they do, however, they originate this way. There are further hierarchical scales about nasal vowels; for example, their number is always the same or less than that of oral vowels, never the reverse, and mergers within nasal vowels occur more often than among oral vowels (see § 9.8).

This typological seriation started with an example between types and proceeded to a discussion of hierarchies within the type. Greenberg has also provided eight implicational laws about voiceless vowels, among them: (1) in languages with stress, every vocalic voiceless segment has the weakest degree of stress; (2) in languages with distinctive vowel length, the existence of voiceless long vowels implies that of voiceless short vowels, but not vice versa; (3) every voiceless vowel is either preceded or followed by a silence or a voiceless plain sound; and (4) low voiceless vowels imply high voiceless vowels. These are typological implicational laws (hypotheses) that have so far stood up under empirical checking.

This kind of seriation and implicational scaling transcends the usual comparative method, although it has a striking resemblance to the principle of *lectio difficilior* in its various manifestations. It provides another important contribution to comparative linguistics: a check on reconstructions. What is truly generic about language must also be part of our reconstructions. We should not posit anything in our unattested protolanguages (diasystems) that contradicts our typological universals. A reconstruction of a vowel system with only nasal or voiceless vowels is consequently impossible. Typology also helps us make guesses about missing parts. If for some reason we have clear but fragmentary evidence for a language with *m* and *ŋ*, it is plausible to assume that it must have had *n* as well; or if a language seems to have affricates, it should also have stops, and so on (see § 6.5).

[16.9 Genealogical Classification of Languages]   The two aspects of language typology—universals and classification—are matched by another division in comparative linguistics: (1) determination of fact and degree of relationship and (2) reconstruction of earlier stages. The first part means classification. Those languages that represent outcomes of one and the same protolanguage are grouped into a family. It was mentioned that comparative linguistics depends on the universal change types, and thus a typological factor is also involved here, although it is generally ignored or not realized. The ultimate task of typology is to determine what structures are possible, and why they are possible to the exclusion of others. In this way typology is hierarchically superior to genetic linguistics. It permits us to understand the general laws of change and the possibilities of change within a given language type. It is this that makes linguistics a true science and not a mere codification of facts, and genetic linguistics of course enjoys the benefits. Otherwise, in actual application, typological classification is of course quite different from the genetic one, because it is based on arbitrary features chosen as bases for syncritical comparison.

The principles of genetic classification have already been treated in the preceding chapter. The basic criterion is simply the sound correspondence. Languages that fit into regular sound correspondences belong to the same family. Subgrouping criteria give then the degree of relationship. Very crudely put, comparison of linguistic categories and systems give typological classification, whereas sound correspondences provide genetic classification (which is the more convincing, the more grammatical elements are involved in the correspondences). Figure 16-4 exhibits the standard criteria for establishing genetic relationship. The lower right-hand corner is the chief area where linguists look for a justification of their decisions.

[16.10]   *Syntax* gets the same evaluation as onomatopoeia in this table. Both are evidently iconic. It can be said that syntax belongs largely to all languages; the more universal any feature is, the less valuable it is for classifica-

Agreement in different parts of language	Can this result accidentally?	Can this result easily from borrowing?	Can this be inherited?	Evidence or proof of relationship?
Agreement in the principles of syntax, morphology, and sound system	Yes	Yes	Yes	No
Agreement in descriptive and onomatopoeic vocabulary	Yes	Yes	Yes	No
Agreement in easily borrowable vocabulary	No	Yes	Yes	No
Multiple agreement in the basic and rather unborrowable vocabulary with *sound correspondences*	No	No	Yes	Yes
Considerable and frequent agreement in grammatical formants (endings, prefixes, auxiliaries) and *sound correspondences*	No	No	Yes	Yes

FIGURE 16-4.   Criteria for establishing genetic relationship. [After A. B. Dolgopol'skij, "Ot Saxary do Kamčatki jazyki iščut rodstvennikov," *Znanie— sila*, **42**:1, 43–46 (1967).]

tion. Any language can be derived from a universal deep structure with omnipotent transformations. Thus the whole notion of syntax is rather limited if not useless for classification. On the other hand, there is no doubt that syntax can also be inherited. But it has not been possible to establish genetic relationship purely on syntactic criteria. Whenever syntactic facts have been retrieved, sound correspondences have also played a part (§§ 19.8–19.11). The fullest treatment of the role of syntax in the question of language relationship (by D. R. Fokos-Fuchs) comes to the conclusion that syntax alone cannot be used, but neither should it be neglected. This is true, of course. The problem is that syntax can be described so many ways, and for no language family do we have commensurate syntaxes as a basis for further study. Take Indo-European as an example. To prove genetic relationship by syntax alone one would have to write a grammar for each language on exactly the same principles and show that a different subgrouping from the use of other criteria would result. Then one would have to show why this grouping is more valid than the others based on different criteria. No such program has been carried out. Rather, all facts of

Proto-Indo-European syntax that have been discovered rest firmly on sound correspondences as well. Note that in Figure 16-4 syntax enters the picture at the lowest row, where it really counts, because it is connected with sound correspondences. Indeed, it is here where evidence for genetic relationship is strongest, and it is a serious mistake to think that proof is even better when sound correspondences are discarded (compare § 8.20). All levels of grammar are intimately tied together, and we have seen that various grammatical facts can condition sound change. There cannot be syntax without sound in the actual functioning of the language. Thus the best target for genetic classification still remains the middle of language. We have to compare higher levels of grammar, but not too high, because then we get into universal grammar. To ensure that we do not float too high, our units of comparison have to be anchored to the lower levels by sound correspondences.

[16.11 Distant Relationship]   'Related' in linguistics means 'relatable'. It is a positive term only, used when the comparative method demonstrates connection. In cases where the method does not work, all that can be said is that at the present time our tools do not cut deeper. Thus because the relationship cannot so far be proved, one says that English and Chinese are unrelated. This does not deny the possibility of ultimate relationship. Indeed there have always been linguists who believe that all languages of the world are related—and relatable. This then converts the classification into families into a vast problem of subgrouping, but as far as the linguistic substance goes there is hardly any difference. In recent years there has been a revival in the study of distant relationship. This means applying the comparative method to some better established families, and if sound correspondences seem to work out, relationship can be postulated. Such hypotheses have been, for example, Indo-Semitic (Indo-European and Hamito-Semitic), Indo-Uralic, and Ural-Altaic, not to mention many cases among the American Indian languages. The Indo-Uralic hypothesis looks particularly strong, because the agreement is very good in pronouns and verbal endings, as well as in some basic vocabulary; for example, Uralic *nime ~ Indo-European *nomṇ > Finnish nime- ~ English name and Uralic *wete ~ Indo-European *wod-ōr/*wed-en- > Finnish vete- ~ English water. But all the above families (and many others as well) have been combined into one superfamily called Nostratic, which reaches from the Sahara to Kamchatka. A table of correspondences for the dentals looks something like Figure 16-5 for a few of the families (all units are actually reconstructed, but asterisks are given only to the Nostratic labels). Korean has also been added to this roster, and then Japanese to Korean. Language relationship is a transitive notion, and this is why Japanese is related to English, if it is to Korean, and if Korean is related to (Ural-)Altaic, and so on. Many scholars also believe that this family can be spotted in the Americas as well, and several so-called cross-Bering comparisons have been made (with little success). The Nostratic hypothesis rests on some 600 vocabulary items, and some of the cross-Bering connections have as much substance behind them. This is much more than in many of the traditional

Nostratic	Altaic	Uralic	Dravidian	PIE	Kartvelian	Hamito-Semitic
*ṭ	t- -t-	t- -tt-	t- -t(t)- ṭ ḍ	t	ṭ	ṭ (t[-p])
*t	t- -d-	t- -t-	t- -t(t)- ṭ ḍ	d	t	t
*d	d- -d-	t- -δ-	t- -t(t)- ṭ ḍ	dh	d	d

(ṭ = glottalized, but Dravidian retroflex)

FIGURE 16-5. Table of the Nostratic dental correspondences. [After V. M. Illič-Svityč, "Sootvestvija smyčnyx v nostratičeskix jazykax," *Ètimologija 1966*, 304–355, 401–410, Moscow, Nauka, 1968.]

American Indian connections. As for cross-Bering comparisons, anthropological and archaeological evidence unambiguously indicates that North America was settled from Asia over a land bridge which has existed from time to time between Siberia and Alaska.

[16.12 Conclusion] Nothing has been said about *areal classification* of languages, but it is not necessary, either, in this connection. There are two types of areal classification: (1) mere geographic and (2) geographic with typological similarity (convergence areas). No line can be drawn between the two types, since geographically close languages are likely to share typological features, and related languages can also be close both in geography and typology. The three modes of classification can thus overlap extensively. 'Oceanic linguistics' is geographic, genetic, and typological; 'Southeast Asian linguistics' is geographic and typological at least (isolating tone languages), but genetic relationship has not been established among all of them. We saw from the Indo-European dialect map (Figure 15-2) that Greek and Latin differ on many points. For cultural reasons, however, they are combined into a 'Classical linguistics'. Socially, the American Indian languages share more or less the same position, and this is why one speaks of an 'American Indian linguistics'. 'African linguistics' is also largely genetic (Bantu) and typological. For cultural and historical reasons there is now even an 'East European linguistics', and so on.

This chapter concentrated on the most elementary principles of language classification, some of which were mentioned in previous chapters. It was regarded more important to treat the principles rather than give classificatory lists, which are easily available in handbooks.

REFERENCES

General: Humboldt 1970 [1836], Steinthal and Misteli 1893, Finck 1910 Horne 1966, Greenberg (ed.) 1963, 1966b, and in Sebeok (ed.) 1963f. vol. 11, Uspenskij

1965, Martinet (ed.) 1968, Graur (ed.) 3.493-682; **16.2** Robins in Sebeok (ed.) 1963f. vol. 11; **16.3** Hodge 1970; **16.4** Sapir 1921; **16.5** Greenberg 1954, Kroeber 1960, Householder 1960, Voegelin et al. 1960; **16.6** Lounsbury (personal communication); **16.7** Nida 1969, Nida and Taber 1969, Alatis (ed.) 1968, Kazazis 1967, Uspenskij 1965; **16.8** Jakobson 1958, K. Schmidt 1966, Skalička 1967, Kuipers 1968, Greenberg 1969a, Hoenigswald in Greenberg (ed.) 1963, Hodge 1970; **16.9** Brugmann 1884, Kroeber 1913, Hymes 1959, Hjelmslev 1970, Haas 1966, Dolgopol'skij 1967, Martinet (ed.) 1968, Katičić 1970; **16.10** Fokos-Fuchs 1962, Teeter 1964.

16.11 Distant relationship: Swadesh 1963, Dolgopol'skij 1967, "Uslyšat' prošloe," *Znanie -- sila* 7/85:9-12, 8/85:14-16, Illič-Svityč 1967, 1968, 1971f., S. Martin 1966, R. Miller 1967, Janhunen et al. (eds.) 1983, Shevoroshkin and Markey (eds.) 1986.

16.12 The World: Comrie (ed.) 1987, Ruhlen 1987, Martinet (ed.) 1968, Meillet and Cohen (eds.) 1952, Voegelin and Voegelin 1977; **North America:** Powell 1966, Boas 1929, Hoijer 1946, Pinnow 1964, Haas 1966 [1969]; **South America:** Loukotka 1968; **Africa:** Greenberg 1966a; **Oceania:** Dyen 1965b; Lewy 1964, Bastian 1964; **Soviet Union:** Vinogradov (ed.) 1966f.--*Current Trends in Linguistics* (Sebeok ed. 1963f.) assigns the following volumes to the following areas: 1 (Russia and East Europe), 2 (East Asia, South East Asia), 4 (Ibero-America, Caribbean), 5 (South Asia), 6 (South West Asia, North Africa), 7 (Sub-Saharan Africa), 8 (Oceania), 9 (Western Europe), and 10 (North America).

CHAPTER 17

PHILOLOGY AND ETYMOLOGY

> *The chapter presents the parents of genetic linguistics—philology and etymology. Genetic linguistics when connected with the history and culture of particular speakers is still as relevant as ever.*

[17.1 Complementarity of Goals and Schools]   Genetic linguistics grew out of philology in the nineteenth century, and, in fact, in England the name 'philology' has remained in use for the former until our own day. In America one can already meet students of linguistics who have never heard the term. The purpose of this chapter is to reverse this trend and to show the place of philology in genetic linguistics.

In philology, language serves as a means toward the understanding of a particular culture. Philology has been directed mainly toward written documents produced by past cultures. It studies language as used by a people or an individual in a given historical environment, the ultimate goal being the understanding of the human aspects. Since the evidence is often fragmentary, one has to work with true human probabilities. Genetic linguistics, on the other hand, elevated language into an end in itself, and language change and reconstruction was studied as if languages were independent organisms. When genetic linguistics gave rise to descriptive linguistics, the separation between language and its users became even more pronounced. Those who study language as an autonomous sign system have strived to establish mathematical certainties and have accused the philologists of 'losing sight of the reality'. The philologists also, even if they acknowledge a certain usefulness in the 'linguistic exercises of symbolic logic', maintain that this is after all not 'the true reality of language'. As often with such scholarly controversies of taste and objectives of study, the underlying reason is the complementarity of the aspects (as in units vs. rules, comparative method vs. internal reconstruction, typology vs. description, and so on). Both sides are justified and necessary, although this is not agreed to in either of the partisan camps. In this unfortunate division, the Neogrammarian emphasis on the independent linguistic side has led to a historical linguistics without history, a development in which notational apparatus is taken as an insight into change itself. Chapter 6 has all the machinery for this approach, although warning was sounded throughout against this pitfall, which is ubiquitous (see § 9.2). Because the basic principles were laid down by the Neogrammarians—and they certainly deserve full credit—textbooks have unintentionally (one should hope) led students into thinking that everything in genetic linguistics has been done.

This is why restatements like those in Chapter 6 have enjoyed such an enthusiastic reception; they *look* different, at least. At the opposite pole, the controversy led to a historical linguistics that acknowledges only the human mind with its individual intuitions as the driving force of change. Linguistic change is just history of the expressions of the mind, that is, art history in its widest sense. Grammar is but part of literary history, which itself belongs integrally to culture history. Aesthetics is the sole ruler of philology. This position is known as the *idealist* school of linguistics. The appeal of the idealist position is reflected clearly in the German term of abuse for the sterile mechanistic (Neogrammarian in the negative sense) approach to language, *Lautschieber*, that is, 'sound shifter', known even among laymen. It has already been mentioned that this mechanical approach is merely being continued as rule manipulation.

Polarization into opposite camps is quite common in the sciences. Two general principles are mainly responsible for this, and A. Kaplan has called them (1) the drunkard's search and (2) the law of the instrument. The first principle says that it is easier to look for a lost key under a street lamp because "it is lighter there" than where it was actually lost. And the second can be exemplified as follows: give a small boy a hammer, and he will find that everything he encounters needs pounding. It is indeed often good strategy to start the investigation "where it is lighter"; and it is no wonder that the scientist formulates problems in such a way that what is needed for their solution are those very techniques at which he is most skilled. There is often considerable pressure from the scholarly community or school as well. If the linguist is aesthetically inclined, he might see all of language in that light; if he has been trained to observe sound shifts, he finds this the most significant line to follow. On the other hand, if his background encompasses rule writing, he finds mere rules everywhere and denies other parts of language. We have all heard stories of doctors who always prescribe the same medicine no matter what the ailment is. The beneficial effect of the law of the instrument is that scholars can ride their ideas to the utmost, until others pull them back. The danger is that one does not listen to others, but brands them as unscientific (or something more colorful); the price for being trained one way is trained incapacity to do things otherwise. It is clear that in their behavior both the philologists and the formalists are identical. They have different lamps and different hammers, but they certainly find that the same objects need their pounding. Actually the philologists are rarely worsted in this battle; the real stalemate is reached among different schools of structuralism (including the generative-transformational approach) where the small-boy behavior is strongest: the cry "My indoctrination can beat your indoctrination" stands for "My father can beat your father," even when the hammers of both parties chip away about as inefficiently.

Structuralism has not only pervaded linguistics, but also other areas connected somehow with philology (ethnology, sociology, philosophy, and so on). Particularly influenced has been literary criticism, which has always been closely allied with philology. The tendency to consider a literary work independently of the total culture has been strong. Structuralism has now tended to become synonymous with narrow-mindedness. The practitioners of this kind of structuralism refer often to one of the main figures of the structuralist movement, Claude Lévi-Strauss. But Lévi-Strauss has dissociated himself from this narrow concept of structuralism; he sees no structural method in most of the works on literary criticism that invoke structuralism. As there is no structural analysis without constant leaning on ethnography, he cannot understand how one could study a work within the framework of the structural approach without having secured in advance all the information given by history, biography, and philology for the interpretation. The analysis of literary works with the structural method illuminates much, but this method just adds to and does not replace the traditional ones. An investigation that wants to be positive uses all the possible methods and means. We should not fall prey so easily to pseudo-philosophical nonsense. Here Lévi-Strauss could be speaking for the linguists as well.

It is highly important for a student of linguistics to be aware of this point, because in most cases he will be drawn into one school of thought, and from that perspective it is impossible to see splits in doctrine, for example, how philology separates from genetic linguistics, and how both sides develop various schools that feud among themselves. The eye and the fingernail develop ultimately from one single cell, but what would an eye be without the rest of the body? As in behavioral sciences in general, linguistic training should include an appreciation of a great number of different techniques, and the linguist should always be ready to ask himself whether it would not be better to use his head instead of a formula.

[17.2 The Necessity of Philology and Its Reintroduction into Linguistics]

The simple truth is that philology and genetic linguistics need each other, if they want to be relevant and to do justice to the complexity of a natural language in its natural setting. The best results have been gained by those linguists who can handle both sides. Serious mistakes have occurred when both parties have taken the achievements of the other side at face value. To determine past linguistic structures the linguist must use the most precise philology possible. He cannot be content with mere philological approximations. He always needs the most up-to-date philological achievements, especially if he works with "dead" languages. Fortunately, at the side of a historical linguistics without history, a modern philology has sprung up. Classical philologists used language as a key to the culture and to its written documents. From the semiotic point of view their main interest was pragmatic, the relation between signs and their users (§ 1.16). Now anthropological linguistics and sociolinguistics have reintroduced the human aspect to linguistics. The old priority has been partially reversed. The speech community and the culture is used to understand linguistic variation and change (§§ 1.18–1.20, 1.25; Chapters 3, 9), as was seen throughout Part II, especially in Chapter 9. This is the sociolinguistic contribution. Anthropological linguistics continues the priorities of the old philology by asking that linguistics be relevant and explain something beyond mere language. Humanistic concern is back where it belongs. Similarly, mathematics for the sake of mere mathematics is of limited appeal in the humanities or other sciences, but as an aid it is rather central. This does not deny the possibility of a mathematical study of language or its usefulness, and many would indeed like to define linguistics this way. But for genetic linguistics it would have little to offer, because language changes when it is used by people.

[17.3 Philology As a Composite Puzzle]   To see how linguistic evidence is often not enough for interpretation, let us look at a hypothetical example which comes close to many cases actually recorded in history. A stone inscription is found in Asia Minor. Many scholars study a tracing of it, and ultimately the following hypotheses are suggested for its interpretation: (1) it is a recipe written in Oneida; (2) it is a recipe written in Lydian, a local language; (3) it gives instructions to build a steam engine; (4) it gives instructions to build a locomotive; (5) it is a sailor's letter home; and (6) it records a treaty between two local communities. That the language should be Oneida is highly unlikely on geographical grounds and the suggestion can be discarded right away. (If the language is unmistakenly Oneida or Iroquoian, one would immediately suspect a hoax.) In addition, cooking recipes are not normally inscribed in stone. Instructions for a steam engine are theoretically possible, since the Greeks toyed with them in Alexandria at least, but locomotives are completely unaccept-able, since their origin is unambiguously recorded. Now, if we know that the stone is a boulder that weighs three tons, it could not possibly be a letter, but it could very well be a treaty. In order to unravel everything as far as possible one would now bring to bear the method of epigraphy, as well as the history of the area known independently from this document and any evidence from com-parative linguistics, if the language would seem to have known relatives. The cultural and historical aspects must match those of linguistics. When all parts fit in perfectly, we have a solution. In essence this is simply what philology is: the clearing of the channels of communication across the ages.

[17.4 Etymology As Prime Philology for Genetic Linguistics]   A particular branch of philology is etymology, the scientifically controlled study of the histories of words. It is part of lexicology but is closely connected with genetic linguistics, because any historical grammar or reconstruction must be based on a careful checking of all the etymological equations. Etymology is a historical undertaking par excellence with potentially unlimited appeal and value for the culture historian as well. It is a good balance against isolationism in genetic linguistics. A basic knowledge of it is a must for any student of language if he wants to use etymological dictionaries in his own field efficiently, even if he would not do reconstructions or etymological histories himself.

As a discipline etymology is older than Western linguistics, and it meant literally the science of true meanings. It was incorrectly believed that the earliest (ascertainable) meaning of a word was the only correct one. Change was looked on as mere corruption, even though man was taken to be above the other primates; that is, change was recognized and interpreted at will. After dialect geography announced that each word has its own history, etymology received an immense boost, although it has never returned to the mainstream of genetic linguistics. But without it the groundwork of both historical grammars and reconstructions is inadequate. In fact, the preceding chapters have included considerable etymological detail, since etymology is the application of the notions of Parts II and III to single words or semantic groups. In particular, Chapter 7 (on semantic change) underlined the historical coincidences in linguistic change, but this was no less true of analogy and borrowing which characteristically affect single words. Etymology displays the same division as historical versus comparative linguistics. Comparative linguistics gives us a starting point for mapping rules that parallel historical change. Etymology can concentrate on the origin of the word (counterpart to Part III) or its history (counterpart to Part II). Both sides are complementary, not unlike the distinction between units (starting points) and rules (derivatory history). Historical gaps are often such that much of the history of a word is known but not its origin, or else the origin is clear but the history contains uncertainties.

[17.5 The Role of History]   Sometimes, through good luck, we have historical attestation of the origin; this is most often true of relatively recent times. Thus *grog* 'a mixture of rum and water' was named after Old Grog, itself a metonymic nickname for Admiral Vernon (1684–1757), because he wore a grogram cloak. *Sandwich* is likewise named after John Montagu, the fourth Earl of Sandwich, who is said to have resorted to this kind of a meal in order not to have to leave the gaming table. Russian *vokzal* 'railway station', appearing first in print in 1777, derives from English *Vauxhall*, an enormously fashionable pleasure garden and recreation spot near London, whose name reflects Falkes Hall, after the thirteenth-century holder of the manor, Falkes de Bréauté. The difficulty lies in explaining how a word for 'pleasure garden' could come to mean 'railway station'. For one thing, the English were world leaders in developing and constructing railroads; for another, the architecture of beer halls and early railroad depots was very similar, and railroad stations have always been characteristic loafing places. This kind of exact historical detail is usually lacking, even for very recent times; but it solves a difficult etymological puzzle that would remain opaque indeed in the absence of such detailed knowledge of history.

The most 'obvious' explanation can be wrong. Today many speakers would explain *bulldog* as 'a dog that is like a bull', and by stretching one's imagination one could find a certain similarity. History shows that the compound is not iconic but indexical, because this kind of dog was bred for bull-baiting, a sport that has died out. Russian *samojed* 'Samoyed' is not the obvious 'self-eater', but rather represents Lapp *Sāme-jennam* 'Lapland'. The Samoyeds once lived west of the Ural mountains, and as late as the eleventh century they occupied parts of the Onega region in Karelia. People and countries get named in a rather "haphazard" fashion. *Russia* is named after the Swedes who founded the kingdom; the original meaning of the form survives in Finnish *Ruotsi* 'Sweden' and in the place-names containing *Roslags* on the coastal area of Uppland. This stretch north of Stockholm was a political unit named *Roslagen*, home of the expeditions to the East. All are derived from Old Norse *róþsmenn* or *róþskarlar* 'rowers, seamen'. In a similar way *Normandy* in France is from *norþmenn* 'northerners', a name that reflects another Scandinavian invasion and settlement (A.D. 911). Similarly, *France* is named after the Franks, a tribe of Germanic invaders, and *Lombardy* in Italy is a modern form of *Langobardia*, named after the Langobards ('long-beards'), a Germanic tribe that invaded Italy and settled in the area (A.D. 568). *Finland* and *Finn* refer originally to Lapps (compare OE *finnas*, Norwegian *finner* 'Lapps'; in addition, the word *Lapp* is perhaps of Finnish origin). At times the transferred meanings are startling, as in Modern Greek *Rōmioí* 'Greeks', derived from *Rōma* 'Constantinople', which became the capital of the Roman empire in 330.

The Finnish adjective *säntillinen* 'punctual' would seem to be connected with *sääntö* 'rule'. There are many other pairs that differ in the length of the radical vowel, for example, *viileä* 'cool' ~ *vilu* 'cold, chill', *riippua* 'hang' (intr.) ~ *ripustaa* 'hang' (trans.) and *kääppä* ~ *käpälä* 'paw'. The connection with *sääntö* becomes less certain with the revelation that dialects and older Finnish also have *santillinen*, with a back vowel. This itself does not disqualify the etymology, since there are pairs with both back and front vowels, for example, *raisu* ~ *räisy* 'quick, boisterous', *loka* ~ *lökä* 'dirt', and *tollo* ~ *töllö* 'simpleton'. But the base of the adjective seems to be an adverb *santilleen/säntilleen* 'at the proper time', and the correct explanation is obvious in terms of Catholic Finland in the Middle Ages, when the calendar was known by the names of the saints assigned to the days. The base form *santti* is a borrowing from Swedish *sankt*, itself ultimately from Latin *sanctus* 'saint', and it survives in dialects in folkloristic contexts. To do something *santilleen* meant thus to do it on the right saint's day, at the right time. The base *santti/säntti* has in turn borrowed the meaning of the adverb and adjective and means 'a punctual or particular person' (compare *fast*, Figure 7-4:C, § 7.9). Change of religion (the Reformation) accounts for the loss of the base word in its primary functions; the connection of *säntillinen* and *sääntö* has no historical foundation, although for many speakers it might have some folk-etymological meaning (similar form, similar meaning).

The European words for 'moustache' can be traced back to Italian *mostaccio* in the West and to Greek *moustáki* (*ou* = [u]) in the Balkans. The word *mústaks* [müstaks], apparently 'upper lip', occurs once in Greek (Plutarch, A.D. 100), and once it was suggested that this might be the etymon of *moustáki* and the Italian word; scholars have repeated this suggestion as though it were obvious and self-validating, despite serious problems. Most importantly, there is no way of relating the vowels of the first syllables; Greek *mústaks*, if borrowed around the end of the first century, would have given Italian **mistacchi* and Greek **mistáki*. When a scholar (Maher) was finally sufficiently bothered by the difficulties and improbabilities of the standard etymology, and reinvestigated the words, a much more plausible account was formulated. The Italian word comes from *mustum* 'new wine', in a derivative *mustāceus* 'wine-doused', a name of a cookie as well as metaphorically of the moustache (attested in the seventh century). The original meaning survives in the diminutive *mostacciolo*, a spiced cake, and the Italian displays the formal scheme *mosto–mostaccio–mostacciolo*. Greek *moustáki* is a borrowing from Latin and has originally nothing to do with Doric *mústaks* 'upper lip', although the two words were mixed up in the learned circles. Italian *mostaccio* survives only in a metaphorical meaning, 'snout' (vulgar for 'face'). For the original meaning the Greek shape was borrowed back as *mostacchio* or *mustacchio* (see § 8.8). This account fits quite well with what we know about naming the moustache: culinary terms are quite common, for example, *soupstrainers*. And of course borrowing back and forth can occur; compare English *sport*, originally from French, which has borrowed it back. That scholars make and keep false connections like the *mústaks* etymology shows that they are human, and sometimes folk-etymologize in the fashion of naïve speakers (as in *sääntö/säntillinen* above).

Apparently all languages have cases of the above kind (§§ 5.5, 7.8). Words that derive from different sources can become psychologically connected, and words that ultimately come from the same source can be completely separated in the speaker's conciousness. A good case is *dough* ~ *figure/fiction* ~ (*para*)*dise* (§ 8.12). The original root **dheigh-* meant 'mold, give shape'. In Germanic, it gave *dough* (food preparation), in Iranian and Latin, 'to mold clay' (Iranian **pari-daiza-* 'molded around', that is, 'walled garden'). When these two words finally reached English their meanings had already shifted, Persian through Greek into a narrower, and Latin into a more abstract and general one. Knowledge of earlier building practices is necessary to see that German *Wand* 'wall' is likewise connected with *winden* 'to wind, twist', because mud walls had a wicker frame armature (wattle) made out of saplings, willow, or the like.

It has become clear that evidence from the material culture, archaeology, and history may be crucial in linguistic explanations (and vice versa, of course).

[17.6 The Adjustment of Origin and History to Each Other] One of the objections of the classical philologists to genetic linguistics, which was becoming independent at the beginning of the nineteenth century, was the neglect of syntax by the linguists. Syntax was the central area for the Classicists, and language was always studied in the context of full texts well integrated with the total culture. Here they were completely right, as was shown by semantic change, which depends heavily on both the cultural and the syntactic context. Let us review another case where syntax and semantics meet. In general, the Latin accusative is the case that is continued by the Romance nouns, or more precisely, the oblique stem that had melted together with the accusative. In some instances, however, the Latin nominative unmistakably survives, as in Italian *moglie* 'wife', *uomo* 'man', and *rè* 'king'; and in religious meanings *suora* 'sister', *frate* 'brother', and *prete* 'priest'. These words denote persons who occur frequently as subjects in sentences, and as titles/vocatives; for both functions

Latin used the nominative in these words. Latin (nom.) *serpēns/serpentem* (acc.) 'snake' survives in both cases in Italian: *serpe/serpente*. The first (the old nominative) apparently derives from the biblical context of paradise. The snake is admittedly not a person, but it is personal, since it speaks. Only the nominative *serpēns* occurs in the Vulgate. A few other words like *lampa* 'lamp', *tempèsta* 'storm', and some (often foreign) birds like *struzzo* 'ostrich' also continue the nominative, because the nominative survives as various types of subject. The area where the Latin nominative is chosen for survival (see § 22.5) is the intersection of the syntactic notion of 'subject/agent' and the semantic notion of 'animacy'. To understand when personification like *serpēns* > *serpe* and the other cases take place, we need the total culture as the background: here, (1) a religious literary legacy, (2) geographic distance from Africa and knowledge of the distribution of fauna in the world, and (3) that natural phenomena occupy subject position in Indo-European (wind, rain, lightning, and so on). All these cases are examples of syntactic petrification, and such change can never be predicted totally, nor is it ever perfectly regular (see § 7.13). Note also similar splits from English, for example, the *shade/shadow* types (§ 5.8) and an adjective like *glad* which occurs only in predicative position: *I am glad*, but not **a glad boy*. Thus it is not surprising that the fringes of a feature 'animacy' (i.e., subject position) would attract a few stray forms like *lampa*, *tempèsta*, and *struzzo*. *Lampa* goes with the natural phenomena and characteristically occupies the subject position like *tempèsta* and is thus different from other pieces of furniture, and *struzzo* would occur more likely in sentences like 'The ostrich is a big bird that lives in Africa', and so on.

Many scholars would derive *serpe* from an accusative *serpem*, which would presuppose a Latin nominative *serps* or *serpis*. The object here is to push the difficulties of historical derivation to the starting point (without caring what happens there). Here the principle of reconstruction that says that protoforms must be reconstructed in such a way as to allow a simple derivation of the occurring forms is pushed too far. In this approach one relies blindly on the sound correspondences, which makes the starting point (or protolanguage) a repository of all the difficulties. These difficulties are expressed in a multitude of coexisting forms. Whenever there is a formal problem of derivation, one manipulates the starting point. Linguistic literature and even handbooks are full of this shortsighted procedure, which is actually based on the implicit assumption that there is only one kind of change, regular sound change in phonetic environments. Germanic verbs cognate to *can* have a vowel between the velar and the nasal against the 'regular' velar-nasal-vowel (§ 8.12). The problem is within Germanic, which has both forms (typified by *know/can*; compare *serpe/serpente*). The most widely encountered solution in handbooks reconstructs a Proto-Indo-European shape **gonə-* (attested in Germanic) next to **ǵnō-* (attested everywhere, Germanic included). Now the Germanic problem is solved, but Proto-Indo-European has acquired a monstrosity; linguists get away with it, because the speakers cannot protest any longer. One has to use typological expectations and synchronize both the origin and the history for a maximal fit. As it happens, *can* is plainly an analogical formation; *serps* is not only not attested in Classical Latin, it is extremely unlikely from the Indo-European side as well. Now, the fact that Venantius Fortunatus, a fifth-century author from Northern Italy, actually once writes *serps* cannot be taken at face value. Given the literary prestige of Latin and the gap between it and the spoken vernacular, both amply attested, it is very likely that Fortunatus is the first recorded scholar 'to make sense' out of *serpe* by creating the expected nominative *serps*. This is a case of hypercorrection for him, since the mapping relations between the two varieties were known to him. A sociolinguistic explanation based on the attested tug-of-war between a prestige norm and a vernacular colloquial form is superior to mere speculation about unlikely Latin words.

[17.7 Principles of Investigation (Some Rules of Thumb)] The question arises: How much should one rely on hard-and-fast rules and sound correspondences in identifying two words as etymologically identical? And how much value should one put on each of the two sides, phonetic and semantic? The answer is simple, although not very useful for application: the ingenuity of the etymologist and his power of invention and combination cannot be replaced by mechanical rules. The etymologist like any other archaeologist or historian may stumble on his subject matter accidentally. Since chance and intuition play such an important role, any kind of radicalism and narrow-mindedness is even more dangerous than in other sciences. The playing chips are simply what has been learned in the preceding chapters (Parts I–IV). A few guidelines can be repeated here. One has to pay constant attention to three aspects: (1) phonetics (sound correspondences), (2) morphology (word formation), and (3) semantics. (1) and (3) correlate strongly with the comparative method, (2) with internal reconstruction, as we saw above (Chapter 12). The following principles can be listed:

1. If the apparent connection between two words contains phonetic difficulties, the linguist should look elsewhere for a more economic solution. Often indeed a better explanation is to be found; but the question is very subtle indeed. We saw above (§ 17.5) cases where history overran deceptively obvious solutions with no phonological problems. To the contrary, many scholars have not wanted to combine Germanic *nut* (OE *hnutu*) with Latin *nux*, because the forms seem to be **knud-* and **nuk-*, respectively. But if Latin is taken as **dnuk-*, this is in metathesis relation with **knud-*. The forms could now be connected, although it is not clear which one represents the original shape. In the same vein, Latin *quattuor* 'four' is problematic both in its *-a-* and long *-tt-* in relation to the reconstructed **kʷetwor-*, but still there is no reason to go and look for other connections for the word.
2. Etymology has to satisfy the well-known rules of word formation; if there are clashes, look elsewhere for a better solution. We have seen this principle already in determining the direction of borrowing (§ 8.6), and in the

embedding of *mostaccio* in the derivational scale between *mosto* and *mostacciolo*.

3. If in an apparent connection one must assume an unusual semantic development, go back to 1 and 2, and often the solution is found there. Handbooks traditionally treat Welsh *blif* 'catapult' as a cognate of Greek *bállō* 'I throw'. Semantically the change is in itself unremarkable, but such a technical meaning in Welsh invites closer scrutiny. Since all the related ballistic terminology is actually borrowed from Greek (catapult, ballist, scorpion), in this case one would have to assume at least a Welsh loan translation. Now checking the phonetic side, *blif* should come from Proto-Indo-European *$g^w l\bar{e}mo$-* with a root shape *$g^w l\bar{e}$-*. Such a shape is nowhere attested; the Greek root comes from *$g^w el\partial$-*. Further, a derivative in *-mo-* is not expected as a tool noun. Hence the best guess is that the whole word is a borrowing from Greek. The best candidate would be a Greek verbal noun *blêma* 'throwing'. This, however, is attested late (Euripides) and refers to a throw of dice only. Thus there is no certain solution, but the assumption of borrowing is definitely the better hypothesis, inasmuch as we know that there were Greek colonies in the South of Gaul where the borrowing could have taken place.

4. If it seems that a word is guaranteed for the protolanguage, its (alleged) absence in any of the daughter languages requires an explanation. A search often finds the reason, or the missing form itself. The Indo-European word for 'mouse' is missing in Romance. We know that Latin had *mūs/mūris*, which should have given, for example, Italian **mure* or **muro*. But these would apparently have clashed with the outcome of *mūrus* 'wall', which provides reason enough for replacement by *talpa* 'mole', giving *topo* 'mouse'. The Indo-European words for 'kidney', German *Niere* (OHG *nioro*), English *kidney* < ME (*kid-*)*nere*, Praeneste *nefrōnēs* and Lanuvian *nebrundinēs*, and Greek *nephrós* warrant a base *$neg^w hro$-*. It is noteworthy that Latin is not represented, although two of its closest relatives (Praeneste, Lanuvium) are. The Latin word is *rēn*, generally regarded as of unknown origin. But it has at least the same *r-n* as the other words, and a metathesis *$neg^w hro$-* > *$reg^w hno$-* > **rēno-* easily shows how it could have happened. The vowel stem **rēno-* was then replaced by a consonant stem *rēn-* by analogy to *liēn* 'spleen', which is also responsible for a by-form *riēn* (compare *nux* above).

5. Various kinds of tests can be performed using a dialect map. For example, if a word is somehow guaranteed for the protolanguage, adjacent dialects should show the greatest resemblance. And if the word is not a loan, it is likely to be paralleled in formation in one of the contiguous areas. In short, studio etymologies often break down completely when taken to the linguistic map.

[17.8 The Uniqueness and Complexity of Solutions]   The cases presented above are all rather simple or represent simple parts of bigger configurations (note, however, the complexity of the 'moustache' case). But it is easy to appreciate what the situation can be when all the change types and historical gaps are thoroughly shuffled. One of the consequences is that each language has a substantial number of unexplained words, and that certain words have many competing explanations. The French word *weekend* is perfectly explained, *aveugle* 'blind' has two candidates (Latin *ab oculīs* 'off eyes', or *albus* + *oculus* 'white-eye'), and *rêver* 'to dream' has had some twenty-seven different suggested explanations. Basically, however, only one can be correct, unless a certain amount of contamination has occurred between two or more rival candidates. When dictionaries have to list rival hypotheses, it would be commendable if they gave an order of preference, but they rarely do. All dictionaries contain mistakes or inadequacies, and the cases presented in this chapter were chosen largely from among those that improve on the standard explanations. But even if the reader knows the methods of genetic linguistics, he cannot solve questions where he has doubts, because dictionaries cannot possibly give all the historical and other information necessary for reinterpretation. It is interesting that there has to be a certain amount of complexity as a challenge, before etymology becomes palatable to the practitioners. Historical grammars use only the perfectly clear cases, and the beginner might miss the point that these clear cases provide the frame for attacking more complex problems.

[17.9 The Service of Etymology for Comparison]   What has been shown above is that etymology (and philology) form an integral part of genetic linguistics, both in historical and comparative aspects. Etymological screening is an obligatory prerequisite for reconstruction, to keep the protolanguage from becoming burdened by the debris of our ignorance and high-handedness. The elimination of English *can* and Welsh *blif* (and dozens of other similar forms) as inheritances has a far-reaching consequence for Proto-Indo-European morphophonemics. The corresponding roots are *$\hat{g}n\bar{o}$-* and *$g^w el\partial$-*, NOT *$\hat{g}on\partial$-* and *$g^w l\bar{e}$-*. A doubtful mechanism of alternation in the place of vowel within the root, *CeRC ~ CReC*, can be eliminated altogether. By adjusting the starting points and the derivatory histories for a maximal fit, we get precision for reconstructions (see § 9.18).

Although experimentation is impossible in history, later independent finds often confirm an earlier analysis (see § 1.24). These take on the function of the experiment in other sciences. In etymology, principle 4 serves this end. The fact that the reconstructed Proto-Indo-European *$neg^w hro$-* 'kidney' was found after all, in a mangled form, in Latin *rēn* reconfirms our faith in the predictive power of reconstruction (see § 18.17).

[17.10 The Blending of Philology into Other Disciplines]   One of the areas of philology is textual criticism, which is also concerned with origin and derivation (history), but based on the text as a unit, not on the word (§§ 2.17, 2.18). As a parallel from folklore we have the historic-geographic method of folklore investigation, which studies folk tales (legends, games, riddles, ballads, and so on). A large number of variants is necessary with many component parts. The distribution of the components on the map and the internal seriation between variants can give hints toward establishing an approximate original, its age and place of origin, and the vicissitudes of the story. The similarity to dialect geography is obvious—even the principle that each tale or item has its own history. There is even a parallel in naming: areal linguistics is known as the Italian school and the historic-geographic method as the Finnish method of folklore investigation.

This short note is a final reminder that philology blends into nonlinguistic aspects of culture. We must, however, content ourselves with this introduction to the subject, having come full circle back to where we started the chapter (see § 21.2).

REFERENCES

General: Bréal 1893, Gamillscheg 1927, Hockett 1948a, Guiraud 1964, Ross 1965, Malkiel 1968, Schulze 1966 -- Pisani 1975, R. Schmitt (ed.) 1977, Mayrhofer et al. (eds.) 1980, Trier 1981, Ahlqvist (ed.) 1982, Meier 1986 -- Malkiel 1976, Bammesberger (ed.) 1983; **17.1** Kaplan 1964, Starosta 1969, Garvin 1970, Vossler 1904, R. Hall 1963, Piaget 1968, Lane (ed.) 1970, Ehrmann (ed.) 1970; **17.2** Reid 1956, Hymes 1968a; **17.4** Szemerényi 1962, in Rix (ed.) 1975; **17.5** Malkiel 1968, Maher 1977, Nirvi 1969; **17.6** Szemerényi 1962, in Rix (ed.) 1975, Maher 1977, 1969d, R. Hall 1969, Romeo 1969; **17.7** Bréal 1893, Szemerényi 1962, in Rix (ed.) 1975; **17.8** Malkiel 1968; **17.9** Anttila 1969b; **17.10** K. Krohn 1926.

CHAPTER 18

RECONSTRUCTING PHONOLOGY

> *This chapter is a complement to Part III, as it gives a summary of the interlocking factors in the application of the methods for reconstruction. It concentrates on how to begin a reconstruction and how to polish it by assigning phonetic value to the units.*

[18.1 The Domain of Reconstruction] By now it has become clear that there is a difference between the comparative method and linguistic reconstruction, which is often called comparative linguistics. The common term 'comparative' is apparently the reason for widespread confusion among students. The comparative method can be used for establishing a pandialectal grammar in a synchronic setting, without any diachronic inference. It is the prime method in reconstruction, of course, but not the sole one; in addition, internal reconstruction can be used (or sometimes must be used). Ultimately, actual reconstruction must include considerations discussed in Chapters 14–17. The methods are just general guiding principles and their results must be postedited in various ways and adapted to other evidence or general (universal) expectations.

The comparative method has a rather curious relationship with reconstruction. In the case of obvious dialect cohesion, the corresponding sets of units have synchronic reality and one does not speak of reconstruction. If, on the other hand, the correspondences between languages remain vague, we can posit distant relationship or borrowing, but reconstruction is impossible. The domain of reconstruction is the area where relationship is neither too close nor too remote.

[18.2 Matching and Correspondence] So far we have assumed that it is relatively simple to segment and to know what sound corresponds to what. But this is not always so easy, especially in the initial stages of reconstruction. In the beginning everything is very provisional, because borrowings, analogical creations, conditioning environments, and so on, can be detected gradually. Thus what appeared to be clear correspondences at first glance are often not exactly that. The term *matching* will refer to such tentative correspondences. Thus when one starts looking to see whether English and French are related, one works out matchings between them, for example, French *ž*–English *dž*, *l–l*, *t–t*, *š–tš* (§ 11.2), *p–f* (*père–father, poisson–fish*), *p–p* (*paternel–paternal, pure–pure*), and so on. There are at least two occurrences of each, which makes the matchings systematic or nonrandom. Of these only *p–f* would turn out to

336   LINGUISTIC RECONSTRUCTION: A SYNTHESIS

be a real correspondence for reconstruction purposes; that is, both languages
have regular phonetic outcomes from a single phoneme in the protolanguage.
The other sets would remain as matchings, because they are due to borrowings
in English or in both languages (*paternal*). The value of matchings is that they
allow the linguist freedom for analytic operations without commitment to any
ultimate historical explanation. This is necessary, because the final explanation
is rarely (or never) apparent at the beginning.

[18.3]   One way to start a reconstruction is to take some basic vocabulary
and to try to match every sound sequence systematically (at least two occurrences). Let us use Gothic and Old English, the two "earliest" varieties of Germanic
attested in texts, choosing the cardinals from one to ten as the basis. If sounds
cannot be matched within these numerals, additional material has to be brought
in from the rest of the vocabulary. If this additional material introduces sequences
which remain unmatched, further items must be admitted until the circle can
be closed so that every sequence recurs and no sounds remain unaccounted for.
For Gothic and Old English we can start out from

	GOTHIC	OE	ADDITIONAL ITEMS
I.	*ains*	*ān* ⎫	*tains–tān* 'twig'
II.	*twai*	*twā* ⎭	
III.	*þrija*	*þrēo*	*frija–frēo* 'free'
IV.	*fidwōr*	*fēower*	*augō–ēage* 'eye', *laun–lēan* 'reward'
			dragan–dragan 'pull', *land–land*
V.	*fimf*	*fīf*	
VI.	*saihs*	*siex*	*wairs–wiers* 'worse'
VII.	*sibun*	*seofon*	*filu–feolu* 'much'
VIII.	*ahtau*	*eahta*	*aiþþau–eþþa* 'or', *waila–wel* 'well'
			kalds–ceald 'cold', *haurn–horn*
IX.	*niun*	*nigon*	*fisks–fisc* 'fish'
X.	*taihun*	*tīen*	

There is always a danger of positing too many zeros for the matchings, and
this is why one can start with bigger sequences, for example, matching -*ains*
with -*ān* in I. Here, however, *ai* matches *ā* also in II, and *n–n* recurs many times
among the numerals so that a matching *s–Ø* is rather obvious. But in III it is
better to match *ija–ēo*, rather than *i–ēo* + *j–Ø* + *a–Ø*, or *i–ē* + *j–Ø* + *a–o*, and
so on. It is too early to find where such zeros fit in best. We can now extract the
following matchings:

I.	1.	*ai–ā*	
	2.	*n–n*	See pairs in VII, IX, and X
	3.	*s–Ø*	
II.	4.	*t–t*	See pairs in IV, VI, and VIII
	5.	*w–w*	

III.	6.	þ–þ	VIII for þ
	7.	r–r	IV
	8.	ija–ēo	
IV.	9.	f–f	V, VII, IX
	10.	ō–e	
	11.	au–ēa	[No matching for -id- and -ēo-]
	12.	g–g	
	13.	a–a	
	14.	d–d	
	15.	iu–ēo	kiusan–cēosan 'choose', triu–trēo 'tree'
	16.	k–c	
	17.	s–s	VII and IX
V.			[No matching for the medial. Closest material is nasal followed by voiceless spirant]
	18.	VN–V̄	munþs–mūþ 'mouth' (see § 4.16)
	19.	m–m	lamb–lamb
	20.	u–u	fulls–full, un—un-
VI.	21.	ai–io	
	22.	hs–x	wahsjan–weaxan 'grow' and VIII
	23.	ē–ǣ	mērjan–mǣran 'preach', swēs–swǣs 'one's own'
	24.	j–Ø	
	25.	a–ea	
VII.	26.	u–o	
	27.	b–b	bileiban–belīfan 'remain'
	28.	b–f	
	29.	i–e	lisan–lesan 'gather'
	30.	ei–ī	-leiþan–līþan 'go' and IX for u–o
	31.	i–eo	
	32.	l–l	
VIII.	33.	h–h	
	34.	au–a	
	35.	ai–e	
	36.	au–o	saurga–sorg 'sorrow' and VIII
	37.	a–Ø	
IX.	38.	i–i	[OE -g- cannot be matched with Gothic Ø]
X.			[Gothic -aihu- and OE -īe- remain unmatched]

Four pairs of elements could thus not be matched at all:

IV.	-id-	-ēo-
V.	-im-	-ī-
IX.	-Ø-	-g-
X.	-aihu-	-īe-

In spite of the obvious close relationship between Gothic and Old English four sequences remain without a match. But, otherwise, the situation is clear: there must be a genetic relationship underlying the matchings, and now one would carry on with the comparative method to see which matchings can be combined into one proto-unit. The great diversity of vowel matchings especially is due to the various Old English umlaut phenomena, and it would eventually come out that these matchings are indeed environmentally conditioned correspondences. When the linguist starts to talk about correspondences he is already making definite historical claims (e.g., borrowings have been weeded out, clusters versus single units have been decided, and so on).

[18.4]   The ease with which one can establish a closed circle of matchings within some kind of basic vocabulary is a quick practical measure both of the degree of genetic relationship, and of the possibility of additional reconstruction. Of course the *significance of matchings* depends on (1) the length of the words, (2) the phonemic inventories, and (3) the number of words. If we have just a few matchings in a few short forms or suffixes in languages with "poor" inventories, we do not have a good case for relationship, and further comparative work looks unpromising.

[18.5]   *Distant relationship* is generally posited on the basis of matchings that remain matchings. Let us check one case that has been suggested as a possible instance of nonrelatability. Schleicher stated once that, with modern (nineteenth century) evidence only, German and Russian could probably not be shown to be related. These two languages do, however, have a certain similarity of grammar that would make them better candidates for relationship than German and French or Russian and French. Schleicher was, of course, stressing the benefits of early written records for reconstructing the Indo-European protolanguage. Let us now see what the situation actually is by taking the 500 most frequent words in Russian and German as a corpus (including German words outside that list if they seem to match a Russian one in the list). These words should include vocabulary items that are basic to the society in which the language is spoken. Ignoring Russian palatalization and German voicing of *s* or devoicing of *g*, we get (among others) the following matchings (note that the glosses provide the same material between Russian and English as well):

RUSSIAN–GERMAN

1. *t–d*   *tam–dort* 'there', *brat–Bruder* 'brother', *ty–du* 'thou', *tri–drei* 'three', *togda–dann* 'then', (e)*tot–der/dies-* 'that/this'
2. *t–t*   *stojat'–stehen* 'stand', *mat'–Mutter* 'mother'
3. *d–t*   *den'–Tag* 'day', *segodnja–heute* 'today'
4. *d–ts*   *sidet'–sitzen* 'sit', *desjat'–zehn* 'ten', *serdce–Herz* 'heart'
5. *d–s*   *voda–Wasser* 'water', *edim–wir essen* 'we eat'
6. *s–s*   *syn–Sohn* 'son', *est'–essen* 'eat', *sidet'–sitzen* 'sit', *sest'–setzen* 'set'
7. *s–h*   *segodnja–heute* 'today', *serdce–Herz* 'heart'
8. *ž–g*   *možno–möglich* 'possible', *ležat'–liegen* 'lie'

9. *tš–xt*   *moč'–Macht* 'power (might)', *noč'–Nacht* 'night'
10. *p–f*   *pjat'–fünf* 'five', *pro–für* 'for', *polnyj–voll* 'full'
11. *b–b*   *brat–Bruder* 'brother', *ljubit'–lieben* 'love', *byt'–ich bin* 'be'
12. *k–v*   *kto–wer* 'who', *kotoryj–welch* 'which', *kogda–wann* 'when'
13. *v–v*   *voda–Wasser* 'water', *dva–zwei* 'two'
14. *v–Ø*   *dver'–Tür/Tor* 'door', *tvoj–dein* 'your'
15. *l–l*   *ljubit'–lieben* 'love', *ležat'–liegen* 'lie', *polnyj–voll* 'full'
16. *m–m*   *moj–mein* 'my', *moč'–Macht* 'power', *mat'–Mutter* 'mother'
17. *n–n*   *ne–nein/nicht* 'not', *ničto–nichts* 'nothing', *syn–Sohn* 'son', *nos–Nase* 'nose', *nu–nun* 'now'
18. *r–r*   *tri–drei* 'three', *pro–für* 'for', *brat–Bruder* 'brother', *serdce–Herz* 'heart'
19. *e–e*   6
20. *a–u*   1, 2
21. *o–a*   9, 17
22. *o–o*   10 and *solnce–Sonne* 'sun'
23. *e–ai*   17 and *celyj–heil* 'whole', *xleb–Laib* 'bread'
24. *e–a*   3 and *vera–wahr* 'true'
25. *u–i*   11 and *sjuda–hier* 'here'

Not only do matchings occur among lexical items, but also in pronouns and the like (which are short forms):

m-	*m-*	'1st sg.'
t-/tv-	*d-*	'2nd sg.'
n-	*n-*	'negation'
to-	*da-/de-*	'(th-) deictic'
k(o)-	*wa-/we-*	'(wh-) question'
-eš'	*-(e)st*	'2nd sg. pres.'
-et	*-(e)t*	'3rd sg. pres.'
-em	*-en*	'1st pl. pres.'
-ete	*-(e)t*	'2nd pl. pres.'

We have confirmation of these matchings among basic vocabulary (kinship terms, lower numeral, basic actions, and the like). There are also similar irregularities, for example, the nasals in *em–bin* 'I am'; matchings in structurally similar categories are strong evidence for relationship. The list of matching items could be extended (e.g., *novyj–neu* 'new', *mnoga–manch* 'many', *rabotat'–arbeiten* 'work', *ljudi–Leute* 'people', *knjaz–König* 'prince/king', *volja–wollen* 'want/will', all among the 500 most frequent words in both languages). Actually, 3 is an accidental matching of a kind that could not be spotted at this stage, nor could many loans. Only those forms that are too similar betray borrowing of some kind, for example, *minuta–Minute* 'minute', *istorija–Historie* 'history', *partija–Partei* 'party', *massa–Masse* 'mass', *plan–Plan* 'plan', *xarakter–Charakter* 'character', and so on.

[18.6] These matchings show that Russian and German are plausibly relatable on the basis of contemporary evidence and that Schleicher was too cautious. Indeed, a similar test between Russian and French also yields a positive result, although a meager one. No actual reconstruction is readily possible in either case, but the evidence for distant relationship is substantial. Thus the matchings between Russian and German and Russian and French give tangible reality to the possibility of ascertaining distant relationship even in cases of languages with no recorded history.

Two ways of using basic vocabulary as the starting point of comparative work have been presented. A third practical beginning is the glottochronological list (the Swadesh list), whose items were originally selected so as to minimize the likelihood of borrowings (§§ 22.13, 22.14). It gives the linguist two hundred items among which matchings should show up, if they occur at all.

[18.7 The Method Deadlocked by External Forces]   The above matchings between Gothic and Old English were a promising start for further application of the comparative method; those between Russian and German indicated some limitation for further reconstruction, owing to the attrition of time, and thus allowed us only the hypothesis of distant relationship without the possibility of exact reconstruction. The method stalls because time has allowed too many changes to accumulate. But typological constraints may in turn frustrate the perfectly clear results of the method (see § 16.8). Let us look at a problem in Tai linguistics. The typology of the Southeast Asian languages poses various problems, but we shall observe two matchings in word-final position between Saek, a language in the Nakhon Phonom area at the Laotian border, and Siamese (Thai). Between these two, final n's match,

Saek	ki $\boxed{n}$ ^{1}	lii $\boxed{n}$ ^{6}	vi $\boxed{n}$ ^{2}	$r\varepsilon$ $\boxed{n}$ ^{2}	vee $\boxed{n}$ ^{2} etc.
Siamese	ki $\boxed{n}$ ^{1}	li $\boxed{n}$ ^{4}	fo $\boxed{n}$ ^{5}	he $\boxed{n}$ ^{5}	$khw\varepsilon\varepsilon$ $\boxed{n}$ ^{5}
	'eat'	'tongue'	'rain'	'see'	'hang up'

and, in fact, correspond, and one would reconstruct an *n. In addition, there is also

Saek	$\textipa{n}\varepsilon$ $\boxed{l}$ ^{2}	rii $\boxed{l}$ ^{2}	va $\boxed{l}$ ^{1}	$y\mathfrak{ɔ}\mathfrak{ɔ}$ $\boxed{l}$ ^{6}	ruu $\boxed{l}$ ^{6} etc.
Siamese	he $\boxed{n}$ ^{5}	hi $\boxed{n}$ ^{5}	fa $\boxed{n}$ ^{1}	$kh\mathfrak{ɔ}\mathfrak{ɔ}$ $\boxed{n}$ ^{4}	$r\mathfrak{ɔ}\mathfrak{ɔ}$ $\boxed{n}$ ^{4}
	'civet cat'	'stone'	'slash'	'hammer'	'hot'

This set l–n contrasts with n–n, and thus needs a separate label. Since Siamese does not have final l at all, *l would be the perfect choice. Certainly the outcomes of both languages can unambiguously be derived from it. But such an *l goes heavily against the "areal grain," because no language has, or is known to have, had, a final $-l$ in the immediate typological area. Saek is completely alone in having it. It is rather staggering to think that it alone would have retained the *l. Although such inheritance is theoretically possible, it is typologically so unnerving that some linguists have not taken the final step of making the matching *l–n* a correspondence. As a matching, it still waits for the ultimate commitment of the linguists, a real explanation that fits best into the total situation. One does not want to go against areal typology without some persuasive justification.

Internal reconstruction also can gradually clash more and more with typological expectations. In laryngeal theory (Chapter 12) we saw a very good example of this: by multiplying laryngeals, the number of vowels could be reduced to one, and in some analyses even to none. But here the method has been pushed beyond the acceptable 'reality' of linguistic universals (for some linguists), and linguists should be extra careful what they ultimately do in such a borderline area where the method works fine but clashes with universals.

[18.8 Phonetic Reconstruction]   The strict application of the comparative method gives us units that contrast with other units, since the method groups together all noncontrasting sets. But the linguist has to pick out the symbols for the proto-units himself (Chapter 11). Two schools of thought have developed as regards the *reality* of the reconstructed sound units. The one is the formulaist (or algebraist) position, which accepts the abstract relational result of the method. For the formulaists a reconstructed sound is merely an ideal notation with no claim for perceptual reality; in fact, the reconstruction of parent forms is a logical, not a historical operation. It is not reconstruction at all, merely construction. The method gives us the network of phonemes with no phonetic reality whatsoever. The other is the realist position, which can maintain that reconstruction might even be so real that the vanished speakers would understand most of it if there were a way to make such an experiment. As in so many other linguistic controversies, the truth lies most of the time between the two poles. Actually the positivist (realist) side wins clearly over the negativist (formulaist); indeed, many of those linguists who maintain a negativist position in theory are actually positivists in practice. On the other hand, positivists sometimes have to acknowledge cases where only formulas can be posited, because reconstructions are always full of gaps. When discussing Grimm's and Verner's laws we started out from plain (voiceless), voiced, and "voiced aspirate" stops, for example, **t*, **d*, and **dh* (§§ 4.9, 4.10, 6.3, 11.3). The first two series should be rather good approximations of the actual Proto-Indo-European phonemes, whereas the phonetic features of **dh*, and so on, have remained in doubt. The notation (e.g., **dh*) is a shorthand symbol for sets that contrast with the other reconstructed series; in other words, in this spot the reconstruction remains on the formulaic level. This exception is, of course, a challenge, and linguists who do not want to leave the question unanswered generally assume murmur as the distinctive phonetic characteristic; but this assumption is far less certain than the guesses about **t*, **d*, and so on.

[18.9]   In phonemic analysis one starts from phonetics to get to the phonemes (Chapter 10). In reconstruction one often makes phonetic inferences only after the phonemes have been established, by relying on universal expectations or naturalness of systems. This is largely due to the formulaic slogan that one can reconstruct only phonemes. One also sees statements that the allophones of the protolanguage are represented by all the noncontrasting sets of correspondences between the daughter languages. This is, of course, a direct analog, but need not be true of the protostage, although in some cases such an inference seems to be correct. The Proto-Indo-European phonetic difference between consonantal (R) and syllabic (R) resonants apparently represents real allophonic variation in the protolanguage (§§ 11.7, 11.12, 11.14). The issue is so obvious that most handbooks use allophonic writing for this. The reason here is that the sets are phonetically different although they do not contrast when the method is applied. Allophonic writing is a compromise between the two aspects (phonetics and noncontrastiveness).

[18.10]   One should note that phonetics has great heuristic value in the actual analysis, that is, in the application of the comparative method. Sets that contain the same or similar sounds are likely candidates for inclusion into the same protophoneme. We saw this in the Germanic reconstruction (§§ 11.5–11.7), where sets were arranged according to the phonetics contained in them. We saw also that this phonetics helped determine the choice of the symbols for the reconstructed units. This is the general approach in reconstruction. Phonetics does enter into the initial stages in an implicit manner, and as a final touch to the reconstruction one returns to it explicitly. In phonetic reconstruction, as in any other kind of reconstruction, one tries to minimize the steps in derivation. For derivation one needs the subgrouping (family tree), and this is why phonetic reconstruction must be done as a final touch. One simply distributes the actual phonetics of the sets of correspondence to the proper branches of the tree. Figure 18-1 shows a family tree for four languages. A set of correspondences A–B–C–D has been aligned with the proper branches. But before we can proceed we have to paraphrase briefly two basic principles of the algebra of classes, namely, *Boolean algebra*.

Here we need only the basic notions of addition and multiplication of classes. If we define a class that contains all women, and another that encompasses all Americans, the addition of the two yields a class that contains *either* women *or* Americans. If we let A represent the class of all women and B that of all Americans (Figure 18-1), we can present the sum of them as in stage 2, A + B. There is an overlap in the middle—obviously those members that belong to both classes, who are both American and women. This overlap is the product or intersection of the two classes. Addition is an either–or relation, multiplication *both–and*. The peanut-shaped shaded figure A + B represents the sum of the two classes A and B. The checkered elliptical leaf shape in the middle is the intersection. The two facing crescents represent non-American women (horizontal lines) and American men (vertical lines), but the crescents are part of the sum. A sum need not contain an intersection; for example, the sum of a class of all stones and all songs is a class with either stones or songs, without any

$(A + B)(C + D)$

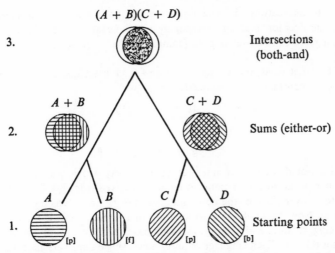

3.　Intersections (both-and)

$A + B$　　$C + D$

2.　Sums (either-or)

A　B　C　D

1.　Starting points
　[p]　[f]　[p]　[b]

FIGURE 18-1. Application of Boolean algebra in the reconstruction of phonetics and semantics (§ 20.7).

intersection. It seems that all students are implicitly aware of these Boolean notions of addition and multiplication; the former gives disjunctive definitions, the latter conjunctive. The phoneme as a family of sounds, say English /k/ as a class of [k, k̑, kʰ, and so on] (see § 10.2, Figure 10-1), is disjunctively defined: /k/ is either [k] or [k̑] and so on, that is, a sum. Conjunctive definition gives the bundle of distinctive features; that is, /k/ is an intersection of [voiceless], [velar], and [closure] (both–and). Striving after conjunctive definitions is central to linguistics (see § 20.7).

Now we are ready to go back to stage 1 in Figure 18-1 and the set A–B–C–D. Let us assign the value p–f–p–b to it, which is simple enough for exemplification. When one ascends the tree one takes the sum of what occurs below for each node. Thus for stage 2 we get A + B and C + D. The shaded areas represent now: horizontal-line crescent = [closure], checkered leaf = [labial] + [voiceless], vertical-line crescent = [friction], rising-line crescent = [voiceless], diamond-checkered leaf = [labial] + [closure], and falling-line crescent = [voice]. But we need not dissect this far because we need just the sums. Since the tree continues higher up, we carry both sums to the next node (for better legibility we round off the peanut shapes into circles). When we reach the top node we take the intersection of A + B and C + D, the shaded leaf shape, which means [labial] + [closure] + [voiceless], that is, *p. The right-facing crescent ([friction]) and the left-facing one ([voice]) were discarded. The result is the obvious one, obtainable through intuition, but Boolean algebra makes it explicit. Because the method handles one protosound at a time, it does not give the answer all by itself. One still has to consider each intersection in relation to other intersections; that is, the contributing factors are (1) subgrouping, (2) intersections, and (3) relations between intersections. The last point allows a considerable share in the decision making to typology and language universals, so mere Boolean algebra can be overweighed (compare the Saek–Siamese case).

[18.11]   Let us assume we have a case of three languages that show a set *g–r–h*. Let us consider three possible trees:

I   II   III

g   r   h   g   r   h   g   r   h

In case I it would come to an intersection right away. If *r* is assumed to have been uvular [R] at an earlier point, it could be derived from [ɣ]. Continuancy wins (2 to 1) over closure; the best candidates are **ɣ* or **g* (voicing also wins out 2 to 1). Now we would have to look at other intersections. If there is one with voicing, closure, and velarity, that one has a better claim for **g*, and we pick **ɣ* for this one. Each language requires now a single step, Verschärfung (*g*), 'rhotacism' (*ɣ > r*), and devoicing (*h*). In case II continuancy occurs over the deepest split which makes **ɣ* more likely at the outset, and in III velarity has the same position making **g* a good candidate, since spirantization would occur only once in the subgroup *r–h*. Here we see clearly the importance of comparing the intersections. In every case if there exists another set with (velar) stops throughout, **ɣ* must be chosen for *g–r–h*.

[18.12]   If no obvious intersection is obtainable, as between *p* and *ŋ* (if such a set occurred somewhere), phonetic reconstruction would have to be based on typological guesswork. Such guesses may of course turn out to be rather accurate. The Russian–German matching no. 12, *k–v*, would seem to be without an obvious intersection. Thus one might try to posit a straight combination **kv* as the starting point. This of course *is* the intersection, because the unit is *both k and v*, and the result comes rather close to the ultimate Proto-Indo-European reconstruction **kʷ*. Further, *k* and *v* are not as incompatible as it would seem at first blush, since Finnish has paradigmatic alternation between them in one environment at least (§ 10.13). In short, one can say that the assignment of phonetic value to the reconstructed proto-units plays an important role in establishing "reality," but it does not add anything to the relational network. Both the positivists and the negativists are right.

[18.13 Phonetic and Internal Reconstruction]   Phonetic inferences are also possible in internal reconstruction. Greek has the following stop sets (columns):

p   t   k   p   before   (*a, o*, consonant)
p   t   k   t   (*i, e*)
p   t   k   k   (*u*)

Internal reconstruction gives an invariant starting point for each set; for the first three there is no problem, and thus the fourth one cannot use any of the |p, t, k|. It contrasts with all of them. It would seem that a coarticulated *|k͡p| would be the best guess. If areal constraints would make that unlikely, one would perhaps resort to a labiovelar *|kʷ| (which it is in Indo-European terms). When all the normal stop positions are already occupied, one can use a "blunt" intersection of the features (compare Russian–German k–v, reflexes of the same proto-unit). Phonetic reconstruction can also aim at an intermediate stage between the starting point and the surface variation. In Finnish consonant gradation (involving single stops), we have the following alternations:

$$
\begin{array}{lll}
p\text{–}v & t\text{–}d & k\text{–}\emptyset \\
p\text{–}m & t\text{–}l & k\text{–}j \\
& t\text{–}r & k\text{–}v \\
& t\text{–}n & k\text{–}\eta
\end{array}
$$

All are environmentally conditioned within each articulatory set, justifying thus reconstruction of *p, *t, and *k. But the weak grade diversity is now a perfect target for Boolean algebra with phonetic features, as exemplified above. The basic features labial, dental, and velar are given "from above" (first columns), and this leaves us with two others to be worked out. Zero (in k–∅) has no phonetic feature, so it has to be excluded. All other outcomes share voice, and all except d continuancy. A single exception is outweighed by the otherwise perfect regularity, and the intersections of the three features give us *β, *ð, and *γ. The assumption of such a unified stage of the weak grade gives a natural phonetic explanation for the various assimilations yielding the attested sounds. The labial *β assimilates only to the labial nasal m, but not to preceding liquids, because of the greater articulatory difference. The dental *ð assimilates also to the liquids, because both share articulation in the dental region. The velar *γ assimilates to flanking lip-rounding, because [γ] and [u] have quite similar tongue positions, and also to flanking dental-palatal tongue position (j = [y]), and is lost elsewhere. Ultimately, then, all such spirants merge with other continuants (v, l, r, j, and nasals).

The only sore spot in this analysis is the stop d. But we here have the possibility

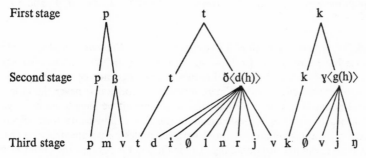

FIGURE 18-2. Derivation trees for Finnish consonant gradation.

of checking our inferences (see §§ 11.8, 11.9). If possible, one should always consult any earlier evidence, and earliest Finnish records show that *d* was a spirant, written *dh* or *đ*, and that instead of a *v* for the velar *γ there was a written *gh* or *g*. In fact, one Western dialect still retains [ð] for *d*; some other Finnish dialects do not have *d* at all; instead various "continuants" occur (*j*, *v*, *l*, flap *ř*) or else *Ø*. The variant *d* of Standard Finnish is thus a late spelling pronunciation (on the Swedish model). We have been able to posit a unified phonetic stage for the weak grade and get the relative chronology given in Figure 18-2. (The outcomes of the second-stage spirants do not necessarily represent direct continuations as seemingly implied by the lines. Some are no doubt transition sounds filling the gaps left by the loss of the spirants. But such transition sounds generally observe "natural phonetics" from the environment.)

[18.14 Inverted Reconstruction]   The derivation trees for the Finnish consonant gradation show one interesting fact. To get at the voiced spirants (the right-hand nodes in the middle row), we used information "from above" (first row) and "from below" (third row). One speaks of reconstruction when one makes inferences from below into earlier stages, and of inverted reconstruction, if there is evidence from a higher node with respect to the one which is our target. Thus in reconstructing Proto-Germanic, information from Proto-Indo-European reconstructed on a wider scale may prove very useful indeed. Such inverted information is always used when our target of investigation is a lower node in an otherwise rather well-established family tree; e.g. in trying to retrieve Pre-Greek we use the attested Greek evidence plus our expectations from Proto-Indo-European. We see also that inverted reconstruction is part of what is known as confirmation, or comparative checking, with further independent material. But since this evidence is drawn right into the primary analysis, it is of course not called checking. When it was said that Latin *serps* is highly unlikely from the Indo-European side (§ 17.6), a principle of inverted reconstruction was being used. It is natural that such triangulation from above and below will often lead to a correct solution that would otherwise have taken much more labor, if it were possible at all. The unmatched sets between Gothic and Old English (§ 18.3) can be explained quite easily in terms of Proto-Indo-European, through the reconstructions *kʷetwores '4', *penkʷe '5', *newṇ '9', and **dekm̥* '10'.

[18.15 Overall Conclusion on Reconstruction]   Chapter 11 and many other sections have already shown how one continues with the method after some initial indication of success. All this cannot and need not be repeated here. It has also become clear that the mere mechanistic method is never the ultimate goal, although it is a valuable guideline and often all we have to go by. Figure 18-3 characterizes the reconstruction process in a flow-chart form. Such a chart is very approximate only, and here resembles corporate structure charts more than computer programming. The main point is perhaps the optimization of the match between units and rules. Here one often has to go back and forth

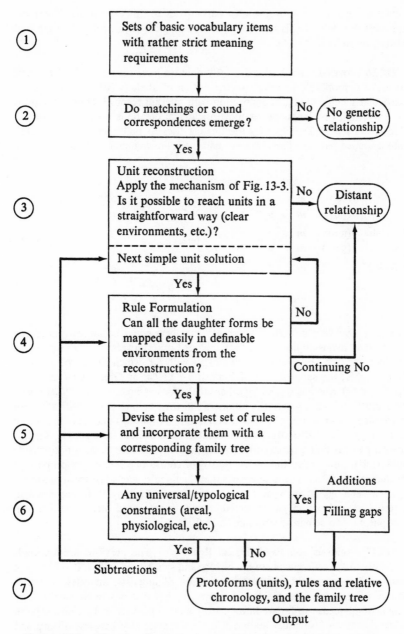

FIGURE 18-3. Flow chart for the basic steps in the reconstruction procedure.

between steps 3 and 4; step 6 also participates in this extensively. The most eloquent example of this has been the etymological adjustment of origin and history of an item (§ 17.6).

[18.16 Analysis and Analogy]   By now we have seen enough of analysis to make it profitable to return to the notion of analogy (Chapter 5). This is particularly enlightening in connection with internal reconstruction, because it occurs within one language, as most analogical creations do (if borrowing is discarded; see § 9.2). Typically the linguist tries to pull aberrant forms back into a unified pattern. Thus we have had the following configurations:

			STRAIGHT SETS						VARIANT SETS			
English	(sg.)	m	p	s	f	(etc.)	vs.	f	θ	s	(etc.)
	(pl.)	m	p	s	f			v	$\eth$	z	
Finnish	(nom.)	m	p	v	r	(etc.)	vs.	p	t	k	(etc.)
	(gen.)	m	p	v	r			v	d	$\emptyset$	
Greek		m	p	t	k			p			
		m	p	t	k	(etc.)	vs.	t			
		m	p	t	k			k			

We have also seen how the "aberrant" members could be unified under one "expected" invariant unit. If the "straightened-out" unit clashes with a previous straight one (e.g., English f–v as $*f$ clashes with f–f, which should be an $*f$ by better rights; the same is true of Finnish p–v as $*p$, or Greek p–t–k as either $*p$, $*t$, or $*k$), one has to choose other labels, for example, English $*f_2$, Finnish $*p_2$, and Greek $*k^w$, where the numbers can then be interpreted with different chronology, and so on. The above tabulation shows the same relational setup as analogy, which also attacks forms that get out of line, for example, English /owŏz/ *oaths* is being replaced by /owθs/ (analogy, of course, does not provide subscripts). This proportion in analysis is of course one side of the proportion in change (see § 9.2). The difference is that the linguist gets a historical pre-form, whereas analogy gives a new synchronic form. Analogy is future-oriented, internal reconstruction past-oriented. But both are based on clashes between morphemic and semantic structure (see § 9.19).

[18.17 Analysis and Psychological Reality]   The previous section leads us finally to the difference between history and synchronic reality. Psychological reality has become the ultimate justification of linguistic analyses, and it is indeed a fine goal. The problem, however, is that it is not really workable in linguistics, because so far we know hardly anything about it. It seems to be to some degree an individual matter. Clearly the boundary between history and synchrony is different for different persons. It seems that most English speakers do not connect *bleak* and *bleach* synchronically, although the connection between *speak* and *speech* is more apparent. The alternations in *bake* and *batch* are quite compatible, although now most speakers store these items separately. Internal reconstruction rakes up all such possible connections, whereas speakers give them up much more readily than linguists usually believe. This is not just a peculiarity of English (e.g., *drink/drench, sing/singe, cook/kitchen*, and so on), but it is quite general of linguistic change (see § 6.24). When such pairs are pointed out to "naïve" speakers, their native linguistic reality is likely to change at one blow to incorporate such new information. Memory or brain storage is on a much more extravagant scale than we would like to think; even the most "obvious" cases can be stored separately. Many examples could be cited from various languages, but the following one from Modern Greek is one of the clearest. A linguist (Kazazis) had been speaking Greek as his first language for some thirty years and had practiced linguistics for some ten (in the United States). He had never made a conscious connection between *petô* 'I fly' and *petô* 'I throw', although the two verbs have identical conjugational paradigms. Then it came to him in a flash that the second *petô* is obviously a causative of the first, i.e. 'I cause to fly', and that formally it is one and the same verb. This also shows admirably how the difference between homophony and polysemy rests ultimately with the individual speaker (see Figure 7-4:C, §§ 7.9, 9.3). Here a case of homophony became instantaneously one of polysemy, both \/.

Linguists of various language backgrounds repeat such experiences all the time, and it reveals an interesting fact: once you have linguistic training, you spoil your native intuitions as a normal naïve speaker, and you cannot write a psychologically real grammar for a normal speaker. Linguists are not normal speakers when they write grammars (see § 6.15). On the other hand, if you are a naïve speaker, you cannot write grammars at all. This is why a psychologically real grammar may be quite impossible to achieve through introspection (see §§ 1.10, 6.25), and psycholinguistic tests have not yet contributed anything. Then, too, perfect history without gaps is certainly beyond our grasp. We are lucky in that in spite of this, linguistics, especially genetic linguistics, passes for the most exact humanistic science (see § 1.24). (See §13.9)

It has been emphasized throughout this book that history provides extra complications for analysis, leading to the frequently heard dogma that no firm conclusions are possible in historical and comparative linguistics. This is totally misleading. If it is true that all languages are fundamentally alike (Chapter 16), then it cannot be questioned that philological linguists are in a position to reconstruct some of the intuitions of native speakers long dead (see Chapters 7, 17, 20). On the other hand, serious mistakes can be made by linguists (who presumably have native speaker intuition) in writing the grammar of their own language, because the grammar one writes is limited by the grammarian's ability to recall and recognize all the relevant variants of, for example, a common sentence type. Thus sampling error interferes as seriously with the correctness of a (say, generative) grammar as of a comparative grammar. The difference is one of degree only, not of principle, and consequently all of linguistics has to use the same methods in parallel situations (see Figure 1-7).

350   Linguistic Reconstruction: A Synthesis

REFERENCES

General: Bonfante 1945, 1946; **18.2** Dyen (private communication), Swadesh 1963, Schramm 1967; **18.7** Gedney 1967, Schlerath 1987; **18.8** Allen 1951, Hoenigswald 1965 -- Glottalic reinterpretation of Proto-Indo-European stops: Gamkrelidze and Ivanov 1984, Vennemann in Fisiak (ed.) 1985, (ed.) 1987; **18.11** R. Hall 1960; **18.13** Hoenigswald 1960b; **18.14** Hockett 1958; **18.16** Bolinger 1968; **18.17** Hass 1969, Raffler Engel 1970, Maher 1970a, Jucquois 1970, Katičić 1970.

CHAPTER 19

RECONSTRUCTING GRAMMAR

*A few characteristic possibilities of grammatical recon-
struction are discussed as partial case studies. The ultimate
prerequisite for grammatical reconstruction—the use of
total grammars as the starting point—is impossible in an
introduction.*

MORPHOLOGY

[19.1 Morphology As Applied Phonology]   Relatively little need be said
about reconstructing morphology in this introduction. As it will turn out, the
basic procedure has already been dealt with; comparative morphology is simply
applied phonology. Of course, it must be remembered that the reconstruction of
phonology is not possible on the basis of mere sound, since meaning plays an
equally important role. Because comparative phonology is based on a triangulation from sound and meaning into grammar (see Figures 1-1, 1-2), it is quite
natural that it leads into morphology, since words are generally used to begin
with. Observing the right sequence of the sound correspondences, we have to
reconstruct Proto-Indo-European *esti 'he is', *bherō 'I carry', and *agō 'I
drive' (Figure 11-6). Other verb forms would follow with equal facility, *esmi
'I am' and *bhereti 'he carries', and so on for dozens of other verbal and
related nominal forms. Once we have enough such forms we can more or less
forget how we got them and apply normal linguistic analysis, which is of course
language-internal. By contrasting forms and meanings one tries to see whether
these forms can be cut into smaller units; for example, the setup

	'BE'	'CARRY'
1st sg.	esmi	bherō
3rd sg.	esti	bhereti

provides at once a third singular *-ti (see also Sanskrit *aniti*, § 12.5) and a first
singular *-mi. In this partial paradigm of 'carry' the subtraction of *-ti leaves
a stem *bhere-, but additional evidence would show that the root here is just
*bher-, so that *bher-e- is the present stem. Now, whenever this *-e- occurs,
the first singular is *-ō and not *-mi; *o is a morphophonemic alternant of
*-e- (as *e ~ *o ablaut), which leaves length as '1st sg.': *bher-o-H (*-o- also
occurs in 1st pl. *bher-o-mes and 3rd pl. *bher-o-nti). Because of the a–a correspondence in the perfect, for example, Greek *oîda*:Sanskrit *véda* 'I know', one

351

can further identify the *H as probably or possibly *A (see § 16.3). Chapters 10 and 12 have already shown how morphophonemic analysis, alias internal reconstruction, combines morphs into invariant morphemes, or even into canonical forms such as by rewriting *esti as *Eesti (with an initial consonant; § 12.4).

[19.2]   This normal analysis now yields morpheme boundaries and the sequences of morpheme slots, for example, *es-ti, *bher-e-ti with ROOT + [e +]ti. We get systematic inferences about *morpheme order*, that is, word internal syntax. There is always the danger that any particular combination of morphemes never occurred in the protolanguage, even if it is present in the daughter languages. But it still means that our sequential formula for combination is valid, since it must be responsible for the independent combinations in these daughters. The problem here is that reconstruction is always positive; we have no sure way of reconstructing the absence of something, except for trivialities like being certain that there was no word for airplane in Proto-Indo-European.

This is how one continues the reconstruction of morphology. It is simply internal reconstruction and normal synchronic linguistic analysis, once the comparative method has provided enough substance to be handled. The difference from synchrony is that the results are far less certain, but in the previous chapter it was pointed out that even synchronic analysis often violates native psychological reality. Again we have reached a juncture with direct access to descriptive linguistics; those who want to brush up their knowledge of linguistic analysis have to refer to the references given (for § 1.1).

[19.3 Relative Chronology and Morphological Types]   In addition to relative chronology of individual sound changes, inferences can be made about the relative age of whole morphological categories. With a combination of variation and productivity one can often reach at least tentative conclusions. A comparison of short selections from English and Finnish will exemplify the method. English has the following ways of deriving verbs from nouns or adjectives:

A.	red	redden	B.	foul	defile
	fast	fasten		doom	deem
	loose	loosen		full	fill
	soft	soften		whole	heal
C.	wreath	wreathe		smoke	smoke
	glass	glaze		cause	cause
	safe	save		brush	brush
				free	free
D.	fish	fish		cool	cool
	color	color		an X	to X

Types A–C are no longer productive; type D is, with no formal difference between noun and verb. Similarly, nominal derivatives like *song* from *sing* and *bond* from *bind* are unproductive as opposed to nouns like *a run, a slip*, and so on. Suffixes like *gift* from *give*, *birth* from *bear*, and *filth* from *foul*, are also limited in their range of combination. Among causatives an unproductive type E contrasts with an analytic one F:

E.		F.	
drink	drench	laugh	make laugh
sit	set	run	(make) run
lie	lay	X	make X
fall	fell		

In fact, the synchronic connection between the columns in E has broken down and is purely historical. The analytical type is unlimited (e.g., *make sit*, and *make lie*). In English, then, generally, the more productive a type is, the less variation or fusion it has. The plural formations repeat this principle, for example, *ox-en* (A), *mice* (B), *calve-s* (C), and *faith-s* (D). *Calves* has the analytic/ agglutinative plural marker, but the variation *f ~ v* and the unproductivity of it makes the type older than *faith-s*, for example. Note that by the same token *warmth* should be later than *filth*, for example, because it has less variation than the latter (*-th* normally carries umlaut). It should be one of the last forms created before the suffix lost its productivity altogether.

We have, of course, seen (§§ 4.2, 4.5) how the umlaut and other alternation phenomena are almost always due to the loss of a suffix (B, C). Now we can also match type D *a fish–to fish* with a plural type *a sheep–many sheep*. There is no alternation and no suffix. Is *sheep* then a recent type also? No, because it is not productive. It is peculiar to a few animal names, particularly in hunting or catching situations; that is, they are now virtually mass nouns like *water*. This is a semantic area that correlates well with earlier "cultural" practices.

[19.4]   In contrast to English, Finnish does not have a scale that equates alternation with nonproductivity:

A. NOUN
  sylke- 'saliva'
  tuule- 'wind'
  kuse- 'urine'
  tuke- 'support'
  sula- 'liquid, unfrozen'
  lohko- 'portion, section'
  tahto- 'want'

VERB
  sylke- 'spit' (§ 10.13)
  tuule- 'blow'
  kuse- 'urinate' (§§ 8.3, 9.3)
  tuke- 'support'
  sula- 'melt'
  lohko- 'split, partition'
  tahto- 'want' (§§ 4.23, 10.13)

B. STEM 1
  sure- 'to mourn'
  pure- 'to bite'
  sana- 'word'
  liittä- 'to join'

STEM 2
  sur-u- 'sorrow'
  pur-u- 'chewed pulp'
  sano- 'to say'
  liitto- 'alliance'

pit-kä- 'long' (§ 6.10)	*pite-X-* 'to become longer'
pakka- 'pack'	*pakka-X-* 'to pack'
täyte- 'full'	*täyttä-* 'to fill'
jää- 'to remain'	*jä-ttä-* 'to leave'

C. NO CONSONANT GRADATION

peti 'bed'	*pupu* 'bunny'
muki 'mug'	*laku* 'licorice'
auto 'car'	*kapu* 'captain'

D. VOICED STOPS AND CLUSTERS

jodi 'iodine' (§ 10.12)	*abbedissa* 'abbess'
grogi 'drink' (§ 17.5)	*struktuuri* 'structure'
jobi 'job'	*frekvenssi* 'frequency'
geeni 'gene'	*agglutinaatio* 'agglutination'

E.

DOMAIN	PERFORMER	ADJECTIVE	GLOSS
kritiikki	*kriitikko*	*kriittinen*	'critical'
epiikka	*eepikko*	*eeppinen*	'epic'
etiikka	*eetikko*	*eettinen*	'ethical'
logiikka	*loogikko*	*looginen*	'logical'
-VCVV-	*-VVCV-*	*-VVC(C)-*	

Finnish has a rich derivational apparatus, a few instances of which are given in B, without indication of the direction of derivation. In general, nouns and verbs, verbs and causatives have different stems. In opposition to this type we have A, which is a curious anomaly indeed; there is no difference between the nominal and the verbal stem. We have already seen, however, that the verbs show consonant gradation in some cases where the nouns do not (§ 10.13). Otherwise consonant gradation prevails in A and B, but is absent in C, where the meanings represent objects of material culture (typical of loans), slang words, and hypocoristic words (second column). Type D is characterized by much more technical semantics (plus some slang: *jobi*) correlated with the phonetic peculiarity of voiced stops and complicated consonant clusters. Such stops belong only to innovative dialects and are not used by all social or regional dialects. This type is thus a clear newcomer. And so is E, which displays the most complicated kind of alternation in which consonant length is coupled with vowel length (except that voiced stops do not alternate). The extremely technical meanings point to recent date, and the type is productive for such Greek terminology.

The Finnish situation thus shows relative growth of suffixing (A to B) and lessening of consonant gradation (A and B to C), as well as formal features which are integrally tied to the functioning of the language (D and E—a kind of derivational consonant gradation with gratuitous vocalic complications as well). Although much in the evaluation of both English and Finnish alternation matches, there are some characteristic differences. First of all, the existence of alternations or derivatory suffixes alone does not guarantee the chronology. One also needs information on productivity and semantics. English started with stem variation and ended up without it (*a fish–to fish*, D), Finnish is the reverse (A is clearly a relic, the list here including practically all the existing stems of this type). In the plural, however, English showed an old type without variation (*one fish–two fish*). Finnish consonant gradation is alternation belonging to the oldest types, and then again a recent peripheral pattern (E) has similar alternation. An inference that one would be likely to draw from the English and Finnish configurations is that English has lost flectional apparatus and that Finnish has acquired it. Basically this is quite correct, with the difference that for English the time span here is about a thousand years, for Finnish perhaps four thousand. We shall not present the comparative and documentary evidence that confirms our analysis, because the purpose was to show what kind of inferences can be made from internal evidence. Moreover, much of the English material has, in fact, been mentioned earlier.

Finally, it should be noted that these inferences about relative chronology concern morphological types or patterns only and not the individual members or items, because any word can analogically shift types (e.g., English *cow* from B to D or *oath* from C to D). Such shifts occur usually toward the more productive (newer) types. These rather systematic inferences concerning the relative chronology of morpheme types are quite parallel to the reconstruction of the sequences of morpheme slots. In the latter case we also faced the uncertainty of not knowing whether any particular morpheme had in fact been combined with some other morpheme in the protolanguage (to which the slots themselves can be assigned).

SYNTAX

[19.5 Syntactic Change]   It has been generally agreed that the unit of speech is the sentence (only now is this conception changing in favor of a whole text, a discourse, as the basic unit; see §§ 19.8–19.11, 20.1–20.6). So far relatively little has been said about sentences and syntactic change in general. First of all, there is the practical problem of space: to characterize syntactic change one would first have to present a great deal of background information. It has always been easier to present change in terms of the various units that build up a sentence, because without units there would be no sentences either. This is a simple and obvious point that is easily forgotten. The arbitrariness of the linguistic sign resides in these building blocks of the sentence and not in the purely syntactic rules, which are heavily iconic. Because syntactic change is analogical it interferes heavily with reconstruction. This creates the following paradox: since syntax is iconic, it is an important factor in change (which is largely iconic) but a peripheral aspect in reconstruction (which requires symbolic factors). Both aspects have already been mentioned. The first has been implicit all along, in the absence of neat compartments of change. Syntax is deeply involved in analogical change, in semantic change, in figures of speech, in borrowing, and so on. It can be the conditioning factor or the conditioned part of sound change. To repeat all these passages here would give material for a separate chapter. It has been noted already that chapter divisions are rather arbitrary practical matters which are likely to do violence to the interconnections of language or linguistics.

The main analogical forces in syntax are reinterpretation or reanalysis, that is, emphasis or fading. We also know these notions under the terms 'elaboration' and 'simplification'. Ellipsis can automatically give a new part of speech (e.g., *daily paper* > *daily*; see § 7.8). Loss of pause can create a conjunction like *I know that*; *You will come* > *I know that you will come*. A question in between ('self-question') can give 'because': Latin *Nōn es eques. Quārē? Nōn sunt tibī mīlia centum.* 'You are not a knight. For what reason? You do not have a hundred thousand'. *Quārē* fades into 'because' and gives later French *car*. Similarly, *I ask you: Whether? Will you come or no(t)?* results in *whether* functioning only as a conjunction. A loss of pause in sentences like *Then he smiled, a shy nervous smile* gives a transitive verb whose object is formally related to an intransitive verb. Semantic fading gives a periphrastic perfect from concrete cases like *I have a cake baked* > *I have baked a cake* in Romance and Germanic (as well as other tenses; § 19.10). We shall see below how similar reinterpretation can engulf independent particles into verbs or pronouns.

Whole sentences get petrified; for example, Latin *quam vīs* 'as you wish' > 'however' and *nox* 'it is night' > 'by night'; English *willy-nilly* from 'whether I want or not want' (i.e., *will-I-ne-will-I*; see § 9.8); and French *peut-être* 'perhaps' < 'can be' (compare *maybe*). These examples show that syntactic derivation was stored as a lump and became an arbitrary linguistic sign. For this to happen, the phrase has to be frequent (see § 9.8). Syntax can remain unchanged even if the outer form is eroded by sound change. In the English type D (§ 19.3) the noun and verb were formally different (as in *help–helpe*). The original French genitive survives, for example, in street names like *la Rue Monsieur le Prince*, the syntactic mode appropriate for the genitive but without the original genitive ending (compare Finnish type A; § 19.4). We shall see below a case in which the same form can be suppressed if it occurs more than once with exactly the same meaning. In the French sentence *Vous savez que je vous ai toujours respecté et vous porté une vive affection*, the *vous* has to be repeated in the last two clauses, because it represents the accusative (e.g., *je le respecte*) and the dative (e.g., *je lui porte*), respectively.

One reason mere syntactic change seems to have been neglected is that there is no independent syntactic change at all. Syntactic change is only a different aspect of the various types that we have seen already (see § 7.13). In using syntactic notation to describe change we are looking at change from a new angle (compare phonemes to rules). This has always been taken into account in etymological research, where everything is considered. We shall see that syntactic reconstruction is largely applied morphology. (See in particular §§ 9.16–9.18.) (§11.21f.)

[19.6   Internal Reconstruction and Syntax]   In the beginning of this chapter we saw that the application of internal reconstruction to morphology was in principle no different from phonology, in that imbalance and irregularity were evaluated against regularity (see § 18.16). Taking unproductive types as the irregular ones, we reached certain conclusions about relative chronology, which is always a by-product of internal reconstruction. In that case, however, reconstruction as such was not possible, only relative chronology. To see how internal reconstruction can work in syntax let us go back to the Finnish material of § 5.17. Now, in Finnish we have a sentence *pojat menevät* 'the boys go' which is formally the reverse of *menevät pojat* 'the going boys'. Word order seems to make the difference between a normal sentence and a nominal phrase, which is not at all infrequent in the languages of the world (compare Indo-European *-nt- both in the third person plural and the present participle, for example, Latin *feru-nt* 'they carry' and *fere-nt-ēs* 'the carrying ones'). The singular of the nominal phrase is as expected, *menevä poika* 'the/a going boy', but the third singular verb phrase *poika menee* does not fit, even though the word order is the expected one. The relational setup is thus

3rd pl. noun phrase XY $X'Y'$
                                      vs.   in the sg.
3rd pl. verb phrase YX $Y'Z$

The plural and the singular match perfectly except for the Z (*menee*). We have often seen that such irregularities are prime targets for analysis, exactly like analogy (§ 18.16). We have immediate success here, since archaic and poetic Finnish goes *poika menevi* in the singular. A *v* shows up where expected, and Z can be replaced by X'', in which only the final vowel deviates from the pattern. Now it would be very attractive to be able to combine -*va* and -*vi*, and the simplest way is to posit grammatical conditioning of sound change: a final -*a* in predicative position yields -*i*. And now X'' can finally join the pattern as X'. Predicative position is rather prone to provide change (see § 4.24), and it is quite common for a nominal sentence to give a verbal tense. The participle became first a verb syntactically, and then (with sound changes) also semantically. Earlier we saw that the accusative singular of the participle produced an uninflected form (§ 5.17). (§11.27)

Thus this evidence, and that in the Finnish type A, support each other: both point to a lack of differentiation between noun and verb in Pre-Finnish (§ 19.4). And indeed comparative evidence makes it likely that this was true of Proto-Uralic.

[19.7   The Value of Numbers for Syntactic Protorules]   The iconicity of syntactic rules has led to the question of how much evidence one needs to justify a syntactic rule for the protolanguage. A widespread rule of thumb has been that chance could easily result in two languages showing a particular rule, but that when three agree, the feature can be assigned to the protolanguage. Greek and

Latin have compound verbs with more or less idiomatic meanings, for example, Greek *en-ktḗsasthai* 'to acquire possessions in a foreign country' (to buy in) and *hupo-thésthai* 'to take a mortgage (to place under), Latin *oc-cídere* 'to kill' (to strike against), and *con-surgere* 'to rise up together'; these can be repeated in the discourse without the preverb, but the meaning undergoes no modification. We have here a kind of syntactic ellipsis or haplology (*AB 'X'* ... *AB 'X'* > *AB 'X'* ... *B 'X'*). Now Latin could perhaps have borrowed this rule from Greek; but it is very unlikely, because it occurs in the earliest legal language of both languages. According to the three-witness requirement, we could not assign this deletion rule to Proto-Indo-European. But when we see that Hittite has the same rule (e.g., *[appa] pai* 'gives back' and *[ser] sarnikmi* 'I make restitution') we have the third witness, and the rule can be assumed for Indo-European. Counting the number of witnesses is not a reliable criterion, however; a deletion of the above kind would seem to be quite natural in any language having similar verbal compounds. In syntax one needs the total situation far more urgently than in other areas of grammar, and below we shall see that even a single witness can be crucial (=internal evidence; cf. §§11.26-30).

[19.8 Proto-Indo-European Pronouns and Hittite Sentence Connectives]
On the basis of the following evidence it was easy to reconstruct a Proto-Indo-European nonpersonal demonstrative (anaphoric) pronoun (which shows relative and personal usage as well):

	PIE	SKT	GREEK	LITH.	GO.	OE
nom. sg. masc.	*so	sá[s]	ho	[tàs]	sa	sē [þe]
acc. sg. masc.	*tom	tám	tón	tą̃	þan[a]	þone
gen. sg. masc.	*tosyo	tásya	toîo	[tõ]	þis	þæs
dat. sg masc.	*tosmōi	tásmāi	[tôi]	tamui	þamma	þæm
nom./acc. sg. neuter	*tod	tád	tó	ta[ī]	þat[a]	þæt
nom. pl. masc.	*toi	té	toí [hoi]	tiẽ	þai	þā

In Greek and English, it subsequently yields a definite article. This is a selection of course, but it is sufficient to provide the necessary information about the Proto-Indo-European paradigm. Parts that violate sound correspondences are bracketed and typically represent analogical formations. Spotting them is part of reconstruction and it is possible when the paradigm starts to emerge. Three "irregularities" or deviations from the normal nominal paradigm can be noted: (1) the initial *s-* in the nom. masc. sg. vs. *t-* in the other cases, (2) lack of a nom. sg. masc. ending, which is *-s* elsewhere, and (3) a formative *-sm-* in the dative. Retention of these features must now be considered older than their lack (on the basis of seriation). Thus the initial *t-* and final *-s* in Lithuanian *tàs* become quite understandable as innovations, as does the late Sanskrit *-s*. Old English also levels out in favor of the oblique stem: *þe*. Some dialects of Greek go the other way, extending the *s*-form into the plural: *hoi.* The omission of *-sm-* in Greek is also clearly leveling, and the Lithuanian genitive *tõ* takes its ending from the noun. There is considerable give and take between the pronoun and the noun in the Indo-European languages, and on the whole the developments can be spotted by plotting the various paradigms side by side. Suffice it to say that the sound correspondences and the paradigmatic relations enable us to reconstruct the pronoun as given. This is the classical Proto-Indo-European reconstruction from the morphological side.

[19.9]   Pronouns are shifters (indexical); they refer to something else in the discourse, especially an anaphoric pronoun. Thus one would expect that syntax is strongly involved. Indeed, once one has reconstructed pronouns, syntax is automatically implied. In the oldest stages of Sanskrit, Greek, and Germanic these pronouns tend to occur at or toward the beginning of the sentence. We could accordingly suspect that such a word order existed in the protolanguage. But it is Hittite that turns the suspicion into probability. Hittite does not have such an anaphoric pronoun at all. It has sentence connectives *su* 'and' (unchanged subject), *ta* 'and (then)' (change of subject), and *nu* 'and (now)'. Practically every sentence in a given discourse, except for the first, begins with one of these. Then there are enclitic pronouns for the third person, *-as* 'he', *-an* 'him', *-at* 'it', *-e* 'they', and *-us* 'them', which can be attached to particles other than the sentence connectives, for example, *-wa(r)-* 'direct quotation': *nu-war-as* 'and now he said: "..."', or *nu-smas-an* 'and you him'. But when no other particles intervene we get the following conglomerates of the sentence connective plus the enclitic pronoun:

nas	*tas*	*sas*	'and he' (nom. masc. sg.)
nan	*tan*	*san*	'and him' (acc. masc. sg.)
nat	*tat*	—	'and it' (neut. sg.)
ne	—	*se*	'and they' (nom. masc. pl.)

The formal similarity of the last two columns to the pronoun **so-/*to-* is obvious. There must be a historical connection. The best inference is that the Indo-European pronoun is a fusion of the earlier sentence connective plus the enclitic pronoun (isogloss 24 in Figure 15-2). It is now possible to see a natural reason for the reinterpretation of **so* as a nominative (no change in subject), and the less frequent combinations **t(o) + os* and **s(o)-om* were lost. (But Old Latin has *sum* 'him', *sam* 'her', and *sōs* 'them'!) The principles of linguistic change tell us how much easier it is to merge independent units rather than split them: for example, English *not* could not have split into *nān wiht*, so the development must have been the reverse (§ 9.8). The Hittite facts have to be interpreted as the *lectio difficilior*, and we see how syntax has crystallized into morphology. Earlier we saw how particular sentences can freeze into adverbs, that is, words (*willy-nilly*).

[19.10   Sentence Connectives and Tense/Mood]   Some Indo-European languages show so-called primary (I) vs. secondary (II) personal endings; for example:

	I	II
1st sg.	-mi	-m
2nd sg.	-si	-s
3rd sg.	-ti	-t
3rd pl.	-nti	-nt

The relation between these endings is best known through the difference between a present *bhére-ti* 'he carries' and an imperfect *é-bhere-t* 'he was carrying'. Sanskrit has also a verbal form called 'injunctive' which does not indicate either tense or mood, for example, (*má*) *bharat* 'he (may not) carry' (*mé bhere-t*). When one lines up all these forms one gets a clear segmentation of forms:

SANSKRIT	PROTO-INDO-EUROPEAN
bhára-t-i	*bhére-t-i*
á-bhara-t	*é-bhere-t*
bhára-t-u (imperative 3rd sg.)	*bhére-t-u*
má bhara-t	*mé bhere-t*

Generally, prefixes and suffixes exclude each other, and it is quite obvious that the *-i* of the primary endings is a temporal suffix added to the person marker. Against this complementarity of suffixes and prefixes we have a type with both, as in Sanskrit *prá-bharat-i* 'he carries forward' (*pró-bhere-t-i*). In the earliest attested Indo-European a pre-verb like *pro* is still a free word, whereas the *-i* is not; in many languages it is obligatory. It looks as if the verb had incorporated the particle *-i* not unlike the Indo-European enclitic pronouns incorporated the sentence connectives. Old Irish does indeed bear this out; all prefixes require secondary endings (known as conjunct), for example, from 'carry' > 'take' (*ni-beir* 'he does not take', *do-beir* 'he gives'):

PRIMARY (ABSOLUTE)		SECONDARY (CONJUNCT)
1st sg.	biru	-biur
2nd sg.	biri	-bir
3rd sg.	berid	-beir
3rd pl.	berait	-berat

The highly complex Irish syntax turns out to be a fossilization of Indo-European at the time of free tense and mood particles. Syntactically, the Irish verb is clear in Proto-Indo-European terms, although sound change has disturbed the appearance, for example:

*tó   bheret > do-beir   /do¹beŕ/
*tó me bheret > do-m-beir   /domˡv̆eŕ/⎞
*nú me bheret > no-m-beir   /nomˡv̆eŕ/⎠"infixed" pronoun
    *bheret i   > berid   /ˡbeŕiδ'/
    *bheret i me > beirthium   /ˡbeŕθ'imʷ/ ("suffixed" pronoun)

In a similar way Romance developed single tenses (e.g., the future) out of
analytic phrases, and also infixed pronouns. Portuguese retains the original
Latin state of affairs most clearly, as in *fābulāre habeō > falar hei > falarei* 'I
will speak'. This is directly parallel to French *parlerai* 'I will speak', which is
an unbreakable single word. In Portuguese, however, pronouns can still occur
between the infinitival part and the present forms of *haver*: *lembrar-me-ei* 'I
will remember' and *chamá-lo-ei* 'I will call him' (the orthography is conventional, compare Brazilian *chamal-o-(h)ei*). Portuguese further has a compound
future with the above components in a different order: *hei-de lho dizer* or
hei-de dizer-lho 'I will say to him'. Such a situation is very similar to the Irish
development (compare Oneida in §16.3). The Proto-Indo-European imperfect
prefix *é is presumably another adverb, as is *mḗ 'don't'. Once the tense or
mood is fully specified, the discourse continues with injunctives, which indicate
person and number only. And these injunctives are linked to the previous sentences by sentence connectives.

The analysis of these two interrelated syntactic problems from Indo-European
—pronouns and sentence connectives, and sentence connectives and injunctives
—was based on the seriation method. This means that internal criteria were
used to single out apparent relics, and these relics were combined for Proto-
Indo-European. The crucial evidence came from Hittite and Old Irish for the
connectives and from Sanskrit and Old Irish for the injunctive, although the
complexities of the Irish evidence for connectives were not elaborated upon (e.g.,
the so-called 'dummy' prefixes like *no-* < *nu*) (see isogloss 15 in Figure 15-2).

[19.11 Indeterminacy of Historical Order] Syntactic reconstruction shows
best results when it can be connected with morphology that contains clear
sound correspondences. This has been anticipated (§§ 16.9, 16.10). Syntactic
reconstruction makes the correspondences on the morphemic level much more
meaningful. It does not replace the work done in other areas of grammar, but
adds to it. Abstract syntactic rules alone are inconclusive for genetic connection.
Of course, rules can be written counter to the actual history. In the case of the
preverb deletion in Latin, Greek, and Hittite it is descriptively obligatory to
start from the richer form *AB ... AB* being reduced to *AB ... B*; the same
would be possible for the injunctive as well; that is, a sequence

$$\text{VERB} + \text{PERSON} + \begin{Bmatrix} \text{TENSE} \\ \text{MOOD} \end{Bmatrix} \dots V + P + \begin{Bmatrix} T \\ M \end{Bmatrix}$$

is reduced to

$$V + P + \begin{Bmatrix} T \\ M \end{Bmatrix} \ldots V + P,$$

if the tense or mood remains the same. For Proto-Indo-European one would be tempted to write such a rule if semantics were taken as syntax-dependent. This shows how easy it is to devise all kinds of rules which probably do not reflect history, for the injunctive is clearly the original verbal form, ousted by those verbs that incorporated temporal and modal particles. History shows accretion of forms, but typical syntactic rules would treat this as deletion.

Of course history can go both ways. Languages may develop complicated congruence phenomena or lose them (often with much of inflection in general). Germanic developed a complicated adjective inflection, which has now been lost in English. The Finnish congruence between adjective and noun in case and number is also an innovation. One cannot predict the direction of change in advance without evaluating the total evidence at hand.

[19.12 Conclusion]   We see now a dilemma between synchronic theory and reconstruction. Synchronic models are based on the directionality of meaning to sound (§ 10.6). Semantics is the very reason of language, but it does not work as a starting point in the study of languages attested only through documents, or in reconstruction. Linguistics as an empirical science must comprise adequate and coherent theory building and exact empirical testing methods. As far as syntax is concerned, generative-transformational grammar meets the theoretical requirements better than any other school, but very little or no attention has been paid to the testing of hypotheses. This is left to the intuitions of the analysts (compare § 18.17), or is brushed aside as a matter of "performance." Thus it is obvious that generative grammar is hardly suitable for reconstruction, because no informants or native intuition are available. Only philology can help here, because it handles the total pragmatic context systematically and serves as an approximate empirical checking.

The comparative linguist must work with a model maximally complete, coherent, consistent, and explicit in its deductive hypothesis formation, but this model must be testable and found probable. A pure aprioristic position is useless in comparative linguistics, because here one is always right in advance. Comparative linguistics needs discovery procedures, and this is the end to which its methods explicitly serve (§ 9.19). These methods operate between theory and philological investigation (Part IV). Syntactic reconstruction is an evaluation of probabilities (not a calculus with exact numerical values; compare § 21.14) based on the following factors: (1) the spread of the phenomenon among the languages used (compare § 19.7), (2) formal correspondences, (3) semantic correspondences, (4) the results of internal reconstruction (compare § 19.6), (5) the fit of the individual phenomenon in the framework of the total reconstruction (e.g., § 19.10), and (6) the typological constraints. Without parallels from the living languages any reconstruction remains doubtful (compare

§§ 6.5, 18.7, 19.10, 21.14, 21.20). Very important are implicational universals of the type that the reconstruction of a phenomenon *a* makes the reconstruction of the phenomenon *b* probable (compare § 16.8).
By necessity the directionality in syntactic reconstruction is thus from sounds to forms to case syntax, and so on (§ 20.2; compare §§ 22.1, 22.2). Note that ultimately this procedure can indeed reach discourse analysis as was exemplified by the Indo-European sentence connectives (§§ 19.8–19.10). The reconstruction of morphology is also often impossible without syntax (§§ 19.5, 19.6, 19.9, 19.10), although morphology need not always be fossilized syntax.

REFERENCES

General: Havers 1931, Fokos-Fuchs 1962, Katičić 1970; **19.1** Krahe 1970, Szemerényi 1970; **19.2** Hymes 1956, Dressler 1969a; **19.5** Bréal 1964, Porzig 1924, Havers 1931, Allen 1951, Watkins 1965, Skrelina 1968, R. Hall 1968, Szemerényi 1968, Traugott 1965, 1969; **19.6** Anttila in Sebeok (ed.) 1963f. vol. 11; **19.7** Watkins 1966; **19.8-19.9** Sturtevant 1939, Szemerényi 1970; **19.10** Meid 1968ab, Kiparsky 1968b --Cowgill in Rix (ed.) 1975, in Schlerath (ed.) 1985, McCone in Schlerath (ed.) 1985, Ahlqvist 1985; **19.12** Dressler 1971.

19.5-19.12 Historical syntax: Hawkins 1983, Li (ed.) 1975, (ed.) 1977 -- Givón 1971, Terho Itkonen 1976, Steever et al. (eds.) 1976, Lightfoot 1979, Cram 1979, Woolford in K. Hill (ed.) 1979, S. Wolfe 1981, Fisiak (ed.) 1984, A. Harris 1985, Hock 1986:309-79, Wanner 1987, D. Stein 1988 -- Norman and L. Campbell 1978, L. Campbell and Mithun 1980, Ramat (ed.) 1980, Hock 1985a, 1986:611-17. (See also p. 263)

CHAPTER 20

RECONSTRUCTING SEMOLOGY/SEMANTICS

> *Because of the impossibility of providing a complete language-specific semology, the chapter can only delineate methods and procedures that point the way. The border between universal semantics and language-specific semology cannot be drawn with partial evidence; thus only the term 'semantic' will be used.*

[20.1 Comparative Method and Morphology/Syntax/Semantics]   Because syntax is so extensively iconic, the comparative method with its sets of correspondences cannot be applied explicitly. Syntactic rules of two languages correspond easily, for example, word order XY in language 1 with word order YX in language 2. This alone does not tell much; it could be quite accidental. Similarly, a participle in one language may correspond to a relative clause in another, as in *a running boy* vs. *a boy who runs*. These are common patterns that even exist side by side in one language. Now the fact that transformational or mapping rules can be written relating the syntax of two languages need have no historical validity whatsoever. Syntactic rules must be tied with some arbitrary features to carry historical conviction. A good example comes from Indo-European case syntax, where we have the following correspondences between Latin and Greek:

	'OF'	'FROM'	'WITH'	'IN'	'FOR/TO'
Latin	GEN	ABL	ABL	ABL	DAT
Greek	GEN	GEN	DAT	DAT	DAT

The morphological units spelled with small capitals represent forms that are connected with sound correspondences; that is, a Latin genitive corresponds in this sense to the Greek genitive, although it does not mean that the two cases have the same function in both languages. On the contrary, the case correspondences have a different range for the three Latin cases and the two Greek ones (see § 7.2). The glosses are a translation shorthand for the syntactic-semantic environments. The sets represent "pure" cases without prepositions. One can now note that syntax and semantics play a role in the environments of the morphological sets (which themselves are reconstructed on the basis of sound correspondences). The configuration suggests immediately that at least the 'of' set and the 'for/to' set contrast; then one should see whether all those sets having

364

Latin ABL belong together, or whether the Greek with only GEN and DAT allows us to predict the Latin. Since the 'with' and 'in' sets are formally the same these are the most likely candidates for being the same. First of all, the 'in' set is rather limited in both languages, which normally use the preposition *in* + the 'in' set for the meaning 'in'. Seriation would hold that a productive form marked twice analytically is the younger one. But then both languages have also a few forms that are not the same as the Latin ablative or the Greek dative, respectively (e.g., Latin "ablative" *mediā urbe* 'in the center of the city', or *Carthāgine* 'in Carthage' vs. the "genitive" *Rōmae* 'in Rome', or an "-*ī*" case in *domī* 'at home'; *rūrī* 'in the countryside' and Greek "dative" *Delphoîs* 'in Delphoi'; and *kúklōi* 'in a circle' [both normally with the additional *en* 'in'] vs. *oíkoi* 'at home' or *ekeî* 'there'). These formal differences, which are clearly relics, are now added to the relic peculiarity of the lack of *in* 'in'. The indication thus is that the 'in' set does not point toward unity with the 'with' set at all, and they cannot be combined.

[20.2]   In fact, all the sets contrast with each other because they carry the different meanings as indicated. We see that our method is quite different from that in phonology, after all. Here we have to know meanings to predict the forms, because meanings are the environments. In phonology we had to predict sounds in the environments of other sounds. We used the meanings to give us the forms for analysis, but in the actual analysis such meanings could be pushed into the background. Here we are clearly coming back to meaning. To reconstruct the actual case morphemes, we would use vague meanings such as 'a grammatical suffix with local meaning'. This would be enough background for the comparative method, which would let the sound correspondences ferret out protoforms, if possible. Here we have come back to the link between meaning and form, the basic makeup of the linguistic sign. This same buildup provided the forms for the comparative method, and we see once more that different parts of language are indissociable and complementary in a natural situation. The linguist's vivisection does not always do justice to the joints. The small selection of Latin and Greek above is extremely simplified because the cases can be formally quite different (in the different declensions). This is why the labels GEN, ABL, and so on, do not represent form alone, but also syntactic-semantic equivalences (slots as it were). This is why the members of these case correspondences (GEN, DAT, and so on) also represent higher levels of grammatical hierarchy (sounds → forms → case syntax). Thus our task is not the reconstruction of single case forms for each set, after all, as would seem from the table; that would not be possible with these languages. The reconstruction results in a series of semantic cases, that is, 'of', 'from', 'with', 'in' and 'for/to'. (The actual forms are a different matter.) It is expedient to assume that the protolanguage had such categories, since the phonology and morphology establish clear protoforms. Although reconstruction is based on both form and meaning, we once more get an indication that both sides obey the laws of independent structures.

[20.3]   This small selection from case syntax is typical: it takes so much exposition compared with the final yield. It was also chosen so that a further comparative check would be possible from Indo-European languages not used in this analysis. Having made the inference that five semantic cases can be assumed for the protolanguage on the basis of five case correspondences in five semantic-syntactic environments, it is also likely that there was a more uniform formal representation of the five semantic cases (in particular the 'in' case had relic forms clearly pointing to extra forms). Otherwise it would be difficult to understand the almost haphazard formal case representation between Latin and Greek. If, on the other hand, we assume that there was a richer case system as a starting point, it is easy to see how the number of cases would be reduced with the expansion of prepositions; the history of English is another good case in point. Although only the 'in' case was mentioned as co-occurring with a preposition *in* (*in/en*), this is true of others as well, for example, *with* (*cum/sún* = *syn*) and *from* (*dē/apó*). Cases without prepositions look older (restricted relics).

The evidence from other languages confirms our guesses quite well. Sanskrit has five local cases: genitive 'of', ablative 'from', instrumental 'with', locative 'in', and dative 'for/to', although an ablative separate from the genitive exists in one declension only. In fact, this formal matching with the assumed semantic cases, which could be adduced from other languages as well, proves the issue. We started out from apparent morphology, which turned out to be case syntax and ultimately semantics, that is, structural semantics independent of form. Semantic reconstruction is also heavily applied historical morphology and syntax.

[20.4 Internal Analysis of Apparent Synonyms (Based on Comparative Evidence)]   To anticipate a simple semantic answer let us look at the Indo-European numerals for 'one'. Formally there are two units, **oi(no)-* and **s(e)m-*:

	*OI(NO)-			**S(E)M-*	
Greek	*oínē*	'one' (on dice)		*heîs* < **sems*	'one' (masc.)
	oîos	'alone'			
Latin	*ūnus*	'one'		*sin(gulus)*	'single'
				sem(el)	'once'
San-	*eka*	'one and only'		*sa(kṛt)*	'once'
skrit	*eva*	'all alone, only'			
		(Avestan 'one')			
OE	*ān*,	NE	(*al*)*one*, *on*(*ly*)		
OCS	*inŭ*	'one, another'			

Sanskrit represents here Indo-Iranian and the selection is limited to forms clearly meaning 'one' (except perhaps for Latin *singulus*). Since exact synonyms are rather rare in a language, the next step is to see whether the formal difference represents a semantic difference as well. Are there other forms available with compatible semantics that would show more about the semantic range of the forms? Indo-Iranian has compounds with *sa-*, for example, Sanskrit *sa-joṣa* 'having one will' or 'having the same will, whose will is the same'. The meaning 'one and the same' is suggested by other occurrences: the full grade *sam* means 'together', as in *san-dhi* 'putting together'. Greek agrees quite well with Indo-Iranian, for example, *há-ma* 'together' and *hom-ós* 'common' (sometimes without the *h-*, as in *á-lokhos* 'having the same bed', i.e., 'wife'). Glosses like 'one, same, together' have already hinted that Germanic *same* also contains the **som-* reflected in Greek 'common'. Sanskrit, in fact, displays the exact counterpart to Germanic *same* and Greek *homós*: *samá* 'same', and an enclitic *sama* 'any, every'. The form recurs in Germanic 'together', German *zu-sam-men*, and Swedish *till-sam-mans*; compare further German *sam-meln* and Swedish *sam-la* 'to gather'. Latin *sim-ul* 'together', *sim-ilis* 'like', Russian *sam-yj* 'same', and the prepositions/adverbs German/Swedish *samt* 'with' and Balto-Slavic (e.g., OCS *sŭ*) 'with' further expand the reflexes for this semantic area. But clearest of all is the Scandinavian preverb *sam-* 'together', as in Swedish *sam-tal* 'conversation' and *sam-arbete* 'joint work, collaboration'.

But even for the numeral, Germanic has reflexes of **s(e)m-*. Old English has a pronominal adjective *sum* 'a certain one, one, a; some'. In Modern English, it can mean unspecified (greater) number or quantity, as in *some twenty people*, but as a suffix it means a specified (smallish) number, as in *threesome*, that is, 'three together [as one]'. The meanings of OE *ān* 'one, a certain one; the same; only, alone' partially overlap with those of *sum*, but this is hardly surprising, since we are dealing with a sphere of 'unity'. *Sum* occurs in what is practically paradigmatic alternation with a derivative of *ān* (*ǣn-ig* > *any*), as in *Do you have some bread? No, I don't have any*.

Other languages and additional forms could be adduced, but this is enough for retrieving one interesting point. Proto-Indo-European apparently had two notions of unity, 'one-alone' and 'one-together'; the importance of the distinction is borne out by the different roots to express it. Of course many languages do express these aspects by derivatives of 'one', for example, Finnish *yksi* 'one', *yksi-n* 'alone', and *yhde-ssä* 'together' ('in one'). In Indo-European such derivations also occur: Latin *ūnitās* 'unity', a together meaning from the alone word, and *singulus* 'single', an alone meaning from the together word. The meaning 'same' fits in quite naturally with 'together', since it means 'something must be taken together with what was known or mentioned before'; it is another side of a known unity. That the words like *ān* > *one* or Russian *odin* also mean 'same' (*They live in one house*, compare *álokhos* above) is a natural phenomenon, but Old Church Slavic shows a meaning 'another' for *inŭ*, which is 'not the same', that is, clear contrast.

[20.5]   Now it is clear that even a numeral like 'one' can be semantically very complex, because it overlaps the pronominal sphere. The question is whether the singulative and the collective unity have other formal expressions in Indo-European. Indeed they do. Consider, for example, the singulative suffix *-(i)ōn and the collective *-(i)ā-, in a Greek name like Plát-ōn 'the flat-faced one', hēgem-ṓn 'leader', Latin Cat-ō(nem) 'the sly one', and Greek sophíā 'wisdom', Latin miseria 'misery'. Greek has clear syntactic reflexes in pántes hoi ánthrōpoi 'all the people' and autòs ho híppos 'the horse itself' (singulative) vs. hoi pántes ánthrōpoi 'the people all together' and ho autòs híppos 'the same horse' (collective). Here word order (Pronoun-Article-Noun vs. A–P–N) differentiates the semantic units we have delineated through different words and derivatory suffixes. It is quite well known that the feminine singular and neuter plural are formally identical in Indo-European (*-[i]ā-), and these can be taken as representing an original collective, which implies plurality as unity. Thus Greek hēníā 'reins' occurs both as nominative plural neuter and as nominative singular feminine, and Rigvedic tánā as nominative plural 'descendants' and as feminine singular 'offspring'. This collective -ā contrasts with the singulative -s (nom. sg. masc.), for example, OCS nog-a 'foot'/Lith. nag-à 'hoof' vs. Greek ónuk-s 'claw', Greek phorá 'produce, fruit' vs. phóro-s 'tribute, payment', phoró-s 'bearing (favorable) wind', and Sanskrit hímā 'winter' vs. himá-s 'cold, frost'. Support for this collective/plural comes also from the fact that a neuter plural subject is combined with a singular predicate in Greek ([pl.] tà zôia [sg.] trékhei 'living things move'), earliest Avestan, and sometimes in Vedic Sanskrit as well. In Baltic the third plural verb was lost altogether and this 'collective singular' usage was generalized.

[20.6]   The purpose of this demonstration was to show that one can continue combining morphological and syntactic evidence for semantic reconstruction. Gaps and mistakes would not be identifiable at this point. As a final conjecture let us look at another possibility in this semantic sphere of unity (we shall take the following forms at face value for the moment). Swedish has two compounds for 'the present time' : nu-tid and sam-tid, that is, with 'now' and 'one-together'. German has corresponding Jetzt-zeit, also 'now-time' and Gegen-wart 'presence', in which the first part is the same as in English again. The meanings of again include 'once more' and 'back into a former position', and an obsolete 'back'. Such meanings come into the area of 'same', that is, repetitions of earlier things, even if against/gegen normally mean togetherness of a hostile nature. Is it really possible to combine meanings 'one, now, again, back' into one semantic unit? We would not take these as variants of one semantic unit in Modern Germanic, but is it possible for earlier times? It would seem so; Oneida has such a unity sememe with exactly the variants mentioned, expressed, for example, by the s- in Skanyataliyo (§ 16.7), although in certain environments another morpheme is used.

But German Gegenwart acquired temporal significance first in the eighteenth century; and Jetztzeit was coined in 1807, Swedish nutid being formed after the latter. Thus the possibilities explored above diminish substantially. The moral of this is that in semantic reconstruction it is easy to go too far, even though each step can be perfectly substantiated or paralleled from another language.

Let us refer back to the buildup of anaphoric pronouns from sentence connectives (§§ 19.8, 19.9). The notion of 'sameness' is inherent in *nu, which means 'carry on, add this sentence to the preceding ones, the same discourse continues'. Since it appears that *to 'and' was used with a *change* of subject, the attractive hypothesis emerges that the mystery *-sm- in local cases of the anaphoric pronoun is actually the zero grade of *sem-, that is, *to-sm-ōi 'and to this same one, to the aforementioned'—the *-sm- in effect canceling the change of subject usually associated with *to, and contributing to the simplification of what presumably was a very complex set of paradigms. Once more we come back to syntax. Reconstructing structural semantics is very complex indeed. We cannot expect easy results, since there are great difficulties in reaching agreement on semantic structure even in synchronic situations. Reconstruction is many more times difficult.

[20.7 Semantic Reconstruction and Boolean Algebra]   In the reconstruction through the formal representation of semantic cases, Boolean algebra was not possible because the target turned out to be the connection of meaning to form. In the case of 'one-alone' and 'one-together' the intersection 'one' did not yield the best reconstruction for both forms either, because again the crucial point was the linkup of the linguistic sign, and 'one' turned out to be a conditioned variant of 'alone' and 'together', respectively, to use common language terminology. Thus in semantic reconstruction we face the problem of deciding when an intersection is a variant or the underlying unit. The one-alone and one-together case is paralleled in phonology; for example, the [v] of *to grieve* and *to dive* is an intersecting variant of both |f| and |v| (see § 12.4). Similarly, in Finnish, the -*i* of *nappi* 'button' and *sappi* 'gall' are variants of |i| and |e|, respectively (compare [gen.] *napin* and *sapen*). Sememes can be defined rather like phonemes. A disjunctive definition of the meanings of Oneida *s*- would give preference to the actual surface variants (e.g., either 'back', or 'now', or 'again', or 'one'), whereas a conjunctive definition produces underlying 'unity' (§ 20.6); the latter is preferable (see § 18.10). Here the intersection gives the unit and not a variant. Boolean algebra can often be used as a guideline (Figure 18-1), when we want to get a common derivation point for different but 'relatable' meanings in different environments or languages.

[20.8]   English *story* 'narrative' and *stor(e)y* 'floor in a building' could ultimately be one polysemous word, if a common denominator (intersection) and its environment could be found. Indeed, some dictionaries connect the two, pointing out that a story is a structured whole that proceeds step by step, or that it is built up of layers. But here we happen to know for certain that the two words are etymologically distinct. This suggested combination shows the dangers of trying to push the analysis too far. This is, in a way, analytic (inductive) folk etymology; it is surprisingly easy to devise abstract meanings to cover any two meanings (see §17.5). Etymological literature is full of such mistakes. Finnish *lokki* 'gull' and *lokki* 'pulley' would at best have an intersection 'hovering in the air', which is obviously absurd, and the words must thus be regarded as homophones only. Independent evidence tells us that this is the correct interpretation. English *board* (1) 'flat (long) piece of wood', (2) 'food' (*room and board*), and (3) 'committee, body of people', presents a formidable problem on purely internal evidence, but if we know *the groaning board* or that Swedish *bord* means 'table' (*smörgåsbord* § 8.6), the metonymic chain is obvious. We see the intersecting indexical joints 'board', 'a board used as a piece of furniture', 'what is put on the board', and 'those who sit around the board for some purpose'. Internal seriation shows that one meaning could be taken as original, the others as conditioned variants. The intersection of the meanings of French *fille* is 'woman' (§ 7.12). This would give a starting point for *jeune fille* 'girl' at least, although not so easily for (*ma*) *fille* 'daughter', both of which are syntactically marked. Semantic derivation would at least suggest that 'prostitute' is not original, and the pronominal combination of *ma fille* seems to be hierarchically deeper than a compound *jeune fille* (see §§ 20.16, 21.17). The intersection 'woman' is not historically accurate, but seriation might have pointed toward the correct origin, Latin *fīlia* 'daughter'.

[20.9]   Translation into the linguists' own language can obscure the issue and strengthen apparent homophony. Thus Greek *tréphō* is usually listed under two meanings, (1) 'rear, bring up, cause to grow' and (2) 'curdle, congeal'. Close observation of the Greek passages shows that these are variants of one meaning: 'to favor the tendencies inherent in the matter, to allow growth'. When you let children have their biological way they will grow up, when you let milk take its course, it will curdle, and so on. Here the intersection of the two meanings gives the simplest solution, and the example shows that the danger of missing legitimate intersections of meanings is about as great as trying to create illegitimate ones. Semantics is notoriously an area where common sense cannot be replaced by mechanical reconstruction steps.

[20.10]   But the principles of Figure 18-1 can serve as guidelines. English *sheep* and Sanskrit *chāga* 'goat' share the protoform *$sk\acute{e}g^{w}o$-. In addition, both languages have reflexes of a word *owi- 'sheep' (*ewe*; Figure 11-6). Because of the latter, the meaning '*sheep' for *$sk\acute{e}g^{w}o$- is unlikely, but could it have been a straight intersection 'small cattle' covering both sheep and goats? We do not know, because some kind of a goat is also possible. Note that we do the same thing here as in phonetic reconstruction: we compare intersections. Since *owi- 'sheep' has a better claim for 'sheep' (the evidence goes well beyond Sanskrit and English), we would have to find something nearby (see §§ 18.10, 18.11). All over the world we have similar problems with domesticated animals. Shifts occur between them very easily, which means that all we need is the context and that *the context need not be elevated into a protomeaning* (see *fille* above). If in American Indian languages the same form can mean either 'cow', 'goat', or 'dog', it does not justify a reconstruction '*domestic animal' in itself. In northern Eurasia the same form can mean either 'dog' or 'reindeer', but a reconstruction '*sledge-pulling animal' would be wrong, because this could have been no more than the characteristic context for metonymic shifts.

[20.11]   Let us assume that a linguist has compiled various reflexes of Proto-Indo-European *pont- with the meaning 'road' in Indic and Balto-Slavic, 'sea' in Greek, 'bridge' in Latin, and 'ford' in Armenian. There seems to be a division between terrestial and aquatic usage. Now, if we take Greek *póntos* as a natural metaphor in the Greek geographic setting, the remaining 'bridge' and 'ford' are stretches of a road negotiating water. All this would now seem to point toward '*road' as the original meaning. But note that while this reconstruction is possible in principle, it has too many iconic and indexical shifts (two *totum pro parte*), and the reconstruction relies heavily on a disjunctive definition (Figure 18-1:2), that is, the sum of variants. What would be a common intersection (Figure 18-1:3) which would not specify whether the route goes above or through the water, or on land? One such meaning is 'passage' in general. Such an intersection is by far more natural than the one devised for the two *stories*, but is it still the same as '*domestic animal' above, that is, various kinds of passages? Yes, it could be the same; the intersection is not enough to prove such a meaning, even if it is an attractive hypothesis. Here we are lucky in that Vedic Sanskrit supplies independent evidence (independent because it was not used in the reconstruction). In Vedic, the word *pánthās* contrasts with various other words for 'road'; it is something unpaved, not used by wheeled vehicles, a stretch between two points implying labor, uncertainty, and danger. And it is not limited to land and water; the birds have theirs as well. Thus a meaning 'passage, crossing' fits the situation quite well. But Iranian, both Ancient and later, turns out to have the meaning 'path', and now one would notice that this occurs also in Indic (and Greek *pátos*). 'Path' is the concrete counterpart of 'passage, crossing' and can be taken as the original meaning, because it seems to be rather usual that 'road' develops into more abstract meanings. English *way* is etymologically the same as *wain/wagon* (see §§ 11.7, 11.8) and meant originally a road passable by carriages, although now it can mean any mode of doing things. Thus it is no wonder that we get the meaning 'sea' in Greek; note OE *hron-rād* (§ 7.8) and Swedish *stråt* 'passage (over water)', and German *Wasserstrasse* 'waterway' (from a loanword meaning 'paved [road]' in Latin) (compare *street*). And finally, note that 'path' as the original meaning is supported by Germanic *path*, which is evidently an Iranian loan, since it does not show Grimm's law.

[20.12]   The principle of constructing derivational trees with the least number of steps is more inconclusive with semantic features than with other linguistic units, although the same procedure holds as for phonetic reconstruction (Figure 18-1). The danger lies in pushing the analysis too far, thus distorting the true historical state of affairs (which may never be available to us anyway). The same danger lurks of course in synchronic analysis, in which linguists are prone to combine forms beyond the actual psychological reality of the naïve speakers (e.g., *bake/batch*; § 18.17). But when the unknowns of history are combined with the present unknowns of semantics, we have to be content with the few methodological approaches and gains we have established so far. One should note particularly the parallelism between phonetic and semantic features (Figures 1-3-1-5) in reconstruction (Figure 18-1), as well as the similarities in their respective relative difficulties.

[20.13 Context and Semantic Reconstruction]   The discussion in this chapter has turned on the notion of context, both linguistic and cultural. Semantic reconstruction consists of making inferences about the most likely semantic changes and using this information to establish earlier stages. (Chapter 7 showed the importance of contexts.) This is why unraveling semantic change consists primarily of spotting contexts that show that two variants are conditioned members of the same unit. The case of Latin *prōclīvis* 'easy' and *prōclīvis* 'difficult' is a very good example of this (§§ 7.3–7.5). The application of all the possible shifts described in Chapter 7 in connection with the total cultural or archaeological evidence provides the means of making inferences about contexts. The inferences can then be processed in connection with family trees and Boolean algebra. One of the prime tasks of semantic reconstruction is to see whether two apparent homophones are in fact polysemous (see § 18.17). Like so many other linguistic notions, homophony and polysemy are relative concepts (like, for example, competence/performance).

[20.14 Word Meanings and Protoculture]   Once the protomeanings for the reconstructed word of a language family have been determined as accurately as possible, we can use these as a window to the protoculture and possibly to its geographic environment. Such cultural reconstruction from vocabulary is very complicated and requires a delicate touch and sensitivity in the interpretation of cumulative evidence. Collaboration between archaeologists and linguists is desirable, because each side tends to apply the findings of the other too simplistically.

For Proto-Indo-European we can reconstruct the numerals from one to ten exactly, and numerous body parts (head, face, ear, eye, mouth, tooth, nose, arm, elbow, hips, arse, penis, foot; blood, heart, liver, milt, lungs, and so on). These words do not tell anything about culture, but they provide sound correspondences, which may be useful in spotting loans in the more technical areas. Reconstructed flora and fauna include barley, birch, beech, aspen, oak, yew, alder; dog, cattle, ox (and yoke), cow, sheep, lamb, wool, horse (and wheel), mare, pig, goat, wolf, bear, fox, mouse, snake, eagle, crane, goose, duck, salmon, otter, beaver, fly, bee, louse, flea, and so on. The kinship terms include words for father, mother, husband, wife, brother, sister, son, daughter, daughter-in-law, mother of husband, father of husband, brother of husband, sister of husband, and wife of husband's brother. There are only a few indications of terms for the blood relations of the wife. A hypothesis that posits a patriarchal joint family, which the wife entered upon marriage, gives an attractive interpretation for this. For wider social organization, it seems likely that there was an elected military and religious leader, a king, for a smallish collection of clans. As for religion, we can reconstruct the personification of natural phenomena (e.g., sky, dawn, fire, and water). As a social ritual there was a reception of guests during which they partook of "fire and water," (i.e., a meal). At such meals heroic poetry was recited, and the art of the poet was apparently looked upon as a craft (that is, he was a carpenter of words). Careful scrutiny of shared vocabulary has led to rather substantial glimpses of Proto-Indo-European culture (e.g., in the areas of law and economy), but here we must be content with these few hints.

[20.15]   This cultural reconstruction is similar to making inferences about cultural diffusion through borrowing (§§ 8.9, 8.10). A borrowed word does not necessarily mean that the corresponding item was also borrowed. A reconstructed meaning does not necessarily mirror the exact reference in the protolanguage; our reconstructed oak may quite well have been a beech, for example. Plant and animal names have been taken as evidence about the possible geographic areas of the protolanguage. Matching such names against the findings of paleobotany and paleozoology might be expected to give the original home automatically. However, it has not turned out to be so easy, because of linguistic indeterminacies and archaeological gaps. The whole doctrine of making cultural inferences from linguistic evidence, known as *linguistic paleontology*, has rarely enjoyed particularly high repute. But in any case it remains true that linguistic paleontology very neatly provides assumptions to be tested.

[20.16 Relative Chronology of Concepts]   The morphological treatment of words incidentally reveals the relative chronology of culture concepts. When the relative chronology of morphological types is looked at from the point of view of meaning, we see, for example, that the older English types occur frequently with cattle, as in *sheep/sheep, ox/oxen, cow/kine,* and *calf/calves* (§ 19.3, and note the zero plurals for game animals). This shows the importance of cattle breeding in the earlier culture. In contrast, the basic electronics terminology does not contain these types; cattle breeding, then, seems to be older than electronics. Of course nonlinguistic evidence confirms this assumption completely.

The overall makeup of the linguistic sign can be used for the same kinds of inference as morphophonemic alternation. Symbolic (unmotivated) unanalyzable forms (e.g., English *bow, arrow, spear, wheel, plough, king,* and *knife*) belong to an older layer than clearly iconic (motivated) formations (e.g., *railroad, battleship, submarine,* and *attorney general*), which are built out of symbolic parts. Place-names can be important in this connection, because the longer an area has been settled by the same speakers the more time has there been for wear, which often makes iconic compounds into symbolic isolates (compare *York,* § 9.8). Thus many Nootka village names are unanalyzable, whereas for less-settled tribes, such as the Paiute and Ojibwa, place-names are readily interpreted. The Hupa call Mt. Shasta (in northern California) *nin-nis-ʾan lak-gai* 'white mountain', whereas the Yana have a single unanalyzable term for it, *waᶜgaluʾ*. The inference is that the Athabaskan-speaking Hupa are newcomers in California compared to the Yana.

Most languages yield readily to such inferences. The fact that Seneca (an Iroquois language) has unanalyzable roots with the meanings 'to be in water' (*-o-*; compare Oneida *kahy-ó-kwas*, § 16.2), 'to fetch water' (*-jɛ-*), and 'depth of water' (**-hnot-*) seems to show prolonged association with water. Similarly, the unanalyzable roots for the snowsnake (**-hwas-*) and hoop and javelin games (**-ket-*) point to the antiquity of these games among the Seneca. The Iroquois religious system has two components, (northern) shamanistic rituals pertaining to a hunting environment and (southern) agricultural ceremonies. Both sections have been regarded as the earlier one. Now, the linguistic evidence unambiguously supports the greater age of the shamanistic complex, because its terminology is comprised mainly of unanalyzable roots, whereas the agricultural area makes use of descriptive compounds.

Among the dangers and uncertainties in this method, only positive evidence counts. That is, the fact that a meaning is represented by regular morphology (*cow/cows* § 19.4) or an iconic compound (*top cow* § 7.6 and *mere-hengest* § 7.8) does not mean that the item cannot be old. Then, borrowings give unanalyzable forms that can be very recent (*squaw* and *wigwam*). And further, a form may change meanings, so that the semantic inference we are making belongs to another notion altogether (for example, *meat* would appear to belong to 'flesh', but actually it once represented 'food', see § 7.13). All this shows once again that for ultimate solutions various principles must be synchronized and fitted with care, and with sensitivity for such puzzles.

[20.17 Conclusion]   Chapter 18 is notably different from 19 and 20, because in phonological reconstruction it is easiest to separate units for analysis. Chapters 19 and 20, on the other hand, form a tight-knit unit in which morphology, syntax, and semantics are inextricably interrelated. Because grammatical and syntactic reconstruction requires such an enormous amount of background information on the languages used, as well as long practice, only brief hints could be supplied in this introduction. Even so, the essential guidelines have been described, and if the student wants to continue in this particular area, he has to develop the necessary ability for "scientifically trained fantasy" himself, without which syntactic and semantic reconstruction is a mere game on paper.

REFERENCES

General: Benveniste 1954; **20.1** Hoenigswald 1960a; **20.5** Lehmann 1958, Maher 1965, 1977; **20.8-20.11** Benveniste 1954; **20.13** Maher 1977; **20.14** Schrader 1883, Sapir 1912, Krahe 1970, Thieme 1953 and in Sebeok (ed.) 1963f. vol. 11, Dressler 1965, Scherer (ed.) 1968, R. Schmitt 1967, Benveniste 1969, Cardona et al. (eds.) 1970, Friedrich 1970; **20.15** Tovar 1954, Swadesh 1959; **20.16** Sapir 1916, Chafe 1964. (See p. 388)

PART V

CONCLUSION:
LINGUISTICS AS PART
OF ANTHROPOLOGY

CHAPTER 21

CHANGE AND RECONSTRUCTION
IN CULTURE AND LINGUISTICS

The study of (genetic) linguistics leads naturally to anthropology. Parallels are drawn between the two with regard to change and reconstruction.

[21.1 Summary]   The preceding parts have concentrated on linguistic change and reconstruction, that is, genetic linguistics. Genetic linguistics was not considered in isolation, however; its relation to synchronic linguistics has been duly considered throughout. In fact, synchronic linguistics alone is not sufficient background for treating change, since cultural and historical information is often indispensable for reaching the proper understanding of change. Language does not exist in a vacuum; it is used in concrete cultural and historical circumstances. Anthropologists and other social scientists may feel that culture has been under-emphasized. If this is true there is no harm done; they already know this aspect of the field and can add the necessary linguistic emphasis here. If linguists also were to join in the complaint, the matter would be rather serious. Such a complaint seems unlikely, however; linguistics has lately concentrated heavily on language-internal factors of change, whereas this treatment has paid attention to the dangers and inadequacies of such a narrow conception of linguistic change. Hence this book attempts not only to give a balanced view of genetic linguistics in itself but also of genetic linguistics as tailored for the needs of the 1970s. One of the timely theses is that linguistics is too important to be left to linguists alone, which is one more reason an introduction should avoid the school feuds and idiosyncratic terminologies of the different camps. Rather than issuing propaganda for the flashy notations of particular schools, the book presents what must be known and accounted for no matter what notation or theoretical framework the student will ultimately adopt. Notation alone is no insight, and to minimize notational dazzle a noncommittal position has been adopted for the book, the purpose of which is to explain genetic linguistics rather than to proselytize for any linguistic school. If a particular theory cannot handle the facts presented, it is immediate evidence for the inadequacy of the theory.

[21.2 Linguistics and the Study of Man]   Both psychology and anthropology have recognized linguistics as a methodological model and as the most precise of these particular sciences. The sociologists acknowledge the "cruel truth" that awareness of language can do more for them than sociology can do for

377

linguistic studies. The issue is not that simple, however, since it is exactly sociological information that is crucial in understanding linguistic change (Chapter 9). Language is necessary for sociologists and society for linguists; the truth of course is that the best results for all social sciences are secured by well-planned cooperation. Thus one must pay equal attention both to the autonomy and to the integration of the social sciences. Linguistics has secured a central position in these interdisciplinary studies, largely because of its unusually regular self-contained patterning and because of its central role in the totality of culture (although the former has led to the dangerous tendency of looking only into language-internal facts in studying change). Language is a constituent of culture and functions as a substructure. Therefore it iₒ easier to abstract linguistics from the remainder of culture and define it separately than vice versa. One does not usually realize that even mathematics is firmly rooted in ordinary language, since it is verbal activity presupposing language. Money and economics can also be viewed as a language, because the circulation of money is one kind of sending messages. This is part of wider communication (for example, social intercourse), and in all these areas linguistic models are useful. Because social life is not conceivable without the existence of communicative signs, semiotics is part of sociology. Linguistics is the study of verbal messages, which makes linguistics a small hierarchical part of sociology after all. And of course the wider end of semiotics leads into biology and neural systems (Chapter 22).

[21.3 Culture and Biology]   Man is an end point in a biological line of evolution; with the stress on his animal nature he is a mere hairless ape. Far more attention has been given to the obvious fact that man is different from other forms of life: he is the language animal, the cultural animal, the tool-making animal, the human animal, the political animal, or the divine animal. None of these components should be forgotten; man is both an animal and a carrier of culture. Language is a property of the human species, but so is culture. The psychic unity of mankind must also have a biological foundation. Culture did not "triumph" over biology, resulting in a superorganic extension of the organic foundation. Neither of these is mutually exclusive or independent. Culture is an aspect of man's biological difference from other species. It depends on an organ, the brain. It is a result of natural selection, exactly like the "social systems" found in other species. The tool-making animal needed mind to survive, and language and culture gave the perfect combination for that. The brain is as much a consequence as a cause of culture, and culture is both the producer and the product of human nature. Culture needed better and better brains, and better brains could expand culture. Behavior evolved with the structure; thus one cannot separate an organic from a superorganic. Man seems to have a species-specific basic grammar and a specific repertoire of behavior (a grammar of behavior), which both have biological limits, although there is no end to fantasy. Our genes determine our ability to learn a language and a culture (or languages and cultures), but they do not determine just what is said or acted. Universal processes do not necessarily produce uniform results. The genes may quite well contain the universal laws of culture as well and not just a naked capacity. Culture is a refined replacement of instincts; in fact, in many ways it becomes instinct by constant drilling of the young. Like instinct, it is unconscious and automatic to such a great degree that it does not require thought for its operation; certain stimuli automatically produce the "correct" response. Culture thus has all the benefits of instincts without their high cost of rigidity. Culture habits can be changed within a generation, if changes in the environment warrant new adaptation; there is no need to wait thousands of years for natural selection to do the same. There are actually cases where societies have sat down and reorganized cultures. In this sense cultural behavior is a means of biological adaptation and serves biological needs. Culture is an organ of change to keep the human species "unchanged", that is, alive, to put it bluntly (§§ 1.17, 22.6). Of course, this means that natural selection is still operative, but guided by culture.

CHANGE

[21.4 Synchrony and Diachrony]   Culture can be interpreted synchronically and diachronically. Like language, every culture is a result of historical development, whether it is studied as a functional system of composite parts (§ 22.6), or atomistically as a description of ethnographic facts. Before studying change one must of course identify the social and cultural system. The problem is that cultural facts are not easily broken up and given precise taxonomies, not to speak of the much more difficult task of structural analysis. In structural comparison linguistics has been an appropriate model for culture, because in it culture is taken as a system of communication (the silent language, grammar of behavior, body language, and so on). Unfortunately, this is not the place to go into these problems. Suffice it to give one parallel between culture and language. Let us take an example from clothing (fashion often exemplifies cultural change in introductions to anthropology). If one imitates the way someone else dresses, which is a common occurrence, we have a parallel to spelling spelling (§§ 2.6, 2.15). When there is a need to use a certain type of clothing, as for diving or space exploration, we have a parallel to pronunciation spelling, spelling after the stark need (§ 2.16). And finally, spelling pronunciation is equivalent to the consequence of wearing false breasts, padded shoulders, and so on; outsiders take these at face value, which of course is the characteristic prelude to spelling pronunciation. Parallels need not be exact to give important insights both ways, and they may lead to new discoveries (see § 9.16).

[21.5 Study, Traces, and Processes of Change]   The cultural and social evolutionists believe that they have been successful in establishing unilinear schemes of social evolution, parallel to the development of man from infant to adult. A scale of evolution from primitive to sophisticated with three basic categories (savagery, barbarism, and civilization) was very popular in the nineteenth century. Every society was supposed to have risen through the same hierarchy (unless it was still standing on the lowest rung). Such typological schemes are untenable today as are so many other earlier ones (Chapter 16, § 21.11). But the essence of such notions is salvaged by neo-evolutionism, which makes use of a typology better suited to the enormously complex phenomena.

[21.6]   Still, change is always characteristic of man's life in organized communities. It is essential to orderly persistence, and not only to revolutions (extremely abrupt discontinuous changes). Changes may pile up and lead to elaboration and specialization, or innovations may simplify the structure. This is parallel to rule addition and rule loss through additions. Culture may also be reinterpreted. Changes may be brought about through internal factors (innovations), or external (e.g., conquest); environment, borrowing, and spontaneous mutation are basic. It is very rare to have a single cause, and the identification of causes is difficult because full experimentation is not possible. The factors are often intricately interwoven. The implications of the following short and unusually straightforward example should be self-explanatory. Pueblo life in San Ildefonso, New Mexico, was deteriorating just before World War I. An anthropologist chose the pottery of the best craftswoman for promotion in the outside world. Once by accident (see § 7.3) two pots turned black instead of red. Such a mutation would have been fatal (self-eliminating) in the local community, but it found an ecological niche in the outside society, because the customers were not bound by tradition in this area (note the maxim that it is difficult to be a prophet in one's own country; see § 2.9). The firing of black pots was then accepted by other potters as well. The acceptance of the black pots was an accident, too, made possible by cultural contact. The "benefits" of the innovation remained, of course, with the home economy as well.

[21.7]   Human matter cannot be presumed to have a neutral attitude toward change. Social action is always purposive, and the direction of change may well reflect the desired direction of change. Some anthropologists operate with the notion of 'strain toward consistency', which implies that habits that do not fit together get eliminated. This has not found general acceptance, although one does speak of basic orientations in culture and themes in their ideologies (compare §§ 9.13, 9.16, 22.6). (Also Chapter 23)

[21.8]   When the fit between cultural norms or suppositions and actual behavior (i.e., the deep structure and the surface structure) becomes rather loose, one can expect restructuring toward the actual behavior, for example, "bringing laws up to date." This is of course another vague parallel, but it is instructive in that here also the change creeps into the underlying structure from the surface (compare § 9.16).

[21.9 The Interrelation Between Culture and Language Change]   To understand linguistic change we must see it as part of cultural change. Linguistic change is sociolinguistic change, as has been seen. Since culture generally does not lend itself to the precise segmentation and comparison necessary to establish genetic relations, linguistics as the oldest cultural science can help. No cultural aspect can be studied without reference to the linguistic signs used for it. Examples show also that linguistic change tends to be accelerated when the culture of the speakers undergoes rapid changes; for example, the Norman conquest of England brought in loanwords, new spelling, and it was at this time that loss of grammatical endings was most rapid (in the literary tradition at least). All this is summed up as the transition from Old to Middle English. When the culture of a people is relatively static or slow to change, linguistic change tends to slow down also. An often cited example of this is Lithuanian, whose speakers led the same kind of life for millennia. Certainly such correlation is not random, even if individual cases might not seem to comply.

[21.10]   It has been observed that the nomadic way of life often corresponds with lack of great dialectal variation, even when the area occupied by such speakers is large. Thus, roughly, the European societies have undergone change through various forms of states, organized religions, and the industrial revolution; the Indo-European languages do seem to have changed more rapidly than, say, the Turkic ones. Dialectal stratification is the basis of internal change, and correlates with social evolution as well. The Paleolithic hunting and gathering societies had low population density, no fixed abodes, and autonomy of the social units. There was no specialization of labor and no stratification in society, and consequently no social or prestige dialects, but equality of single ones. There were different dialects, of course, but they were all taken as equal, as is still true in the Paleolithic way of life. Father, mother, children, aunts, uncles can all speak different dialects. People branch into different tribes and get together occasionally for such matters as the arrangement of new marriages. With the Neolithic economy of planned food production, population increased; the social unit remained about the same size, but it was still rather mobile because of the slash-and-burn method of agriculture. Surplus people branched off to found new settlements. The family-tree model is appropriate here. But branching off often meant marriage in another community, and thus the wave theory is also operative. The Neolithic social unit remained self-sufficient and without prestige dialects until urban revolution produced a stratified society and prestige dialects, and apparently much faster change in language. Note that prestige is one factor in addition to the Paleo- and Neolithic variations along the scales of sex and age. Ecological influence finds its way into the grammar; for example, hunters occasionally have to stay away from their families, which encourages development of hunting tabus and other sex-linked linguistic features.

[21.11]   Linguists have noticed that the Malayo-Polynesian languages have apparently changed much less than the Indo-European ones during the same time (e.g., the last five millennia). And in fact we are once again dealing with small Paleo- ~ Neolithic communities without much social stratification.

It seems thus quite likely that socioeconomic factors correlate with change (see Müller, § 16.3). In the Soviet Union, N. Y. Marr took this hypothesis too far when he correlated language with the Marxist doctrine of social evolution through the following stages: primitive horde, slave-holding, feudal, capitalist, socialist, and communist (see § 21.5). Of course Russian did not change with the revolution, except for new vocabulary.

[21.12]   If culture can influence language, especially in its vocabulary, then maybe language can influence culture as well. What is meant is not the success of certain orators or demagogues in influencing the course of history, but the possibility that the very structure of language (and not what is said) has an influence. The so-called *Sapir-Whorf hypothesis* states that language *is* culture; it mediates action; culture is stated in language; action is described in language. According to this conception language becomes a molder of thoughts, cultures, and philosophies. Language is supposed to direct our perception, so that speakers of different languages experience the world differently. Whorf highlighted his arguments by speculating on the differences that Aristotle's philosophy would have shown if he had been a Hopi Indian, since the relations expressed in Hopi are quite different from those in the standard average European languages. There is no agreement as to how far the hypothesis is valid.

[21.13 Diffusion and Duplication of Culture Elements]   Cultural diffusion shows many parallels to linguistic borrowing, and in fact the latter is often a consequence of the former. Those who are most unhappy with their own culture will accept new things more easily. Other things being equal, tangible objects (tools, utensils, and ornaments) are borrowed more easily than abstract notions (see § 8.2). The process of acculturation shows the same phases as borrowing: (1) the initial acceptance of the cultural element, (2) its dissemination to other members of the society, and (3) the modifications by which it is finally embedded to the preexisting culture matrix. Cultures easily tolerate duplication of function, at least temporarily, whether this is due to borrowing or invention. Such duplication is an essential accompaniment of culture change, which is true of linguistic change as well. The old and new forms exist side by side until one wins out or both differentiate into different domains. The car replaced the horse only gradually, and there remain environments for the latter only; earlier, the railroad had interfered with the horse. Now each mode of locomotion has its own characteristic environment. Relics are pushed into secondary functions (see § 5.15): horse coaches are still used for ceremonial purposes by the Queen of England, and horseback riding is now mainly a sport, as are hunting, skiing, archery, and even nudism. When the Kwakiutl borrowed the steel knife, stone knives were preserved in the salmon-cutting ritual. Candles have similar ritualistic overtones; Roman numerals still occur in conventional uses like chapter headings; and the Old English (black letter) script may find its way into certain books of poetry, wedding invitations, and so on. Many pagan customs found a place in the Christian structure, such as the traditions associated with Christmas and Easter to a large degree. In a vanishing bilingual situation the obsolescent language has considerable stylistic value: nostalgic, comic, or the like (for the parallels in language see especially §§ 5.15, 7.9, 8.8). A sound change produces often mere "decor," as in the umlaut in *mȳs-i, before it is made grammatical use of, as in mȳs (§§ 4.5, 5.21). Similarly, many technological and scientific inventions have been toys before becoming part of utilitarian systems, for example, electricity and rockets (compare § 9.16).

RECONSTRUCTION

[21.14 The Comparative Method in Anthropology] Culture is extensively indexical with respect to man's biological needs; that is, it is part of man (§ 21.3), and thus actual reconstruction has no solid basis. There is nothing like the comparative method in linguistics, which gives good approximations of earlier *forms* at least, or like the actual skeletons of paleontology. Culture everywhere serves the realities of the human condition: two-handedness, biological aging, the male–female dichotomy, the long period of infants' helplessness, and so on. Consequently the comparative method in anthropology is quite different from that in linguistics (Chapter 11). It is directed toward ferreting out cultural universals, toward distinguishing those functions of man that are inborn from those that are acquired. The procedure is known as cross-cultural comparison; it is syncritical comparison that lines up an intersection from all cultures (see §§ 18.8–18.11, 20.7–20.12). This intersection shows the nature of human nature, the regularities within man; these are either universal truths or at least statistical probabilities. But once statistical probabilities are drawn in, the danger of loose interpretation arises, and indeed features occurring in less than half of the world's cultures have been taken as universal, which is highly doubtful.

Cross-cultural comparison is the basis for anthropologists' generalizations about culturally regulated human behavior. For example, comparison of religious behavior among various cultural groups illuminates the functions of religion as a whole, which are difficult to isolate by studying a single society. Cross-cultural comparison itself is not explanation, and it should not be taken as a disguised form of scientific experiment leading to explanation. It is indispensable for the exposition of the cultural argument. But even if it does not prove anything, it gives deep insight into the nature of culture. Note that the comparative method in linguistics also exposes certain possibilities without giving final answers, because the linguist has to postedit the results of the method.

[21.15 The Historical Method] Since the common core of culture is universal, the attention is drawn to contrasts rather than similarities. This is true in linguistics as well. The study of contrasts gives us functional alternatives; that is, what is the range of possible structures capable of fulfilling a given (universal) function? And the study of individual cases leads to the reconstruction of the long-term cultural history of a society. This is the so-called historical method, which concentrates on well-defined small geographical areas. The method implies a detailed study of customs in relation to the total culture and their relation to, and distribution among, the neighboring tribes. The method is thus culture-internal with glimpses into neighboring geography. It is dialect geography with cultural items. The comparative method studies the results of historical growth, the historical method the processes of growth. The two are complementary and essential for understanding societies and their institutions.

[21.16 Seriation and Stratigraphy]   The historical method is of course seriation and stratigraphy. *Cultural seriation* is based on the often-contested assumption that human development has normally proceeded from simple to complex. Thus simpler forms of a cultural element are often interpreted as of greater age than the complex ones. The Nootka totem pole consisting of a single carved figure is thus older than the more elaborate poles of the Haida and Tsimshian, with superimposed figures (see § 22.8). The unorganized shamanistic practices of the Eastern Cree and some other Algonkian tribes may well represent an older stratum of religion than the more elaborate medicine lodge of the Ojibwa and Menomini (see § 20.16). The gradient need not be from simple to elaborate, but any other logical sequence; for example, realistic picture signs might develop into geometric designs (see § 1.12). Here the scale is from the logically prior to the logically secondary. *Typological seriation* is particularly clear in (archaeological) artifacts, where mere inspection may give the direction of development. We are all familiar with series depicting how a box-like automobile becomes more and more streamlined every year. Pots and axes may show the same development and thus provide relative footholds for dating.

[21.17]   Another kind of seriation is *cultural association*. Elements and complexes of culture are always interconnected. Some complexes presuppose others, and thus one can make inferences about relative chronology. The art of dressing skins among the Plains Indians is older than making buffalo-skin tepees. The widespread Eskimo design in bone or ivory of a dot and a circle or concentric circles is later than the drill with which these designs must be made. Borrowing may of course disturb our associative inferences very badly, exactly as in comparative linguistics. Older elements can be embedded into newer complexes (or vice versa), for example, superstitions and pagan rituals in Christianity, or whaling adventures among Nootka family legends. The firmer the association between two elements, the older the connection; or the more frequently an element is associated with others, the older it is. For example, Christianity enters into more cultural areas than do trains. Similarly, loanwords fall into different hierarchical levels in respect to the grammatical rules to which they are subject (see §§ 10.16, 10.17, 19.4).

[21.18]   Stratigraphy enters the *age-and-area hypothesis*. The notion of the culture area is a handy means of organizing vast amounts of data on maps.

CHANGE AND RECONSTRUCTION IN CULTURE AND LINGUISTICS 385

Thus for food areas in North America we get caribou, buffalo, salmon, wild seeds, Eastern maize, and intensive agriculture. Each element has its chracteristic area. There is, of course, some overlapping at the peripheries. With a sufficient number of diagnostic elements culture areas can be defined as intersections of the elements. It is assumed that the culture center is the place for superior productivity, and when the center mantains itself for some time it tends to radiate culture content into surrounding zones. Relative age can now be posited as in dialect geography (see §§ 14.5–14.7, 17.10, 21.21f.).

[21.19] A theory related to the age-and-area hypothesis is the *Kulturkreis-lehre* (doctrine of culture circles). This is the study of cultural similarities which are apparently not determined by the material element or institution. Granted that most people have houses of some kind, it is not automatically given that they should be round or rectangular, have two doors and five windows, display certain decorations in the eaves, and so on. If there is matching in these arbitrary accompaniments, historical connection is assumed and the qualitative criterion has been successful. But still the houses of two peoples might accidentally have the same qualitative features. What excludes chance is the quantitative piling up of qualitative agreements in various parts of culture (e.g., building, weapons, religion, and music). This method comes close to the comparative method in linguistics, because it is based on signs (culture elements) which contain arbitrary ingredients, and the arbitrary part can of course point more readily to genetic relation, as it does in language. But there is a wide distance between the solid comparative method and the much less definite *Kulturkreislehre*. If borrowing can be ruled out, there is, however, a certain parallelism between culture area, diffusion (i.e., borrowing), and linguistic areal classification (dialect geography) versus Kulturkreis, inheritance (i.e., migration), and linguistic genetic classification.

[21.20 Living Paradigms in Reconstruction] One requirement of linguistic reconstruction is that typological or universal facts (known from present-day languages) cannot be violated. When the methods give us a few footholds (e.g., in the form of relational phonemes), we can fill out the rest from our experience with modern languages (e.g., phonetic reconstruction) (see §§ 16.8, 18.7). Archaeology and history face the same situation. Excavation yields the mere (relational) house posts, and one has to infer the missing parts from the ground plan and other possible debris. Material objects are often all one has to make inferences about the rest of culture. We have already seen how this is possible with linguistic signs (§ 20.13). One can grasp the concept of truths like the Pythagorean theorem or the comparative method, one can explain realities like thunder and lightning, but one must *understand* historical deeds and movements, personalities, and works of art. Conception, explanation, and understanding are important factors in historical study, but the last one is a crucial "step into the irrational." To understand means to be able to set oneself into the assumed circumstances and to see the (mental) relations of things. "To understand oneself one must understand others, and to understand others, one must look into oneself" is Schiller's variant of the principle of syncritical comparison in ethnology. We study history in order to make the present understandable through the past, but the past would be inaccessible to us, if we could not use our own experience to interpret the traces of past life and societies. In other words, synchrony, diachrony, and syncrisis are intimately connected, as in linguistics (see Figure 1-7). (§23.1)

[21.21]   Thus, using the *living paradigms* offered by the Eskimos or the Papuans, anthropologists can supply rather realistic detail for the life of the Ice Age mammoth hunters of northern Europe, or of the Neolithic peasants penetrating into the European virgin forests. The folklore of modern gathering communities may give clues to earlier rituals. The way such communities make and use tools brings life to archaeological finds. As in linguistics, all theories must be checked against "living paradigms." And without such present-day examples much would remain incomprehensible. The psychic unity of mankind serves as a typological check on reconstruction, even if alone it does not carry historical meaning other than species specification in relation to other primates.

[21.22 Migration Theory]   Linguistic subgrouping and the geographical distribution of the languages yield information on the direction of population movements as well as on time depth. There are just two principles of making inferences about time past. Either great differences, or wide geographical spread between languages requires time. We have already seen how place-names may be worn beyond analyzability (§ 20.15), which also indicates passage of time. Inferences about migration rest on two postulates: (1) The area of origin of related languages is contiguous, and (2) the probabilities of different reconstructed migrations are in an inverse relation to the number of reconstructed language movements that each requires. The first assumption of course gives a reason to look for a unified home in the case of discontinuous languages rather than taking the existing distribution as the original one. We are working with probabilities only, because islands like Sardinia may quite well make the protolanguage discontinuous. The postulate of least moves is of course the general principle of simplicity we have seen in rule writing and other derivation schemes (e.g., subgrouping and drawing family trees). Migration theory uses these family trees once more for population movements. It is much more likely that a node in a tree "moved" once rather than many times; for example, it is more probable that the modern Indic languages differentiated in India after the speakers of one protolanguage came there once (which may have taken centuries or more), rather than that each language came with its own migration (see § 15.2). We choose the one move necessitated by the protolanguage against a dozen or more.

[21.23]   Without going into a rigorous step-by-step demonstration of the method implied by the migration theory, let us refer to one more diagnostic criterion. The area where the related languages are mosi differentiated is the original area of the protolanguage. Sapir's metaphor of the "center of gravity" of a language family (borrowed from botany) is helpful in understanding the method. Through Blackfoot, Arapaho, and Cheyenne, the Algonkian family shows great diversity in the West compared to the rather unified Central and Eastern languages around the Great Lakes and on the Atlantic; whatever the exact relation of Wiyot and Yurok (in California) is to Algonkian, they certainly agree by showing even greater diversity. An attractive inference is that this language situation shows a west–east movement of the peoples. Similarly, the Athabaskan languages show deep boundaries in the North (with Haida and Tlingit as well), against the greater homogeneity on the Pacific and in the Southwest. The migrations must have gone from north to south. The greatest diversity of Eskimo-Aleut in Alaska, compared to Canada and Greenland, points to migration toward the East. English is a good test case. Dialectal differences are far greater in England and Scotland than in North America, South Africa, or Australia. Thus one would infer that the original home is England as compared with the other areas, and we know this to be true.

[21.24]   Of course history can play tricks on us, and this is why one has to remember that the method yields probabilities only. But these are very valuable for ethnology when used together with other nonlinguistic evidence. Modern mobility and immigration interferes with the method, but in such cases we generally have documentation to go by. When one finds the Russian colony in California, one would presumably guess that it came from Russia, or from Russian Alaska. But simplest derivations are not necessarily always right historically. The colony is known to have moved first to China, from there to Brazil, and then to California. Unless loanwords record such routes (see Figure 8-4), mere migration theory is powerless. Every historical method has its weaknesses, of course.

[21.25 Conclusion]   The few basic characteristics presented in this chapter cannot do justice to the enormous complexity of the factors involved. It is wrong to expect simple answers. Let us conclude with a quotation of Sapir: "It is a comfortable procedure to attach oneself unreservedly or primarily to a single mode of historical inference and wilfully to neglect all others as of little moment, but the clean-cut constructions of the doctrinaire never coincide with the actualities of history" (1916). Sapir identified a malady that was to plague historical linguistics fifty years later.

REFERENCES

General: Kroeber 1935, 1944, (ed.) 1953, 1963ac, Rice (ed.) 1931, Carroll 1953, Beals and Hoijer 1965, Pike 1967, Jakobson 1969, Hallowell 1956, Henle (ed.) 1965, Hoijer (ed.) 1954, *Current Trends in Linguistics* vol. 12 (Sebeok ed.), Barnett 1983; see also the selections in the Bobbs-Merrill Reprint Series in Social

Sciences; **21.2** Voegelin and Harris 1947, White (ed.) 1956, E. Hall 1959, Fast 1970, Birdwhistell 1970, Bouissac 1970; **21.3** Lenneberg 1960, L.A. White 1959, Steiner 1969, Wescott 1969, Fox 1970, Woolfson 1970; **21.4** Kroeber 1919, L.A. White 1945; **21.5** L.A. White 1945, Eisenstadt 1968, W. Moore 1968, Service 1968, E. Vogt 1968; **21.6** E. Hall 1959; **21.7-21.8** Oliver 1964; **21.9** Hoijer 1948, Holmberg 1954; **21.10** W. Miller 1967, Maher 1970b; **21.12** Whorf 1956, Hörmann 1970, Shands 1970; **21.14-21.15** Irving 1949, Eggan 1954, Leach 1968; **21.16** Paor 1967, Deetz 1967, Sapir 1916, Romney 1957; **21.17** Sapir 1916; **21.18** Ehrich and Henderson 1968; **21.19** W. Schmidt 1939, Greenberg 1957; **21.20-21.21** Childe 1951; **21.22-21.23** Sapir 1916, Dyen 1956, Romney 1957, Diebold 1960, Rouse 1986.

Reconstructing semantics and protoculture (Chapter 20; see also p. 374): Gamkrelidze and Ivanov 1984 (see also *Journal of Indo-European Studies* 13:1-2 [1985]), Dyen see Hockett 1985, Diebold 1985, particularly Diebold, Lehmann, both in Skomal and Polomé (eds.) 1987, Meid (ed.) 1987; *Studien zur Ethnogenese.* Rheinisch-Westfälische Akademie der Wissenschaften, Abhandlungen 72. Opladen, Westfälischer Verlag 1985.

CHAPTER 22

GENETIC LINGUISTICS AND BIOLOGICAL GENETICS

A comparison is made between the phenomena of language and biology from the point of view of change and reconstruction. Existence is change.

[22.1 The Genetic Code and Language]   One of the recent striking findings of molecular biology is the structure of the genetic code, which revolves around compounds known as DNA. These are nucleic acids whose immense molecules are arranged in double helices. When the strings separate, each helix attracts the missing part of the original double helix, thus providing exact copies of the original. A DNA molecule must contain all the information for all the details of the future plant or animal. How this staggering requirement is met is not known. DNA is built out of four nucleotides (A, G, T, C), and this gives a four-letter alphabet of life, combined according to the "grammar of life," as yet undiscovered. (Curiously, this matches the number of mythical cardinal humors: blood, phlegm, choler, and melancholy.) The order of the letters is significant, as well as certain bracketing, that is, commas or "spaces." A DNA code word, a *codon*, consists of three letters. The message in DNA is taken up by another nucleic acid molecule, RNA, and this single-stranded messenger takes it into the protoplasm, where the transfer RNA each bring their own amino acids, which form proteins according to the message in the first RNA. In spite of the attractive chemistry, all this is pure witchcraft, that is, beyond our understanding. How does DNA regulate growth and specialization of cells of the same genetic inheritance? How does it determine a bird's song? We do not know. But one parallel to language is obvious: we have a deep structure, DNA, and rules, RNA, that take the message to an ultimate surface structure. And, indeed, geneticists have freely used linguistic terminology; S. K. Šaumjan in Russia uses the biological terms genotype and phenotype as the counterparts of deep and surface structure. DNA is subject to mutations, the equivalent of deletion and metathesis. An alphabetic unit can also produce a different result in different positions of the genetic message, that is, contextual meaning. Now it seems that there is one crucial difference compared with language: the message goes one way only, from DNA to RNA, which would be parallel to a grammar for a speaker only. Such grammars have indeed been popular in linguistics around the late 1960s. But it now seems certain that certain cancer-producing viruses, consisting of only RNA and a protein sheath, may make their own DNA once they invade a host cell. This message from the RNA stays permanently in the host cell, and cancer is passed on during cell division. This evidence makes the DNA–RNA relations more similar to language, where the machinery is habitually used both ways (Figure 1-1). Note also the curious facts of regeneration. When the posterior half of a planarian develops a new front part, it will include the brains as well. The rear end develops its own future control mechanism (§ 5.7).

[22.2]   The parallels are startling, though not perfect. One could find more; for example, is a grammar of rules only, with no units, a "virus" or a "cancerous grammar"? A more important question is this: Does genetics support the view that deep structure is after all the place for determining genetic relationship of languages? (§ 16.10). The answer is apparently no, because note that the alphabetic compartments are reversed in language and the genetic code. The chemical alphabet occurs in the deep structure, the acoustic one in language in the surface structure. In genetics the "arbitrariness" lies in the fact that a particular combination of the nucleotides is connected with a particular meaning (e.g., man, cat, worm, and so on). Similarity in DNA cannot be random; it means closer historical connection. Since all forms of life are related, the matter is one of subgrouping, and it works out as expected; for example, the primates have closely related DNA as well as similar physical shape, and so on down the hierarchy. It would seem that DNA parallels support the position presented in the preceding chapters exactly. Of course such parallels do not necessarily have any validity whatsoever. But they are so striking that one can raise the question whether the isomorphism between genetic and verbal codes results from a mere convergence of similar needs, or whether the verbal code was imposed directly on the molecular structural principles (see § 21.3). Language is in part at least a molecular endowment of man, and both the genetic code and language are anticipatory models of the future (see § 1.16).

[22.3]   A biologist and a linguist, C. D. Darlington and L. F. Brosnahan, have tried to show that genetic factors do, in fact, interfere with the sounds of a language. A preference for particular sounds is supposed to depend on a statistically predominant combination of genes in a mating group. Since gene combinations in population recombine constantly, genetic drift would now explain sound shift as well. The authors have plotted various genes and sounds of Europe and claim to be able to show more than chance correlation between them. Thus the distribution of the O-type blood gene at a frequency of 60 per cent or more in Europe covers roughly the same area as the existence of the dental fricative. The distribution of this spirant, however, includes both past and present spread, and there are other flexibilities as well. So far such a theory of genetic dominance as deciding the preference for certain sounds has not found acceptance, either in biology or in linguistics.

CHANGE

[22.4 Direction and Mechanism of Change]   According to the second law of thermodynamics, all natural (chemical and physical) processes tend to proceed toward increased entropy, that is, greater chaos. In other words, they tend to run down. Organic matter (life) is sharply the reverse, because in it order tends to increase. The general trend of biological evolution is toward organisms of greater efficiency as a whole, and this is achieved by more and more complex synorganization and interdependence of parts. Cells can either be independent units or collaborate to complex ends. This is in a way a parallel to language, where various components and units can be studied in isolation, but where ultimately everything is combined for reaching one end, that of providing a flexible means for communication. Language and biology share complicated synorganization in their systems. Life, like language, is complex, self-reproducing, and self-varying matter, and both inherently reside in the same structure and imply each other. Mutation is an accidental affair; it takes place in all directions, but it provides the raw material for evolution. Natural selection converts accident into apparent design and determines its direction. Those mutations that improve the fit of the organism to its environment usually make the organism more fecund and favored (selected) for survival; others will be ultimately rejected. New and old forms can exist side by side for a long time, if the mutation is not fatal outright; or, with isolation, both can survive in different environments. Evolution has also been vexed by the problem of whether change comes from within or from without. Gene mutations do come from within, but the future of such changes is mediated by natural selection. Adaptation to the environment is the main causative agent of organic evolution. In this sense, evolutionary changes come from the environment, that is, interaction between inheritance and environment. No organism is without a genotype (deep structure), and no genotype can exist outside an environment, that is, a continuum of space and time.

[22.5]   The parallels to the above in linguistic change are obvious. In the previous chapters we have seen that linguistic change is a complex phenomenon in which both internal and external causes must be recognized. In environmental factors the social ones are the most important, and social factors are of course further anchored in a particular society, a particular age, and a particular historical event. Social factors play a role in human evolution as well, because various incest tabus and marriage systems either prohibit or encourage exchange of genes between particular individuals. A linguistic innovation is either accepted or rejected by the speakers, or both can be preserved in different environments, for example, *once/one's, mead/meadow, my/mine, metal/mettle* etc. (§§ 5.7–5.9, 7.9). Also linguistic change is subject to *choice*, a kind of Darwinian selection. The speakers can choose to change or not to change, and this is clearest in situations with social motivation. One can sometimes choose one's group membership and linguistic solidarity. The universality of change (§ 9.1) makes no change very baffling indeed, and language does not stay put as long as biology can (for example the ant has remained practically the same for some fifty million years). Choice is still a force that governs both change and no change, and in language of course there may be no change in grammar even if there is in phonology. But over rather short stretches (some one hundred years or so) language always changes somehow. However, in language there does not seem to be any improvement or progress in organization; that is, language retains its basic structure (Figures 1-1, 1-2). There is an efficiency factor, however, in that areas vital for the community will be matched by language. The language of the Aymara is adapted to the importance of the potato, that of the Arabs to the camel, and that of the Eskimos to snow. Thus a language will increase its efficiency for any particular cultural situation by developing new vocabulary or syntactic patterns, without violating the universal laws of language design. The implications of this are explicit in the cultural-relativistic slogan that every language is as good as any other for the society that uses it; that is, the Aymara have a rich vocabulary for potatoes, and the Western languages for airplane screws and nuts. The same seems to be true of organisms as well: they all are well fitted for the environments they live in. Of course, languages can borrow from each other to meet specific needs; organisms cannot: a bird cannot borrow the burrowing and eating habits of a worm. Only man has been successful in this; he has borrowed underwater travel from the fish (submarines), armor from the rhinoceros (tanks), flying from the birds (airplanes), and so on. Ultimately, all this is possible only through language.

[22.6 Teleology, Mentalism, and Function]   Even if the genetic code and the mechanism of natural selection explain one side of biological evolution, it is not enough for understanding life, or the mind. No notion of awareness of existence can be extended from physics or chemistry into biology; a non-mechanistic factor must be involved, and most biologists agree on this point. Parapsychology, the study of extrasensory perception and psychokinesis, is an established fact, although still a disquieting one for many scientists (who believe that they have open minds). Its statistical proofs are impeccable. On the other hand, statistics shows unequivocally that man cannot exist. Mere evolutionary accidents would never have produced man. Biologists have had to return to Aristotle's final causes, which are goal-directed, purposive, and self-regulating. It is not enough to ask how or for what reason; rather, it is legitimate to ask for what purpose (§ 9.1). It is the nature of the organism to be oriented toward the change that occurs. The earlier monistic views based either on matter or on mind alone are inadequate. This has changed into a both–and attitude and the beginnings of psychosomatic biology.

Language is also a teleological or goal-directed system. It maintains a certain dynamic equilibrium for functioning through time, providing a vehicle for anticipation, initiative, and foresight (§ 21.3). This is quite typical of functional systems. It can be briefly mentioned here that the notion of function is applicable where the following conditions are fulfilled: (1) the object of study can be taken as a system forming a unitary whole (which is not to say a monolithic lump); (2) the unitary whole can be ordered as a differentiated complex so that it is possible to talk about part–whole relationships; and (3) the parts are elements that contribute to fulfilling the purpose for which the ordered whole has been set up, that is, the parts must help maintain the whole in a persisting or enduring state. Phonology alone can satisfy these criteria, since its parts, distinctive features (or units) and rules, ensure speech synthesis (see § 9.15); the same is true of other parts of language, or of culture in general, although such a notion of function was originally borrowed from biology. Keeping the necessary homeostasis, that is, functioning, the language has to change to stay the same, to continue to fill its purpose. One of the factors here is the psychological-mental one of one meaning–one form, shortcuts in particular environments, whether grammatical or cultural. And then of course one cannot predict which mechanism will be chosen for new nomination when it is needed, or even without a need (see § 9.5). As it turns out, the psychological factors of biological evolution are completely beyond our grasp, at least so far, whereas they are on the whole understandable where linguistic change is concerned. No doubt much more will be found out in the future.

RECONSTRUCTION

[22.7 The Influence of Evolution on Linguistics]   Geology was an important model for biological evolution, and comparative anatomy was an explicit guide for the founder of Indo-European comparative grammar, Franz Bopp. He formulated (comparative) linguistics as a natural science, and looked on languages as natural organisms (in their morphology), which were subject to sickness, mutilation, and decay. In half a century a compromise was struck: in its method linguistics is a natural science; but in its object, a social science. It is consequently understandable why historical explanation became elaborately genetic (§ 1.24); by preference every science was taken from the historical point of view. It should be noted that all this happened well before Darwin. (Cf. Chapter 23)

[22.8 Subgrouping, Seriation, and the Comparative Method]   The biologist looks at the results of evolution and then reconstructs the total picture of derivation that will best fit the facts. Independent confirmation sometimes is available in the form of fossils, which will help fill out the details. Since all forms of life are related, the central question is subgrouping, that is, drawing a family tree on the basis of common innovations. The actual method is firmly based on seriation and syncritical analysis, because the historical connection is given in advance. Syncrisis gives us the shared innovations. Thus looking at the situation of man, we compare him with that form most similar to him, the ape, and take the intersection. Thereafter we can expand the area to all primates, then to all mammals, and so on. Since seriation is given by the principle of life which develops into more complex organizations, we can establish the branchings, and get relative chronology. We arrive at the well-known hierarchy of taxonomy: species, genus, family, order, class, phylum, and kingdom. (The kingdoms are animals, plants, viruses, and so on down the scale.) In biology, subgrouping coincides with typology. Syncrisis thus sifts the shared characteristics, seriation orders them, and the "confusion" of descriptive facts is turned into history. Schleicher phrased the same principle for language, in that one need only convert the side-by-side arrangement of systems (e.g., man and fish) into the successive stages of evolution (fish first). We have seen how seriation works in making inferences about relative chronology in linguistics (§ 14.7). There is also a biological equivalent of the comparative method, although it does not come out as explicitly as the corresponding one in linguistics: there is certain *form* (e.g., a bone structure in mammals) which carries a *function* (i.e., meaning, say, locomotion); but the form may be environmentally conditioned (e.g., the leg, the wing [of a bat], and the flipper [of a dolphin]—these three are conditioned by land, air, and water, respectively, and thus they are variants of one mammalian protoform).

[22.9]   What makes linguistic reconstruction possible is the *irreversibility of* (sound) *change*, and the same is true of evolution. Thus all terrestial animals that have become secondarily adapted to aquatic life retain many features that betray their stay on land. The superficial similarity between whales and fishes is a case of convergence, owing to the strong environmental selection. Mammals, of course, ultimately came from water, that is, as fishes do. We have seen the same phenomenon in a language family, which is the parallel to the life family. Loans can be spotted by their sound contours, which betray earlier habitats. Many Indo-European words converge in English, and sometimes it is quite easy to spot their origin, for example, *raise, hale, dentist,* and *genotype* (§ 8.12). In this sense, it can be said that after considerable further evolution the "whale" was "borrowed" back into water.

Mammalian flippers point to the interesting parallel that "rule addition," that is, adaptation, can ultimately lead to loss, which is true of language as well (§§ 5.16, 6.14, 6.15). For example, the snake ultimately adapted to crawling and lost its legs altogether by "rule addition" (compare end of § 6.15).

[22.10]   Physical appearance that is out of line from the expected seriation reveals "loans" geographically. Sometimes the distribution of certain genes or gene combinations shows distinct spatial orderliness in the form of statistical averages that produce a gradient over the map. These gradient steps are called *clines*. For example, skin color, dependent on the presence of a complex organic molecule called melanin, has a general distribution of darker at the equator and lighter in the north, or away from the equator. This is similar to the "cline" in French dialect geography with *k–tš–š* from south to north, that is, decrease in obstruction (see § 14.6). The reason apparently is that heavy pigmentation protects against radiation and thus has survival value. Where there is less sun to cope with, pigmentation decreased accordingly, because all evidence points to dark as the original color. If these hypotheses are true, the distribution of skin color clines on the map automatically reveal certain movements ("borrowings"). Thus it is apparent that the New World was populated later than the Old (although darker pigmentation has developed around the equator in the New World also), that the majority of the Indonesian population are latecomers, that the Eskimo have been in the north a shorter time than the Scandinavians, and so on. In short, this locates disjoint seriation. Often there is other evidence to support such reasoning.

[22.11] This leads to the question of using *diversity for relative chronology* as in migration theory (§§ 21.22, 21.23). The area of greatest diversity is the one of longer settlement. Thus the racial diversity of man in the Old World points to oldest settlements there, because this way we need to posit fewer large-scale migrations. Mutations take time to pile up, and where they have exerted their influence most, the most time has flown by. In language we could use similar seriation in that diversity represents an older state of affairs. For example, a dialect with *cow/kine* is "older" than one with *cow/cows* (§§ 14.7, 19.3, 19.4); but note the case of Finnish type E, which is the latest arrival (§ 19.4). And indeed, the same danger lurks in biology as well, in the form of adaptive radiation. A famous example is Darwin's ground finches, from the Galapagos Islands, songbirds derived from some New World species. The islands provided a perfect evolutionary setting, without competitors or predators. The normal seed-feeding mode of life was of limited use on the islands, and those variants that could take advantage of un-finch-like sources of food would flourish. The group now consists of seed-eaters, omnivorous ground-eaters, insect-eaters, leaf- and bud-eaters, and a woodpecker type—four genera and fourteen separate species. Although the birds are still very similar, they have developed beaks that are adapted to these different modes of food gathering. On the mainland there were no such low-pressure niches available, and no such differentiation has occurred. Reconstruction is a very delicate puzzle game indeed. Note that the filling of ecological niches by various forms of life has a certain similarity to filling the holes in phonological patterns (§ 9.6). When genetic drift alters a single species in the same environment, there is often the difficulty in deciding when it becomes a new species. The same problem recurs in linguistics—for example, the boundary between Old and Middle English (see § 21.9).

[22.12 Decay Dating—Glottochronology] We have seen that some of the methods of reconstruction are the same for language, culture and biology, notably stratigraphy and (typological) seriation. Dendrochronology, dating by the year rings of trees, is also a kind of stratigraphy or seriation, because the tree fingerprints the sequence of fat and lean years. In a way this is parallel to how the whales have recorded their stay on land. Atomic physics has made available a chronological method of very wide application in archaeology. Owing to the bombardment of the upper atmosphere by cosmic rays from outer space, some atoms of the nitrogen isotype ^{14}N are converted into atoms of the carbon isotype ^{14}C, which is radioactive. This mixes with the ordinary carbon ^{12}C contained in the carbon dioxide of the atmosphere, which is absorbed by living organic matter. The proportion of ^{14}C and ^{12}C is constant, and the proportion absorbed by organisms is the same as that in the atmosphere. Once an organism dies it ceases to take in carbon. Because ^{14}C is radioactive, it decays (reverts back to nitrogen) at a steady rate: half of the original quantity takes some 5,600 years to "evaporate." The ratio ^{14}C to ^{12}C in the sample tells when the organism died. There are of course many problems with this method, but this is the basic principle.

[22.13]   Genetic linguistics has its own decay dating, known as *glotto-chronology*. One of its underlying assumptions is that some items of the vocabulary are better preserved than others: lower numerals, pronouns, body parts, natural objects, basic actions, and so on—items referred to as the basic core vocabulary. Words that are intimately tied with cultural items suffer loss with the items themselves; for example, the vocabulary of falconry went with the practice (any dead metaphors surviving today are synchronically unanalyzable). Another assumption is that the rate of attrition in the core vocabulary is constant, so that about 81 per cent of the original two-hundred-item core vocabulary set would be preserved after a thousand years. The time of separation, t, is now equal to the logarithm of the percentage of cognates, c, divided by twice the logarithm of the percentage of cognates retained after a thousand years of separation, r:

$$t = \frac{\log c}{2 \log r}$$

The cognates are decided through strict observance of meaning; for example, 'animal' between English and German comes out as *animal/Tier*, that is, no cognation, even though *Tier* can be etymologically aligned with English *deer* (§ 7.12). Generally, inspection and matchings are used, because inaccuracies can be expected to cancel each other out.

Glottochronology has often been equated with *lexicostatistics*, but it is advisable to take the latter as a wider field of statistics in the service of historical vocabulary studies, including stylostatistics for determining disputed authorship. Stylostatistics can also be used for establishing relative chronology within the output of one author. But the prime function of lexicostatistics is the determination of the degree of lexical relationship among related languages. This can be expressed in dips calculated, for example, by the formula

$$d = 14 \frac{\log c}{2 \log r}$$

or by other similar means. When used for lexicostatistical subgrouping such a method tells relative closeness only, and its potential value is great for language families not yet worked out in detail by the conventional methods. For many languages only word lists are available, so a lexicostatistical subgrouping gives a useful interim result and may give valuable hints for the other methods as well. There is a certain parallel to biological subgrouping ascertained by counting the agreements between DNA of the various forms of life. Although the method yields numerical indices (compare Figure 16-2) between languages, these need not be interpreted to the letter, if nonnumerical evidence points to the contrary. As always in historical investigation, one-sided rigidity must be avoided. Note that low numerical values mean diversity, and such figures can be used for migration theory. If low figures cluster in one geographic area, it means older settlement (see §21.22).

[22.14]   Of the three uses of lexicostatistics, (1) time depth (glottochronology), (2) subgrouping, and (3) genetic relationship, the first has run into the most difficulty. With greater and greater time depth the percentage of cognates diminishes rather rapidly; an example that shows the even millennia from the nomographic curve with an assumed retention rate of 81 per cent follows:

millennia	1	2	3	4	5	6	7	8	9
percentage of shared vocabulary	66	43	29	18	12	8	5	3	2

It is clear that spotting the cognates and loans after nine thousand years can be rather haphazard, especially in view of the extensive phonological changes that must be expected for such a time depth. Critical break-off points are the 3,000- to 4,000-year range, with a time span of less than 1,000 years, say, 500 at least (note that the comparative method obeys similar limitations, § 18.1). On the other hand, distant relationship is a real phenomenon, and on the whole glottochronology agrees with our notions, which were independently established. The difficulties of spotting cognates can be seen clearly in English *be/future*, and *wright/organ* (§ 8.12). Of course, glottochronological work requires that the meanings be the same, which helps. It is generally required that time depth be speculated upon only after comparative work. Point 3 does not mean that lexicostatistics alone would prove genetic relationship. But the basic core vocabulary is very valuable in giving a quick elicitation list for those items where loans are least likely, and thus one can start comparative work conveniently from here (see § 18.6). It is clear that lexicostatistics is supplementary to other methods, both as a preliminary starting point and in the final subgrouping and chronological inferences.

Problems abound in every sector of the method, both in its basis and its application (but of course this is true to differing degrees of the traditional methods also). It is difficult to devise a universal, basic core vocabulary; for example, how prevalent are 'snow', or even 'animal', 'tree', 'kill', and 'know' as generic terms? Of course, there is no sharp dichotomy between basic and nonbasic; once more we have a continuum that is broken up for practical reasons (as in competence/performance). The two-hundred or so "words" in the list do not all have the same probability for being replaced; rather, each meaning has its own. Without going into all its shortcomings, it can be stated that the method is still rather effective. In particular, it makes our intuitions about time spans and basic vocabularies maximally explicit (see § 18.10). In at least half the cases it has given reasonable results, which is more than certain proposed universals in culture can claim (see § 21.14). Of course, there are cases where a strong literary tradition, contact, or strong tabu effects have distorted results of the method. The method is not without value, but neither is it omnipotent. Although claims about chronology are weak, further inquiry is justified by the results so far. Lexicostatistics must contribute to and draw from the general theory of culture change, and the numerical expressions of linguistic, cultural, and biological distance should be correlated. We have returned to an area where more has to be found out about language typology (how to pick out the basic vocabulary) and the influence of society, for example, how it affects the rate of change (see §§ 21.9–21.11), or the formation of tabus. No area of genetic linguistics is settled for good. The student meets new challenges everywhere.

REFERENCES

General: Hockett 1948b, Kroeber 1963b, Beals and Hoijer 1965, Zipf 1965, Lenneberg 1967, Spuhler (ed.) 1967, Jakobson 1969; **22.1** Crick 1962, 1966 Nirenberg 1963, Yanofsky 1967, Beadle and Beadle 1967, Baltimore et al. 1970; **22.2** Chao 1967; **22.3** Darlington 1947, 1955, Brosnahan 1960, 1961, Hogben 1956; **22.5** Greenberg 1959, Hymes 1961; **22.6** Emmet 1958, Segerstråle 1968; **22.7** Hoenigswald 1963, Maher 1966, Neumann 1967; **22.10** Huxley 1953, Brosnahan 1961, Brace and Montagu 1965; **22.12** Paor 1967, Deetz 1967; **22.13-22.14** Kroeber and Chrétien 1937, Swadesh 1951, 1952, 1955, Lees 1953, Gudschinsky 1956, Arndt 1959, Hymes 1960, Dyen 1962, 1964, 1965ab, Dyen et al. 1967, Martinet (ed.) 1968, D. Sankoff 1970, Lees 1953, Chrétien 1962, Bergsland and Vogt 1962, Teeter 1963, Fodor 1965, H. Vogt 1965, L. Campbell 1977, Hymes and Sherzer, Rea, and Hattori in Sebeok (ed.) 1963f. vol. 11, Embleton 1986.

CHAPTER 23

GENETIC LINGUISTICS AND METATHEORY

In the late 1950s there arose discussion about the two cultures (humanities vs. sciences) and a corresponding metascientific treatment in the philosophy of science. Although linguists are generally unaware of it, this touches their field in a significant way, since it determines the structure of explanation relevant to their métier.

[23.1 Positivism vs. Hermeneutics]   The dominating philosophy of science, particularly in the Anglo-Saxon world, has been what is known as *positivism*. It takes the so-called deductive-nomological (nomic, or covering law) explanation as the model for all sciences. Everything is supposed to be reducible to the laws of nature, which would explain the space-time aspects of all phenomena. Observation is the crucial activity of the analyst, and the explanation resorted to is strictly deterministic in that prediction IS explanation.   The only causality acknowledged is that of natural laws (nomicity).   Various notions of empiricalness and experimentation get further confused by linguists so that, for example, the transformational-generative grammarians felt confident in proclaiming linguistics an empirical science quite on a par with physics and chemistry, with every speech act providing a basis for experimenting with one's own intuitive reactions.   What seems to have aided this particular position is that positivists generally take logic as pure science; and formal linguistics and logic are close enough.

Human rule-governed goal-directed and goal-intended action must, however, be conceptually understood, not chemically explained. We have to do with intuition, conceptual analysis, normative rules, pattern congruity, history as interpretation (with abduction), and in general self-reflection (agent's knowledge, not observer's as above), the lack of which indeed defines positivism. This domain (known under names like the human(istic), cultural, moral, or social sciences; *hermeneutics* or *Geisteswissenschaften*) requires a different mode of explanation, namely (philosophical) explication or understanding (*Verstehen*; Einfühlung, empathy, appreciation).   In fact, self-knowledge is incompatible with natural-science causality; and philosophical analysis must belong to hermeneutic explication.   Thus formal logic is fully hermeneutic and not natural science (as taught by most linguists).   Logic is not something "eternal" like the natural laws, but is tied to situation, use, or the pragmatic context (cf. abduction §§9.16, 23.4); in other words, history is the primary frame.   Hermeneutic explication starts with pre-understanding, and this becomes honed into more and more explicit theoretical knowledge; practical experience comes before theory.   Pre-understanding is of course also culture-dependent.   Psychoanalysis is often compared with historical alienation (changes pile up and alienate participants and us from the original unity); they clearly show the difference between positivism and hermeneutics. In these the causal factors that have produced the "disturbance" are to be eliminated through understanding (cf. §21.20, 23.10). This cannot be done with natural causes.

As it happens linguistics is a singularly pure hermeneutic discipline ("science") of non-empirical nature, since it is tied with conceptual analysis, not with prediction of spatiotemporal events of language use. It defines what is a correct utterance in language L. Speakers of English know for certain that the article precedes its head noun, for example *the head*. If a grammarian observed a sequence *head the* (cf. Swedish *huvud-et*, Rumanian *cap-ul*), he would discard it as an incorrect utterance. Here object and observer are to a crucial degree the same (insider's knowledge), which is not true in natural science where, for example, a similar irregularity in the behavior of snowflakes could not be ignored, but would rather work toward changing our conception of the laws (outsider's knowledge). When we add the factors or mechanisms that contribute to the occurrence of linguistic behavior, whether they be biological, psychological, or social-historical, we find, surprisingly, that linguistics becomes in fact doubly hermeneutic (as the preceding chapters have amply implied), that is, both in respect to the conceptual system of norms and its use in context.

[23.2] The positivist (classical) picture of the world implied the elimination of all notion of purpose, as the future was described as a mechanistic result of antecedent conditions. It also removed the concept of man as a free agent, and the result was the same kind of determinism everywhere. The *unity of science* program followed this stance (and linguistics was included). Unfortunately, the very existence of human sciences was denied. Positivists have in fact watered their requirement down to an expectation: ultimately all sciences will be explained through covering laws. Of course the embarrassing fact remains that to date not a single covering-law explanation exists in history (or human sciences in general). The viable position is that positivism is wrong (as a universal theory), and that one must accept the complementarity of the methods. General (dynamic) field theory maintains a certain parallelism or isomorphism between cosmic, molecular, and social structures, but this can be done only by denying the positivistic thesis. The principles involved extend to man-made objects, and thus also to language (cf. §23.9).

The militantly doctrinaire reductionism which axiomatically prescribes that all the relevant macro-information about nature must be, and eventually will be, derived completely from adding up and piecing together all the individual micro-information about the smallest sample units, is in fact antiquated in its own domain. This claim had to be gradually given up when electrodynamism, thermodynamics, quantum theory, and the uncertainty principle entered the scene. Thus physical sciences themselves do not give (linguists) reason for espousal of mere covering-law models; rather, modern physics teaches that the observer is drawn into the act of observation. The notion of a detached observer is an illusion. The mind is an integral part of the world and all the mental processes interact with what is observed. The scientist cannot know anything about anything without getting involved with what he observes. Furthermore, the physicist must also understand what he is doing (to what end and why). The crucial filter even here is thus hermeneutics. One has to accept a scale from physico-chemical laws to biological laws to sociological-cultural laws, and thus one sees that biology is the best parallel to genetic linguistics (at least a strong analogy), since it has to tackle the question of evolution (Chapter 22). Change is negligible in the physical world, but it is a must where mind or meaning is involved. IF one wants to make claims about the unity of science, its anchoring point is at the opposite end of the gradience: Hermeneutics is the general theory, and natural science is a limiting case thereof, since what it deals with presents only a small section of reality. There is also a kind of approach to physical reality that does not raise the causal question, namely so-called protophysics, which analyzes those ideal rules of measurement that make empirical physics possible; thus protophysics constitutes the logical precondition of empirical physics (not to speak of various popularizations uniting particle physics with Eastern mysticism). The unifying principles for their part represent dynamic field notions, which, in mental life and psychology, are known under the terms of gestalt conceptions. A comparative examination of field dynamics in physics and the experimental data of the gestalt school shows that the same tendency toward symmetry which is the supreme law of the dynamics underlying organization in the physical world is also the most fundamental law of the dynamics of perceptual and cognitive organization, with the functioning of both similarity and contiguity (cf. §§1.11, 1.17, 7.2) in both perception and thought being a special case of this law. And this law holds for both open and closed systems. But this is at a level at which linguists have not had much reason to dwell. Genetic linguistics deals with history and human action, and here hermeneutics is the only viable metatheory, because we have maximally open systems in which (mechanistic) prediction is impossible.

[23.3 The Primacy of History]   Ever since Saussure, students have been misled with a statement that *synchrony* is primary over *diachrony* (although he acknowledged that historical linguistics is more fun). Historical linguistics tends to be appended as a necessary evil, and too often it is not required at all, because synchronic (descriptive, structural) linguistics is taken as theoretical linguistics (§§1.1, 1.18), and linguists love theory. But there is no such real (or theoretical) dichotomy at all. The distinction is a practical one and pertains to linguistics, not the essence of language itself. It is of course easier to start from synchrony, because in it language can be taken in a stripped-down version. The moment we include individual differences between speakers, the play between older and newer items, and the dimension of the future -- as we must -- we step into diachrony. Historical linguistics is privileged in that it encompasses description as a cut in the history of the language, whereas description does not include history in any relevant sense. Paradoxical is that the future plays such an important role. A language cannot be nailed down in its entirety as a historical product. The dimension of future adds unrealized possibilities and potentialities for our purview, and these are not there as real facts. We cannot experience future with any determination.

To study it we have to study it as the past, in its relation towards the future (which we already know as past). That is, the chronological cut under study, C, has as its future B, which from our vantage point, A, is already past. In genetic explanation (§1.24) the earlier state of affairs (B) does not explain causally ("from behind") the existing state (A), but from the point of view of future ("from in front"): the later point (B, A) in fact establishes the possibilities of the earlier state (C, B). In a strict synchronic mode one would not know about real possibilities at all, because they have to be realized by speakers in history (cf. the symbol as a purpose in potential future, §§1.10, 1.16). A synchronic explanation is in fact impossible, because for any explanation one has to refer to something else (cf. §23.10). In this way descriptive linguistics explains speech, not language. The moment one wants to account for why a language is the way it is, one has to resort to genetic explanation, as in history in general. We do not reduce forces to causes but we observe facts in their finalistic development. The question in human activity is 'for what purpose', that is, not 'Why did Brutus murder Caesar?', but 'For what purpose would I have murdered Caesar?' Answering questions of 'for what purpose?' we explain the earlier state of affairs by a later one, gaining deeper understanding of the facts. The important point is that the state of affairs is explained by its evolution with more exact understanding. The possibility is manifested and the openness of the system vindicated. Change is now just creation, use of language; history is an integral part of the object, not an addition to description. In natural objects we can separate being/existence from becoming to a reasonable degree, but not in cultural objects, or cultural activity where becoming is the very essence of existence. Language use is (re)interpreted tradition. In short, only historical linguistics does justice to our real experience with language and the essence of language. This does of course not deny synchrony. A synchronic-structural treatment of a given language state is the only reasonable one for description, although the description of a culture object belongs to a phase in its becoming. There is no contradiction between description and history. As Hermann Paul said, linguistics is really historical linguistics.

[23.4 Teleology]   The previous section brought us to strong requirements of history and final causation. The mode of explanation necessary in this domain is known as teleology. There is incredible opposition to teleological explanation in linguistics, which means that most linguists deny the very essence of language. Teleology does not entail some mysterious pull of the future, but rather belongs to a doctrine of the potency of present possibilities. This fact is reflected in the very nature of the symbol. It is essentially a purpose (cf. §1.16) with an embryonic reality endowed with the power of growth. When the sign system is used the symbols tend to make themselves more and more definite; they determine a time dimension in which the process unfolds. Symbols are used for a purpose, or more generally, all sign types exist solely in order to be used (as tokens). When we talk about *use as*, we of course are talking about a goal. Thus the creation and replication of types (i.e., speech acts) is goal-directed. Whereas sign-production is goal-directed only for types/symbols, sign-interpretation is that for all signs (one strives to retrieve the meaning intended or otherwise produced). Symbolic types exist only where there is life (cf. Chapter 22), and they are manipulated by individuals to produce new meanings -- and they probably constitute the form of consciousness found in human life. As far as *language* goes, both sign-action and sign-interpretation are purely teleological. The symbol does of course also incorporate habits (of interpretation and action). But habits, as laws and generals, do not consist in any particular acts that happen to instantiate them. They operate in agreement with final causation: specific manifestations of habits are the results of a certain type that would tend to occur even if the circumstances of their occurrence varied. Habits as intellectual entities manifest rationality and are hence subject to final causes and govern acts by making them conform to and manifest a general pattern.

Linguists usually refer to structures as systems held together by parts-wholes dynamics. This is correct as far as it goes, if we do not think that such structures cohere on the basis of natural-science determinism like chemical compounds (efficient causation). Final and efficient causation are hierarchically ordered, and both need each other. The latter is that kind of causation in which parts compose the whole, while the former is that kind of causation whereby the whole calls out its parts. Both directions are teleological forces. Note that a notion like that of a natural class comes under final causation, because its members owe their existence as members of the class to a common final cause, the defining idea of the class (and *nature* originally meant 'birth'). That functioning structures can change is due to the fact that efficient causation is subject to evolution, and this evolution is again teleological: the conformity of particular efficient causes to laws of efficient causation is itself an example of final causation. Or, in more general terms, the relation of law, as a cause, to the action of force, as its effect, is final (or ideal) causation, not efficient causation. Typically again, primary hermeneutic ingredients lie behind the positivistic bastions.

There is a distinction between *acting for* a purpose (goal-intention) and *existing for* a purpose (goal-direction). The latter case includes organs or artifacts that have been selected to fulfill a function; that is, the existence of the organ is teleologically explained. This is true of biological units like the heart or grammatical structures like phonological rules or syntactic structures (of a particular kind). This is known as teleology of function, the former as teleology of purpose. The important point is that functional analysis belongs within teleology, that is, the function is also essentially a historical concept, contrary to what is usually stated. So is selection, a key concept in sign-behavior and even in linguistic analysis; it can only be understood under final causation (because it is an aspect of sign types [selection from an *inventory*], see above).

Social forces show clearly *teleology of purpose*. Speakers choose to modify their language to assimilate it to other people's norms. When centralization is adopted as the sign of 'Vineyarder' (§9.11), it is enhanced. The idea of group membership is adopted first (cf. §13.9); it calls out an effect in pronunciation. Similarly, avoidance of homophony is opted for by speakers because they want to be understood without noticeable complications. Homophony can be avoided for example by grammatical conditioning of sound change (§§4.22-26, 5.12-13) or lexical replacement (§§9.3-4). But this already involves *teleology of function*, because parts get selected for an efficient result (§§4.24, 5.12). The distinction between the two kinds of teleology may not always be that relevant, but it does not deny that teleology is the main force. The main manifestation of this force has been phrased here as 'one meaning, one form' (§§5.21, 7.9).

The difference in status between a pattern in the making and a pattern once established is particularly pronounced in language structure. This applies not only to change and its stable result but also to language acquisition. The child learning its native language has as its goal the acquisition of the patterns that make that language. While the goal is still unreached, the process is subordinated to teleological considerations: final causes call out the parts of the whole. The process is obviously gradual. Once the patterns have been learned, however, their fulfillment in adult speech changes character: the structure switches to efficient causes, the parts compose the whole (cf. the comparative method in §13.9). The syllogism used in all learning (and thus in all change) is the abductive one, from the vantage point of perception under the human hermeneutic imperative (cf. §§9.16-18, 11.27; this time pointing toward law, not case as above):

ABDUCTIVE The surprising fact, *C*, is observed.
SYLLOGISM But if *A* were true, *C* would be a matter of course.
--------- -- -- --
Hence, there is reason to suspect that *A* is true.

Thus *A* cannot be abduced or conjectured until its content is already present in the premise. Abduction is indeed the first explanatory phase of scientific inquiry; it suggests that something may be. Similarly, the explanation of (linguistic and other) actions (and variation) rely on the practical syllogism:

PRACTICAL *X* intends to achieve *G*.
SYLLOGISM *X* believes that unless he does *A*, he will not achieve *G*.
--------- -- -- --
Therefore *X* sets himself to do *A*.

Here one has to reach the intention behind the action, and we see the same kind of leakage from the premises into the conclusion as in the abductive syllogism (this is indicated by the broken line), the premises entail the conclusion. The deductive-nomological inference does not allow it; there is total independence between the two components.

[23.5] We have seen a number of rather central terms that fall under final causation and teleological considerations (or history in general). This is of course no surprise for concepts such as 'development, flux, growth, creation', but rather startling for 'symbol, type, general, law, function, structure, selection, natural class, acquisition, use' (sign-production and sign-interpretation), 'habit', as well as 'description' (since it is pointless without a relative goal). These terms define pragmatics as well, and thus logic gets included, since it is tied to the historical context, and since it changes with time. That is logical which it is necessary to admit in order to render the universe intelligible (§23.7), and, as abduction shows, it is a random and fallible matter. It is clear that synchronic linguistics cannot be talked about without the above terms. The theoretical primacy of history is thus vindicated. And we can draw the following balance: Language and its development are always teleological. A purpose or other final cause is also the essence of mental phenomena, and it is mind that makes meaning. Change is the *telos* of language. It is also the very essence of meaning. Functionally put: language has to change to stay the same (§§21.7, 22.6). There is a descending hierarchy from hermeneutics to semiotics to teleology.

[23.6 Rational Explanation]   There is a crucial difference between actions and events. The former are (to some degree at least) controled by agents, the latter include forces of nature like rainfall or erosion (cf. §1.24). Both crucially involve change; that is, change is the prime notion. In linguistics one often just *talks* about events, because the agents remain largely unknown (§§23.7, 23.9), and because this is shorthand for *historical* events. We have "real" history only when (the) mind is involved. Autonomous linguistics systemizes linguistic norms and answers what-questions (about correct sentences; §§23.1-2), whereas causal linguistics investigates the causation of behavior which conforms to or violates those norms (answering how-questions of sentence perception, production, acquisition, and change through time). Human (including linguistic) action falls under non-nomic (§§23.1-2), teleological (§§23.4-5), and representational causation. The concept of mental representation assures an analogy between language and thought and leads to (a) definition(s) of "cognitive structures, models, or maps" which somehow represent prior experiences and allow for action in the present or for the future. All goal-directed organisms (life) possess representations of their goals and environments, but it is only with human beings that this comes to full fruition and consciousness. This is symbol behavior, sign-action (§§1.10, 1.16, 23.3). Mental representation elucidates the specific nature of human behavior and of its causation. The agent's reasons for acting are analogous to drawing conclusions from acceptable premises (cf. §23.4). For the same reason, the construction of common-sense beliefs and the simulation of behavior by computer programs are instances of *explication.* Similarly, the construal of reasons explains why actions, although caused, are nevertheless felt to be *understood* in a way physical events are not, and could not be. At every turn we abut hermeneutic imperatives.

Human action manifests practical necessity in that if one has a definite goal and believes that an action necessary for achieving it is at one's disposal, one must perform the action (cf. 'acting for', §23.4) -- if one is a rational person (and if the action does not interfere with moral or other value systems and free will). This is (2) in the following set-up:

ACTIONIST	(1) G[oal] & B[elief]		(2) A
SYLLOGISMS	---- -- -- --------	and	===
	A[ction]		A*

We have (1) a mental representation of a necessary action (A) derived from one's goals and beliefs ($G\&B$), and then (2) the move from thought to action, from A to the spatiotemporal action A^*. The connection between belief and action is *conceptual* (and this is again the reason for the broken line in (1); it represents a valid inference under the *norm*, cf. §23.4). Beliefs for their part become established largely through the forces of abduction.

Human behavior issues from the agent's goals and beliefs. The former are prompted by free will and/or by external circumstances and have the role of a 'dynamic cause' in bringing about the action, whereas the belief, comprising semantic memory, mental representation, etc., acts as a 'static cause'. Actions are typically rational, that is, adequate in the light of goals and beliefs, and thus rationality assumes the role of causality in the pretheoretical sense of making things happen. Within rationality one can distinguish between socially valid rationality principles and their individual-psychological internalizations (=reasons). A rational action is a solution to a problem, namely an attempt to eliminate a contradiction (cf. hermeneutic elimination of "disturbance" §23.1, abduction in general §23.4, and dissonance theory §23.10). The domain where non-nomic rationality as a basis of explanation cannot in any way be dispensed with is historical change (and scientific progress).

[23.7] Pragmatics is use of language (and sentences) in context, and thus falls within the theory of action, employing mainly conscious rationality. Semantics, in contrast, remains largely within the concept of correctness, except for word-formation, which must resort to rational explanation (we cannot predict the exact relation in, e.g., *London bus* ['to, from, in', etc.], or metaphorical naming, etc.). Sociolinguistic correlates rest on unconscious rationality, because the speakers need not be aware of the relevant variables. The correlation of centralization in Martha's Vineyard with middle-aged fishermen and others with a positive attitude toward the island could be made *intelligible*, understandable (§§9.10-11). Such attitudes are (static) causes of change (see also §§3.3, 3.7), and sociolinguistic facts of this kind fall under the concept of empathy (or the method of *Verstehen*) as in history in general. Language acquisition for its part displays strong and clear goals in context. The learners ("agents") have to solve problems encountered rationally, and individual differences must be explained with some kind of (non-nomic) "historical understanding". Even "crazy" solutions (through abduction) can be understood as rational (which is quite parallel to irrational neurotic behavior). We understand the rationality afterwards, and deduction brings out the earlier abductions (in that sense we do have historical explanation). The analysis of *formation* as *4-mation* leading to *twomation* was reasonable in the context (§5.5), and certainly a perceived problem was solved (as with *sparrow grass*, etc.). Apparently at one time somebody felt it a defect that Finnish did not have feminine gender morphemes like the neighboring Indo-European languages (Swedish, Russian). The solution was to cut the Baltic loan *tytär* 'daughter' in two: *ty-tär*! This now yields the "missing" item, which happens to be of the same structure as *-ton* '-less' (cf. §11.19); for example, based on the masculine *ope-tta-ja* 'learn'-causative-agent = 'teacher', we get *opettaja-tar* (the genitive is *opettaja-ttare-n*). However crazy this is, it can be made intelligible, and only by showing that the action was rational. This is how reanalysis and extension (analogy) work. It can/must be understood through empathy.

The essence of language change is that a reasonable (local) solution in one part of structure can lead to complications elsewhere. This is phrased as the tug-of-war between sound change and analogy, or more generally between form and meaning. This is how morphosyntactic change works under the primacy of the cognitive (meaning) side. When the one-to-many relations between form and meaning are felt to be problematic, one can expect a move toward one-to-one symbolization. This teleological force has been called in this book 'one meaning -- one form' (this can also be called the basic principle of [representational] iconicity or *isomorphism*), and the notation ∧∨I has been used for it (§§5.14, 5.21, 6.23, 7.9, 9.3-4). This is quite directly relatable to the actionist framework, to the (generalized) language user's rational behavior. The general goal is clearly isomorphism, I, that is, ∧ > I, ∧ > I,I, ∨ > I,I, ∨ > I. Action involves change, but also no-change as part of controling the world, the state of affairs. Note now that the analogical/ morphological resistance to sound change falls under the same kind of rationality. Consider the Greek future *lūsō* (§5.12). It shows functional (teleological) motivation to prevent I > ∧ (two allomorphs for the future) and I,I > ∨ (merger of the present and the future). The most common type of semantic change, I > ∨ (Fig. 7-4A.) would now at first blush seem to be a serious counter-example, serious, because this is the heart of language use. But form, or the linguistic sign, must be conceived widely enough to include the contexts. Contexts are parts of the signs, and since the totality is primary and the sign is derived from it, the contexts make signs formally different, and they are so experienced. Often in fact such cases are reinterpreted as pure homophony on the level of the "naked" sign (i.e., without its context), for example *cold* (weather) vs. *cold* (illness), *flower/flour*, *metal/mettle* (§7.9), whether spelling enhances this or not (in languages with a tradition like English).

[**23.8**] It is important to note that acts of speaking and acts of understanding speech must be explained through the same rationality principles (social control), although the acts remain distinct. The former are explained by attributing suitable rationality principles to the speaker, and the latter are simulated by these very same acts of attributing those principles to the speaker. Simulation is of course re-enactment, hermeneutic anamnesis, verification-in-principle, and hence explanation. Guessing is solving a problem, which is so clear in language acquisition, which relies on abduction. Perception is already unconscious proto-abduction, whereas conscious actions rely largely on the practical syllogism, which was introduced to provide the human sciences an explanation model in its own right as an alternative to the deductive-nomological model of the natural sciences. Rational explanation is a related model that combines many of the strains mentioned in that it also covers areas of unconscious behavior, and there is now a trend in cognitive psychology in that (Humean) causality is losing ground in favor of unconscious rationality. It seems that rational explanation is in fact THE explanatory model of human sciences. It can further assume the functions both of nomic and of non-nomic explanation (cf. §23.2); it is for this reason that the natural-science methods had to be transgressed in the first place. One can note that rationality as explanation was propounded already by the founders of modern linguistics (von Humboldt, Whitney).

[23.9 Invisible-Hand Explanation] The more one descends the conscious, teleological, non-nomic levels of human behavior toward the "lower" reaches occupied by subconscious automatic subactions, the more does the degree of nomicity increase. But this gradual shift from non-nomic to nomic teleology cannot really be formalized. And the minimal linguistic subactions, that is, instances of phonetic variation, seem to be governed by some sort of statistical causation. They become important (for change) only when social value is attached to them (§9.11). In general, the social context of causation of actions is the most powerful filter which forces individuals to maintain social institutions and common beliefs. The (quasi-)nomic aspect of human, including linguistic, behavior largely coincides with institutional behavior. The rationality principles for their part have introduced the collective aspect of rational action that an individual agent makes use of. In fact, it makes sense to speak of rational actions as performed by a collective agent. Linguistic change belongs here, because of its social control, for example for the survival of innovations and mental grammars abduced by children. The community seems to change its language. We in fact regularly talk about languages themselves as being agents, or changes as events, forgetting or overlooking that they are *historical* events.

In social sciences and economics where one has to deal with mass effects there has arisen the question whether phenomena can be the result of human actions, but not the goal of their intentions (e.g., inflation, population growth, traffic jams, and language). Phenomena of this kind would fall between natural events and human actions (§23.1). The Scottish moral philosophers of the 18th century worked on these and (Adam Smith) coined the term *invisible hand* working behind them. The collective consequences (A_c) of individual actions (A_i) become telescoped into a final product (a collective aggregate):

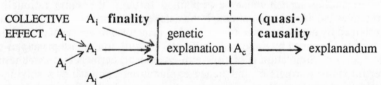

Collective behavior and its explanation shows how each causal factor enters into the process and contributes to bringing about the final outcome. This is of course genetic explanation (typical historical explanation and called 'conjectural history' by the Scots), which is characterized by the lack of reliable laws and the ensuing unpredictability of the explanandum-events. This way invisible-hand explanations are hypothetical reconstructions. And intentions generate the explanandum. Thus all the crucial explanatory forces remain on the finalistic (teleological) side; matter is effete mind. An order is explained as the causal consequence of intentional actions performed according to similar rationality principles (maxims). The quasi-causal nomic teleology is a practical way of talking about the events as events, the final structures (cf. §23.5). One area in which this comes out is, for example, *drift* (§9.13, p. 200), clearly a series of such actions. Here the nomicity of a diachronic universal turns out to be a diachronic aggregate of (collective) rational actions (cf. §23.5). The statistical nomicity of a drift is due to the fact that people are likely to choose more rational options over less rational ones in similar situations. Compare the traffic jam: for each individual it is reasonable to reduce speed rather than to collide, and this can lead to a collective (total) standstill.

[**23.10 Pattern Explanation**]   The representation of signs requires 'frozen action' as a foundation of semiotic and pragmatic meaning. The meaning of a sentence is explicated in terms of its verification-in-principle. This entails that the crucial notion is that of a *coherent story*. Meaning is thus (re)enactment (anamnesis; §13.9), and identical to hermeneutics and historical investigation in general. In interpretation social conventions and experience come through memory into the act whose goal is to re-enact the original goal or intention. Explanation thus looks backward and forward. All 'living' systems that unfold in time require anamnestic-proleptic coherence. Coherence is the crucial notion in all structuralism, for example, in language use and change as constant systematization (and all these concepts fall under final causation). Abduction is the main (psychological) tool for bringing about coherence and intelligibility (§23.6). In collective behavior there is a constant urge to eliminate inconsistency, as, for example, analyzed by the proponents of the *theory of cognitive dissonance*, which says that people more or less consciously know an indefinite number of psychological implications, for example, 'If X, then Y'. Now 'X and not-Y' constitutes a disturbing inconsistency, which must be solved, for example either by changing 'X' into 'not-X' or by changing 'not-Y' into 'Y'. Even when this manipulation of 'reality' leads to neurotic behavior, it is in its own domain rational and logical (cf. §21.20). In general one manipulates meaning until there is a fit (sense constancy). Again, structurally this is akin to hermeneutic removal of disturbance (§§23.1, 23.6).

One usually thinks that scientific activity consists in first noting correlations between observable phenomena and then in postulating such unobservable causal mechanisms as could produce, and thus explain, the correlations. *Correlational* models are very uncertain, and in language work mainly in low levels, for example pronunciation (e.g., §§3.3, 9.10-11). *Postulational* (analytic) models of language often lead to positing outlandish deep structures (e.g., §§6.5-22). But there is a third type of causal model, called *synthetic*, which reverses the direction of research by going from the 'inside' to the 'outside' (cf. hermeneutics again), or from known causes to less well known effects (cf. invisible-hand explanation). The importance of synthetic models has been largely overlooked since they cannot be used in natural sciences. The role of rationality becomes more and more pronounced as one moves from correlational via postulational to synthetic models of linguistic behavior. The embarrassing fact in linguistics is that the correlational models are inadequate at the sentence level or above, and they also mistake probability for causality. Large-scale postulational modes are also unfeasible, and all such attempts turn out to be synthetic in disguise. Artificial intelligence now develops synthetic models, but it is not clear to all that the method derives from social philosophy (§23.9). It has to be *social*, because the explanation of people's actions is at issue, and it has to be *philosophy*, because the method employed, intuition-with-reflection is philosophical in character (§23.1).

A synthetic model developed within American social science and cultural anthropology is known as *pattern explanation*. It specifies the place of the problematic item in the pattern and classifies its status deeper and deeper until it fits the pattern. Objectivity lies in the totality which often decides which alternatives must be chosen. The explanans and explanandum are on the same level of generality, and no general laws appear out of necessity, but part-whole relations of equal particularization. The whole explanation is a description of particularity (be it a belief, norm, or law), and usually even in linguistics one's own description IS explanation. Pattern explanation is appropriate when the *relations* between the facts are important and can be rather directly observed, and these relations are not of logical implication. All explanation relates something to something else, and from this vantage point deductive-nomological explanation is (again) a limiting case of pattern explanation, which for its part is a variant of the hermeneutic spiral, since patterns are rarely finished, data come in piecemeal, and experimentation is not possible (§§21.1-2). In fact, the case study methods falling under pattern explanation are far superior to the deductive-nomological model, because of their primary focus on particular histories and because the generalities arise for the description of particularities. They include both the particular and the universal (history) within a science; they exhibit the universal within the particular without segregation and permit easy shifting from one into the other. This way one avoids grand hierarchical jumps by working with concatenations of indexical chains (= contexts).

The explanatory force of pattern explanations resides in revealing the coherence between apparently disconnected or even inconsistent facts. It creates a fit between the parts and eliminates inconsistency. We are back in dissonance theory, and the hermeneutic imperative. The same striving after consistency characterizes both researchers and research objects, and this guarantees the general adequacy of pattern explanations. Any use of rational explanation (§23.6) for its part implies a pattern explanation or a synthetic model. These combine the best of all possible worlds (producing a welcome balance to the effects of historical gaps): they are easy to construct for the purposes of data collection, and they are more interesting than the other alternatives because they are much larger in scope.

[23.11 Philology and Etymology]   Pattern explanation (§23.10) turns out to be identical to philological concerns worked out earlier in Europe within the humanities (and note that linguistics is usually placed either within social sciences or humanities; its methods cannot come from natural sciences)(§§1.20, 1.24, Chapter 17). Philology has also always served as a paragon of hermeneutics (§§23.1-2). It is not a mere listing of facts, since the necessary encyclopedic frame must be understood as a general concept dealing with generalized knowledge. In this way the common character (the universal in the individual) is typical of philology, whose higher aim is the historical reconstruction of the whole (knowledge) as well as its parts, and the study of the ideas stamped into it (anamnesis again). Philology shows the case study aspects in a well-tested form. And linguistics must be theoretically philological, and it is thus a limiting case of the latter (dealing with just the mere stripped-down tool aspects of language). Language in context (and history) is much more interesting as part of a composite puzzle (§§1.20, 17.3, 17.10, 21). One now hears pleas for a theory of sociohistory. But philology always provided such a theory, and so did the theory of history. Both work by providing "order into chaos", another variant of the theme of creating consistency.

If philology and historical writing in general provide coherent stories, etymological work supplies "short stories". There is no conceptual difference between the two, just a difference in the size of the chunks under study.

[23.12 Conclusion]   The main body of this book was opened with a mere reminder of what historical explanation involves (§§1.24-25), and it was closed with one timid reference to understanding and hermeneutics under a positivist characterization of them as requiring a crucial "step into the irrational" (§21.20, p. 385). This chapter (and cf. §13.9) has now set the record straight by drawing the irrational into the concept of rationality. This chapter has dealt with a large number of variations on the theme of explanation within history and the human (hermeneutic) sciences. At many points the explication encountered so-called limiting cases, and in each such case (genetic) linguistics sided with history and hermeneutics. In (genetic) linguistics we also solve the unusual, the strange, bringing it into conscious awareness (= hermeneutic reflection). Theoretical linguistics is genetic linguistics; synchronic linguistics is descriptive linguistics.

REFERENCES

General: Esa Itkonen 1983 (also for all individual sections), Martin 1977, Porter 1981, v. Wright 1971, Lass 1980, Lightfoot 1979; 23.1-2 Esa Itkonen 1978; 23.3 Coseriu 1980; 23.4 Shapiro 1985, Short 1981, Lass in Koopman et al. (eds.) 1987, Vincent, Anttila both in Fisiak (ed.) 1978, Campbell and Ringen 1981, Adamska-Sałaciak 1986; 23.5 Shapiro 1985; 23.6-8 Esa Itkonen 1984, Stevenson et al. (eds.) 1986, Hollis and Lukes (ed.) 1982; 23.9 Keller 1985; 23.10 Diesing 1972, Kaplan 1964, Hörmann 1976; 23.11 Ahlqvist (ed.) 1982, Romaine 1982, Becker 1982.

BIBLIOGRAPHY

Adamska-Sałaciak, Arleta. 1986. *Teleological explanations in diachronic phonology*. University of Poznań dissertation.

Ahlqvist, Anders. 1985. "The relative endings of the Old Irish simple verb," *Ériu* 36.137-42.

----- (ed.). 1982. *Papers from the fifth international conference on historical linguistics*. Amsterdam, Benjamins.

Alatis, James E. (ed.). 1968. *Contrastive linguistics and its pedagogical implications* (19th Round Table Meeting). Washington, D.C., Georgetown University Press.

----- (ed.). 1969. *Linguistics and the teaching of Standard English to speakers of other languages or dialects* (20th Round Table Meeting). Washington, D.C., Georgetown University Press.

----- (ed.). 1970. *Bilingualism and language contact: anthropological, linguistic, psychological, and sociological aspects* (21st Round Table Meeting). Washington, D.C., Georgetown University Press.

Allen, W. S. 1951. "Phonetics and comparative linguistics," *Archivum Linguisticum* 3.126-36.

-----. 1953. "Relationship in comparative linguistics," *Transactions of the Philological Society*, 52-108.

Andersen, Henning. 1966. *Tenues and mediae in the Slavic languages: a historical investigation.* Cambridge, Mass., Harvard University dissertation.

-----. 1969. "A study in diachronic morphophonemics: the Ukrainian prefixes," *Language* 45.807-30.

-----. 1972. "Diphthongization," *Language* 48.11-50.

-----. 1973. "Abductive and deductive change," *Language* 49.765-93. [Also in Baldi and Werth (eds.) 1978:313-47.]

----- (ed.). 1985. *Sandhi phenomena in the languages of Europe*. New York and The Hague, Mouton.

Anderson, John M. and Charles Jones (eds.). 1974. *Historical linguistics I-II.* Amsterdam, North-Holland.

Anshen, Frank. 1970. "A sociolinguistic analysis of a sound change," *Language Sciences* 9.20-21 (February).

Anttila, Raimo. 1968. "The relation between internal reconstruction and the comparative method," *Ural-Altaische Jahrbücher* 40.159-73.

-----. 1969a. *Uusimman äännehistorian suunnasta ja luonteesta*. Publications of the Phonetics Department of the University of Turku 5.

-----. 1969b. *Proto-Indo-European schwebeablaut*. Berkeley and Los Angeles, University of California Press.

413

-----. 1975. *The indexical element in morphology.* Innsbrücker Beiträge zur Sprachwissenschaft, Reihe Vorträge 12. Innsbruck, Sprachwissenschaftliches Institut.

-----. 1977a. "Toward a semiotic analysis of expressive vocabulary," *Semiosis* 5.27-40.

-----. 1977b. *Analogy.* The Hague, Mouton.

-----. 1980. "Language and the semiotics of perception," *The signifying animal*, 263-83. See Savan 1980.

Anttila, Raimo, and Warren A. Brewer. 1977. *Analogy: a basic bibliography.* Amsterdam, Benjamins.

Anttila, Raimo, and Eeva Uotila. 1984. "Finnish *ovela* 'sly, cunning' and the Baltic Finnic outer local cases," *Ural-Altaische Jahrbücher* 56.121-28.

Arens, Hans. 1969. *Sprachwissenschaft. Der Gang ihrer Entwicklung von der Antike bis zur Gegenwart.*[2] Freiburg and Munich, Karl Alber.

Arlotto, Anthony. 1972. *Introduction to historical linguistics.* Boston, Houghton Mifflin. [Washington, University Press of America 1981.]

Armstrong, Edward G. 1986. "Uniform numbers," *American Journal of Semiotics* 4.99-127.

Arndt, Walter W. 1959. "The performance of glottochronology in Germanic," *Language* 35.180-92.

Aron, Albert W. 1930. "The gender of English loan-words in colloquial American German," *Language Monographs* 7.11-28 (December). Baltimore, Linguistic Society of America.

Austerlitz, Robert. 1968. "L'Ouralien," in Martinet (ed.) 1331-87.

Axmanova, Ol'ga S. 1966. *Slovar' lingvističeskix terminov.* Moscow, Sovetskaja Enciklopedija.

Bach, Adolf. 1934. *Deutsche Mundartforschung. Ihre Wege, Ergebnisse und Aufgaben.* Heidelberg, Carl Winter.

-----. 1956. *Geschichte der deutschen Sprache.*[6] Heidelberg, Quelle & Meyer.

Bailey, Charles-James N. 1969. "The integration of linguistic theory: internal reconstruction and the comparative method in descriptive linguistics," *Working Papers in Linguistics* 2.85-122 (March). Department of Linguistics, University of Hawaii, Honolulu. [Also in Stockwell and Macaulay (eds.) 22-31.]

-----. 1973. *Variation and linguistic theory.* Arlington, Center for Applied Linguistics.

-----. 1982. "The garden path that historical linguists went astray on," *Language and Communication* 2.151-60.

-----. 1983. "An apparent paradox concerning the nature of language," *Language and Communication* 3.205-18.

-----. 1985. *On the yin and yang of language.* Ann Arbor, Karoma.

Baldi, Philip, and Ronald H. Werth (eds.). 1978. *Readings in historical phonology.* University Park and London, Pennsylvania State University Press.

Baltimore, David, et al. 1970. "Viral RNA-dependent DNA polymerase," *Nature* 226.1209-13 (June 27).

Bammesberger, Alfred (ed.). 1983. *Das etymologische Wörterbuch. Fragen der Konzeption und Gestaltung.* Eichstätter Beiträge 8. Regensburg, Friedrich Pustet.

----- (ed.). 1988. *Die Laryngaltheorie und die Rekonstruktion des indogermanischen Laut- und Formensystems.* Heidelberg, Carl Winter.

Barber, E. J. W. 1974. *Archaeological decipherment: a handbook.* Princeton, Princeton University Press.

Barnett, H. G. 1983. *Qualitative science.* New York, Vantage Press.

Bàrtoli, Matteo. 1925. *Introduzione alla neolinguistica.* Geneva, Olschki.

Bastian, Otto. 1964. *Die europäischen Sprachen.* Dalp-Taschenbücher. Bern and Munich, Francke.

Baugh, Albert C., and Thomas Cable. 1978. *A history of the English language.* Englewood Cliffs, N.J., Prentice-Hall.

Beadle, George, and Muriel Beadle. 1967. *The language of life.* Garden City, N.Y., Doubleday.

Beals, Ralph L., and Harry Hoijer. 1965. *An introduction to anthropology.*[3] New York, Macmillan.

Becker, Alton. 1982. "Modern philology," *Forum linguisticum* 7.27-41.

Becker, Henrik. 1948. *Der Sprachbund.* Leipzig, Humboldt-Bücherei.

Bendix, Edward H. 1966. *Componential analysis of general vocabulary: the semantic structure of a set of verbs in English, Hindi, Japanese.* IJAL Publication 41 [40]. Bloomington, Indiana University.

Benediktsson, Hreinn. 1970. "Aspects of historical phonology," *The Nordic languages and modern linguistics* (Hreinn Benediktsson, ed.) 87-142. Reykjavík, Vísindafélag Íslendinga.

Bennett, Hobart. 1969. "Manifestations of i-umlaut in Old English, " *Linguistics* 50.5-26.

Bennett, William H. 1968. "The operation and relative chronology of Verner's law," *Language* 44.219-23.

Bentele, Günter. 1984. *Zeichen und Entwicklung. Vorbelegung zu einer genetischen Semiotik.* Tübingen, Narr.

Benveniste, Émile. 1939. "La nature du signe linguistique," *Acta Linguistica* 1.23-29. [Also in *Readings in linguistics* (E. Hamp et al., eds.) 2.104-108 (1966). Chicago, University of Chicago Press.]

-----. 1954. "Problèmes sémantiques de la reconstruction," *Word* 10.251-64.

-----. 1969. *Le vocabulaire des institutions indo-européennes.* 2 vols. Paris, Minuit. [English transl. Coral Gables, Fla., University of Miami Press 1973.]

Bergmann, Rolf. 1980. "Methodische Probleme der Lautverschiebungsdiskussion," *Sprachwissenschaft* 5.1-14.

Bergsland, Knut, and Hans Vogt. 1962. "On the validity of glottochronology," *Current Anthropology* 3.115-53.

Bernštejn, S. B. 1961. *Očerk sravnitel'noj grammatiki slavjanskix jazykov.* Moscow, Nauka.

Best, Karl-Heinz. 1973. *Probleme der Analogieforschung.* Munich, Hueber.

Beveridge, W. I. B. 1950. *The art of scientific investigation.* New York, Vintage Books.

Bhat, D. N. Shankara. 1968. "Is sound change gradual?," *Linguistics* 42.5-18.

Bickerton, Derek. 1973. "The nature of a creole continuum," *Language* 49.640-69.

-----. 1975. *Dynamics of a creole system.* London and New York, Cambridge University Press.

Biggs, Bruce. 1965. "Direct and indirect inheritance in Rotuman," *Lingua* 14.383-445.

Birdwhistell, Ray L. 1970. *Kinesics and context: essays on body motion communication.* Philadelphia, University of Pennsylvania Press.

Birnbaum, Henrik, and Jaan Puhvel (eds.). 1966. *Ancient Indo-European dialects.* Berkeley and Los Angeles, University of California Press.

Blansitt, Edward L., Jr. (ed.). 1967. *Tagmemic theory, current research in tagmemic description, grammatical analysis* (18th Round Table Meeting). Washington, D.C., Georgetown University Press.

Bloch, Bernard. 1948. "A set of postulates for phonemic analysis," *Language* 24.3-46. [Bobbs-Merrill Language-5.]

Bloomfield, Leonard. 1933. *Language.* New York, Holt.

Blount, Ben G., and Mary Sanches (eds.). 1977. *Sociocultural dimensions of language change.* New York, Academic Press.

Boas, Franz. 1929. "Classification of American Indian languages," *Language* 5.1-7.

-----. 1966. *Race, language, and culture.* New York, Macmillan (Free Press).

Bocheński, I. M. 1965. *The methods of contemporary thought* (transl. by Peter Caws). New York, Harper & Row.

Bolinger, Dwight L. 1949. "The sign is not arbitrary, " *Boletín del Instituto Caro y Cuervo* 5.52-62. Bogotá.

-----. 1968. *Aspects of language.* New York, Harcourt.

Bonfante, Giuliano. 1945. "On reconstruction and linguistic method," *Word* 1. 83-94, 132-61.

-----. 1946. "Additional notes on reconstruction," *Word* 2.155-56.

Boretzky, Norbert. 1977. *Historische Sprachwissenschaft.* Hamburg, Rowohlt.

-----. 1983. *Kreolsprachen, Substrate und Sprachwandel.* Wiesbaden, Harrassowitz.

Bottiglioni, Gino. 1954. "Linguistic geography: achievements, methods and orientations," *Word* 10. 375-87.

Bouissac, Paul A. R. 1970. "The circus as a multimedia language," *Language Sciences* 11.1-7 (August).

Brace, C. Loring, and M. F. Ashley Montagu. 1965. *Man's evolution, an introduction to physical anthropology.* New York, Macmillan.

Bréal, Michel. 1893. "On the canons of etymological investigation," *Transactions of the American Philological Association* 24.17-28.

-----. 1964 [1897]. *Semantics: studies in the science of meaning* (transl. by Nina Cust). New York, Dover.

Bremer, Otto. 1894. "Relative Sprachchronologie," *Indogermanische Forschungen* 4.8-31.

Brend, Ruth M. 1970. "Tagmemic theory: an annotated bibliography," *Journal of English Linguistics* 4.7-45.

Bright, William (ed.). 1966. *Sociolinguistics.* The Hague, Mouton.

Bright, William, and A. K. Ramanujan. 1964. "Sociolinguistic variation and language change," in Lunt (ed.) 1107-13.

Brosnahan, L. F. 1960. "Language and evolution," *Lingua* 9.225-36.

-----. 1961. *The sounds of language.* Cambridge, Heffer & Sons.

Brugmann, Karl. 1884. "Zur Frage nach den Verwandtschaftsverhältnissen der indogermanischen Sprachen," *Internationale Zeitschrift für allgemeine Sprachwissenschaft* 1.226-56.

Burling, Robbins. 1970. *Man's many voices. Language in its cultural setting.* New York, Holt.

Bynon, Theodora. 1977. *Historical linguistics.* Cambridge and New York, Cambridge University Press.

Cairns, Charles E. 1969. "Markedness, neutralization, and universal redundancy rules," *Language* 45.863-85.

Campbell, Brenton. 1969. "Metaphor, metonymy, and literalness," *General Linguistics* 9.149-66.

Campbell, Lyle. 1977. *Quichean linguistic prehistory.* Berkeley and Los Angeles, University of California Press.

-----. 1986. "Claims about syntactic change and Finnish historical syntax," *Journal of the Atlantic Provinces Linguistic Association* 8.72-93.

Campbell, Lyle, and Marianne Mithun. 1980. "The priorities and pitfalls of syntactic reconstruction," *Folia Linguistica Historica* 1.19-40.

Campbell, Lyle, and Jon Ringen. 1980. "Teleology and the explanation of sound change," *Phonologica 1980* (W. U. Dressler et al., eds.) 57-68. Innsbruck, Sprachwissenschaftliches Institut.

Campbell, Lyle, et al. 1986. "Meso-America as a linguistic area," *Language* 62.530-70.

Cardona, George, et al. (eds.). 1970. *Indo-European and Indo-Europeans.* Philadelphia, University of Pennsylvania Press.

Carroll, John B. 1953. *The study of language. A survey of linguistics and related disciplines in America.* Cambridge, Mass., Harvard University Press.

Chafe, Wallace L. 1959. "Internal reconstruction in Seneca," *Language* 35.477-95.

-----. 1962. "Phonetics, semantics, and language," *Language* 38.335-44.

-----. 1964. "Linguistic evidence for the relative age of Iroquois religious practices," *Southwestern Journal of Anthropology* 20.278-85.

-----. 1967. "Language as symbolization," *Language* 43.57-91.

-----. 1968. "The ordering of phonological rules," *International Journal of American Linguistics* 34.115-36.

-----. 1970. *Meaning and the structure of language.* Chicago, University of Chicago Press.

Chambers, J. K., and Peter Trudgill. 1980. *Dialectology.* Cambridge, Cambridge University Press.

Chao, Yuen Ren. 1967. "Chemical analogies in Chinese grammatical structure," *To honor Roman Jakobson* 1.447-51. The Hague, Mouton.

-----. 1968. *Language and symbolic systems.* New York, Cambridge University Press.

418   BIBLIOGRAPHY

Chen, Matthew Y. 1976. "Relative chronology: three methods of reconstruction," *Journal of Linguistics* 12.209-58.
Chen, Matthew, and Hsin-I Hsieh. 1971. "The time variable in phonological change," *Journal of Linguistics* 7.1-13.
Childe, Gordon V. 1951. *Man makes himself*. New York, New American Library.
Chomsky, Noam, and Morris Halle. 1968. *The sound pattern of English*. New York, Harper & Row.
Chrétien, C. Douglas. 1962. "The mathematical models of glottochronology," *Language* 38.11-37.
-----. 1963. "Shared innovations and subgrouping," *International Journal of American Linguistics* 29.66-68.
Christie, William, Jr. (ed.). 1976. *Current progress in historical linguistics*. Amsterdam, North-Holland.
Churchward, C. Maxwell. 1940. *Rotuman grammar and dictionary*. Sydney, Australasian Medical Publishing Company Ltd. for the Methodist Church of Australasia, Dept. of Overseas Missions.
Coates, Richard. 1987. "Pragmatic sources of analogical reformation," *Journal of Linguistics* 23.319-40.
Coates, William Ames. 1968. "Near-homonymy as a factor in language change," *Language* 44.467-79.
van Coetsem, Frans, and Linda R. Waugh (eds.). 1980. *Contributions to historical linguistics*. Leiden, Brill.
Cohen, David. 1969. "Why the Slavic 'second palatalization' comes first," *Papers from the fifth regional meeting of the Chicago Linguistic Society*, 306-13. Department of Linguistics, University of Chicago.
Cohen, Marcel. 1958. *La grande invention de l'écriture et son évolution*. 3 vols. Paris, Imprimérie nationale.
Collinder, Björn. 1937-39. "Das Wort als phonetische Einheit," *Språkvetenskapliga sällskapet i Uppsala förhandlingar* 63-75 [Also in *Sprachverwandtschaft und Wahrscheinlichkeit*. Acta Univ. Ups. Studia Uralica et Altaica 1964:205-17.]
-----. 1955, 1957, 1960. *A handbook of the Uralic languages*. 3 pts. Stockholm, Almqvist & Wiksell.
-----. 1965. *An introduction to the Uralic languages*. Berkeley and Los Angeles, University of California Press.
Collinge, N. E. 1985. *The laws of Indo-European*. Amsterdam, Benjamins.
Comrie, Bernard (ed.). 1987. *The world's major languages*. London and Sydney, Croom Helm.
Cook, Walter A. 1969. *Introduction to tagmemic analysis*. New York, Holt.
Coseriu, Eugenio. 1958. *Sincronía, diacronía, e historia: el problema del cambio lingüístico*. Universidad de la República. Facultad de Humanidades y Ciencias. Investigaciones y estudios 2. Montevideo. [Repr. Tübingen 1969, Madrid 1974; German transl. Munich., Fink 1974.]
-----. 1964. "Pour une sémantique diachronique structurale," *Travaux de linguistique et de littérature* II:1.139-86. Centre de Philologie et de Littératures Romanes, Université de Strasbourg. Paris, Klincksieck.
-----. 1980. "Vom Primat der Geschichte," *Sprachwissenschaft* 5.125-45.

-----. 1988. *Einführung in die allgemeine Sprachwissenschaft*. Tübingen, Francke.

Costello, John R. 1982. "The absolute construction in Indo-European: a syntagmemic reconstruction," *Journal of Indo-European Studies* 10.236-52.

-----. 1983. *Syntactic change and syntactic reconstruction*. Arlington, Summer Institute of Linguistics and University of Texas at Arlington.

Cram, David. 1979. "Catastrophe theory and syntactic change in Celtic," *University of East Anglia papers in linguistics* 9.1-10.

Crick, F. H. C. 1962. "The genetic code," *Scientific American*, 3-10 (October). [Scientific American Reprints 123.]

-----. 1966. "The genetic code: III," *Scientific American*, 55-62 (October).

Crystal, David. 1985. *A dictionary of linguistics and phonetics*.² Oxford and New York, Blackwell (and Deutsch).

Dahlstedt, Karl-Hampus. 1970. "The dilemmas of dialectology," *The Nordic languages and modern linguistics*, 158-84. See Benediktsson.

Darlington, C. D. 1947. "The genetic component of language," *Heredity* 1.269-86.

-----. 1955. "The genetic component of language," *Nature* 175.178.

Davenport, Michael, et al. (eds.). 1983. *Current topics in English historical linguistics*. Odense, Odense University Press.

Day, Richard R. (ed.). 1980. *Issues in English creoles*. Heidelberg, J. Groos.

Dearing, Vinton A. 1959. *A manual of textual analysis*. Berkeley and Los Angeles, University of California Press.

DeCamp, D., and I. Hancock (eds.). 1974. *Pidgins and creoles: current trends and prospects*. Washington, D.C., Georgetown University Press.

Deetz, James. 1967. *Invitation to archaeology*. Garden City, N.Y., The Natural History Press.

Denes, Peter B., and Elliot N. Pinson. 1963. *The speech chain*. Bell Telephone Laboratories. Baltimore, Waverly Press.

Deroy, Louis. 1956. *L'emprunt linguistique*. Paris, Les Belles Lettres (Bibliothèque de la Faculté de philosophie et lettres de l'Université de Liège 141).

Devoto, Giacomo. 1969. "Il metodo comparativo classico e le correnti linguistiche attuali," in Graur (ed.) 1.123-49.

Diebold, A. Richard, Jr. 1960. "Determining the centers of dispersal of language groups," *International Journal of American Linguistics* 26.1-10.

-----. 1985. *The evolution of Indo-European nomenclature for salmonid fish: the case of 'huchen' (Hucho spp.)*. Journal of Indo-European Studies, Monograph 5.

Dinneen, Francis P. 1968. "Analogy, langue and parole," *Lingua* 21.98-103.

Diringer, David. 1968. *The alphabet* (with Reinhold Regensburger).³ 2 vols. New York, Funk & Wagnalls.

Doerfer, Gerhard. 1967. "Homologe und analoge Verwandtschaft," *Indogermanische Forschungen* 72.22-26.

Dolgopol'skij, A. B. 1967. "Ot Saxary do Kamčatki jazyki iščut rodstvennikov," *Znanie--sila* 42:1.43-46.

420   BIBLIOGRAPHY

Dressler, Wolfgang. 1965. "Methodische Vorfragen bei der Bestimmung der 'Urheimat'," *Die Sprache* 11.25-60.
-----. 1969a. "Eine textsyntaktische Regel der idg. Wortstellung," *Zeitschrift für vergleichende Sprachforschung* 83.1-25.
-----. 1969b. "Die Erhaltung der Redundanz (lateinische Beispiele für ein wenig beachtetes Prinzip der Sprachentwicklung)," *Studia classica et orientalia Antonino Pagliaro oblata* 2.73-84. Istituto di Glottologia della Università di Roma.
-----. 1971. "Über die Rekonstrucktion der indogermanischen Syntax," *Zeitschrift für vergleichende Sprachforschung* 85.5-22.
-----. 1985. *Morphonology: the dynamics of derivation.* Ann Arbor, Karoma.
Dunkel, George. 1981. "Typology versus reconstruction," *Bono homini donum* (Yoël L. Arbeitman and Allan R. Bomhard, eds.) 559-70. Amsterdam, Benjamins.
Dyen, Isidore. 1956. "Language distribution and migration theory," *Language* 32.611-26.
-----. 1962. "The lexicostatistically determined relationship of a language group," *International Journal of American Linguistics* 28.153-61.
-----. 1963. "Why phonetic change is regular," *Language* 39.631-37.
-----. 1964. "On the validity of comparative lexicostatistics," in Lunt (ed.) 239-52.
-----. 1965a. "Lexicostatistics in comparative linguistics," *Lingua* 13.230-39.
-----. 1965b. *A lexicostatistical classification of the Austronesian languages.* IJAL Memoir 19. Bloomington, Indiana University.
-----. 1969. "Reconstruction, the comparative method, and the protolanguage uniformity assumption," *Language* 45.499-518.
Dyen, Isidore, et al. 1967. "Language divergence and estimated word retention rate," *Language* 43.150-71.
Ebeling, C. L. 1962. *Linguistic units.* The Hague, Mouton.
Eco, Umberto, and Thomas A. Sebeok (eds.). 1983. *The sign of three. Dupin, Holmes, Peirce.* Bloomington, Indiana University Press.
Eggan, Fred. 1954. "Social anthropology and the method of controlled comparison," *American Anthropologist* 56.743-63. [Bobbs-Merrill A-57.]
Ehrich, Robert W., and Gerald M. Henderson. 1968. "Culture area," *International encyclopedia of the social sciences* 3.563-68. New York, Macmillan (Free Press).
Ehrmann, Jacques (ed.). 1970. *Structuralism.* Garden City, N.Y., Doubleday.
Eisenstadt, Shmuel N. 1968. "Social evolution," *International encyclopedia of the social sciences* 5.228-34. New York, Macmillan (Free Press).
Ellis, Jeffrey. 1966. *Towards a general comparative linguistics.* The Hague, Mouton.
Embleton, Sheila M. 1986. *Statistics in historical linguistics.* Bochum, Brockmeyer.
Emeneau, Murray B. 1956. "India as a linguistic area," *Language* 32.3-16.
Emmet, Dorothy. 1958. *Function, purpose, and powers.* New York, Macmillan.
Esper, Erwin A. 1966. "Social transmission of an artificial language," *Language* 42.575-80.

Fairbanks, Gordon H. 1969. "Language split," *Glossa* 3.49-66.
Fasold, Ralph W. 1969. "Tense and the form 'be' in Black English," *Language* 45.763-76.
-----. 1970. "Two models of socially significant linguistic variation," *Language* 46.551-63.
-----. 1984. *The sociolinguistics of society*. Oxford, Blackwell.
Fast, Julius. 1970. *Body language*. New York, Evans. [Pocket Books 1971.]
Ferguson, Charles A. 1959. "Diglossia," *Word* 15. 325-40.
Finck, Franz N. 1910. *Die Haupttypen des Sprachbaus*. Leipzig, Teubner.
Fischer, John L. 1958. "Social influences in the choice of a linguistic variant," *Word* 14.47-56. [Also in Hymes (ed.), 1964:483-88.]
Fishman, Joshua A. (ed.). 1968. *Readings in the sociology of language*. The Hague, Mouton.
-----. 1985. "Why did Yiddish change?," *Diachronica* 2.67-82.
Fisiak, Jacek (ed.). 1978. *Recent developments in historical phonology*. The Hague, Mouton.
----- (ed.). 1980. *Historical morphology*. The Hague, Mouton.
----- (ed.). 1984. *Historical syntax*. Berlin, Mouton.
----- (ed.). 1985a. *Historical semantics. Historical word-formation*. Berlin, Mouton.
----- (ed.). 1985b. *Papers from the sixth international conference on historical linguistics*. Amsterdam, Benjamins.
Fodor, István. 1965. *The rate of linguistic change*. The Hague, Mouton.
Fokos-Fuchs, D. R. 1962. *Rolle der Syntax in der Frage nach Sprachverwandtschaft*. Ural-Altaische Bibliothek 11. Wiesbaden, Harrassowitz.
Fónagy, I. 1956-57. "Über den Verlauf des Lautwandels," *Acta Linguistica Hungarica* 6.173-278.
-----. 1967. "Variation und Lautwandel," *Phonologie der Gegenwart* (Josef Hamm, ed.) 100-123. Graz, H. Böhlaus Nachf.
Fox, Robin. 1967. *Kinship and marriage, an anthropological perspective*. Baltimore, Penguin.
-----. 1970. "The cultural animal," *Encounter* 35:1.31-42.
Francescato, Giuseppe. 1965. "Structural comparison, diasystems, and dialectology," *Zeitschrift für romanische Philologie* 81.484-91.
Francis, W. Nelson. 1983. *Dialectology: an introduction*. London and New York, Longman.
Frey, Leonard H. 1966. *Readings in Early English language history*. New York, Odyssey Press.
Friedrich, Paul. 1970. *Proto-Indo-European trees*. Chicago, University of Chicago Press.
Fudge, E. C. 1969. "Mutation rules and ordering in phonology," *Journal of Linguistics* 5.23-38.
Gamillscheg, E. 1927. "Zur Methodik der etymologischen Forschung," *Zeitschrift für französische Sprache und Literatur* 50.216-98.
-----. 1928. *Die Sprachgeographie und ihre Ergebnisse für die allgemeine Sprachwissenschaft*. Bielefeld, Velhagen.

422   BIBLIOGRAPHY

Gamkrelidze, T. V., and Vjačeslav V. Ivanov. 1984. *Indoevropejskij jazyk i indoevropejcy*. 2 vols. Tbilisi, Izdatel'stvo Tbiliskogo Universiteta. [English translation, Berlin, Mouton de Gruyter 1988; summary in *Soviet anthropology and archaeology* Summer 1983:51-96.]

Garvin, Paul L. 1970. "Moderation in linguistic theory," *Language Sciences* 9.1-3 (February).

Gaur, Albertine. 1984. *A history of writing*. London, The British Library.

Gedney, William J. 1967. "Future directions in comparative Tai linguistics," Paper read at UCLA.

Gelb, I. J. 1963. *A study of writing*. Rev. ed. Chicago, University of Chicago Press.

Giacalone Ramat, Anna, et al. (eds.). 1987. *Papers from the seventh international conference on historical linguistics*. Amsterdam, Benjamins.

Giglioli, Pier Paolo (ed.). 1972. *Language and social context*. Harmondsworth, Penguin.

Givón, Talmy. 1971. "Historical syntax and synchronic morphology. An archaeologist's field trip," *Papers from the seventh regional meeting of the Chicago Linguistic Society*, 394-415. Department of Linguistics, University of Chicago.

Gleason, H. A., Jr. 1961. *An introduction to descriptive linguistics*. Rev. ed. New York, Holt.

-----. 1964. "The organization of language: a stratificational view," *Monograph series on languages and linguistics* 17.75-95. Washington, D.C., Georgetown University Press.

Goodenough, Ward H. 1956. "Componential analysis and the study of meaning," *Language* 32.195-216. [Bobbs-Merrill A-91.]

Goossens, Jan. 1969. *Strukturelle Sprachgeographie. Eine Einführung in Methodik und Ergebnisse*. Heidelberg, Carl Winter.

Götze, Albrecht. 1923. "Relative Chronologie von Lauterscheinungen im Italischen," *Indogermanische Forschungen* 41.78-149.

Grace, George W. 1969. "Speaking of linguistic change," *Working papers in linguistics* 3.101-116. Department of Linguistics, University of Hawaii, Honolulu.

Graur, A., et al. (eds.). 1969-70. *Actes du Xe congrès international des linguistes, Bucarest 1967*. 4 vols. Bucharest, Éditions de l'Académie.

Greenberg, Joseph H. 1954. "A quantitative approach to the morphological typology of language," *Method and perspective in anthropology: papers in honor of Wilson D. Wallis* (Robert F. Spencer, ed.) 192-220. Minneapolis, University of Minnesota Press. [Also in *International Journal of American Linguistics* 26.178-94 (1960).]

-----. 1957. *Essays in Linguistics*. Chicago, University of Chicago Press.

-----. 1959. "Language and evolution," *Evolution and anthropology: a centennial appraisal* (Betty J. Meggers, ed.), 61-75. Washington, D.C., The Anthropological Society of Washington. [Bobbs-Merrill A-95.]

----- (ed.). 1963. *Universals of language*. Cambridge, Mass., M.I.T. Press.

-----. 1966a. *Languages of Africa*.[2] Bloomington, Indiana University Press.

-----. 1966b. "Language universals," in Sebeok (ed.) 3.61-112.

-----. 1969a. "Some methods of dynamic comparison in linguistics," *Substance and structure of language* (Jaan Puhvel, ed.) 147-203. Berkeley and Los Angeles, University of California Press.

-----. 1969b. "The theoretical significance of the relation of frequency to semantic features in a case language (Russian)," *Linguistic Society of America Meeting Handbook*, 126-27 (December). Washington, D.C., Center for Applied Linguistics.

Greenough, James B., and George L. Kittredge. 1929. *Words and their ways in English speech*. New York, Macmillan. Paperback, 1961. [Chapters 15 and 20 in Bobbs-Merrill Language-31.]

Gudschinsky, Sarah. 1956. "The ABC's of lexicostatistics," *Word* 12.175-210. [Bobbs-Merrill A-97, and Hymes (ed.) 1964:612-23.]

Guiraud, Pierre. 1955. *La sémantique*. (Que sais-je?) No. 655. Paris, Presses Universitaires de France.

-----. 1964. *L'étymologie*. (Que sais-je?) No. 1122. Paris, Presses Universitaires de France.

Gumperz, John J. 1958. "Dialect differences and social stratification in a North Indian village," *American Anthropologist* 60.668-82. [Bobbs-Merrill A-98.]

-----. 1961. "Speech variation and the study of Indian civilization," *American Anthropologist* 63.976-88.

-----. 1968. "The speech community," *International encyclopedia of the social sciences* 9.381-86. New York, Macmillan (Free Press).

Haas, Mary R. 1966. "Historical linguistics and the genetic relationship of languages," in Sebeok (ed.) 3.112-53. [Expanded version *The prehistory of languages*, The Hague, Mouton 1969.]

Haiman, John. 1980. "The iconicity of grammar: isomorphism and motivation," *Language* 56.515-40.

----- (ed.) 1985. *Iconicity in syntax*. Amsterdam, Benjamins.

Hakulinen, Lauri. 1961. *The structure and development of the Finnish language* (transl. by John Atkinson). Bloomington, Indiana University Press.

Hall, Edward T. 1959. *The silent language*. Greenwich, Conn., Fawcett Publications.

Hall, Robert A., Jr. 1950. "The reconstruction of Proto-Romance," *Language* 26.6-27. [Also in *Readings in linguistics* (Martin Joos, ed.) 1.303-314 (1958). University of Chicago Press.]

-----. 1958. "Creolized languages and 'genetic relationships'," *Word* 14.367-73.

-----. 1960. "On realism in reconstruction," *Language* 36.203-206.

-----. 1963. *Idealism in Romance linguistics*. Ithaca, Cornell University Press.

-----. 1964. *Introductory linguistics*. Philadelphia, Chilton Books.

-----. 1966. *Pidgin and creole languages*. Ithaca, Cornell University Press.

-----.1968. "Comparative reconstruction in Romance syntax," *Acta Linguistica Hafniensia* 11.81-88.

-----. 1969. "Italian *serpe, serpente* again," *Language Sciences* 8.27-28 (December).

Halldórsson, Halldór. 1970. "Determining the lending language." See Benediktsson 365-78.

Halle, Morris. 1962. "Phonology and generative grammar," *Word* 18.54-72.

Hallowell, A. Irving. 1956. "The structural and functional dimensions of a human existence," *The Quarterly Review of Biology* 31.88-101. [Bobbs-Merrill A-105.]

Hammarström, Göran. 1966. *Linguistische Einheiten im Rahmen der Modernen Sprachwissenschaft.* Kommunikation und Kybernetik in Einzeldarstellungen 5. New York, Springer.

Hammerich, Louis L. 1954. "The Russian stratum in Alaskan Eskimo," *Word* 10.401-428.

Harris, Alice C. 1985. *Diachronic syntax: the Kartvelian case.* New York, Academic Press.

Harris, James W. 1969. "Sound change in Spanish and the theory of markedness," *Language* 45.538-52.

Harris, Martin, and Paolo Ramat (eds.). 1987. *Historical development of auxiliaries.* Berlin, Mouton de Gruyter.

Harris, Roy. 1986. *The origin of writing.* London, Duckworth.

Harris, Zellig S. 1951. *Structural linguistics.* Chicago, University of Chicago Press.

Hass, Wilbur A. 1969. "The psychological reality of different types of phonological change," *Papers from the fifth regional meeting of the Chicago Linguistic Society,* 343-47. Department of Linguistics, University of Chicago.

Hattori, Shirô, et al. (eds.). 1983. *Proceedings of the XIIIth international congress of linguists.* Tokyo, Proceedings Publishing Committee.

Haugen, Einar. 1950. "The analysis of linguistic borrowing," *Language* 26.210-31.[Also in Lass (ed.) 1969:58-81.]

Havers, Wilhelm. 1931. *Handbuch der erklärenden Syntax. Ein Versuch zur Erforschung der Bedingungen und Triebkräfte in Syntax und Stilistik.* Heidelberg, Carl Winter.

Havránek, Bohuslav. 1966. "Zur Problematik der Sprachmischung," *Travaux linguistiques de Prague* 2.81-98.

Hawkins, John A. 1983. *Word order universals.* New York, Academic Press.

Heine, Bernd. 1973. *Pidgin-Sprachen im Bantu-Bereich.* Kölner Beiträge zur Afrikanistik 3. Berlin, Reimer.

Heine, Bernd, and Ulrike Claudi. 1986. *On the rise of grammatical categories. Some examples from Maa.* Kölner Beiträge zur Afrikanistik 13. Berlin, Reimer.

Heine, Bernd, and Mechthild Reh. 1984. *Grammaticalization and reanalysis in African languages.* Hamburg, Buske.

Henle, Paul (ed.). 1965. *Language, thought and culture.* Ann Arbor, University of Michigan Press.

Herbert, Robert K. 1986. *Language universals, markedness theory, and natural phonetic processes.* Berlin, Mouton de Gruyter.

Herman, L., and M. S. Herman. 1958. *Foreign dialects: a manual for actors, directors, and writers.* New York, Theater Arts Books.

Hermann, Eduard. 1907. "Über das Rekonstruieren," *Zeitschrift für vergleichende Sprachforschung* 41.1-64.
-----. 1931. *Lautgesetz und Analogie*. Abhandlungen der Gesellschaft der Wissenschaften zu Göttingen, Phil.-Hist. Klasse, Neue Folge, Band 23:3.
Hill, Archibald A. 1936. "Phonetic and phonemic change," *Language* 12.15-22.
----- (ed.). 1969. *Linguistics today*. New York, Basic Books.
Hill, Kenneth C. (ed.) 1979. *The genesis of language*. Ann Arbor, Karoma.
Hjelmslev, Louis. 1963. *Prolegomena to a theory of language* (transl. by Francis J. Whitfield). Madison, University of Wisconsin Press.
-----. 1970. *Language: an introduction* (transl. by Francis J. Whitfield). Madison, University of Wisconsin Press.
Hock, Hans Henrich. 1985a. "Yes, Virginia, syntactic reconstruction is possible," *Studies in the Linguistic Sciences* 15.49-60.
-----. 1985b. "Regular metathesis," *Linguistics* 23.529-46.
-----. 1986. *Principles of historical linguistics*. Berlin and New York, Mouton de Gruyter.
Hockett, Charles F. 1948a. "Implications of Bloomfield's Algonkian studies," *Language* 24.117-31. [Also in *Readings in linguistics* (Martin Joos, ed.) 1.281-89 (1958). Chicago, University of Chicago Press, and Hymes (ed.) 1964:599-611.]
-----. 1948b. "Biophysics, linguistics, and the unity of science," *American Scientist* 36.558-72. [Bobbs-Merrill A-115.]
-----. 1958. *A course in modern linguistics*. New York, Macmillan.
-----. 1960. "The origin of speech," *Scientific American* 3-11 (September). [Scientific American Reprints 603.]
-----. 1961. "Linguistic elements and their relations," *Language* 37.29-53.
-----. 1965. "Sound change," *Language* 41.185-204.
-----. 1967. "Where the tongue slips, there slip I," *To honor Roman Jakobson* 2.910-36. The Hague, Mouton.
-----. 1985. "Knowledge of the past," *Linguistics and philosophy* (A. Makkai and A. K. Melby, eds.) 317-41. Amsterdam, Benjamins.
Hockett, Charles F., and Robert Ascher. 1964. "The human revolution," *Current Anthropology* 5.135-68. [Bobbs-Merrill A-306.]
Hodge, Carleton T. 1970. "The linguistic cycle," *Language Sciences* 13.1-7 (December).
Hoenigswald, Henry M. 1946. "Sound change and linguistic structure," *Language* 22.138-43. [Bobbs-Merrill Language-48.]
-----. 1950. "The principal step in comparative grammar," *Language* 26.357-64. [Bobbs-Merrill Language-49, and *Readings in linguistics* (Martin Joos, ed.) 1.298-302 (1958). Chicago, University of Chicago Press.]
-----. 1955. "Change, analogical and semantic," *Indian Linguistics* 16.233-36.
-----. 1960a. *Language change and linguistic reconstruction*. Chicago, University of Chicago Press.
-----. 1960b. "Phonetic similarity in internal reconstruction," *Language* 36.191-92.
-----. 1963. "On the history of the comparative method," *Anthropological Linguistics* 5.1-11.

426   BIBLIOGRAPHY

-----. 1964a. "Allophones, allomorphs, and conditioned change," in Lunt (ed.) 645-49.

-----. 1964b. "Graduality, sporadicity, and the minor sound change processes," *Phonetica* 11.202-215.

-----. 1965. "Phonetic reconstruction," *Proceedings of the fifth international congress of phonetic sciences* (E. Zwirner, ed.) 25-42. Basel, Karger.

-----. 1966. "Criteria for the subgrouping of languages," in Birnbaum and Puhvel (eds.) 1-12.

Höfler, Otto. 1958. *Die zweite Lautverschiebung bei Ostgermanen und Westgermanen.* Tübingen, Niemeyer.

Hofmann, J. B., and H. Rubenbauer. 1963. *Wörterbuch der grammatischen und metrischen Terminologie.* Heidelberg, Carl Winter.

Hofstra, Tette. 1985. *Ostseefinnisch und Germanisch: frühe Lehnbeziehungen im nördlichen Ostseeraum im Lichte der Forschung seit 1961.* Groningen.

Hogben, L. 1956. "Human biology and human speech," *British Journal of Preventive Medicine* 10.63-74.

Hogg, Richard M. 1979. "Analogy and phonology," *Journal of Linguistics* 15.55-85.

Hoijer, Harry. 1939. "Chiricahua loan-words from Spanish," *Language* 15.110-15.

-----. 1946. "Introduction" to *Linguistic structures of native America.* Viking Fund Publications in Anthropology 6.9-29. [Bobbs-Merrill A-118.]

-----. 1948. "Linguistic and cultural change," *Language* 24.335-45. [Also in Hymes (ed.), 1964:455-66.]

----- (ed.). 1954. *Language in culture.* Chicago, University of Chicago Press.

Holland, Gary B. 1986. "Nominal sentences and the origin of absolute constructions in Indo-European," *Zeitschrift für vergleichende Sprachwissenschaft* 99.163-93.

Hollis, Martin, and Steven Lukes (eds.). 1982. *Rationality and relativism.* Oxford, Blackwell.

Holmberg, Allan R. 1954. "Adventures in culture change," *Method and perspective in anthropology* (Robert F. Spencer, ed.), 103-113, Minneapolis, University of Minnesota Press. [Bobbs-Merrill A-119.]

Hombert, Jean-Marie, et al. 1979. "Phonetic explanation for the development of tones," *Language* 55.37-58.

Hořejší, Vladimír. 1964. "Chronologie relative et linguistique structural," *Travaux linguistiques de Prague* 1.107-110.

Hörmann, Hans. 1970. *Psycholinguistics. An introduction to research and theory* (transl. from rev. ed. by H. H. Stern). New York, Springer.

-----. 1976. *Meinen und Verstehen.* Frankfurt, Suhrkamp. [English transl. Berlin, Springer 1981.]

Horne, Kibbey M. 1966. *Language typology: 19th and 20th century views.* Washington, D.C., Georgetown University Press.

Householder, Fred W. 1960. "First thoughts on syntactic indices," *International Journal of American Linguistics* 26.195-97.

Houston, Susan. 1969. "A sociolinguistic consideration of the Black English children in northern Florida," *Language* 45.599-607.

-----. 1970. "Competence and performance in Child Black English," *Language Sciences* 12.9-14 (October).

Humboldt, Wilhelm von. 1970 [1836]. *Linguistic variability and intellectual development* (transl. by George C. Buck and Frithjof A. Raven). Coral Gables, Fla., University of Miami Press.

Huntley, D. G. 1968. "Two cases of analogical feature substitution in Slavic," *Language* 44.501-506.

Huxley, Julian. 1953. *Evolution in action*. London, Chatto & Windus.

Hyman, Larry M. 1970a. "How concrete is phonology?," *Language* 46.58-76.

-----. 1970b. "The role of borrowing in the justification of phonological grammars," *Studies in African Linguistics* (UCLA) 1.1-48.

Hymes, Dell H. 1956. "Na-Dené and positional analysis of categories," *American Anthropologist* 58.624-38.

-----. 1959. "Genetic classification: retrospect and prospect," *Anthropological Linguistics* 1.50-66. [Bobbs-Merrill A-125.]

-----. 1960. "Lexicostatistics so far," *Current Anthropology* 1.3-44. [Bobbs-Merrill A-126.]

-----. 1961. "Functions of speech: an evolutionary approach," *Anthropology and education* (Frederick C. Gruber, ed.), 55-83. Philadelphia, University of Pennsylvania Press. [Bobbs-Merrill A-124.]

----- (ed.). 1964. *Language in culture and society. A reader in linguistics and anthropology*. New York, Harper & Row.

-----. 1968a. "Linguistics: the field," *International encyclopedia of the social sciences* 9.351-71. New York, Macmillan (Free Press).

-----. 1968b. "Sociolinguistics," *Language Sciences* 1.23-26 (May).

----- (ed.). 1971. *Pidginization and creolization of languages*. Cambridge, Cambridge University Press.

Illič-Svityč, V. M. 1967. "Materialy k sravnitel'nomu slovarju nostratičeskix jazykov," *Étimologija 1965*, 321-73. Moscow, Nauka.

-----. 1968. "Sootvestvija smyčnyx v nostratičeskix jazykax," *Étimologija 1966*, 304-355, 401-410. Moscow, Nauka.

-----. 1971, 1976, 1984. *Opyt sravnenija nostratičeskix jazykov*. (V. A. Dybo, ed.). 3 vols. Moscow, Nauka.

Irving, John A. 1949. "The comparative method and the nature of human nature," *Philosophy and Phenomenological Research* 9.545-57.

Itkonen, Erkki. 1941. "Über den Charakter des ostlappischen Stufenwechselsystems," *Finnisch-Ugrische Forschungen* 27.137-67.

-----. 1946. *Struktur und Entwicklung der ostlappischen Quantitätssysteme*. Mémoires de la Société Finno-Ougrienne 88. Helsinki, Suomalais-ugrilainen Seura.

-----. 1966. *Kieli ja sen tutkimus*. Helsinki and Porvoo, Söderström.

Itkonen, Esa. 1978. *Grammatical theory and metascience*. Amsterdam, Benjamins.

-----. 1983. *Causality in linguistic theory*. Bloomington, Indiana University Press/London and Canberra, Croom Helm.

-----. 1984. "On the 'rationalist' conception of linguistic change," *Diachronica* 1.203-16.

Itkonen, Terho. 1970. "Ovatko äänteenmuutokset vähittäisiä vai harppauksellisia?," *Virittäjä* 74.411-38.

------. 1976. "Syntaktisten vaikutusyhteyksien luonteesta," *Virittäjä* 80.52-81.

Itkonen, T. I. 1958. *Koltan- ja kuolanlapin sanakirja* (Wörterbuch des Kolta- und Kolalappischen). 2 vols. Lexica Societatis Fenno-Ugricae 15. Helsinki, Suomalais-ugrilainen Seura.

Ivić, Milka. 1965. *Trends in linguistics.* The Hague, Mouton.

Jacobsohn, Hermann. 1922. *Arier und Ugrofinnen.* Göttingen, Vandenhoeck & Ruprecht.

Jakobson, Roman. 1949. The phonemic and grammatical aspects of language in their interrelation," *Proceedings of the sixth international congress of linguists* (Michel Lejeune, ed.) 5-18. Paris, Klincksieck.

------. 1958. "Typological studies and their contribution to historical linguistics," *Proceedings of the eighth international congress of linguists* (Eva Sivertsen, ed.) 17-35. Oslo, University Press.

------. 1965. "Quest for the essence of language," *Diogenes* 51.21-37.

------. 1968. *Child language, aphasia and phonological universals* (transl. by Allan R. Keiler). The Hague, Mouton.

------. 1969. "Linguistics in its relation to other sciences," in Graur (ed.) 1.75-122.

Janert, Klaus Ludwig. 1961. "Studien zu den Aśoka-Inschriften. III," *Nachrichten der Akademie der Wissenschaften zu Göttingen.* I. Phil.-Hist. Klasse, No. 1. 1-25.

Janhunen, Juha, et al. (eds.). 1983. *Symposium saeculare societatis fenno- ugricae.* Mémoires de la Société Finno-Ougrienne 185. Helsinki, Suomalais-ugrilainen Seura.

Jeffers, Robert J., and Ilse Lehiste. 1979. *Principles and methods for historical linguistics.* Cambridge, Mass., M.I.T. Press.

Jensen, Hans. 1969. *Die Schrift.*[3] Berlin, VEB deutscher Verlage der Wissenschaften. [English transl. London, Allen & Unwin 1970.]

Jespersen, Otto. 1941. *Efficiency in linguistic change.* Det Kgl. Danske Videnskabernes Selskab. Hist.-fil. Meddelelser 27:4.

------. 1956. *Growth and structure of the English language.* Oxford, Blackwell.

------. 1964. *Language, its nature, development and origin.* New York, Norton.

Joki, Aulis J. 1973. *Uralier und Indogermanen. Die älteren Berührungen zwischen den uralischen und indogermanischen Sprachen.* Mémoires de la Société Finno-Ougrienne 151. Helsinki, Suomalais-ugrilainen Seura.

Joos, Martin. 1952. "The Medieval sibilants," *Language* 28.222-31. [Also in *Readings in linguistics* (Martin Joos, ed.) 1.377-78 (1958). Chicago, University of Chicago Press.]

------. 1962. *The five clocks.* IJAL Publication 22. Bloomington, Indiana University.

Joseph, Brian D. 1983. *The synchrony and diachrony of the Balkan infinitive: a study in areal, general, and historical linguistics.* Cambridge, Cambridge University Press.

Jucquois, Guy. 1970. "La théorie de la racine en indo-européen," *La Linguistique* 6.69-102, 8.73-103 (1972).

Kahre, Annette. 1985. *Studien zum morphosemantischen Sprachwandel.* Frankfurt, Peter Lang.

Kalima, Jalo. 1915. *Die ostseefinnischen Lehnwörter im Russischen.* Helsinki, Suomalaisen Kirjallisuuden Seura.

-----. 1936. *Itämerensuomalaisten kielten balttilaiset lainasanat.* Helsinki, Suomalaisen Kirjallisuuden Seura.

Kaplan, Abraham. 1964. *The conduct of inquiry. Methodology for behavioral science.* San Francisco, Chandler Publishing Co.

Kastovsky, Dieter, et al. (eds.). 1988. *Luick revisited.* Tübingen, Narr.

Katičić, Radoslav. 1966. "Der Entsprechungsbegriff in der vergleichenden Laut- und Formenlehre," *Indogermanische Forschungen* 71.203-20.

-----. 1970. *A contribution to the general theory of comparative linguistics.* The Hague, Mouton.

Kay, Paul, and C. McDaniel. 1979. "On the logic of variable rules," *Language in Society* 8.151-89.

Kazazis, Kostas. 1967. "On a generative grammar of the Balkan languages," *Foundations of Language* 3.117-23.

-----. 1968. "Sunday Greek," *Papers from the fourth regional meeting of the Chicago Linguistic Society,* 130-40. Department of Linguistics, University of Chicago.

-----. 1970. "The relative importance of parents and peers in first-language acquisition," *General Linguistics* 10.111-20.

-----. 1972. "The status of Turkisms in the present-day Balkan languages," *Aspects of the Balkans: continuity and change* (H. Birnbaum and S. Vryonis, eds.) 87-116. The Hague, Mouton.

Keiler, Allan R. 1970. *A phonological study of the Indo-European laryngeals.* The Hague, Mouton.

Keller, Rudi. 1985. "Towards a theory of linguistic change," *Linguistic Dynamics* (Thomas T. Ballmer, ed.) 211-37. Berlin, Mouton de Gruyter.

Kent, Roland G. 1936. "Assimilation and dissimilation," *Language* 12.245-58.

Kettunen, Lauri. 1962. *Eestin kielen äännehistoria.*[3] Suomalaisen Kirjallisuuden Seuran Toimituksia 156. Helsinki.

Keyser, Samuel Jay. 1963. "Review of The pronunciation of English in the Atlantic states, by Hans Kurath and Raven I. McDavid," *Language* 39.303-16.

King, Robert D. 1967. "Functional load and sound change," *Language* 43.831-52.

-----. 1969a. "Push chains and drag chains," *Glossa* 3.3-21.

-----. 1969b. *Historical linguistics and generative grammar.* Englewood Cliffs, N.J., Prentice-Hall.

Kiparsky, Paul. 1965. *Phonological change.* Cambridge, Mass., M.I.T. dissertation.

-----. 1968a. "Linguistic universals and linguistic change," *Universals in linguistic theory* (Emmon Bach and Robert T. Harms, eds.) 170-202. New York, Holt.

-----. 1968b. "Tense and mood in Indo-European syntax," *Foundations of Language* 4.30-57.

-----. 1982. *Explanation in phonology*. Dordrecht, Foris.

Kirn, Paul. 1963. *Einführung in die Geschichtswissenschaft*. Sammlung Göschen 270. Berlin, de Gruyter.

Knight, Thomas S. 1965. *Charles Peirce*. New York, Washington Square Press.

Knobloch, Johann. 1961f. *Sprachwissenschaftliches Wörterbuch*. Heidelberg, Carl Winter.

Koch, Walter A. 1970. *Zur Theorie des Lautwandels*. Hildesheim/New York, Olms.

Kohler, Klaus J. 1967. "Structural dialectology," *Zeitschrift für Mundartforschung* 34.40-44.

Koivulehto, Jorma. 1970. "Suomen *laiva*-sanasta," *Virittäjä* 74.178-83.

-----. 1981. "Reflexe des germ. /ē¹/ im Finnischen und die Datierung der germanisch-finnischen Lehnbeziehungen," *Beiträge zur Geschichte der deutschen Sprache und Literatur* 103.167-203, 333-76.

Koopman, W. F., et al. (eds.). 1987. *Explanation and linguistic change*. Amsterdam, Benjamins.

Korhonen, Mikko. 1969. "Die Entwicklung der morphologischen Methode," *Finnisch-Ugrische Forschungen* 37.203-362.

-----. 1979. "Entwicklungstendenzen des finnisch-ugrischen Kasussystems," *Finnisch-Ugrische Forschungen* 43.1-21.

Kraft, V. 1955. "Geschichtsforschung als exakte Wissenschaft," *Anzeiger der Österreichischen Akademie der Wissenschaften* 19.239-51.

Krahe, Hans. 1970. *Einleitung in das vergleichende Sprachstudium* (ed. by Wolfgang Meid). Innsbruck, Sprachwissenschaftliches Institut.

Krámský, Jiří. 1969. *The word as a linguistic unit*. The Hague, Mouton.

Kroeber, A. L. 1913. "The determination of linguistic relationship," *Anthropos* 8.389-401.

-----. 1919. "On the principle of order in civilization as exemplified by changes of fashion," *American Anthropologist* 21.235-63. [Bobbs-Merrill A-137.]

-----. 1935. "History and science in anthropology," *American Anthropologist* 37.539-69. [Bobbs-Merrill A-136.]

-----. 1944. *Configuration of culture growth*. Berkeley and Los Angeles, University of California Press.

----- (ed.). 1953. *Anthropology today. An encyclopedic inventory*. Chicago, University of Chicago Press.

-----. 1960. "On typological indices I: ranking of languages," *International Journal of American Linguistics* 26.171-77.

-----. 1963a. *Anthropology: culture patterns and processes*. New York, Harcourt.

-----. 1963b. *Anthropology: biology and race*. New York, Harcourt.

-----. 1963c. *An anthropologist looks at history*. Berkeley and Los Angeles, University of California Press.

Kroeber, A. L., and C. D. Chrétien. 1937. "Quantitative classification of Indo-European languages," *Language* 13.83-103.

Krohn, Kaarle. 1926. *Die folkloristische Arbeitsmethode*. Cambridge, Mass., Harvard University Press. [English transl. Austin, University of Texas Press 1971.]

Krohn, Robert K. 1969. *English vowels*. Ann Arbor, University of Michigan dissertation; University Microfilms 70-4123.

Kronasser, Heinz. 1952. *Handbuch der Semasiologie*. Heidelberg, Carl Winter.

Kuipers, Aert H. 1968. "Unique types and typological universals," *Pratidānam* (J. C. Heesterman et al., eds.) 68-88. The Hague, Mouton.

Kurath, Hans. 1972. *Studies in area linguistics*. Bloomington and London, Indiana University Press.

Kurath, Hans, and Raven I. McDavid, Jr. 1961. *The pronunciation of English in the Atlantic states*. Ann Arbor, University of Michigan Press.

Kuryłowicz, Jerzy. 1945-1949. "La nature des procès dits 'analogiques'," *Acta Linguistica* 5.15-37. [Also in *Readings in linguistics* (E. Hamp et al. eds.) 2.158-74 (1966). Chicago, University of Chicago Press.]

-----. 1964. "On the methods of internal reconstruction," in Lunt (ed.) 9-36.

-----. 1968. "A remark on Lachmann's law," *Harvard Studies in Classical Philology* 72. 295-99.

Labov, William. 1963. "The social motivation of a sound change," *Word* 19.273-309.

-----. 1964. "Phonological correlates of social stratification," *The ethnography of communication* (J. J. Gumperz and D. H. Hymes, eds.) 164-76. *American Anthropologist* 66:6, pt. 2.

-----. 1965. "On the mechanism of linguistic change," *Monograph Series on Languages and Linguistics* 18.91-114. Washington, D.C., Georgetown University Press.

-----. 1966. *The social stratification of English in New York City*. Washington, D.C., Center for Applied Linguistics.

-----. 1969. "Contraction, deletion, and inherent variability of the English copula," *Language* 45., 715-62.

-----. 1970. "The study of language in its social setting," *Studium Generale* 23.30-87.

-----. 1972. "The internal evolution of linguistic rules," in Stockwell and Macaulay (eds.) 101-71.

Labov, William, et al. 1972. *A quantitative study of sound change in progress*. 2 vols. NSF GS-3287. Philadelphia, The U.S. Regional Survey.

Ladefoged, Peter. 1982. *A course in phonetics*.[2] New York, Harcourt Brace Jovanovich.

Lamb, Sydney M. 1964. "The sememic approach to structural semantics," *The ethnography of communication* (J. J. Gumperz and D. H. Hymes, eds.) 57-78. *American Anthropologist* 66:3, pt. 2.

-----. 1966. *Outline of stratificational grammar*. Washington, D.C., Georgetown University Press.

Lane, Michael (ed.). 1970. *Introduction to structuralism.* New York, Basic Books.

Langhoff, Stephan. 1980. *Gestaltlinguistik.* Frankfurt, Peter Lang.

Lanham, Richard A. 1969. *A handlist of rhetorical terms.* Berkeley and Los Angeles, University of California Press.

Lass, Roger (ed.). 1969. *Approaches to English historical linguistics: an anthology.* New York, Holt.

-----. 1980. *On explaining language change.* Cambridge, Cambridge University Press.

Lausberg, Heinrich. 1967. *Elemente der literarischen Rhetorik.*³ Munich, Hueber.

Leach, Edmund R. 1968. "The comparative method in anthropology," *International encyclopedia of the social sciences* 1.339-45. New York, Macmillan (Free Press).

Le Bourdelle, H., et al. (eds.). 1980. *L'emprunt linguistique. Cahiers de l'Institut de Linguistique de Louvain* 6:1-2.

Leed, Richard L. 1970. "Distinctive features and analogy," *Lingua* 26.1-24.

Lees, Robert B. 1953. "The basis of glottochronology," *Language* 29.113-27.

Lehmann, Christian. 1974. "Isomorphismus im sprachlichen Zeichen," *Struktura* 8.98-123.

-----. 1982. *Thoughts on grammaticalization. A programmatic sketch.* Vol. 1. Cologne, Institute of Linguistics.

Lehmann, Winfred P. 1958. "On earlier stages of the Indo-European nominal inflection," *Language* 34.179-202.

-----. 1962. *Historical linguistics: an introduction.* New York, Holt. [2nd ed. 1973.]

-----. 1964. "Types of sound change," in Lunt (ed.) 658-62.

-----. 1971. "Grammatischer Wechsel and current phonological discussion" *Generative studies in historical linguistics* (Mária Tsiapera, ed.) 9-43. Current Inquiry into Language & Linguistics 2. Edmonton/Champaign, Linguistic Research, Inc.

-----. 1974. *Proto-Indo-European syntax.* Austin, University of Texas Press.

Lehmann, Winfred P., and Yakov Malkiel (eds.). 1982. *Perspectives on historical linguistics.* Amsterdam, Benjamins.

Lehrer, Adrienne. 1969. "Semantic cuisine," *Journal of Linguistics* 5.39-55.

Lenneberg, Eric H. 1960. "Language, evolution, and purposive behavior," *Culture in history: essays in honor of Paul Radin* (S. Diamond, ed.) 869-93. New York, Columbia University Press. [Bobbs-Merrill A-142.]

-----. 1967. *Biological foundations of language.* New York, Wiley.

Leppik, Merle. 1968. "On the non-phonological character of consonant gradation in Proto-Fennic," *Sovetskoe Finno-Ugrovedenie* 4.1-12.

Lepschy, Giulio C. 1970. *A survey of structural linguistics.* London, Faber & Faber.

Leumann, Manu. 1927. "Zum Mechanismus des Bedeutungswandels," *Indogermanische Forschungen* 45.105-108.

Lewy, Ernst. 1964. *Der Bau der europäischen Sprachen.*² Tübingen, Niemeyer.

Li, Charles N. (ed.). 1975. *Word order and word order change.* Austin, University of Texas Press.

----- (ed.). 1977. *Mechanisms of syntactic change.* Austin, University of Texas Press.

Lieberson, Stanley (ed.). 1967. *Explorations in sociolinguistics.* IJAL Publication 44. Bloomington, Indiana University.

Lightfoot, David W. 1979. *Principles of diachronic syntax.* Cambridge, Cambridge University Press.

Liljencrants, Johan, and Björn Lindblom. 1972. "Numerical simulation of vowel quality systems: the role of perceptual contrast," *Language* 48.839-62.

Lindblom, Björn E. F. 1972. "Phonetics and description of language," *Proceedings of the seventh international congress of phonetic sciences* (André Rigault and René Charbonneau, eds.) 63-97. The Hague, Mouton.

Lindeman, Fredrik Otto. 1970. *Einführung in die Laryngaltheorie.* Sammlung Göschen 1247/1247a. Berlin, de Gruyter.

Lindroth, Hjalmar. 1937. "Das Sprachgefühl, ein vernachlässigter Begriff," *Indogermanische Forschungen* 55.1-16.

Locke, John L. 1983. *Phonological acquisition and change.* New York, Academic Press.

Loflin, Marvin D. 1969. "Negro Nonstandard and Standard English: same or different deep structure?," *Orbis* 18.74-91.

Loman, Bengt. 1970. "Social variation in the syntax of spoken Swedish." See Benediktsson 211-34.

Loukotka, Čestmír. 1968. *Classification of South American Indian languages* (J. Wilbert, ed.). Reference Series 7, Los Angeles, UCLA Latin American Center.

Lounsbury, Floyd G. 1964. "The structural analysis of kinship semantics," in Lunt (ed.) 1073-93.

Lüdtke, Helmut (ed.). 1980. *Kommunikationstheoretische Grundlagen des Sprachwandels.* Berlin and New York, de Gruyter.

Lunt, Horace (ed.). *Proceedings of the ninth international congress of linguists.* The Hague, Mouton.

Luria, A. R. 1967. "Problems and facts of neurolinguistics," *To honor Roman Jakobson* 2.1213-27. The Hague, Mouton.

Lyons, John. 1968. *Introduction to theoretical linguistics.* New York, Cambridge University Press.

----- (ed.). 1970. *New horizons in linguistics.* Baltimore, Penguin.

Maas, Paul. 1958. *Textual criticism* (transl. by Barbara Flower). New York, Oxford University Press.

Maher, J. Peter. 1965. *Indo-European origins of some Slavic grammatical categories.* Bloomington, Indiana University dissertation; University Microfilms 66-1474.

-----. 1966. "More on the history of the comparative method: the tradition of Darwinism in August Schleicher's work," *Anthropological Linguistics* 8.1-12.

-----. 1969a. "English-speakers' awareness of the distinctive features," *Language Sciences* 5.14 (April).

-----. 1969b. "Italian *serpe*: why not *serpente?," *Language Sciences* 6.5-8 (August), 8.30-35 (December).

-----. 1970a. "A note on the English passive with reference to some general questions of theory," *Language Sciences* 13.30-31 (December).

-----. 1970b. "Sociological reality in linguistic theories" (manuscript).

-----. 1972. "Distinctive-feature rhyme in German folk versification," *Language Sciences* 19.19-20 (February).

-----. 1977. *Papers on language theory and history I*. Amsterdam, Benjamins.

Maher, J. Peter, et al. (eds.). 1982. *Papers from the third international conference on historical linguistics*. Amsterdam, Benjamins.

Malkiel, Yakov. 1967. "Multiple versus simple causation in linguistic change," *To honor Roman Jakobson* 2.1228-46. The Hague, Mouton.

-----. 1968. *Essays on linguistic themes*. Berkeley and Los Angeles, University of California Press.

-----. 1976. *Etymological dictionaries. A tentative typology*. Chicago, University of Chicago Press.

Malmberg, Bertil. 1963a. *Phonetics*. New York, Dover.

-----. 1963b. *Structural linguistics and human communication*. Kommunikation und Kybernetik in Einzeldarstellungen 2. New York, Academic Press (Berlin, Springer).

-----. 1969. "Synchronie et diachronie," in Graur (ed.) 1.13-36.

Mańczak, Witold. 1958. "Tendences générales des changements analogiques," *Lingua* 7.298-325, 387-420.

-----. 1968. "Le développement phonétique irrégulier dû à la fréquence en russe," *Lingua* 21.287-93.

-----. 1969. *Le développement phonétique des langues romanes et la fréquence*. Kraków, Nakładen Uniwersytetu Jagiellońskiego.

Marchand, James W. 1956. "Internal reconstruction of phonemic split," *Language* 32.245-53.

Markey, Thomas L. 1985. "On suppletion," *Diachronica* 2.51-66.

Marouzeau, J. 1961. *Lexique de la terminologie linguistique* (français, allemand, anglais, italien).[3] Paris, Geuthner.

Martin, Rex. 1977. *Historical explanation: reenactment and practical inference*. Ithaca and London, Cornell University Press.

Martin, Samuel E. 1966. "Lexical evidence relating Korean to Japanese," *Language* 42.185-251.

Martinet, André. 1958. "Function, structure and sound change," *Word* 8.1-32.

-----. 1964. *Économie des changements phonétiques*.[2] Bern, Francke.

----- (ed.). 1968. *Le langage*. Encyclopédie de la Pléiade 25. Paris, Gallimard.

Matthews, Peter H. 1972. *Inflectional morphology: a theoretical study based on aspects of Latin verb conjugation*. Cambridge, Cambridge University Press.

Mayerthaler, Willi. 1981. *Morphologische Natürlichkeit*. Wiesbaden, Athenaion. [English transl. Ann Arbor, Karoma 1988.]

Mayrhofer, Manfred, et al. (eds.). 1980. *Lautgeschichte und Etymologie*. Wiesbaden, Reichert.

Meid, Wolfgang. 1968a. *Indogermanisch und Keltisch*. Innsbrucker Beiträge zur Kulturwissenschaft, Sonderheft 25. Innsbruck, Sprachwissenschaftliches Institut.

-----. 1968b. "Indo-European and Celtic," *Scottish Studies* 12.45-56.

----- (ed.).1987. *Studien zum indogermanischen Wortschatz*. Innsbruck, Sprachwissenschaftliches Institut.

Meier, Harri. 1986. *Prinzipien der etymologische Forschung. Romanistische Einblicke*. Heidelberg, Carl Winter.

Meillet, Antoine. 1926. *Linguistique historique et linguistique générale*.[2] Paris, Champion.

-----. 1967a. *The comparative method in historical linguistics* (transl. by Gordon B. Ford, Jr.). Paris, Champion.

-----. 1967b. *The Indo-European dialects* (transl. by Samuel N. Rosenberg). University, Ala., University of Alabama Press.

Meillet, Antoine, and Marcel Cohen (eds.). 1952. *Les langues du monde*. New ed. Paris, Champion.

Meisel, Jürgen M. (ed.) 1977. *Langues en contact -- pidgins -- creoles -- languages in contact*. Tübingen, Narr.

Meisinger, Othmar. 1932. *Vergleichende Wortkunde. Beiträge zur Bedeutungslehre*. Munich, Beck'sche Verlagsbuchhandlung.

Menner, Robert J. 1936. "The conflict of homonyms in English," *Language* 12.229-44.

-----. 1945. "Multiple meaning and change of meaning in English," *Language* 21.59-76.

Merrell, Floyd. 1987. "Of position papers, paradigms, and paradoxes," *Semiotica* 65.191-223.

Miller, Roy Andrew. 1967. "Old Japanese phonology and the Korean-Japanese relationship," *Language* 43.278-302.

Miller, Wick R. 1967. "Shoshoni dialectology," Paper delivered at the Linguistic Society of America meeting, December.

Moore, Samuel. 1927. "Loss of final *n* in inflectional syllables of Middle English," *Language* 3.232-59.

-----. 1928. "Earliest morphological changes in Middle English," *Language* 4.238-66.

Moore, Wilbert E. 1968. "Social change," *International encyclopedia of the social sciences* 14.365-75. New York, Macmillan (Free Press).

Moulton, William G. 1954. "The stops and spirants of early Germanic," *Language* 30.1-42. [Bobbs-Merrill Language-68.]

-----. 1960. "The short vowel systems of Northern Switzerland. A study in structural dialectology," *Word* 16.155-82.

-----. 1961. "Lautwandel durch innere Kausalität: die ostschweizerische Vokalspaltung," *Zeitschrift für Mundartforschung* 28.227-51.

-----. 1967. "Types of phonemic change," *To honor Roman Jakobson* 2.1393-1407. The Hague, Mouton.

-----. 1968."Structural dialectology," *Language* 44.451-66.

-----. 1970. "Opportunities in dialectology." See Benediktsson 143-57.

Mounin, Georges. 1967. *Histoire de la linguistique des origines au XXᵉ siècle*. Paris, Presses Universitaires de France.

436   BIBLIOGRAPHY

Mueller, Hugo J. (ed.). 1954. *Bilingualism and mixed languages. The spectrographic analysis of speech, language and culture* (5th Round Table Meeting). Washington, D.C., Georgetown University Press.

Mühlhäusler, Peter. 1984. "Tracing the roots of Pidgin German," *Language and Communication* 4.27-57.

-----. 1986. *Pidgin and creole languages.* Oxford, Blackwell.

Muysken, Pieter and Norval Smith (eds.). 1986. *Substrata versus universals in creole genesis.* Amsterdam, Benjamins.

Nash, Rose. 1968. *Multilingual lexicon of linguistics and philology: English, Russian, German, French.* Coral Gables, Fla., University of Miami Press.

Nelde, Peter Hans (ed.). 1980. *Sprachkontakt und Sprachkonflikt/Languages in contact and conflict.* Wiesbaden, Steiner.

Nelde, Peter Hans, et al. (eds.). 1986. *Language contact in Europe.* Tübingen, Niemeyer.

Neumann, Günter. 1967. *Indogermanische Sprachwissenschaft 1816 und 1966.* Innsbrucker Beiträge zur Kulturwissenschaft, Sonderheft 24. Innsbruck, Sprachwissenschaftliches Institut.

Newman, Paul. 1968. "The reality of morphophonemes," *Language* 44.507-15.

Newton, B. E. 1971. "Ordering paradoxes in phonology," *Journal of Linguistics* 7.31-53.

Nida, Eugene A. 1969. "Science of translation," *Language* 45.483-98.

Nida, Eugene A., and Harold W. Fehderau. 1970. "Indigenous pidgins and koinés," *International Journal of American Linguistics* 36.146-55.

Nida, Eugene A., and Charles R. Taber. 1969. *The theory and practice of translation.* Helps for Translators 8. Leiden, Brill.

Nielsen, Niels Åge. 1952. "La théorie des substrats et la linguistique structurale," *Acta Linguistica* 7.1-7.

Nirenberg, Marshall W. 1963. "The genetic code: II," *Scientific American,* 2-12 (March). [Scientific American Reprints 153.]

Nirvi, R. E. 1969. "Muuan keskiaikaista perinnettä kuvasteleva sanaperhe," *Acta Universitatis Tamperensis,* Ser. A:26. Suomen kielen laitoksen julkaisuja 1.102-13. Tampere.

Norman, William, and Lyle Campbell. 1978. "Toward a Proto-Mayan syntax: a comparative perspective on grammar," *Papers in Mayan linguistics* (Nora C. England, ed.) 136-56. Miscellaneous Publications in Anthropology 6. Columbia, Museum of Anthropology, University of Missouri.

Nurse, Derek. 1987. "Toward a typology of diachronic phonological change in Bantu languages," *Journal of the Atlantic Provinces Linguistic Association* 9.100-22.

Nyman, Martti. 1987. "Is the Paradigm Economy Principle relevant?," *Journal of Linguistics* 23.251-67.

Oertel, Hanns. 1901. *Lectures on the study of language.* New York, Scribner (London, Arnold).

Ogden, C. K. 1968. *Basic English: international second language.* Rev. ed. by E. C. Graham and L. W. Lockwood. New York, Harcourt.

Ogden, C. K., and I. A. Richards. 1923. *The meaning of meaning.* New York, Harcourt.

O'Grady, William, and Michael Dobrovolsky (eds.). 1987. *Contemporary linguistic analysis: an introduction.* Toronto, Copp Clark Pitman.

Öhman, Suzanne. 1951. *Wortinhalt und Weltbild: Vergleichende und methodologische Studien zu Bedeutungslehre und Wortfeldtheorie.* Stockholm, Norstedt.

Okell, John. 1965. "Nissaya Burmese, a case of systematic adaptation to a foreign grammar and syntax," *Lingua* 15.186-227.

Oldfield, R. C., and J. C. Marshall (eds.). 1968. *Language. Selected readings.* Baltimore, Penguin.

Oliver, Douglas L. 1964. *Invitation to anthropology, a guide to basic concepts.* Garden City, N. Y., American Museum of Natural History (The Natural History Press).

Onishi, Masao. 1969. "Linguistic behavior as the course of phonetic changes," in Graur (ed.) 1.488-94.

Palmer, Leonard. 1972. *Descriptive and comparative linguistics: a critical introduction..* London, Faber and Faber.

Paor, Liam de. 1967. *Archaeology, an illustrated introduction.* Baltimore, Penguin.

Patterson, William T. 1968. "On the genealogical structure of the Spanish vocabulary," *Word* 24.309-39.

Paul, Hermann. 1920. *Prinzipien der Sprachgeschichte.*[5] Halle, Niemeyer.

Peirce, Charles Sanders. 1955. *Philosophical writings of Peirce* (ed. by Justus Buchler). New York, Dover.

Penzl, Herbert. 1957. "The evidence for phonemic changes," *Studies presented to Joshua Whatmough* (Ernst Pulgram, ed.), 193-208. The Hague, Mouton. [Also in Lass (ed.), 1969:10-24.]

Petrovici, Emil 1957. *Kann das Phonemsystem einer Sprache durch fremden Einfluss umgestaltet werden?* The Hague, Mouton.

-----. 1969. "Interpénétration des systèmes linguistiques," in Graur (ed.) 1.37-73.

Petyt, K. M. 1980. *The study of dialect. An introduction to dialectology.* London, Deutsch.

Piaget, Jean. 1968. *Le structuralisme.*[3] (Que sais-je?) No. 1311. Paris, Presses Universitaires de France. [The English version, *Structuralism*, transl. and ed. by Chaninah Maschler. New York, Harper & Row, 1971.]

Pike, Kenneth L. 1947. "Grammatical prerequisites to phonemic analysis," *Word* 3.155-72. [Bobbs-Merrill Language-72.]

-----. 1957. *Axioms and procedures for reconstruction in comparative linguistics:--an experimental syllabus.* Rev. ed. Santa Ana, Summer Institute of Linguistics.

-----. 1967. *Language in relation to a unified theory of the structure of human behavior.*[2] The Hague, Mouton.

Pilati, Leona Lampi. 1969. "The Fox dialect: the influence of Finnish on a local American English dialect," *Neuphilologische Mitteilungen* 70.145-58.

Pinnow, Heinz-Jürgen. 1964. *Die nordamerikanischen Indianersprachen: ein Überblick über ihren Bau und ihre Besonderheiten.* Wiesbaden, Harrassowitz.

Pisani, Vittore. 1966. "Entstehung von Einzelsprachen aus Sprachbünden," *Kratylos* 11.125-41.

-----. 1975. *Die Etymologie. Geschichte -- Fragen -- Methode.* Munich, Fink.

Plank, Frans. 1979. "Ikonisierung und De-Ikonisierung als Prinzipien des Sprachwandels," *Sprachwissenschaft* 4.121-58.

Porter, Dale H. 1981. *The emergence of the past. A theory of historical explanation.* Chicago and London, University of Chicago Press.

Porzig, Walter. 1924. "Aufgaben der indogermanischen Syntax," *Stand und Aufgaben der Sprachwissenschaft: Festschrift für Wilhelm Streitberg* (J. Friedrich et al, eds.), 126-51. Heidelberg, Carl Winter.

-----. 1954. *Die Gliederung des indogermanischen Sprachgebiets.* Heidelberg, Carl Winter.

Posner, Rebecca. 1983. "The origins and affinities of French Creoles: new perspectives," *Language and Communication* 3.191-201.

Posner, Roland (ed.). 1980. *Ikonismus in den natürlichen Sprachen. Zeitschrift für Semiotik* 2:1-2.

Posti, Lauri. 1942. *Grundzüge der livischen Lautgeschichte.* Mémoires de la Société Finno-Ougrienne 85. Helsinki, Suomalais-ugrilainen Seura.

-----. 1948. "Till frågan om brytning och omljud," *Språkvetenskapliga sällskapets in Uppsala förhandlingar* 1946-48. *Uppsala Universitets Årsskrifter* 13.39-59.

-----. 1953. "From Pre-Finnic to late Proto-Finnic," *Finnisch-Ugrische Forschungen* 31.1-91.

Powell, J. W. 1966. *Indian linguistic families* (Preston Holder, ed.). Lincoln, University of Nebraska Press.

Pulgram, Ernst. 1951. "Phoneme and grapheme: a parallel," *Word* 7.15-20. [Bobbs-Merrill Language-76.]

-----. 1953. "Family tree, wave theory and dialectology," *Orbis* 2.67-72.

-----. 1959. "Proto-Indo-European reality and reconstuction," *Language* 35.421-26.

-----. 1961. "The nature and use of proto-languages," *Lingua* 10.18-37.

-----. 1964. "Proto-languages as proto-diasystems: Proto-Romance," *Word* 20. 373-83.

-----. 1965. "Graphic and phonic systems: figurae and signs," *Word* 21.208-24.

Raffler Engel, Walburga von. 1970. "The LAD, our underlying unconscious, and more on 'felt sets'," *Language Sciences* 13.15-18 (December).

Ramanujan, A. K. 1968. "The structure of variation: a study in caste dialect," *Structure and change in Indian society* (Milton Singer and Bernard Cohn, eds.) 461-74. Viking Fund Publications in Anthropology 47. Chicago, Aldine.

Ramat, Paolo (ed.). 1980. *Linguistic reconstruction and Indo-European syntax.* Amsterdam, Benjamins.

Rauch, Irmengard, and Gerald F. Carr (eds.). 1983. *Language change.* Bloomington, Indiana University Press.

Raun, Alo. 1968. "Native speaker and distinctive features," *Lingua* 21.346-50.

Ravila, Paavo. 1952. "Onomatopoieettisten ja deskriptiivisten sanojen asema kielen äännesysteemissä," *Virittäjä* 56.262-74.

Reddy, Michael J. 1969. "A semantic approach to metaphor," *Papers from the fifth regional meeting of the Chicago Linguistic Society*, 240-51. Department of Linguistics, University of Chicago.

Reichstein, Ruth. 1960. "Étude des variations sociales et géographiques des faits linguistiques," *Word* 16.55-99.

Reid, T. B. W. 1956. "Linguistics, structuralism and philology," *Archivum Linguisticum* 8.28-37.

Rice, Stuart A. (ed.). 1931. *Methods in social science. A case book.* Chicago, University of Chicago Press.

Risch, Ernst. 1966. "Historisch-vergleichende Sprachbetrachtung und Dialektgeographie," *Kratylos* 11.142-55.

Rix, Helmut (ed.). 1975. *Flexion und Wortbildung.* Wiesbaden, Reichert.

Robins, R. H. 1964. *General linguistics, an introductory survey.* London, Longmans (Bloomington, Indiana University Press).

-----. 1967. *A short history of linguistics.* Bloomington, Indiana University Press.

Rohlfs, Gerhard. 1922-23. "Apul. *ku*, kalabr. *mu* und der Verlust des Infinitivs in Unteritalien," *Zeitschrift für romanische Philologie* 42.211-23.

Romaine, Suzanne. 1982. *Socio-historical linguistics: its status and methodology.* Cambridge and New York, Cambridge University Press.

Romeo, Luigi. 1969. "Italian *serpente*: why also *serpe?*," *Language Sciences* 8.28-30 (December).

Romney, A. Kimball. 1957. "The genetic model and Uto-Aztecan time perspective," *Davidson Journal of Anthropology* 3.35-41. [Bobbs-Merrill A-192.]

Ross, A. S. C. 1965. *Etymology.* London, Methuen.

Rouse, Irving. 1986. *Migrations in prehistory. Inferring population movement from cultural remains.* New Haven and London, Yale University Press.

Ruhlen, Merritt. 1987. *A guide to the world's languages. Volume 1: Classification.* London, Arnold/Stanford, Stanford University Press.

Samarin, William J. 1985. "Plurigenesis in pidginization," *Journal of Historical Linguistics and Philology* 2.100-19.

Sampson, Geoffrey. 1985. *Writing systems: a linguistic introduction.* Stanford, Stanford University Press.

Samuels, M. L. 1972. *Linguistic evolution with special reference to English.* Cambridge, Cambridge University Press.

Sankoff, David. 1970. "On the rate of replacement of word-meaning relationships," *Language* 46.564-69.

----- (ed.). 1978. *Linguistic variation: models and methods.* New York, Academic Press.

----- (ed.). 1986. *Diversity and diachrony.* Amsterdam and Philadelphia, Benjamins.

Sankoff, David, and William Labov. 1979. "On the use of variable rules," *Language in Society* 8.189-223.

Sankoff, Gillian. 1980. *The social life of language.* Philadelphia, University of Pennsylvania Press.

Sapir, Edward. 1912. "Language and environment," *American Anthropologist* 14.226-42. [Bobbs-Merrill A-199.]

-----.1916. *Time perspective in aboriginal American culture.* Memoir 90, Anthropological Series No. 13. Geological Survey, Department of Mines. Ottawa. [Also in *Selected writings of Edward Sapir* (David G. Mandelbaum, ed.) 389-462 (1949). Berkeley and Los Angeles, University of California Press.]

-----. 1921. *Language.* New York, Harcourt.

Saporta, Sol. 1965. "Ordered rules, dialect differences, and historical processes," *Language* 41.218-24.

Saussure, Ferdinand de. 1879. *Mémoire sur le système primitif des voyelles dans les langues indo-européennes.* Leipzig, Teubner.

-----. 1959. *Course in general linguistics* (transl. by Wade Baskin). New York, Philosophical Library.

Savan, David. 1980. "Abduction and semiotics," *The signifying animal* (I. Rauch and G. F. Carr, eds.) 252-62. Bloomington, Indiana University Press.

Scancarelli, Janine. 1986. "Interpretation in context: a cause of semantic change," *Cahiers de l'Institut de Linguistique de Louvain* 12.167-82.

Schane, Sanford A. 1971. "The phoneme revisited," *Language* 47.503-21.

Scherer, Anton (ed.). 1968. *Die Urheimat der Indogermanen.* Darmstadt, Wissenschaftliche Buchgesellschaft.

Schlerath, Bernfried (ed.). 1985. *Grammatische Kategorien, Funktion und Geschichte.* Wiesbaden, Reichert.

-----. 1987. "On the reality and status of a reconstructed language," *Journal of Indo-European Studies* 15.41-6.

Schmidt, K. H. 1966. "Historische Sprachvergleichung und ihre typologische Ergänzung," *Zeitschrift der Deutschen Morgenländischen Gesellschaft* 116.8-22.

Schmidt, Wilhelm. 1939. *The cultural historical method of ethnology* (transl. by S. A. Sieber). New York, Fortuny's.

Schmitt, Rüdiger. 1967. *Dichtung und Dichtersprache in indogermanischer Zeit.* Wiesbaden, Harrassowitz.

----- (ed.). 1977. *Etymologie.* Darmstadt, Wissenschaftliche Buchgesellschaft.

Schrader, Otto. 1883. *Sprachvergleichung und Urgeschichte.* Jena, Costenoble.

Schramm, Gene M. 1967. "The correspondence of distinctive oppositions in distantly related languages," *To honor Roman Jakobson* 3.1769-74. The Hague, Mouton.

Schuchardt, Hugo. 1917. "Sprachverwandtschaft," *Sitzungsberichte der Berliner Akademie der Wissenschaften* 37.518-29. [Also in *Brevier* 1928:189-204, see below.]

-----. 1928. *Hugo Schuchardt-Brevier* (Leo Spitzer, ed.).[2] Halle, Niemeyer.

Schulze, Wilhelm. 1966. *Kleine Schriften* (Wilhelm Wissmann, ed.).[2] Göttingen, Vandenhoeck & Ruprecht.

Ščur, G. S. 1966. "On system in diachrony and a comparative-historical study of cognate languages," *Kratylos* 11.178-89.

Sebeok, Thomas A. (ed.). 1963f. *Current trends in linguistics* 12 vols. The Hague, Mouton.

-----. 1968. "Zoosemiotics: a guide to its literature," *Language Sciences* 3.7-14 (December).

----- (ed.). 1968. *Animal communication*. Bloomington, Indiana University Press.

Segerstråle, Sven. 1968. *Elämän arvoitus*. Helsinki and Porvoo, Söderström.

Senn, Alfred. 1953. "Die Beziehungen des Baltischen zum Slavischen und Germanischen," *Zeitschrift für vergleichende Sprachforschung* 71.162-88.

Šerech, Yury. 1954. "Toward a historical dialectology: its delimitation of the history of literary language," *Orbis* 3.43-57.

Service, Elman R. 1968. "Cultural evolution," *International encyclopedia of the social sciences* 5.221-28. New York, Macmillan (Free Press).

Sgall, Petr. 1964. "Zur Frage der Ebenen im Sprachsystem," *Travaux linguistiques de Prague* 1.95-106.

Shands, Harley C. 1970. "Language: medium or operator?," *Language Sciences* 11.11-15 (August).

Shapiro, Michael. 1969. *Aspects of Russian morphology, a semiotic investigation*. Cambridge, Mass., Slavica Publishers.

-----. 1972. "Consonant syncope in Russian," *The Slavic word* (Dean S. Worth, ed.) 404-25. The Hague, Mouton.

-----. 1983. *The sense of grammar*. Bloomington, Indiana University Press.

-----. 1985. "Teleology, semeiosis, and linguistic change," *Diachronica* 2.1-34.

Shapiro, Michael, and Marianne Shapiro. 1976. *Hierarchy and the structure of tropes*. Bloomington, Indiana University Press.

Shevoroshkin, Vitalij V., and Thomas L. Markey (eds. and transl.). 1986. *Typology, relationship and time. A collection of papers on language change and relationship by Soviet linguists*. Ann Arbor, Karoma.

Short, Thomas L. 1981. "Peirce's concept of final causation," *Transactions of the Charles S. Peirce Society* 17.369-82.

Sieberer, Anton. 1964. *Lautwandel und seine Triebkräfte*. Vienna, Notring.

Sigurd, Bengt. 1966. "Generative grammar and historical linguistics," *Acta Linguistica Hafniensia* 10.34-48.

-----. 1970. "The phonemic principle and transformational grammar," *Language Sciences* 11.15-18 (August).

Skalička, V. 1967. "Sprachtypologie und Sprachentwicklung," *To honor Roman Jakobson* 3.1827-31. The Hague, Mouton.

Skomal, Susan N., and Edgar C. Polomé (eds.). 1987. **PIE: The archaeology of a linguistic problem*. Washington, D.C., Institute for the Study of Man.

Skrelina, L. M. 1968. "De l'économie de certains changements grammaticaux en ancien français," *La Linguistique* 1/1968:61-78.

Smalley, William A. 1963. *Manual of articulatory phonetics*. Rev. ed. Tarrytown, N. Y., Practical Anthropology.

Söhngen, Gottlieb. 1962. *Analogie und Metapher*. Munich, K. A. Freiburg.

Sørensen, Hans Christian. 1968. "The problem of linguistic basic elements," *Acta Linguistica Hafniensia* 11.67-80.

Southworth, Franklin C. 1964. "Family-tree diagrams," *Language* 40.557-65.

Specht, Franz. 1952. "Nochmals: die äussere Sprachform als Ausdruck der seelischen Einstellung," *Zeitschrift für vergleichende Sprachforschung* 70.1-8.

Sperber, Hans. 1930. *Einführung in die Bedeutungslehre*. Bonn, Schroeder.

Spuhler, J. N. (ed.). 1967. *Genetic diversity and human behavior*. Viking Fund Publications in Anthropology 45. New York, Wenner-Gren Foundation.

Stampe, David. 1969. "The acquisition of phonetic representation," *Papers from the fifth regional meeting of the Chicago Linguistic Society*, 443-54. Department of Linguistics, University of Chicago.

Starosta, Stanley. 1969. "Linguistics and anti-science," *Working Papers in Linguistics* 11.91-127 (December). Department of Linguistics, University of Hawaii, Honolulu. [The final expanded version in *Philippine Journal of Linguistics* 2.13-27 (June 1971).]

Steever, S., et al. (eds.). 1976. *Papers from the parasession on syntax*. Department of Linguistics, University of Chicago.

Stein, Dieter. 1988. *Natural syntactic change*. Berlin, Mouton de Gruyter.

Stein, Gabriele. 1970. "Zur Typologie der Suffixentstehung (Französisch, Englisch, Deutsch)," *Indogermanische Forschungen* 75.131-65.

Steiner, George. 1969. "The language animal," *Encounter* 33:2.7-24 (August).

Steinthal, Heymann, and F. Misteli. 1893. *Charakteristik der hauptsächlichsten Typen des Sprachbaues*. Berlin, Dümmler.

Stern, Gustaf. 1931. *Meaning and change of meaning* (with special reference to the English language). Bloomington, Indiana University Press.

Stern, Theodore. 1957. "Drum and whistle 'languages': an analysis of speech surrogates," *American Anthropologist* 59.487-506. [Bobbs-Merrill A-215.]

Stevenson, Leslie, et al. (eds.). 1986. *Mind, causation, and action*. Oxford and New York, Blackwell.

Stevick, R. D. 1963. "The biological model and historical linguistics," *Language* 39.159-69.

Stockwell, Robert P., and Ronald S. K. Macaulay (eds.). 1972. *Linguistic change and generative theory*. Bloomington, Indiana University Press.

Strunk, Klaus. 1976. *Lachmanns Regel für das Lateinische. Eine Revision*. Göttingen, Vandenhoeck and Ruprecht.

Sturtevant, Edgar H. 1939. "The pronoun **so*, **sā*, **tod* and the Indo-Hittite hypothesis," *Language* 15.11-19.

-----. 1947. *An introduction to linguistic science*. New Haven, Yale University Press.

-----. 1961. *Linguistic change*. Chicago, University of Chicago Press.

Swadesh, Morris. 1951. "Diffusional cumulation and archaic residue as historical explanations," *Southwestern Journal of Anthropology* 7.1-21. [Also in Hymes (ed.) 1964:624-37, Bobbs-Merrill A-220.]

-----. 1952. "Lexicostatistic dating of prehistoric ethnic contacts," *Proceedings of the American Philosophical Society* 96.452-63.

-----. 1955. "Towards greater accuracy in lexicostatistic dating," *International Journal of American Linguistics* 21.121-37.

-----. 1959. "Linguistics as an instrument of prehistory," *Southwestern Journal of Anthropology* 15.20-35. [Also in Hymes (ed.) 1964:575-84, Bobbs-Merrill A-221.]

-----. 1963. "A punchcard system of cognate hunting," *International Journal of American Linguistics* 29.283-88.

Szemerényi, Oswald. 1962. "Principles of etymological research in the Indo-European languages," *Innsbrucker Beiträge zur Kulturwissenschaft*, Sonderheft 15.175-212. Innsbruck, Sprachwissenschaftliches Institut.

-----. 1964. "Structuralism and substratum," *Lingua* 13.1-29.

-----. 1968. "Methodology of genetic linguistics," *Enzyklopädie der geisteswissenschaftlichen Arbeitsmethoden* 4.3-38. Munich, Oldenbourg.

-----. 1970. *Einführung in die vergleichende Sprachwissenschaft.* Darmstadt, Wissenschaftliche Buchgesellschaft.

Tabouret-Keller, Andrée. 1969. "La motivation des emprunts. Un example pris sur le vif de l'apparition d'un sabir," *La Linguistique* 1/1969:25-60.

Tauli, Valter. 1956. "The origin of affixes," *Finnisch-Ugrische Forschungen* 32.170-225.

-----. 1968. *Introduction to a theory of language planning.* Acta Univ. Upsaliensis, Studia Philol. Scandinavicae Upsaliensia 6. Uppsala, Almqvist & Wiksell.

Teeter, Karl V. 1963. "Lexicostatistics and genetic relationship," *Language* 39.638-48.

-----. 1964. "Algonkian languages and genetic relationship," in Lunt (ed.) 1026-34.

Thieme, Paul. 1953. *Die Heimat der indogermanischen Gemeinsprache.* Akademie der Wissenschaften und der Literatur. Abhandlungen der Geistes- und Sozialwissenschaftlichen Klasse, No. 11. Wiesbaden, Steiner. [For a summary see "The Indo-European language," *Scientific American*, 63-74 (October 1958).]

-----. 1964. "The comparative method for reconstruction in linguistics," in Hymes (ed.) 585-98.

Thomason, Sarah Grey, and Terrence Kaufman. 1987. *Language contact, creolization, and genetic linguistics.* Berkeley and Los Angeles, University of California Press.

Thompson, Laurence C., and M. Terry Thompson. 1969. "Metathesis as a grammatical device," *International Journal of American Linguistics* 35.213-19.

Thorndike, E. L. 1947. "Semantic change," *American Journal of Psychology* 40.588-97.

Thumb, A., and K. Marbe. 1901. *Experimentelle Untersuchungen über die psychologischen Grundlagen der sprachlichen Analogiebildungen.* Leipzig, Engelmann. [Amsterdam, Benjamins 1978.]

Todd, Loreto. 1974. *Pidgins and creoles.* London and Boston, Routledge and Kegan Paul.

Todorov, Tzvetan. 1967. "Tropes et figures," *To honor Roman Jakobson* 3.2006-23. The Hague, Mouton.

Tovar, Antonio. 1954. "Linguistics and prehistory," *Word* 10.333-50.

Traugott, Elizabeth Closs. 1965. "Diachronic syntax and generative grammar," *Language* 41.402-15. [Rev. version in Lass (ed.) 1969:311-24.]

—----. 1969. "Toward a grammar of syntactic change," *Lingua* 23.1-27.

Traugott, Elizabeth Closs, et al. (eds.). 1980. *Papers from the fourth international conference on historical linguistics*. Amsterdam, Benjamins.

Trier, Jost. 1981. *Wege der Etymologie*. (Hans Schwarz, ed.) Berlin, Erich Schmidt.

Trnka, Bohumil. 1964. "On the linguistic sign and the multilevel organization of language," *Travaux linguistiques de Prague* 1.33-40.

—----. 1967. "Words, semantemes, and sememes," *To honor Roman Jakobson* 3.2050-54. The Hague, Mouton.

—----. 1968. "On analogy," *Zeitschrift für Phonetik, Sprachwissenschaft, und Kommunikationsforschung* 21.345-51.

Trudgill, Peter. 1983. *On dialect. Social and geographical perspectives*. New York and London, New York University Press.

—----. 1986. *Dialects in contact*. Oxford, Blackwell.

Ullmann, Stephen. 1959. *The principles of semantics*.[2] Glasgow, Glasgow University Publications 84.

—----. 1962. *Semantics, an introduction to the science of meaning*. Oxford, Blackwell.

Uotila, Eeva. 1986. "Baltic impetus on the Baltic Finnic diphthongs," *Finnisch-Ugrische Forschungen* 47.206-22.

Ureland, P. Sture (ed.) 1980. *Sprachvariation und Sprachwandel*. Tübingen, Niemeyer.

Uspenskij, B. A. 1965. *Strukturnaja tipologija jazykov*. Moscow, Nauka. [The 1962 Russian precursor to this work has been translated as *Principles of structural typology*, The Hague, Mouton (1968); it lacks a bibliography.]

Vachek, Josef. 1962. "On the interplay of external and internal factors in the development of language," *Lingua* 11.433-48.

—----. 1966. *The linguistic school of Prague*. Bloomington, Indiana University Press.

—----. 1968. "A note on future prospects of diachronistic language research," *Lingua* 21.483-93.

Valdman, Albert (ed.) 1977. *Pidgin and creole linguistics*. Bloomington, Indiana University Press.

Valdman, A., and A. Highfield (eds.) 1980. *Theoretical orientations in creole studies*. New York, Academic Press.

Valesio, Paolo. 1969. "Icons and patterns in the structure of language," in Graur (ed.) 1.383-88.

Vendryes, J. 1925. *Language, a linguistic introduction to history* (transl. by Paul Radin). London, Routledge & Kegan Paul.

Venezky, Richard L. 1970. *The structure of English orthography*. The Hague, Mouton.

Vennemann, Theo. 1968. *German phonology*. Los Angeles, University of California dissertation; University Microfilms 69-11,920.

-----. 1970. "The German velar nasal: a case for abstract phonology," *Phonetica* 22.65-81.

-----. 1972. "Historical German phonology and the theory of marking," in Stockwell and Macaulay (eds.) 230-74.

----- (ed.). 1987. *The new sound of Indo-European*. Berlin, Mouton de Gruyter.

-----. 1988. *Preference laws for syllable structure and the explanation of sound change*. Berlin, Mouton de Gruyter.

Versteegh, Kees. 1984. *Pidginization and creolization: the case of Arabic*. Amsterdam, Benjamins.

Vinogradov, V. V., et al. (eds.). 1966. *Jazyki narodov SSSR*. 5 vols. Moscow, Nauka.

Voegelin, C. F. 1945. "Influence of area on American Indian linguistics," *Word* 1.54-58. [Also in Hymes (ed.) 1964:638-41.]

Voegelin, C. F., and Z. S. Harris. 1947. "The scope of linguistics," *American Anthropologist* 49.588-600. [Bobbs-Merrill A-108.]

Voegelin, C. F., and F. M. Voegelin. 1977. *Classification and index of the world's languages*. New York, Elsevier.

Voegelin, C. F., et al. 1960. "Typology of density ranges I: introduction," *International Journal of American Linguistics* 26.198-205.

Vogt, Evon Z. 1968. "Culture change," *International encyclopedia of the social sciences* 3,554-58. New York, Macmillan (Free Press).

Vogt, Hans. 1954. "Contact of languages," *Word* 10.365-74.

-----. 1965. "Some remarks on glottochronological word-lists," *Norsk Tidsskrift for Sprogvidenskap* 20.28-37.

Voorhoeve, Jan. 1973. "Historical and linguistic evidence in favor of the relexification theory in the formation of creoles," *Language in Society* 2.133-45.

Vossler, Karl. 1904. *Positivismus und Idealismus in der Sprachwissenschaft*. Heidelberg, Carl Winter.

Voyles, Joseph B. 1967. "Simplicity, ordered rules, and the First Sound Shift," *Language* 43.636-60.

Walther, Elisabeth. 1979. *Allgemeine Zeichenlehre. Einführung in die Grundlagen der Semiotik.*² Stuttgart, Deutsche Verlags-Anstalt.

Wang, William S.-Y. 1969. "Competing changes as a cause of residue," *Language* 45.9-25.

----- (ed.). 1977. *The lexicon in phonological change*. The Hague and New York, Mouton.

Wanner, Dieter. 1987. *The development of clitic pronouns in the Romance languages I*. Berlin, Mouton de Gruyter.

Wartburg, Walther von. 1931. *Das Ineinandergreifen von deskriptiver und historischer Sprachwissenschaft*. Berichte über die Verhandlungen der sächsischen Akademie der Wissenschaften zu Leipzig, Phil.-Hist. Klasse 83.

-----. 1969. *Problems and methods in linguistics* (Rev. ed. with Stephen Ullmann, transl. by Joyce M. H. Reid). New York, Barnes & Noble.

Watkins, Calvert. 1965. "Lat. *nox* 'by night': a problem in syntactic reconstruction," *Symbolae linguisticae in honorem Georgii Kuryłowicz*, 351-58. Wrocław, Polska Akademija Nauk.

-----. 1966. "An Indo-European construction in Greek and Latin," *Harvard Studies in Classical Philology* 71.115-19.

-----. 1970. "A further remark on Lachmann's law," *Harvard Studies in Classical Philology* 74.55-65.

Weidert, Alfons. 1987. *Tibeto-Burman tonology*. Amsterdam, Benjamins.

Weijnen, A. A. 1969. "Lautgeschichte und Wortfrequenz," in Graur (ed.) 1.454-62.

Weinreich, Uriel. 1954. "Is a structural dialectology possible?," *Word* 10.388-400.

-----. 1958. "On the compatibility of genetic relationship and convergent development," *Word* 14.374-79.

-----. 1968. *Languages in contact, findings and problems*. The Hague, Mouton.

Weinreich, Uriel, et al. 1968. "Empirical foundations for a theory of language change," *Directions for historical linguistics* (W. P. Lehmann and Yakov Malkiel, eds.) 95-195. Austin, University of Texas Press.

Welmers, William E. 1970. "Language change and language relationships in Africa," *Language Sciences* 12.1-8 (October).

Wescott, Roger W. 1969. *The divine animal*. New York, Funk & Wagnalls.

-----. 1971. "Linguistic iconism," *Language* 47.416-28.

Wheeler, Benjamin Ide. 1887. *Analogy and the scope of its application in language*. Ithaca, Cornell University Press (Wilson & Son). [Johnson Reprint Corporation 1965.]

Whitaker, Harry Allen. 1969. *On the representation of language in the human brain: problems in the neurology of language and the linguistic analysis of aphasia*. Los Angeles, University of California dissertation; University Microfilms 70-8252. [Final version as *Current Inquiry into Language and Linguistics* 3. Edmonton/Champaign, Linguistic Research, Inc., 1971.]

White, Leslie A. 1945. "History, evolutionism, and functionalism: three types of interpretation of culture," *Southwestern Journal of Anthropology* 1.221-48. [Bobbs-Merrill A-236.]

-----. 1959. "The concept of culture," *American Anthropologist* 61.227-51. [Bobbs-Merrill A-238.]

White, Lynn, Jr. (ed.). 1956. *Frontiers of knowledge in the study of man*. New York, Harper & Row.

Whorf, Benjamin Lee. 1956. *Language, thought and reality* (selected writings edited by John B. Carroll). Cambridge, Mass., M.I.T. Press.

Wickman, Bo. 1958-60. "Some problems concerning metaphony, especially Livonian," *Språkvetenskapliga sällskapets i Uppsala förhandlingar*, Jan. 1958 - Dec. 1960:25-48.

Wiegand, Herbert Ernst. 1970. "Onomasiologie und Semasiologie," *Germanistische Linguistik* 3/70:243-384.

Wildgen, Wolfgang. 1985. *Archetypensemantik. Grundlagen für eine dynamische Semantik auf der Basis der Katastrophentheorie.* Tübingen, Narr.

Winter, Werner (ed.). 1965. *Evidence for laryngeals.*[2] The Hague, Mouton.

Wolfe, Patricia Booker. 1972. *Linguistic change and the great vowel shift in English.* Berkeley and Los Angeles, University of California Press.

Wolfe, Susan J. 1981. "Generative models for syntactic change," *Forum linguisticum* 7.141-67.

Wolfram, Walter A. 1969. *A sociolinguistic description of Detroit Negro speech.* Washington, D.C., Center for Applied Linguistics.

-----. 1970. "Underlying representations in Black English phonology," *Language Sciences* 10.7-12 (April).

Woolford, Ellen, and William Washabaugh (eds.). 1983. *The social context of creolization.* Ann Arbor, Karoma.

Woolfson, A. Peter. 1970. "An examination of Sapir's concept of language in the light of ethological theory and Piagetian developmental psychology," *Language Sciences* 11.8-10 (August).

von Wright, Georg Henrik. 1971. *Explanation and understanding.* London, Routledge and Kegan Paul.

Wurzel, Wolfgang Ullrich. 1984. *Flexionsmorphologie und Natürlichkeit.* Berlin, Akademie-Verlag.

-----. 1985. "Zur Determiniertheit morphologischer Erscheinungen -- Ein Zwischenbericht," *Acta Linguistica Academicae Scientarum Hungaricae* 34(1-2):151-68.

Yannay, Igal. 1970. *The quadriliteral verb in the Hebrew language.* Los Angeles, University of California dissertation; University Microfilms 71-3852.

Yanofsky, Charles. 1967. "Gene structure and protein structure," *Scientific American* 80-94 (May).

Zawadowski, Leon. 1967. "A classification of signs and semantic systems," *To honor Roman Jakobson* 3.2333-54. The Hague, Mouton.

Zeps, Valdis J. 1967. "A synchronic and diachronic order of rules: mutations of velars in Old Church Slavonic," *Approaches in linguistic methodology* (Irmengard Rauch and Charles T. Scott, eds.) 145-51. Madison, University of Wisconsin Press.

Zipf, George K. 1965. *The psycho-biology of language: an introduction to dynamic philology.* Cambridge, Mass., M.I.T. Press.

INDEX

descriptive prerequisite, 3
determinatives, 33
determinism, 399, 403
Devanagari, 40
development, 404
devoicing, 117, 195, 196, 199-200
diachronic aggregate, 409
diachronic correspondence, 129, 153, 195, 198
diachronic linguistics, 20
diachronic universal, 409
diachrony, 21, 202-203, 401-402
diacritic features, 211, 226-27, 257
diacritic signs, xi-xii
diagrammatic representation of lexical vs. grammatical meanings, 17, 196
diagrams: xi-xiii, 16-17, 50, 170; between different languages, 255, 258, 285-86; showing distinctive-feature hierarchies, 195-96
dialect, xv, 289
dialect boundary, 290
dialect cohesion, 283-84, 292
dialect correspondence, 47-50, 58
dialect geography: 182-83, 289-99, 304-309; in the service of comparative linguistics, 306
dialect variation, 255, 282-84
dialectology, 47, 54
diaphoneme, 283, 284, 292, 293-94
diasystem, 292, 298-99, 317
diatopicality, 21
dicent, x
differentiation, 107, 143-45, 170, 382
diffusion, 155
diglossia, 52
directionality, 166, 258, 362-63, 389-90
discovery procedures, 202-203, 362
disjunctive definition, 343, 369, 370
dissimilation, 71, 74-75
dissonance theory, 406, 409, 410
distant relationship, 320-321, 338, 397
distinctive features: 6-9, 115, 158, 195-96, 245; shown diagrammatically, 195-96
distribution of phonemes, 167
division of linguistics, 20-22
Dravidian, 321
drag (pull) chain, 112, 186
drift, 194, 200, 252, 254, 352, 409
drum and whistle speech, 39
drunkard's search, 324
Dutch, 57
dynamic cause, 406
dynamic field theory, 400, 401

ease of articulation, 189, 198
ecological influence, 381
effect, 131, 408
efficiency: 392; of comparative method, 286
Egyptian (writing), 38, 39, 45

Einfühlung, 399
elaboration, 143-44
ellipsis, xv, 138, 142, 143-44
empathy, 399, 406
empirical science, 24, 399
encyclopedic frame, 411
English, xii, xiii-xiv, 9-11, 14, 17, 26, 33-37, 40, 41, 42, 51, 57-59, 64-80 passim, 84-97 passim, 101, 102, 104, 108, 109, 110, 114-15, 119, 125, 126, 127, 136, 137, 140-49 passim, 151, 155, 158-62 passim, 164-65, 169, 172, 176, 177, 184, 187, 188, 190-91, 196, 201, 203, 208, 209, 210, 214-18, 219, 226-27, 229-42, 247, 249, 267, 297, 311-14 passim, 318, 320, 327, 329, 333, 335, 352-53, 355, 356, 366-67, 368-73 passim, 387, 394, 396, 400, 407
entailment, 404
entelechy, 193
entropy, 391
environment: xiii, 61, 231, 233, 235, 247, 248, 256, 405; in evolution, 391, in syntax-semantics, 364-65, 366
epigraphy, 43
Eskimo (Inuktitut), 10, 162, 311, 314-15, 392
Eskimo-Aleut, 387
Esperanto, 175, 176
Estonian, 79, 80, 82, 91, 97, 98, 100, 102, 116, 120, 139, 201, 211, 224, 261, 262, 280, 301
étalon language, 316, 317
Etruscan, 23
etymology, 326-33, 410-11
euphemism, 139-40, 145-46
European Pidgin Romance, 175
evidence: 112; of change and variation, 35-37; for syntactic rules, 357-58
evolution: 20, 153, 401, 402, 403; and linguistics, 393
exception features, 225
exceptions, 64, 86, 127, 218, 225
excessive shortness, 184
excrescence, 67-69, 70, 72, 80
existence, 402
existing for, 403
experience, 285, 286, 405, 409
experimentation, 24, 333, 383, 399, 410
explanation: 24, 84, 126, 131, 197, 285, 383, 404, 407; covering-law, 399; deductive-nomological, 399, 407, 410; genetic, 25, 180, 402, 408; historical, ix, 24-25, 112, 129, 180, 393, 406, 411; invisible-hand, 408-409; nomic, 399, 408; non-nomic, 408; of actions, 410; of change, 179-81; pattern, 285, 286, 409-411; prediction as, 399; rational, 405-408, 410; synchronic, 402; teleological, 402-405

linear relationship, 19
lingua franca, 175
linguistic collocation, 138
linguistic cycle, 317
linguistic paleontology, 373
linguistic sign: 6, 13, 365; arbitrariness of, 13-14, 19, 255; its meaning-sound linkup, 100-102, 255, 302-303; one-to-many, 100-101; one-to-one, 98, 133; in reconstruction, 365
linguistic variation, 141, 404
linguistics. *See* autonomous, causal, comparative, descriptive, genetic, historical, structural, synchronic, and theoretical
linguistics and social science, 377-78, 399, 408, 410, 411
literary criticism, 324-25
literature, 22
Lithuanian, 66, 74, 85, 116, 158, 160, 162, 246, 358-59, 368, 381
Livian, 64, 80, 84, 301, 303
loan (word): 126-27, 138, 155-58, 162-69, 227-28, 241, 281, 285, 339, 384; spotting of, 394
loan translation, 140, 144, 156, 169
loanblend, 156
loanshift, 156
logic, 399, 404-405
logical possibility, 259
logogram, 33
logography, 32, 38
logology, 41
logosyllabic, 38
loss: 69; as conditioning, 64; of marking, 127, 143, 153, 188; of motivation, 138-39, 202-203
Low German, 165, 172, 231, 241, 290, 299
Lude, 149, 172, 177, 301
Luwian, 38

Macedonian, 284
Malay(an), 75, 311
Malayo-Polynesian, 381
Mansi (Vogul), 301
mapping relation, 50, 159, 166, 167, 253, 278-80, 283, 297
mapping rules, 224-25, 255-56, 303, 364
Marathi, 172
marginal language, 176
Mari. *See* Cheremis
markedness: 102, 112, 125; as cause of change, 188-89; positive and negative, 126-27; and rule change, 125-27; reversal of, 127, 199
Martha's Vineyard, 191-92, 403, 406
matching: 50, 335-41; patterns in syntax, 260-61; significance of, 257, 258; 338; texts, 259

maximal differentiation, 186
Mayan, 162
Mazatec, 316
meaning: 142; as a factor of change, 76; essence of, 405; requirements for, 234
mechanism, 400
mechanisms of change, 179-81, 195
Melanesian Pidgin English, 175, 176
memory, 101, 107, 129, 181, 187, 349
mental representation, 405-406
merger, xiii, 69-70, 103, 130, 151, 186
metaphony. *See* umlaut
metaphor, 16, 28, 140, 141-42, 144, 152
metathesis, 63, 71, 75, 98, 113
methods: application of, 219; aspects of, 213; domain of, 278-84; ingredients of, 229, 278-79; interlocking of, 273; order of, 266, 274-77, 280; penetration of, 274-77; priority of, 274-75; reality of, 278; of science, 197; structure of, 278-84. *See also* deadlocks on methods; limitations on comparative method
metonymy, 141-42, 144
Middle English, 35-36, 59, 69, 70, 80, 86, 90, 93, 94, 96, 119, 140-41, 150, 332, 381
Middle High German, 81-82, 86, 185, 237
Middle Indic, 78
migration theory, 386-87
minimal pairs, 62, 167, 208-212, 215, 218, 219-22, 251
misspellings, 36
mixed language, 171-72
mixing the levels, 78
model: 131; correlational, 409; as icon, 307; postulational, 409; synthetic, 409
monograms, 41
moral philosophers, 408
moral sciences, 399
Mordvin, 164, 167-68, 301
morpheme: 6; order, 352
morphological analysis, 351-52
morphological change and reconstruction, 261-63, 351-52
morphophoneme, 5-6, 214, 278-80
morphophonemic alternation (variation), xii-xiii, 60, 81, 264-70, 345-46
morphophonemic analysis, 114-15, 213-28, 229, 264-65, 267, 278-81
morphophonemic conditioning: 116, 221; of sound change, 70, 81-84, 94, 97-98, 99, 101, 180
morphophonemic process, 64
morphophonemic rules, 85
morphophonemic writing, 34-35
morphophonemics, 251
morpho(pho)nology, 214
morphosyntax, 259, 260
Morse code, 40
motivated compounds, 140

In the CURRENT ISSUES IN LINGUISTIC THEORY (CILT) series (Series Editor: E.F. Konrad Koerner) the following volumes have been published thus far, and will be published during 1989:

1. KOERNER, E.F. Konrad (ed.): *THE TRANSFORMATIONAL-GENERATIVE PARADIGM AND MODERN LINGUISTIC THEORY*. Amsterdam, 1975.
2. WEIDERT, Alfons: *Componential Analysis of Lushai Phonology*. Amsterdam, 1975.
3. MAHER, J. Peter: *Papers on Language Theory and History I: Creation and Tradition in Language*. Foreword by Raimo Anttila. Amsterdam, 1977.
4. HOPPER, Paul J. (ed.): *STUDIES IN DESCRIPTIVE AND HISTORICAL LINGUISTICS: Festschrift for Winfred P. Lehmann*. Amsterdam, 1977. Out of print.
5. ITKONEN, Esa: *Grammatical Theory and Metascience: A critical investigation into the methodological and philosophical foundations of 'autonomous' linguistics*. Amsterdam, 1978.
6. ANTTILA, Raimo: *Historical and Comparative Linguistics*. Amsterdam/Philadelphia, 1989.
7. MEISEL, Jürgen M. & Martin D. PAM (eds): *LINEAR ORDER AND GENERATIVE THEORY*. Amsterdam, 1979.
8. WILBUR, Terence H.: *Prolegomena to a Grammar of Basque*. Amsterdam, 1979.
9. HOLLIEN, Harry & Patricia (eds): *CURRENT ISSUES IN THE PHONETIC SCIENCES, Proceedings of the IPS-77 Congress, Miami Beach, Fla., 17-19 December 1977*. Amsterdam, 1979. 2 vols.
10. PRIDEAUX, Gary (ed.): *PERSPECTIVES IN EXPERIMENTAL LINGUISTICS. Papers from the University of Alberta Conference on Experimental Linguistics, Edmonton, 13-14 Oct. 1978*. Amsterdam, 1979.
11. BROGYANYI, Bela (ed.): *STUDIES IN DIACHRONIC, SYNCHRONIC, AND TYPOLOGICAL LINGUISTICS: Festschrift for Oswald Szemerényi on the Occasion of his 65th Birthday*. Amsterdam, 1980.
12. FISIAK, Jacek (ed.): *THEORETICAL ISSUES IN CONTRASTIVE LINGUISTICS*. Amsterdam, 1980.
13. MAHER, J. Peter with coll. of Allan R. Bomhard & E.F. Konrad Koerner (ed.): *PAPERS FROM THE THIRD INTERNATIONAL CONFERENCE ON HISTORICAL LINGUISTICS, Hamburg, August 22-26, 1977*. Amsterdam, 1982.
14. TRAUGOTT, Elizabeth C., Rebecca LaBRUM, Susan SHEPHERD (eds): *PAPERS FROM THE FOURTH INTERNATIONAL CONFERENCE ON HISTORICAL LINGUISTICS, Stanford, March 26-30, 1980*. Amsterdam, 1980.
15. ANDERSON, John (ed.): *LANGUAGE FORM AND LINGUISTIC VARIATION. Papers dedicated to Angus McIntosh*. Amsterdam, 1982.
16. ARBEITMAN, Yoël & Allan R. BOMHARD (eds): *BONO HOMINI DONUM: Essays in Historical Linguistics, in Memory of J. Alexander Kerns*. Amsterdam, 1981.
17. LIEB, Hans-Heinrich: *Integrational Linguistics*. 6 volumes. Amsterdam, 1984-1986. Vol. I available; Vol. 2-6 n.y.p.
18. IZZO, Herbert J. (ed.): *ITALIC AND ROMANCE. Linguistic Studies in Honor of Ernst Pulgram*. Amsterdam, 1980.
19. RAMAT, Paolo et al. (eds): *LINGUISTIC RECONSTRUCTION AND INDO-EUROPEAN SYNTAX. Proceedings of the Coll. of the 'Indogermanische Gesellschaft' Univ. of Pavia, 6-7 Sept. 1979*. Amsterdam, 1980.
20. NORRICK, Neal R.: *Semiotic Principles in Semantic Theory*. Amsterdam, 1981.
21. AHLQVIST, Anders (ed.): *PAPERS FROM THE FIFTH INTERNATIONAL CONFERENCE ON HISTORICAL LINGUISTICS, Galway, April 6-10, 1981*. Amsterdam, 1982.

22. UNTERMANN, Jürgen & Bela BROGYANYI (eds): *DAS GERMANISCHE UND DIE REKONSTRUKTION DER INDOGERMANISCHE GRUNDSPRACHE.* Akten, Proceedings from the Colloquium of the Indogermanische Gesellschaft, Freiburg, 26-27 February 1981. Amsterdam, 1984.

23. DANIELSEN, Niels: *Papers in Theoretical Linguistics.* Amsterdam, n.y.p.

24. LEHMANN, Winfred P. & Yakov MALKIEL (eds): *PERSPECTIVES ON HISTORICAL LINGUISTICS.* Papers from a conference held at the meeting of the Language Theory Division, Modern Language Ass., San Francisco, 27-30 December 1979. Amsterdam, 1982.

25. ANDERSEN, Paul Kent: *Word Order Typology and Comparative Constructions.* Amsterdam, 1983.

26. BALDI, Philip (ed.) *PAPERS FROM THE XIIth LINGUISTIC SYMPOSIUM ON ROMANCE LANGUAGES, University Park, April 1-3, 1982.* Amsterdam, 1984.

27. BOMHARD, Alan: *Toward Proto-Nostratic.* Amsterdam, 1984.

28. BYNON, James: *CURRENT PROGRESS IN AFROASIATIC LINGUISTICS: Papers of the Third International Hamito-Semitic Congress, London, 1978.* Amsterdam, 1984.

29. PAPROTTÉ, Wolf & René DIRVEN (eds): *THE UBIQUITY OF METAPHOR: Metaphor in Language and Thought.* Amsterdam, 1985.

30. HALL, Robert A., Jr.: *Proto-Romance Morphology.* Amsterdam, 1984.

31. GUILLAUME, Gustave: *Foundations for a Science of Language.* Translated and with an introd. by Walter Hirtle and John Hewson. Amsterdam, 1984.

32. COPELAND, James E. (ed.): *NEW DIRECTIONS IN LINGUISTICS AND SEMIOTICS.* Houston/Amsterdam, 1984. No rights for US/Can. *Customers from USA and Canada: please order from Rice University.*

33. VERSTEEGH, Kees: *Pidginization and Creolization: The Case of Arabic.* Amsterdam, 1984.

34. FISIAK, Jacek (ed.): *PAPERS FROM THE VIth INTERNATIONAL CONFERENCE ON HISTORICAL LINGUISTICS, Poznan, 22-26 August 1983.* Amsterdam, 1985.

35. COLLINGE, N.E.: *The Laws of Indo-European.* Amsterdam, 1985.

36. KING, Larry D. & Catherine A. MALEY (eds): *SELECTED PAPERS FROM THE XIIIth LINGUISTICS SYMPOSIUM ON ROMANCE LANGUAGES.* Amsterdam, 1985.

37. GRIFFEN, T.D.: *Aspects of Dynamic Phonology.* Amsterdam, 1985.

38. BROGYANYI, Bela & Thomas KRÖMMELBEIN (eds): *GERMANIC DIALECTS: LINGUISTIC AND PHILOLOGICAL INVESTIGATIONS.* Amsterdam, 1986.

39. BENSON, James D., Michael J. CUMMINGS & William S. GREAVES (eds): *LINGUISTICS IN A SYSTEMIC PERSPECTIVE.* Amsterdam, 1988.

40. FRIES, Peter Howard and Nancy (eds): *TOWARD AN UNDERSTANDING OF LANGUAGE: CHARLES C. FRIES IN PERSPECTIVE.* Amsterdam, 1985.

41. EATON, Roger, et al. (eds): *PAPERS FROM THE 4th INTERNATIONAL CONFERENCE ON ENGLISH HISTORICAL LINGUISTICS.* Amsterdam, 1985.

42. MAKKAI, Adam & Alan K. MELBY (eds): *LINGUISTICS AND PHILOSOPHY. Essays in honor of Rulon S. Wells.* Amsterdam, 1985.

43. AKAMATSU, Tsutomu: *The Theory of Neutralization and the Archiphoneme in Functional Phonology.* Amsterdam, 1988.

44. JUNGRAITHMAYR, Herrmann & Walter W. MUELLER (eds): *PROCEEDINGS OF THE FOURTH INTERNATIONAL HAMITO-SEMITIC CONGRESS.* Amsterdam, 1987.

45. KOOPMAN, W.F., F.C. VAN DER LEEK, O. FISCHER & R. EATON (eds): *EXPLANATION AND LINGUISTIC CHANGE*. Amsterdam, 1987.
46. PRIDEAUX, Gary D., and William J. BAKER: *STRATEGIES AND STRUCTURES: The Processing of Relative Clauses*. Amsterdam, 1986.
47. LEHMANN, Winfred P.: *LANGUAGE TYPOLOGY 1985. Papers from the Linguistic Typology Symposium, Moscow, 9-13 Dec. 1985.* Amsterdam, 1986.
48. RAMAT, Anna Giacalone (ed.): *PROCEEDINGS OF THE VII INTERNATIONAL CONFERENCE ON HISTORICAL LINGUISTICS, Pavia 9-13 September 1985.* Amsterdam, 1987.
49. WAUGH, Linda R. & Stephen RUDY (eds): *NEW VISTAS IN GRAMMAR: Invariance and Variation.* Amsterdam/Philadelphia, 1989. n.y.p.
50. RUDZKA-OSTYN, Brygida (ed.): *TOPICS IN COGNITIVE LINGUISTICS.* Amsterdam/Philadelphia, 1988.
51. CHATTERJEE, Ranjit: *Aspect and Meaning in Slavic and Indic.* Amsterdam/Philadelphia, 1988.
52. FASOLD, Ralph & Deborah SCHIFFRIN (eds): *LANGUAGE CHANGE AND VARIATION.* Amsterdam/Philadelphia, 1989.
53. SANKOFF, David (ed.): *DIVERSITY AND DIACHRONY.* Amsterdam, 1986.
54. WEIDERT, Alfons: *Tibeto-Burman Tonology. A Comparative Analysis.* Amsterdam, 1987.
55. HALL, Robert A. Jr.: *Linguistics and Pseudo-Linguistics.* Amsterdam, 1987.
56. HOCKETT, Charles F.: *Refurbishing our Foundations. Elementary Linguistics from an Advanced Point of View.* Amsterdam, 1987.
57. BUBENIK, Vít: *Hellenistic and Roman Greece as a Sociolinguistic Area.* Amsterdam/Philadelphia, 1989.
58. ARBEITMAN, Yoël L.: *FUCUS. A Semitic/Afrasian Gathering in Remembrance of Albert Ehrman.* Amsterdam/Philadelphia, 1988.
59. VOORST, Jan van: *Event Structure.* Amsterdam/Philadelphia, 1988.
60. KIRSCHNER, Carl and Janet DECESARIS (eds): *STUDIES IN ROMANCE LINGUISTICS.* Amsterdam/Philadelphia, 1989. n.y.p.
61. CORRIGAN, Roberta, Fred ECKMAN and Michael NOONAN (eds): *LINGUISTIC CATEGORIZATION.* Amsterdam/Philadelphia, 1989. n.y.p.
62. FRAJZYNGIER, Zygmunt (ed.): *CURRENT PROGRESS IN CHADIC LINGUISTICS.* Amsterdam/Philadelphia, 1989. n.y.p.